Using PageMaker® 5 for Windows™
Special Edition

SHARYN VENIT

que

Screen reproductions in this book were created with Collage Plus from Inner Media, Inc., Hollis, NH.

Using PageMaker 5 for Windows, Special Edition, is based on PageMaker Version 5.0. Commands and functions detailed in this book may work with other versions in which the pertinent features are available.

Publisher: David P. Ewing

Associate Publisher: Rick Ranucci

Operations Manager: Sheila Cunningham

Publishing Plan Manager: Thomas H. Bennett

Marketing Manager: Ray Robinson

Book Designer: Scott Cook

CREDITS

Title Manager
Shelley O'Hara

Product Director
Kathie-Jo Arnoff

Production Editor
Anne Owen

Editors
Tracy L. Barr
William A. Barton
Fran Blauw
Jane A. Cramer
Virginia Noble
Susan Pink
Christine Prakel
Joy M. Preacher
Kathy Simpson

Acquisitions Editor
Patricia J. Brooks

Technical Editor
Maire Mascow

Production Team
Jeff Baker
Claudia Bell
Danielle Bird
Julie Brown
Jodie Cantwell
Laurie Casey
Brad Chinn
Brook Farling
Heather Kaufman
Bob LaRoche
Jay Lesandrini
Caroline Roop
Linda Seifert
Sandra Shay
Tina Trettin
Johnna VanHoose
Michelle Worthington

Composed in *Cheltenham* and *MCPdigital* by Que Corporation

ABOUT THE AUTHOR

Sharyn Venit began working in the publishing industry as a proofreader and layout artist when page proofs were delivered on galleys and pasted up manually. She learned letterpress techniques ("...as an art form") in 1979, and she has directed the publication departments of several software companies. Her rich background in all aspects of publishing is reflected in this book and her other writings—more than ten books and hundreds of articles about using computers for publishing. Her articles have appeared in national magazines, including *PC Computing*, *PC Magazine*, *PC Week*, and *Publish!*. Her articles include reviews of laser printers and typesetters, page layout applications, drawing applications, and word processing software. She designed and produced the original *PageMaker Classroom* training materials for Aldus Corporation. Venit is one of the founders of TechArt, Inc., a graphic design and production shop in San Francisco, and a company where PageMaker has been a primary tool since it was first introduced in 1985.

ACKNOWLEDGMENTS

My greatest appreciation goes to Diane Burns, my business partner and coauthor on the first two editions of this book, whose enthusiasm and patience helped carry us through all the trials and who helped celebrate the many triumphs that we experienced as pioneers in desktop publishing. Many of the tips you will find throughout this book are fruits of the lessons Diane and I learned in trying to deliver camera-ready copy—on time—to diverse and demanding clients at TechArt.

This book would not have been possible without the help and cooperation of TechArt's clients and staff, including the following: Aldus Corporation; American Electronics Association; Ben Bowermeister, Aldus Corporation; David Park Brown, TechArt San Francisco; Chris Chenard; Laurie Deutsch, McCutchen, Doyle, and Brown and Enerson; Leticia Gueverra, TechArt San Francisco; Ike Computer Company; Judy Jacobson, Aldus Corporation; Know How, Inc.; Denise Lever, TechArt San Francisco; Sam Louie, TechArt San Francisco; Grace Moore, TechArt San Francisco; Laura Murphy, TechArt San Francisco; National Association of Professional Women (NAPW); Barry Owen; Pacific Heights; Shana Penn, stylist; Susan Robinson-Equitz, TechArt San Francisco; Emily Rosenberg, Venture Development Service; Mike Sherwood, Aldus Corporation; Robert Sheridan; David Smith, designer; TechArt San Francisco; Thompson and Company; and Zablocki Printing Company.

Special thanks to Reyna Cowan, Berkeley, California, for her extensive writing and editing of text and preparing of figures for the second and third editions of this book, and to Lisa Pletka for her help in developing the illustrations for the third and fourth editions.

I am especially grateful for all the support I felt from my contacts at Que for this fourth edition, including Shelley O'Hara for suggesting we make this a Special Edition; Patty Brooks for lining up the resources needed to keep us on schedule; Anne Owen for sweating through several edit rounds with me; Kathie-Jo Arnoff for her real encouragement, for seeing the value in the content, and for lobbying in favor of the color pages. Thanks also to the production staff for creating these beautiful page layouts *in PageMaker*.

Finally, thanks to Marie Mascow for her technical review and helpful comments, and to all the other editors whose careful reads and probing questions made this such a great book!

Trademarks

All terms mentioned in this book that are known to be trademarks or service marks have been appropriately capitalized. Que cannot attest to the accuracy of this information. Use of a term in this book should not be regarded as affecting the validity of any trademark or service mark.

CONTENTS AT A GLANCE

CONTENTS AT A GLANCE

TABLE OF CONTENTS

III Advanced Techniques

IV Publication Design

V Examples of Publications Created Using PageMaker

Introduction

PageMaker, by Aldus Corporation, is one of the most sophisticated page-layout programs for microcomputers on the market today. First released for the Macintosh computer in July 1985, and later for IBM ATs, AT compatibles, and IBM PS/2 computers, PageMaker is credited with starting the desktop publishing revolution. This book discusses using PageMaker 5.0 under Microsoft Windows 3.1 on IBM PCs and compatibles.

Desktop publishing uses personal computers to produce typeset-quality text and clean graphic images, merge the text and graphics on the same page, and then print full pages on a high-resolution laser printer or typesetter. With desktop publishing, you eliminate the need for rulers, ink pens, blue lines, boards, wax, tape, screens, and knives as you produce camera-ready pages for offset printing or photocopier reproduction.

PageMaker is an especially easy-to-use desktop publishing program. With it, you perform all your production tasks on a screen that displays an exact image of your page as it will be printed. (Some font types require additional soft fonts or cartridges for you to print what you see on-screen.) Because of the program's power and sophistication, almost any user can produce professional publications with a minimum investment in equipment and software.

Why a Book about PageMaker?

Although PageMaker basics are easy to learn, developing efficient operating techniques can take months. Moreover, the fact that the *program* is capable of producing beautiful publications doesn't guarantee that every *user* is capable of producing beautiful documents without getting advice from professional designers or studying graphic design.

This book is not intended as a substitute for the excellent Aldus documentation. Instead, *Using PageMaker 5 for Windows*, Special Edition, is a practical guide that goes beyond the basics of the manual and provides practical examples and hints for using the program in a production environment, including many time-saving tips. This book offers tips to help you design and produce a wide variety of documents, ranging from short brochures and fliers to full-length books and reports.

Who Should Use This Book?

No matter what your background and experience, you will need to learn new methods and terms when you enter the world of desktop publishing. This book brings together the special vocabularies of the typesetter, designer, word processor, and computer operator to explain clearly the concepts from these disciplines, which are merged in desktop publishing applications.

Using PageMaker 5 for Windows, Special Edition, helps solve the problems of the less experienced user. This book is also intended for professional designers, typesetters, publishers, corporate publishing department personnel, and independent publishers who already are using or considering using PageMaker. The numerous examples demonstrate the wide range of possibilities with PageMaker. By studying these examples and tips, users can improve the appearance of their documents, as well as reduce the document's overall production time.

Although this book is addressed specifically to IBM and compatible MS-DOS system users, those persons using PageMaker on the Apple Macintosh also will find these examples and suggestions useful. For a book specifically about PageMaker on the Mac, refer to Que's *The Ultimate PageMaker 5 Book for the Mac*, Special Edition.

What Is in This Book?

PageMaker 5.0 offers many more features than previous versions. For instance, you now can rotate, skew, or mirror text or graphics at any angle. You can open multiple publications—and perform global searches or spelling checks on more than one publication at a time. You can also print process color separations, create libraries of commonly used elements, and link imported text and graphics through Windows 3.1's Object Linking and Embedding feature (OLE). A Control palette is now available for quickly changing the location, size, or other attributes of a selected object. PageMaker 5.0 incorporates Aldus Additions—a submenu of handy utilities that let you run scripted sequences of steps, build signatures for offset printing, and rearrange the sequence of pages. These capabilities and other new or enhanced features of PageMaker 5.0 are described in *Using PageMaker 5 for Windows*, Special Edition.

Part I of the book (Chapters 1 through 3) introduces desktop publishing and PageMaker to new users. Part II (Chapters 4 through 10) addresses PageMaker's basic features and describes the steps involved in producing a publication. Part III (Chapters 11 through 14) describes advanced techniques that are not essential for simple publications but offer tremendous design and productivity aids for professional publishers. Part IV (Chapters 15 through 16) offers specific advice about defining the type specifications and designing and producing different types of publications. Part V (Chapters 17 through 21) presents examples of publications produced by PageMaker and highlights specific design and production tips.

This new Special Edition also includes a 30-minute tutorial to give beginners a kick-start, a step summary for many procedures to give experienced users a hint of how to use features with which they are less familiar, and a handy tear-out reference card of keyboard shortcuts.

If you already are using PageMaker on the PC (or on the Macintosh), you may want to skim Parts I and II, looking for tips and new feature descriptions (highlighted by a *5* icon in the margin); review Parts III and IV more carefully to find the many new features and production tips offered in these chapters; and use Part V as a reference when you have a specific production problem.

Part I: Getting Started

The first three chapters introduce PageMaker to beginners. Chapter 1, "Introducing PageMaker and Desktop Publishing," defines desktop publishing and describes PageMaker's basic functions. After comparing PageMaker with word processing and graphics programs, the chapter describes the final form of a page created in PageMaker and gives an overview of the production process.

Chapter 2, "PageMaker: A First Look," shows how to start PageMaker and offers descriptions of the opening screens and menu commands. This chapter also offers a quick summary of the steps necessary to produce a complete PageMaker publication.

Chapter 3 is a 30-minute Tutorial that walks beginners through an overview of PageMaker's basic procedures: starting Windows and PageMaker, opening a new publication, placing text and graphics, inserting pages, formatting the text, saving and printing the publication, and quitting PageMaker.

Part II: The Production Process with PageMaker

The information in Part II (Chapters 4 through 10) lays a solid foundation for using PageMaker to create publications. Chapter 4, "Starting a New Publication," describes how to open a PageMaker publication, define the page size and other publication-wide variables, and save the publication as a template or as a new document.

Chapter 5, "Creating Page Layouts," presents detailed instructions and tips for laying out a document page-by-page and step-by-step. This chapter illustrates how to use PageMaker's ruler line, master page grid, and automatic page numbering capability. The chapter offers specific tips on building a publication and creating layouts that call for mixed formats (such as different numbers of columns from page to page). This chapter also introduces Object Linking and Embedding (OLE)— a new feature of Windows 3.1 that is supported by new commands in PageMaker 5.0.

Chapter 6, "Adding Text," discusses the methods of placing text on a page in PageMaker (for example, typing directly on the page, typing in PageMaker's Story Editor, or importing text from other sources), and distinguishes between formatting in a word processing program and formatting in PageMaker.

Chapter 7, "Editing Text," describes how to edit or change the *content* of the text, including PageMaker's spelling checker and global search feature.

Chapter 8, "Formatting Text," demonstrates the techniques you use to format or change the *look* of text in PageMaker, including changing paragraph formats (alignment and spacing) and character formats (font, leading, and kerning).

Chapter 9, "Working with Graphics," describes PageMaker's built-in graphics tools and tells how to bring in graphics created in other programs. You learn how to scale and crop graphics and how to position graphics on a page. You also see the difference between object-oriented and bit-mapped graphics.

Chapter 10, "Printing," takes you through the steps involved in printing with different printers, including Apple's LaserWriter, Hewlett-Packard's LaserJet, and Linotronic typesetters. You learn how to work with multiple printers and how to print thumbnails and tabloid-size newspapers.

Part III: Advanced Techniques

Chapters 11 through 14 describe more advanced techniques and offer tips that are not required in producing simple publications but are needed for creating more complex page layouts and for solving problems.

Chapter 11, "Creating Special Effects and Complex Layouts," describes how to work with objects in layers, how to wrap text around graphics, and how to anchor graphics within the text. The chapter also describes PageMaker 5.0's new Multiple Paste command (for pasting multiple copies of the same object at specified intervals on a page) and transformation features (rotating, skewing, or mirroring text or graphics at any angle). This chapter also includes a description of PageMaker's Table Editor and the process of importing tables.

Chapter 12, "Creating Color Publications," introduces you to PageMaker's color capabilities, including PageMaker 5.0's capability to print process color separations. You learn how to produce a camera-ready color document using PageMaker's color overlay feature, and how to add new dimensions to your publication with spot or process color.

Chapter 13, "Special Considerations in Printing," describes how to print a publication to disk (instead of on paper), how to manage fonts to minimize printing problems, how to work with large picture files, and how to prepare publications for printing at a service bureau. The chapter describes PageMaker 5.0's new Aldus Addition called Build Booklet, which enables you to print page spreads adjacent to one another. You also learn how to diagnose problems in printing.

Chapter 14, "Managing Large Documents," describes how to manage large documents using PageMaker capabilities for displaying publication information, associating a series of PageMaker publications through the Book command, and generating a table of contents and index. Here you find a description of PageMaker 5.0's new Library feature. This chapter also offers suggestions for organizing your disk files and managing files in work groups.

Part IV: Publication Design

Part IV (Chapters 15 and 16) focuses on design decisions and efficient procedures in creating and applying design specifications.

Chapter 15, "PageMaker as a Design Tool," explores the process of designing with PageMaker, including developing a series of design alternatives for a single document and using master pages and templates to standardize a series of documents. This chapter offers special tips on creating design specifications for files from different sources, including word processors and graphics programs. In this chapter, you also find tips about preparing pages for the offset printer, including photographs and color separations.

Chapter 16, "Typography," begins with a discussion from the typographer's view of a document—specifically, how to select fonts for a document. You learn what fonts, font sizes, and font styles are available for your printer before you start the design process. You also learn how to work with a limited font selection. The chapter contains definitions and illustrations of leading and kerning, and gives special tips on copy fitting.

Part V: Examples of Publications Created Using PageMaker

Part V (Chapters 17 through 21) offers numerous examples of different types of documents. These examples illustrate specific design principles and production tips that are given in Part II. The examples also demonstrate the range of fonts available with different printers.

Chapter 17, "Creating Business Reports, Books, and Manuals," describes some specific design and production ideas that you can use in creating reports, manuals, and books.

Chapter 18, "Creating Newsletters and Similar Publications," covers design features and production problems for documents that use columns, have *interrupted* text (text that is continued several pages later), and share some other characteristics.

Chapter 19, "Creating Overhead Transparencies, Slides, and Handouts," uses examples to show how to work with these "presentation" materials. Graphics play a major role in this type of publication.

Chapter 20, "Creating Brochures, Price Lists, and Directories," provides examples of these common publications. They are promotional materials—but come in a wide variety of formats.

Chapter 21, "Creating Fliers and Display Ads," explains how to approach these short documents that often come in nonstandard sizes.

Reference

The Reference topics at the end of the book are organized in three appendixes.

Appendix A, "System Setup," describes the basic hardware requirements for running PageMaker, and describes some of the additional hardware that you might find in a professional desktop publishing environment. Here you learn how to install PageMaker, how to install new fonts, and how to download fonts to the printer.

Appendix B, "Quick Review: Summaries of Steps," provides quick summaries of the steps involved in many procedures. This appendix serves as a quick reminder for experienced users of how to use features they don't use often enough to remember in detail, or as a quick reference for adventurous new users who want to try a feature without reading the detailed descriptions in Chapters 1 through 10.

Appendix C, "Keyboard Shortcuts," lists PageMaker's keyboard shortcuts and the keys you type in order to produce special characters on a page or to search for special characters in the text. The same information is repeated on the inside front and back covers of the book.

A Glossary includes terms used in PageMaker's menus and dialog boxes as well as traditional terms used in typesetting, design, and printing.

Command Card: Views of the Control Palette

Finally, PageMaker 5.0's new Control palette is illustrated and described on a handy tear-out reference card at the back of the book, showing how the palette changes depending on what kind of object is selected.

Summary

Enjoy *Using PageMaker 5 for Windows*, Special Edition, and make use of the many helpful tips in this book. You will profit by applying these tips to your desktop publishing projects; you will reduce the amount of time needed to put together your documents, and you will reduce the number of mistakes you make. These tips can help you create attractive and professional publications that fulfill your objectives.

Getting Started

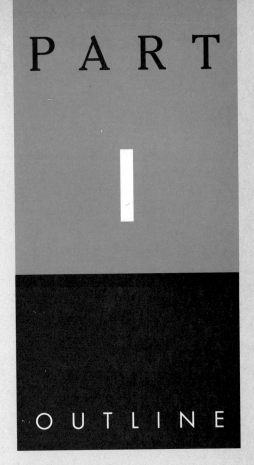

Part I introduces PageMaker's outstanding features and the basic steps of the production process. You get an overview of desktop publishing, as well as a description of PageMaker's features and how the program fits in with other applications you may be using. You are introduced to PageMaker's publication window, menus, and palettes.

Part I also includes a quick tutorial that takes you through the basic steps of creating a publication—without the detailed explanations of every feature, which follow in Part II.

Introducing PageMaker and Desktop Publishing

PageMaker is a page-layout program with which you can compose a complete publication—including text and graphics—and preview full pages on-screen before printing the publication on a high-resolution printer or typesetter. In combining text and graphics created in PageMaker or imported from other software programs, PageMaker's tools and commands enable you to perform the functions of the layout artist's tools and materials: typeset galleys of text, photographic reproductions of line art, halftones of photographs, pens, pressure-sensitive tapes, knives, wax, blue lines, boards, and acetate overlays. PageMaker also incorporates the functions of a word processor, including automatic indexing, automatic generation of tables of contents, search and replace operations, and spelling checks.

System Requirements

 PageMaker runs in the Microsoft Windows environment on a Personal Computer AT or compatible system. Although PageMaker can run on a 286 system, Aldus recommends using a 386 or 486 system for faster operation. PageMaker's 3 1/2-inch disk version runs on the IBM PS/2 and portable computers that can run under the Windows 3.1 or greater environment. You must have at least the following software and hardware in order to run PageMaker 5.0:

- DOS version 3.3 or later (version 5.0 or later is recommended)

- Microsoft Windows version 3.1 or later

- A minimum of 4M of memory (Aldus recommends 8M)

- A VGA monitor (Aldus recommends Super VGA)

- A hard disk with at least 20M for storage (Aldus recommends 40M—up to 12M is required simply to install PageMaker along with all filters and tutorial files)

Appendix A describes in more detail the equipment requirements for running PageMaker.

Created by Aldus Corporation in 1985 for the Macintosh computer and LaserWriter printer, PageMaker helped launch the desktop publishing revolution. This book tells you how to use PageMaker version 5.0 for desktop publishing with Microsoft Windows version 3.1 or greater on your IBM PC and compatibles. You also find tips and suggestions that you can apply to using PageMaker on Macintosh computers.

 This chapter is an introduction for readers who are not already familiar with PageMaker and desktop publishing. If you are familiar with other desktop publishing applications, skip to Chapter 4 for an overview of how PageMaker works. If you are familiar with version 4.0 of Page-Maker, skip ahead in this chapter to the section "New Features of PageMaker 5.0." You then can skim Chapters 4 through 14 to look for the version 5.0 icon in the margin next to paragraphs that describe new features.

Beginners may need to turn to other references concerning the Windows operating environment and DOS to find information not presented in this book. For more information about Windows, refer to Que's *Using Windows 3.1*, Special Edition; for more information about DOS, refer to *Using MS-DOS 5*, Special Edition.

In this chapter, you see how desktop publishing has evolved from technological breakthroughs in a number of fields and how desktop publishing is changing the way printed pages are produced in many communication areas. You learn about PageMaker's basic capabilities by examining a page that was produced using PageMaker and several other programs. You also get an overview of the production process, from assembling a team to printing the final copy. Later chapters provide more details and tips concerning the steps described in this chapter.

A Brief History of Desktop Publishing

The term *desktop publishing* did not exist before 1985. The phrase was coined by the founder of Aldus Corporation and one of PageMaker's designers, Paul Brainerd. The term quickly caught on as a way to describe the combined results of technological changes in the computer and publishing industries.

First, the cost of microcomputer equipment, including the storage required for on-screen graphics data, has dropped steadily over time as the technology has improved and demand has increased. New breakthroughs in laser technology also drastically reduced the price of high-resolution printers and imagesetters. To take advantage of the new laser printers, type manufacturers began designing new typefaces or adapting traditional typeface designs for the desktop publisher. Software developers realized that these breakthroughs in hardware technology opened the way for the creation of programs, such as Page-Maker, that merge text and graphics directly on-screen. These developments formed the basis of complete publishing systems assembled for extremely low prices (see fig. 1.1).

This combination of capabilities embodied in PageMaker has had a tremendous impact on typesetters, designers, professional publishers, corporate publications departments, and small businesses (as well as those who dream of producing their own great novels). You can understand the significance of these capabilities in a society where *information* is the main product. Measured in terms of the number of people involved in production, the United States produces more information than manufactured goods. Each person probably spends more time consuming information than consuming tangible items, such as food or clothes.

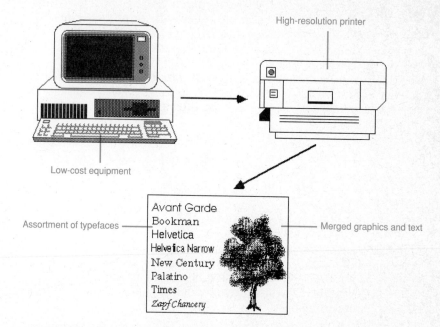

High-resolution printer

Fig. 1.1

Elements of desktop publishing.

Low-cost equipment

Assortment of typefaces —

Avant Garde
Bookman
Helvetica
Helvetica Narrow
New Century
Palatino
Times
Zapf Chancery

— Merged graphics and text

A tremendous amount of information is generated daily. With so much information bombarding us, how can we consume and digest facts important to us? When reading a publication, how can you absorb all the information you need to know as quickly as possible? How can an author or publisher catch the reader's attention? The answer, of course, is to design the information to invite the reader's attention, to include headings and subheadings that make skimming the material for key points easy, and to include illustrations that can convey complex ideas much more quickly than words.

Desktop publishing enables you to create the kinds of effective, eye-catching publications that you need in this information age. The fact that desktop publishing programs are personal computer applications means that many individuals and businesses already have desktop publishing facilities. Even though these users may not consider themselves publishers, they are beginning to realize that these new capabilities have the potential of making all printed communications more effective.

FROM HERE...

For Related Information

▶▶ Installing PageMaker," p. 897.

PageMaker Features

Up to this point, this chapter has discussed desktop publishing in general. But what about PageMaker itself? What is PageMaker, and how is PageMaker similar to and different from other programs you are using on your computer? PageMaker is primarily a page-composition program: it enables you to compose pages using elements created in other programs and in PageMaker. Figure 1.2 shows examples of several types of publications you can produce by using PageMaker.

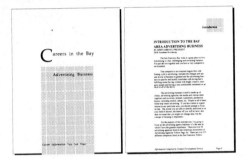

Books and Reports

Forms

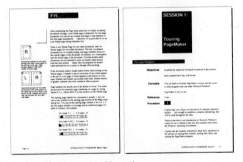

Manuals

Directories

Newsletters

Resumes

Fig. 1.2

Publications produced by using PageMaker.

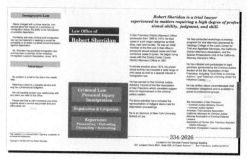

Brochures

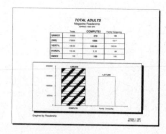

Overhead Transparencies

Fig. 1.2

Continued.

Advertisements

You can type text directly into PageMaker, or you can type text using your word processor and then import that text into PageMaker. You can create simple graphics directly in PageMaker, and you can bring in graphics that were created using a graphics program such as CorelDRAW!, Aldus FreeHand, Micrographx Designer, Windows Draw, or PC Paintbrush. After the graphics are in PageMaker, you easily can move the graphics around on the page, change their sizes and shapes, add color, duplicate the graphics, or delete them.

Table 1.1 lists basic PageMaker features, and table 1.2 itemizes some of the major new features that have been added in PageMaker 5.0. The remainder of this section describes these and other PageMaker features as they compare to other packages you already may be using.

Table 1.1 Basic Features of PageMaker

- View full pages or page spreads on-screen
- Type text or import text from other sources
- Draw graphics or import graphics from other sources
- Wrap text around graphics, and adjust the shape of the graphic boundary
- Layer text and graphics on top of each other
- Create master pages that set the basic grid and content of all pages
- Work with text in Story view to access PageMaker's word processing features
- Apply extensive typographic controls
- Format text using style sheets as a productivity tool
- Access a wide range of fonts
- Adjust the contrast and brightness of imported bit-mapped images
- Add spot color in PageMaker, or import full-color images
- Print positive or negative page images, including color separations
- Bleed text or graphics across page boundaries

Table 1.2 Major New Features Added in PageMaker 5.0

- Control palette
- Library palette
- Open multiple publications
- Multiple paste command
- Object Linking and Embedding (OLE) support
- Expanded color support
- Transformations
- Font conversion dialog box

continues

Table 1.2 Continued

■ Aldus Additions, including the following:

  Balance Columns

  Build Booklet

  Bullets and Numbering

  Continuation

  Create Color Library

  Display Pub Info

  Drop Cap

  Edit All Stories

  Edit Tracks

  Expert Kerning

  Find Overset Text

  KeyLiner

  List Styles Used

  Open Template

  Run Script

  Running Headers/Footers

  Sort Pages

  Story Info

  Textblock Info

  Traverse Textblocks

  Zephyr Library

New Features of PageMaker 5.0

This section briefly describes the major new features of PageMaker 5.0, and mentions a few additional features not shown in Table 1.2.

The new *Control palette* is a window that enables you to quickly change the size, location, or other attributes of a selected object without using menus. The new *Library palette* feature enables you to store commonly used elements in a library that you can access quickly by using an on-screen palette.

You now can *open multiple publications* and drag elements from one publication window to another (drag and drop items), and perform global searches or spelling checks on more than one publication at a time. You can use the *Multiple paste command* to paste multiple copies of the same object at specified intervals on a page—a handy feature for creating forms or other publications with repetitive items.

PageMaker now supports *Object Linking and Embedding (OLE)*—a feature of Windows 3.1 that enables you to import text or graphics and automatically activate another application through PageMaker in order to edit the imported object (for example, you can open PC Paintbrush to edit an imported PC Paintbrush bitmap).

Expanded *color support* includes the capability to print process color separations (as well as spot color separations), define colors using standard color systems (in addition to PANTONE), import EPS colors, add base color, and tint.

PageMaker 5.0 offers a full range of *transformations* (as they have been called in illustration packages); you now can rotate, skew, and mirror text or graphics at any angle.

Getting A Quick Start on Transformations

T I P

If you are already familiar with other versions of PageMaker, but would like to try some quick transformations right away, jump to "A Quick Trip through the Control Palette" in Chapter 3, "Quick Start: A 30-Minute Tutorial."

Publications moved from one system to another system that does not share the same fonts will now display a *font conversion* dialog box, listing the names of the fonts in the original document and the fonts that will be substituted on the new system. You can specify font substitutions as temporary or permanent.

Aldus Additions have been added—a submenu of commands that activate add-on programs. Although you can expect to be able to create your own additions or to buy additions for special functions in the near future, Aldus supplies a starting set of additions, which may include some of the following:

■ *Balance Columns*. Adjusts the lengths of selected columns of text to vertically align the bottom lines.

■ *Build booklet*. Prints pages as *spreads*—side-by side pairs appropriate for creating signatures or facing-page layouts. If you are creating a 4-page 8 1/2-by-11-inch newsletter to be printed on 11-by-17-inch sheets of paper and folded, you could use the Build Booklet addition to print pages 1 and 4 on one side of an 11-by-17-inch sheet, and print pages 2 and 3 on another 11-by-17-inch sheet. This process enables you to create only two camera-ready sheets for final back-to-back reproduction.

■ *Bullets and Numbering*. Adds numbers or bullets (or any character you specify) at the beginning of a specified range of paragraphs).

■ *Continuation*. Adds "Continued on page xx" to the bottom of a text block or "Continued from page x" to the top of a text block, letting PageMaker assign the correct page number for you.

■ *Create Color Library*. Creates a custom color library.

■ *Display Pub Info*. Displays a list of all fonts, links, and styles used in a publication. You can save this information as a text file and print it.

■ *Drop Cap*. Creates a large initial letter at the beginning of a paragraph.

■ *Edit All Stories*. Automatically opens Story Editor windows for every story in a document.

■ *Edit Tracks*. Enables you to edit font-tracking information.

■ *Expert kerning*. Automatically adjusts the spacing between characters.

■ *Find Overset Text*. Jumps to an Actual Size view of the bottom handle of any text block that still has text to be placed.

■ *KeyLiner*. Automatically draws a rectangular box around a selected graphic or text block. Convenient alternative to using the Rectangle tool from the Tool palette.

■ *List Styles Used*. Lists the names of all styles used in selected text and the number of paragraphs using each style. The list is created as a separate text block on the layout.

■ *Open Template*. Creates a new, untitled publication containing preformatted guides, margins, and other publication page components.

■ *Run Script*. Tells PageMaker to execute a series of instructions in a script that automates a series of steps that you would otherwise perform by using the mouse and the keyboard. You can write your own scripts and macros using the scripting language.

■ *Running Headers/Footers.* Creates headers or footers that reflect the content of each page in the active publication; the header or footer text is extracted from text in the selected story.

■ *Sort Pages.* Displays thumbnail views of every page in a publication and changes the sequence of pages by dragging a page from one position to another.

■ *Story Info.* Displays statistics about a selected story: linkage information, number of text blocks, character count, first and last page on which story appears, total area (square inches) and total depth (inches).

■ *Textblock Info.* Displays statistics about a selected text block: linkage information, relative sequence in the group of text blocks that compose a story, character count, total area (square inches) and total depth (inches), and pages on which preceding and next text block appear.

■ *Traverse Textblocks.* Quickly jumps from the current text block to the next or preceding text block in the story, or to the first or last text block in the story.

■ *Zephyr Library.* Stores text or graphics and enables you to access them from floating palette.

PageMaker 5.0 also offers a new Show Pasteboard command, maximum 42-by-42-inch page size, control of printing resolution, many new preferences options, and improved typographic controls.

To accommodate some of these new features, Aldus has changed the location of some commands on the menus between versions 4.0 and 5.0:

■ The Text Rotation command has been deleted from the Element menu and replaced with a Rotate tool in the Tool palette.

■ The Options menu has been renamed the Utilities menu.

■ The Page menu is now the Layout menu.

■ A new command, Guides and Rulers, has been added to the Layout menu to replace several commands that previously appeared on the Options menu (Scroll Bars, Rulers, Snap to Rulers, Zero Lock, Snap to Guide, and Lock Guide).

■ The Display Master Items and Copy Master Guides commands have been moved from the Page menu to the Layout menu.

■ Commands to change the percentage view of a page have been moved from the Page menu to the View submenu under the Layout menu.

■ The Show Pasteboard command has been added.

■ The Target Printer command has been removed from the File menu and now is handled through the Page Setup command and dialog box.

■ The Preferences command has been moved from the Edit menu to the File menu, and new Preferences options have been added.

 Each of these features is described in detail in Chapters 4 through 14. Look for the PageMaker 5.0 icon in the margin next to paragraphs that introduce new features.

PageMaker and Word Processors

If you choose to use a word processor for your initial text entry, or if you will be assembling your publications using text collected from a variety of sources, PageMaker enables you to import text from most word processing applications, as described in Chapter 6. You also can type text directly into PageMaker. Because PageMaker was designed as a graphics-oriented program, versions earlier than version 4.0 were much slower for word processing than true word processing programs, which are designed for speed. For this reason, PageMaker 4.0 introduced the Story Editor—a built-in word processor that enables you to type and edit text as quickly as you can in most word processors. In addition, the Story Editor offers several special word processing functions, including a global Search and Replace feature and a spelling checker. In fact, you now can use PageMaker as a stand-alone word processing package.

On the other hand, if you do not already own a copy of PageMaker but use an advanced word processing package such as WordPerfect 5.1, you may question the wisdom of investing in a page-layout application such as PageMaker when your word processor can do the same thing. Since the dawn of desktop publishing, word processing applications have been evolving to perform more like page-layout applications. Page-layout applications first offered the capability to use different typefaces in a publication, and now most word processors offer that capability. Desktop publishing introduced *WYSIWYG* (What-you-see-is-what-you-get), and now many word processors offer WYSIWYG—especially when run under Microsoft Windows. Page-layout applications enabled you to create and import graphics, and now word processors enable you to create and import graphics. You can expect these two application areas to merge even further as time goes on.

So, why would you invest in a page-layout application that costs $895 (PageMaker) when you can get the same results from your word processor for $495 (WordPerfect and Microsoft Word for Windows)? The following sections detail nine differences that remain between word processing and page-layout applications—nine reasons that designers and typographers choose PageMaker over traditional word processing applications.

Typographic Controls

The text in the page-layout view on the PageMaker screen looks very nearly as it will when you print the page. PageMaker enables you to adjust in fine increments the spacing between characters, words, and lines. You can use this feature to make type fit a given space or to give a page a custom look. The feature is used most often, however, to adjust large fonts in headlines, banners, and logos. In the early days, PageMaker met with heavy criticism for enabling you to adjust leading only in half-point increments; therefore, later versions enable you to adjust leading and point size in 1/10-point increments. A point is 1/72 inch—0.0139 inches. Typographers are accustomed to working with these small numbers.

Word processors, on the other hand, often are designed to measure distance in inches. The old standard on typewriters was six lines per inch. Spacing between lines (*leading*) could be set as single-line, line-and-a-half, or double spacing. Although some word processors enable you to adjust leading in finer increments, their adjustment capabilities do not equal those of PageMaker. Some word processors enable you to expand or condense type by adjusting the spacing between all selected characters—a process called *tracking*. PageMaker offers tracking as well as *kerning*, which is a more complete type of control over spacing between characters.

Irregular Text Wrap

PageMaker offers an automatic text-wrap feature that includes an irregular text-wrap capability—PageMaker can wrap text around the edges of nonrectangular graphics. With a word processor, you can force an irregular wrap by inserting carriage returns manually if you want to paste in the graphic manually (with scissors and glue, for example) on the printed page, but you cannot force text and graphics to overlap or cross rectangular borders. PageMaker has a layering capability so that you can force the text to cross the rectangular bounding box that holds the imported graphic (see the section "Layers" later in this chapter for more information on the layering capability).

Graphics Tools

PageMaker incorporates the basic graphics tools that you find in drawing applications but are not available in most word processors: lines, rectangles, and ovals. PageMaker 5.0 introduces the capability to rotate, skew, and mirror text at any angle (features that are called *transformations* in many graphics applications).

PageMaker offers image-manipulation tools for imported scans such as Image control to change lightness, contrast, and screen pattern. Word processing programs like WordPerfect and Microsoft Word also enable you to create lines or boxes as part of the text, but they cannot create diagonal lines, they do not offer transformations, and they do not have an Ellipse tool. Word processing applications also do not include the Fill capability for solid shapes or a wide variety of line styles.

Layers

Another distinguishing feature is PageMaker's capability to work in layers. You can layer graphics and text on top of each other. The most common use of this Layering feature is to place text on a shaded background, but you also can layer text on top of imported graphics to achieve special effects, as often seen in magazines and newspapers. You can layer graphics on top of one another as well.

Master Pages

Almost all word processors have the capability to create running headers or footers that appear on every page. In some word processing applications, you can include graphics in the headers or footers. PageMaker takes this capability one step further by enabling you to create master pages. A *master page* contains the basic grid and other elements appearing on every page of the publication. You can put text or graphic elements anywhere on a master page—not just in the header or footer—and these elements will appear on every page in the publication.

Bleeds between Pages

Sometimes you see an illustration or a simple graphic element (such as a line or a box) that runs off the edge of a page or crosses from one page to the facing page—a situation known as a *bleed*. Bleeds are possible with PageMaker, and are limited only by your output device; currently, bleeds are impossible with any word processing applications, however.

Color Separations

Some word processing applications (such as Microsoft Word) enable you to apply different colors within a document for printing on a color printer. These applications do not enable you (as does PageMaker) to print the color separations necessary for offset printing in color, however.

Efficiency

The final pages printed from a word processing application and Page-Maker may look the same. If you plan to produce a large volume of complex page layouts, however, you should compare time spent producing a page using a word processing application versus using PageMaker. Page-layout applications compete heavily on efficiency; factors such as screen-redraw speed and the number of steps required to position a graphic affect the purchase decision for many publishers. Word processors, on the other hand, still compete primarily on their text-handling features; the capability to incorporate graphics and to create complex page layouts is just icing on the cake. If your publications often include graphics, consider using PageMaker rather than your word processor to save a lot of time and trouble in the page layout process.

Furthermore, PageMaker 5.0 comes with an Aldus addition called Build Booklet that enables you print to print *signatures*—facing-page spreads printed adjacent to each other in the sequence required for offset printing.

Printing Speeds

Word processors originally were designed to print words only. To keep a good share of the market from switching to page-layout applications, word processing programs more recently have added the capability to create and import graphics. Word processors, however, haven't yet provided the capability to print pages with graphics quickly—a PageMaker capability that appeals to professional publishers who produce hundreds of pages a day.

PageMaker and Graphics Programs

You can draw simple graphics, such as lines, boxes, and circles, directly in PageMaker; or you can bring in graphics from other programs (as described in Chapter 9). Graphic images that have been brought into PageMaker can be scaled and cropped to fit the allotted space on individual pages. Like most drawing programs, PageMaker has menus of available lines and fill patterns for graphic objects, and you can now define custom line widths. Another major enhancement offered with PageMaker 5.0 is the capability to rotate, skew, or mirror text or graphics at any angle. This feature eliminates the need to use a graphics application as previously required in order to create these special effects with text. PageMaker also enables you to add color to your graphic images, as described in Chapter 12.

If you are accustomed to using a graphics program as a stand-alone package to produce one-page documents such as fliers and advertisements, you should know that PageMaker offers additional benefits. Most drawing programs accommodate some form of text entry but do not handle text formatting, such as columnar layouts and tabular data, as readily as PageMaker does. Furthermore, most graphics programs do not handle multiple pages. By working directly with a draw or paint program, however, you can use some of the more sophisticated features not offered directly in PageMaker, such as airbrush effects, blends, and pixel-by-pixel image manipulation. You also can use a paint program to clean up images that have been digitized with a scanner. You then can import these images into PageMaker.

The Final PageMaker Publication

A completed PageMaker publication can be composed of text and graphics created entirely in PageMaker or created with elements brought in from other programs. Figure 1.3 shows a typical page created by using PageMaker. The text was typed in a word processing program (Microsoft Word). The text then was moved into PageMaker with the PageMaker's Place command. The bar graph was created in 1-2-3. The graphic logo—a globe—was created in a drawing program (Windows Draw). A scanned image was modified using PC Paintbrush before the image was placed on the PageMaker page. Some of the short text elements, such as the banner text across the top of the page, were typed directly into PageMaker. Other text, such as the headline, was modified using PageMaker's Style Sheet option. Hairline rules and boxes were added with PageMaker's graphics tools. Running footers and automatic page numbering were set up on the publication's master page—the page that contains the basic grid and other elements that appear on every page of the publication.

Figure 1.3 shows you what is possible with PageMaker. The rest of the book shows you how to create such a publication. (See Chapter 12 for a description of working with color in PageMaker.)

For Related Information

▶▶ "Importing Text by Using the Place Command," p. 232.

▶▶ "Using Graphics Supported by PageMaker," p. 352.

FROM HERE...

PageMaker and the Publishing Cycle

PageMaker brings together functions that at one time were divided among many people at different locations. Before desktop publishing, for example, a typist may have typed the text of a newsletter and sent the file, on paper or on disk, to the typesetter for formatting and type-setting. Meanwhile, the graphics department may have used a computer or pens and ink to create the graphic images for an outside service to photostat to the correct size. Eventually, the galleys of type and the reproductions of the figures would reach a drafting table, where the layout artist would use knives and wax to trim the paper and paste it down on boards into final pages.

With PageMaker, the same person can type the text, draw the graphics, and compose the pages on-screen. Just because one person is performing all the steps does not mean that the steps themselves are much different. The person responsible for the entire production, however, may be strong in some areas and weak in others. Many desktop publishing departments, therefore, still divide the desktop publishing tasks among different people. When the production team is small (as is common in desktop environments), weak spots still can develop in the production cycle—areas in which no one on the team has experience. This book provides tips in areas of expertise where you and your team may be lacking.

Division of Responsibilities

Even if one person produces the publication, responsibilities still can be divided conceptually among different publishing roles: production manager, author, editor, copy editor, designer, illustrator, and production crew.

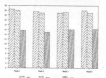

Bylines

Ground-Breaking for New Headquarters Announced

It was all pomp and fanfare at the groundbreaking ceremonies for BMI's new corporate head-

quarters, held last Wednesday at the site on which the 27-story building will rise.

In attendance was BMI's entire Board of Directors, including Chairman Stephen W. Olsen, as well as a contingent of local dignitaries headed by the Mayor of Minneapolis and his wife. A cheering crowd of 1000 looked on, and all BMI employees were given the day off so that they could attend.

"This is an important day in the history of our company," Olsen said after he turned over a

symbolic pile of dirt with a gold-plated spade. "Our spectacular growth has been making headlines for years. Now we will have a consolidated home that represents the status we have achieved in the management consulting industry."

After presenting Olsen with a key to the city of Minneapolis, the Mayor commented, "As the leader of this great city, nothing is more exciting for me than to see another beautiful skyscraper thrust upward to signify to the world that Minneapolis is as dynamic and vibrant as ever."

Festive music was provided during the ceremony by the Edina High School Marching Band under the direction of Michael Lindstrom. Local circus performers also entertained, and a picnic lunch was provided for company employees. Blue skies and a warm breeze kept the party alive well into the afternoon.

One BMI Plaza seems destined to become as famous as BMI itself, because the new building will be revolutionary in many ways. The design, by Dennis Wedlick of R.G. Nystrom Associates of Chicago, echoes the Pompidou Center in Paris and

Quarterly Sales

the new headquarters of Lloyd's of London. Most of the building's pipes, ducts, and elevators will be installed on the outside of the structure, allowing large open spaces inside.

A seven story atrium with cascading waterfalls and a lake will take advantage of this unusual plan because, as Chairman Olsen said at Wednesday+s ceremony, "We want our employees to work in a beautiful and comfortable environment."

Building services will include three cafeterias, a health club with a rooftop running track available to all employees, and an in-house travel agency. One BMI Plaza will also be what is currently known as a "smart building." Computers will manage all the climate control functions, and every floor will be wired for extensive interoffice computer communication.

Bergman foresees no potential glitches in the construction

Fig. 1.3

A page created by using PageMaker.

The production manager oversees the entire project, makes sure that everyone else involved meets the schedule, or adjusts the schedule as needed. The production manager also should make sure that efficient file-management procedures are followed throughout the project, as described in Chapters 17 through 21.

The author delivers complete, accurate text, probably on a disk. An author also can format the text if he or she knows the final design specifications.

An editor then reviews the text and graphics to be sure that the publication is clear and complete. A good editor will highlight or revise wordy phrases, redundancies, repetitive statements, and words that are used incorrectly. The editors also may be responsible for tone and content. Even after one or more review cycles, a copy editor often reads the text and graphics for grammatical, typographical, and formatting errors and makes sure that all references to figures or other sections or pages of the publication are accurate.

The designer determines the overall appearance of the pages: paper size and orientation, margins, and basic grid structure. The designer specifies the typefaces, sizes, and styles to be used in the publication and also may specify fill patterns or treatments for all illustrations. The illustrator produces the graphics files that will be placed on the page. In some cases, the illustrator may be the author or the designer.

Finally, the production crew includes anyone who sits at the computer and uses PageMaker to assemble the pages. The production crew also may format the text if the author has not done the formatting.

As stated previously, these responsibilities may be performed by one person or divided among several people, depending on the situation. A knowledge of these functions will help you more easily produce high-quality work with PageMaker.

Steps in the Production Process

Whether you are producing a layout from design to final camera-ready mechanicals on your own or working with a team, an overview of all the steps involved in a typical production cycle will help you to set up an efficient production schedule. A quick overview of the steps involved in producing a document follows—from verifying that you have all the necessary disk files, to printing the final copy. Later chapters provide more details and tips on how to execute each step.

The steps for creating a document with PageMaker fall into three areas:

- Designing and planning your document
- Creating the text and graphics with PageMaker or other applications
- Producing and printing the final page layouts in PageMaker

Once you understand the basic steps in creating a document, you can fit the detailed steps explained in the rest of this book into the overall process. The following overview of the steps involved in producing a document includes references to other chapters in which the steps are discussed in more detail.

The steps outlined here do not necessarily occur sequentially or in the order shown. Some steps can take place simultaneously, and some projects will call for a slightly different sequence. A typical production sequence showing relationships among the following steps is shown in a flow chart in figure 1.4.

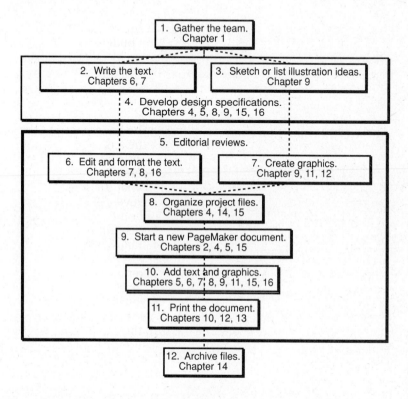

Fig. 1.4

A typical production schedule.

The typical steps in the production process are the following:

1. Gather the team.

   Identify the division of responsibilities, and prepare the production schedule. The team can include the client ordering the work as well as the production group, or a "team" may be simply the talents of one individual who sketches a single timetable.

2. Write the text.

   You can do this by using PageMaker's Story Editor or a word processor. You can import text from almost any word processor into PageMaker. Even if the authors are not using the same type of computer you will be using with PageMaker, you can convert or telecommunicate almost any text before the final PageMaker stage. Working with text is described in Chapters 6 and 7.

3. Sketch or list illustration ideas.

It's important to collect some ideas about the illustrations early in the project cycle, and to match them with the capabilities of your software, your laser printer, and the final inks and paper to be used in publishing. Make sure that your ideas are feasible and affordable within your environment before you start illustrating or commissioning illustrations, which may require a lot of time and can be a major portion of your production budget. Consulting with your commercial printer on illustration ideas and design specifications can save you money and time. Talk with your printer early on in the production process.

4. Develop design specifications.

Designing a document requires planning the appearance of the *page* (paper size, margins, and grid) and the appearance of the *type* (text formatting). Designing often is performed after the text is written, because the design may be affected by the content and structure of the text. If the authors know what the design specifications are before they write the text, however, they can participate in the production by setting tabs and other paragraph format requirements in the word processing files as they go along. Traditionally, design specifications have been handwritten or typed and illustrated as rough pencil sketches with penciled lines indicating text position. You can use PageMaker as a design tool for developing specifications, however (see Chapters 15 and 16). Before you begin individual page layout, you can set up the page design on a master page (see Chapter 5) or in a template document (Chapter 15). You then can capture the type specifications in a style sheet (Chapter 8). This step includes deciding what type of printer you will use for the final production, because the choice of printer affects your type specifications (Chapters 10 and 16).

So at some point in the project—using paper and pen or a computer—the designer develops the design specifications, including the following:

■ Typefaces, sizes, and styles for different elements within the text

■ Basic text format

Will the paragraphs have a first-line indentation? How much space will be left between paragraphs? Will the text be justified? Will headings be flush left or centered?

■ Basic page layout or grid

Includes page size, margins, orientation, number of columns, and positions of other nonprinting guides. Some of this information is required before you start a new PageMaker publication.

■ Final (maximum) size of illustrations, as well as typefaces, sizes, and styles to be used within the illustrations and in the captions

■ Final page count or the range of pages expected to be filled

This count will help you to decide whether to divide a long publication into smaller publications or sections, to determine how to divide the publication, and to estimate the printing costs. The page count traditionally has been performed after the text is written because the design may be affected by the content and structure of the text. Often, the authors know the design specifications (including page count) before writing the text, enabling them to participate in the production process by setting tabs and other format requirements.

5. Editorial reviews.

Have one or more editors read the text for the following purposes:

■ Accuracy and completeness of content

■ Grammar and consistency of usage

■ Marking text according to design specifications

■ Verifying that the text on the final page layouts has been set in the correct format

Most professionals find that one person cannot read on all these levels at one sitting, and there can be more than one editorial reader, each with a different specialty. If you have only one reader, these readings should be done separately. Very often these readings are performed at different stages during production, and they can occur before or after the text is placed in PageMaker.

6. Edit and format the text.

You can do this with the word processor, or edit and format the text in PageMaker in step 10. A design editor usually marks the author's unformatted printed manuscript for formatting according to the design specifications. With PageMaker, you can format text by using the Style Sheet feature (see Chapter 8). This feature simplifies the process of formatting text. The designer can describe in detail each different format only once for entry into a PageMaker style sheet. The text then can be marked up with simple style names that can be applied by using the Style palette or menu commands in PageMaker.

7. Create graphics.

You can draw simple shapes—lines, boxes, polygons, and circles—in PageMaker, but you also can import more complicated graphics or other graphic formats (including black-and-white or color halftone images and color illustrations) that were created by using other programs (see Chapter 9). Create the illustrations by using the graphics program best suited for each, as follows:

■ Scanners can digitize photographs or line drawings that can be manipulated using software like Aldus PhotoStyler, Micrografx Picture Publisher, or Computer Presentations ColorLab. Scanned images also can be traced, creating fine line art using drawing programs such as Aldus FreeHand.

■ Paint-type programs such as PC PaintBrush and Windows Paint are best suited for creating bitmap fine art illustration—original artwork that is never modified or edited.

■ PostScript-type drawing packages, like Micrografx Designer, CorelDRAW!, Arts & Letters, Adobe Illustrator, or Aldus FreeHand, are best suited for line art and technical illustrations. These types of programs can also be used to create original artwork or trace existing digitized images.

■ Spreadsheets or graphing programs are most efficient for graphs that are derived from tables of numbers.

■ Some illustrations or graphic elements can be created directly in PageMaker.

8. Organize your project files.

Set up a single directory on the hard disk for this document or publication; move all text and graphics files into that directory. (You can group several small projects into a single directory.) A quick summary of this book's recommendations about file organization follows (from Chapter 14):

■ Decide on the conventions you will use in naming all new files created during the project.

■ Copy all your source files onto one hard disk drive.

■ Keep a backup version of all files, and back up files regularly.

■ Keep all files related to one document in a single directory.

These few steps are worth taking before you begin assembling text and graphics on a page. Spending time on these preliminaries can save you hours over the life of a large project. You can easily apply these simple steps to small projects as well. Chapter 14 offers more detailed suggestions about organizing large projects and working in networked environments.

9. Start a new PageMaker document.

After the text and graphics have been prepared in other programs, you start PageMaker and begin building the document. In this step, you may begin with a new file for each document, or you may use PageMaker to create a template file that embodies the design specifications for the entire publication (if the publication requires more than one file). The template can include a style sheet and elements on the numbered pages as well as on the master page.

Master pages are nonprinting pages that automatically format document pages. Any item you position on a master page will appear on all other pages in the document associated with that master page. The master pages can include running heads, footers, and any other elements that appear on every page. Master pages also can contain the *underlying grid*—a baseline grid for text plus a matrix of margin guides, column guides, and ruler guides that appear on-screen but are not printed. You can use this grid to align objects consistently on all pages of the document (see Chapters 5 and 15). The elements set on the master pages can be changed on individual pages of the document as you are working.

See Chapters 5 and 15 for information about building master pages and templates. Other details of this step and the next two steps are the subject of the rest of this book.

10. Add text and graphics.

On each page of the document, you use the Place command to get text and graphics from other programs (see Chapters 5, 6, and 9). You can add other text and graphic elements using PageMaker's tools. With PageMaker, you can arrange text in columns and jump text from one page to another, including nonsequential pages. You can easily move text and graphics around on the page, change their sizes and shapes to fit the space allowed on individual pages, duplicate them, or delete them. You can use the automatic features to wrap text around graphics or anchor specific graphics frames to captions within the text (see Chapter 11).

You can edit the text using all of the normal editing commands, such as Copy, Cut, and Paste. By using PageMaker's Story Editor, you have the advantage of fast screen display and the capability to easily scroll through each story. PageMaker also enables you to perform functions normally associated with word processing only, such as finding and changing text (global Search and Replace), checking spelling, and adding words to a custom dictionary (Chapter 7). You also can adjust the hyphenation and justification specifications to change the appearance of the text.

You can use commands in the Type menu to format text or to create a style sheet to simplify and speed up the process of formatting text (see Chapter 8). PageMaker offers a wide range of typographic controls that you can apply to text, including customization of kerning and tracking tables.

Besides normal page-layout activities such as positioning, sizing, and cropping pictures, PageMaker enables you to rotate, skew, and mirror text and graphics (see Chapter 11). You also can adjust the contrast and brightness settings of images, and select from one of several screen patterns for halftone printing (see Chapter 9).

You can create colors and apply them to selected text, lines, or box frames or backgrounds; you then can print color separations for spot-color printing or process-color printing (see Chapter 12).

11. Print the publication.

You should expect to print a document many times before you print the final version. Even if you have thoroughly edited the text and graphics before placing them on a page, you still need to print drafts of the PageMaker version of the pages to review for format and alignment. PageMaker is a WYSIWYG program: what you see (on-screen) is what you get (on the printed page). Minor differences always exist, however, between the screen and the printed page because of the differences in resolution. You cannot see these minor discrepancies until you print the document. You can find detailed information about printing in Chapter 10.

After each draft printing, there will be the normal rounds of proofing, and you will repeat many of the steps outlined in this section as the text and graphics are corrected and massaged until the document is perfect.

Lastly, you will print the final camera-ready masters (including color separations). You can print these masters on a laser printer at 300 to 600 dots-per-inch resolution, or you can print them at higher resolutions on an imagesetter. In most cases, the final document will be reproduced from the single final copy printed from PageMaker. You can reproduce this master copy simply by using a photocopier, or you can offset print it from camera-ready masters produced by PageMaker. You can print PageMaker pages as negatives on film and you can print color separations directly from PageMaker, thereby saving steps normally left to the off-set print shop. Chapter 10 describes PageMaker's printing capabilities.

12. Archive files.

   When the project is finished, copy all files related to that publication onto one or more floppy disks or a removable hard disk for archiving. Save the disk files until the publication has been reproduced and distributed—or longer if the publication will be revised for later editions. (Don't forget to save files while you work on them; if your hard disk fails, you will need a backup copy of your work.) Chapter 14 offers suggestions for backup procedures.

Some of these steps are essential for any PageMaker production. Other steps, such as designing a publication from scratch, are considered advanced. If you are new to design, you probably should start with small projects that mimic other publication designs. After you learn how to use PageMaker's basic features (described in Chapters 4 through 10) and try building a few pages, you can tackle the advanced topics covered in Chapters 11 through 16. Table 1.3 indicates the level of each step and lists the chapters that provide information about each step.

Table 1.3 Steps, Levels, and References for Production Process

Step	Level	Chapter
1. Gather the team	Basic	Chapter 1 (this section)
2. Write the text	Basic	Chapters 6 and 7
3. List illustration ideas	Advanced	Chapters 9-15
4. Develop design specifications	Advanced	Chapters 15 and 16
5. Editorial review	Basic	(not in this book)
6. Edit and format the text	Basic Advanced	Chapters 6, 7, 8 Chapters 8 and 16
7. Create graphics	Basic Advanced	Chapter 9 Chapters 11-14
8. Organize your project files	Basic Advanced	Chapter 2 Chapter 14

Step	Level	Chapter
9. Start a new PageMaker document	Basic Advanced	Chapters 4 and 5 Chapter 15
10. Add text and graphics	Basic Advanced	Chapters 4-9, 12, 14 Chapter 11
11. Print the publication	Basic Advanced	Chapter 10 Chapter 13
12. Archive files	Basic	Chapter 14

See Chapter 14 for more tips on managing large projects or publication departments.

Quality, Economy, and Deadline

More than almost any other business or activity, publishing is ruled by deadlines. You cannot send out June's news in July, for example. When the published document is part of a larger product package, the marketing or distribution group probably will want the publications finished as soon as the product is ready for shipment, even though you cannot write the text until the product is complete. For these reasons, the publication department usually is pushed to complete everything as quickly as possible. Professionals often must struggle to maintain the highest quality in their productions. In the end, you will find that no publication is ever perfect in the eyes of those who work on it.

When you produced your business reports with a word processor and a letter-quality printer, you probably spent more time editing the content of the publication than you spent formatting the pages. With desktop publishing, you may find that the reverse is true; you may spend more time formatting than editing.

You may spend more time formatting especially if your production group includes professional designers or typesetters who will not tolerate inconsistencies and misalignments. During the final stages, you will discover that what you see on a 72-dpi screen is not exactly what you get when you print with a 300-dpi laser printer, let alone on a 2400-dpi imagesetter. You then may have to make fine adjustments to the file to get exactly what you want.

You probably will need to print your publication more than once during the final production stages, so plan for several printings as part of the production schedule. Remember that printing time can be significant when you are producing a 400-page book with graphics.

Desktop Publishing: The Melting Pot

As you probably have inferred already, desktop publishing merges traditions from four disciplines: typesetting, graphic design, printing, and computing. Each discipline has its own set of technical terms and standards. Professionals from these fields find that they need to add a few terms to their vocabularies to "speak" desktop publishing. Users are discovering, for example, that terms such as *spot*, *dot*, and *pixel* can mean the same thing and that each area of expertise has something to teach the others.

Typesetting Traditions

In the past, most electronic typesetters worked with codes: one code set the typeface, another set the style, another set the size, and so on. The disadvantage of the code-based systems was that they were difficult to learn. Furthermore, older typesetting machines lacked the capability of previewing exactly how the text would look when printed; the typesetters had to print the text through the photochemical typesetting device to find any errors in the coding.

On the other hand, some people argue that the advantage of traditional typesetting is precision. Most typesetting systems enable you to set the spacing between lines and letters in finer increments than is possible with PageMaker (which offers increments in type size and leading as small as 1/10 point). Typesetters may need to slightly adjust their demands and expectations to match the capabilities of desktop publishing systems, but desktop publishing does not have to mean inferior typographic quality. PageMaker also can accomplish some text layout feats—such as irregular text wrap and rotated, skewed, or mirrored text—that are much more difficult with traditional typesetting equipment. Chapters 5 and 16 describe PageMaker's typographic controls in detail, and Chapter 11 shows some special effects with text.

Although menu-driven systems such as PageMaker can be slower than typesetting machines, some typesetters welcome desktop publishing's low-cost WYSIWYG screens, short learning curve, and economical printing options. At the same time, desktop publishers can learn something from typesetters. The typesetter can tell you how many words or characters of a certain typeface and size will fit in a given space, for example. You learn several copy-fitting tricks in Chapter 16.

Design Traditions

Professional designers take pride in their ability to take a client's tastes and ideas and translate them into beautiful finished products. In the past, the process of transferring design ideas to paper has been painstaking and time-consuming, as reflected in the fees charged for design services.

With PageMaker, you can quickly rough out design ideas and deliver what looks like finished work rather than the traditional penciled sketches of the preliminary stages. In many cases, the efforts of producing a design idea with PageMaker are not lost, because the files can be fine-tuned for final production. Furthermore, files can be duplicated and modified for other publications in the same series or for similar publications in another series. In the long run, the efficiency of designing with desktop-publishing techniques can be passed on to clients in the form of lower design fees.

Initially, some professional designers may balk at the idea of using a computer for such creative tasks (not to mention the lower billing amounts that result). These factors, however, can increase demand for design services at all levels.

The fact that even amateurs can produce attractive designs with PageMaker seems a bit frightening to professionals. Good design, however, always will require the knowledge and skills of the design trade. Chapters 15 and 16 offer specific ideas about designing publications in PageMaker. You learn some of these design principles in Chapters 17 through 21, in addition to production methods that help you match the designer's tradition of excellence with the business community's demand for expediency.

Printing Traditions

Not long ago, to make multiple copies of a publication, you had to take your masters to an offset printer to get the best results. More recently, some copy equipment has been improved to the point of producing good-quality reproductions. In either case, the result depended on the condition of the original page. You needed clean, clear, black images on white paper.

Now, laser printers print the entire image, including gray scales, directly on any color paper you choose. You can print hundreds of "originals" for immediate distribution. If you take the same image to an offset printer, however, you may find that the camera used in the printing process does not see the image the same way you do. In later chapters, you learn how to prepare your master for offset printing. You also learn the vocabulary you need to communicate with the printer, who is accustomed to dealing with graphics professionals. Chapter 12 specifically discusses the issues involved in preparing publications to be printed in color.

Computing Traditions

The final elements in the desktop publishing melting pot come directly from the computer industry. *Pixels* and *screen fonts*, *ports* and *baud rates*, *icons* and *menus* are terms that you will become familiar with as you move from the other trades and into desktop publishing.

Throughout this book, you find production tips for getting the most out of your computer, using PageMaker commands, using Windows commands, and implementing other procedures unique to computer operation. You also learn the importance of developing good "housekeeping" habits for your disk files, just as many designers practice good housekeeping with the papers and tools in their studios. See Chapters 8 and 16 for more information about typography. See Chapters 15 and 16 for specific ideas about design. See Chapters 17 through 21 for additional tips on design and production methods used by professionals. See Chapter 12 for information about preparing a document for offset printing.

Summary

The process of putting text and graphics on a page is changing drastically and quickly, thanks to the revolution called desktop publishing. PageMaker holds an important position in this new field and has helped to transform the appearance of a wide range of printed communications. Some people believe that desktop publishing with personal computers has revolutionized our communications as significantly as Gutenberg's press did in the fifteenth century. In the end, of course, the real impact of this revolution will not be on the production methods alone, but also on the readers, who will benefit from the clearly formatted and illustrated publications.

Electronic publishing systems bring together the features and capabilities that were once dispersed among different professional specialties. The rest of this book helps you identify the different tasks associated with a full publishing project. It also shows you how to update your current designs and production procedures to take advantage of the capabilities of PageMaker 5.0 under Windows. This book helps you understand the basic vocabulary of desktop publishing applications, distinguish between the different types of programs used in desktop publishing, identify the possible sources of text and graphics in any document produced using PageMaker, and determine your software and hardware needs.

PageMaker: A First Look

This chapter presents the basic steps in starting PageMaker after you have installed it on your system. Appendix A describes equipment configurations and the installation process in detail. In this chapter, you see how Windows works, and you learn to use PageMaker efficiently.

If you have not yet installed PageMaker on your system, see Appendix A for instructions. If someone else has installed PageMaker on your system, you can complete the steps while you read this chapter. If you are new to both Windows and PageMaker, you should read the entire chapter before going on to the rest of the book. If you have used PageMaker on a Macintosh system, simply review the first part of this chapter to learn how Windows works on an MS-DOS system.

Starting PageMaker

After PageMaker is installed, you can start the program from DOS or Windows. This section explains how to start PageMaker from Windows or before Windows is started.

Starting PageMaker from the Windows Program Manager

Before you can start PageMaker from Windows, you must start Windows. On most systems, you just type **win** and press Enter at the C: prompt under DOS. (If this does not work on your system, check with the person who set up Windows for you, or with someone who has used Windows on your system.) Then follow these steps to start PageMaker from the Windows Program Manager:

1. Open the Windows Program Manager.

    Double-click the Program Manager icon to open that window (if it is not already open). Or, from any Windows application, choose Switch To from the Control menu and select Program Manager from the list of active applications. The Windows Program Manager window is displayed, containing the Aldus program group icon (see fig. 2.1).

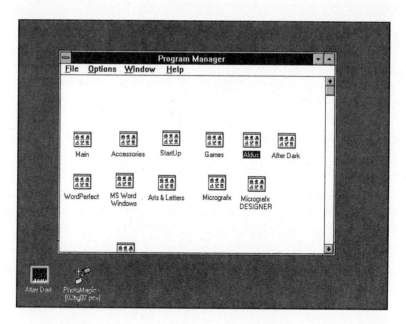

Fig. 2.1

The Program Manager window with the Aldus program group icon selected.

2. Double-click the Aldus program group icon to open the Aldus program group window.

    If you accepted the normal defaults in installing PageMaker, the Aldus program group icon will appear in the Program Manager window. When you double-click the Aldus icon, the Aldus program group window is displayed, containing the PageMaker 5.0 icon (see fig. 2.2).

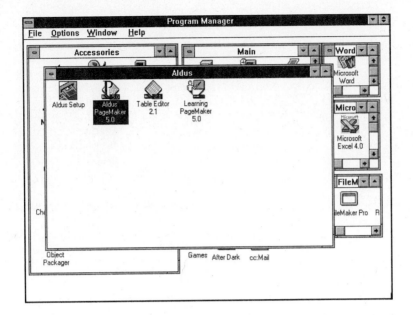

Fig. 2.2

The Aldus
program group
window showing
the PageMaker
5.0 icon.

3. To start PageMaker, double-click the PageMaker application icon.

   PageMaker displays the opening screen (see fig. 2.5, later in this
   chapter).

Starting PageMaker from the Windows File Manager

You can start PageMaker from the File Manager if it is already open on
your screen and more readily accessible than the Aldus program group
icon. (Otherwise, the procedure involves more steps than in the following section.) This alternative is handy if you want to open a document
at the same time, as you can see from the following steps.

To start PageMaker from the File Manager, follow these steps:

1. Open the Windows File Manager (if it isn't already open) by
   double-clicking the File Manager icon.

   The File Manager icon is normally located in the Main program
   group under the Program Manager.

2. Click the PM5 directory icon in the left half of the window.

   The PageMaker directory contents are displayed in the right half
   of the window (see fig. 2.3).

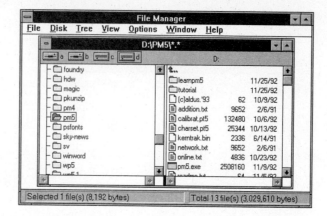

Fig. 2.3

The File
Manager
window with the
PageMaker
directory
contents
displayed.

3. Double-click the PageMaker application named PM5.EXE in the
   right half of the window.

To open a document and PageMaker at the same time, follow these
steps:

1. Open the Windows File Manager.

2. Click the directory icon for the PageMaker document (the name of
   the directory in which the PageMaker document is saved) in the
   left half of the window.

   The directory's contents are displayed in the right half of the
   window.

3. Double-click the PageMaker document in the right half of the
   window.

Starting PageMaker with
the Run Command

If you cannot find an icon that represents PageMaker, if you prefer to
type commands rather than look for icons, or if you are conscientious
about saving memory by opening as few windows as possible (see
"Memory and System Resource Management" in Chapter 14), start
PageMaker with the Run command from the Windows File Manager or
Program Manager. Follow these steps:

1. Open the Windows File Manager or Program Manager.

2. Choose Run from the File menu.

3. Type **pm5.exe** in the Run dialog box, as shown in figure 2.4, and press Enter or click OK.

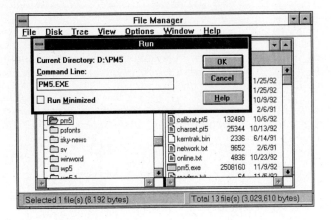

Fig. 2.4

The Run dialog box executing PageMaker.

The preceding steps start PageMaker if the AUTOEXEC.BAT file includes the PageMaker directory in the PATH statement. Otherwise, you need to type the full path before the program name, such as **c:\pm5\pm5.exe**.

You also can open a publication directly by choosing the Run command from the File menu and typing one of the following:

> **pm5** *filename*
>
> **pm5 c:**subdirectoryname****filename
>
> **c:\pm5\pm5.exe c:**subdirectoryname****filename

In the preceding lines, you supply the name of your publication file and, if needed, the name of the subdirectory where the file is located.

Starting PageMaker from DOS

If your PATH statement in the AUTOEXEC.BAT file includes a line that lists the directories for Windows and PageMaker, such as PATH C:\PM5;C:\DOS;C:\WINDOWS, you can start PageMaker from any directory by typing **win PM5**.

Remember that during the installation process you were prompted to change your AUTOEXEC.BAT file. If you let the program change the file, the preceding line was added to your PATH. If you did not OK the change, you can add the line yourself by using a text editor, or you can start Windows and PageMaker directly from DOS by typing full path names:

c:\windows\win.exe c:\pm5\pm5.exe

If you have created a PageMaker document and saved it in the current directory on disk, you can start PageMaker and open that document in one step from DOS. Type **win pm5** *filename*, where *filename* is the name of the file you want to open.

If the file is not in the current directory, you can include the directory path in the command. Type **win pm5 c:***subdirectoryname******filename*.

Starting PageMaker and Windows at the Same Time

You can have PageMaker start up automatically whenever you start Windows by adding the PageMaker application icon to the Startup program group under the Program Manager. (Refer to the Windows User's Manual.)

Whatever method you use, when you start the PageMaker program, the opening screen displays the Aldus logo and information about your version of PageMaker. The opening screen fades to a new screen that contains your name and PageMaker serial number, and then changes to a new publication window. A row of menu names is displayed along the top of the screen (see fig. 2.5).

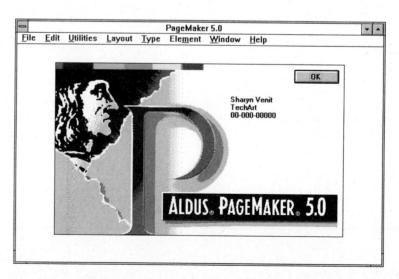

Fig. 2.5

PageMaker's opening screen.

The following sections describe basic program operations, using the opening screen as a reference.

For Related Information

▶▶ "Memory and System Resource Management," p. 624.

▶▶ "Organizing Your Disk Files," p. 627.

▶▶ "System Setup," p. 891.

FROM HERE...

Using Pull-Down Menus

One of the advantages of Windows on the PC is that you are not forced to enter obscure, hard-to-remember commands through the keyboard. Instead, Windows lets you choose commands from lists on pull-down menus. Menu names appear on the menu bar at the top of the screen. When you position the pointer on a menu name and hold down the mouse button, the menu drops down the screen to show all the commands under that menu. You choose a command by dragging the pointer down until the command is highlighted and then releasing the mouse button.

You can use one of three techniques to close a pull-down menu without choosing a command. You can click the mouse on the menu name or anywhere else on-screen. You can press the Escape (Esc) key to close the menu but keep the menu bar active so that you can choose another menu by using the keyboard. You can press Alt or F10 to close the menu and return to the application window.

You can choose a menu command quickly with the mouse by pointing to a menu name, holding the mouse button down and dragging to the command name, and releasing the mouse button when the command is highlighted. If you have already opened the menu (using any of the techniques described in the preceding paragraph), you can just position the pointer on the command name and click.

Note that commands appear gray on the menus when they are not available. See each command description, throughout this book, for conditions under which each command is available.

Keyboard Shortcuts

Menus make finding a command easy, but using a menu is usually slower than entering a keyboard command. For this reason, Windows offers standard keyboard alternatives. (PageMaker requires a mouse for full use of all features, but this alternative can come in handy if your mouse breaks and you want to save your work before turning your system off.)

You can open a menu by holding down the Alt key and typing the underlined letter of the menu name. For example, pressing Alt+E opens the Edit menu. You can also press either Alt or F10 to activate the menu bar, use the right- and left-arrow keys to highlight a menu name, and press Enter to open the highlighted menu.

You can choose a menu command by typing the underlined letter in the command name on the menu. For example, when the Edit menu is open, you can choose the Copy command by simply pressing C. You can highlight a command on an open menu by pressing the down-arrow key until the command is highlighted and then pressing Enter to activate the command.

Besides the Windows keyboard commands, most commands commonly used in PageMaker have their own keyboard alternatives that do not require you to open the menu first. Often you can execute a command by holding down the Control (Ctrl) key while pressing another key. These keyboard shortcuts are shown next to the command names on the menus. A caret (^) before a letter represents the Ctrl key. For example, the keyboard alternative to the Type Specs command on the Type menu is Ctrl+T (see fig. 2.6). It is easy to remember the keyboard shortcuts for the commands you use most often. If you have used PageMaker on a Macintosh system, you will notice that the Ctrl key is the PC's equivalent of the Command key (⌘) on the Macintosh.

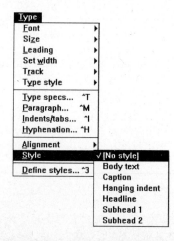

To execute a command, hold down the Ctrl key while you press the letter shown. Command shortcuts also can include the function keys and the Shift key.

Other Symbols on the Menus

A black, right-pointing triangle (►) next to a command name means that a submenu appears when you choose that command. When you choose one of these commands, a secondary menu pops out. You can click the mouse on the selection you want or type the underlined letter in the command name on the submenu.

A check mark in front of a command indicates an on/off option. The feature is turned on if it is checked; you can turn off the feature by selecting the command. The feature is turned off if it is not checked; you can turn on the feature by selecting the command.

An ellipsis (...) following a command indicates that a dialog box asking you for more information will be displayed after you select the command. The dialog box also gives you a chance to cancel the command.

Making Entries in Dialog Boxes

As noted, a command followed by an ellipsis (...) yields a dialog box. Dialog boxes may also be displayed with error messages, warning messages, or information messages in response to actions you attempt in PageMaker or under Windows. Some dialog boxes are like windows in that you can move them on-screen (by dragging the title bar or choosing the Move command from the Control menu in the dialog box). Dialog boxes that are the result of commands offer a variety of options (see fig. 2.7). These options work the same way in most dialog boxes under Windows. This section explains how to make entries in a dialog box with either the mouse or the keyboard.

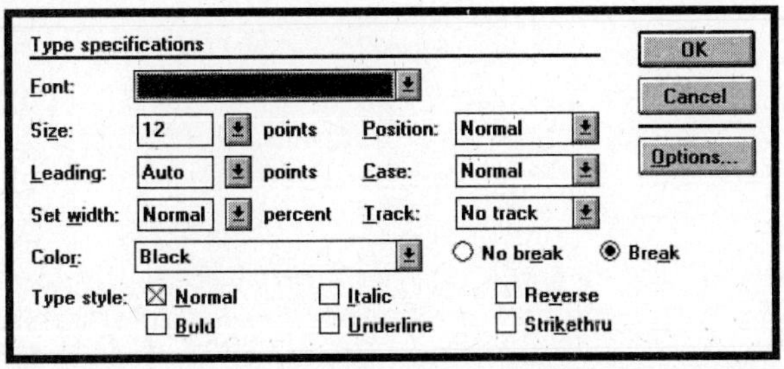

Fig. 2.7

The Type Specifications dialog box showing several types of entries.

Click an option button (a circular button, sometimes called a radio button) or its label to make a selection from a list of mutually exclusive options. Or hold down the Alt key and type the underlined letter in the button label. A third alternative is to press the Tab key to move through the controls, and then use the arrow keys to select from the list of options. The selected option shows a black dot in the circular option button.

Click a check box or its label to make one or more selections from a nonexclusive list of options. Or hold down the Alt key and type the underlined letter in the check box label. Another alternative is to press the Tab key to move through the controls, and then press the space bar to activate or deactivate the check box when it is highlighted.

Use the Tab key to move to a text box and type a value, or click the text box and type a value. Alternatively, hold down the Alt key, press the underlined letter in the text box label, and type a value. When a text box is active, a flashing vertical text-insertion point appears in the box, or the current text entry is highlighted.

To select a name in a list box, click the name. Scroll bars are available if the list box contains more entries than will fit in one view. You can also highlight a name in a list box by pressing the Tab key until you activate the list box. Or you can hold down the Alt key, press the underlined letter in the entry label, and use the arrow keys to highlight the entry.

Click a drop-down list indicator (a down-pointing arrow) to display a drop-down list, and then click a selection in the list. Alternatively, you can use the Tab key to move to the selection (or hold down Alt and press the underlined letter in the entry name), and then use the up- and down-arrow keys to scroll through the list, viewing choices one by one in the text area. In some cases, the drop-down list closes when you press the arrow keys, but the selection shown in the entry area changes each time you press an arrow key. In other cases, the drop-down list might remain open as you press the arrow keys, and you can close it (after making your selection with the arrow keys) by pressing the Tab key.

Command buttons initiate actions that might close a dialog box or open another one. Click OK to close the dialog box with your changes recorded, or click Cancel to close the box without recording any changes. The currently selected command button is outlined in a darker border than the rest. You can activate any command button by clicking on it; you can activate the currently selected command button by pressing the Enter key.

You can also hold down the Alt key and press the underlined letter in the command button name. For example, press Alt+Y for Yes, and Alt+N for No. Click Cancel or press Esc to cancel the command and ignore any changes you have made in the dialog box. Or you can use the Tab key to highlight any of the command buttons, and then press Enter or the space bar to activate the highlighted choice.

A command button that shows a command name followed by an ellipsis (...) will open another dialog box. A command button that includes greater-than signs (>>) will expand the current dialog box. Unavailable command buttons are dimmed.

The basic techniques for working with all PageMaker dialog boxes are the same. Specific dialog box entries and their meanings are described throughout this book. The following list summarizes mouse operations in a dialog box:

- Click an option button to make a selection from a mutually exclusive list.

- Click a check box to make a selection from a nonexclusive list.

- Tab to or click a text entry box; then type a value.

- Click a name in a list to select the name.

- Click a down-pointing arrow to display a drop-down list; then click a selection from the list.

- Click OK to close the dialog box with changes.

- Click Cancel to close the dialog box without recording any changes.

Press Alt+Click To Close All Open Dialog Boxes at Once T I P

Sometimes you will open two or more dialog boxes at once to get to a particular option. For example, if you want to change the graphics resolution through the Print command, you need to click OK four times to close all the dialog boxes. To close all the boxes at once, hold down the Alt key while you click OK or Cancel.

Opening a Publication

From the File menu, you can choose the New command to create a new publication or the Open command to open an old one (see fig. 2.8). The following sections show you how to open both new and existing PageMaker documents.

Fig. 2.8

The File menu
with the Open
command
selected.

Opening Multiple Publication Windows

PageMaker 5.0 introduces the capability to open more than one
publication at a time. You can use New or Open as many times as
you like (limited only by the amount of memory available), without closing the currently open publication(s). You also can drag
an element from one document window to another, thereby copying the element from one publication to the other without having
to use the Copy and Paste commands or the Place command.

Creating a New Publication

You use the New command from the File menu to start a publication
from scratch. This command displays the Page Setup dialog box (see
fig. 2.9). Use this box to specify characteristics of the publication.
These options are explained in Chapter 4.

The Page Setup dialog box appears when you create a new document
or use the Page Setup command from the File menu. You can make
changes to the page setup before the document is open, or you can
keep PageMaker's defaults and simply click OK. After you close the
Page Setup dialog box, PageMaker displays the blank page 1 of the
untitled new document (see fig. 2.10).

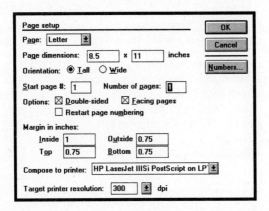

Fig. 2.9

The Page Setup
dialog box.

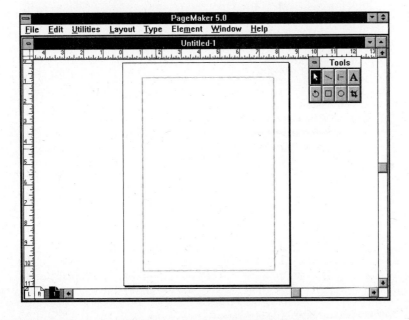

Fig. 2.10

The blank page
1 of a new
document.

Opening an Existing Publication

You use the Open command to open a template or publication that
already exists. (PageMaker comes with a set of templates that you
can use as starting points in creating your own publications; see
"Using Templates" in Chapter 15.) When you use the Open command,
PageMaker displays the Open Publication dialog box, showing the list
of PageMaker files on your disk. To choose the name of the file you
want to open, first find the file name in the window (see fig. 2.11).
Follow these steps:

1. If the list of file names is longer than fits in the window, scroll bars appear at the right of the list, and you can click on an arrow to scroll up or down the list.

2. Click [. .] at the top of the Directories list to view the list at the next higher directory level. Click a directory name (shown in brackets) to view the list at the next lower directory level (see fig. 2.11). Double-click a directory name to view files in a sub-directory. If the directories list is longer than fits in the window, scroll bars appear at the right of the list, and you can click on an arrow to scroll up or down the list.

3. To view files on another drive, click the down-pointing arrow under Drives to display a drop-down list, and click [-A-], [-B-], or [-C-] to view the lists of files on other drives.

4. Click Cancel to stop the Open command.

5. Click the file name to highlight the file. To open a copy of the document, click Copy in the Open dialog box to make a duplicate of the file as you are opening it; then click Open on the File menu. Or, to open the original publication, you can just double-click the file name. PageMaker displays the page that was displayed when the file was last saved.

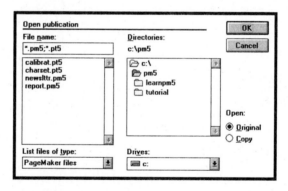

Fig. 2.11

Finding a file name in the Open Publication dialog box.

For Related Information

▶▶ "Opening a Publication," p. 133.

▶▶ "Using Packaged Templates," p. 668.

Examining the Publication Window

After a new or an old publication is open, PageMaker displays pages in the document window, also called the publication window (see fig. 2.12). The publication window is actually a second window within the application window. A quick look at the different elements of the publication window can give you an idea of the versatility of PageMaker.

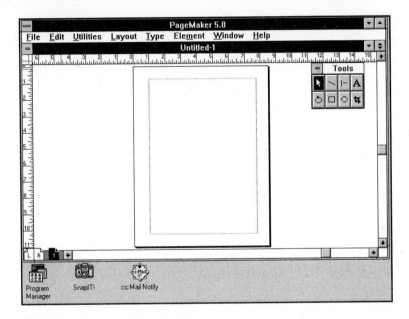

Fig. 2.12

The publication window.

The top title bar—the title bar of the application window—shows the name of the program (PageMaker 5.0), with the Control menu box on the left, and the maximize and minimize arrows on the right. All are standard features of any window in Microsoft Windows, and they are described later in this chapter. Pull-down menu names on the menu bar indicate PageMaker's command categories. The second title bar—the title bar of the document window—shows the publication name, the Control menu box, and the maximize and minimize arrows for that window. In figure 2.12, the toolbox appears as a movable window containing graphics and text tools.

The page image shows the outline of the edges of the paper, and the nonprinting guides on the page indicate margins, columns, or grid lines. The surrounding area serves as a pasteboard for storing text and graphics that have not been positioned on the page. The pointer shows the current position of the mouse, used to select commands and objects on the page or pasteboard.

The scroll bars and rulers can be turned on or off. The page icons at the bottom of the screen show your location in the document; the current page number is highlighted. You click a page icon to turn to that page. The L and R pages are master pages. If you are working under the full Windows program, the icon for the Program Manager appears at the lower-left corner of the screen.

Examining the Toolbox

You open or close PageMaker's toolbox by choosing Toolbox from the Window menu; Toolbox is a toggle command that shows a check mark when the toolbox is displayed. The toolbox is much like a conventional artist's collection of drawing tools (see fig. 2.13). Pens, rulers, protractors, and knives are replaced by icons, which you select to perform the artist's work. For example, the Line tool draws lines at any angle, and the Constrained-Line tool draws lines at any angle divisible by 45 degrees.

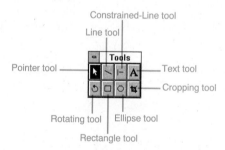

Fig. 2.13

The toolbox.

The Pointer tool selects objects, and the Text tool edits and types text. With the Rotating tool (new in version 5.0), you can rotate text or graphics at any angle. You use the Rectangle tool to create square or rectangular boxes (with squared or rounded corners), and the Ellipse tool to draw circles or ovals. You use the Cropping tool to trim edges from graphics that you bring in from other programs.

To select any tool in the toolbox, click the tool or use the keyboard shortcuts shown in table 2.1. With any tool selected, you can press F9 to toggle between that tool and the Pointer tool.

Table 2.1 Keyboard Shortcuts for the Toolbox

Keys	Tool
Shift+F2	Line tool
Shift+F3	Constrained-Line tool
Shift+F4	Text tool
Shift+F5	Rotating tool
Shift+F6	Rectangle tool
Shift+F7	Ellipse tool
Shift+F8	Cropping tool
F9	Toggle to Pointer tool from any other tool

The use of the Pointer tool for selecting, moving, and resizing objects is described in Chapter 5. The Text tool is described in Chapters 5, 6, and 7. The graphics created with tools from the toolbox are covered in Chapter 9, as is the Cropping tool. The Rotating tool is described in Chapter 11.

The toolbox is a separate window. You can drag the window by its title bar to any position on-screen. You can also close the window by double-clicking the Control menu icon at the upper-left corner of the toolbox, or by choosing the Toolbox command on the Window menu. To redisplay the toolbox after you close the window, choose the Toolbox command again. Because the Story Editor is used for text editing only, the toolbox is displayed in Layout view only.

Examining the Control Palette

You open or close PageMaker's Control palette (new in version 5.0) by choosing Control Palette from the Window menu; Control Palette is a toggle command that shows a check mark when the palette is displayed. The Control palette displays information about the currently selected element on a page. This information will change dynamically as you move, scale, or otherwise alter an active element. You can change the specifications by making entries directly through the Control palette.

The Control palette provides a quick method for modifying many attributes that can be changed also through menus and dialog boxes; the information can be changed in any of these areas. The Control palette is by far the fastest way to view or change values. As a result, you just go into a dialog box when you want to change other variables not shown in the Control palette, or when the Control palette is not displayed.

You can move the Control palette anywhere on-screen by clicking and dragging its "title" bar (at the left edge of the palette). The contents of the palette vary depending on the type of object selected, but there are three basic views: Layout view, Character view, and Paragraph view (as shown in figure 2.14).

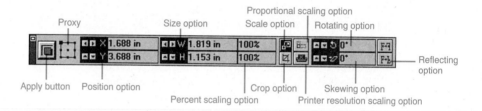

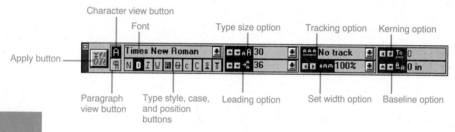

Fig. 2.14

The Control palette in Layout view (top), Character view (middle), and Paragraph view (bottom).

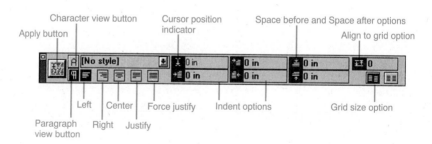

Working with the Control palette in Layout view is described in Chapter 5. Working with the Control palette in Character and Paragraph views is described in Chapter 8.

Examining the Styles Palette

You open or close PageMaker's Styles palette by choosing Style Palette from the Window menu; Style Palette is a toggle command that shows a check mark when the palette is displayed. The Styles palette enables you to apply formats to text easily, as an alternative to applying character and paragraph formats with the commands from the Type menu, or applying styles through the Style submenu of the Type menu. To apply a style sheet, select the text you want to format, and then click the appropriate style name in the Styles palette (see fig. 2.15). The Styles palette is not active unless the text I-beam pointer (I) has been clicked in a text box.

Fig. 2.15

The Styles palette.

You use the Styles palette also to edit style sheet specifications. Hold down the Ctrl key and click a style name in the palette to display the Edit Style dialog box for that style sheet. This is an alternative to choosing Define Styles on the Type menu, clicking the style name, and clicking the Edit button to display the Edit Style dialog box.

Examining the Colors Palette

You open or close PageMaker's Colors palette by choosing Color Palette from the Window menu; Color Palette is a toggle command that shows a check mark when the palette is displayed. The Colors palette provides a convenient way of applying color to text, graphics, lines, and fills and borders of rectangles and ellipses (see fig. 2.16).

Fig. 2.16

The Colors
palette.

To apply colors, select an object, choose one of the icons for line or fill
at the top of the Colors palette, and choose a color. The palette lists all
the colors that were created for the document with the Define Colors
command on the Element menu, plus colors imported as part of a color
EPS file.

The Colors palette may be used also to open the Edit Color dialog box.
To display that dialog box, hold down the Ctrl key and click the name
of a color in the palette. This is an alternative to choosing Define Colors
on the Element menu.

Examining the Library Palette

PageMaker 5.0 adds a Library palette feature as a convenient way to
handle text or graphic objects you use repeatedly. You can store, organize, search for, and retrieve items by using this palette. You open or
close the Library palette by choosing Library Palette from the Window
menu (see fig. 2.17); Library Palette is a toggle command that shows a
check mark when the palette is displayed.

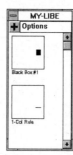

Fig. 2.17

The Library
palette.

When the Library palette is open, you can add elements to the library
by selecting them in the document window in PageMaker and then
clicking the plus sign in the palette; or you can use the Copy command
to copy selected objects in PageMaker or any Windows application and

then click the plus sign in the palette. You copy an element from the Library onto a page or onto the Pasteboard by dragging it from the palette.

Examining the Pasteboard

The area surrounding the page edges shown in Layout view is the *pasteboard*—a nonprinting area for storing text and graphics (see fig. 2.18). You can use the pasteboard also as a work area. The "pasteboard" is a metaphor for the traditional graphic artist's table: you can put text and graphics on it that you are not using at the moment or that you want to work on before placing them on the page.

The width of the pasteboard is determined by the width of your pages and the width of the facing-page spread. The pasteboard extends the width of one page off each side of a facing-page spread, or two page widths from the zero point (that is, the left corner) of a single-page display. There is only one pasteboard in PageMaker—changing pages keeps the same view of the pasteboard. (PageMaker is unlike some other applications that have a separate pasteboard surrounding each page spread.)

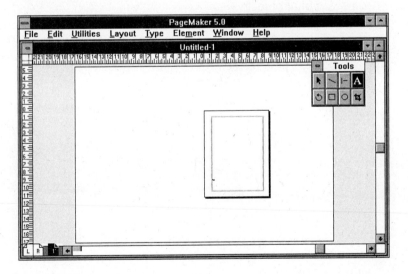

Fig. 2.18

The pasteboard surrounding each page in Layout view.

You can view the page and the full pasteboard by choosing Show Pasteboard from the View submenu of the Lay-out menu (refer to fig. 2.18). Show Pasteboard is a new command introduced with version 5.0.

Examining the Menus

PageMaker menus function the same way that standard Windows pull-down menus function, as described earlier in this chapter. The menus are divided logically into commands that relate to one another. Furthermore, the commands on each menu are grouped into categories, separated by black lines.

The File Menu

The File menu, shown in figure 2.19, includes commands that relate to the entire document or to other files. Some of these commands are common to most Windows applications, such as New, Open, Close, Save, Save As, Page Setup, Print, and Exit. PageMaker adds a Revert command that lets you cancel any changes you made to the document since you last saved it. The File menu also provides an Export command for exporting text from PageMaker into a separate text file, a Place command for importing text and graphics files into PageMaker, a Links command for linking imported graphics files, and a Book command for linking several PageMaker documents into a longer publication. With the Preferences command, you can define how your screen displays text, graphics, and measurements. You use Preferences also to control PANOSE font matching (a new feature of PageMaker 5.0).

File	
New...	^N
Open...	^O
Close	
Save	^S
Save as...	
Revert	
Export...	
Place...	^D
Links...	Sh^D
Book...	
Preferences...	
Page setup...	
Print...	^P
Exit	^Q

Fig. 2.19

The File menu.

The Edit Menu

The Edit menu, shown in figure 2.20, includes commands common to most Windows programs, such as Undo, Cut, Copy, Paste, Clear, and Select All. PageMaker 5.0 adds a Multiple Paste command plus Object Linking and Embedding (OLE) commands (Paste Link, Paste Special,

Insert Object, and Edit Original). You use the Edit Story command to switch to Story view for faster text editing and to access the spelling checker and the global search commands.

Fig. 2.20

The Edit menu.

The Utilities Menu

The Utilities menu, shown in figure 2.21, includes PageMaker 5.0's new Aldus Additions submenu of new features (described in the section "New Features of PageMaker 5.0" in Chapter 1). The Utilities menu also provides global search commands (Find, Find Next, and Change) and the Spelling command for checking spelling, as well as commands for creating an index and table of contents. These commands are only available in the Story Editor.

Fig. 2.21

The Utilities menu.

The Layout Menu

The Layout menu, shown in figure 2.22, includes the View submenu of commands for changing the size of the page view in the document window, the Guides and Rulers submenu of commands for displaying or activating guides and rulers, and the Column Guides command for setting column guides. Commands on the Layout menu also add, delete, and move to specific pages; and hide, display, or copy master page items on the current page. The last command on this menu, Autoflow, lets you control how text flows into the document when you use the Place command.

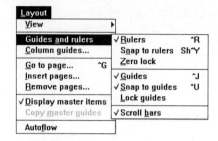

Fig. 2.22

The Layout menu,
with the Guides
and Rulers
submenu
displayed.

The Type Menu

The commands on the Type menu affect the appearance of text
(see fig. 2.23).

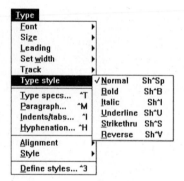

Fig. 2.23

The Type menu.

The Element Menu

The Element menu offers commands that enable you to modify the
color, weight, or style of lines and the color or pattern of fills for graphics drawn with PageMaker's tools (see fig. 2.24). With the second group
of commands, you can change the layering sequence of overlapping
elements, or remove transformations from an object that has been rotated, skewed, or mirrored. Commands in the third group control how
text wraps around graphics, control the contrast and brightness of
imported halftone images, and create rounded corners on rectangles.
The next two commands define colors or restore original color to an
imported color graphic, and the last two commands control how imported graphics are linked to the PageMaker document.

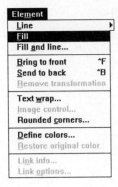

Fig. 2.24

The Element
menu.

The Window Menu

The Window menu, shown in figure 2.25, offers three commands that
are basic Windows options: Arrange Icons aligns the icons of document
windows that have been minimized and appear at the bottom of the
application window; Tile automatically sizes all the windows so that
they touch each another and fill the screen; and Cascade shows windows layered on top of each other. Commands on this menu display or
hide the five palettes available with PageMaker 5.0: Style, Color, Control, Library, and the toolbox. In addition, the Window menu lists the
names of all open publications so that you can choose a different
document from the menu (as an alternative to clicking the document
window).

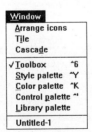

Fig. 2.25

The Window
menu.

The Help Menu

With the Help menu, shown in figure 2.26, you can access on-line help,
go through the PageMaker tutorial, and see what version of the program you are using and how it has been installed (including what filters
and additions are installed). The commands on this menu have been
reworked considerably for version 5.0, and they are described in detail
in the section "Getting Help" later in this chapter.

Fig. 2.26

The Help menu.

NOTE   The quickest way to find information about a specific command is through the index at the back of this book.

Controlling a Window

You can control a window—open it, close it, move it, size it, or reduce it to an icon—by using commands on the Control menu or by clicking or dragging special areas along the edges of the window, as described in the next sections. Not all windows offer every alternative described here. Some dialog boxes, for example, cannot be moved, and only windows that represent programs or documents can be reduced to an icon. You usually can guess what a window will allow by looking for the symbols in the window's frame (see fig. 2.27).

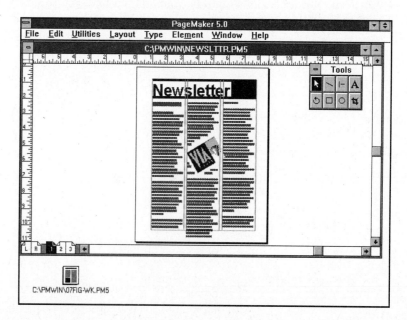

Fig. 2.27

The Publication window with one document reduced to an icon while another publication remains open.

The upper-left corner of most windows shows a small square with a thin bar: the Control menu icon. You open the Control menu with the mouse, or from the keyboard by pressing Alt+space bar (to open the application window's Control menu) or Alt+hyphen (to open the document window's Control menu).

The Control menu lists the commands that are accessible from any program running under Windows (see fig. 2.28). These commands control the screen display by moving, sizing, closing, or switching between windows. The Clipboard command displays the contents of the clipboard.

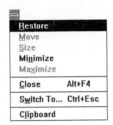

Fig. 2.28

The Control menu.

In addition, the Control menu for applications other than PageMaker might list one or more of the following commands: Next, Edit, Settings, and Fonts. All these commands are explained in your Windows manual.

Activating a Window

If more than one window is open on-screen, you can activate a window by clicking anywhere on it. If you cannot see the window—or if you don't want to use the mouse—you can cycle through the different application windows that are open by pressing Alt+Esc. Cycle through different document windows by pressing Ctrl+F6 or Ctrl+Tab.

The Control menu also includes the Switch To command, which allows you to switch between running applications and rearranging windows and icons on the desktop.

Closing a Window

You can close a window under Windows with the Close command on the Control menu (which you open by clicking on the Control menu box at the upper-left corner of the window) or by double-clicking on the Control menu box itself. You can close a window also from within

PageMaker (and most Windows applications) by choosing Close or Exit from the File menu. Usually, if both Close and Exit are listed on the File menu, the Close command closes the current document window, and the Exit command quits the application.

With the Close command on the Control menu, you can close a window and also exit the program that is running in that window. When you use this command, most programs (including PageMaker) prompt you to save the file.

To close a window without exiting the program that is currently running, use the Minimize command on the Control menu or click the down-pointing arrow in the upper-right corner of the window. When you choose Minimize, the selected window closes and is replaced by an icon at the bottom of the screen (see fig. 2.29). The window you most recently clicked is the one selected and is displayed on top of other windows. To change any icon back to an open window, double-click the icon or drag the window.

Fig. 2.29

An icon resulting from the use of the Minimize command.

Moving a Window

You can move a window by dragging the title bar, or by choosing the Move command on the Control menu and then using the arrow keys to move the window.

When two or more windows are displayed, you can rearrange them with the Move command. Choose Move from the Control menu of the first window you want to move. Then click the second window. The two windows change places.

Changing the Size of a Window

You can use the mouse to resize any window that shows a thin gray frame. Place the pointer on the edge of the window and hold down the mouse button; the pointer changes to a two-headed arrow. Click the window's border or corner that you want to resize, and then drag the pointer up or down. The highlighted borders mark the position of the window. When the window is in the correct location, release the mouse button (see fig. 2.30).

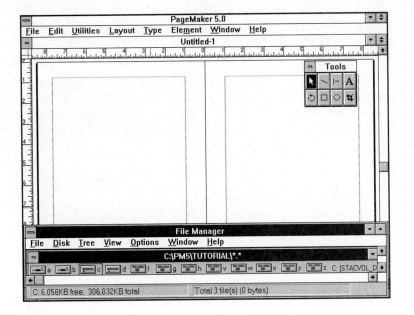

Fig. 2.30

Changing the
size of a window
with more than
one window
on-screen.

If two or more windows are open on-screen, you can adjust the size
of each by using the Size command on the Control menu. When you
choose Size, the pointer changes to a four-headed arrow. By using the
arrow keys on your keyboard, you can position and size the windows.

To enlarge a window so that it completely fills the screen, you can use
one of the following techniques: choose the Maximize command on the
Control menu, click the Maximize button that shows an up-pointing
arrow in the upper-right corner of the window, or double-click the title
bar. If a Window has already been maximized, a Restore button displays up and down arrows at the upper-right corner of the window;
clicking the Restore button returns the window to the size it was before
being maximized. Or you can just double-click the title bar to return
the maximized window to its previous size.

To reduce a window to an icon at the bottom of the screen, click the
Minimize box at the upper-right corner of the window. You can open
the window again by double-clicking on the minimized icon that shows
the window name. Minimized icons will not be visible if the active window is enlarged to cover the bottom of the screen; you might have to
reduce the size of the large window in order to access the minimized
icons.

Using Scroll Bars To Change the View within a Window

Scroll bars can be found in windows and in many dialog boxes that offer lists, whether in PageMaker or any other application. To move the view in the window or in the list in small increments, click a scroll arrow. Click the gray area of a scroll bar (on either side of the scroll box) to move the view in the window up or down in larger increments. Drag the scroll box to move any distance, or put the mouse pointer over a scroll arrow and hold down the mouse button to scroll continuously. The position of the scroll box on the scroll bar indicates the relative position in a window. For example, if the scroll box is in the center of a scroll bar, you are viewing the center of that window's contents.

Arranging Multiple Windows with Commands on the Window Menu

The Window menu includes three commands that are common to most Windows applications. These are particularly useful in PageMaker 5.0, which not only lets you open multiple story windows but also lets you open more than one PageMaker publication at a time. This means that you can end up with many windows open at once, or with many windows reduced to icons on-screen.

The Arrange Icons command arranges in neat rows all the icons in the current open window—a useful aid if you have moved the icons or deleted some of them, creating a "disorderly" array. The Cascade command arranges all open document windows (in Layout view) or story windows (in Story view) overlapped so that only their title bars are visible (see fig. 2.31). To cascade all open story windows in all open publications at once, hold down the Shift key and choose Cascade from the Window menu.

The Tile command arranges all open windows "tiled" next to each other so that you can see all of each window (see fig. 2.32). Tiling is especially useful when you want to compare the publications or drag elements from one publication window to another.

FROM HERE...

For Related Information

▸▸ "Working with Pages," p. 172.

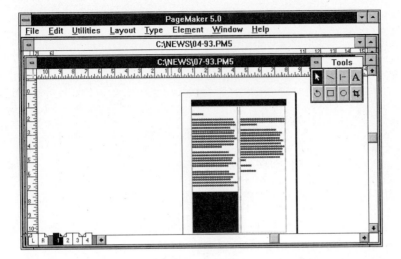

Fig. 2.31

Windows
arranged with
the Cascade
command.

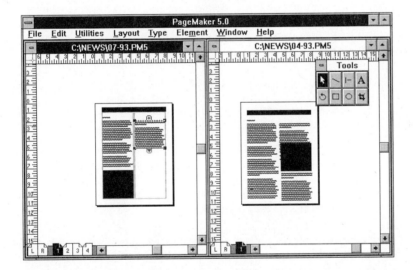

Fig. 2.32

Two windows
arranged
with the Tile
command.

Getting Help

PageMaker offers a list of on-line help topics that are available from the
Help menu if the PM5.HLP file is in the Aldus directory. PageMaker Help
is compatible with the standard Windows 3.1 Help system, and you can
add your own annotations to the Help information that comes with
PageMaker.

When you click the Help menu, as shown in figure 2.33, you can choose
Contents, Search, Shortcuts, or Using PageMaker Help to get informa-
tion about how PageMaker works. You use the Learning PageMaker 5.0
command to access the tutorial that comes with PageMaker, and the
About PageMaker command to get information about your version of
PageMaker and how it has been installed.

Fig. 2.33

The Help menu.

Contents Command

The Contents command displays the on-screen Help table of contents
(see fig. 2.34). Click a topic to view a second list of the topics covered
under your selected topic, each with a folder icon (see fig. 2.35). Click a
folder in this second list to expand a list of subtopics that shows more
folders or document icons. When you click a document icon in a help
list, you see detailed information on the topic (see fig. 2.36).

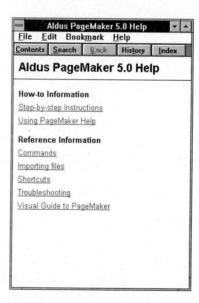

Fig. 2.34

The main Help
screen.

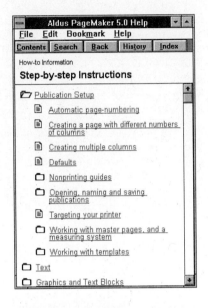

Fig. 2.35

A secondary
level of help
topics.

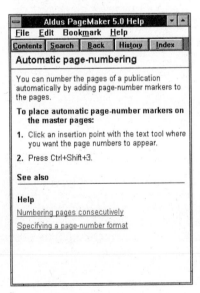

Fig. 2.36

A detailed help
topic.

To help your searching, the top of the Help screen contains several
buttons. By using the mouse, you can click Contents, which lists the
general topics; Search, which finds a topic by keyword; Back, which
returns you to the preceding screen; History, which lets you jump to
any of the last 40 Help screens you have viewed; and Index, which lists
all topics alphabetically in a second Help window.

When a Help window is open, you can double-click the Control menu box to return to the document window, or click the Minimize button to change the Help window to an icon at the bottom of the screen. If you minimize the Help window, you can activate it easily and return to the same view of help topics by double-clicking the icon. (You might have to change the size of the PageMaker application window to see minimized icons at the bottom of the screen.)

When a Help window is active, you can use commands on the File menu to open other help documents, print the Help screen, set up a printer, or exit Help. You can use commands on the Edit menu to copy text and annotate (add notes to) a Help screen. The Bookmark menu lists commands and topics you want to reference frequently. You can use the Define command on that menu to add any existing topic in PageMaker Help to the Bookmark menu.

Context-Sensitive Help

You can press Shift+F1 in Layout view or Story view in PageMaker, and, after the cursor changes to a question mark (?), choose a menu command to open the Help screen describing that command. You can get specific help also from within any dialog box by holding down the Shift key and clicking with the right (secondary) mouse button in the background of the dialog box.

The Shortcuts Command

The Shortcuts command on the Help menu lists keyboard shortcuts. This aid is especially useful in gradually accelerating your speed as you work with PageMaker, once you become familiar with the basic commands and features. Most people have a rapid learning curve when they first try a product, and then they reach a plateau where they stop learning new methods, sticking with the ones they have learned even though those methods might not be the fastest. It's a good idea to check this list of shortcuts periodically to find faster ways of working.

About PageMaker Command

The About PageMaker command tells you what version of the program you are using (see fig. 2.37). Knowing the version of your program is important if you use the telephone hot line offered by Aldus to resolve any problems you may have with the program. This service, available to registered owners, is well worth the subscription fee if you plan to do a great deal of production with PageMaker.

The serial number, along with other information, can be found in the
PageMaker Environment window (see fig. 2.38). To access this window,
hold down the Ctrl key and choose About PageMaker from the Help
menu. Knowing the version of your program and your serial number is
important if you use PageMaker's technical support to resolve program
problems. Again, this service, which is available to registered owners,
is worth the subscription fee if you will be doing a great deal of production with PageMaker.

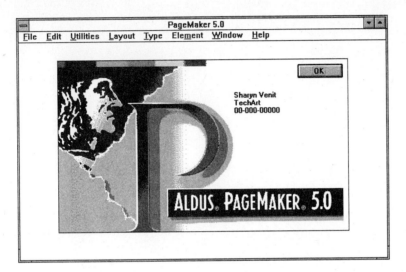

Fig. 2.37

The About
PageMaker
dialog box.

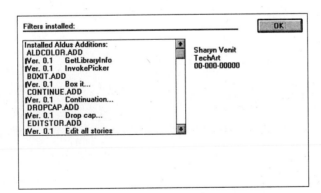

Fig. 2.38

The PageMaker
Environment
window.

Summary

You should now be familiar with some of the basic concepts and terminology you will encounter in learning PageMaker. The best way to learn PageMaker is to use it. If you have never used PageMaker, go through the tutorial in the next chapter to get a quick overview of the program's features. No matter what your level of experience, you can find many useful tips throughout this book for using PageMaker efficiently.

Quick Start: A 30-Minute Tutorial

This tutorial requires between 30 and 60 minutes; it takes you through the basic steps of starting PageMaker, starting a document, placing text and graphics, adding pages, changing views, changing type specifications, saving the file, printing the file, and exiting PageMaker. The tutorial gives you a good overview of PageMaker's most essential features and provides you with the basic skills needed to create simple publications. The steps are presented in their shortest form, with references to other places in the book where the same procedures are explained in detail. You also can use PageMaker's Help menu at any time to answer questions, as described in the section "Getting Help" in Chapter 2.

Using Your Own Files

To go through this tutorial, you should have PageMaker 5.0 and its tutorial files installed on your computer. If you do not have these files, you can try the same steps by placing whatever text files and graphics files are on your system. If you place your own text and graphics, the pages will not look exactly the same as those created in this tutorial (see fig. 3.1). You still should be able to follow the steps, however.

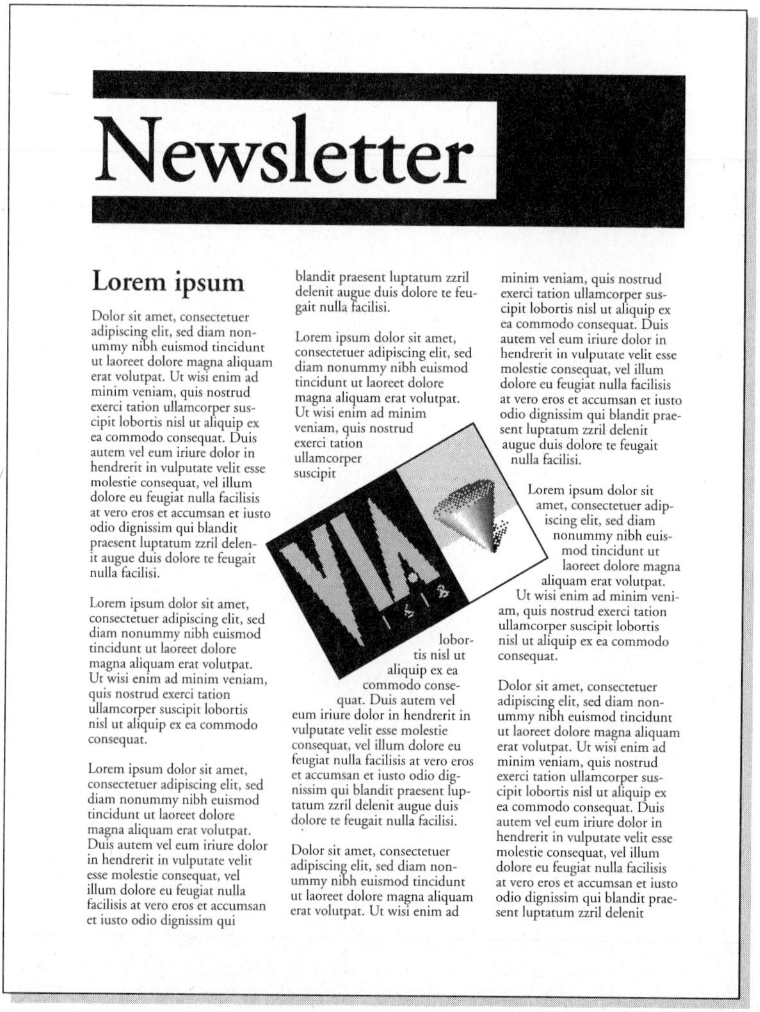

Newsletter

Lorem ipsum

Dolor sit amet, consectetuer adipiscing elit, sed diam nonummy nibh euismod tincidunt ut laoreet dolore magna aliquam erat volutpat. Ut wisi enim ad minim veniam, quis nostrud exerci tation ullamcorper suscipit lobortis nisl ut aliquip ex ea commodo consequat. Duis autem vel eum iriure dolor in hendrerit in vulputate velit esse molestie consequat, vel illum dolore eu feugiat nulla facilisis at vero eros et accumsan et iusto odio dignissim qui blandit praesent luptatum zzril delenit augue duis dolore te feugait nulla facilisi.

Lorem ipsum dolor sit amet, consectetuer adipiscing elit, sed diam nonummy nibh euismod tincidunt ut laoreet dolore magna aliquam erat volutpat. Ut wisi enim ad minim veniam, quis nostrud exerci tation ullamcorper suscipit lobortis nisl ut aliquip ex ea commodo consequat.

Lorem ipsum dolor sit amet, consectetuer adipiscing elit, sed diam nonummy nibh euismod tincidunt ut laoreet dolore magna aliquam erat volutpat. Duis autem vel eum iriure dolor in hendrerit in vulputate velit esse molestie consequat, vel illum dolore eu feugiat nulla facilisis at vero eros et accumsan et iusto odio dignissim qui blandit praesent luptatum zzril delenit augue duis dolore te feugait nulla facilisi.

Lorem ipsum dolor sit amet, consectetuer adipiscing elit, sed diam nonummy nibh euismod tincidunt ut laoreet dolore magna aliquam erat volutpat. Ut wisi enim ad minim veniam, quis nostrud exerci tation ullamcorper suscipit lobortis nisl ut aliquip ex ea commodo consequat. Duis autem vel eum iriure dolor in hendrerit in vulputate velit esse molestie consequat, vel illum dolore eu feugiat nulla facilisis at vero eros et accumsan et iusto odio dignissim qui blandit praesent luptatum zzril delenit augue duis dolore te feugait nulla facilisi.

Dolor sit amet, consectetuer adipiscing elit, sed diam nonummy nibh euismod tincidunt ut laoreet dolore magna aliquam erat volutpat. Ut wisi enim ad minim veniam, quis nostrud exerci tation ullamcorper suscipit lobortis nisl ut aliquip ex ea commodo consequat. Duis autem vel eum iriure dolor in hendrerit in vulputate velit esse molestie consequat, vel illum dolore eu feugiat nulla facilisis at vero eros et accumsan et iusto odio dignissim qui blandit praesent luptatum zzril delenit augue duis dolore te feugait nulla facilisi.

Lorem ipsum dolor sit amet, consectetuer adipiscing elit, sed diam nonummy nibh euismod tincidunt ut laoreet dolore magna aliquam erat volutpat. Ut wisi enim ad minim veniam, quis nostrud exerci tation ullamcorper suscipit lobortis nisl ut aliquip ex ea commodo consequat.

Dolor sit amet, consectetuer adipiscing elit, sed diam nonummy nibh euismod tincidunt ut laoreet dolore magna aliquam erat volutpat. Ut wisi enim ad minim veniam, quis nostrud exerci tation ullamcorper suscipit lobortis nisl ut aliquip ex ea commodo consequat. Duis autem vel eum iriure dolor in hendrerit in vulputate velit esse molestie consequat, vel illum dolore eu feugiat nulla facilisis at vero eros et accumsan et iusto odio dignissim qui blandit praesent luptatum zzril delenit

Fig. 3.1

The newsletter produced in this tutorial.

Before you begin this tutorial, you need to be familiar with the basic operations for the mouse and Windows. If you are not familiar with these operations, review the procedures explained in the sections "Using Pull-Down Menus," "Making Entries in Dialog Boxes," and "Controlling a Window" in Chapter 2.

Taking Breaks from the Tutorial

T I P

If you want to take breaks during this tutorial, it's best to choose a place where a new section starts. If you need to quit PageMaker in the middle of the tutorial, stop at one of the steps where you save the file and choose Exit from the File menu. When you want to resume the tutorial, start PageMaker, choose Open from the File menu, and double-click the file named NEWSLTTR.PM5.

Starting PageMaker from the Windows Program Manager

After PageMaker is installed, you can start the program from DOS or Windows. This section explains how to start PageMaker from the Windows Program Manager. The section "Starting PageMaker" in Chapter 2 describes this procedure in more detail, as well as other methods of starting PageMaker.

Before you can start PageMaker from Windows, you must start Windows. On most systems, you can start Windows by typing **win** and pressing Enter at the C: prompt under DOS. (If this process does not work on your system, check with the person who set up Windows for you, or with someone who has used Windows on your system.) Then follow these steps:

1. Open the Windows Program Manager.

   Double-click the Program Manager icon to open that window (if it is not already open). Or, from any Windows application, choose Switch To from the Control menu and select the Program Manager from the list of active applications (see fig. 3.2).

2. Double-click the Aldus program group icon to open the Aldus program group window (see fig. 3.3).

   If you accepted the normal defaults in installing PageMaker, you will find a program group icon named Aldus in the Windows Program Manager. Otherwise, use one of the other techniques described in Chapter 2 to start PageMaker.

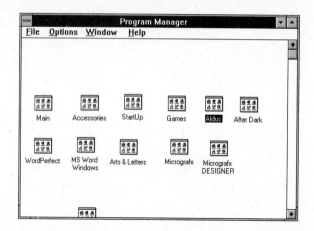

Fig. 3.2

The Microsoft
Windows
Program Man-
ager with the
Aldus program
group icon.

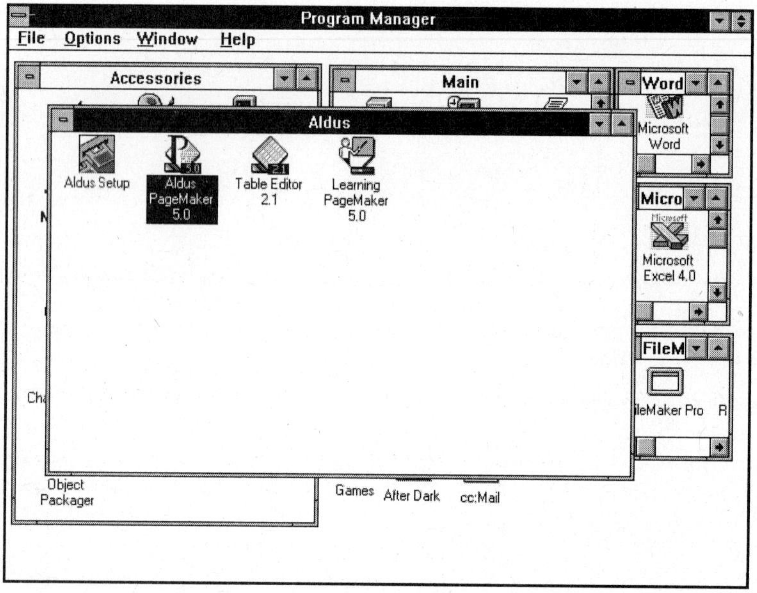

Fig. 3.3

The Aldus
program group
window showing
the PageMaker
5.0 icon.

3. Double-click the PageMaker application icon.

   PageMaker displays the opening screen shown in figure 3.4. This
   screen first shows copyright information, then changes to show
   the name of the registered user and the serial number. The Aldus
   information window then closes, and only the menus remain at
   the top of the screen.

Fig. 3.4

PageMaker's opening screen showing the version number and copyright information.

Opening a New Document

To open a new document, follow these steps:

1. Choose New from the File menu to start a new publication.

   The Page Setup dialog box appears when you create a new publication (see fig. 3.5). You use this dialog box to specify the size of the sheets of paper you want to use, orientation of the printed image, text margins, number of pages, starting page number, and whether you will print and bind the publication as a two-sided publication. In addition, you can specify the target printer, printing resolution, and page number format.

   The Page Setup dialog box is described in detail in the section "Entering Page Setup Specifications" in Chapter 4.

2. For now, leave all the default settings as shown in figure 3.5 (with your own printer shown in the bottom of the dialog box) and click OK.

   PageMaker displays a blank page with the default setting for column guides (see fig. 3.6). The margin guides and page size shown in this display are described in detail in Chapter 4. The menus and all other elements of this display are explained in the sections "Examining the Publication Window" and "Examining the Menus" in Chapter 2. If you haven't already reviewed that chapter's description of this screen, you may want to do so now, but you don't need to know anything about the display in order to proceed with the next steps.

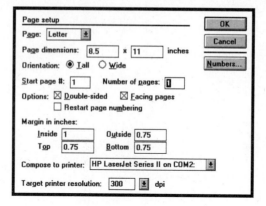

Fig. 3.5

The Page Setup
dialog box with
default settings.

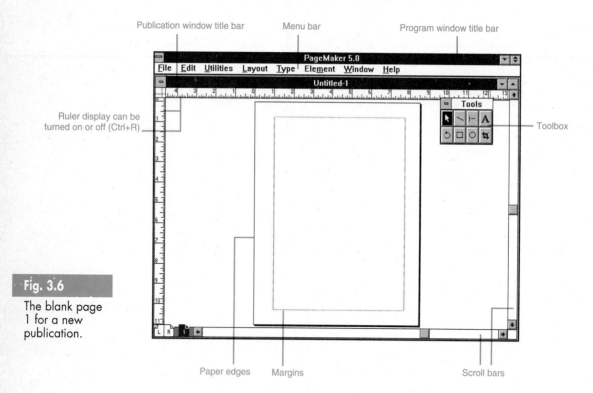

Publication window title bar   Menu bar   Program window title bar

Ruler display can be
turned on or off (Ctrl+R)

Toolbox

Fig. 3.6

The blank page
1 for a new
publication.

Paper edges   Margins   Scroll bars

You can begin building the publication immediately by bringing in text
and graphics you have prepared in other programs. For these tasks,
you use the Place command on the File menu, or PageMaker's built-in
graphics and text tools. These steps are covered next in this tutorial,
and they are described in Chapters 5 through 9 in detail.

Typing Text

For a full discussion of all the methods of adding text, refer to Chapter 5. Following are the simplest steps for typing text on the page:

1. Choose the Text tool by clicking the letter *A* in the upper right corner of the toolbox (see fig. 3.7).

Fig. 3.7

The toolbox with the Text tool selected.

The pointer changes to an I-beam (ɪ). You position the I-beam on the page or pasteboard, and click or drag to tell PageMaker where you want the next text you type to appear.

2. Position the I-beam near the upper left corner of the page margins and click.

Be sure to click within the margins—not simply at the top corner of the edge of the page (see fig. 3.8).

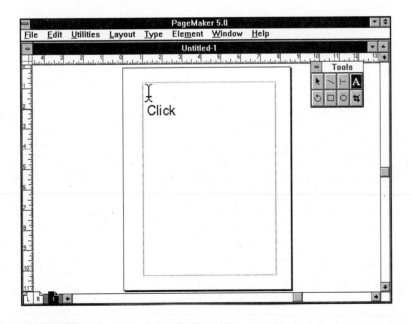

Fig. 3.8

Clicking within the margins near the upper left corner.

A blinking vertical line appears at the left margin, indicating where the next typed text will appear. Notice that the text cursor automatically "snaps" to the column guide, even if you don't position the I-beam exactly at the margin. See the section "Using Guides To Align Objects" in Chapter 5 for an explanation of the snap-to effect.

3. Type the word **Newsletter**.

What you should see on-screen is a small gray bar near the upper left corner of the page. This is the word you have just typed, but it is shown *greeked* (grayed) because it is a small point size (12-point Times is the default) and you are looking at a reduced view of a full 8 1/2-by-11-inch page on your screen (see fig. 3.9). In the next step, you enlarge the view so that you can read the text.

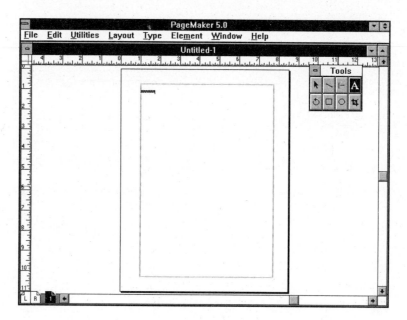

4. Choose Actual Size from the View submenu of the Layout menu.

The display changes to show a closer view of the upper left corner of the page, where the word Newsletter is clearly readable, as shown in figure 3.10. (Other methods of changing the view of the page, including keyboard and mouse shortcuts, are explained in the section "Changing the View of a Page in the Layout Window" in Chapter 5.)

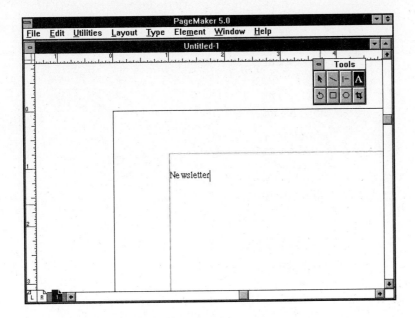

Fig. 3.10

The word
Newsletter in
Actual Size view.

Don't worry if you have typed the word incorrectly. Just go on
with the next steps. (If you want to correct your error now,
Chapter 7 describes how to edit text.)

5. Choose Select All from the Edit menu.

   The text becomes highlighted (shown in reverse video) on-screen.
   This does not affect the way the text will print, but only indicates
   that the text is selected (see fig. 3.11). If this step does not result
   in highlighted text, be sure that the Text tool is selected on the
   toolbox, and click anywhere within the word Newsletter. Then
   try this step again.

   Many other methods of selecting text are described in the section
   "Selecting Text" in Chapter 6.

6. Choose Bold from the Type Style submenu of the Type menu.

   The text becomes bold (thicker) on-screen. If this does not happen, be sure that the text is still highlighted (selected). If it is not,
   go back to step 5. If step 5 does not result in highlighted text, be
   sure that the Text tool is selected on the toolbox, and double-click
   anywhere within the word Newsletter. Then try this step again.

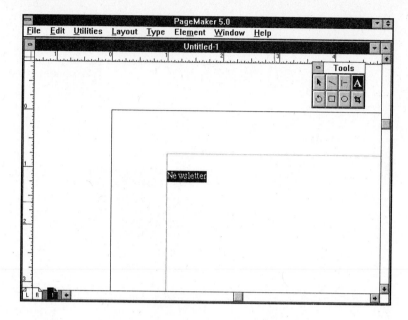

Fig. 3.11

The word
Newsletter
highlighted,
showing that it
is selected.

7. Choose 72 from the Size submenu of the Type menu.

   The list of available type sizes depends on the fonts you have
   installed and the printer you are using. If 72 is not listed on the
   Size submenu, choose Other and type **72** in the Type Size dialog
   box. Then click OK to close it. If, for some reason, you cannot
   enter 72 by either of these methods, just choose the largest type
   size available on your system. The text is enlarged, some of it
   extending off the screen display (see fig. 3.12).

8. Choose Fit in Window from the View submenu of the Layout
   menu.

   When you return to a view of the whole page, the enlarged text is
   clearly readable (see fig. 3.13). Only smaller type sizes are greeked
   (grayed) in reduced views. To change the size in which text is
   greeked on-screen, see the section "Changing Preferences" in
   Chapter 4.

Fig. 3.12

The word
Newsletter
enlarged and
bold.

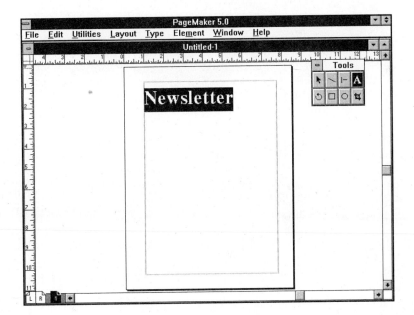

Fig. 3.13

The word
Newsletter in
Fit in Window
view.

Saving the Publication the First Time

To save the publication the first time, follow these steps:

1. Choose Save from the File menu.

   PageMaker displays the Save Publication As dialog box, as shown in figure 3.14.

2. Type the name of the file.

   The name Newsletter appears in figure 3.14, but you can use any name you like (up to eight characters). Don't add an extension; PageMaker supplies the extension PM5 automatically, identifying the file as a PageMaker 5.0 publication.

   In this case, you are saving the publication to the current directory. You can choose another directory if you like. The section "Saving a Document or Template" in Chapter 4 describes the various options for saving a document.

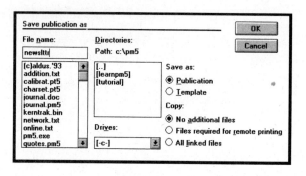

3. Click OK to close the Save Publication As dialog box and save the publication.

The preceding steps create a document file on the hard disk. This file remains unchanged until the next time you use the Save command. Meanwhile, any new work you do is held in the computer memory (RAM), and PageMaker saves interim (temporary) versions of your work on disk. Chapter 4 describes how PageMaker saves files and handles interim versions.

Drawing with PageMaker's Graphics Tools

In this section, you use two graphics tools to draw a line and rectangle as part of the banner for the newsletter. Follow these steps:

1. Click the Constrained-Line tool on the toolbox (see fig. 3.15).

    Two line tools are on the toolbox: the Line tool, which draws lines at any angle; and the Constrained-Line tool, which draws lines at any angle divisible by 45 degrees. In this case, you use the Constrained-Line tool (see fig. 3.15), but it doesn't matter which one you choose here. See the section "Drawing Straight Lines" in Chapter 9.

Fig. 3.15

The Constrained-Line tool selected on the toolbox.

    The I-beam now changes to a crossbar. All of PageMaker's drawing tools work the same way. You first move the mouse to position the crossbar on the page or pasteboard, and then hold down the mouse button as you drag the crossbar. The object appears on-screen as you drag. As long as you press the mouse button, you can keep adjusting the size of the object. When you release the mouse button, the graphic is set.

2. To create a straight line across the top of the page, position the crossbar at the upper left corner of the margins, hold down the mouse button, drag across to the upper right corner of the margins, and release the mouse button.

    The line shows as a solid black line at the top margin, framed by two small square "handles" indicating that the line is selected (see fig. 3.16). Do not click the mouse again until after the next step, or you will deselect the line. (If you do, simply skip the next step, or see Chapter 5 or 9 to learn how to select graphics on a page.)

    Don't worry if you have drawn the line incorrectly—too short or too long. Just go on with the next steps. (If you want to correct your error now, Chapter 9 explains how to edit lines. To change the size or position of a completed graphic, you must switch to the Pointer tool.)

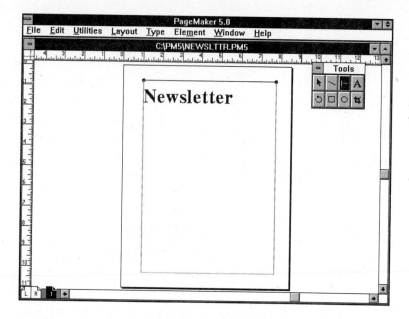

Fig. 3.16

Small squares
or "handles"
displayed at the
ends of the line.

3. Choose 12pt (12-point type) from the Line submenu of the
   Element menu (see fig. 3.17).

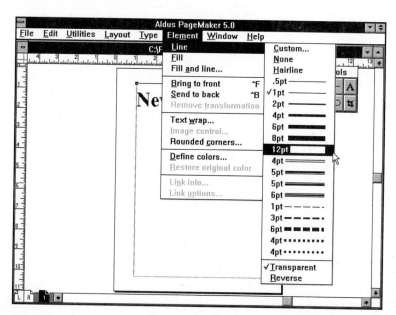

Fig. 3.17

The Line submenu
of the Element
menu with
12-point type
selected.

The line changes to a wider black strip at the top of the page (see fig. 3.18, which illustrates the next step).

If the line overlaps the word Newsletter, you can move that text down by choosing the Pointer tool on the toolbox, clicking the text to select it, and dragging the text down a bit. These techniques are described in Chapters 5 and 6. If you are learning PageMaker and Windows for the first time, leave any minor improvements to the newsletter's appearance until later. Just go on with the next steps now.

4. Click the Rectangle tool on the toolbox (see fig. 3.18).

The pointer remains a crossbar.

Fig. 3.18

The Rectangle tool selected on the toolbox.

5. Position the crossbar at the upper right corner of the margins, hold down the mouse button, and drag diagonally down and to the left, stopping near the bottom of the letter r in Newsletter.

The rectangle appears as you drag the mouse. When you release the mouse button, the rectangle is framed by eight square handles indicating that it is selected (see fig. 3.19). Do not click the mouse again until after the next step, or you will deselect the line. (If you do, simply skip the next step, or see Chapter 5 or 9 to learn how to select graphics on a page.)

Fig. 3.19

The rectangle
displaying eight
handles, one at
each corner and
one in the center
of each side.

Don't worry if you have drawn the rectangle incorrectly. Just go
on with the next steps. (If you want to correct your error now,
Chapter 9 explains how to change rectangles.)

6. Choose Solid from the Fill submenu of the Element menu (see
   fig. 3.20).

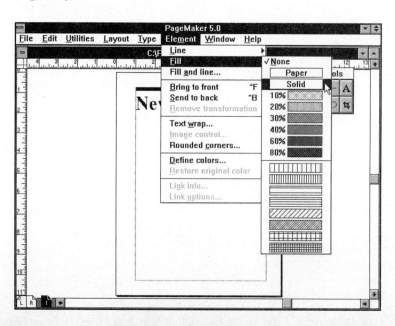

Fig. 3.20

The Fill submenu
of the Element
menu with Solid
selected.

The rectangle changes to a solid black shape at the top of the page (see fig. 3.21).

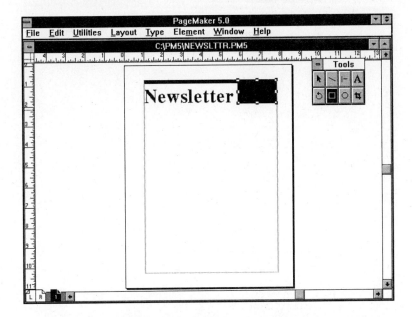

The newsletter banner.

In the next steps, you copy the solid line at the top of the banner and move the copy just below the word Newsletter.

7. Choose the Pointer tool by clicking the arrow at the upper left of the toolbox.

8. Click the solid line at the top of the banner.

   The line displays the small handles at each end to show that the line is selected (see fig. 3.22). If this does not happen, try again. Be sure that you are clicking on the line itself (not on the rectangle or the text of the banner) and that you are using the Pointer tool.

9. From the Edit menu, first choose Copy and then choose Paste.

   A second line appears, slightly offset from the first. The small handles show that the second line is selected (see fig. 3.23).

10. Position the pointer over the second line and hold down the mouse button. Drag the line below the word Newsletter and position the line between the margins and at the bottom of the rectangle. Then release the mouse button (see fig. 3.24).

Fig. 3.22

The line selected at the top of the banner, showing handles at each end.

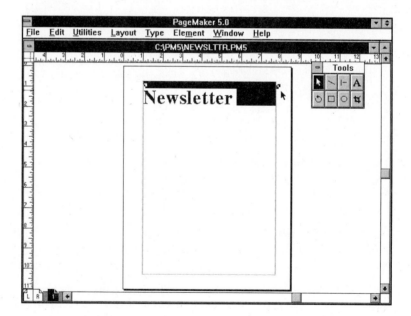

Fig. 3.23

The second line, slightly offset from the first.

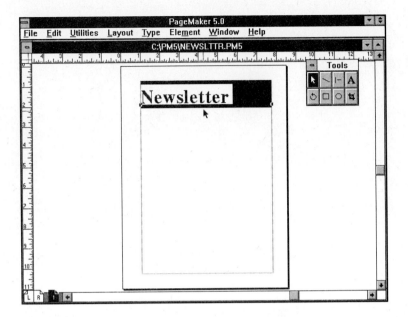

Fig. 3.24

The newsletter
banner.

If your newsletter banner does not look exactly like that shown in figure 3.24, simply go on with the next steps and leave any fine-tuning for later. If the bottom of the rectangle does not reach to the top of the line when you position it below the word `Newslet-ter`, you can change the size of the rectangle with techniques described in Chapter 9. You will use the same technique later in this tutorial to size an imported graphic.

Of course, a real newsletter banner usually contains the date, volume, and issue number, along with a subheading to indicate what the newsletter is about or where it is published. In the interest of keeping this tutorial short, you next learn how to place text and a graphic.

11. Choose Save from the File menu, or use the keyboard shortcut Ctrl+S.

It's a good idea to save your work often. After you have saved your work the first time, PageMaker does not display a dialog box in response to the Save command. The program simply saves the publication by replacing the previously saved version with whatever changes you have made since that last save.

Changing the Number of Columns

Until now, you have been working with one column, but a newsletter often has two or more columns. In this section, you change the number of columns before placing text on the page. You want the number of columns to be the same on every page, so to make this change, you turn to the master pages first. This way, you have to set the number of columns only once, instead of setting them once for each page. Follow these steps:

1. Click the L and R page icons at the bottom left corner of the screen. (Both letters are selected when you click either of them.)

   The display changes to show two facing pages. These are the master pages (see fig. 3.25). Master pages are described in detail in Chapter 5.

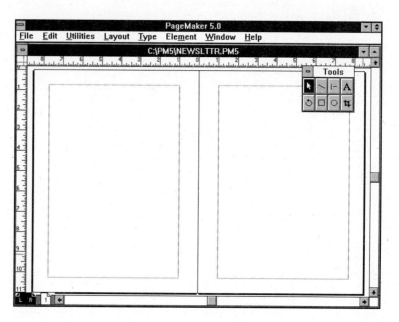

Fig. 3.25

The master pages
displayed as two
facing pages.

2. Choose Column Guides from the Layout menu.

   PageMaker displays the Column Guides dialog box.

3. Type **3** as the number of columns (see fig. 3.26).

   Leave all other entries in this dialog box unchanged. Chapter 5 explains in detail how to change column guides.

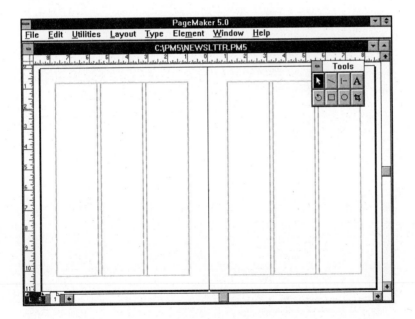

Fig. 3.26

The Column Guides dialog box with 3 entered as the number of columns.

4. Click OK to close the Column Guides dialog box.

   The master pages now show three columns on each page (see fig. 3.27).

Fig. 3.27

The master pages showing three columns.

5. Click the icon for page 1 at the bottom left corner of the screen.

   PageMaker now shows page 1 with three column guides (see fig. 3.28). The master page guides appear on every page of the publication (unless you choose to change them on individual pages).

Fig. 3.28

Page 1 showing three column guides.

Notice that changing the page to three columns does not affect the width of the word Newsletter in the banner. Changing column guides does not affect text that is already on the page.

Placing Text

In this section, you import text that has been created in another program—a word processor. Using a word processor to type text and then import it to PageMaker is common in many production settings. The reason is that writers often use different systems, not necessarily under Microsoft Windows, to create the text and then pass it along to the production department, which uses PageMaker. Follow these steps:

1. Choose Place from the File menu.

   It doesn't matter which tool you use in this step. PageMaker displays the Place Document dialog box, showing the list of text files and graphics files that can be placed from the current directory (see fig. 3.29).

   Don't worry if the list on your screen is different from the list shown in figure 3.29. If your list is different, see "Using Your Own Files" following the next step.

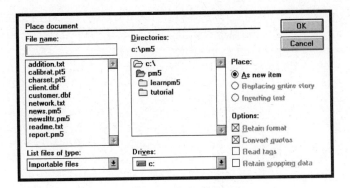

Fig. 3.29

The Place
Document dialog
box showing text
files and
graphics files in
the current
directory.

2. Double-click the directory name TUTORIAL in the list in the
middle of the Place Document dialog box. Then double-click the
directory name LESSON1 to view the files in that directory (see
fig. 3.30).

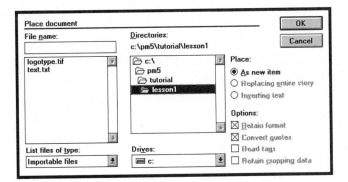

Fig. 3.30

The Place
Document dialog
box showing text
files and
graphics files in
the LESSON1
directory.

Using Your Own Files

In step 2, you change directories and find the file you want to
place. If you have not loaded the tutorial files that come with
PageMaker 5.0, you can use the same technique to change
directories and find any other text file on your system, or
you can place the README.TXT file in the PM5 directory.
What you want to do is place almost any text file on your
system, but preferably one that is about two pages long (because more time is needed to compose longer text files).

3. Double-click the file named TEXT.TXT.

Because this file is an unformatted (ASCII) text file, PageMaker displays the Text-Only Import Filter dialog box (see fig. 3.31).

Text-only import filter, v1.5   [OK]
Remove extra carriage returns: [Cancel]
☐ At end of every line
☐ Between paragraphs
☐ But keep tables, lists and indents as is
☐ Replace [3] or more spaces with a tab
☐ Monospace, import as Courier
☒ No conversion, import as is
◉ DOS text file (ASCII)
○ Windows text file (ANSI)

Using Your Own Files

If you are placing some other text file that has been formatted, the Text-Only Import Filter dialog box will not appear. In that case, just skip to step 5. If you are placing a file that is not recognized by PageMaker, a dialog box appears asking you to specify the type of file. Choose a file type or choose a different file, if necessary.

4. Click OK in the Text-Only Import Filter dialog box without making any changes.

PageMaker returns to the display of page 1, and the mouse pointer changes to a "loaded" text-placement icon (see fig. 3.32). Be careful not to click the mouse until step 5. If your loaded text icon looks different—that is, it appears as a curved line with an arrow—then Autoflow has been selected on the Layout menu. Deselect Autoflow (by choosing that command from the Layout menu) before going to the next step. The Autoflow option is explained in Chapter 6.

5. Position the loaded text icon at the top of the first column, below the banner, and click (see fig. 3.32).

The text flows to the bottom of the first column (see fig. 3.33). Notice that the text is framed in handles or *windowshades*, indicating that the text is selected. The down-pointing arrow in the bottom windowshade indicates that there is more text to be placed.

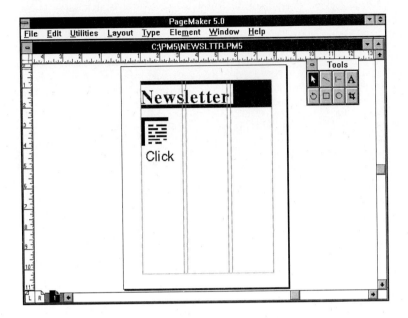

Fig. 3.32

Clicking the loaded text icon at the top of the first column, below the banner.

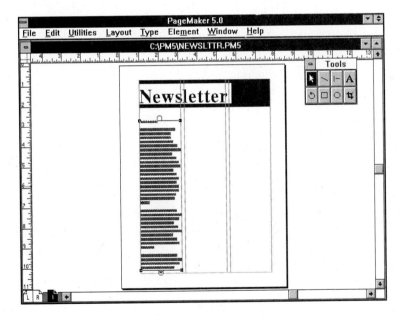

Fig. 3.33

The first column filled with text.

Using Your Own Files

If your text does not fill the column and the bottom windowshade does not show a down-pointing arrow, the text file is too short to fill the column. In this case, click the small empty square at the bottom of the text block and drag the windowshade up several lines to shorten the text block before going to the next step. A down-pointing arrow should appear when you release the mouse button.

6. To save your work before going on, choose Save from the File menu, or use the keyboard shortcut Ctrl+S.

Continuing Text to the Next Column

To continue text to the next column, follow these steps:

1. Click the down-pointing arrow in the small square of the bottom handle in the first column (see fig. 3.34).

   If the text is not framed in handles, it is not selected. To select the text and display the handles, choose the Pointer tool on the toolbox and click once anywhere on the text. If the bottom handle does not show a down-pointing arrow, see the preceding "Using Your Own Files" information for a solution.

   The pointer changes to a loaded text icon, as shown in figure 3.35.

2. Position the loaded text icon at the top of the second column, below the banner, and click (see fig. 3.35).

   The text flows into the second column (see fig. 3.36). In this case, the text didn't quite reach the bottom of the column. The empty square in the center of the bottom windowshade indicates that there is no more text to place.

   In the next steps, you place the same text file again, filling up the third column and continuing to a second page if you want to. Because the next few steps repeat those in the preceding section on placing text, fewer details and illustrations are provided here.

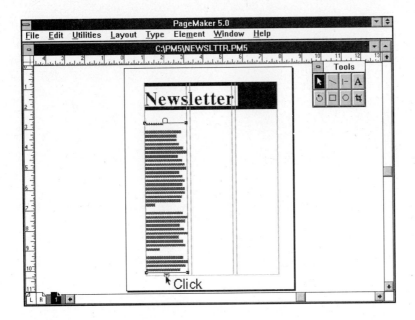

Fig. 3.34

Click the down-
pointing arrow
in the bottom
handle.

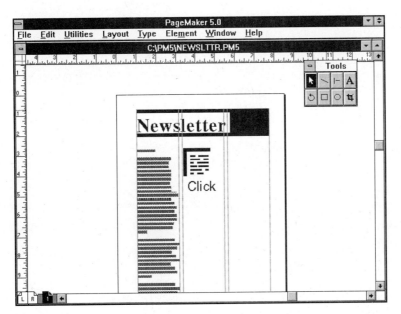

Fig. 3.35

Click the loaded
text icon at the
top of the second
column.

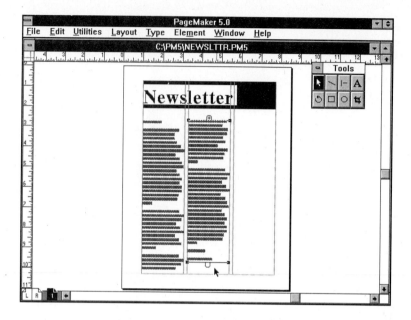

Fig. 3.36

The second column filled with text.

Using Your Own Files

Don't worry if the text on your screen is different from that shown in figure 3.36. If you are placing a longer file, the text will fill the entire second column and end with a down-pointing arrow in the bottom windowshade. Continue placing the text in the third column by using the same technique described in steps 1 and 2. Then go to step 3 if the text does not fill the third column entirely, and place the text again, starting just below where your text ends in the third column. When the text fills the third column and a down-pointing arrow appears in the bottom handle, go to step 7.

3. Choose Place from the File menu.

   PageMaker displays the Place Document dialog box, showing the list of text files and graphics files that can be placed from the current directory. This directory should be the same as the previous directory from which you placed text (refer to fig. 3.30).

4. Double-click the file named TEXT.TXT.

   PageMaker displays the Text-Only Import Filter dialog box (refer to fig. 3.31).

5. Click OK in the Text-Only Import Filter dialog box without making any changes.

PageMaker returns to the display of page 1, and the mouse pointer changes to a loaded text icon, as shown in figure 3.37.

6. Position the text icon at the top of the third column, below the banner, and click (see fig. 3.37).

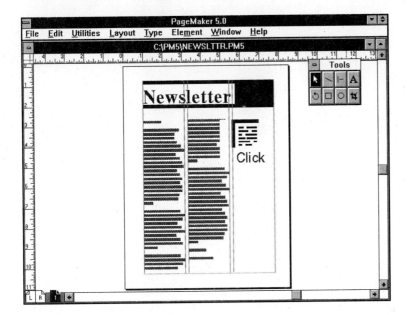

Fig. 3.37

Click the loaded text icon at the top of the third column, below the banner.

The text flows to the bottom of the third column (see fig. 3.38).

The first page is now filled with text, but the down-pointing arrow at the bottom of the third column indicates that there is still more text to be placed. You will need to get the loaded text icon again before adding a new page.

NOTE If you don't want to learn how to add new pages and place text from one page to another, you can skip the next section and go directly to the section "Placing a Graphic."

7. Click the down-pointing arrow at the bottom of the third column (see fig. 3.39).

Remember that if the text is not framed in handles, it is not selected. To select the text and display the handles, choose the Pointer tool on the toolbox and click once anywhere on the text. If the bottom handle does not show a down-pointing arrow, refer to the preceding section.

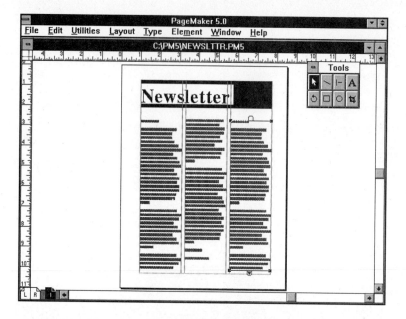

Fig. 3.38

The third column filled with text.

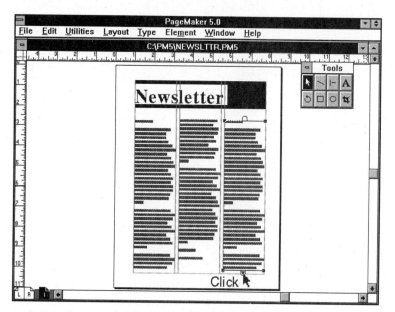

Fig. 3.39

Click the down-pointing arrow at the bottom of the third column.

The pointer becomes a loaded text icon. You can choose commands from the menus with the loaded text icon, but don't click the mouse on the page.

Inserting a Page

To insert a page, follow these steps:

1. Choose Insert Pages from the Layout menu.

   PageMaker displays the Insert Pages dialog box, with the default of two pages being inserted after the current page (see fig. 3.40).

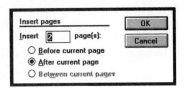

Fig. 3.40

The Insert Pages dialog box.

2. Click OK without making any changes in the Insert Pages dialog box.

   The display changes to show two blank, facing pages. Notice that the page icons at the bottom of the screen now show 2 and 3 (see fig. 3.41).

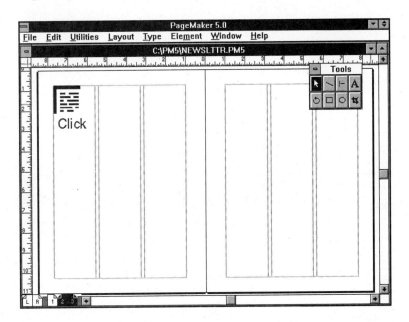

Fig. 3.41

Click the text icon at the top of page 2.

The reason that page 2 does not face page 1 is that in a facing-page layout the even-numbered pages (such as 2) are always on the left of the odd-numbered pages (such as 3). Page 1 has no facing page. In a bound publication, page 1 might face the inside of the front cover, the back of the title page, or the last even-numbered page of the table of contents or preface.

3. At the top of the first column of page 2 (the left-facing page), click the text icon (refer to fig. 3.41).

    The pointer should still be a loaded text icon when you take this step. If it is not, you will need to go back to page 1 (by clicking the page 1 icon at the bottom left of the screen), click the Pointer tool on the text in the third column to select it, click the down-pointing arrow at the bottom of the third column, click the page 2 icon at the bottom of the page, and then repeat this step.

    In this case, the text stops short of filling the column (see fig. 3.42).

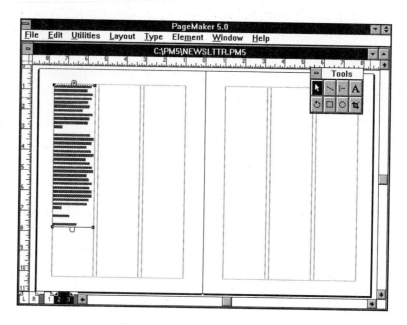

Fig. 3.42

The first column partially filled with text.

Using Your Own Files

If you are placing a different file that is longer, the text will fill the entire column and end with a down-pointing arrow in the bottom windowshade. Continue placing the text in the second and third columns. If you like, continue placing text on page 3, using the technique described in the preceding section. Or just leave the text as is and go on to the next steps.

4. Click the page 1 icon at the bottom left of the screen to return to page 1.

5. To save your work before going on, choose Save from the File menu, or use the keyboard shortcut Ctrl+S.

Placing a Graphic

In this section, you place a graphic on page 1. You can place the graphic directly on top of the text in the center of the page (where you want it to end up), but instead you place the graphic just below the margin at the bottom of the page. This action makes it easier for you to see the handles, scale the graphic before moving it onto the page, and match the width of the graphic to the column. Follow these steps:

1. Choose Place from the File menu.

   PageMaker displays the Place Document dialog box, showing the list of text files and graphics files that can be placed from the current directory. This directory should be the same as the previous directory from which you placed text (refer to fig. 3.30).

Using Your Own Files

Again, don't worry if the list on your screen is different from the one shown in figure 3.30. If you have not loaded the tutorial files that come with PageMaker 5.0, you can use the technique described earlier in the section "Placing Text" to change directories and find any other graphics file on your system. For this tutorial, you can place almost any graphics file on your system.

112

2. Double-click the file named LOGOTYPE.TIF.

   The pointer changes to a graphic placement icon. In this case, the icon is a square containing an X, as shown in figure 3.43. This icon indicates that the file is in a TIF file format (TIFF). (Other file formats and their placement icons are described in Chapter 9.)

3. Position the graphic icon at the left margin, just below the bottom margin, and click (see fig. 3.43).

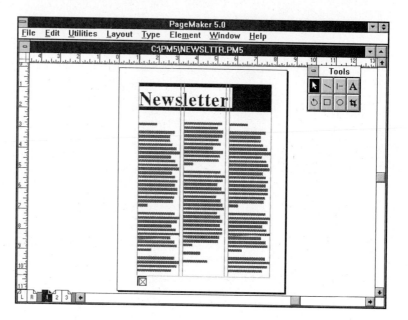

Fig. 3.43

The graphic icon positioned at the left margin and below the bottom margin.

The graphic appears at the bottom of the page (see fig. 3.44). Don't worry if you placed some other graphic of a different size; you learn how to scale the graphic in the next steps.

4. Position the pointer over the graphic and click the secondary mouse button—usually the rightmost button on the mouse.

   You now see an Actual Size view of the area where the mouse was located when you clicked (see fig. 3.45). If this step doesn't work, be sure that you clicked the graphic, not a menu or the toolbox. This shortcut and others for changing views of the page are described in the section "Changing the View of a Page in the Layout Window" in Chapter 5.

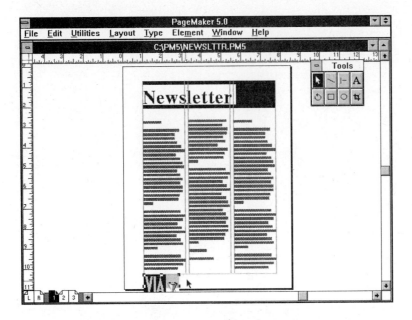

Fig. 3.44

The graphic appearing at the bottom of the page.

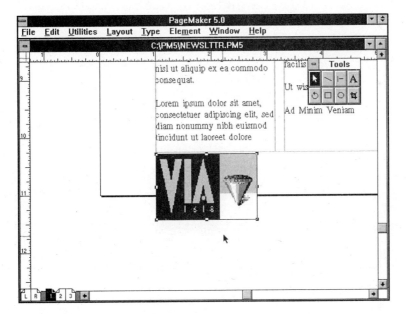

Fig. 3.45

The lower left corner of the page in Actual Size view.

Using Your Own Files

If you placed a different graphic that is larger, you might
need to use one of the commands from the View submenu of
the Layout menu so that you can zoom out to a 75 percent or
50 percent view of the page and see all the handles.

5. Hold down the Shift key as you position the pointer over the small
handle at the lower right corner of the graphic and drag the corner until the width of the graphic matches the width of the column (see fig. 3.46).

Holding down the Shift key as you drag the corner ensures that
the graphic will be scaled proportionally. You must hold down the
Shift key before you begin dragging. If the graphic does not display eight small handles, it is not selected. To display the handles,
you must first select the graphic with the Pointer tool.

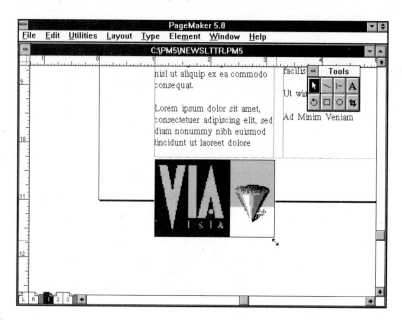

Fig. 3.46

The graphic
scaled propor-
tionally to fit the
width of the
column.

Release the mouse button (and the Shift key) when the graphic is
the width of the first column.

6. Click the secondary mouse button to switch back to Fit in Window view.

   If the first click does not put you in Fit in Window view, perhaps you were not already in Actual Size view. Click the secondary mouse button again.

7. Position the pointer over the graphic and hold down the mouse button as you drag the graphic to the center of the second column on the page (see fig. 3.47).

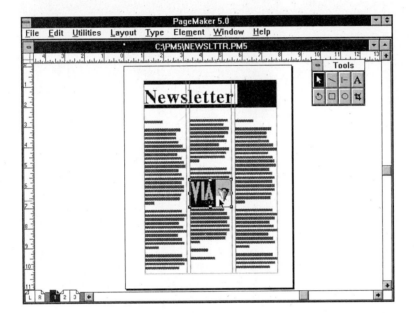

Fig. 3.47

The graphic dragged to the center of the second column.

8. Position the pointer over the graphic and click the secondary mouse button to jump to an Actual Size view of the graphic again (see fig. 3.48).

9. Position the pointer over the graphic and hold down the mouse button as you drag the graphic up and down a bit on the page.

   The graphic becomes slightly transparent, and you can see text under it. In the next steps, you force the text to wrap around the graphic.

10. With the graphic still selected, choose Text Wrap from the Element menu.

    PageMaker displays the Text Wrap dialog box, as shown in figure 3.49.

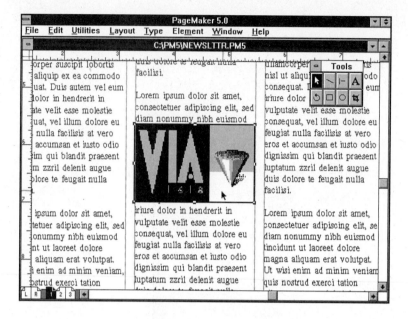

Fig. 3.48

Actual Size view
of the graphic.

11. Click the second Wrap option in the Text Wrap dialog box (see
    fig. 3.49).

    Notice that the third Text Flow option is automatically selected in
    the dialog box (see fig. 3.49).

Fig. 3.49

The Text Wrap
dialog box with
the second Wrap
option selected.

12. Click OK to close the Text Wrap dialog box.

    The text shifts to flow above and below the graphic. You can see
    a second set of handles now, at the corners of a dotted-line rect-
    angle that frames the graphic. This rectangle shows the limits of
    the text offset—the distance between the text and the graphic—as
    defined in the Text Wrap dialog box (see fig. 3.50). The section

"Wrapping Text around Graphics" in Chapter 11 explains how to manipulate the handles on the text-wrap border to create irregular text wrap.

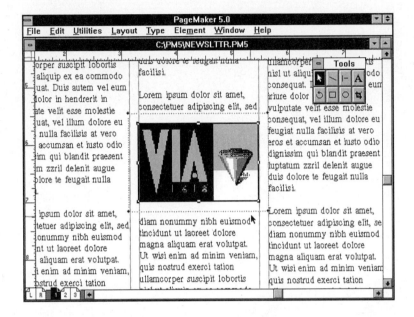

Fig. 3.50

Text wrapped around the graphic.

13. To save your work before going on, choose Save from the File menu, or use the keyboard shortcut Ctrl+S.

Formatting Text

To change the format of the imported text, follow these steps:

1. Position the pointer near the upper left corner of the screen. Hold down the Alt key while you hold down the mouse button and drag to the bottom center of the window.

   The mouse pointer should change to a hand—the "grabber hand"—when you press the mouse button while holding down the Alt key. If this does not happen and you inadvertently move the text block from the first column on the page, choose Undo from the Edit menu immediately. The goal is to move to an Actual Size view of the beginning of the first text block. Use the scroll bars if necessary to make your screen look like that in figure 3.51.

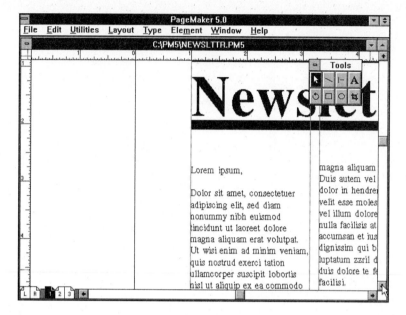

Fig. 3.51

The page
dragged down
and to the right.

T   I   P   **A Short Lesson in Greek**

Now that you can see the text up close, you may think that it is in some strange language (if you placed the same file used in this tutorial). This text is what typographers call "Greek" text, although it actually looks like Latin. *Greek text* is an old standard series of characters, repeated over and over, used to set "dummy" text for sample layouts or to measure the number of characters per inch in different type sizes and fonts. Remember that in PageMaker, text is also said to be *greeked* when small fonts appear in gray in reduced views. Of course, the text does not really appear in the Greek language in either of these cases.

2. Select the Text tool by clicking the letter *A* in the upper right corner of the toolbox.

   The pointer changes to an I-beam. You use the Text tool to select individual characters within a text block.

3. Position the I-beam over the first character in the first line of text. Then hold down the mouse button as you drag from the left to the right to select the first line of text.

The selected text is highlighted (see fig. 3.52). If the text is not highlighted (as shown in figure 3.52), try selecting the text again. Be sure that the I-beam is within the text block (not in the margin) before you hold down the mouse button. If you have trouble getting the first letter of the text, try dragging from the last character in the line to the first character.

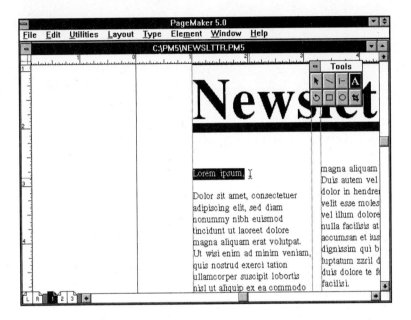

Fig. 3.52

The selected (highlighted) text.

Using Your Own Files

If you placed different text and your first line is more than 20 characters long, shorten your selection to 20 characters.

4. Choose Type Specs from the Type menu.

   PageMaker displays the Type Specifications dialog box (see fig. 3.53).

5. Select (or type) 24 in the Size entry box and then click Bold at the bottom of the dialog box.

   You can type a number in the Size entry box, or you can select a number from the drop-down list that appears when you choose Size (refer to fig. 3.53). For a complete explanation of how to make entries in dialog boxes, see the section "Making Entries in Dialog Boxes" in Chapter 2.

Fig. 3.53

The Type
Specifications
dialog box with
Bold selected
and the Size
pull-down
menu open.

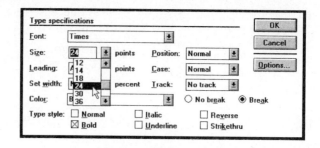

You can choose a different font if you like. The list of fonts in the
Font drop-down list depends on what fonts are installed on your
system. See the section "Font Management" in Chapter 13 for
more information on installing fonts.

6. Click OK to close the Type Specifications dialog box.

   The screen shows the selected text larger and bolder (see
   fig. 3.54).

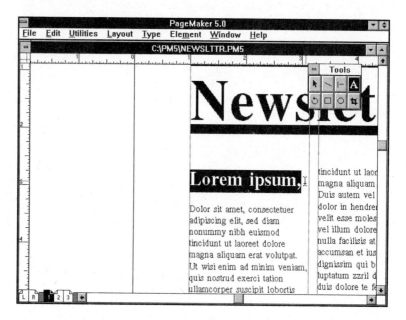

Fig. 3.54

The selected text
shown larger and
bolder.

In the next steps, you make a specific change to the imported text.
If you imported a different text file, you can use the same technique to make any change to your text.

7. Click the I-beam once at the end of the first line, just after the comma.

   This step removes the highlighting from the whole line (deselects it) and positions the text-insertion point (the cursor) after the comma, as shown in figure 3.55.

   Lorem ipsum,

   Using Your Own Files

   If you placed different text and the first paragraph was more than 20 characters (or more than the characters you se-lected and enlarged), position the cursor after the last en-larged character and press Enter to create a new paragraph. Then skip the next step.

8. Press the Backspace key to delete the comma.

   The cursor moves left, and the comma is deleted.

9. To return to Fit in Window view, click the secondary mouse button anywhere on the page.

   The enlarged headline is now readable in Fit in Window view if your screen has a high enough resolution. Otherwise, the headline appears in gray (greeked), as shown in figure 3.56.

   Notice that the text in the second column now extends beyond the bottom margin. This happened because you inserted the graphic in that column. Chapter 6 explains in detail how to adjust the length of text blocks. For now, just leave the text as is and go to the next section on printing the page.

10. Choose Save from the File menu.

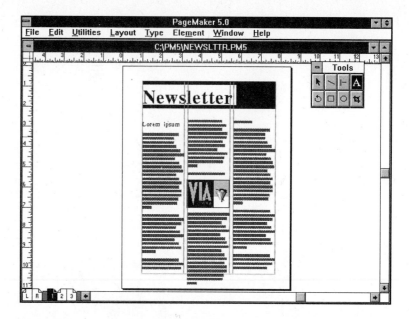

Fig. 3.56

Fit in Window
view of the
newsletter.

Printing the Publication

You can print the page if a printer is hooked up to your system. If you
do not want to print the page, skip to the next section, "A Quick Trip
through the Control Palette," or to the last section, "Exiting PageMaker
and Windows." To print the page, follow these steps:

1. Choose Print from the File menu.

   PageMaker displays the Print Document dialog box.

2. Press the Tab key until the Ranges area is highlighted, and type 1
   to print page 1 only (see fig. 3.57).

3. Click the Print button to close the dialog box and begin printing.

   For this section of the tutorial, you should have PageMaker already set up to print to your current printer. If you are not ready
   to print your publication, refer to Chapter 10, which describes in
   detail how to set up a printer and print a publication. The final
   printout of page 1 appears in figure 3.58.

4. Choose Save from the File menu.

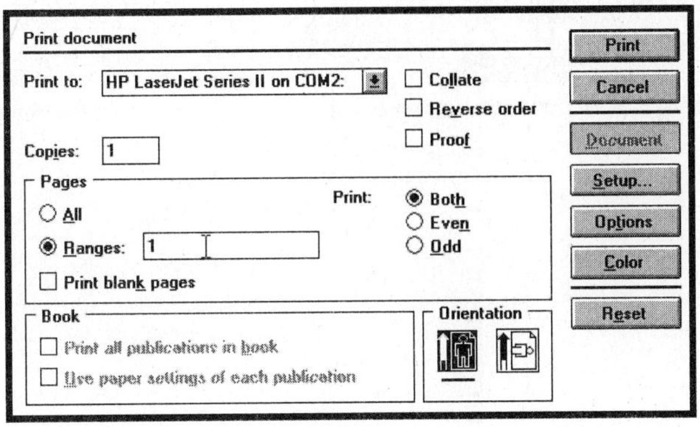

Fig. 3.57

The Print Document dialog box set to print page 1 only.

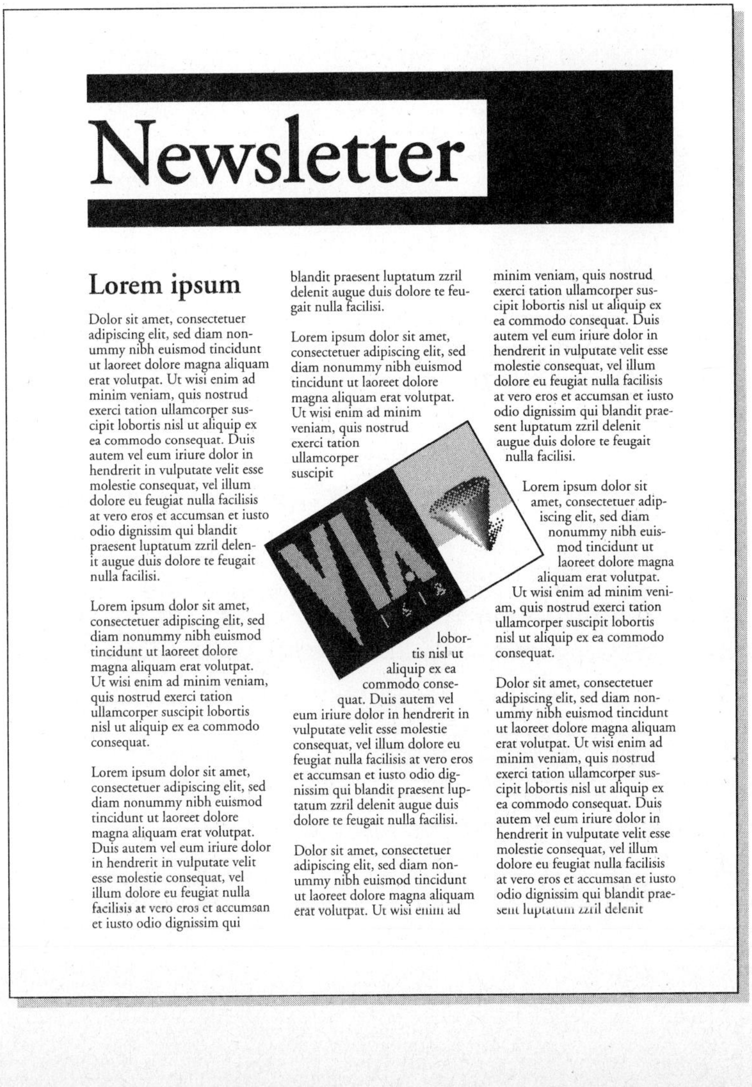

Newsletter

Lorem ipsum

Dolor sit amet, consectetuer adipiscing elit, sed diam nonummy nibh euismod tincidunt ut laoreet dolore magna aliquam erat volutpat. Ut wisi enim ad minim veniam, quis nostrud exerci tation ullamcorper suscipit lobortis nisl ut aliquip ex ea commodo consequat. Duis autem vel eum iriure dolor in hendrerit in vulputate velit esse molestie consequat, vel illum dolore eu feugiat nulla facilisis at vero eros et accumsan et iusto odio dignissim qui blandit praesent luptatum zzril delenit augue duis dolore te feugait nulla facilisi.

Lorem ipsum dolor sit amet, consectetuer adipiscing elit, sed diam nonummy nibh euismod tincidunt ut laoreet dolore magna aliquam erat volutpat. Ut wisi enim ad minim veniam, quis nostrud exerci tation ullamcorper suscipit lobortis nisl ut aliquip ex ea commodo consequat.

Lorem ipsum dolor sit amet, consectetuer adipiscing elit, sed diam nonummy nibh euismod tincidunt ut laoreet dolore magna aliquam erat volutpat. Duis autem vel eum iriure dolor in hendrerit in vulputate velit esse molestie consequat, vel illum dolore eu feugiat nulla facilisis at vero eros et accumsan et iusto odio dignissim qui blandit praesent luptatum zzril delenit augue duis dolore te feugait nulla facilisi.

Lorem ipsum dolor sit amet, consectetuer adipiscing elit, sed diam nonummy nibh euismod tincidunt ut laoreet dolore magna aliquam erat volutpat. Ut wisi enim ad minim veniam, quis nostrud exerci tation ullamcorper suscipit

lobortis nisl ut aliquip ex ea commodo consequat. Duis autem vel eum iriure dolor in hendrerit in vulputate velit esse molestie consequat, vel illum dolore eu feugiat nulla facilisis at vero eros et accumsan et iusto odio dignissim qui blandit praesent luptatum zzril delenit augue duis dolore te feugait nulla facilisi.

Dolor sit amet, consectetuer adipiscing elit, sed diam nonummy nibh euismod tincidunt ut laoreet dolore magna aliquam erat volutpat. Ut wisi enim ad minim veniam, quis nostrud exerci tation ullamcorper suscipit lobortis nisl ut aliquip ex ea commodo consequat. Duis autem vel eum iriure dolor in hendrerit in vulputate velit esse molestie consequat, vel illum dolore eu feugiat nulla facilisis at vero eros et accumsan et iusto odio dignissim qui blandit praesent luptatum zzril delenit augue duis dolore te feugait nulla facilisi.

Lorem ipsum dolor sit amet, consectetuer adipiscing elit, sed diam nonummy nibh euismod tincidunt ut laoreet dolore magna aliquam erat volutpat. Ut wisi enim ad minim veniam, quis nostrud exerci tation ullamcorper suscipit lobortis nisl ut aliquip ex ea commodo consequat.

Dolor sit amet, consectetuer adipiscing elit, sed diam nonummy nibh euismod tincidunt ut laoreet dolore magna aliquam erat volutpat. Ut wisi enim ad minim veniam, quis nostrud exerci tation ullamcorper suscipit lobortis nisl ut aliquip ex ea commodo consequat. Duis autem vel eum iriure dolor in hendrerit in vulputate velit esse molestie consequat, vel illum dolore eu feugiat nulla facilisis at vero eros et accumsan et iusto odio dignissim qui blandit praesent luptatum zzril delenit

Fig. 3.58

The finished page.

A Quick Trip through the Control Palette

The steps in this section are optional; you can create whole publications without ever using the Control palette, which is a new feature added in PageMaker 5.0. Here you use the Control palette for the one category of features you cannot get to any other way: transformations (rotating and skewing). If you do not want to try using these features now, skip to the last section, "Exiting PageMaker and Windows."

If you are already familiar with PageMaker, you may be especially interested in these features. If that is the case, use the Rectangle tool to draw a rectangle and then follow these steps:

1. Choose Control Palette from the Window menu (if the palette is not already displayed).

    The appearance of the Control palette changes, depending on what is selected. Various appearances of the Control palette are described in the section "Examining the Control Palette" in Chapter 2. If the Text tool is still selected and the cursor is positioned within the text block (as you left it earlier), the Control palette will be displayed in Character view (see fig. 3.59).

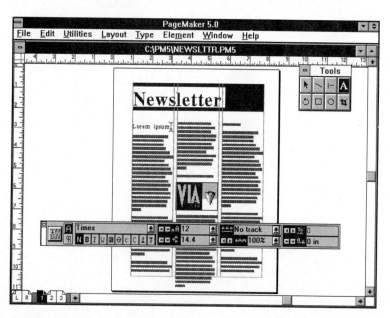

Fig. 3.59

The Control palette displayed in Character view.

2. Choose the Pointer tool by clicking the arrow at the upper left corner of the toolbox.

3. To select the graphic in the center of the page, click the Pointer tool on the graphic.

    The selected graphic displays handles, and the Control palette changes to Layout view (see fig. 3.60).

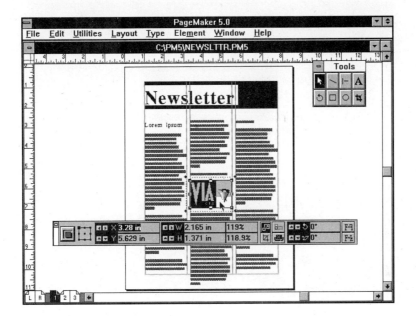

Fig. 3.60

The graphic selected with the Pointer tool.

You can change the position of the graphic by pressing the Tab key until the X or Y value is highlighted and then entering a new value. You can alter the size of the graphic by highlighting the W or H value and entering a new value. Try these changes on your own if you like. In the next steps, you jump right to the exciting new transformation capabilities of PageMaker 5.0.

4. Press the Tab key until the 0° at the far right (next to the rotation symbol) is highlighted. Then type **30** (see fig. 3.61).

5. Press Enter for the change to take effect on the page.

    The selected graphic is rotated 30 degrees, and the text shifts to fit around the new shape (see fig. 3.62).

Fig. 3.61

A rotation value
of 30 degrees
entered in the
Control palette.

Rotation value

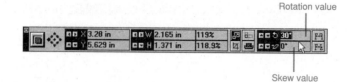

Skew value

Fig. 3.62

The text shifted to
fit around the
rotated graphic.

6. Press Tab again to move to the skew value (below the rotation value). Type **30** and press Enter again.

   The selected graphic is skewed 30 degrees, as well as rotated. Again, the text shifts to fit around the new shape of the graphic (see fig. 3.63).

If you have time, use the Control palette to make other changes on the page you have created. Practice what you have learned by changing other type specifications, or try to adjust the length of the text in the second column. Use this book as a reference in answering questions as they come up. When you are ready to end your session, go on with the steps in the following section.

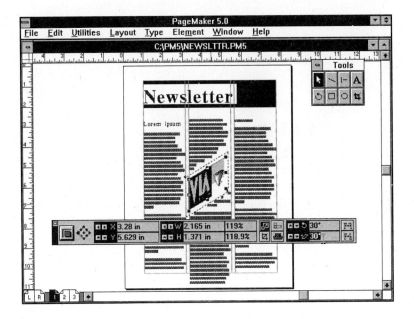

Fig. 3.63

A skew value
of 30 degrees
entered in the
Control palette.

Exiting PageMaker and Windows

If you want to close the current publication but keep working in PageMaker, stop after step 1. If you want to exit PageMaker but keep working in Windows, skip to step 2 and stop there. If you want to exit PageMaker and Windows, skip to step 2 and go on with step 3. Following are the steps:

1. To close the current publication, choose Close from the File menu.

    If you have recently saved your document, PageMaker simply closes the publication. If you have not saved your document since you made changes, PageMaker displays a dialog box asking whether you want to save the document before you close it. See the section "Closing a Document Window" in Chapter 4.

    Now you can go on working in PageMaker. You can choose New or Open from the File menu (to open a new or an existing PageMaker publication or template), or you can choose any of the available commands from the menus when no publication is open (and thereby change the defaults for your system). These procedures are explained in Chapter 4.

128

2. To exit PageMaker, choose Exit from the File menu.

In the Windows environment, you can run other programs without closing PageMaker. When you do want to leave PageMaker, however, you can use the Exit command on the File menu, or the Close command on the Control menu of the application window. PageMaker verifies that you have saved your current document. If you have not saved the current document, PageMaker displays a dialog box asking whether you want to save your changes as well as close PageMaker (see Chapter 4).

When you leave PageMaker, you return to Windows opening screen or to a full-screen view of the other windows that are open.

3. To leave the Windows program, choose Close from the Control menu of the Windows Program Manager window.

The Windows program always asks you to confirm in a dialog box whether you want to end the session.

Summary

This tutorial has taken you through all the basic steps in creating and printing a publication in PageMaker. You can begin building new publications on your own, using this book simply as a reference in solving the problems you encounter. A better approach, however, is to review Chapter 2 carefully (if you haven't already) and to look at Chapters 4 and 5 for an overview of the recommended, detailed steps in building a publication from scratch. Chapter 14 offers many useful suggestions if you will be creating large publications or working on large projects with many other people. Chapters 15 and 16 provide useful design tips as well as efficiency tips.

The Production Process with PageMaker

PART

II

OUTLINE

Part II describes the production process in detail. You learn about the tools for creating text and graphics in PageMaker, and the various methods of bringing text and graphics from other applications into PageMaker.

Part II also teaches you how to edit and format text and graphics in PageMaker and how to print black-and-white publications.

In short, Part II describes all the essential aspects of the production process involved in using PageMaker. More advanced features are described in Part III.

Starting a New Publication

I n this chapter, the initial setup steps in the page-layout process are isolated and described in detail. These steps include starting a new document, defining the page size and margins, and saving a new publication onto disk. The chapter guides you through the following procedures:

- Opening a new PageMaker publication

- Entering page-layout specifications in the Page Setup dialog box

- Defining your preferences for the on-screen page display

- Saving the new document as either a publication or a template

If you have never used PageMaker, carefully review this chapter and the next five chapters, and try creating a few short, simple publications before launching your first major publishing project. After you become familiar with the operations described in Chapters 1 through 10, you can take on the advanced features described in Part III of this book (Chapters 11 through 14).

This chapter builds on the first two chapters, and assumes that you are familiar with the basic operations described in Chapter 2. The Introduction and Chapter 1 of this book summarize the overall sequence of creating a PageMaker document. Chapter 2 describes the basics of working with Microsoft Windows and examines PageMaker's opening screen and menus. If you have never used PageMaker before, it would be a good idea to go through Chapter 3 as well, which presents a quick tutorial to take you through the full page-layout process in about 30 minutes.

This chapter describes the initial setup procedures only, and you could skip it (for now) if you are starting with a template or an existing publication. The next chapter explains how to add elements—guides, text, and graphics—to a page. Chapters 6 and 9 explain how to use other programs to prepare text and graphics before starting to build a PageMaker publication and how to import the text and graphics into PageMaker. Chapters 6, 7, 8, and 9 also describe how to use Page-Maker's tools in creating and editing your imported text and graphics.

The procedures in this chapter are described mainly from a production perspective, assuming that you already know the design specifications for your publication and that your task is to build the publication according to those specifications. In Chapter 15, several of these procedures are reviewed from a designer's perspective. The examples in Part V (Chapters 17 through 21) show basic design principles applied to PageMaker publications.

Understanding PageMaker Terms

Many terms describing the elements in a PageMaker publication are discussed in Part I of this book. The following paragraphs summarize those key terms used in this chapter.

A PageMaker file is called a *publication* and is composed of numbered pages and master pages. *Numbered pages* are those pages of the document you print. *Master pages* contain nonprinting guides (margin guides, column guides, ruler guides) that help you position items consistently on document pages. Master pages also can contain text and graphics items that print repeatedly on multiple document pages, such as page numbers or logos.

Pages are displayed in *Layout view* exactly as they appear when printed. In Layout view, you can use the area beyond the paper's edges as a *pasteboard* for storing elements you have not yet positioned on a page. You can view, type, and edit text more quickly, however, in *Story view*, where text is displayed in only one font and graphics are displayed as gray boxes.

The fundamental element of text in PageMaker is the *text block*. Text blocks can be chained together to direct the flow of text from page to page or from block to block on the same page. Text flows automatically if you set *Autoflow* to On for imported text. PageMaker also enables you to connect a series of text blocks manually. The stream of text that flows through a chain of text blocks is called a *story*.

Imported graphics also can be stored as part of the PageMaker publication or *linked* to the publication at the time of printing, as described in Chapter 13. A series of PageMaker publications can be associated and printed together as a *book*, as described in Chapter 14.

The Glossary at the back of this book defines these and other terms related to PageMaker or to document production and design in general.

Opening a Publication

You can create a new document in PageMaker by starting the program, choosing New from the File menu, making the appropriate entries in the Page Setup dialog box, and then positioning items on the first page of the new publication. If the document you want to create is similar to other documents you already have created, you may save time by opening the similar document, modifying that document, and saving the modified document under a different name. These two options (starting with a blank publication or cloning an existing publication), outlined briefly in the sections that follow, are covered in more detail in Chapter 2. The remainder of the chapter describes the steps used in creating a publication from scratch.

Starting a New PageMaker Publication

Chapter 2 describes several different ways to start PageMaker (or any application) in Microsoft Windows. This and the following sections assume that you have already installed PageMaker and started Windows. The steps that follow are described in detail in Chapter 2:

1. Open the Windows Program Manager.

2. Double-click the Aldus program group icon.

3. Double-click the PageMaker 5.0 application icon.

4. Choose the New command from the File menu to start a new publication.

The Page Setup dialog box appears after you follow the preceding steps to create a new publication. (The Page Setup dialog box is discussed in detail later in this chapter.)

Opening an Existing PageMaker Publication

To open an existing PageMaker publication, choose the Open command from the File menu. After you choose the Open command, PageMaker displays the Open Publication dialog box, which contains a list of the PageMaker files on your hard disk.

To choose the file you want to open, find the file name in the window at the left in the dialog box shown in figure 4.1. (This procedure was summarized in Chapter 2, but some new twists are added here and in the next section.)

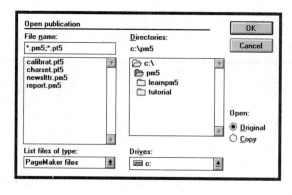

Fig. 4.1

Finding a file name in the Open Publication dialog box.

If the file name you want is not visible, use the following techniques to find the file in the dialog box. If the list of file names is longer than fits in the window, scroll bars appear at the right of the list, and you can click an arrow to scroll up or down the list. Click c:\ at the top of the Directories list to view the list at the next higher directory level. Click a directory name to view the list at the next lower directory level. Double-click a directory name to view files in a subdirectory. If the directories list is longer than fits in the window, scroll bars appear at the right of the list, and you can click an arrow to scroll up or down the list. To view files on another drive, click the down-pointing arrow under Drives to display a drop-down list, and click a:, b:, or c: to view the lists of files on other drives.

If you still cannot find the file, then perhaps it was saved using a nonstandard file extension. Normally, PageMaker automatically adds the extension PM5 for publications, or PT5 for templates. To find files with other extensions, change PageMaker Files in the List Files of Type area of the Open Publication dialog box to All Files. If all else fails, click Cancel to stop the Open command if you cannot find the file name; you can use the New command to start a new publication as described in the previous section.

After you locate the publication file you want to open, just double-click the file name to open the original (or a copy if it is a template, as described in Chapter 15). If you want to open a copy of the publication, click the file name to select it, click the Open Copy radio button, then click OK to open the duplicate publication. In either case, the publication opens to the same page that was open in the original when you last saved it.

Starting a New Publication from a Template

T I P

A template is a PageMaker document that has already been set up with basic elements common to all publications that are started from that template. PageMaker comes with an assortment of templates for use in common business publications, such as Avery labels, brochures, calendars, invoices, manuals, newsletters, and so on. Chapter 15 describes how to create your own custom templates. You save a great deal of time by starting from a custom template that matches frequently used designs, instead of using the New command to create every publication.

Whenever you transfer any publication from one PC to another, OLE (Object Linking and Embedding) objects transfer, but their links to the source application are broken. Relinking is necessary if you want to edit the objects, and the source application must be available on the new platform. (For more information, see the section "Managing Linked Text and Graphics" in Chapter 13.)

Opening Publications Created in PageMaker 4.0 or Earlier Versions

To open a publication created in PageMaker 4.0, you must first change the initial entry in the List Files of Type area of the Open Publication dialog box from PageMaker Files to Older PageMaker Files so Page-Maker will search for files with extensions other than PM5. Use the same procedures as described in the previous section to locate the file through the dialog box. When you do find the file, double-click to open it. PageMaker first converts the publication to a version 5.0 docment— displaying a dialog box that shows the progress of the conversion (which can take some time if the publication is very long or includes many graphics). PageMaker then opens the converted document as an untitled publication.

Although PageMaker 5.0 can open files saved in version 4.0, version 5.0 cannot open files created in earlier versions of PageMaker. To open files created in versions of PageMaker earlier than version 4.0, you must first open the files in PageMaker 4.0, save them, and then open them in version 5.0. PageMaker 5.0 then converts the newly converted version 4.0 publication into version 5.0 format and opens it as an "Untitled" publication.

T I P **Running Two Versions of PageMaker Simultaneously**

If you plan to keep two versions of PageMaker on your system, you may need to follow special instructions in installing PageMaker 5.0 to make sure that the two versions don't attempt to share the same resources. If you want to run the two versions at the same time, launch PageMaker 5.0 first for the best results.

CAUTION: PageMaker 5.0 includes new tracking algorithms. Converting a publication from PageMaker 4.0 to PageMaker 5.0 can result in changes to the line breaks if anything but "No Track" was specified in the original publication. Review each page carefully to be sure text hasn't been forced beyond the margins or into other unexpected areas.

Transferring a Macintosh Publication to the PC

PageMaker publications created on a Macintosh can be transferred to a PC (and vice versa). You can make such transfers through a network such as AppleShare, Ethernet, or TOPS or via telecommunications methods, using modems or a direct cable and the appropriate software, such as MacLink Plus by DataViz, LapLink Plus by Travelling Software, or TOPS by Centram Inc. Transfer the PageMaker files in a binary format (an option offered by the file transfer application). Transfer any linked graphic documents as well, preferably using software that offers the option of converting Macintosh graphics formats to their PC-equivalents (and vice versa). Store all linked files in the same directory as the publication.

You also can transfer publications by using either special software or file disk drives that enable your PC to read Macintosh disks. MatchMaker by Micro Solutions Computer Products and the Copy II PC Deluxe Option Board by Central Point Software are examples of such file disk drives. DOS Mounter is a software program that lets you read PC disks on a Macintosh.

If the Macintosh publication was originally created in PageMaker 4.0, the document must first be converted to a 5.0 publication on the Macintosh to be opened by PageMaker 5.0 on the PC after the file is transferred. In transferring the publication to the PC, you also must give the publication a valid DOS name. Use the extension PM5 when you name the file.

Another alternative is to transfer a PageMaker 4.0 publication from the Macintosh to the PC, giving the file a valid DOS name with the extension PM4, and then open the document in PageMaker 4.0 on the PC, and save the file in PC PageMaker 4.0 format. Then you can open the document and convert it to PageMaker 5.0, as discussed in the preceding section.

In switching documents between the two platforms, PageMaker converts the text, PageMaker formatting, PageMaker graphics, all bit-mapped graphics, EPS graphics, low-resolution screen versions of scanned images, Macintosh PICT graphics, and graphics with a complete copy stored in the publication. Macintosh PICT graphics are converted to Windows metafiles. Imported draw-type graphics created in other formats appear on-screen and print as X-filled boxes on the PC, but they reappear when you transfer the publication back to the Macintosh.

PageMaker knows if a transferred publication has links, but it does not transfer linked graphics or text files. You must transfer the linked files separately, as described earlier, and relink them. Macintosh subscriber links are broken when you transfer a publication to the PC, but you can still print the publication and the figures on the PC. PageMaker preserves the link information, however, and you can still update the subscriber after the publication is transferred back to the Macintosh.

After you transfer a publication from the PC to the Macintosh, OLE (Object Linking and Embedding) objects transfer, but the links to the source application are broken. Relinking is necessary if you want to edit the objects after you transfer the publication back to the PC.

Type specifications are transferred if you use the same type of printer on both systems—such as a PostScript printer. If the printers are different or if the same fonts are not available, text formatting changes as you transfer a publication from one platform to another. After you open the publication for the first time on the new platform, the PANOSE Font

Matching Results dialog box appears, enabling you to view and change PageMaker's proposed font substitutions (see fig. 4.2). If you make no changes, PageMaker uses the default font but saves the original specifications in case you transfer the publication back to its original platform. (See "PANOSE Font Matching" later in this chapter for more on this topic.)

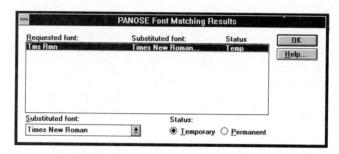

Fig. 4.2

The PANOSE
Font Matching
Results
dialog box.

T I P   **Knowing When To Reassign Fonts**

Reassign fonts if you are permanently moving a publication from one platform to another and do not plan to install the same fonts and printer used on the original system. Otherwise, if you are moving a publication back and forth between two platforms—to distribute work between members of a work group using different systems or to collect graphics created on different systems into one publication—do all your text formatting on the platform to be used for the final printing, and do not reassign fonts if you move the publication to other platforms temporarily. (See the section "PANOSE Font Matching" later in this chapter for more information on font mapping.)

After you have opened a publication, you can add to or edit the document by using any of the techniques described in the rest of this chapter and in Chapters 5 through 9. The next section describes how to start a new publication from scratch.

FROM HERE...

For Related Information

◄◄ "Opening a Publication," p. 53.

▶▶ "Managing Fonts," p. 592.

▶▶ "Managing Linked Text and Graphics Documents," p. 597.

▶▶ "Building a Template," p. 675.

Entering Page Setup Specifications

After you begin creating a publication by using the New command on the File menu, PageMaker displays the Page Setup dialog box (see fig. 4.3). You use this box to specify the size of the sheets of paper you want to use, the orientation of the printed image, the text margins, the number of pages, the starting page number, and whether you intend to print and bind the publication as a two-sided publication. You also can specify the target printer, printing resolution, and the page number format.

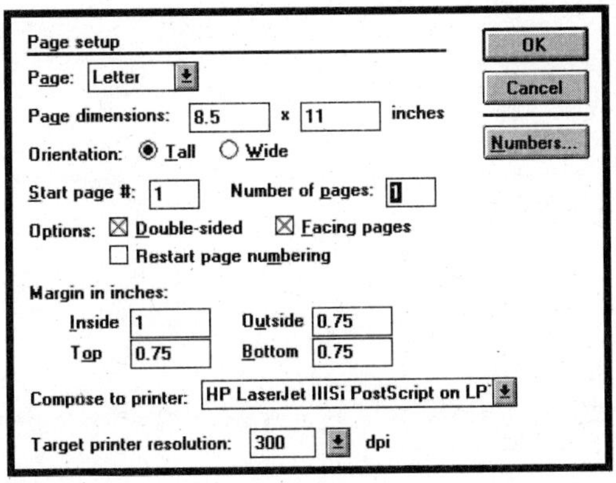

Fig. 4.3

The Page Setup dialog box, showing the default settings.

Figure 4.4 shows how the settings in the Page Setup dialog box affect a page as displayed on-screen. The Page Dimensions are defined in solid lines; the Orientation is Tall. The inside margin measure is applied to the right margin of left-hand pages and the left margin of right-hand pages. The dashed lines on the inside and outside margins indicate that a column guide is on the margin. The top and bottom margins are shown as dotted lines.

At any time during the production process, you can change the Page Setup options by using the Page Setup command on the File menu. The following sections explain what happens when you change these settings after you have started building the publication.

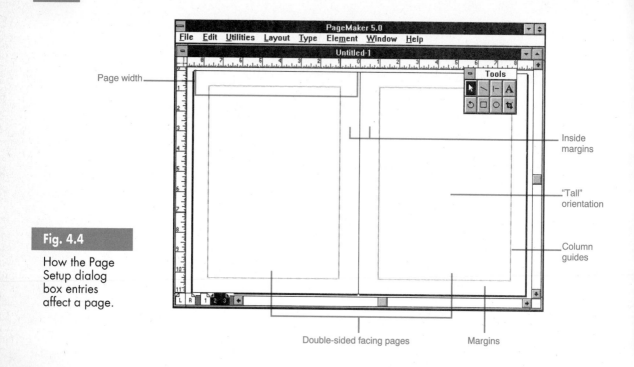

Page width

Inside margins

"Tall" orientation

Column guides

Fig. 4.4

How the Page Setup dialog box entries affect a page.

Double-sided facing pages   Margins

T I P   Determining the Page Dimensions Before You Start

Plan the design of your publication carefully before making your selections in the Page Setup dialog box. The page's size, orientation, and margins are essential elements of its design specifications. Changing these settings after you have started building a publication may require moving text and graphics that already have been placed on pages.

T I P   Changing the Defaults for Page Setup

If you choose the Page Setup command while no document is open, you can change the defaults that appear in the New dialog box after you choose the New command. Use this method to change the paper size and orientation, single-sided/double-sided/facing-page settings, or margins to the values you use most frequently in your publications. If your publications have many different specifications, however, create instead templates that capture these values for each type of publication (as described in Chapter 15).

Using the Keyboard To Make Dialog Box Entries— A Reminder

Throughout this book, you are given instructions for making dialog box selections by using the mouse. Most dialog boxes offer keyboard alternatives as well, as described in the section "Making Dialog Box Entries" in Chapter 2. To move the cursor to any field in a dialog box, hold the Alt key and press the letter that is underscored in the field's title. The letter *a* is underscored in the word Page, for example, so you can move to the Page field of the Page Setup dialog box by holding the Alt key and pressing A (Alt+A). To view a drop-down list attached to a dialog box option, keep holding the Alt key and press the down-arrow key. To make a selection from a drop-down list, release the Alt key and press the up- or down-arrow key to choose an item from the list. In some cases, the drop-down list closes after you press the arrow keys, but the selection shown in the field changes each time you press an arrow key. In other cases, the drop-down list remains open as you press the arrow keys, and you close it after making your selection with the arrow keys by pressing the Tab key.

Similarly, you can move to any text box entry in a dialog box by holding the Alt key and typing the letter underscored in the field name. You then can type the new text. You also can select radio buttons or check boxes by holding the Alt key and typing the underscored letter in the button or box name. You can toggle (select or deselect) check boxes by holding the Alt key and typing the underscored letter in the box name.

Specifying Page Size

In the Page Setup dialog box, PageMaker 5.0 offers 14 predefined page sizes that match the standard American and European paper sizes (see table 4.1). You can, however, specify any size up to 42 by 42 inches. (This maximum size has been increased in version 5.0 from the 17-by-22-inch limit of earlier versions, but 17 by 22 inches is still the limit for facing pages to be displayed on-screen.) You specify page size by clicking the arrow to the right of the current page size to display the drop-down list of Letter, Legal, Tabloid, European standards, and Custom size options.

If you choose one of the standard sizes, PageMaker fills in the dimensions automatically. Alternatively, you can enter any dimension (up to the 42-by-42-inch maximum) by pressing the Tab key to move to the dimension boxes and typing new values. If you follow this procedure, the Custom option appears in the Page field. You can enter most measurements in increments as fine as .001.

Table 4.1 Standard Paper Sizes in PageMaker

Option	Size
Letter	8 1/2 by 11 inches
Legal	8 1/2 by 14 inches
Tabloid	11 by 17 inches
A4	210 by 297 millimeters (8.268 by 11.693 inches)
A3	297 by 420 millimeters (11.693 by 16.535 inches)
A5	148 by 210 millimeters (5.827 by 8.268 inches)
B5	176 by 250 millimeters (6.929 by 9.842 inches)
Magazine	8.375 (8 3/8) by 10.875 (10 7/8) inches
Magazine narrow	8.125 (8 1/8) by 10.875 inches
Magazine wide	9 by 10.875 inches
Magazine broad	10 by 12 inches
Compact disk	4.722 by 4.75 inches
Letterhalf	5 1/2 by 8 1/2 inches
Legalhalf	7 by 8 1/2 inches
Custom	Any size up to 42 by 42 inches

Overriding the Unit of Measure

You can override the current unit of measure in the Page Setup dialog box (or any dialog box) by entering a one-character abbreviation for the unit of measure you want to specify (see table 4.2). Changing the unit of measure does not affect any text or graphics already on the page. To specify inches, enter **i** after the number (for example, **0.75i**). To specify millimeters, type **m** after the number (as in **19.06m**). To specify picas and points, enter a **p** between the number of picas and the number of points (for instance, **4p6**). To specify picas only, enter a **p** after the number. To specify points only, type a **p** before the number. To specify ciceros, enter a **c** between the number of ciceros and the number of points (as in **4c2.8**).

The unit of measure shown on the publication ruler line (displayed by the keyboard shortcut Ctrl+R) always reflects the current unit of measure, as set with the Preferences command on the File menu, regardless of the unit of measure you enter in a dialog box (see "Setting Preferences" later in this chapter).

Table 4.2 Equivalent Measures:
Inches, Millimeters, Picas and Points, and Ciceros

Size	Inches	Millimeters	Picas	Ciceros
	.04	1		
	.167		1p0	
	.177			1c0
	.25	6.36	1p6	1c4.9
	.5	12.7	3p0	2c9.9
	.75	19.06	4p6	4c2.8
	1	25.4	6p0	5c7.8
A5	5.827	148	34p11.6	32c10.7
B5	6.929	250	41p6.9	39c 1.4
A4, A5	8.268	210	49p7.3	46c8
Letter, Legal	8.5	215.9	51p0	47c11.7
B5	9.842	176	59p.07	55c6.7
Letter, Tabloid	11	279.4	66p0	62c1.1
A4	11.693	297	70p1.9	66c
Legal	14	355.6	84p0	79c0.3
A3	16.535	420	99p2.6	93c4
Tabloid	17	431.8	102p0	95c11.5

The page size you specify in the Page Setup dialog box is not necessarily the same as the size of the sheets of paper that you feed into a laser printer. The size you choose here dictates the measurements of the page border on-screen. You can specify Tabloid size, for example, but actually print the publication pages in sections on 8 1/2-by-11-inch sheets by using the Print command's Tile option, which is explained in Chapter 10. Figure 4.5 shows how 12-by-22-inch pages can be printed in four pieces on 8 1/2-by-11-inch paper by using the Print command's Tile option.

If you choose a page size smaller than that of the sheets of paper on which you print, PageMaker prints the image in the center of the paper. You can use the Printer's Marks option in the Print Command dialog box to print crop marks that indicate the final trim size on the larger paper (see fig. 4.6).

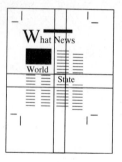

Fig. 4.5

A page printed by using the Tile option.

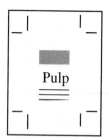

Fig. 4.6

Crop marks printed around a page layout smaller than the paper on which it is printed.

> **CAUTION:** You can use the Page Setup command to change the page size after you open a publication, but PageMaker does not reposition existing text and graphics to match the new page size. On single-sided pages, PageMaker maintains the position of text and graphics relative to the top-left margin corner. On facing pages, PageMaker centers the new page outline behind the text and graphics of the old page. If the new page is smaller than the old page, text and graphics spill over into the pasteboard. You must manually reposition text and graphics on each page to fit the new page size and margins.

Setting Page Orientation

The width and length of each page also is affected by the Orientation option in the Page Setup dialog box. You can orient your pages to print Tall or Wide by clicking the appropriate button. The most common page size and orientation for business publications is Tall, 8 1/2 by 11 inches. Figure 4.7 shows examples of the following variations in page size and orientation:

A. An 8 1/2-by-11-inch page with Tall orientation, printed one sheet per page

B. An 8 1/2-by-11-inch page with Wide orientation, printed one sheet per page

C. An 11-by-17-inch (tabloid) page with Tall orientation, printed four tiled sheets per page

D. An 11-by-17-inch page with Wide orientation, printed four tiled sheets per page

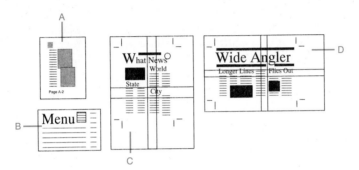

Fig. 4.7

Examples of page size and orientation settings.

> **CAUTION:** You can use the Page Setup command to change the page's orientation after you open a publication, but PageMaker does not reposition existing text and graphics to match the new orientation. Text and graphics spill over into the pasteboard if they do not fit the new orientation, and you must reposition text and graphics individually on each page to adjust these elements to fit the new orientation.

Designating the Number of Pages

PageMaker is set by default to create a one-page publication. You can, however, designate the exact number of pages you want in a publication. Before you start building the publication, type a number in the Number of Pages text box of the Page Setup dialog box. If you do not know the exact number of pages in the finished publication, you can add or delete pages as you work by using the Insert Pages or Remove Pages commands on the Layout menu. (You cannot use the Page Setup dialog box to change the number of pages after you open a new publication.) If you place text with the Autoflow option set to On, as described in Chapter 6, PageMaker inserts additional pages as needed to accommodate the placed text.

A PageMaker publication can be up to 999 pages long, but working with smaller files is more efficient. In long files, response time is slow when you turn pages or make text edits that carry over to subsequent pages. Dividing a long publication into sections or chapters is good practice, therefore, because you can work faster on smaller files. Another advantage is that you can set up a different running header and running footer for each chapter. (Running headers and footers usually are entered on the master pages, so they cannot be changed in the middle of a file.) The Book command, described in Chapter 14, enables you to associate, or connect, a series of separate PageMaker documents together as chapters in a book.

Another important consideration in determining the number of pages in a single file is the size of the final publication in bytes. To be able to back up your publications on floppy disks for storage and transport, you must keep the sizes of your files within the following limits:

> 360K for double-sided double-density 5 1/4-inch disks
>
> 1.2M for double-sided high-density 5 1/4-inch disks
>
> 720K for double-sided double-density 3 1/2-inch disks
>
> 1.44M for double-sided high-density 3 1/2-inch disks

Other alternatives are to use a compacting program to make files smaller for storage and transport or to use removable hard drives for storing and transporting large files.

Even if you have unlimited disk space on a file server, keeping individual publication files small for printing is a good idea. As you print a file to the Print Spooler in Windows, you actually create a temporary print file that requires space on the hard disk. If the publication is very large, and sufficient free space is not available on your hard disk, you may need to print the publication one page at a time. (See the section "Diagnosing Problems in Printing" in Chapter 13.)

You can use the Book command (described in Chapter 14) to assemble several PageMaker publications into one publication to print or generate a table of contents or an index.

Checking the File Size as You Work

If you are creating large publications, save your file frequently as you work. Periodically use the Save As command, and then open the Windows File Manager window to see how large your publication is. You must use the Save As command to update the file size, date, and time last modified in the Windows File Manager window if simultaneously running PageMaker. If the file size does not appear next to the files listed in the File Manager window, choose All File Details from the View menu in order to view the size and time last modified.

PageMaker also stores "ghost" memories of deleted elements or pages if you use the Save command to save your publication. Using the Save As command reclaims this stored space in a publication reduced in size by editing, cutting, pasting, or deleting pages. You can reclaim as much as 40 percent of the publication's size. (You can use the Preferences command, described later in this chapter, to make the Save command act like the Save As command, but each Save operation is slower.)

Assigning a Starting Page Number

You can start a publication with any page number up to 9999 by typing a number in the Number of Pages text box in the Page Setup dialog box. If you fill one file with 999 pages, the maximum number possible, for example, you can continue building a second file that starts with page 1000. You also can specify the starting page number for publications divided into sections, with the first section starting on page 1 and the second section starting on page 20.

You can use the Page Setup command to change the starting page number of the publication at any time. PageMaker then renumbers all the pages in the publication. Be aware, however, that if you change a double-sided publication that starts on an odd-numbered page so that it now starts on an even-numbered page, or vice versa, its left-hand pages become right-hand pages. You must make adjustments for facing pages that formerly had elements that "bled" across the inside margins from one page to another and for pages that previously were inserted to force subsequent pages onto the left or right side.

Controlling Left-Hand and Right-Hand Page Positions

T I P

If preparing a publication for double-sided printing, make sure that you account for and print every page, including blank left-hand pages inserted to force new sections or chapters to start on right-hand pages. Having a numbered sheet for every page of the publication also helps whoever is printing or copying the publication before binding.

Selecting a Format for Page Numbers

Click the Numbers button in the Page Setup dialog box if you want to use special page number formats. The Page Numbering dialog box, as shown in figure 4.8, offers five format choices: Arabic Numeral (the default), Upper or Lower Roman numerals (uppercase and lowercase, respectively), and Upper Alphabetic or Lower Alphabetic characters (also upper- or lowercase).

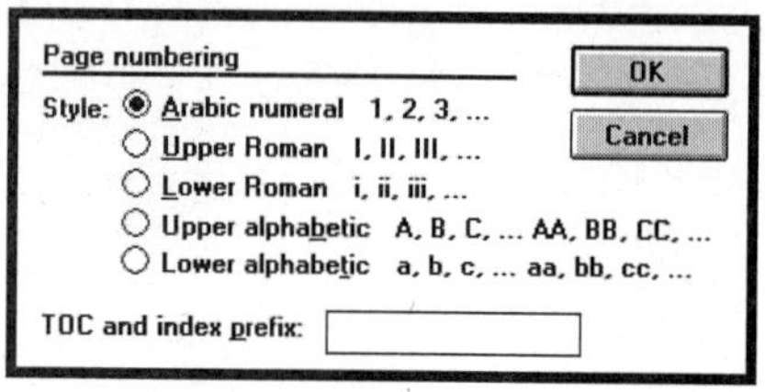

Fig. 4.8

The Page
Numbering
dialog box.

You also can enter a prefix in the TOC and Index Prefix text box. The prefix then appears on all page numbers in the automatically generated table of contents and index. This prefix does not appear on each page, however, unless you type it as part of the page number on the master pages, as described in the section "Adding Master Page Elements" in Chapter 5.

Working with Double-Sided Publications

You can create a double-sided publication by selecting the Double-sided check box in the Options section of the Page Setup dialog box. The Double-sided option does not cause pages to be printed on both sides of the paper as the paper comes out of the laser printer—for that, you use the Duplex option in the Print dialog box, described in Chapter 10. You use the Double-sided option in the Page Setup dialog box if you want to reproduce the final pages as a two-sided publication, using either a duplex printer or xerographic or offset printing equipment. Figure 4.9 shows several pages of a double-sided publication.

After you choose the Double-sided option, PageMaker applies the mea-sure specified for the inside margin to the left margin of odd-numbered pages and to the right margin of even-numbered pages. The inside mar-gin often is set wider than the outside margin to accommodate binding. Double-sided publications have two master pages: one for even-numbered, or left-hand, pages and one for odd-numbered, or right-hand, pages. You can set up different running headers and running footers for left-hand and right-hand pages. Figure 4.10 shows the screen display for a single-sided publication. Figure 4.11 shows the screen display for a double-sided publication. Table 4.3 describes the differences between single- and double-sided publications.

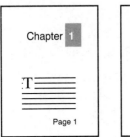 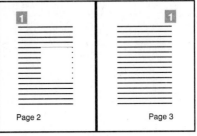

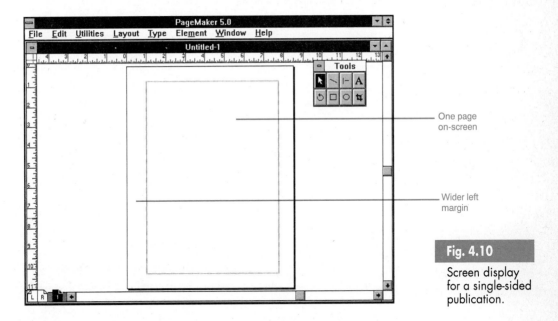

One page on-screen

Wider left margin

If you select both the Facing Pages option and the Double-sided option in the Page Setup dialog box (and your pages are no larger than 11 by 17 inches), you can simultaneously view on-screen those pages that face one another in double-sided publications. This feature is especially useful if you design pages with graphics that bleed across the inside margin or you want to make sure that a two-page layout is balanced (see Chapter 15).

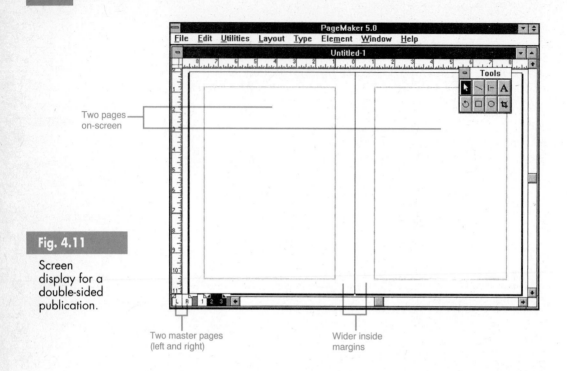

Two pages on-screen

Fig. 4.11

Screen display for a double-sided publication.

Two master pages (left and right)

Wider inside margins

Table 4.3 Single-Sided versus Double-Sided Publications

Single-Sided Publications	Double-Sided Publications
One page displayed at a time	Option of viewing one page at a time or two facing pages; option of "bleeding" an illustration across two pages
One master page or grid for all pages of the publication	Two master pages: one for left-hand (even-numbered) pages and one for right-hand (odd numbered) pages
Same running headers and different running footers on every page	Option of having headers and footers on left- and right-hand pages
Left margin usually wider to accommodate binding	Inside margins usually wider to accommodate binding

You can use the Page Setup command to change the Double-sided and Facing Pages options after you open a publication. If the publication is

double-sided and you change it to single-sided, the inside margin specification becomes the left margin on all pages, and the outside margin
becomes the right margin. If the publication is single-sided and you
change it to double-sided, the left margin becomes the inside margin,
and the right margin becomes the outside margin. If the publication has
facing pages and you turn off this option, text and graphics that bleed
across facing pages remain anchored to the left-facing page and spill
into the pasteboard; you must reposition text and graphics individually
on each page to fit the new page size and margins.

Using the Double-Sided Option for Single-Sided Publications

T I P

You can reduce the time you spend turning pages in a long, single-
sided publication by setting up the document as a double-sided
publication and viewing facing pages as you work. If the right and
left margins are equal, you can print the publication as a double-
sided publication with identical left and right master pages. If the
left and right margins are not equal, you must turn off the Double-
sided option before printing the final pages.

You can set up a double-sided publication as a single-sided publication
if the inside and outside margins are the same and the master pages are
identical. In most cases, however, use the Double-sided option for any
publication you plan to make double-sided, and turn off the Facing
Pages option if you want to work on one page at a time.

While setting up the master pages, however, always work with the Facing Pages option turned on. This practice helps you align running headers and footers and horizontal guides on the two pages.

Work Faster by Using Facing Pages

T I P

You also can use the Facing Pages option as an efficiency tool.
Laying out and changing pages can be done more quickly if you
can see two pages at the same time.

T   I   P   **Turn Off the Facing Pages Option for Extensive Pasteboard Use**

If your page layouts are not affected by what is on the facing pages of a double-sided publication, and you expect to use the pasteboard extensively as a work area during production, turn off the Facing Pages option and work on one page at a time. With the Facing Pages option turned off, you can see more of the pasteboard on either side of the page in reduced views such as Fit in Window.

Restarting Page Numbers

Choose the Restart Page Numbering option in the Page Setup dialog box if you want the page numbering of the publication always to begin with the page number specified in the Start Page # text box. Do not choose the Restart Page Numbering box if this publication is part of a "book" with continuous page numbering, assembled by using PageMaker's Book command as described in Chapter 14.

Specifying Page Margins

You enter measurements for the page margins in the Page Setup dialog box by clicking (or tabbing to) the text boxes for the four margins and typing numeric values. The page margins entered in the Page Setup dialog box affect all pages of a publication, and this setting cannot be altered for individual pages. To change the text margins on individual pages, you must move the column guides, as described in the section "Moving Guides" in Chapter 5.

Margins are measured from the edges of the page; that is, margins are measured from the page size, which is not necessarily the paper size (as explained earlier in this chapter). Margins reflect the limits for text and column settings on numbered pages, not the limits for headers and footers and other master-page elements. Sometimes graphics on individual pages are allowed to extend beyond the margins as part of the page design (see fig. 4.12). Margins also must be within the image area of your target printer—the LaserJet, for example, does not print nearer than 0.5 inch to the edge of a page.

The margins are displayed in the Page Setup dialog box in the unit of measure specified by the Preferences command in the File menu (see "Setting Preferences" later in this chapter). You can enter any number, including decimals, to specify margins. If the unit of measure is specified as picas and points, you must include a *p* to separate the pica units from the points. You can enter a measurement of 4 picas and zero points, for example, as either 4 or 4p0, as shown in figure 4.13. You also can enter abbreviations to specify measurements in any unit, regardless of the one currently displayed, as discussed in the tip "Overriding the Unit of Measure" earlier in this chapter.

Fig. 4.12

Margins defining the text area limits but not confining the header and footer.

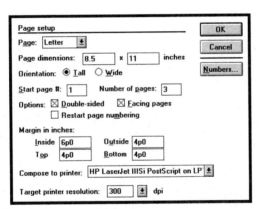

Fig. 4.13

Overriding the current unit of measure (inches) by entering margins in picas in the Page Setup dialog box.

NOTE
As is true for page size and orientation, you can use the Page Setup command to change the margins after you open a publication, but PageMaker does not reposition existing text and graphics to match the new margins. PageMaker maintains the position of text and graphics relative to the top-left margin corner. You must manually reposition text and graphics to fit the new margins on each page, including any text positioned by using the old column guides.

Specifying the Target Printer and Resolution

The Page Setup dialog box shows which printer currently is the target printer. If the specified printer is not the printer you intend to use for your final publication, you should change the target printer before you start building your publication; your target printer selection can affect your choice of fonts and sizes, the resolution of text and graphics, and the print area available.

Change the target printer by selecting a new printer from the Compose to Printer drop-down list of installed printers in the Page Setup dialog box. (PageMaker 5.0 has eliminated the Printer Setup command on the File menu.) You also can select a different printer in the Print dialog box before you print, as described in Chapter 10. Both lists of printers include all printers installed through the Windows Control Panel (also in Chapter 10). Not all printers installed through Windows, however, must necessarily be connected to your current system in order for you to compose a publication. You can, for example, prepare a publication for final printing on a PostScript printer that is not hooked to your computer by choosing that printer in the Page Setup dialog box, and then print drafts on a non-PostScript printer that is connected to your system by specifying the draft printer in the Print dialog box.

If you have more than one type of printer installed on your system, however, or you use a font cartridge system (especially if you have more than one cartridge)—or both—you should always define the target printer you intend to use for final printouts *before* you start a new publication, and you should stick with that setting throughout the production cycle. Otherwise, when you change target printers in the Page Setup dialog box, PageMaker asks you whether to reformat the publication for the new printer. If you answer Yes, PageMaker changes the publication file itself—changing fonts and adjusting letter spacing if necessary to match the new printer's capabilities. If you don't want to change the publication itself, you can still print to any other printer by specifying a different printer in the Print dialog box (described in Chapter 10), in which case the publication is temporarily adjusted by PageMaker to print to the draft printer, but the publication file remains as set up for the target printer as specified in the Page Setup dialog box.

PageMaker 5.0 also enables you to specify the resolution (dots per inch) used in the final printing. PageMaker uses this information to *magic-stretch* bitmapped images. (For details, see the section "Editing Imported Graphics" in Chapter 9.)

Lower Resolutions Save Time and Space

T I P

Higher resolutions that print more dots per inch generally look better but also require more printer memory and may even take longer to print. If you print your publications on high-quality glossy stock, you probably want to specify the actual resolution of the imagesetter used to print the final, camera-ready copy. Otherwise, you can specify lower resolutions than the printer can handle and still get good results. Many professionals, for example, scan and print images at 150 dots per inch to save time and space without losing much in quality, even if they print their final copy at 2,400 dots per inch on an imagesetter.

For a discussion of the differences among printers, the methods available for installing and selecting printers, and the ways printers can affect your publication's design and production, see Chapter 10.

Closing the Page Setup Dialog Box

After you enter initial specifications in the Page Setup dialog box and click OK, PageMaker displays a blank page showing the default setting for column guides (refer to fig. 4.10). This page is page 1 of your publication. You can begin building a publication immediately by using the Place command to import text and graphics prepared in other programs or by using PageMaker's built-in graphics and text tools. These procedures are described in detail in Chapters 5 through 9.

For Related Information

FROM HERE...

▶▶ "Working with Pages," p. 172.

▶▶ "Specifying Text Flow," p. 240.

▶▶ "Installing the Printer," p. 399.

▶▶ "Building a Template," p. 675.

Changing Preferences

Before adding text and graphics to the first page of your newly created publication, you may want to begin by setting your preferences
for how PageMaker displays elements on-screen and by defining the
document's master pages so that you can fit each page layout into an
overall grid system. (Remember, however, that you can change your
Preferences settings at any time without affecting any of the work you
have done in building pages. If you're on a self-imposed crash course in
learning PageMaker now, you can skip to "Saving a Document or Template" at the end of this chapter.)

To customize the way PageMaker displays elements on-screen, choose
the Preferences command on the File menu. If you use the Preferences
command when no publication is open, your selections apply to all new
publications. If you use the Preferences command when a publication is
open, your choices apply to that publication only.

The Preferences dialog box shows the first set of options you can customize (see fig. 4.14). You are most likely to change these particular
preferences periodically as you work. You are more likely to retain the
settings of those preferences accessed through the Other button and
the Map Fonts button throughout a project.

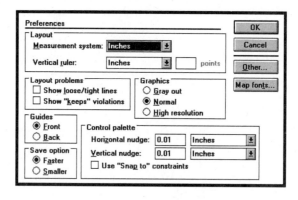

The Preferences
dialog box.

Steps involving the Preferences dialog box are described in the following sections as using the mouse. Remember, however, that you also can
use the keyboard to make dialog box entries, as described in Chapter 2
and summarized in the tip "Using the Keyboard To Make Dialog Box
Entries" earlier in this chapter.

Specifying Layout Ruler Units

You can set the preferred Measurement System in the Preferences dialog box to Inches, Inches Decimal, Millimeters, Picas (and points), or Ciceros by clicking the arrow to the right of the currently selected measurement system to display a drop-down list of systems. Drag the mouse down the list to select the system you want to use in your publication. This setting determines the unit of measure displayed on the horizontal ruler and in most dialog boxes that show measurements (such as the Page Setup dialog box). Remember, however, that you can enter a measurement in any unit by using the abbreviations described in the section "Overriding the Unit of Measure," earlier in this chapter.

You can choose a different unit of measure for the Vertical Ruler by clicking the arrow to the right of the currently selected measurement system for the vertical ruler to display a drop-down list of systems. Drag the mouse down this list to select the system you want for the vertical ruler. If you choose Custom, you can force tick marks on the vertical ruler to match the leading of your text, by entering in the Points field to the right of the Vertical Ruler field the exact number of points between tick marks. If Snap To Rulers is turned on in the Guides and Rulers submenu of the Layout menu, PageMaker aligns the baselines of selected text to the vertical ruler's tick marks.

You can change the preferred unit of measure at any time without affecting the publication itself—only the ruler lines and other displays that show measurements change. You may choose to work with one unit of measure throughout the production, or you may want to switch among the different units (for example, using picas for margins and columns and inches for scaling figures).

The number of increments displayed along the ruler line varies, depending on the size in which you currently are viewing the page. As mentioned in Chapter 2 and detailed in Chapter 5, you can view pages in five different scales, from 200% Size to Fit in Window view. The ruler line shows finer increments of measure in enlarged views (such as 200% Size) than in reduced views.

Displaying Layout Problems

You can set PageMaker to help you spot layout problems by selecting one or both check boxes in the Layout Problems area of the Preferences dialog box. If you select Show Loose/Tight Lines, PageMaker highlights lines of text that contain too much or too little spacing between words and letters as a result of hyphenation and justification. PageMaker bases its evaluation on the spacing limits you set in the Spacing Attributes dialog box (see Chapter 8).

If you select Show "Keeps" Violations, PageMaker highlights lines that violate the Widow, Orphan, or Keep-With-Next controls that you set in the Paragraph Specifications dialog box (see Chapter 8). Violations result when PageMaker cannot reconcile all the preferences you have set for Spacing, Keep-With-Next, and so on. For example, if you have a heading near the bottom of the page set up to "keep with next" paragraph, and the next paragraph is only three lines long but set up with widow and orphan control and three lines will not fit on the page, PageMaker will be forced to violate either the keep-with-next or the widow/orphan control specification.

You may be able to resolve the problem by changing the paragraph spacing, line spacing, word spacing, letter spacing, manually extending the text block below the page margin, or by using other methods described in Chapter 8. You can also correct these problems by editing the text—literally changing the words.

Displaying Graphics

You can choose to view graphics normally, to gray them out, or to display them at high resolution by selecting one of the three radio buttons in the Graphics area of the Preferences dialog box. Graying out graphics reduces screen redraw time (whenever you turn pages or change views of a page), while displaying graphics at high resolution increases redraw time. At high-resolution, the graphics are displayed in sharper detail and also can be displayed in color. These options affect the screen display only—not how graphics print. To display the high-resolution version of linked graphics files, the graphic's link must be updated or the graphic must be stored as part of the publication (as described later in this chapter and in Chapters 9 and 13).

Displaying Guides on Top or Bottom Layer

You can set nonprinting guides (margin guides, column guides, and ruler guides) to display in front of or in back of printing elements on-screen by selecting the radio buttons for Front or Back in the Preferences dialog box. This choice determines the layer on which these elements can be selected. If Front is selected, the pointer most easily selects the guide when positioned over a guide that overlaps text or a graphic. If Back is selected, you can more easily select the graphics or text that meet or overlap the guide, so you minimize the risk of accidentally moving a guide. In any case, you can always select objects on successive layers by holding the Ctrl key as you click the pointer tool over the area where several objects—including guides—overlap.

Choosing Different Save Options

You can make the Save command run faster by selecting the Faster radio button at the bottom left of the dialog box. Choosing the Faster option may make files larger, however, by including "ghost" memories of elements or pages you deleted. Under this option, PageMaker simply appends mini-saved versions of the publication file to the end of the saved publication file.

You can make the Save command act like the Save As command instead, which clears any mini-saved versions and creates a new version of your publication file. This results in files that are as much as 40 percent smaller than under the Faster option, but saving a file takes a little longer and uses more memory each time you choose Save. You can select this option by clicking the Smaller radio button at the bottom left of the dialog box.

Faster or Smaller—Suit Yourself

Remember that you can set Preferences for all publications by making your selections when no publications are open, and you can set them for individual publications by making your selections with a publication open. If you have enough disk space available, then keep Faster as the default preference for all publications. Change the preference to Smaller only for the final save of a publication—just before archiving the publication (or use the Save As command, which has the same effect).

If disk space is limited, change the default to Smaller for all publications. You can always change it to Faster for individual publications when the slower Save creates a noticeable productivity loss or aggravates your patience during heavy edit cycles.

Adjusting Control Palette Preferences

PageMaker 5.0 introduces a Control palette through which you can make many adjustments to a selected object without opening a dialog box, including "nudge" an object to move it in fixed increments. In the

Preferences dialog box, you can specify the number and unit of measure to be used as the Horizontal and Vertical nudge amount when you click the nudge buttons in the Control palette. Nudge buttons are described in Chapter 5, in the section "Using the Control Palette in Layout View," and in Chapter 8, in the section "Using the Control Palette To Change Character Attributes."

Select Use "Snap to" Constraints to make values entered in the Control palette snap to the nearest ruler tick mark of a nonprinting guide when you use the nudge buttons. This option works in conjunction with commands on the Guides and Rulers submenu on the Layout menu. If the option is selected and you have Snap to Rulers turned on and Snap to Guides turned off, Control palette values snap to ruler tick marks but not to margins, column guides, or ruler guides when you use the nudge buttons.

FROM HERE...

For Related Information

◀◀ "Making Entries in Dialog Boxes," p. 51.

▶▶ "Controlling Breaks," p. 316.

▶▶ "Importing Graphics Created in Other Programs," p. 363.

▶▶ "Managing Linked Text and Graphics Documents," p. 597.

Setting Up Other Options

Select the Other button in the Preferences dialog box to display the Other Preferences dialog box, as shown in figure 4.15, which includes options that affect the appearance of text in the story editor and on the printed page, plus options related to how graphics are stored in the PageMaker publication, PPD (PostScript Printer Description) file names, and how PageMaker displays pages when flowing text.

Autoflow

If you select the Display All Pages check box, PageMaker displays each page of the publication as that page is created when text is placed by using the Autoflow feature (see Chapter 6). Otherwise, PageMaker places all the text and then displays only the last page added.

Printer Name

You can select the Display PPD Name check box to display the PPD file
name rather than the full printer name or nickname in the Printer lists
in the Print dialog box and the Page Setup dialog box. Selecting this
option can decrease the amount of time PageMaker takes to display
these dialog boxes.

Bitmap Image Preferences

You also can determine in the Other Preferences dialog box the amount
of memory used to create *internal bitmaps*—the screen displays of
graphic images that PageMaker creates when Normal is selected in the
Graphics area of the Preferences dialog box (as described earlier in this
chapter). Lower values for Size of Internal Bitmap save disk space,
memory, and screen redraw time, but lowers the display resolution of
any imported graphics larger than this value. This setting does not
affect how the graphics print, however, unless PageMaker cannot find
the linked file when printing.

The Auto Include Images Under value sets the minimum file size for
which PageMaker prompts you whether to include an imported image
as part of the PageMaker publication or to link the image as an external
file. You can set this to a small value and link every imported file—but
remember that you must move all linked graphics along with the publication for transport or archiving. If you set this to a high value, smaller
files are included as part of the PageMaker publication file, which
makes the PageMaker file larger but reduces the number of external
files you must keep track of.

T I P   **Linking All Graphics To Incorporate Changes**

If you plan to update imported graphics frequently, you can set the Auto Include Images Under option to a low value so that PageMaker detects when an imported image has been changed and prompts you to update the links (as explained in Chapters 9 and 13).

Text Preferences

If you select the Use Typographer's Quotes check box in the Text area of the Other Preferences dialog box, PageMaker displays open and close quotation marks (", ", ', ') instead of foot and inch marks (', ") when you use the quotation mark/apostrophe key on the keyboard. This setting affects only those characters typed after the preference is selected and does not retroactively change text that has already been typed.

You cannot type foot and inch marks when this option is selected. If the option is not selected, you can create open and close double quotation marks (", ") and single quotation marks (', ') by pressing Ctrl+Shift+[, Ctrl+Shift+], Ctrl+[, and Ctrl+], respectively. (These and other special characters are discussed in Chapter 6 and are listed in Appendix C, as well as on the inside front and back covers of this book.)

Selecting the Preserve Line Spacing in TrueType radio button preserves the line spacing, or leading, of TrueType fonts and adjusts the character height as necessary if you type a character with an accent above it. Selecting the Preserve Character Shape in TrueType radio button preserves the character height of TrueType fonts, regardless of the line spacing—in which case, you may need to adjust the leading manually (as described under "Specifying Leading" in Chapter 8) to compensate for special conditions, such as accents above letters.

In reduced views, such as Fit in Window view, PageMaker displays small-sized type as gray bars to reduce the time required for the screen refresh if you change views. These gray bars are called *greeked text*. The default setting for greeked text is nine pixels, which means that if the text is nine pixels or smaller in the chosen view, the text is greeked. By typing a number in the Greek Text Below text box, you can set the default smaller to reduce or eliminate greeking or higher to increase the amount of greeking. Greeking affects the screen display only—not how text prints.

Text Display in the Story Editor

You can select the font and size for text displayed in Story view in the Story Editor area of the dialog box. The Font and Size options display drop-down lists that restrict the range of choices to fonts and sizes that facilitate a fast screen display. You make selections by selecting the arrows to the right of the values for Size and Font to display their drop-down lists of choices. You then drag the mouse down the list to highlight your selection. Your choices appear in the Font and Size text boxes.

You also can choose to Display Style Names next to each paragraph and Display ¶ (that is, display hidden characters, such as spaces, tabs, and the paragraph character at the end of each paragraph) by selecting those check boxes.

See Appendix C for a list of special characters and how to type them.

For Related Information

▶▶ "Typing Text in Layout View," p. 225.

▶▶ "Specifying Text Flow," p. 240.

FROM HERE...

PANOSE Font Matching

If you select the Map Fonts button in the Preferences dialog box, you access the PANOSE Font Matching dialog box, a feature new to PageMaker 5.0 (see fig. 4.16). In earlier versions, when you opened a publication that used fonts that were not available on the current system, PageMaker substituted Courier for any missing font. In PageMaker 5.0, PageMaker tries to match the missing font with the most similar font on the current system. Before making substitutions, PageMaker displays a dialog box showing which fonts it has chosen as substitutes for the missing fonts. This dialog box enables you to specify how PageMaker is to handle fonts if you open a publication using fonts unavailable on the current system. (Select the Help button in the dialog box if you need information on how PANOSE Font Matching works.)

You can turn font matching off entirely by deselecting the Allow Font Matching check box (selected as the default setting). PageMaker displays a screen showing the results of font matching after you open a document on a different system unless the Show Mapping Results check box also is deselected. You also can set in this dialog box the Substitution Tolerance—which determines exactly how close a substituted font must match the original font's size and other characteristics—and select the preferred substitution font (Default Font) to be used when no close matches can be found.

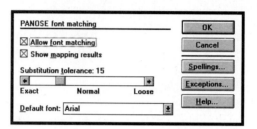

Fig. 4.16

The PANOSE Font Matching dialog box.

Select the Spellings button in the PANOSE Font Matching dialog box to view a list of Alternate Spellings for Windows fonts and their equivalents on the Macintosh. (You also can select Help from the Alternate Spellings dialog box.) Select Add to add new pairings of font names for the two platforms. Select Remove to delete a pair of font names. Select Change to change the spellings used in a pair of font names. Click OK to return to the PANOSE Font Matching dialog box.

Select the Exceptions button in the PANOSE Font Matching dialog box to add alternative substitutions when the preferred substitution font is not available. (You can click Help from the Matching Exceptions dialog box as well.) Select Add to add new pairings of font names for the two platforms. Select Remove to delete a pair of font names. Select Change to change the spellings used in a pair of names. Click OK to return to the PANOSE Font Matching dialog box.

See the section "Transferring a Publication from the Macintosh to the PC" earlier in this chapter for examples of using the PANOSE Font Matching dialog box when opening a publication.

For Related Information

FROM HERE...

▶▶ "Opening a Publication with Missing Fonts," p. 593.

Saving a Document or Template

Save your files often by using the Save command from the File menu or by typing Ctrl+S. As you work on a document, your work is stored in the computer's memory (RAM)—a temporary work area that is "erased" whenever the computer is turned off or after you quit an application. Each time you save the document, the version in memory is copied to the disk. If the power fails or something else forces you to restart the computer, anything in the computer's memory is erased, but whatever you saved on disk is preserved.

PageMaker's built-in recovery program (for recovering from power failures or causes for quitting PageMaker unexpectedly) is more sophisticated than those of other desktop publishing programs. PageMaker saves on disk *interim versions* of the document every time you insert, remove, turn a page, or touch the icon on the current page. These interim versions do not replace the latest version you saved on disk but are available if you must reopen a document after a system failure. When you restart PageMaker and open the publication that you were working on when the system failed, PageMaker asks if you want to open the saved disk version or the last interim version of the publication.

The first time you use the Save command on a new document, the Save Publication As dialog box appears in which you can specify the name of the document and the disk drive or directory in which you want to store the document file (see fig. 4.17). This dialog box is common to most Windows applications.

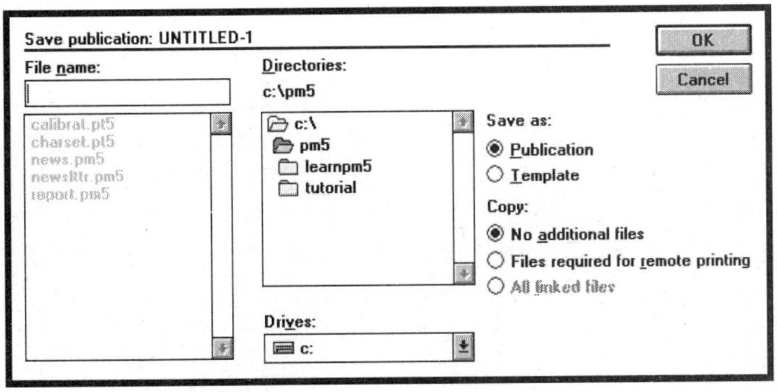

Fig. 4.17

The Save
Publication As
dialog box.

Use the first eight characters of the name you assign to the document to distinguish between chapters or versions of similar documents. After you assign a new document its eight-character name, PageMaker adds the extension PM5 (for Publications) or PT5 (for Templates). If you type your own extension as part of the name, PageMaker does not override your entry—but the program only looks for files with the PM5 and PT5 extensions after you next choose the Open command, unless you tell PageMaker to look for other extensions (by specifying All Files in the List Files of Type area of the Open dialog box). Accepting PageMaker's extension assignment, however, usually is more efficient in the long run.

In the bottom right area of the Save Publication As dialog box you can click Copy Files Required for Remote Printing, or All Linked Files, to copy linked graphics files that have already been placed in the publication to the specified directory. These options are normally used with the Save as command after the publication is complete and all files have been placed (see Tip under next section heading). The default is to Copy No Additional Files.

After you name and save a document, the Save command saves your updated versions of the publication without displaying the dialog box again. You can use the Save As command, however, to display the dialog box and change the name or location of the publication (as described in the following section).

T I P

Saving All Open Publications Simultaneously

PageMaker 5.0 enables you to open more than one publication at a time. You also can save all open publications simultaneously by holding the Shift key while opening the File menu, and then choosing Save All.

If you use PageMaker's Revert command to cancel your current edits and revert to the last saved version, you return to the version you most recently saved by using the Save or Save As command. Interim versions saved by PageMaker are ignored by the Revert command.

Become accustomed to saving your work at regular intervals—not just at the end of a work session. The keyboard shortcut (Ctrl+S) makes saving your document easy.

When To Save a Document

Make sure that you save your document under any of the following circumstances:

- ◼ After you finish a page—and before turning to another page.
- ◼ After you finish importing a long text file into a PageMaker publication.

- After you finish placing, sizing, and cropping a graphic.
- As you are working—every five minutes or so.
- Before you print a document or part of a document.
- Before you globally change type specs or formats.
- After you make any changes to the master pages.
- Before leaving your computer, using the phone, or pausing.
- OFTEN!

At least once a week, back up your hard disk files to floppy disks in case of hard disk failure.

You can save a PageMaker template to use as the basis for starting other documents. Type the PT5 extension as part of the file name, or select the Template radio button in the Save As area of the Save dialog box. The next time you open that file and save it, PageMaker displays the Save dialog box so that you can rename the template file as a document.

Saving with a Changed Name, Format, or Drive/Directory Location

Use the Save As command from the File menu to save an existing document under a different name. This feature is useful if you want to create a new document based on the existing one. You could start a February newsletter, for example, by opening the file for the January newsletter, called V01-N01, and saving it under a new name, such as V01-N02. (See Chapter 15 for suggestions about creating templates instead of copying complete documents.)

You also can use the Save As command to move the document to a different directory or onto a disk in a different disk drive. This capability is useful if you want to make an updated version of a document without changing the name or modified date (recorded by the system) of the original version, thereby creating a backup version. You could, for example, start the second revision of a heavily edited report by opening the file for the first version (perhaps stored on a network file server) and saving it to a different disk drive (your own hard disk).

You also can use the Save As command to save the document in a different format (as a template rather than a document). After finishing the first newsletter in a series, for example, you can save the newsletter as a document (to store as an archive), and then use Save As to create a template (for use in subsequent issues).

T I P

Using Save As To Make a Publication File Smaller

Remember that you can set your preferences for saving documents Faster or Smaller, as described in the section "Using Different Save Options" earlier in this chapter. If you selected the Faster option, which makes your files larger than they need to be, you can force a file to be smaller by using the Save As command.

The dialog box displayed by the Save As command is the same as the Save Publication As dialog box that is displayed when you first use the Save command (described earlier in this chapter), and is common to most Windows applications (refer to fig. 4.17).

Using Save As To Copy Linked Graphics

One way to ensure that all the linked files are stored in the same directory as the publication is to place all graphics in the publication and then choose Save As from the File menu. In the Save As dialog box, click Copy Files Required for Remote Printing (which also copies special files such as the track-kerning resource file that is needed in printing) or Copy All Linked Files (to include all linked graphics whether or not they are already included as part of the publication).

You can also use the Save As command and these options to copy a publication and its linked files onto a disk for transport to another system, as described under "Changing Systems and Using Service Bureaus" in Chapter 14.

Closing a Document Window

You can close one PageMaker file without leaving PageMaker altogether by using the Close command on the File menu. You also can close the current publication by double-clicking the Control menu icon of the document window or by choosing Close from the Control Box menu.

If you saved your document, PageMaker simply closes the publication. If you have not saved your document since making changes, PageMaker displays a dialog box asking whether you want to save the document before you close it (see fig. 4.18).

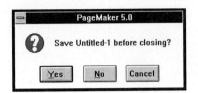

Fig. 4.18

A warning dialog box appears when you close a document without saving changes.

Click Yes, press Enter, or type **y** to save the changed document or to display the Save As dialog box; click No or type **N** to ignore the changes; or click Cancel to cancel the Close command and keep the document open. You also can use the Tab key to highlight any of the buttons and then press Enter to activate the highlighted choice.

Quitting PageMaker

In the Windows environment, you can run other programs without closing PageMaker. If you do want to leave PageMaker, however, you can use the Exit command from the File menu or the Close command on the Control menu of the application window. PageMaker verifies that you have saved your current document. If you have not saved the current document, PageMaker displays a dialog box asking whether you want to save your changes as well as close PageMaker (refer to fig. 4.18).

After you leave PageMaker, you return to a view of any other application windows that remain open. To leave Windows, choose the Close command on the Control menu of the Windows Program Manager window. The Windows program always asks you in a dialog box to confirm that you want to end the session.

For Related Information

▶▶ "Building a Template," p. 675.

FROM HERE...

Summary

This chapter has explained how to start a new publication or open an existing one, how to change the preferences for how elements are displayed on-screen, as well as for other options, and how to save the publication. The next chapter describes how to create a master grid for the publication, and discusses the basic methods of selecting and moving elements on a page.

Together, Chapters 4 through 10 present the commands and steps required for a complete production cycle, except for the design process. Part III describes more advanced features of PageMaker; Part IV offers basic guidelines to help you design your own publications; and Part V provides examples of publications designed for efficient production, usefulness, and pleasing appearance.

Creating Page Layouts

C hapter 4 takes you through the process of starting a new publication, entering Page Setup specifications for page size and margins, changing the default Preferences for how pages are displayed on-screen, and saving your work as either a publication or a template. In this chapter, you continue building the publication, learning how to set up master pages that will affect the whole publication, and you receive tips on developing efficient procedures. You are also introduced to adding and editing text and graphics, and using the basic commands and tools that are common in working with both text and graphics. (The procedures for adding and editing text and graphics are described in greater detail in Chapters 6 through 9.)

In this chapter, you learn to change the view of the current page, add and remove pages, turn pages, and sort pages (a new feature of PageMaker 5.0). You begin setting up a master page with a page layout grid and running headers or footers with page numbers. You learn how to use rulers and guides to help position elements on a page, and how to select and move elements with the Pointer tool and the Text tool. You learn how to use the mouse and the Control palette to move or scale objects on a page, how to arrange elements in layers, and how to use the Edit menu commands—Cut, Copy, Paste, and Undo—that are common to most Windows applications.

Working with Pages

While building a publication, you can use the Layout menu commands to move around on a page, to add or delete pages, or to turn from one page to another. The Layout menu commands are described in the following sections.

Changing the View of a Page in the Layout Window

Often, you can see only a part of a page or a document on-screen. In PageMaker, you have three ways available to move the page image around the screen: you can use the Scroll bars to scroll vertically and horizontally; you can use the grabber hand to move the image in any direction; you can use the View command's submenu of the Layout menu to jump to enlarged views of a particular area or reduce the page image to a smaller size. All the View submenu commands have keyboard equivalents or mouse shortcuts. These techniques are described later.

To jump the Text tool (the I-beam) from one place to another within a text block (and thereby jump to a new view of the page), use the keyboard shortcuts described in Chapter 7 (table 7.1 under "Inserting Text").

Using the Scroll bars

PageMaker's Scroll bars operate the way other Scroll bars work under Windows. To move the on-screen image in small increments, click on an arrow. Click in the gray area of a Scroll bar (shown white in figure 5.1) to jump in one direction or another in the window in larger fixed increments. Drag the Scroll box in the Scroll bar to move any distance. The position of the Scroll box on the Scroll bar indicates the position of the screen image relative to the whole page and the pasteboard.

Fig. 5.1

A PageMaker
scroll bar.

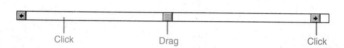

Click   Drag   Click

The distance the image moves depends on the view you are using. The increments are smaller in enlarged views, such as 200 percent, than in reduced views, such as Fit in Window.

To turn off the Scroll bars so that they aren't displayed, select the Scroll Bars command from the Guides and Rulers submenu of the Layout menu. You then can see more of the page, and you can use any of the following techniques to move around on-screen. When the Scroll bars are turned off, the page icons are also hidden, so you cannot easily know which page you are viewing or jump to another page by clicking an icon with the mouse, but you can use the Go to Page command on the Layout menu to change pages.

To turn on the Scroll bars, select the Scroll Bars command again. This on/off switch shows a check mark next to the command when the Scroll bars are turned on.

Using the Grabber Hand

In any view, you can use the grabber hand to drag the image in any direction. Hold down the Alt key while you press the main mouse button. When the pointer changes to a hand, you can drag the pointer in any direction to move the page image on-screen (see fig. 5.2). If you hold down both the Alt key and the Shift key, the grabber hand moves either horizontally or vertically—not diagonally.

Fig. 5.2

The grabber hand.

Moving Around on the Page

T I P

The quickest way to move around the page on-screen for diagonal or small movements is to use the grabber hand.

Using the View Submenu

The View submenu of the Layout menu offers eight commands for changing your view of the page and shows the keyboard shortcuts to the right of the commands. You can get a Show Pasteboard view, which displays all the pasteboard, by choosing Show Pasteboard (a menu command added in PageMaker 5.0 that was previously only

available by holding down the Shift key when you chose Fit in Window)
(see fig. 5.3). You can force all pages in the publication to the same
view by holding Ctrl+Alt and choosing any view from the View
submenu.

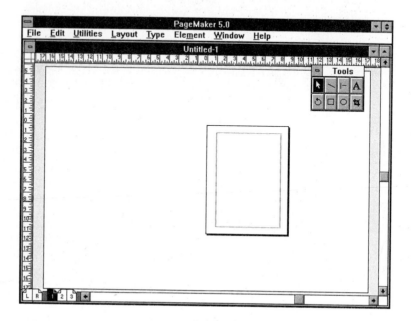

Fig. 5.3

Press
Ctrl+Shift+W
to get a wider
view of the
pasteboard area.

In addition to using the Ctrl key shortcuts for commands on the View
submenu, you can use the mouse to quickly change views of the page.
You can turn to a Fit in Window view of any page, regardless of the
view in which the page was left last, by holding down the Shift key as
you click the mouse on a page icon. This method also works if you click
on the icon for the current page.

Click the secondary mouse button to switch to an Actual Size view of
the pointer's position on the page or to toggle between Actual Size and
Fit in Window. The same toggle action is possible by using the main
mouse button while holding the Ctrl+Alt keys. (See the Microsoft Windows installation guide for information about specifying the primary
and secondary mouse buttons.)

Hold down the Shift key and click the secondary mouse button to
switch to a 200% Size view of the pointer's position or to toggle between 200% Size and Actual Size. The same toggle action is possible
using the main mouse button while holding the Ctrl+Alt+Shift keys.

PageMaker 5.0 adds the capability to magnify up to 800% to get custom
page views. Press Ctrl+Spacebar and drag to enlarge the view of the

area to 800%. Press Ctrl+Alt+Spacebar and click or drag to reduce the view in fixed increments to as small as 25%.

Table 5.1 summarizes the shortcuts for each command on the View submenu.

Table 5.1 Shortcuts for View Submenu Commands

Command	Shortcut
Fit in Window	Ctrl+W; or Shift+clicking on a page icon at bottom of window; or Toggle between Fit in Window and Actual Size by clicking secondary mouse button; or Ctrl+Alt+clicking main mouse button
Show Pasteboard	Ctrl+Shift+W
25% Size	Ctrl+0
50% Size	Ctrl+5
75% Size	Ctrl+7
Actual Size	Ctrl+1, or use the mouse to toggle (see Fit in Window and 200% Size)
200% Size	Ctrl+2; or toggle between 200% Size and Actual Size by holding the Shift key and clicking the secondary mouse button; or Ctrl+Alt+Shift+clicking the main mouse button
400% Size	Ctrl+4
Ctrl+Alt+any view	Forces all pages in the publication to the same view
Custom Page Views	Ctrl+Spacebar+Drag to enlarge up to 800%; Ctrl+Alt+Spacebar+Drag to reduce view

Changing Views of the Page

Get into the habit of using the secondary mouse button to toggle between Actual Size and Fit in Window, and using the Shift key with the secondary mouse button to toggle between Actual Size and 200% Size, rather than opening the Layout menu and then the View submenu and choosing a command. Remember to position the pointer at the spot you want to see before you click to enlarge the view.

continues

Changing Views of the Page (continued)

This method is also helpful for moving around on the page. For example, toggling from Actual Size to Fit in Window and back to Actual Size of another part of the page can be faster than using the Scroll bars or the grabber hand when moving diagonally for long distances.

T   I   P   **Starting a Page in the Fit in Window View**

Start building each page by working in the Fit in Window view, letting the snap-to effect of the guides help you place text and graphics from other programs. To type or edit text or to draw graphics with PageMaker's tools, change to Actual Size, 75% Size, or 50% Size. Change to 200% Size to work with small type (eight points or fewer) and to align graphics and text precisely without using guides.

T   I   P   **Saving Pages in Different Views**

Some layout artists save the finished pages in their publications in Fit in Window view and the unfinished pages in a close-up view of where they left off with that page. This way, the layout artist can page through a publication quickly, making finishing touches after the first complete run-through. (Each page is displayed in its last view.)

Inserting and Removing Pages

While you are working, you can insert and delete pages by using the Insert Pages and Remove Pages commands on the Layout menu. With either command, you enter the number of pages to be inserted or deleted (see fig. 5.4).

The page count displayed in the Page Setup dialog box reflects page insertions and deletions in the publication. "Specifying Text Flow" in Chapter 6 describes how to flow text from one page to another when you are using the Insert Pages command, and how to insert pages automatically with the Autoflow option.

Insert pages

Insert ☐ page(s):

OK

Cancel

○ Before current page
◉ After current page
○ Between current pages

Fig. 5.4

Inserting new pages.

When you delete pages, PageMaker warns you that you cannot restore their contents. If you delete a block of text from the middle of a multipage flow of text from the same source, PageMaker preserves the link between adjacent blocks, but the content of the deleted text block is lost. For example, before a block of text is deleted, the text in figure 5.5 flows through three columns. After the middle block of text is deleted, the text flows from the first column to the third column. To delete pages without losing their contents, you can use the Pointer tool to select all the page contents, drag the contents to the pasteboard area, and then delete the pages.

 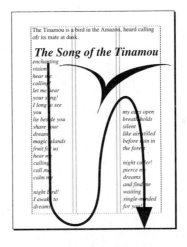

Fig. 5.5

The chain between adjacent text blocks is preserved after text deletion.

If you insert pages between two facing pages, any elements that extend across the boundaries between the two pages remain on the left-hand page. If you delete a left-hand page from a facing-page set and some elements overlap both pages, PageMaker deletes those elements. If you delete pages so that two new facing pages have more than 40 ruler guides (the maximum allowed for a pair of facing pages), PageMaker deletes some of the ruler guides on the right-hand page.

If you insert an odd number of pages into a double-sided facing-page layout, elements that were formerly set up to bleed from the left-hand to the right-hand page of a pair bleed onto the pasteboard. In figure 5.6, for example, elements bleed across pages 2 and 3. When a new page is inserted, the elements bleed from page 3 (the old page 2) onto the pasteboard, and the connection with page 4 (the old page 3) is lost (see fig. 5.7).

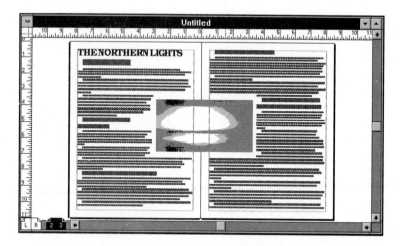

Fig. 5.6

Before one page is inserted between two facing pages, the figure bleeds across pages 2 and 3.

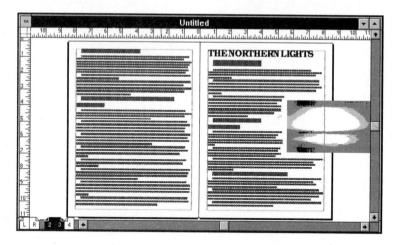

Fig. 5.7

After one page is inserted, the figure bleeds onto the pasteboard.

PageMaker has two methods for forcing a left-hand (even-numbered) page to become a right-hand (odd-numbered) page. You can insert a blank page in front of the left-hand page. Alternatively, if you are working with a publication consisting of many sections, you can make each section a separate file, each of which starts with an odd-numbered page. Figure 5.8 illustrates these two methods.

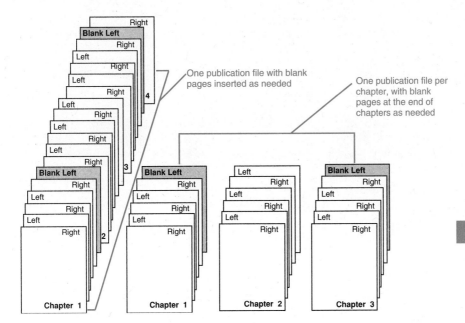

One publication file with blank pages inserted as needed

One publication file per chapter, with blank pages at the end of chapters as needed

Fig. 5.8

Two ways of forcing new sections to start on right-hand pages.

Turning Pages

You can move from page to page by clicking on the page icons at the bottom of the screen in Layout view if the Scroll bars are displayed (see fig. 5.9).

Fig. 5.9

Scrolling through the page icons in large publications.

If the publication is so large that all the page icons cannot fit on the bottom of the screen at one time, you can click on the arrows that appear at each end of the page icons. Use one of the following methods:

■ To scroll one page icon at a time in the direction of the arrow, position the mouse pointer on the arrow and click the main mouse button once.

■ To keep the page icons scrolling, hold down the mouse button on an arrow.

■ To jump half the number of page icons shown, place the mouse pointer over the scroll arrow and click with the secondary mouse button.

■ To jump to the beginning or end of the page icon list, click on the third mouse button or hold down the Ctrl key and click once on an arrow.

You can also jump to other parts of the publication by using the Go To Page command on the Layout menu, or you can use keyboard shortcuts to jump one page forward or backward at a time. Use one of the following methods:

■ To jump forward one page (or two pages in a double-sided publication with facing pages), press F12.

■ To jump backward one page (or two pages in a double-sided publication with facing pages), press F11.

Changing Pages by Moving the Text Tool

You can change pages by using the keyboard shortcuts for jumping through an article with the Text tool. In other words, you can jump to the end of an article in order to jump to the page on which the article ends. With the Text tool selected and the I-beam placed within a block of text, you press Ctrl+PgUp to jump to the beginning of that text file. To jump to the end of a text file, you press Ctrl+PgDn.

You also can use the new Aldus Addition added in PageMaker 5.0, *Traverse Textblocks*, to quickly jump from the current text block to the next or previous text block in the story, or to the first or last text block in the story (see the section "Traversing Textblocks" in Chapter 6).

Scrolling through Pages Automatically—An On-Screen Slide Show

You can have PageMaker page through a publication automatically, displaying pages sequentially like a continuous slide show, by holding the Shift key as you choose Go To Page from the Layout menu. Click the mouse button to stop the slide show. This is a good way to review an entire publication quickly, or to find a particular page when you don't know its number (but can recognize the layout).

You can also use this feature to create a live "slide show" for a presentation. Turn the Scroll bars off by choosing Scroll Bars from the Guides and Rulers submenu of the Layout menu, and set each page to a close-up view of the presentation material.

You can control the speed at which pages are turned by adding the following line to the ALDUS.INI file (using the Windows Notepad or any text editor and saving the file in "text only" format):

SlideTimer=x

where x is the number of seconds each page is displayed.

Sorting Pages

One of the new Aldus Additions introduced by PageMaker 5.0 is called *Sort Pages*. This command displays thumbnail views of every page in a publication; you can change the sequence of pages by dragging a page from one position to another.

Choose Sort Pages from the Aldus Additions submenu of the Utilities menu. PageMaker displays the PageSorter window with a thumbnail of each page in the publication and the page number below each one (see fig. 5.10). You can move pages or facing-page spreads by dragging a page from one position to another. When you move a page, the new page number is shown at the left below the page, and the old page number sequence is shown at the right (see fig. 5.11).

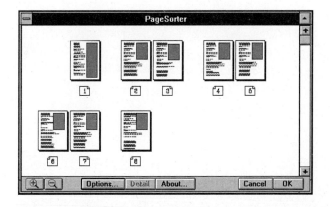

Fig. 5.10

PageSorter window before pages are moved.

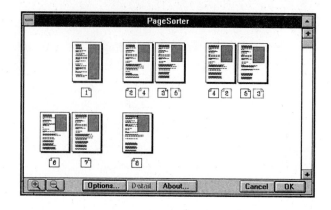

Fig. 5.11

PageSorter window after pages are moved.

If the pages are displayed in facing-page spreads in the PageSorter window, you can move spreads from one position to another, but you cannot move individual pages between two pages of a spread or move one of the pages from a spread to another position. If you want more flexibility in moving pages, click the Options button at the bottom of the PageSorter window, and turn Facing Pages off (see fig. 5.12). The display changes to show individual pages that can be moved to any sequence (see fig. 5.13).

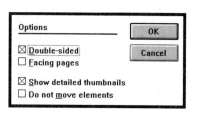

Fig. 5.12

PageSorter Options dialog box with Facing Pages turned off.

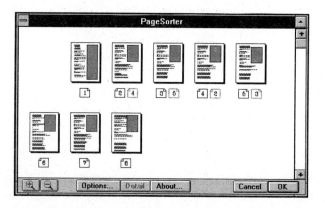

Fig. 5.13

PageSorter window display when the Facing Pages option is turned off.

You can also turn on or off Double Sided display in the PageSorter Options dialog box. When on, the PageSorter display shows a blank space to the left of the first page of a publication that starts with an odd-numbered page. You can turn off Show Detailed Thumbnails to get a faster display of pages in the PageSorter window. When this option is off, each page shows as a gray rectangle, but you can still get a detailed view of a page by clicking on it in the PageSorter window and clicking the Detail button at the bottom of the window.

Normally, if you have specified different inside and outside margins for a double-sided publication, PageMaker maintains the same position of all elements on the page relative to the margins by moving them on pages whose margins change when the pages are rearranged. Click Do Not Move Elements to keep all elements in the same position relative to the page, as opposed to relative to margins.

For Related Information

◀◀ "Controlling a Window," p. 68.

▶▶ "Specifying Text Flow," p. 240.

▶▶ "Traversing Textblocks," p. 267.

▶▶ "Inserting Text," p. 276.

FROM HERE...

Adding Master-Page Elements

PageMaker divides publications into two types of pages: master pages and numbered pages. Any text, graphics, or guides that you set on a master page appear on every page in the publication. Any text, graphics, or guides that you set on a numbered page are printed on that page only. If your publication is longer than two pages, you can save time by making basic settings on master pages.

Figure 5.14 shows elements that usually are on master pages. These elements include column guides, running headers and footers, and nonprinting guides, which define the basic grid system underlying the publication's design. Settings made on the master pages can be changed on individual pages when necessary. You can move column guides, suppress running headers and footers, hide all guides, or call the original master page settings back to the current page display.

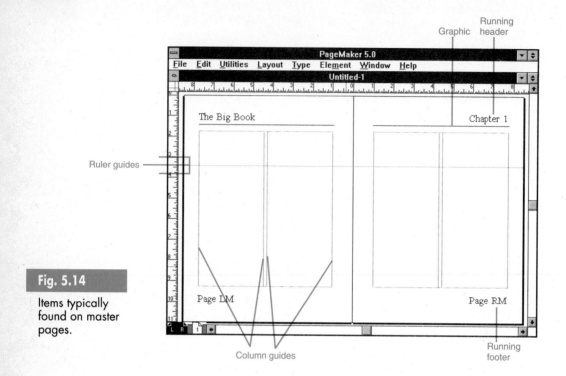

Fig. 5.14

Items typically
found on master
pages.

To turn to a master page, click on the page icon for the left or right
master page. These icons are displayed at the bottom left of the screen.
You can also use the Go To Page command on the Layout menu and
choose the left or right master page in the dialog box. When on the
master page, you can use the techniques described in this chapter to
set the column guides and other grid lines.

Left and right master pages have different effects on numbered pages.
Elements set up on the right-hand master page appear on every page of
a single-sided publication but only on odd-numbered pages of double-
sided publications. Elements set up on the left-hand master page appear on all even-numbered pages of double-sided publications. If you
select the Double Sided and Facing Pages options in the Page Setup
dialog box, you can work on both master pages at the same time because master pages appear on-screen simultaneously.

The following sequence of steps is typical for building a master page:

1. Set the column guides.

2. Display the ruler and position guides that are part of the grid,
    including horizontal guides for positioning the running headers
    and footers on the master pages.

3. Type the running header between the column guides, and then drag the running header to the top of the page.

4. Add graphic elements common to all pages.

5. Type the running footer between the column guides, and then drag the running footer to the bottom of the page.

An example of a master page appears in figure 5.14.

Creating a Master Grid of Columns and Rulers Guides

You usually think of a grid as a matrix of evenly spaced lines, like quadrille rules, but in publishing the basic grid is defined by the page margins and column guides for a publication. Professional designers often use much more elaborate grid systems, as described in Chapter 15. The grid can include ruler guides as well as graphic elements, such as hairline rules between columns. The principle used in designing a grid for master pages is to identify all the basic elements—nonprinting guides as well as text and graphics—that appear on every page throughout the publication.

Figure 5.15 shows some examples of grid systems used in a book, a manual, and a newsletter. For a more complete discussion of using the grid system in design, see "Creating a Grid System" in Chapter 15. Chapters 17 through 21 provide examples of grids used in various publications, including those shown in figure 5.15.

The grid for left-hand pages may differ from that for right-hand pages. More likely, however, the grid itself will be the same on all pages; only the text of the running headers and footers differs between pages. The following sections describe how to use the Column Guides command, how to set up other guides, and how to use other commands on the Layout menu to set up your master grids (see fig. 5.16).

Setting Column Guides

PageMaker's default setting is for one column. With the Column Guides command on the Layout menu, you can call up a dialog box to change this number (see fig. 5.17). You can use this command to set up columns on each page individually, but it is more efficient to set them up on the master pages if most of the pages in your publication have the same number of columns.

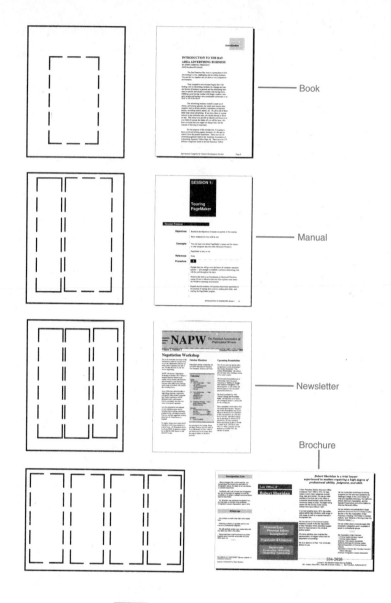

Book

Manual

Newsletter

Brochure

Fig. 5.15

Examples of grid systems and their uses.

Fig. 5.16

The Layout menu commands used to set up nonprinting guides.

If you have set the publication to be double-sided (in the Page Setup dialog box described earlier), you can set the same number of columns and space between columns on both master pages, or you can check the box beside Set Left and Right Pages Separately to make the dialog box display separate entries for left and right pages. Use the mouse or the Tab key to select the current entries in the boxes beside Number of Columns and Space Between Columns, and then type new values.

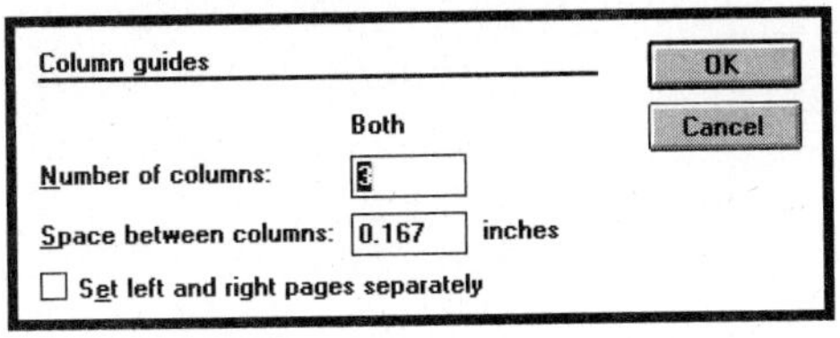

Fig. 5.17

The Column Guides dialog box.

The space between columns is given or entered in the unit of measure currently selected through the Preferences command on the File menu. If you have set up inches as the default unit of measure but like to enter gutter widths in picas, you can use the abbreviation system described in the tip "Overriding the Unit of Measure" under "Specifying Page Size" in Chapter 4. You, for example, can type **1p6** to get a gutter width of one pica and six points.

All columns on a page must have the same amount of space between them. You can force unequal gutter widths using a trick described in Chapter 11 under "Wrapping Text Around Graphics."

PageMaker imposes a maximum limit of 20 columns per page and a minimum column width of one-half inch. The maximum number of columns allowed on a page, therefore, is determined by the margins of the page and the space between the columns. In practice, you rarely reach this limit because most publications have no more than five columns on a page.

When you first select a number of columns and specify the amount of space you want between the columns, PageMaker takes these figures and divides the page into equal columns between the margins (see fig. 5.18). To make columns unequal, you drag the column guides (see "Moving Guides" later in this chapter). The column guides that you set up on the master pages apply to all numbered pages, but you can change the column guides for individual pages by turning to the numbered page and using the Column Guides command.

Column guides define the width of text that is placed or pasted in the column. Changing column widths—either through the Column Guides command or by dragging the column guides—doesn't affect the width of blocks of text already on the page, only the width of new text placed or pasted into the column. After placing text in a column, you can change the column guides without affecting the text, and you can change the width of the text by dragging the text block handles, as explained in Chapter 6 in the section "Sizing a Text Block with the Pointer Tool."

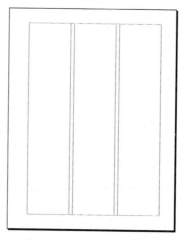

Fig. 5.18

A three-column page division.

T   I   P

Reflowing Text after Changing Column Widths

If you decide to change the column widths after flowing text, you can adjust the text width by changing the width of each text block manually, as described under "Using the Mouse To Move and Resize Elements" and "Using the Control Palette in Layout View" later in this chapter, and under "Sizing a Text Block" in Chapter 6. If, however, you need to adjust many text blocks, it might be faster to select the entire story, use the Cut command on the Edit menu to delete it, and then use the Paste command on the Edit menu to Paste it in the first column and use the Autoflow option to flow the text into subsequent columns, as described in Chapter 6.

Creating Additional Nonprinting Guides

Nonprinting guides include all the various dotted and dashed lines that are displayed in PageMaker's Layout view but are not printed. These nonprinting guides include page margins, column guides, and ruler guides, as shown in figure 5.19. You specify page margins when you use the New command on the File menu to start a new publication, and you can change them by using the Page Setup command. To set up column guides, you use the Column Guides command, which is described in the preceding section.

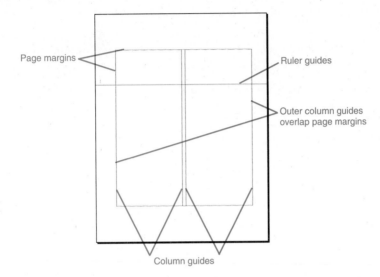

Page margins

Ruler guides

Outer column guides overlap page margins

Column guides

Fig. 5.19

Nonprinting guides.

In addition to the margin and column guides, you can drag up to 40 ruler guides from the ruler lines. Ruler guides are useful for positioning objects on a page but don't directly affect the width of text (as column guides do) or the length of text (as the bottom page margin does). You can create ruler guides on a master page as a grid for positioning objects consistently on document pages, or you can create ruler guides on individual pages of the publication.

A Guide to the Guides

T I P

Only column guides and ruler guides can be moved by dragging them on the page. Only margins and column guides cause text to wrap. Only the bottom page margin affects the length of the columns.

To drag a guide from the ruler line, the horizontal and vertical rulers must be visible at the top and left of the Layout view. If the rulers aren't displayed, choose Rulers (Ctrl+R) from the Guides and Rulers submenu of the Layout menu. Then place the pointer on the ruler line and hold down the mouse button until the pointer changes to a two-headed arrow. Drag the pointer onto the page. Drag from the top ruler line to create horizontal guides; drag from the left ruler line to create vertical guides. The dotted-line marker on the ruler line helps you position the guide, and the numeric position of the guide relative to the zero point is shown in the Control palette (if it is open) as you drag.

Ruler guides that you position on master pages appear on all new or blank numbered pages. Ruler guides that you position on a numbered page are displayed on that page only.

> **CAUTION:** If you have already placed ruler guides or customized column settings on several pages before you define or change the master page elements, those pages retain their original settings and don't pick up the new master settings, unless you use the Copy Master Guides command on the Layout menu.

Moving Guides

You can reposition column guides and ruler guides by dragging them on the page. You can move these guides on numbered pages even if the guides originally were set up on the master page, and you can revert to the original master page guides at any time by choosing Copy Master Guides from the Layout menu. You can move page margins with the Page Setup command only (described in the section "Specifying Page Margins" in Chapter 4).

To move a column guide or ruler guide, put the pointer over the guide and hold down the mouse button. When the pointer changes to a two-headed arrow, you can drag the guide to a new location. Figure 5.20 shows an example of a publication in which the column guides were moved to create custom layouts. The example is taken from Part III of this book. On the left side of the figure, the middle column guides of a two-column layout have been moved to the left to create a narrow left column and a wide right column. In the center example, columns have been arranged to create a wide right column and two narrow columns. In the example on the right, the column guides have been moved to create two columns: a wide left column and a narrow right column.

When you move a column guide to create unequal columns, the word Custom replaces the number of columns you typed in the Column Guides dialog box. You can restore equal columns by choosing the Column Guides command from the Layout menu and entering a number of columns again. If you created equal columns on the master pages and move the column guides on a numbered page, you can restore the master page settings by choosing Copy Master Guides from the Layout menu.

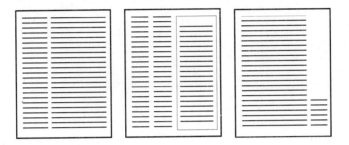

Fig. 5.20

Examples of publications with custom column settings.

Being Precise in Positioning Guides

It is a good practice to use the rulers or the numeric display in the Control palette to help position the column guides precisely. Before moving column guides, display the ruler lines (by choosing the Rulers command from the Guides and Rulers submenu of the Layout menu or pressing Ctrl+R), and the Control palette (by choosing the Control palette command from the Window menu).

T I P

You can remove a ruler guide by dragging the guide off the page. To remove a column guide, however, you must use the Column Guides command and dialog box from the Layout menu.

Changing the Zero Point

The *zero point* is the intersection of the zero points of the two rulers. Usually, the zero point falls at the top left corner of the page. In double-sided publications viewed with the Facing Pages option, the zero point falls at the inside edges of the facing pages.

Before you can change the zero point, the ruler line must be on-screen. To move the zero point, put the pointer on the intersection point of the rulers and hold down the mouse button as you drag the marker to the new zero point location (see fig. 5.21 and fig. 5.22). Crossed lines appear as you drag the zero point, to help you see where the new location will be when you release the mouse. The measures on the ruler line then shift to the new point, as shown in figure 5.23.

Fig. 5.21

Changing the zero point: the pointer at the intersection of the ruler lines.

Fig. 5.22

Changing the zero point: dragging the marker to the new location.

Fig. 5.23

Changing the zero point: the measures on the ruler line shift to the new point.

When To Move the Zero Point

Normally, you only need to move the zero point when you want to print a publication using the Manual Tiling option (described in Chapter 10 in the sections "Entering Paper Printing Options for PostScript Printers" and "Printer Options for PCL Printers"). You might also need to move the zero point if all of the design specifications are given relative to a point other than the top left corner of a page or the top center point of a two-page spread.

With PageMaker 5.0's new Control palette, moving the zero point can be handy when adjusting the size of an object numerically. Position the zero point at the top left corner of the object, and then set the W(idth) and H(eight) values to the exact measurements you want.

The Zero Lock command on the Guides and Rulers submenu of the Layout menu is a toggle command that enables you to lock the zero point so that it cannot be moved accidentally, or to unlock the zero point if it is locked.

Typing Running Headers and Footers

Text entered on the master pages appears on every page of the publication unless the text is suppressed (see the section "Hiding Master-Page Items" later in this chapter). This text can include page numbers as well as running headers and footers that might identify the publication or the chapter. You can type text directly onto the master page, as described here, or you can import it from another source (see "Importing Text with the Place Command" in Chapter 6) or copy it from a Library (see "Creating and Using a Library" in Chapter 14).

To type text directly on a page in PageMaker, first select the Text tool: the letter *A* in the top right corner of the toolbox. When you click the pointer on the Text tool, the mouse pointer changes to an I-beam. Click the I-beam anywhere on the page to set an insertion point, and start typing.

Using Margins To Control Placed Text

T I P

Place the running headers and footers outside the page margins, as shown in figure 5.24. Use the top and bottom margins to define the length of the columns when you place text on numbered pages.

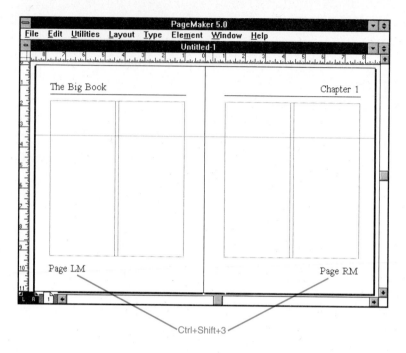

Fig. 5.24

Setting up automatic page numbering by pressing Ctrl+Shift+3.

Chapter 6 describes additional methods of positioning text on a page; Chapter 7 describes how to edit the text; and Chapter 8 describes how to format the text (change the font, style, alignment, and so on).

Numbering Pages Automatically

You can set the starting page number in a publication through the New and Page Setup commands, as described in Chapter 4. To have page numbers print out on publication pages, however, you must insert them as part of the text—usually on the master pages.

You create a page number by pressing Ctrl+Shift+3 (Ctrl+#) while typing with the Text tool. When you press this keystroke combination on a single-sided master page or on a right-facing master page, RM appears at the text-insertion point on the master page. When you type Ctrl+Shift+3 on a left-facing master page, LM appears at the text-insertion point. You can format the page number as you would any other text by selecting the page number with the Text tool and setting type specifications, as described in Chapter 8 in the section "Formatting Text."

Page numbers usually appear in a running header or footer on the master pages, but you can make PageMaker print page numbers anywhere on any page. If you enter the page numbers by pressing Ctrl+Shift+3 on the master pages, on subsequent pages the page numbers appear in the location set on the master pages. You can also set up page numbers by pressing Ctrl+Shift+3 on individual pages within a publication.

Positioning Page Numbers on Numbered Pages

You can suppress master page elements on numbered pages by turning Display Master Items off under the Layout menu. If you want to suppress everything *except* the running header or footer with the page number, try the following method.

Turn to the master page and use the Pointer tool to select the text block that contains the page number; then choose Copy from the Edit menu. Turn to the numbered page, and press Ctrl+Shift+P to paste the copied element in precisely the same position as it was on the master page. (See the sections "Selecting with the Pointer and Text Tools" and "Using the Edit Menu Commands" later in this chapter.)

If the copied text block includes text that you don't want displayed on the numbered page, select the text with the Text tool and use the Type Specs command from the Type menu, and then choose Paper in the color box of the Type Specifications dialog box, or use the Color palette to set the text color to (Paper).

This action ensures that the page number appears in the same position in copied text block as on the master page from which it was copied, but the Paper option for text will not work for some PCL printers. If your printer has this limitation, delete the elements you don't want to print and adjust the position of the text block as necessary.

See also the tip "Suppressing Parts of the Master-Page Elements" later in this chapter.

Adding Graphic Elements to Master Pages

In addition to containing text and guides, master pages can include graphics created in PageMaker or imported from other programs. The grid system, for example, may include hairline rules between columns. You can create or place graphics on a master page the same way you create or place graphics on any page in PageMaker. These techniques are described in Chapter 9.

Positioning Page Numbers Where They Are Easy To Find

The most easily referenced parts of any book are the outer edges of the pages: the top or bottom left of even-numbered pages, and the top or bottom right of odd-numbered pages. Using these four positions makes page numbers and section names easy to find.

You can also use the reverse psychology intentionally: position the page numbers near the inside margin, or in the center of wide pages, to force the readers to view more of the publication than they would otherwise need to see. This is a common practice in magazines, for example, where readers are encouraged to view the advertisements while searching for articles.

Figure 5.25 shows sample master pages from Part III of this book; the example incorporates graphics on the master pages. The pages shown use PageMaker graphics to set off the grid and dummy text.

Fig. 5.25

Master pages
including
graphics from
other programs.

Remember that you use master pages to make specific material appear on all or most pages of a publication. After you are on a numbered page of the publication, you can suppress all or parts of the master-page elements by using one of the techniques described in the following two sections.

When you have set up the master pages, you are ready to begin working on the first numbered page. Use the Place command on the File menu to bring in graphics and text from other programs, or use PageMaker's built-in text and graphics tools, as described in Chapters 6 through 9.

Repeating Elements from One Master Page to Another   T I P

After setting up text and graphics on one master page, you can copy the text and graphics to the second master page in a facing-page publication. To copy the text and graphics to the second master page, follow this procedure: use the Edit menu's Select All command to select the entire group (assuming there is nothing on the pasteboard), and then use the Copy and Paste commands to copy and paste the group on the second master page, and drag the pasted group into position.

For Related Information

FROM HERE...

◄◄ "Assigning a Starting Page Number," p. 147.

◄◄ "Specifying Page Margins," p. 152.

►► "Adding Running Headers or Footers," p. 268.

►► "Entering Document Printing Options," p. 412.

►► "Setting Additional Printing Options for PCL Printers," p. 420.

►► "Wrapping Text around Graphics," p. 443.

►► "Creating a Grid System," p. 683.

Building Individual Pages

Up to this point, you have learned that you should build master pages before creating individual pages, and that you can easily add or remove pages or hide master items on selected pages. The actual steps for adding text to any page are described in Chapter 6, and the steps for adding graphics are described in Chapter 9, but we summarize the basic methods here so you can actually add one or two items to your document now if you are using this chapter as a tutorial, and trying the commands as we describe them.

Summary of Methods for Adding Elements to a Page

■ Select the Text tool and click anywhere on the page to position the text cursor; then begin typing.

■ Select one of the graphics tools from the toolbox (the Rectangle tool, the Line tool, or the Ellipse tool), position the pointer on the page, and hold down the mouse button as you drag the pointer diagonally to create a graphic.

■ Use the Place command on the File menu to import a text or graphic file into PageMaker from another application; then click the pointer on the page to place the imported element.

■ You can use the Copy and Paste commands to copy elements from other Windows applications into PageMaker, or the new OLE commands added in PageMaker 5.0 (Paste Link, Paste Special, and Insert Object).

After you build the master pages as described in the preceding sections, you begin the task of placing text and graphics on each page. A typical sequence of steps for each page is as follows:

1. Verify that the master-page elements are appropriate for the current numbered page. If column guides or ruler guides need to be changed for this page, adjust them as needed before placing text and graphics on the page. Commands that are used in this step include Column Guides, Rulers, and Display Master Items.

2. If your design specifications limit you to one or two variations in text and graphic formats, you can change the default settings to match the most common specifications or set up a style sheet so that each text variation has its own tag. You change the default settings for text and graphics by making menu selections while the Pointer tool is selected. You can read more about style sheets in Chapter 8.

3. Place text and graphics on the page. The following are general guidelines:

   ■ Work in Fit in Window view at first to lay out the entire page. Change to closer views to make fine adjustments.

   ■ Use the Snap to Guides feature to help you position text and graphics against the guides on the page.

■ Use the Drag-Place feature to scale a graphic as you are placing the graphic or to override the column width when placing text (see the section "Using the Drag-Place Feature" in Chapter 6).

4. Save your work often. Press Ctrl+S to execute the Save command or click the current page icon to cause a minisave. For more information on these two alternatives, see the section "Reversing All Changes Made since the Last Save" later in this chapter.

Chapters 6 through 9 explain how to place text and graphics on the pages by using the Place command or PageMaker's text and graphics tools. This sequence of chapters follows one common approach to building a publication: position and format all of the text first, and then add the graphics.

Developing Efficient Procedures

When building a publication, you will find it helpful to study various methods or sequences of operations before deciding on the one that suits you best. The most efficient approach to building a publication varies according to the type of publication you are producing and your own preferences. In some cases, you assemble all the elements on one page at a time, refining every detail of that page layout before you go on to the next page. In other cases, you quickly position all or part of the elements on each page, working through the entire publication once before you go back to make fine adjustments. The question of whether to place text or graphics first also depends on the design of the publication and your personal preference.

In most cases, you should import all the text into the publication before you do any text editing that wasn't done with the word processor. If you are placing unformatted text, be sure that the default paragraph format and type specifications match those specified for the bulk of the text so that you can fit the copy roughly on the pages as you go along. You can change the defaults for text by making selections on the Type menu with the Pointer tool selected from the toolbox, as explained in Chapter 6, or by using style sheets, as explained in Chapter 8.

You should finish placing one whole text file before you start placing another. Placing an entire text file before going on to the next is not a requirement; you can work with as many "loose ends" of overset text as you like. In practice, however, you may find that working with more than two text files at one time is confusing.

Using Guides To Align Objects

Margin guides, column guides, and ruler guides that you create on the master pages will appear on any new blank numbered page in the document (if Display Master Guides is checked on the Layout menu). Margin guides are the same throughout a publication and cannot be varied on individual numbered pages, but column guides and ruler guides can be changed on any page, using the same techniques as described earlier under "Creating a Master Grid." If you change guides on a numbered page, you can always revert to the original master page guides at any time by choosing Copy Master Guides from the Layout menu (described later in this chapter).

Note that in order to move a ruler guide, you should click on it in the margins of the page or where it is not positioned on top of anything else on the page. Otherwise, you might move the object instead of the guide.

Locking Guides

To be sure that you don't move any guide inadvertently, you can use the Lock Guides command from the Guides and Rulers submenu of the Layout menu. The Lock Guides command works like a toggle switch. When the toggle is on, the command is checked on the menu; when the toggle is off, the command is not checked. The Lock Guides setting affects every page of the publication.

Using the Snap-To Effect

Page margins, column guides, and ruler guides help align objects on a page. All three types of guides have a snap-to effect if the optional Snap To Guides effect is turned on (from the Guides and Rulers submenu of the Layout menu). The snap-to effect pulls the pointer, icons, and the edges of a graphic or block of text into position against the guide when you bring the object close to the guide. This capability is extremely useful for aligning objects quickly and precisely, especially when you are working in reduced views such as Fit in Window.

Sometimes, you may prefer to work with the snap-to effect turned off—for example, when you are forcing something into a position outside the basic grid structure. Suppose that you are drawing a hairline rule between two columns. You don't want the crossbar or the rule to snap to either column guide. Turn the snap-to effect off by choosing Snap To Guides from the Guides and Rulers submenu of the Layout menu when the command shows a check mark. (This is a toggle switch; it is checked in the menu when the effect is on, and it is not checked when the effect is off.) Turning Snap To Guides on and off has no effect on text and graphics already on the page.

Hiding Master-Page Items

After building your master pages, you can eliminate all the master guides, text, and graphics from an individual numbered page by turning off the Display Master Items command on the Layout menu. Then use PageMaker's text and graphics tools to add back only the elements you want to use on a selected page.

Suppressing Parts of the Master-Page Elements   T I P

If you want to suppress only some of the master-page elements, you can hide them by covering them with white boxes: rectangles created with PageMaker's Rectangle tool and given a color of white (Paper in the Fill command's submenu) and a line style of None (in the Lines command's submenu). Figure 5.26 provides an example in which a white box at the top of the page hides the running header. This technique doesn't work with all printers; some printers cannot print reverse type or white boxes.

Fig. 5.26

Using a white box to hide the running header.

See also the tip "Positioning Page Numbers on Numbered Pages," in the section "Numbering Pages Automatically," earlier in this chapter.

Copying Master Guides

Suppose that you have suppressed the display of all master elements by turning off the Display Master Items command when a numbered page is displayed on-screen. Or suppose that, on a numbered page, you have moved any of the column guides or ruler guides initially set up on the master pages. With the Copy Master Guides command on the Layout menu, you can restore these guides. The Copy Master Guides command is useful in several situations:

- When you want to restore the master guides after changing them on a numbered page.

- When you want to display the master guides on a page that you built before setting up the master page.

  If you already have placed ruler guides and customized column settings on several pages before you define the master-page elements, those numbered pages retain their original settings and don't pick up the master settings unless you use the Copy Master Guides command.

- When you are using more than one grid system or column layout in a publication.

  If, for example, you want some pages to contain three equal columns and other pages to have a particular custom column setting, you set up the custom columns on the master pages and use the Column Guides command to switch to three columns (see "Creating a Grid System" in Chapter 15 and Example 17.4 in Chapter 17).

Using Rulers To Position Objects on a Page

Use the Rulers command from the Guides and Rulers submenu of the Layout menu (Ctrl+R) to display or hide the horizontal and vertical rulers at the top and left edges of the Layout view. You can use these rulers to help position ruler guides, text, and graphics on the page, to measure distances, or to draw or scale graphics to fit an area.

To display rulers on-screen, select the Rulers command (Ctrl+R). This is a toggle command; the command displays a check mark if the rulers are displayed and no check mark if they are hidden.

The on-screen position of the pointer or an object is indicated by dotted markers on the rulers when you initially create the object or when you click, drag, or scale the object with the pointer, as illustrated in figure 5.27. These markers can be helpful, especially in aligning objects or drawing a graphic to exact size. (You can view or specify an object's position precisely in numerical terms through the Control palette, as described later in this chapter.)

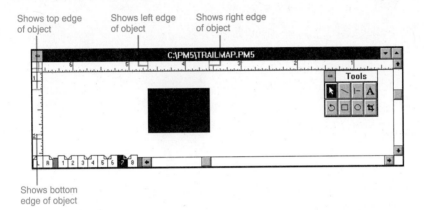

Fig. 5.27

Markers on the ruler line show positions of pointer or objects being moved, cropped, or scaled.

The number of increments displayed along the rulers vary depending on the size in which you are currently viewing the page. Rulers show finer increments of measure in enlarged views, such as 200 percent, than in reduced views.

Choosing the Unit of Measure

T I P

Use the Preferences command from the File menu to set the unit of measure displayed on the rulers. You can change the unit of measure at any time without affecting the document itself; only the rulers and other displays that show measurements will change. You may choose to work with one unit of measure throughout the production, or with different measures (using picas for margins and columns, and inches for scaling figures, for example).

FROM HERE...

For Related Information

▶▶ "Adding Text," p. 225.

▶▶ "Editing Text," p. 275.

▶▶ "Formatting Text," p. 293.

▶▶ "Working with Graphics," p. 351.

▶▶ "Creating a Grid System," p. 683.

Selecting with the Pointer Tool and Text Tool

While you are creating a document in PageMaker, you can use the menu commands, the palettes, or keyboard shortcuts to edit text or to work with graphics. Most of these commands will affect only the object or objects that are selected or active at the time the command is invoked; if nothing is selected at the time the command is used, then nothing happens! This may seem obvious, yet beginners often mistakenly execute a command without first selecting the object for which it is intended. This section describes how to select elements on a page.

Selecting Text Blocks and Graphic Objects with the Pointer Tool

An object is automatically selected or active as soon as it is drawn or placed on a page, or objects can be selected with the Pointer tool. A selected element is framed by *handles*, small black squares at each end of a selected line or eight black squares around a box or ellipse or an imported graphic, or by *windowshades* at the top and bottom of a selected text block.

The three basic methods of selecting objects with the Pointer tool are shown in figures 5.28, 5.29, and 5.30. The following list describes these and several other alternatives:

■ Position the pointer over text or a graphic, and click once to select the text block or graphic. If the handles aren't displayed as
expected, the object may be buried under other objects. Hold
down the Ctrl key and click again to select objects on the next
layer down, or use the Send to Back and Bring to Front commands
to dig out the object, as described later in this chapter (see
fig. 5.28).

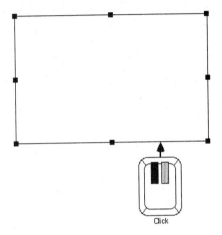

Fig. 5.28

Clicking once to
select text or a
graphic.

■ Hold down the Shift key as you click on several different objects—
one at a time. You can select more than one object at a time this
way, and the objects don't need to be adjacent to each other (see
fig. 5.29).

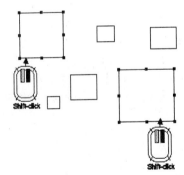

Fig. 5.29

Using Shift+click
to select several
objects.

■ If the objects are adjacent to each other, you can position the Pointer tool in an empty area at one corner of the area to be selected and drag the pointer diagonally to the opposite corner. A selection rectangle will appear as you drag. Objects that are not completely encompassed are not selected (see fig. 5.30).

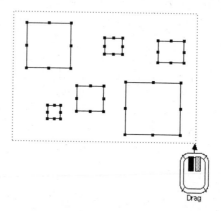

■ You can use a combination of the preceding two methods: holding down the Shift key, clicking to select one object at a time, and dragging to select other groups of objects.

■ Use the Select All command from the Edit menu (Ctrl+A) to select all the elements on the active page, including the pasteboard.

■ Use any of the above methods to select a group of elements, and then hold down the Shift key and click on an active element to *deselect* it from a group.

The multiple-item select feature enables you to select multiple items and perform actions on all those elements at once. When you select multiple elements, for example, you can use commands to move, cut, copy, paste, or delete the elements; send all elements behind; or bring all elements forward.

If an element is hidden by another, PageMaker allows you to activate the hidden element underneath. With the Pointer tool selected, hold down the Ctrl key while clicking where the hidden element is located. If several elements are stacked on one another, successive clicks of the mouse will activate elements from the top to the bottom.

Using the Select All Command

The effect of the Select All command on the Edit menu (Ctrl+A) depends on the current tool selection and pointer position on-screen:

■ If the Pointer tool is selected, the Select All command selects all text blocks, graphics, and lines on the current page and on the pasteboard.

■ If the Text tool is selected and the cursor is positioned in a text box (by positioning the I-beam pointer in the text box and clicking once to position the blinking text cursor), the Select All command selects all of the text in the active text block *and the text in any other text block that is part of the same story.*

Selecting Text with the Text Tool

You can use the Text tool to select portions of text within a block of text or to establish the text insertion point before typing new text. The methods of selecting text and insertion points with the Text tool are shown in figures 5.31, 5.32, and 5.33.

Position the I-beam beside a character, and click the main mouse button to position the cursor with a line of text (see fig. 5.31). Use this method for inserting new text:

1. Double-click a word to select it (see fig. 5.32).

2. Drag the I-beam over the text to select it (see fig. 5.33).

3. Click the Text tool once in a text block, and choose the Select All command from the Edit menu to select the entire story—the current text block plus all linked blocks.

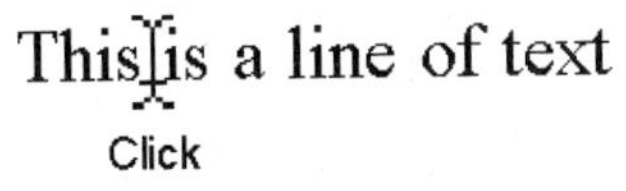

This is a line of text

Click

Fig. 5.31

Positioning the I-beam to select a text insertion point.

Fig. 5.32

Selecting one
word.

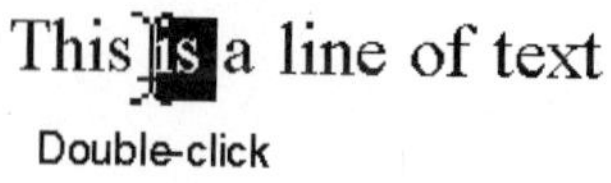

This **is** a line of text

Double-click

Fig. 5.33

Dragging the
I-beam to select
text.

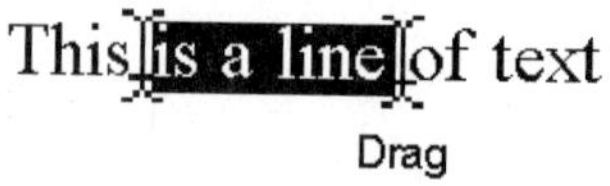

This **is a line** of text

Drag

Use the keyboard shortcuts shown in table 5.2. You can always use the
Shortcuts command under Help menu if you quickly want to find a keyboard shortcut you have forgotten.

Table 5.2 Keystrokes Used To Move the Text Insertion Point	
To Move Text Insertion Point To	**Press**
Beginning of a line	Home
End of a line	End
Beginning of a sentence	Ctrl+Home
End of a sentence	Ctrl+End
Left one character	Left arrow
Right one character	Right arrow
Left one word	Ctrl+left arrow
Right one word	Ctrl+right arrow
Up one line	Up arrow
Down one line	Down arrow
Up one paragraph	Ctrl+up arrow
Down one paragraph	Ctrl+down arrow
Up one screen	PgUp
Down one screen	PgDn
Top of story	Ctrl+PgUp
Bottom of story	Ctrl+PgDn

The Appearance of the Mouse Pointer

The appearance of the mouse pointer changes with what you are doing. Any pointer can be used to select menu commands, toolbox options, page icons, or to use the Scroll bars. The appearance of the pointer also indicates which other functions can be performed.

For example, you use the arrow pointer, which appears whenever the Pointer tool is selected in the toolbox, to select objects on the page. The I-beam appears when the Text tool is selected in the toolbox. Use the I-beam to select portions of a block of text and to position the text insertion point. A crossbar appears when a graphics tool is selected in the toolbox. Use the crossbar to draw lines, boxes, and circles. When the Cropping tool is selected in the toolbox, the pointer changes to the cropping icon. Use this icon to trim the edges of a graphic imported from another program.

The mouse pointer also takes a different appearance when you use the Place command to retrieve text or graphics from other programs. PageMaker has three text icons you can use to import text into PageMaker. Which icon is active depends on whether the Autoflow option is on manual, semiautomatic, or automatic. The pencil icon indicates that you are importing a graphic from a draw program. The paintbrush icon places a graphic from a paint program. When you are placing a scanned image, the pointer becomes a box containing an X. When you are placing EPS (Encapsulated PostScript) files, the pointer becomes the letters *PS*. The hourglass icon is displayed while the program is processing. You must wait until the hourglass changes into one of the other icons before you can continue working.

For Related Information

FROM HERE...

▶▶ "Working with Text Blocks," p. 257.

▶▶ "Selecting Text," p. 277.

▶▶ "Selecting an Object," p. 380.

Using the Pointer Tool To Move and Resize Elements

PageMaker offers different methods for accomplishing the same task. Elements often can be moved or scaled by using the mouse, keyboard shortcuts, or the Control palette. The next sections summarize these various techniques, which are explained in more detail in Chapter 6 (as they relate to text) and Chapter 9 (as they relate to graphics).

Moving an Element with the Pointer Tool

Once a text block or graphic is created or placed in PageMaker, you can change its position on the page by selecting the Pointer tool, clicking on the object, and dragging it by any part except its handles to move it. Hold down the Shift key to constrain the movement of an element horizontally or vertically as you move it.

If you click on an object and drag it immediately, you see only an outline of the object as you move it. If you pause one-half second before you move an element, you see the element and its contents as you move.

Scaling an Element with the Pointer Tool

You can change the size of the object by dragging one of the small black square handles that are displayed when the object is selected. Drag a corner handle to scale both dimensions (horizontal and vertical) at once. Drag a side handle on a rectangle or ellipse or imported graphic when you want to scale only one dimension. When resizing a rectangle or ellipse, you can constrain it to a square or circle by holding down the Shift key as you drag a handle.

To change the length of a line using the mouse, drag one of the handles on either end of the line. Hold down the Shift key to keep the line straight as you resize it or to constrain it to 45-degree angles.

FROM HERE...

For Related Information

▶▶ "Working with Text Blocks," p. 257.

▶▶ "Editing Text in Layout View," p. 279.

▶▶ "Editing Graphics," p. 379.

Using the Control Palette in Layout View

PageMaker 5.0 introduces a Control palette—a window that you can display on-screen that shows information about whatever object is currently selected on the page. You can display or hide the Control palette by choosing the Control palette option from the Window menu, or by typing Ctrl+'. The appearance of the Control palette changes depending on what is selected. Chapter 2 showed the three basic views of the Control palette: Layout view, Character view, and Paragraph view. This section describes the Control palette's Layout view (fig. 5.34) in more detail, as well as some basic operations that apply in all views. The other two views are specifically described in Chapter 8.

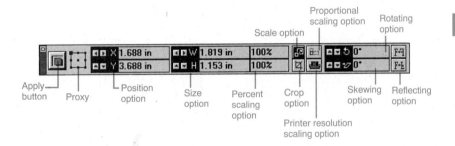

Fig. 5.34

The Control palette in Layout view when an object is selected with the Pointer tool.

Examining General Characteristics of the Control Palette

The Control palette displays information about a selected tool or object or group of objects, and the information changes as you move or scale the object. You can also move, scale, or otherwise change an element by first selecting it and then making entries in the Control palette.

When the Control palette is displayed, you can activate it by simply selecting an object and then clicking on the palette. Once in this palette, as in any dialog box, you can move through the controls by clicking the mouse pointer on a control or pressing the Tab key, or by pressing Shift+Tab to tab in reverse order. These and other keyboard shortcuts are listing in table 5.3.

Table 5.3 Keyboard Shortcuts in the Control Palette

Key	Function
Ctrl+' (close single quote)	Displays or hides the Control palette
Press Ctrl+`	Switches between the Control palette and the publication or story window
Tab	Moves to the next option
Shift+Tab	Moves to the previous option
Arrow key	Depending on which option is active: ■ Moves the cursor between characters in an edit box ■ Moves the selected object by one pixel or ruler increment ■ Moves to another reference point on the proxy ■ Alternates between scaling and cropping
Arrow key	In Layout view only, moves the selected object by the nudge amount or by ruler increments
Ctrl+Arrow key	Increases nudge factor by 10 (x10) (Power Nudge)
Numeric keypad numbers	Chooses a reference point on the proxy
Esc	Displays the last valid value for an option
Enter	Applies changes and moves to the next option
Spacebar	Turns the current button on or off
Shift+F11	Scrolls through valid units of measure in the current option

Make entries in the Control palette by clicking buttons, editing the entry as text, using scrolling arrows (nudge buttons) to select values, or choosing from drop-down lists:

- Click a button to turn it on (highlight it) or off. A change you make by clicking a button takes effect immediately.

- Select from a pull-down menu. Changes made through menus on the Control palette take effect immediately.

- Click a nudge button to increase or decrease a value by a set amount. Hold down the Ctrl key as you click a nudge button to increase the nudge amount by ten times (*power nudge*). The default nudge amount depends on the unit of measure: .01 inch, 1 point (if picas or Ciceros are used), or 1 mm. You can adjust the nudge amounts through the Preferences command (described in Chapter 4). Nudges will also snap to guides, if that option is selected from the Guides and Rulers submenu of the Layout menu.

- Type an entry in a text box, as in any dialog box. While in a text box, press Shift+F11 to cycle through the units of measure available for the option.

- Perform arithmetic on an entry. You can add to, subtract from, multiply, or divide any existing value for an option by using the symbols on the numeric keypad (+, -, *, and /). If the current measure is 4 inches, for example, you can increase it by 1/4 inch by positioning the cursor after the 4 or after the unit of measure and typing **+.25**; you need not enter the unit of measure if it is the same as the current default measure. Similarly, you could increase the 4-inch measure by 2 picas and 3 points by typing **+2p3** after the 4.

Many changes made to the information on the palette are not reflected on the page until you click the Apply button at the left side of the palette (refer to fig. 5.34). To exit the palette and activate all changes, press the Enter key or click the mouse in the document window.

Using the Control Palette To Move and Scale Objects

You can also use the Control palette to change the position and size (and other features) of an object that has been selected with the Pointer tool, such as the rectangle shown in figure 5.35.

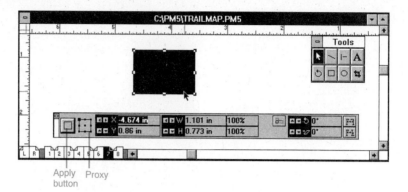

Fig. 5.35

The Control palette when a rectangle is selected.

Apply button   Proxy

When an object is selected with the Pointer tool, the control areas in the Control palette include the following:

- *Apply button.* Displays the changes made to selected objects without exiting the Control palette. The Apply button will change appearances to show whether the current selection includes one object or several objects. If no objects are selected, this area shows the icon for the currently selected tool.

- *Proxy icon.* Represents the selected object. If one point on the proxy appears larger than the others, it indicates the point on the object that you are currently manipulating. You can change the current reference point by clicking on a point on the proxy or on a handle of the selected object. The X and Y coordinates show the position of the current reference point. You can change between moving and resizing by clicking the current reference point on the proxy.

- *X.* The horizontal position of the current reference point of the element relative to the current zero point on the rulers. (Note that the current reference point is the one shown largest in the proxy icon on the Control palette, which is not necessarily the apparent top left corner of the element.) You can see these values change as you move the object or change the reference point, or you can enter values to move the object, or click on one of the arrows to the left of the X to nudge the object (move it) in increments specified through the Preferences command (as described in Chapter 4).

- *Y.* The vertical position of the current reference point of the element relative to the current zero point on the rulers. This value can be changed or nudged as described for the X value.

- *W.* The width of the element in the current unit of measure as well as the percentage of the original width (if the element has been scaled). This value can be changed or nudged as described for the X value.

■ *H*. The height of the element in the current unit of measure as well as the percentage of the original height (if the element has been scaled). This value can be changed or nudged as described for the X value.

■ *Percentage*. Scaling options for width and height. This value changes if you change the width or height or, if you change the percentage value, the width or height changes. The percentage value reflects the percentage the object has been changed from its original size during the current editing session. If you deselect the object to work on other tasks, the percentage will change back to 100 percent.

■ *Proportional-scaling option button*. When turned on, causes PageMaker to retain the original proportions of the height to width when you resize the graphic. The values in the percentage fields change in tandem, regardless of which other value you manipulate in scaling. (Imported graphics can also have picture scaling and cropping options and a printer-resolution scaling option, as described in Chapter 9.)

■ *Rotating, skewing, and reflecting controls at the far right on the palette*. (Transformations are described in Chapter 11.)

You can change the position or the size of an object by selecting the appropriate area in the Control palette and entering a new value, or adding, subtracting, multiplying, or dividing the value. You can enter most measurements in increments as fine as .001 and font sizes from 2 to 720 points.

Click the Apply button, press the Enter key, or click on the document window for the new value to take effect.

Overriding the Unit of Measure   T I P

You can override the current unit of measure in the Control palette (or any dialog box) by entering a one-character abbreviation for the unit of measure you want to specify: *i* for inches (for example, **0.75i**), *m* for millimeters (for example, **19.06m**), *p* for picas and points (for example, **4p6**), *c* for Ciceros (for example, **4c2.8**).

The unit of measure shown in the Control palette always reflects the current unit of measure, as set with the Preferences command on the File menu, regardless of the unit of measure you enter in the palette (see the section "Setting Preferences" in Chapter 4).

For Related Information

◄◄ "Examining the Control Palette," p. 59.

▶▶ "Using the Control Palette in Character View," p. 296.

▶▶ "Using the Control Palette To Change Paragraph Attributes," p. 311.

▶▶ "Editing Graphics," p. 379.

▶▶ "Working with Transformations," p. 504.

Using the Edit Menu Commands

After laying out all the pages with their essential elements, or while you are still building pages, you can use the Edit menu commands to delete, copy, or move text or graphics. The Edit menu commands described in this section are basic editing commands common to all Windows applications, such as Undo, Cut, Copy, Paste, Clear, and Select All. The same keyboard shortcuts are usually applicable across most Windows applications, and PageMaker 5.0 adds Ctrl+key commands that mimic the Command-key shortcuts on the Macintosh (see table 5.4). (The Multiple Paste command, new in PageMaker 5.0, is described in Chapter 11. The Paste Link, Paste Special, Insert Object, and Edit Original commands are described under "Using OLE Commands To Import Graphics" in Chapter 9. The Edit Story command is described in Chapter 7.)

Table 5.4 Keyboard Shortcuts To Edit Menu Commands		
Command	**Macintosh Mimic**	**PC Standard**
Undo	Ctrl+Z	Alt+Bksp
Cut	Ctrl+X	Shift+Del
Copy	Ctrl+C	Ctrl+Ins
Paste	Ctrl+V	Shift+Ins
Clear		Del
Select All		Ctrl+A

You probably will use these commands so often that you will quickly learn the keyboard shortcuts and never need to use the menu to choose them.

Most of these commands affect only the object (or objects) you select at the time you invoke the command. If you select nothing when you give the command, nothing happens. (This statement may seem obvious, but one of the most common mistakes beginners make is to execute a command without first selecting an object.) Basic methods of selecting text or objects were described earlier in this chapter, and additional methods are described under "Working with Text Blocks" in Chapter 6, "Selecting Text" in Chapter 7, and "Selecting Graphic Objects" in Chapter 9.

Deleting and Copying Objects

The Cut, Copy, and Clear commands and the Backspace and Delete keys affect any blocks of text and graphics selected with the Pointer tool, or the phrases of text selected with the Text tool.

First, select the object (or objects) by clicking or dragging the Pointer tool (to select graphics or whole text blocks) or the Text tool (to select parts of text within a block). To remove the selection from the page, from the Edit menu choose the Cut command (Ctrl+X or Shift+Del) or the Clear command (Del). Alternatively, press the Backspace key. To make a copy of the selected object, choose Copy (Ctrl+C or Ctrl+Ins), and then use the Paste command (described later in this chapter under the next two sections).

You can also use these commands to move an object, as an alternative to dragging it with the mouse. Select the object with the Pointer tool or the Text tool, choose the Cut command (Ctrl+X or Shift+Del), and then choose the Paste command.

How the Windows Clipboard Works with the Edit Menu Commands

Both the Cut (Ctrl+X or Shift+Del) and Copy (Ctrl+C or Ctrl+Ins) commands put the selected object (or objects) in the Windows Clipboard. The Cut command removes the selected objects from the page, whereas the Copy command leaves the objects on the page and puts a copy of them in the Clipboard. The Clipboard is a temporary storage area that is active while you are working, but the Clipboard's contents are lost the next time you use the Cut or Copy command or when you leave Windows.

continues

How the Windows Clipboard Works with the Edit Menu Commands (continued)

The Clipboard remains active throughout each Windows session. Suppose, for example, that you use Windows Draw to draw a graphic. You then copy the graphic to the Clipboard and open a PageMaker publication without leaving Windows. With the Paste command, you can pull the graphic from the Clipboard onto the page in PageMaker. However, PageMaker's Place command or one of the OLE commands are more commonly used for importing objects from other applications.

Similarly, you can use the Clipboard to paste selected objects from one PageMaker publication into another, but PageMaker 5.0 lets you open more than one publication at a time, and you can copy elements from one publication to another by dragging them between windows.

When you use the Clear command or the Del or Backspace key, PageMaker removes the selected object from the page; unlike the Cut command, however, PageMaker doesn't put the objects into the Clipboard. The only way to retrieve objects after using the Clear command or the Del or Backspace key is to invoke the Undo command immediately.

To remove objects from a page for indefinite storage and retrieval, save them as a Clipboard file, or move them onto the pasteboard or into a Library (see "Creating and Using a Library" in Chapter 14).

T I P   Viewing the Contents of the Clipboard

Use the Clipboard command from the Control menu to view the current contents of the Clipboard (see fig. 5.36). This feature is helpful when you are ready to use the Cut or Copy command and you want to be sure that whatever is in the Clipboard is "expendable," or before using the Paste command. When the Clipboard window is open, you can use commands on its menus to save the contents into a clipboard file or to open another clipboard file. (See the *Microsoft Windows User's Guide* or use the Help menu on the Clipboard window for more information about the Windows clipboard.)

Note that graphics created with PageMaker's drawing tools are not visible in the Clipboard.

Fig. 5.36

The Clipboard
window with the
File menu open.

Pasting Objects within PageMaker

By using the Paste command (Ctrl+P or Shift+Ins) from the Edit menu, you can retrieve whatever was last put in the Clipboard with the Cut or Copy command and place that element on the page. The pasted object can come from within PageMaker (as described in this section) or from another Windows application (described in the next section).

PageMaker normally positions the pasted object in the same relative position on the current page as the Cut or Copied object was on the source page, offset slightly to the left and down. You can paste an object to the *same* position by pressing Ctrl+Shift+P to paste the object, or control the position of multiple pastes numerically through the Multiple Paste command (described under "Using the Multiple Paste Command" in Chapter 11).

When objects are first pasted on the page, they already are selected; that is, you can see the handles of the pasted graphics and text. If you are pasting a group of objects, you can move the objects as a group by dragging the entire selection immediately after pasting the selection on the page. Otherwise, if you click the pointer off the selection, the object or group is no longer selected.

Move a Pasted Group Immediately after Pasting   T I P

You should move a pasted group of objects into position—or away from other objects—as soon as you paste them on a page, while they are all still selected. Otherwise, if you accidentally click away from them, they become deselected as a group, and you have to select them again carefully to avoid also selecting other objects on the page.

T I P

Drag-Copying Objects between PageMaker Publications

In PageMaker 5.0, you can open more than one PageMaker publication at a time and copy elements by dragging them between windows, thereby eliminating the use of commands described here, and bypassing the Clipboard.

Pasting Objects into PageMaker from Other Applications

As a page layout application, PageMaker has always allowed you to import text and graphics from other applications by using the Place command from the File menu. In addition, Windows has always let you use the Cut or Copy and Paste commands to get objects from one Windows application into another Windows application that supported the same file format. The advantages of using the Edit menu commands are that you can import a portion of another file (instead of the whole file), and you can import some formats that aren't available through the Place command (either because you haven't installed the filter or because the filter doesn't exist). The advantage of the Place command is that you can import files that would be too big or complicated to "fit" through the Windows Clipboard, which is a limited space in memory. The Place command also lets you link imported files to the PageMaker publication, rather than actually importing the entire file.

PageMaker 5.0 adds support for Object Linking and Embedding (OLE) under Windows 3.1. Now, whenever you use the Paste command in PageMaker to paste an object that was cut or copied from another Windows application that also supports OLE (that is, an OLE server application), PageMaker imports the object as an OLE embedded object (unless the object is text). This means that the object can be linked to the publication, just as it can be with the Place command, but OLE adds the advantage of being able to *edit* the imported object by activating the object's original creator (a graphics application, for example) by simply double-clicking on the object in PageMaker.

With OLE, the advantages of using the Place command over the Paste command have become less distinct than they were with earlier versions of Windows and PageMaker. The Place command and the OLE commands are described under "Using Object Linking and Embedding with Text" in Chapter 6 and "Object Linking and Embedding (OLE)" in

Chapter 9 as they relate to graphics. Following are some general guide-lines summarized from those chapters regarding the use of the Place and Paste commands:

- Use the Place command to import text *unless* you want to import just a small portion of a large text file, or you want to import text in a format that PageMaker doesn't recognize through the Place command.

- Use the Place command to import graphics if you will be moving the publication to a Macintosh platform for final printing. Objects that are linked to Windows 3.1 applications will not be editable on the Macintosh.

- Use the Place command to import graphics if you don't have enough memory to run PageMaker and the graphics application at the same time, and you plan to edit the graphics.

- Use the Paste command to import graphics if you expect a lot of edits to the graphics during the production cycle and want to edit while PageMaker is running.

- Use the Paste command if the Place command doesn't seem to work, or if the file seems corrupted when imported, and vice versa: use the Place command if the Paste command doesn't seem to work, or if the file seems corrupted when imported.

Because OLE is new with Windows 3.1 and PageMaker 5.0, try it your-self and see if you prefer it to the Place command.

Undoing Your Most Recent Action

The Undo command on the Edit menu reverses the action taken imme-diately before the command is invoked; that is, immediately after mak-ing a mistake or changing your mind about an edit, you can use the Undo command to reverse that action. You should work cautiously when making major changes to a publication, such as changing the type specifications or formatting a whole block of text or story. Check the results of each action as you go along. The wording of the Undo com-mand itself changes to describe the last action—for instance, Undo Move or Undo Stretch.

If PageMaker cannot reverse your last action, the Edit menu displays the words Cannot Undo in gray instead of the Undo command in black. Some actions you cannot reverse include the commands on the File menu (except Page Setup), Story menu, or Type menu; changes in the screen view; changes to lines or fills; and transformations (rotation, skewing, or reflection).

Reversing All Changes Made Since the Last Save

With the Revert command on the File menu, you can reverse all edits or changes you made since the last time you saved the publication. In other words, you can use the Revert command to restore a publication to the state the publication was in the last time you used the Save or Save As command. If you haven't used either command since the last time you used the Open command, you restore the publication to the condition the publication was in before you opened it. This command is a convenient shortcut to an alternative that is available with almost any application: Close the active document without saving changes, and then reopen the saved version of the document.

PageMaker automatically saves a temporary copy of your file—called a *minisave*—on disk whenever you click a page icon, add or delete a page, or change the page setup. You can revert to the last minisave by holding down the Shift key as you select the Revert command.

T I P   Using the Save and Revert Commands

Save your publications often while you are working. Saving often enables you to use the Revert command to reverse your most recent changes.

FROM HERE...

For Related Information

▶▶ "Working with Text Blocks," p. 257.

▶▶ "Typing and Editing Text in the Story Editor," p. 280.

▶▶ "Importing Graphics Created in Other Programs," p. 363.

▶▶ "Using the Multiple Paste Command," p. 483.

▶▶ "Managing Linked Text and Graphics Documents," p. 597.

▶▶ "Creating and Using a Library," p. 656.

Summary

This chapter explained the sequence of steps that you follow when building any publication with PageMaker:

- Set up the master page elements and nonprinting grid lines.

- Use the guides to arrange text and graphics on each page.

- Use the Pointer and Text tools to select elements on the page.

- Use various techniques to arrange elements on a page.

Chapter 6 explains the process of adding text to the publication by typing it directly into PageMaker or by importing it from other sources. Chapter 6 also explains how to work with text blocks on a page.

Adding Text

Y ou can type text directly into PageMaker, or you can import text from another file into PageMaker. Imported text can come from many sources, including word processing programs or databases and spreadsheets that have been saved in text format. PageMaker also offers a Table Editor, a separate utility you can use to create complex tables that you can import into PageMaker. PageMaker preserves most text formats set by your word processor—for example, type specifications, tabs, and paragraph alignment.

This chapter shows you how to type text into PageMaker and how to import text from word processing programs. You also learn how to control the position and size of text blocks, and you can see how PageMaker handles text formatted in a word processing program. By understanding the capabilities of both PageMaker and your word processor, you can decide whether to do most formatting during the word processing step or later, when working in PageMaker itself.

Chapters 4 and 5 cover the steps that precede typing or placing text into PageMaker, such as setting up column guides. In Chapter 7, you learn how to edit text, changing the words themselves. In Chapter 8, you learn how to change the appearance of the text—by paragraph formatting and setting type specifications—after text is placed on the page in PageMaker.

Typing Text in Layout View

You can use the Text tool in Layout view (that is, the WYSIWYG view of the page) to type short segments of text. Long text entries are more quickly typed in PageMaker's Story Editor or in a word processor and then imported into PageMaker. (See Chapter 1 for a discussion of the differences between PageMaker and word processing programs.) In this section, you see how the Text tool operates as an input device.

The most efficient use of PageMaker's Text tool in Layout view, however, is for editing and formatting text. The Text tool as an editing tool is described in Chapter 7, and its use as a formatting device is described in Chapter 8.

To type text directly on a page in PageMaker, first select the Text tool— the letter *A* in the upper right corner of the toolbox. After you click the Text tool, the mouse pointer changes to an I-beam. Click the I-beam anywhere on the page to set an insertion point, and begin typing (see fig. 6.1).

Fig. 6.1

Starting to type on a PageMaker page.

Click

The position of the typed text varies depending on where you click the I-beam to set the text insertion point. If you click the I-beam on an empty part of the page between two column guides, for example, the text begins at the left column guide and wraps at the right column guide (see fig. 6.2). The text is typed in PageMaker's default format, which usually is flush-left, 12-point Times Roman type.

New typed text snaps to left column guide and wraps at right, insertion point is blinking vertical line|

Fig. 6.2

Typed text.

If you click the I-beam on a page with no column guides, the new typed text wraps at the right margin.

If you click the I-beam within an existing block of text, the typed text is inserted within that text block, at the insertion point. This text has the same format as the text immediately to the left of the insertion point.

If you click the I-beam to position the text insertion point on the pasteboard or beyond the column guides on a page, the typed text begins wherever you click the insertion point, and the text assumes the margin-to-margin width defined in the Page Setup dialog box.

You can create a text box by using the Drag-Type feature, that is, by dragging the I-beam to form a boundary for the text. (This boundary is visible only as you drag the mouse.) The typed text stays within the horizontal limits defined by the boundary, but runs whatever length is required to fit what you type.

If you want to type more text than can fit in the current text block, column, or page, you can use the techniques described later in this chapter to change the size or position of the text block or to create a series of chained text blocks.

Correcting the Problem of Illegible Text

Text is usually very readable in Layout view. Sometimes, however, the text is too jagged on-screen to be readable or the characters seem to pile up and overlap each other, becoming illegible on-screen.

The most common cause of overlapping characters is that the publication has lost track of its target printer. You can fix this by choosing Page Setup from the File menu and selecting a printer in the Compose to Printer area at the bottom of the dialog box. If PageMaker asks whether you want to recompose the publication, click OK.

Another cause of text overlap is that the text block is too narrow to accommodate a long word that cannot be hyphenated by PageMaker, either because the word is not in the dictionary and not handled by PageMaker's hyphenation formulas, or because the hyphenation zone prevents hyphenation (see "Controlling Hyphenation" in Chapter 8). You can either widen the block or hyphenate the word manually.

Other possible reasons for illegible or jagged text on-screen while in Layout view are that you are typing in a screen font or size that is not installed on your system, or that you are using a printer font that is not available for the current target printer.

If the font is not installed on your system but is available for the final printer, don't worry—the font should print correctly even if it looks bad on-screen. If you find it too frustrating to work with a hard-to-read display, however, switch to Story view (see Chapter 7), or install the font on your system in all the sizes you intend to use (see "Installing and Using Fonts" in Appendix A), or use a type manager such as Adobe Type Manager or TrueType fonts (see "Font Management" in Chapter 13).

continues

Correcting the Problem of Illegible Text (continued)

To get the best results, make sure that you use only the fonts available to your final printer. If the font is not available for the current target printer, Windows displays a question mark (?) before the font name as listed in the Type Specifications dialog box and on the Font submenu of the Type menu (described in Chapter 8). The question mark might appear if you change printers or font cartridges while working on a single publication, if you open a publication without activating PageMaker's PANOSE Font Matching feature, or if the fonts have not been installed correctly.

Typing Special Characters

PageMaker uses the ANSI (American National Standards Institute) character set for its standard fonts. You can type most common special characters, including hidden characters that affect formatting, by using the keys shown in table 6.1. These and other characters also can be created by pressing the Alt key as you type the character's ANSI value (see the following section).

How well these characters print depends on the font you choose and the printer you use. Usually, the printed characters match those you see on-screen. If printed and on-screen characters do not match, either the screen version of the font is not installed or the printer font isn't being handled correctly by your type management utility. (See the section "Font Management," in Chapter 13, for more information.)

Table 6.1 Typing Special Characters and Hidden Formatting Characters

Example	Description block	Enter in text dialog box	Enter in
"	typographer's open quotation marks	Ctrl+Shift+[	^{
"	typographer's close quotation marks	Ctrl+Shift+]	^}
'	typographer's single open quotation mark	Ctrl+[	^[
'	typographer's single close quotation mark	Ctrl+]	^]

Example	Description block	Enter in text dialog box	Enter in
LM.RM	page-number marker	Ctrl+Shift+3	^3
•	bullet	Ctrl+Shift+8	^8
®	registered mark	Ctrl+Shift+G	^r
©	copyright mark	Ctrl+Shift+0	^2
¶	paragraph mark	Ctrl+Shift+7	^7
§	section mark	Ctrl+Shift+6	^6
◘	index entry	n/a	^;
	em space	Ctrl+Shift+M	^m
	en space (1/2 em)	Ctrl+Shift+N	^>
	thin space (1/4 em)	Ctrl+Shift+T	^<
	nonbreaking space	Ctrl+Shift+H	^s
-	nonbreaking hyphen	Ctrl+Shift+(hyphen)	^~
-	discretionary (soft) hyphen	Ctrl+(hyphen)	^-
—	em dash	Ctrl+Shift+=	^— Shift+(hyphen)
–	en dash	Ctrl+=	^=
/	nonbreaking slash	Ctrl+Shift+/	^/
→	tab	Tab	^t
↵	soft return	Shift+Enter	^n
¶	end of paragraph	Enter	^p

Making Typographer's Quotes Automatic

T I P

If you know that you always want typographer's quotes (that is, opening and closing quotes that look different from each other), select Use Typographer's Quotes in the Other Preferences dialog box. You access this dialog box by choosing Preferences from the File menu and clicking the Other button in the Preferences dialog box.

Using ANSI Values To Type Special Characters

If the character you want does not appear in table 6.1 (or as an alternative to using the keyboard shortcuts shown in the table), you can hold the Alt key and type the ANSI value for the character. PageMaker comes with a template named charset.pt5 that shows the full ANSI character set, including symbols, and gives the ANSI value for each character (see fig. 6.3).

ALDUS CHARACTER SET PUBLICATION *

Font_____ Character Set____ Printer_____ Driver____

#		#		#		#		#		#	
1	- -	46	.	91	[	136	^	181	µ	226	â
2	- -	47	/	92	\	137	‰	182	¶	227	ã
3	- -	48	0	93	]	138	Š	183	·	228	ä
4	.	49	1	94	^	139	‹	184	,	229	å
5	-	50	2	95	_	140	Œ	185	¹	230	æ
6	- -	51	3	96	˜	141	□	186	º	231	ç
7	- -	52	4	97	a	142	□	187	»	232	è
8	- -	53	5	98	b	143	□	188	¼	233	é
9		54	6	99	c	144	□	189	½	234	ê
10	'	55	7	100	d	145	'	190	¾	235	ë
11	'	56	8	101	e	146	'	191	¿	236	ì
12	- -	57	9	102	f	147	"	192	À	237	í
13		58	:	103	g	148	"	193	Á	238	î
14		59	;	104	h	149	•	194	Â	239	ï
15	/	60	<	105	i	150	–	195	Ã	240	ð
16	-	61	=	106	j	151	—	196	Ä	241	ñ
17	- -	62	>	107	k	152	~	197	Å	242	ò
18		63	?	108	l	153	™	198	Æ	243	ó
19	- -	64	@	109	m	154	š	199	Ç	244	ô
20	- -	65	A	110	n	155	›	200	È	245	õ
21		66	B	111	o	156	œ	201	É	246	ö
22		67	C	112	p	157	□	202	Ê	247	÷
23		68	D	113	q	158	□	203	Ë	248	ø
24	l	69	E	114	r	159	Ÿ	204	Ì	249	ù
25		70	F	115	s	160		205	Í	250	ú
26		71	G	116	t	161	¡	206	Î	251	û
27		72	H	117	u	162	¢	207	Ï	252	ü
28		73	I	118	v	163	£	208	Ð	253	ý
29		74	J	119	w	164	¤	209	Ñ	254	þ
30	- -	75	K	120	x	165	¥	210	Ò	255	ÿ
31		76	L	121	y	166	¦	211	Ó		
32		77	M	122	z	167	§	212	Ô		
33	!	78	N	123	{	168	¨	213	Õ	**Keyboard Shortcuts**	
34	"	79	O	124	|	169	©	214	Ö	C=Control	
35	#	80	P	125	}	170	ª	215	×	S=Shift	
36	$	81	Q	126	~	171	«	216	Ø		
37	%	82	R	127	□	172	¬	217	Ù	CS+=	- -
38	&	83	S	128	□	173		218	Ú	C+=	'
39	'	84	T	129	□	174	®	219	Û	CS+[	'
40	(	85	U	130	,	175	¯	220	Ü	CS+]	'
41	)	86	V	131	ƒ	176	°	221	Ý	C+[	'
42	*	87	W	132	„	177	±	222	Þ	C+]	'
43	+	88	X	133	…	178	²	223	ß	CS+8	·
44	,	89	Y	134	†	179	³	224	à	CS+6	§
45	-	90	Z	135	‡	180	´	225	á		

* See README.TXT for instructions.

Revision: October, 1992

Fig. 6.3

ANSII character set and values, as shown in PageMaker's charset.pt5 template.

To use the template most efficiently, open the file and then select the Text tool from the toolbox. Click the text anywhere, and choose Select All from the Edit menu. Use the Font submenu on the Type menu to set the text to the font you are using in your publication. Finally, choose Print from the File menu to print the list. (The Print command is described in Chapter 10.) Save the printout as a reference whenever you want to type a special character.

To type a special character in PageMaker, click the Text tool at the desired insertion point. Using the printout of charset.pt5 as a guide, find the character you want, and note its corresponding ANSI number. Hold the Alt key as you type the ANSI number on the numeric keypad, adding a zero before the number. Alt+0182, for example, creates the paragraph symbol (¶) shown as 182 on the charset.pt5 printout. You can set the special character in any font or style you like by using the techniques described in Chapter 8.

Typing ANSI Values without a Numeric Keypad

T I P

You can type the ANSI numbers needed for special characters on any keyboard that has a Num Lock key but no numeric keypad. When you press Num Lock to turn it on, the keys shown on the right in the following table are equivalent to the numeric keypad numbers shown on the left:

```
789 789456  uio123 jkl0 m
```

Notice that the "keypad" descends diagonally (right) from the 7-8-9 top row on a QWERTY keyboard.

Adding Bullets or Numbering Lists

PageMaker 5.0 introduces an Aldus Addition called Bullets and Numbering that automatically adds bullets or numbers, followed by a tab, to the beginning of each line in a series. To use this utility, select the Text tool and click the first line that you want bulleted or numbered. Then choose Bullets and Numbering from the Aldus Additions submenu of the Utilities menu to display the Bullets and Numbering dialog box.

You can use the Bullets and Numbering dialog box, as shown in figure 6.4, to bullet or number various parts of a publication. Select the Every Paragraph in Story radio button to number the entire story (that is, every paragraph in the publication, as is often the case in legal documents). Select the Only Those with Style radio button to number all lines set in a particular style (see the section "Using Style Sheets," in

Chapter 8). Select the For [number] Paragraphs from Cursor radio button (and type a number into its text box) to number a specific number of paragraphs from the cursor. Select a bullet type from the buttons at the top of the dialog box. Or select the Numbers button and specify a style for the numbering.

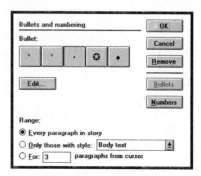

Fig. 6.4

The Bullets and Numbering dialog box.

For Related Information

◀◀ "PageMaker and Word Processors," p. 22.

▶▶ "Editing Text in Layout View," p. 279.

▶▶ "Formatting Text Using Styles in PageMaker," p. 343.

▶▶ "Using the Print Command," p. 410.

▶▶ "Managing Fonts," p. 592.

▶▶ "Installing and Using Fonts," p. 902.

Importing Text by Using the Place Command

In most large projects, you usually begin a publication by preparing the text on a word processor. (Responsibilities are usually divided in such projects so that most authors and editors use word processors, while the production team uses PageMaker.)

You use the Place command on the File menu to import into PageMaker any text typed in a word processor, spreadsheet, or database, text that appears in another PageMaker publication, or data saved as a text-only (ASCII) file from a spreadsheet, database, or noncompatible word processor. If the imported text is from another PageMaker publication or was formatted in a word processing program supported by PageMaker, PageMaker can preserve some of that formatting, saving you from duplicating the work (see the section "Importing Formatted Text," later in this chapter, and Chapter 8 for details).

To place text from an external text file into PageMaker, follow the steps in the next sections.

Determining Where Imported Text Appears

Determine first how you want to place the imported text in the publication—as a new story, replacing an entire existing story, replacing part of a story, or inserted into the story. The next sections describe the steps for each of these options.

Placing Text as a New Story

To place text as a new story, follow these steps:

1. Turn to the page on which you want to place the text. The exact tool you select or where you place the cursor doesn't matter.

2. Choose the Place command from the File menu (see fig. 6.5).

Fig. 6.5

The File menu with the Place command selected.

PageMaker displays the Place Document dialog box, which contains a list of text and graphics files on the current disk, and PageMaker publications. If the name of the file you want does not appear in the list, you can use the techniques described in step 5 to check all the directories and disk drives on your system.

3. Select As New Story in the Place area of the Place Document dialog box (see fig. 6.6).

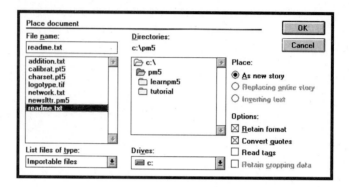

Fig. 6.6

The Place Document dialog box as it appears when the Pointer tool is selected.

The As New Story option in the Place area of the Place Document dialog box is the default and is the only choice available for placing text if the text cursor is not positioned within a text block when you choose the Place command. (The other options under Place are dimmed and cannot be selected.) If the Text tool is selected and the cursor is positioned within a text block before you choose the Place command, the additional text-placing options become available, as described under the following sections and as shown later in figures 6.9 and 6.10.

4. Select the Retain Format check box to keep the formatting that was set in your word processing program. (Formatting is described later in this chapter.) Select the Convert Quotes check box if you want to convert regular quotation marks (as they appear on your keyboard) to typesetting quotation marks (actual opening and closing marks). Select the Read Tags check box if you want PageMaker to read the style tags that you set up in your word processing program. (See Chapter 8 for more information on style tags.)

5. Locate in the Place Document dialog box the name of the text file you want to place (refer to fig. 6.6).

   ■ If the list of file names is longer than fits in the window, scroll bars appear at the right of the list; you can click on an arrow to scroll up or down the list. You can expand or limit the list by choosing from the List Files of Type drop down list: Importable files (all text, graphics, and PageMaker files), PageMaker files (ending in PM5 or PT5), Older PageMaker files (ending in PM4 or PT4), or All files (including files that might not be importable).

   ■ Click C:\ at the top of the Directories list to view the list at the next higher directory level.

■ Click a directory name to view the list at the next lower directory level. Double-click a directory name to view files in a subdirectory. If the directories list is longer than fits in the window, scroll bars appear at the right of the list; you can click on an arrow to scroll up or down the list.

■ To view files on another drive, click the down-pointing arrow under Drives to display a drop-down list, and click a:, b:, or c:, or another drive letter (if you have more than three drives) to view the lists of files on other drives.

Notice that you change directories and disks in the Place Document dialog box by using the same techniques you learned in Chapter 2 for the Open Publication dialog box. The difference is that only PageMaker publications are listed in the Open Publication dialog box, while the Place Document dialog box lists text and graphics files as well.

If the file name still is not displayed after checking all directories and disk drives, either your system does not contain the text file or the file is not recognized by PageMaker. You must install the correct filters for each file format you intend to use by performing the installation procedures described in Appendix A.

6. Select the file you located in step 5 and close the dialog box by double-clicking the file name in the File Name list. (Double-clicking is a shortcut for clicking the file name once to select the file and then clicking OK.)

If you are importing formatted text, you can access a dialog box containing additional options by holding the Shift key as you click OK. (See the section "Importing Formatted Text," later in this chapter.)

If you are importing text in ASCII format, PageMaker displays a dialog box of options for converting the text as the file is imported. (See the section "Importing Unformatted Text," later in this chapter.)

If your text file name does not have an extension representing a word processing program, such as DOC for Microsoft Word documents, a dialog box appears displaying the message Do not know how to place text. Specify the word processing program that the text came from by double-clicking the format. (Table 6.2 in the section "Importing Formatted Text," later in this chapter, lists extensions for different word processing programs.)

If you are importing text from a publication created in PageMaker, the Place PageMaker Stories dialog box is displayed, listing each of the stories in the PageMaker publication. See "Importing Stories from Another PageMaker Publication" later in this chapter.

If the file format is not recognized by PageMaker, the correct filter might not be installed. You must install the correct filters for each file format you intend to use by performing the installation procedures described in Appendix A.

T   I   P   Viewing Your List of Installed Filters

You can view a list of all the filters that you have installed by holding the Ctrl key as you choose the About PageMaker command from the Help menu.

Once any dialog boxes relating to format have been closed, PageMaker runs the text through an import filter and displays on-screen a dialog box indicating the progress of the conversion. Very long text files, or files that include many different text formats or graphics, take longer to convert than shorter, simpler text files.

When placing text as a new story, the pointer changes to either the Manual text flow icon (with horizontal lines representing lines of text) or the Automatic text flow icon (with a curved line representing text flowing through columns or pages), and you proceed with step 7. (Text flow options are discussed in the following section.)

7. Position the text flow icon where you want the text to appear on the page, and then click the mouse.

The text fills the width of the column in which the text is placed or the width of a boundary created by using the Drag-Place method, as described in the section "Using the Drag-Place Feature," later in this chapter. If the Autoflow option (described in the following section) is selected, new pages are inserted by PageMaker as needed to accommodate the flow of text. If Autoflow is not active, text placement stops at the bottom of the column, as shown in figure 6.7, or if the text runs into another object on the page.

If you import text formatted in a word processing program, you can either retain the existing formats or have these formats stripped out as the text is imported by selecting or deselecting the Retain Format check box in the Place Document dialog box. (See step 4 in the preceding set of steps.) If the text is not already formatted in a word processing program, or if PageMaker does not support the word processor and cannot preserve its formatting, the text takes on PageMaker's default formats and type specifications when imported. Figure 6.8 shows examples of formatted and unformatted text placed on a page in PageMaker. (These two options are described in more detail later in this chapter. See also Chapter 8 for additional information about PageMaker's default formats and other methods of formatting text.)

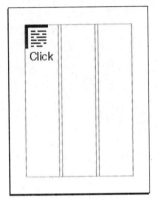 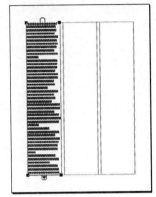

Fig. 6.7

The page before placing text (left) and after placing text (right) by using the manual placing option.

This text was placed in Pagemaker with Retain Format turned off, and has taken on PageMaker's default specifications. All bold, underscore, and italic settings made in the word processing program are lost. Paragraph formatting is also lost.

This text was formatted in Windows Write before being placed in Pagemaker with Retain Format on, and has retained **bold**, underscore, and *italic* settings, paragraph indentation, and justification, as made in the word processing program.

Fig. 6.8

Unformatted text (left) and formatted text (right) placed in PageMaker.

Replacing an Entire Story

To replace an entire story, importing new text files to replace all the text in a series of text blocks that are already positioned on pages in the publication, follow these steps:

1. Select the Text tool from the toolbox, and click the pointer anywhere within a text block that is part of the story.

2. Choose the Place command from the File menu (refer to fig. 6.5).

3. Select Replacing Entire Story in the Place area of the Place Document dialog box. (This radio button is available only if the text tool is selected and the cursor is positioned in a text block before you choose the Place command, as shown in fig. 6.9.)

4. Select the Retain Format, Convert Quotes, and/or Read Tags check boxes as described in step 4 earlier under "Placing Text as a New Story."

5. Follow the procedures for finding the file you want to place as described in step 5 under "Placing the Text as a New Story."

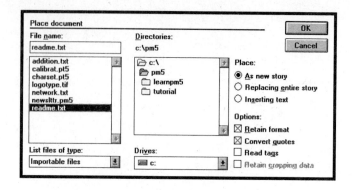

Fig. 6.9

The Place
Document dialog
box as this
dialog box
appears if the
text cursor is
positioned within
a text block.

6. Select the file you located in step 5 and close the dialog box by double-clicking the file name in the File Name list. (Double-clicking is a shortcut for clicking the file name once to select the file and then clicking OK.)

Additional options that vary depending on format of the text are described under step 6 in the earlier section, "Placing the Text as a New Story."

When replacing an existing story, text placement occurs with no further action on your part.

If the placed text results in more text than fits in all the text blocks filled by the story, the last text block in the story displays a down-pointing arrow after the block is selected, and you can continue the flow as described in the section "Working with Text Blocks" later in this chapter.

Replacing Part of a Story

To replace only a selected part of a story, complete the following steps:

1. Select the text to be replaced by using the selection techniques described in the section "Selecting Text by Using the Text Tool" in Chapter 5.

2. Choose the Place command from the File menu (refer to fig. 6.5).

3. Select Replacing Selected Text in the Place area of the Place Document dialog box. (This radio button replaces the Inserting Text button in the dialog box if a section of text is selected, as shown in fig. 6.10.)

```
Place document
File name:                  Directories:              OK
readme.txt                  c:\pm5                    Cancel

addition.txt          [=] c:\              Place:
calibrat.pt5          [=] pm5              (•) As new story
charset.pt5           [=] learnpm5         ( ) Replacing entire story
logotype.tif          [=] tutorial         ( ) Replacing selected text
network.txt
newslttr.pm5                               Options:
readme.txt                                 [X] Retain format
                                           [X] Convert quotes
                                           [ ] Read tags
List files of type:         Drives:        [ ] Retain cropping data
Importable files            [=] c:
```

Fig. 6.10

The Place Document dialog box as this dialog box appears if text is selected.

4. Select the Retain Format, Convert Quotes, and/or Read Tags check boxes as described in step 4 earlier under "Placing Text as a New Story."

5. Follow the procedures for finding the file you want to place as described in step 5 under "Placing the Text as a New Story."

6. Select the file you located in step 5 and close the dialog box by double-clicking the file name in the File Name list. (Double-clicking is a shortcut for clicking the file name once to select the file and then clicking OK.)

Additional options that vary depending on format of the text were described in step 6 in the section "Placing the Text as a New Story" earlier in this chapter.

When replacing selected text, text placement occurs with no further action on your part.

If the placed text results in more text than fits in all the text blocks filled by the story, the last text block in the story displays a down-pointing arrow after the block is selected, and you can continue the flow as described in the section "Working with Text Blocks" later in this chapter.

Inserting Text into a Story

To import text and insert it within a story, complete the following steps:

1. Select the Text tool from the toolbox, and click the pointer within the text at the point where you want to insert the new text.

2. Choose the Place command from the File menu.

3. Select Inserting Text in the Place area of the Place Document dialog box. (This option appears only if the text tool was selected and the cursor was inserted in a text block before choosing the Place command. Refer to fig. 6.9.)

4. Select the Retain Format, Convert Quotes, and/or Read Tags check boxes as described in step 4 earlier under "Placing Text as a New Story."

5. Follow the procedures for finding the file you want to place as described in step 5 under "Placing the Text as a New Story."

6. Select the file you located in step 5 and close the dialog box by double-clicking the file name in the File Name list. (Double-clicking is a shortcut for clicking the file name once to select the file and then clicking OK.)

Additional options that vary depending on format of the text were described under step 6 in the section "Placing the Text as a New Story" earlier in this chapter.

When inserting text within a story, text placement occurs with no further action on your part.

If the placed text results in more text than fits in all the text blocks filled by the story, the last text block in the story displays a down-pointing arrow after the block is selected, and you can continue the flow as described in the section "Working with Text Blocks" later in this chapter.

Specifying Text Flow

PageMaker offers three ways of directing the flow of text imported as a new story: manual flow, automatic flow (or Autoflow), and semiautomatic flow. You can select how you want the text to flow before importing the text, or you can switch between manual, semiautomatic, and automatic text flow after the text flow icon appears.

Using Manual Text Flow

Manual text flow is active when the Autoflow command on the Layout menu is not checked. The text flow icon is composed of horizontal lines representing lines of text. Manual text flows to the bottom of the column or to the first object that blocks the text. The pointer tool is selected when the text stops flowing, and the text appears in a *text block* framed in horizontal lines (called *windowshades*) at the top and bottom. In the middle of each windowshade is a *handle*. If the bottom handle is empty, all of the story has been placed. If the bottom handle contains a down arrow, additional text remains to be placed. To continue placing the text manually, click the handle at the bottom of the text block to reload the text flow icon (this deselects the text block), and then position the loaded text flow icon in a new column or page, and click to continue placing the text (see fig. 6.11).

Fig. 6.11

Text flow icon positioned in next column.

After the page is filled but the last block still shows a down arrow in the bottom handle, you can continue the text to the next page by clicking that handle to display the text flow icon. You then have the following options:

- Click the icon of the page number (in the bottom left corner of the publication window) to which you want to go.
- Select the Go to Page command from the Layout menu.
- Select Insert Pages from the Layout menu to create a new page.

Don't worry that the text flow icon changes to an arrow after you make a menu selection. The loaded text flow icon returns after you are back on a page.

After the next page is displayed, position the text flow icon on the page and click. The text file continues flowing on the page until reaching the bottom margin or another object.

Text placed from a single file remains connected as a story, regardless of how many columns or pages are spanned. Figure 6.12 shows that, if text blocks are chained in a single file, any insertion or deletion of text that is selected by using the Text tool causes the text in chained blocks to move forward or backward to accommodate the change. If a block is selected by using the Pointer tool and then is deleted, the text in that block is deleted, but the positions of chained blocks and the flow between them remain unchanged.

Fig. 6.12

Adding material within chained blocks of text causes surrounding text to shift to make room for the new block.

Using Automatic Text Flow

A more efficient way to continue text from column to column or page to page is to use the Autoflow option. To activate automatic text flow, choose Autoflow from the Layout menu (if that option is not already checked) before using the Place command or before clicking to position text with the loaded text flow icon. The text flow icon shows a curved line representing text flowing through columns or pages. Autoflow places text continuously, wrapping text around previously placed graphics, filling all columns, and adding pages as needed until all the text is placed. Text placement stops if you click the mouse button, after the text runs out, or if the publication reaches 999 pages.

If you stop the automatic text flow by clicking the mouse button, you can extend or shorten the last text block by dragging the bottom windowshade with the pointer tool. You can resume the flow at any time by clicking the down-pointing arrow in the windowshade that marks the bottom of the flowed text after the text is selected by using the Pointer tool. This method yields a loaded text flow icon that you can click at the margin to continue the flow.

In Autoflow mode, text can flow around graphics. By using the Text Wrap command in the Element menu, you can specify how the text wraps around the graphic and where the text flows after wrapping around the graphic. (See Chapter 11 for a discussion of the Text Wrap command.)

Using Semiautomatic Text Flow

To activate semiautomatic text flow, hold down the Shift key while placing text in manual or automatic mode. The text flow icon shows a dotted curved line representing text flowing through columns or pages. After you hold the Shift key to activate semiautomatic flow and click the text flow icon on the page, text flows to the bottom of the current column and stops, but the text flow icon remains loaded and ready for you to position. You then just position and click the icon to continue the flow. The semiautomatic mode changes the text flow mode only temporarily. After you release the Shift key, the flow pattern reverts to manual or automatic at the end of the column, depending on which mode you were in before switching to semiautomatic mode.

Switching between Manual Flow and Autoflow

You can temporarily switch from automatic flow to manual flow by pressing the Ctrl key, just as you can switch from automatic to semiautomatic flow by pressing the Shift key. You can keep Autoflow on, therefore, and switch easily to another option as needed. (If you frequently find your finger growing tired of holding the Ctrl key to use manual flow, however, switch Autoflow off.)

If you usually do not want text to flow automatically, make sure that Autoflow is not checked on the Layout menu before you choose the Place command. If you choose the Place command and see the automatic text flow icon displayed, you can choose Autoflow on the Layout menu to deselect that option before you position and click the loaded text flow icon. After you deselect Autoflow, the manual text flow icon appears. If you use the drag-place feature—holding the mouse and dragging the text flow icon to outline a text block—manual text placement is activated. If you start placing text with Autoflow selected, you can stop the flow by clicking the mouse button and then deselecting the Autoflow option before you continue placing the text.

If you usually want text to flow automatically, make sure that Autoflow is checked on the Layout menu before you choose the Place command. If you choose the Place command and see the manual text flow icon displayed, you can choose Autoflow on the Layout menu before positioning and clicking the icon; the automatic text flow icon appears. If you start placing text with Autoflow deselected, you can change to Autoflow whenever the manual flow stops.

T   I   P   **Using Different Views**

Work in the Fit in Window view while placing text from another program, but work in Actual Size view while typing or editing text. The
text is greeked in the Fit in Window view so that you are unable to
read the letters as you are typing. (To adjust the size of greeked text,
change the size specified in the Preferences dialog box accessed by
the File Preferences command.)

Text may be greeked in the 75% Size and 50% Size views as well,
depending on the resolution of your screen and the point size of
the text.

Using the Drag-Place Feature

Usually, the line length of placed text depends on the width of the column in which you add the text, and the depth of the text block is determined by the bottom margin (unless the text is shorter than the full
page or runs into another object on the page). The drag-place feature is
useful if you want to override the column guides for text, making the
text any width or making it extend beyond the column guides. This
technique also can be used to place a large graphic into a small area
(see Chapter 9). You can use this feature in manual text flow or semiautomatic text flow, but using drag-place overrides automatic text
flow (that is, the text no longer flows to subsequent columns or pages
automatically).

To use the drag-place feature, define the width of the text by holding
the mouse button and dragging the loaded text flow icon diagonally.
An outline of a box appears on the page as you drag the mouse button.
After you release the mouse button, the text you are placing takes on
the dimensions of the box.

Placing Text on the Pasteboard

Usually, you place text from outside files directly into columns in
PageMaker. Under some conditions, however, you may want to place
text on the pasteboard. You may want all the text to fit on one page, for
example, but after you fill the last column, you can see that more text
remains in the source file. You then place the remainder of the text on

the pasteboard to see how much overflow must be accommodated or edited out, as shown in figure 6.13.

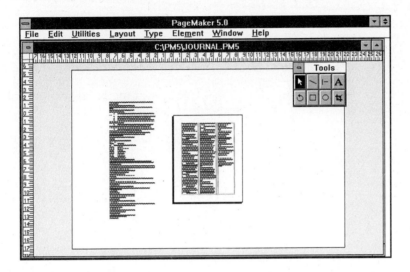

Fig. 6.13

Text flowed onto the pasteboard.

To place text on the pasteboard, choose the Place command—or click on the down-pointing arrow in the bottom windowshade of a text block that has not been placed completely—to display the loaded text flow icon. Then position the loaded text flow icon anywhere beyond the page boundaries displayed in Layout view, and click. Text that you place on the pasteboard assumes the default width, which is determined by the page margins rather than the column guides.

As when using the drag-place feature, you can place text on the pasteboard by using manual text flow or semiautomatic text flow, but placing text on the pasteboard overrides automatic text flow (that is, the text no longer flows to subsequent columns or pages automatically).

CAUTION: Text placed on the pasteboard loses its "overset" status. PageMaker 5.0 introduces an Aldus Addition named Find Overset Text, which is useful for locating the end of any text block that is not yet placed completely or that is too short for the full text of the story. The Find Overset Text utility does not count text placed on the pasteboard as overset text, however, unless still more text is to be flowed from the pasteboard text block.

Importing Stories from Another PageMaker Publication

If you choose a PageMaker publication in the Place Document dialog box, the Place PageMaker Stories dialog box is displayed, showing the first words or characters of each story in the publication (see fig. 6.14). (In earlier versions of PageMaker, you could import stories from another PageMaker publication through the Story menu in the Story Editor, but PageMaker 5 eliminates this restriction.)

Fig. 6.14

The Place PageMaker Stories dialog box.

You can limit or expand the list of stories by specifying the minimum number of characters in the List Stories Over area and clicking Relist. The default is to list stories over 20 characters long.

If you cannot recognize the story you want by the first characters, you can highlight any story by clicking it, and then click the View button to view the full text of the story in a View Story window.

You can place a single story by just double-clicking on the story in the list.

You can select a range of stories by clicking the first one in the range and then Shift+clicking on the last one in the range, or you can click Select All to select all the stories in the publication. You can select more than one story in any order by Ctrl+clicking on each story you want to select, or deselect individual stories by Ctrl+clicking on highlighted stories. If more than one story is highlighted when you click the OK button, the stories are placed as one story in the target publication.

Text imported from another PageMaker publication retains its format, and styles used in the imported text are added to the target publications list of styles.

Using the Place Command To Assemble a Story   T I P

If you have a publication that has been composed of many different stories, but you want them all to be assembled as one story, you can use the Place command to place all the stories from the publication into another publication as one story.

If you want to assemble a single story from many different text files, but you cannot tell until you place the text what order they go in, place them all in one PageMaker publication and arrange the text blocks in the order you want, and then save the first publication and Place it into the final publication, choosing the Select All option in the Place PageMaker Stories dialog box.

Importing Formatted Text

If you select the Retain Format option in the Place Document dialog box, PageMaker preserves the formatting of text from word processing programs such as Windows Write, Microsoft Word, WordPerfect, WordStar, MultiMate, Lotus Manuscript, and XyWrite. In addition, PageMaker reads Rich Text Format (RTF) files and Document Content Architecture (DCA) files such as those created by IBM DisplayWrite3, SAMNA Word, Volkswriter 3, and WordStar 2000. The names of files imported from these programs must have the appropriate extensions so that the files can be recognized and converted correctly when placed in PageMaker by the Place command. Table 6.2 lists several of the most common word processing programs and their extensions as normally assigned by the word processing application. (You also can import data directly from compatible spreadsheets and databases, as described later in this chapter.)

Table 6.2 Extensions for Common Word Processing Programs

Word Processor	Extension
DCAa	DCA or RFT
Windows Write 3.1	WRI
Word (any version)	DOC
WordPerfect 5.1	WP
WordStar 3.3	WS
XyWrite III	XYW
Text-only ASCII files	TXT or ASC

Make sure that you save your word processing files with their normal (default) extensions if you want PageMaker to translate text-formatting commands after you choose the Place command. PageMaker's text-importing capability is file-extension sensitive. If the extension (DOC, TXT, DCA, and so on) does not appear in the Place Document dialog box, another dialog box appears and prompts you for the type of file you are importing (see fig. 6.15). File types listed include only those for which filters have been installed. If you do not see the type of file you want in the list, you can use Aldus Setup to install additional filters (see "Installing PageMaker," in Appendix A).

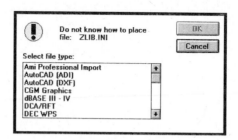

Fig. 6.15

The dialog box that appears if PageMaker cannot recognize a file format.

T I P

Using OLE Commands To Import Formats for Which No PageMaker Filter Is Available

If no filter is available for the type of file you want to import, you can try using Object Linking and Embedding (OLE) commands as described later in this chapter. Note that any word processing application that supports OLE probably has a filter for use with PageMaker, so the main reason that a filter would not be available is that you elected not to install it when you installed PageMaker.

Formatting characteristics that are preserved in PageMaker from most word processors include the following:

- Left margin
- Left and right indents
- First-line indent
- Carriage returns
- Tabs

If your word processor offers different font selections, PageMaker may preserve the font specifications or convert them to equivalent fonts available in PageMaker. If the target printer does not support the type specifications set with that word processor, PageMaker substitutes a close match but remembers the initial specifications and uses them if you switch to a printer that supports them.

The right margin of your text is changed to match PageMaker's column width, and right margin indents are preserved from some word processors. But PageMaker ignores such specialized formatting commands as running headers, running footers, and footnotes.

The example in figure 6.16 demonstrates how PageMaker preserves formats from compatible word processing programs. You can use PageMaker tools to implement any type specifications and formatting options not supported by the word processing program or not preserved in PageMaker (see Chapter 8).

Microsoft Word

This text was typed in Microsoft Word in 10-point Times. This paragraph has no indent. The ruler line was set with a flush-left tab at .5 inches and a decimal tab at 2 inches.

Flush Left   Decimal
text   100.00

Centered Bold Text

Flush Right Italic Text
Bold Italic Text

This paragraph has a normal indent at .25 inches in the word processor.

This paragraph has a reverse or "hanging" indent of .25 inches in the word processor.

Fig. 6.16

Formatted Microsoft Word text placed in PageMaker.

Making Your Own Test File

T I P

If you want to test formatting commands not shown in figure 6.16, you can make your own test file and place the file in PageMaker.

Along with the normal formatting preserved by the import filter, you can control additional options for formatted text by holding the Shift key as you click OK in the Place Document dialog box. A dialog box appears containing formatting options specific to the filter for the type of file you are importing. Figure 6.17, for example, shows the dialog box for the Microsoft Word for Windows import filter.

Fig. 6.17

The Import Filter dialog box that appears after you hold the Shift key and click OK in the Place Document dialog box when placing a Microsoft Word for Windows file.

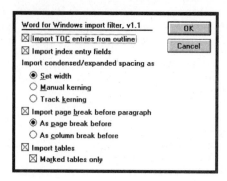

In importing text saved in Word for Windows format, you can convert table of contents (TOC) and index entries from Word into table of contents and index entries in PageMaker. You can convert Word's condensed or expanded spacing to Manual kerning or Track kerning or change it to Set Width spacing. You can convert forced page breaks to page breaks or column breaks. You also can choose to import all tables or marked tables only. (Tables are imported as columns of text separated by tabs.)

T I P   Importing Marked Tables from Word

By default, PageMaker imports only marked tables from Microsoft Word for Windows, enabling you to control which tables are imported. To mark a table in Word for Windows, insert a new line before the table and type **T** or **t** as the only character on the line, and then format the *T* as hidden text.

Importing Unformatted Text

The three common sources of unformatted text are ASCII files from any word processor (including word processing applications on other types of systems, such as mainframe computers), data saved in ASCII format from a spreadsheet or database program, and text that has been telecommunicated through an electronic mailbox facility. You also can convert formatted text to unformatted text by deselecting the Retain Format option in the Place Document dialog box.

If you import ASCII text, PageMaker displays a dialog box that enables you to control how the text is converted (see fig. 6.18). Some sources of unformatted ASCII text force hard carriage returns at the end of every line of text instead of only at the end of each paragraph. You can choose to strip out such extra carriage returns, removing the extra returns at the end of every line and/or between paragraphs. You can specify that tables, lists, and indented lines are to retain carriage returns. You also can opt to replace three or more spaces with a tab character (for tables that were formatted by using spaces) or to import the data in the monospace Courier font. You can also opt for No Conversion, and import the text as is.

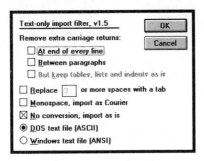

Fig. 6.18

The Text-Only Import Filter dialog box.

PageMaker 5.0 adds the capability to specify whether the file was created in DOS (ASCII format) or Windows (ANSI format).

Initially, unformatted text assumes PageMaker's default type specifications and format. The default specifications also are applied to formatted text files if you place them by deselecting the Retain Format option in the Place Document dialog box.

Choosing Not To Use the Retain Format Option

T I P

If your word processor is not capable of specifying the fonts you want in your publication, adjust the default settings in PageMaker to match the specifications for your publication's text. Place the files without selecting the Retain Format option in the Place Document dialog box.

By changing the default settings first, you can see immediately how the text fills each page. Using this method is better than placing all the text in the wrong font and then using the Select All command to change the type specifications.

If your word processor is not supported directly by PageMaker, you still can place your text files in PageMaker if those files have been saved by using the text-only option most word processors offer. (If your word processor does not offer this option and is not otherwise supported by PageMaker, you may be able to import the files by using OLE commands, as described later in this chapter.)

Text can be telecommunicated from one computer to another directly or through a mailbox facility. If you telecommunicate directly to another computer, you can preserve the formatting setup in many word processing programs. If you send your text through an e-mail (mailbox) facility, however, the e-mail application often forces you to send text in ASCII format (text-only).

You can format telecommunicated text by using your word processing program, or you can place the text in PageMaker to be formatted directly within the program.

Importing Spreadsheet Data as Text

PageMaker includes filters for importing database or spreadsheet data as text. These file names must have the appropriate extensions so that the files can be recognized and converted correctly when placed in PageMaker by the Place command. Table 6.3 lists the formats supported by PageMaker and their normal file name extensions. You also can use OLE commands to import data from these and other programs, as described later in this chapter.

Table 6.3 Spreadsheets and Databases That Can be Placed in PageMaker

Application	Extension
dBASE III+, IV version 1.1-1.5	DBF
Excel 2.1-4.0 Spreadsheets	XLS
Excel 2.1-4.0 Charts	XLC
FoxPro	DBF
Lotus 1-2-3 Spreadsheets	WKS, WK1, or WK3
Lotus 1-2-3 Graphics	PIC
Quattro Spreadsheets	WK1, WKS
Quattro Graphics	PIC
R-Base	DBF
SuperCalc Spreadsheets	WK1, WKS
SuperCalc Graphics	PIC
Symphony Spreadsheets	WRK, WR1
Symphony Graphics	PIC

PageMaker offers the option of importing spreadsheets as text or graphics and of importing the entire spreadsheet or just a range of cells (see fig. 6.19). If you import Microsoft Excel spreadsheet data, for example, you can choose to import it as either text or a graphic. If you select an Excel spreadsheet in the Place Document dialog box, PageMaker displays the Place Excel Range dialog box asking if you want to import the spreadsheet as text or as a graphic. You also can specify a range of cells or a range name. The data is imported as tab-delimited text, with each row of the spreadsheet becoming one line or paragraph in PageMaker, and each column from the spreadsheet separated by tabs in PageMaker. You can specify whether the initial tabs are set as decimal, right, left, or center tabs. You also can specify the number of decimal places to be used in numbers. (See Chapter 9 for information about importing data as a graphic and importing spreadsheet graphics.)

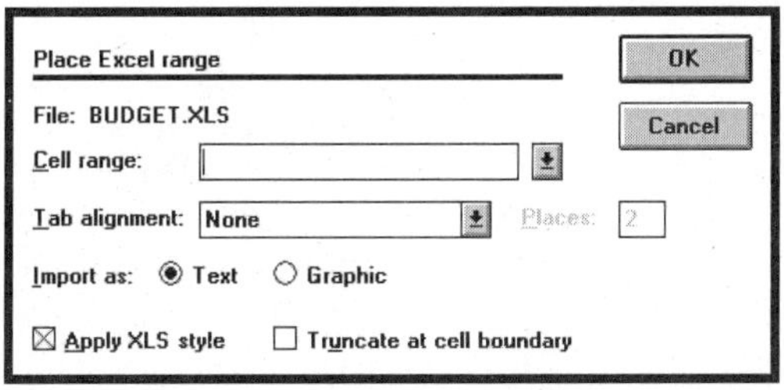

Fig. 6.19

The Place Excel Range dialog box that appears if an Excel spreadsheet is imported.

Importing Data as Text versus Data as a Graphic

T I P

If you import data as text, you can edit the data in PageMaker, but PageMaker does not import all the formatting done in the spreadsheet. If you import the spreadsheet as a graphic, PageMaker retains all the formatting done in the spreadsheet, but you must use the original spreadsheet application to edit the data.

If you import the data as text you also are limited to only 40 columns. Columns that are "hidden" in the spreadsheet are not counted or imported. If the data is imported as a graphic, however, PageMaker supports any number of columns.

PageMaker can preserve the font specified in XLS spreadsheets, such as are created by Excel, and converts the text imported from WKS files to 10-point Courier. You can create a new style named WKS or XLS before importing the data, and PageMaker applies that style to the text, but the import filter overrides the tab settings and makes the column widths the same as in the spreadsheet. (See the section "Using Style Sheets," in Chapter 8.)

T   I   P   **Letting PageMaker Set Tabs for You**

If you import data as text, that data is imported as tab-delimited text, so you can specify whether the initial tabs are set as decimal, right, left, or center tabs. PageMaker matches the tab setting to the original column widths in the spreadsheet. If you plan to format the text in PageMaker in a font larger than that of the original spreadsheet, you may want to widen the columns in the spreadsheet to accommodate the larger font before importing it to PageMaker. Otherwise, you can select all the imported text after it is in PageMaker and change the tabs at the same time that you change the font.

T   I   P   **Importing Date Formats**

PageMaker does not read the date, time, and currency formats directly from the spreadsheet but picks up this information from the WIN.INI file instead. If these formats are different in WIN.INI, and you want to keep the formats used in the spreadsheet, you must update the WIN.INI file. See the Windows manual for more information.

Importing Database Data as Text

If you import a database file with the extension DBF, PageMaker displays a dialog box that enables you to import the data in either directory or catalog format. You also can select the specific fields (columns) in the database that you want to import by selecting from the Fields Available list.

If Directory format is selected, PageMaker imports the data the same way it does spreadsheet data: Each row (record) is a paragraph, each field is separated by a tab, and PageMaker sets tabs that match the widths of the original columns in the database. PageMaker sets the text in 10-point Courier. You can set up a style in advance and select that style for the directory listing. (See the section "Using Style Sheets," in Chapter 8.)

If Catalog format is selected, each field is imported as a separate paragraph, and each record is separated by two carriage returns. You can position the contents of more than one column on a line (such as city, state, and ZIP code) or change the style assigned to a specific field. To make either of these changes, first select a field in the Fields Selected list, and then click the Style button in the Place dBASE File dialog box. You can select from an existing style name that has already been created in your publication, or you can assign a new style name. (PageMaker sets the file in 10-point Courier, but you can change the format after you import the data.) You also can select Keep on Same Line as Previous Field, and Remove Trailing Spaces from Previous Field, as appropriate.

If you do a lot of publishing from large databases, Aldus offers a special version of PageMaker called PageMaker Database Edition, for data-intensive publishing, with added features (not covered in this book) for handling the import of large databases.

Importing Spreadsheet or Database Files Saved in ASCII Format

If the spreadsheet or database program you use is not compatible with PageMaker and does not support OLE (described later in this chapter under "Using Object Linking and Embedding with Text"), you can import text-only versions of the data and then format the data in PageMaker. Most spreadsheet programs and database packages offer the option of saving data as text-only ASCII files, and you can specify whether the data fields are separated by tabs or commas or some other delimiter. If you use the tab character as the delimiter, you can use PageMaker to set tabs on the ruler line, as described in Chapter 8. The data then falls into columns. (You also can import data directly from some spreadsheets and databases in their normal format, as described in the previous sections.)

If the ASCII file uses commas or some other delimiter to separate data elements, you must convert these delimiters to tabs before the data can be arranged in columns in PageMaker. Sometimes the text-only files include quotation marks around fields that happen to use that delimiter (a comma, for example) as part of the data. In either case, you can further prepare the data by using the Change command in the Story Editor window. (See the section "Finding and Changing Text in Story View," in Chapter 7.)

See Examples 3 and 4 in Chapter 20 for a complete description of how spreadsheet or database data can be converted to formatted text in PageMaker.

For Related Information

◄◄ "Selecting Text with the Text Tool," p. 207.

►► "Finding Text in Story View," p. 288.

►► "Formatting Text Using Styles in PageMaker," p. 343.

►► "Importing Spreadsheets as Graphics," p. 370.

►► "Wrapping Text around Graphics," p. 443.

►► "Managing Linked Text and Graphics Documents," p. 597.

Using Object Linking and Embedding with Text

The Paste Link, Paste Special, and Insert Object commands are new in PageMaker 5.0 and are used with Windows 3.1 and subsequent versions that support Object Linking and Embedding (OLE). The Paste command also becomes an OLE command whenever you copy elements from another application that supports OLE and paste them into PageMaker. OLE commands are designed to be used by PageMaker for file formats that it cannot edit. Because PageMaker can edit text easily, most text files cannot be imported using the Paste Link or Paste Special commands, and when you Paste text from another application, by default that text is never OLE-linked or OLE-embedded. The preferred method for importing text is to use the Place command to import text and reserve OLE commands for importing graphics that you expect to update frequently.

OLE commands can be used, however, to import spreadsheet or database data as text. The following procedure briefly summarizes how to import spreadsheet or database data as text into PageMaker by using OLE commands. See also "Importing Spreadsheets as Graphics" in Chapter 9.

To link or embed any object—including spreadsheet or database data—from another application that supports OLE into a PageMaker document, follow these steps:

1. Create your data in the spreadsheet or database application, and then select the data you want to import into PageMaker and choose Copy from the Edit menu.

2. Open a PageMaker publication.

3. Choose Paste Special from the Edit menu, and PageMaker displays a dialog box offering a list of available formats in which the data can be imported.

   Choose Text format in the dialog box to import the data as text. Other format options import the data in a graphic format, as explained in the section "Importing Spreadsheets as Graphics" in Chapter 9.

In Chapter 9, OLE commands are described in detail as the commands relate to graphics, because many options available with these commands apply only to graphics. All the features and restrictions for linked or embedded graphics described in that chapter also apply to linked or embedded text. (See also the section "Managing Linked Text and Graphics Documents," in Chapter 13, for additional information related to these commands.)

For Related Information

◀◀ "Selecting Text with the Text Tool," p. 207.

▶▶ "Understanding Object Linking and Embedding," p. 374.

▶▶ "Managing Linked Text and Graphics Documents," p. 597.

FROM HERE...

Working with Text Blocks

After you select text by clicking the text with the Pointer tool in Layout view, your text appears as a *text block*, framed at the top and bottom by horizontal lines (windowshades). A black *sizing square* is located at each end of a windowshade (see fig. 6.20). In the middle of each windowshade is a handle, which looks like a square. A handle can be empty or can contain a plus sign or a down arrow. The handles disappear if the text block is no longer selected with the Pointer tool or if the Text tool is selected.

Whether typed, placed, or pasted into a publication, text becomes part of a text block on a page. A page can contain any number of text blocks. A full page of single-column text with no graphics may consist of one text block, but a two-column page of text must have at least two text blocks—one in each column. Text can flow from one block to another and from one page to another. Text that is connected in a flow of chained text blocks is called a *story*. A publication can be composed of many different stories or sets of chained text blocks.

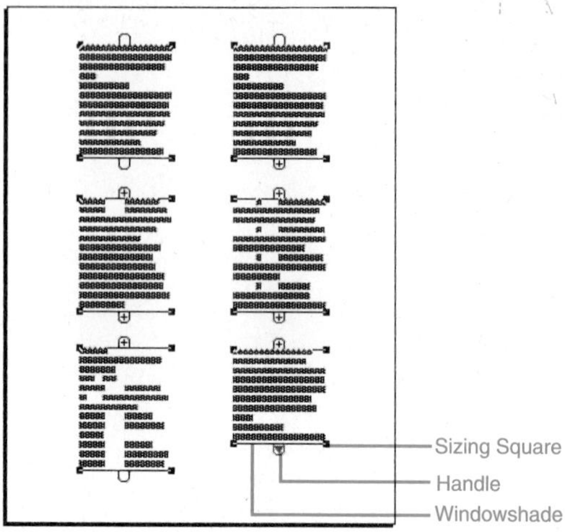

Fig. 6.20

Windowshades and handles on several text blocks.

Sizing Square
Handle
Windowshade

The symbols in the handles indicate whether the displayed text is chained to any other text in a publication. An empty top handle indicates that the block is the beginning of a story. A plus sign (+) in the top handle means that the text is continued from another block—the text at the beginning of this text block is not the beginning of the story. An empty bottom handle indicates that the block is the end of a story. A plus sign in the bottom handle means that another text block is chained to that block. A down arrow in the bottom handle indicates that the story contains overflow (or overset) text that has not yet been positioned on a page or on the pasteboard. You can enlarge the text block or click the bottom handle to display the text flow icon and continue placing text on that page or on other pages.

You can move a block of text, change its size, or break up or combine text blocks by using the techniques described in the following sections.

Moving a Text Block by Using the Pointer Tool

You use the Pointer tool from the toolbox to move a block of text. Click the block anywhere and hold down the mouse button to drag the block in any direction (see figs. 6.21 and 6.22).

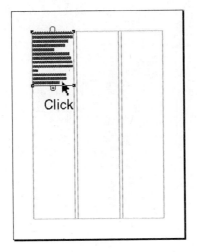

Fig. 6.21

A block of text
ready to be
moved.

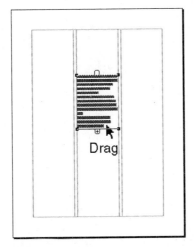

Fig. 6.22

A block of text
after being
moved.

Sizing a Text Block by Using the Pointer Tool

After your text is placed on the page, you can easily change the length of the text block. Use the Pointer tool to select the text block and display the handles; then drag the bottom handle up or down, as shown in figures 6.23 and 6.24. If this text block is connected to others, any extra text flows into the next chained block if you shorten the first block. If you lengthen the block, additional text flows in from the next chained block.

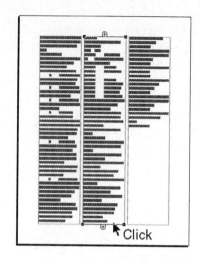

Fig. 6.23

A block of text
before being
shortened.

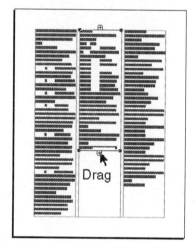

Fig. 6.24

The same block
of text after it is
shortened.

You cannot lengthen a block of text beyond the end of the story. If the
end of the block is the end of all the text—signified by an empty bottom
handle—you cannot drag the bottom handle down any farther.

The width of a text block usually is determined by the column guides
that you set up by using the Column Guides command of the Layout
menu—unless you use the drag-place or drag-type features in placing
or typing text, as described earlier in this chapter. Remember that you
can create a text frame by dragging the mouse to form a box (which is
visible only as you drag the mouse). The typed text then fills in the
shape of the box and stops wherever the box stops. You also can drag
the mouse to create a box to place text in the publication.

After you have typed or placed text in a column, however, you can change the width of the text block. Use the Pointer tool to select the text block, and then drag one of the sizing squares at a corner of either windowshade to the left or right. This is one way to change the width of text that has already been placed on a page if you decide to change the column guides. (See the tip "Reflow Text After Changing Column Widths" in the section "Setting Column Guides," in Chapter 5.)

By dragging a sizing square at the corner of the windowshade, you change the width of the entire text block, and all the text in that block adjusts automatically. If you make a text block narrower, the overflow text flows into the next connected text block or becomes part of the text yet to be flowed. If you make a text block wider, additional text flows in from the next connected block or from the unflowed portion of the text file.

To change the width and the length of a block in one motion, as shown in figure 6.25, follow these steps:

1. Position the pointer over a sizing square at the corner of a windowshade and hold down the mouse button to display a two-headed arrow.

2. Drag the mouse pointer diagonally in the direction you want to change the text block's width and length.

3. Release the mouse button after the text block is in the shape you want.

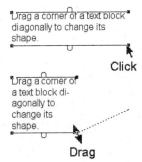

Drag a corner of a text block diagonally to change its shape.

Click

Drag a corner of a text block diagonally to change its shape.

Drag

Fig. 6.25

Dragging a sizing square diagonally to change a text block's width and length.

Notice that you need not change the column guides themselves to change the width of text after the text has been typed or placed in the column. The column guides are necessary only as you are first placing text, and the guides are a part of the publication's grid structure to which you can always return.

Using the Control Palette To Move or Size a Text Block

You also can use the Control palette to change the position and size (as well as other features) of a text block that has been selected by using the Pointer tool. As the section "Using the Control Palette To Move and Scale Objects," in Chapter 4, described, if an object is selected by using the Pointer tool, the control areas in the Control palette include the Apply button, a Proxy icon, X (the horizontal position of the current reference point of the selected text block), Y (the vertical position of the current reference point of the selected text block), W (the width of the text block), H (the height of the text block), percentage-scaling options for width and height, a proportional-scaling option button, and rotating, skewing, and reflecting controls at the far right on the palette. (Transformations—rotating, skewing, and reflecting—are described in the section "Working with Transformations" in Chapter 11.)

You can change the position or the size of a text block by selecting the appropriate area in the Control palette and entering a new value or by adding, subtracting, multiplying, or dividing the value. You can enter most measurements in increments as small as .001 and in font sizes from 2 to 720 points. Click the Apply button or press Enter, or click the document window for the new value to take effect.

Breaking a Column of Text into Several Blocks

A column of text on a page can include more than one text block. You can create several text blocks to accommodate several situations: when a column is composed of text placed from different files, when the text is typed as separate blocks, or when the text deliberately is broken up to accommodate special layout requirements (see fig. 6.26).

Suppose that you want to break into two blocks the text shown in the middle column of figure 6.27. To do so, follow these steps:

1. Select the block to be broken up to display its handles.

2. Drag the bottom handle up to shorten the block.

3. Click the plus sign in the bottom handle to display the text flow icon.

Fig. 6.26

Columns
composed of
several blocks of
text.

4. Click the text flow icon anywhere in the column below the top
   block (see fig. 6.28).

   The text continues flowing as a second block of text, and a space
   is left between the two blocks (see fig. 6.29).

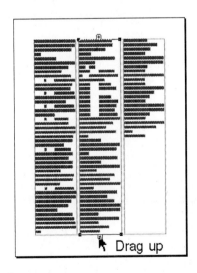

Drag up

Fig. 6.27

The text block
before breaking
it up.

By using this method, you can break text into any number of blocks.
Generally, you do not need to break text into blocks to make room for a
graphic—you can use the automatic text wrap feature described in
Chapter 11. If you want text to wrap around another text block, however, you must break the wrapping text into separate blocks.

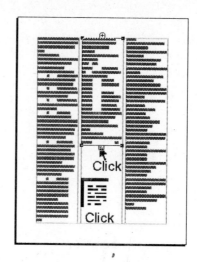

Fig. 6.28

The text flow
icon, ready to
continue placing
text.

Fig. 6.29

The divided text
block.

Merging a Series of Text Blocks

If two or more text blocks already are chained as a story, you can
merge them into one text block by dragging the bottom handle of the
first text block until it contains all the text, as indicated by an empty
bottom handle. If you want to delete a text block from the middle of a
series of chained text blocks, drag the bottom handle of the text block
you want to delete up to meet the top handle. This process squeezes all

the text out of the block and into the next block in the story chain, enabling you to delete the block without losing any text. Then drag the handle of the text block you want to keep downward, expanding the block until all the text fits in that block.

If you want to merge or chain together blocks of text that are not already chained as a single story, you must use the Cut and Paste commands from the Edit menu. If, for example, you want to chain two separate text blocks, you first must merge them into one text block. Use the Text tool or the Select All command to select all the text in the second text block, and choose the Cut command. Then position the text insertion point at the end of the text in the first block, and choose Paste. You then can expand the first text block to display all the text. Alternatively, you can break the block into a series of chained text blocks as described in the preceding section.

You also can cut and paste text between separate stories by working in multiple story windows using the Story Editor, as described in Chapter 7.

Finding and Placing Overset Text

PageMaker 5.0 introduces an Aldus Addition, Find Overset Text, that is useful for locating the end of any text block that has not been placed completely or that is too short for the full text of the story—that is, for locating any text block whose bottom windowshade would show a down-pointing arrow if it were selected with the pointer tool.

After you choose Find Overset Text from the Aldus Additions submenu of the Utilities menu, PageMaker displays an Actual Size view of the bottom handle of the first text block that still has text to be placed. This text block is selected, and the bottom handle displays a down-pointing arrow. (Notice that the Find Overset Text utility does not count text placed on the pasteboard as overset text—unless more text can be flowed from the pasteboard text block.)

After the utility has located a text block with overset text, you can use the Pointer tool to drag the bottom handle of the windowshade to make the text block longer to contain the extra text. You also can click the down-pointing arrow in the handle to display and load the text flow icon and then click the loaded text flow icon at the place on the page where you want the overset text to flow.

Balancing Columns Automatically

PageMaker 5 introduces an Aldus Addition called Balance Columns that calculates the average length of the selected columns and then resizes them to that length. You can opt to align the tops of columns with the top text block or the bottoms of columns with the bottom text block and determine whether to add remaining lines to the first or last column(s) when lines of text cannot be divided equally.

This feature is handy in creating newsletters, magazines, or brochures that often have several columns per page, where the text does not quite fill a whole page.

To balance columns, follow these steps:

1. Use the Pointer tool to select two or more columns within the same story.

2. Choose Balance Columns from the Aldus Additions submenu on the Utilities menu.

3. Click the settings you want in the Balance Columns dialog box, and click OK (see fig. 6.30).

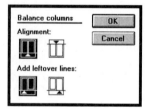

Fig. 6.30

The Balance Columns dialog box.

The Addition changes the length of each column to make them all equal, or within one line difference (see fig. 6.31).

Viewing Text Block and Story Information

PageMaker 5.0 introduces two Aldus Additions that display useful statistics about a selected text block or story. Textblock Info and Story Info are two new commands available from the Aldus Additions submenu of the Utilities menu. You must select a text block before you choose either command.

Fig. 6.31

Three columns
before and after
balancing.

The Textblock Info command displays a dialog box containing statistics about a selected text block: linkage information, relative sequence in the group of text blocks that compose a story, character count, the total area in square inches and total depth in inches, and the pages on which the previous and next text blocks appear (see fig. 6.32, left side).

The Story Info command displays a dialog box containing statistics about a selected story: linkage information, number of text blocks in the story, character count, number of overset characters in the story, the total area in square inches and total depth in inches, and the first and last pages on which the story appears (see fig. 6.32, right side).

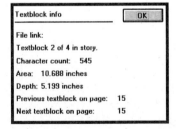

Fig. 6.32

The Textblock
Info (left) and
Story Info (right)
dialog boxes.

Traversing Text Blocks

PageMaker 5.0 introduces an Aldus Addition called Traverse Textblocks, which enables you to quickly move from the current text block to the next or previous text block in the story or to the first or last text block in the story. You must select a text block before choosing the Traverse Textblocks command on the Aldus Additions submenu of the Utilities menu. PageMaker displays a dialog box of options (see fig. 6.33). By selecting the appropriate radio button and clicking OK, you immediately jump to the text block specified. This feature helps you locate text blocks that do not flow continuously from column to column or page to page, as can be the case in a magazine or newsletter layout. The Traverse Textblocks command also is useful for jumping to a different page if the scrollbars are hidden.

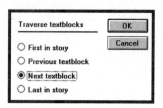

Fig. 6.33

The Traverse Textblocks dialog box.

FROM HERE...

For Related Information

◀◀ "Using the Control Palette To Move and Scale Objects," p. 213.

▶▶ "Wrapping Text around Graphics," p. 443.

Adding Headers, Footers, and Page References

PageMaker 5.0 adds two Aldus Additions that create frequently used text for you: the Continuation Addition adds "Continued on page x" or "Continued from page x" and assigns the correct page number for you. The Running Headers/Footers Addition adds running headers or footers specific to the content of each page. These two additions are described in the next sections.

Adding Running Headers or Footers

The Running Headers/Footers Addition creates headers or footers that reflect the content of each page on which the selected story appears, by extracting text from the selected story. This Addition is useful for adding specific references to a header or footer—such as a section title that changes within one publication. You can also use this Addition in a glossary or index, to show the first or last term on the page. This Addition supplements the headers or footers you might add to the master pages, to appear the same on every page of the publication (see the section "Typing Running Headers and Footers" in Chapter 5.)

You can extract text from a text block for the header or footer, based on search criteria you enter, or you can type your own header or footer text. You can also determine whether the header or footer should fall on left pages or right pages, or both. The following steps take you through this process.

To place a running header or footer, perform the following steps:

1. Select the first text block of a threaded story with the pointer tool.

   The story must include the heading (or text) that you want to appear in the header or footer, formatted with a specific style that distinguishes it from the body text, such as a heading style, if you want the Addition to be able to find the text easily for you. For example, the text block selected in figure 6.34 includes the section title "Open Doors" formatted in Subhead 1 style. You can enter the text of the header or footer manually in step 5.

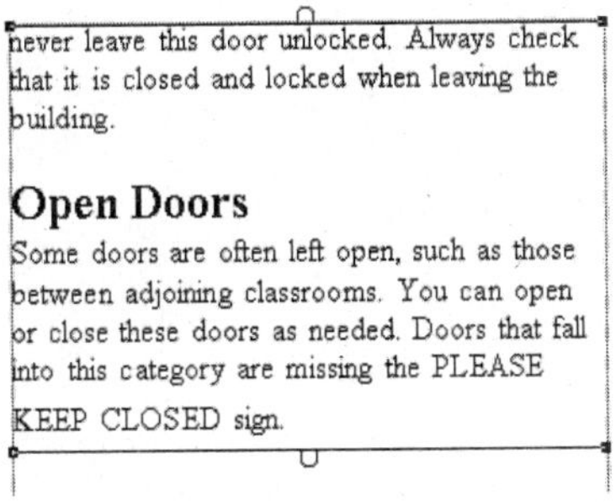

never leave this door unlocked. Always check that it is closed and locked when leaving the building.

Open Doors

Some doors are often left open, such as those between adjoining classrooms. You can open or close these doors as needed. Doors that fall into this category are missing the PLEASE KEEP CLOSED sign.

Fig. 6.34

Selected text block includes the section title "Open Doors" formatted in Subhead 1 style.

2. Choose Running Headers/Footers from the Aldus Additions submenu on the Utilities menu, to display the Running Headers/Footers dialog box (see fig. 6.35).

3. Choose the type of search (first or last occurrence) and the paragraph style to find.

   For example, if you want headings formatted in Subhead 1 style to appear in the header or footer, and the Addition finds two or more Subhead 1 headings on one page, would you want the first or last Subhead 1 heading on a page to appear in the header or footer?

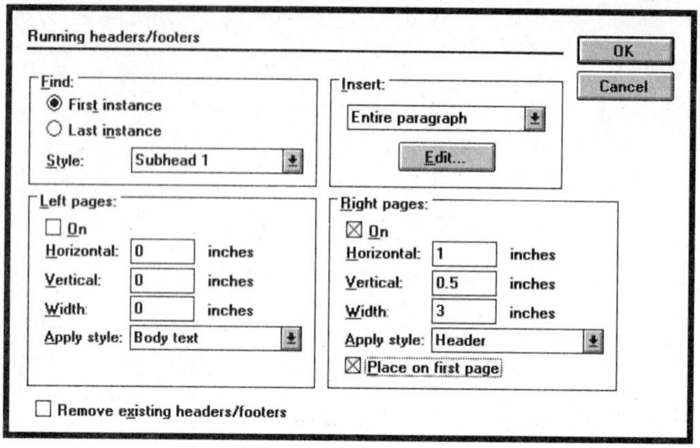

Fig. 6.35

The Running Headers/Footers dialog box.

4. Under Insert, choose the header or footer content from the list or click Edit and create custom instructions (step 5).

   The Addition provides 8 predefined insert options, such as First word, First two words, Entire paragraph, and so on. You can also specify more complex customized headers or footers by using the Addition to rearrange the text copied from the specified paragraphs, insert portions of the text, or insert static repeating text within the running text.

5. If you click Edit in the Running Headers/Footers dialog box, the Create Custom Content dialog box appears. Choose Your Text Plus Paragraph from the drop-down list (see fig. 6.36); then type your custom text in the bottom box of the dialog box (see fig. 6.37). For example, you might add the word "Section:" to appear in the header or footer before the section or procedure name. Delete the "\1" if you do not want the text from the found paragraph included—only your custom text.

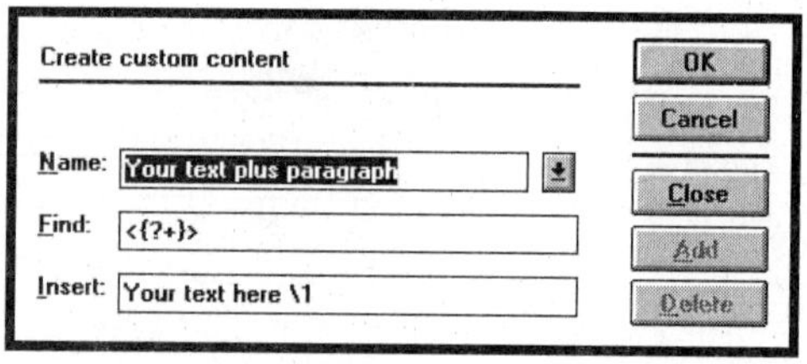

Fig. 6.36

The Create Custom Content dialog box with custom text option.

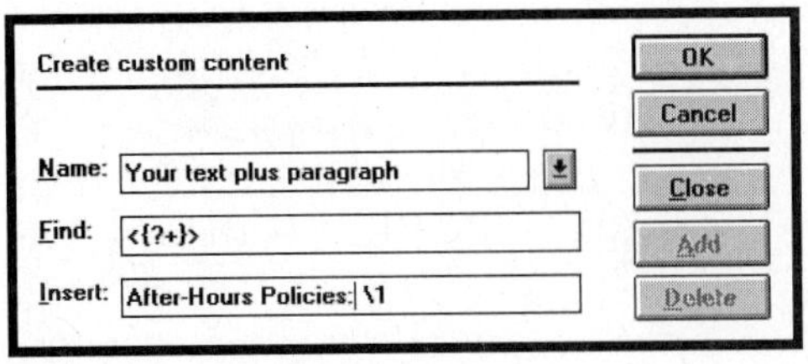

Fig. 6.37

The Create Custom Content dialog box with custom text typed.

---

6. Complete the placement options, including which paragraph style to apply to the header/footer.

   Specify whether the header or footer should appear on left pages or right pages or both, and enter the horizontal and vertical position and width of the text block. The Addition uses the publication's zero point to calculate the placement of the header or footer text blocks. The horizontal measurement locates the text block to the right and down from the zero point; negative numbers locate it to the left and up from the zero point.

   The position you specify here determines whether the text will be a header or a footer—headers being positioned at the top of a page and footers at the bottom.

7. Click OK to close the dialog box.

   The Addition searches the contents of a threaded text story and finds the first (or, optionally, the last) occurrence on each page of text assigned a specific paragraph style. The Addition then inserts all or part of the text in that paragraph as the header or footer for the page (see fig. 6.38).

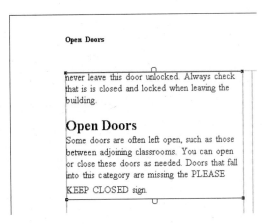

Fig. 6.38

A running header positioned as specified.

> **CAUTION:** If the new header or footer text block overlaps an existing text block with the same paragraph style, the Addition presents a warning. If you click OK to continue the Addition, the existing text blocks may be deleted when the headers or footers are placed.

To delete headers or footers, complete the following steps:

1. Select the text block from which you ran the Addition.

2. Choose Running Headers/Footers from the Aldus Additions submenu on the Utilities menu.

3. Click Remove Existing Headers/Footers to remove any header or footer text that was previously created by the Addition; then click OK. (This does not affect text that has been positioned on the master page.)

The Addition retains the placement value from the last time you ran the Addition. If you have moved the header or footer text blocks, enter the new location measurements of the header or footer to be deleted.

Adding Continuation Page References

The Continuation Addition automatically adds a text block above or below the selected text block with "Continued on page x" or "Continued from page x" and assigns the correct page number for you. The Addition shrinks the selected text block by one line and places a jump-line story with the correct page number before the text block (for Continued from...) or after the text block (for Continued on...). The Addition also creates new styles in your Styles palette called ContFrom and ContOn.

To create and place a Continued statement, follow these steps:

1. Select a text block with the Pointer tool.

2. Choose Continuation from the Aldus Additions submenu on the Utilities menu.

3. In the Continuation Notice dialog box, click the appropriate option to place a jump line on the page (see fig. 6.39). Choose Top of Textblock to add a "Continued from..." line (see fig. 6.40), or choose Bottom of Textblock to add a "Continued on..." line.

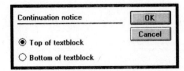

Fig. 6.39

The Continuation Notice dialog box.

Fig. 6.40

A "Continued from..." line.

If you change your layout, page numbers in jump-line stories are not updated automatically—you must manually revise the page numbers or delete the jump-line stories, expand the text blocks by one line, and run the Addition again.

Summary

Importing text into PageMaker is not difficult. You use the Place command to import long text files from other programs. You also can use the Paste command to import text from another Windows applications. You can type text in the Story Editor or use the Text tool from the toolbox to type text directly on a page.

To see how PageMaker handles text after you place the text on a page, you can build a test file by using your word processor. Try placing the test file twice—once with the Retain Format option selected and once with the Retain Format option deselected to see how the situations differ. After you become familiar with how PageMaker handles your files, you can decide intelligently how much preparations you want to make to the text in your word processing program before placing text in PageMaker.

After you place text in PageMaker, you can use the commands and techniques explained in the following chapter to edit the text. How to format text in PageMaker is explained in Chapter 8.

Editing Text

You can type and edit text in Layout view, in which the screen shows exactly what the text will look like when printed. You can also type and edit text in the Story Editor, which displays text quickly in Story view, using a single font that doesn't reflect exactly the text's printed appearance. Story Editor also incorporates features usually associated with word processors, such as global search and a spelling checker.

Chapter 6 shows you how to type or import text onto a page and how to manipulate whole text blocks. This chapter goes on to explain how to edit the text. Chapter 8 takes you one step further, explaining how to format text.

Inserting and Selecting Text

You can replace text and insert new text by entering it at the keyboard, as you do with a word processor. Whether you are working in Layout view or Story view, the methods for inserting the text cursor and selecting text are the same. Earlier chapters mentioned some of these methods, but in this chapter they are explained in detail. (These selection methods and other useful mouse and keyboard shortcuts are repeated in Appendix C and on the inside front and back covers of this book.)

Inserting Text

If you want to insert new text in a text block, position the I-beam pointer where you want the new text to begin. As you type, existing text shifts to make room for the inserted text. You can also replace selected text as you type, as described in the next section.

You can move the text insertion point by using the mouse to move the I-beam pointer when the Text tool is selected and by clicking to position the text insertion point within a text block. You can also move the text insertion point by using the keyboard shortcuts listed in table 7.1.

Table 7.1 Shortcuts for Moving the Text Insertion Point

To Move the Insertion Point	Press
One character at a time to the left or right	Left arrow, Right arrow
One word at a time to the left or right	Ctrl+left arrow, Ctrl+right arrow
One line at a time	Home or up arrow, End or down arrow
One sentence at a time	Ctrl+Home or Ctrl+End
One paragraph at a time	Ctrl+up arrow or Ctrl+down arrow
A fixed distance determined by the view and screen resolution	PgUp or PgDn
To the beginning or end of the story	Ctrl+PgUp, Ctrl+PgDn
To beginning of line	Keypad Home or keypad 7
To end of line	Keypad End or keypad 1
To beginning of sentence	Ctrl+keypad Home or Ctrl+keypad 7
To end of sentence	Ctrl+keypad End or Ctrl+keypad 1
Left one character	Left arrow or keypad 4
Right one character	Right arrow or keypad 6
Left one word	Ctrl+left arrow or Ctrl+keypad 4
Right one word	Ctrl+right arrow or Ctrl+keypad 6
Up one line	Up arrow or keypad 8
Down one line	Down arrow or keypad 2

To Move the Insertion Point	Press
Up one paragraph	Ctrl+up arrow or Ctrl+keypad 8
Down one paragraph	Ctrl+down arrow or Ctrl+keypad 2
Up a screen	Keypad PgUp or keypad 9
Down a screen	Keypad PgDn or keypad 3
To top of story	Ctrl+keypad PgUp or Ctrl+keypad 9
To bottom of story	Ctrl+keypad PgDn or Ctrl+keypad 3

Selecting Text

If you want to replace text, highlight the text to be replaced by dragging the I-beam pointer over it (or by using any of the text selection methods described below). When you begin typing, the highlighted block of text is deleted; you don't have to delete the block before you begin typing. Use these same methods to select text for formatting, as described in Chapter 8.

The most generally applicable method of selecting any amount of text within a block is to drag the I-beam over the text you want. Place the I-beam next to the first part of the text you want to select. Hold down the mouse button as you drag the I-beam to the end of the text to be selected. If necessary, the screen scrolls as you drag the I-beam down a column. When you release the mouse button, the selected text appears in reverse video (see fig. 7.1).

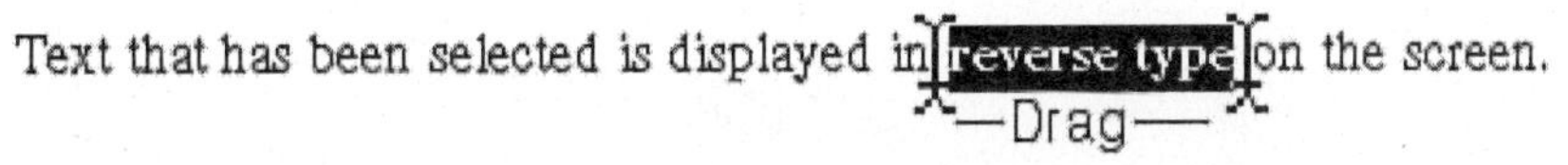

Text that has been selected is displayed in reverse type on the screen.
—Drag—

Fig. 7.1

Selecting text by dragging the I-beam.

You can use many shortcut methods to select text groups, including segments crossing multiple blocks of linked text. These methods, described in table 7.2, involve clicking the mouse alone or with special keys. To select the end of a text file, for example, click the I-beam once to put the text insertion point in front of the first word or character you want to select and press Shift+Ctrl+PgDn.

Table 7.2 Shortcuts for Selecting Text

Selection	Action
Next point of insertion for new text from keyboard	Click between two characters
A range of text character-by-character or line-by-line	Click+drag
Whole word	Double-click
A range of text word by word	Double-click+drag
Whole paragraph	Triple-click
A range of text paragraph-by-paragraph	Triple-click+drag
All the text between two insertion points	Click at one end of text; then move the I-beam and Shift+click at other end of text
A whole story	Click anywhere in the story and type Ctrl+A or choose Select All from the Edit menu

Each of the preceding selection methods sets the anchor point from which the following keyboard commands operate. Keyboard shortcuts work on all standard 101 keyboards. Some clone keyboards and particularly laptop and notebook keyboards will not support all the shortcuts.

Task	Action
Extend or decrease the selection one character at a time	Shift+left arrow or Shift+right arrow
Extend or decrease the selection one word at a time	Shift+Ctrl+left arrow or Shift+Ctrl+right arrow
Extend or decrease the selection one line at a time	Shift+Home or Shift+up arrow; Shift+End or Shift+down arrow
Extend or decrease the selection one sentence at a time	Shift+Ctrl+Home or Shift+Ctrl+End
Extend or decrease the selection one paragraph at a time	Shift+Ctrl+up arrow or Shift+Ctrl+down arrow

Task	Action
Extend or decrease the selection a fixed distance determined by the view and the resolution of your screen	Shift+PgUp or Shift+PgDn
Extend or decrease the selection to the beginning or the end of the article if the article ends or begins on the same page where the cursor is located	Shift+Ctrl+PgUp or Shift+Ctrl+PgDn

Text selection methods and other useful mouse and keyboard short-cuts are repeated in Appendix C and the front and back covers of this book.

Editing Text in Layout View

In Chapter 6, you learned that to move or reshape a whole block of text, you use the pointer tool to select the text. To format or edit text in Layout view, you must select the text with the text tool. If you are new to PageMaker, one of your most common mistakes in editing text will be to use the pointer tool when you need to use the text tool (or vice versa). The difference between the tools is worth repeating as a tip.

Knowing the Difference between the Pointer Tool and the Text Tool

T I P

Use the pointer tool to move, copy, or size whole blocks of text. Use the text tool to edit the content (that is, change or rearrange words) or format the text (as described in Chapter 8).

You select the text tool in Layout view by clicking the large *A* in the toolbox or by using the shortcut, Shift+F4 (see fig. 7.2). When you select the text tool, the pointer changes to an I-beam icon, as shown in figure 7.3. You use the I-beam to position the text-insertion point or to select text already on the page, as described in the following sections.

Fig. 7.2

Select the text
tool by clicking
the large *A* in the
toolbox.

Fig. 7.3

The text tool
I-beam icon.

With the text tool selected, you can use any of the methods described earlier in this chapter to insert the cursor within a text block or to select text. You needn't first select a text block with the pointer tool in order to select text within it using the text tool.

Once text is selected, you can type new text from the keyboard to replace it, or use commands under the Edit menu (described in Chapter 5) to Cut or Copy the selection and Paste it to another location in the publication.

Keystrokes for typing special characters are shown in Table 6.1 in Chapter 6, and these and other useful mouse and keyboard shortcuts are repeated in Appendix C and the inside front and back covers of this book.

For Related Information

◀◀ "Using the Edit Menu Commands," p. 216.

▶▶ "Formatting Text," p. 293.

FROM HERE...

Typing and Editing Text in the Story Editor

PageMaker's Story Editor feature offers several advantages over typing and editing text directly in Layout view. The Story Editor enables you to enter and edit text much more quickly, because the text is displayed in a single screen font that you specify through the Preferences command, as described in Chapter 4. (The Story Editor window doesn't show the WYSIWYG view of the text.) You can use the Story Editor to type or edit text, and you can open more than one story window at a time. In addition, the Story Editor offers a spelling checker and a search and replace feature. These features are described in the following sections.

Displaying the Story Window

Before you can use the Story Editor, a PageMaker publication must be open. When a publication is open, you can use the Story Editor to edit the text of an existing story or to create a new story in Story view—a window on-screen that displays text without showing the formatting which is evident in Layout view. (A story in PageMaker is a single text block or all the text in a chained series of text blocks. Methods of chaining a series of text blocks are described earlier in this chapter.) A publication can include more than one story, and you can open multiple story windows under the Story Editor and view stories from different pages of the publication at the same time.

The five methods that you can use to open a story window are described in the following paragraphs.

1. The quickest way to switch to Story view is to triple-click on a text block with the pointer tool. You can also use the slower method of clicking once on the text block and then choosing Edit Story from the Edit menu (or use the keyboard shortcut Ctrl+E). In either case, the story window opens with the text insertion point at the beginning of the story.

2. With the text tool selected, position the text insertion point within a block of text in Layout view and choose Edit Story from the Edit menu (or use the keyboard shortcut Ctrl+E). The story window opens with the Story view at the text insertion point as selected in Layout view (see fig. 7.4).

   When you are in Story view, the menus at the top of the screen change. The Layout and Element menus aren't available, and a Story menu is added.

3. You can open a new, empty story window by choosing Edit Story from the Edit menu (or by using the keyboard shortcut Ctrl+E) when no text is selected and the text insertion point is not positioned in a text block in Layout view. (The next section describes how to enter text in a new story window.)

   If a story window is already open but hidden behind another story window or the publication window, you can click a visible part of the story window to bring it to the front. Alternatively, you can choose the window by name from the Window menu.

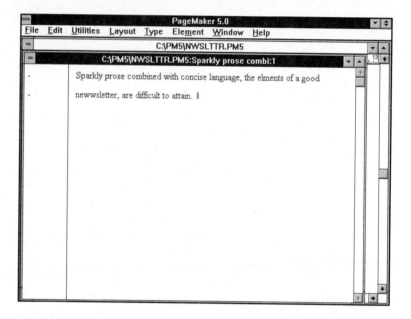

Fig. 7.4

The story
window.

4. You can use the first three methods to open multiple story windows. You can also open a new, empty story window while a story window is displayed by choosing New Story from the Story menu.

5. PageMaker 5.0 adds a new Aldus Addition named Edit All Stories. When you choose Edit All Stories from the Aldus Additions submenu under the Utilities menu, PageMaker automatically opens Story Editor windows for every story in a document.

The display in the story window has several characteristics that distinguish it from the publication window:

■ The text in the story window is displayed in the single font selected through the Preferences dialog box, as described in Chapter 4. Actual page, column, and line breaks aren't displayed in Story view. Inline graphics (graphics that are anchored to the text as described in Chapter 11) are displayed as markers only; actual graphics aren't displayed.

■ Each story window is named with the first few words of the story.

■ The menu bar changes to display the Story menu. The Element and Layout menus aren't available.

■ The toolbox isn't available.

■ You can format text by using the Colors, Styles, and Control palettes or by using commands under the Type menu, but format changes don't appear until you return to Layout view.

- The Display Style Names command from the Story menu enables you to view the assigned styles by name, as displayed in the left column beside the text.

- The Display ¶ command from the Story menu displays special characters such as carriage returns. When you change from Story view to Layout view, any changes made to the text in the story window will be reflected in the publication window. The display in the publication window, however, doesn't change as you work in the story window.

Switching between Story View and Layout View

You can switch between Story view and Layout view by clicking the windows or by choosing the windows by name from the Window menu. Using these methods, you return to the same view of the publication as before you opened the story window. By choosing Edit Layout from the Edit menu (or by using the keyboard shortcut Ctrl+E), you return to Layout view with the text insertion point in the same position as it was in the story window.

Closing the Story Window

You can also change from Story view to Layout view by closing the story window. The fastest way to close the story window is to double-click the Control menu icon in the upper left corner of the story window. You can also close the window by clicking the Control menu icon and choosing Minimize or Close, or by choosing Close Story (Ctrl+Shift+E) from the Story menu (see fig. 7.5).

When you close a new story window that contains new (unplaced) text, PageMaker displays a dialog box asking if you want to Place or Discard the story. If you choose Place, PageMaker displays a loaded text placement icon. You then can place the story in a publication, as described in Chapter 6. If you choose to discard the story, the story window closes and the text isn't saved.

Changing the Display in the Story Window

As described in Chapter 4, you can change your preferences for how the story window displays text. To do this, choose the Preferences command from the File menu, and click Other in the Preferences dialog box. The second dialog box lets you select the font and size for text displayed in Story view. These font and size lists are drop-down lists that restrict the range of choices to fonts and sizes that facilitate fast screen display. You make selections by clicking the arrows to the right of the values for Size and Font to display a drop-down list of choices. You then drag to highlight your choice.

Fig. 7.5

The Story menu.

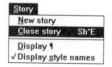

You can also choose to Display Style Names next to each paragraph, and Display ¶ (that is, display hidden characters). These last two options can also be adjusted for an open story window using commands under the Story menu without affecting other defaults or other story windows.

Weird Text in Story View?

You might open the story window and see the text displayed in Greek letters or strange symbols. This can happen if you have removed the font from the system that you formerly used to display text in Story view, or if you open a publication on a system that doesn't have the font you used in Story view. In these cases, PageMaker has to guess which font to use, and it might guess Symbol font or Wingdings.

You can correct this problem by choosing Preferences from the File menu, clicking Other in the first dialog box, and choosing a different font for the story editor in the second dialog box.

Adding Text in the Story Window

You can type text directly in the story window just as you would in any word processor. You can use the mouse to reposition the text insertion point and select text. The text selection methods described earlier in this chapter can be applied to select text in Layout view or in Story view.

You can use the Place command from the File menu to import text or inline graphics. The Import to Story Editor dialog box is the same as the Place command dialog box in Layout view, which is described in Chapter 6. The only difference between the Place command in the two views is that in Layout view, it can result in a loaded text or graphics icon, and in Story view, it simply positions the imported text or graphics at the text insertion point as part of the story.

Imported graphics are represented by a graphics marker in the story window. You cannot view, resize, or crop the graphic until you return to Layout view.

Placing Text versus Placing Graphics in Story View   T I P

Note that if you select a range of text in Story view and use the Place command to import text, the imported text replaces the selected text. You cannot, however, replace selected text with an imported graphic. In order to import a graphic, you must position the cursor between two characters within the text. If a range of text is selected, you will not be allowed to place a file with a graphic format.

You can use the Export command from the File menu to export text from the Story Editor to an external text file. You can also export text from Layout view, as described later in this chapter.

Changing Text in Story View

When a story window is active, the Find, Find Next, and Change commands are available on the Utilities menu (see fig. 7.6). You can search for and change text (words or phrases and nonprinting characters) and text attributes (by style names or fonts, styles, and sizes). You can search all stories in a publication at the same time, or you can search the current story or selected text. PageMaker 5.0 adds the capability to open more than one publication at a time, and the Find and Change commands now offer the option of searching all stories in all open publications.

Fig. 7.6

The Utilities menu with Change active.

To search text for a phrase or specific text format that you want to replace with a new phrase or format, follow these steps:

1. Choose the Change command from the Utilities menu, or use the keyboard shortcut, Ctrl+9. When you choose the Change command, the Change dialog box appears (see fig. 7.7).

Fig. 7.7

The Change dialog box.

2. In the Change dialog box, type the phrase you want to find in the Find What text box (refer to fig. 7.7).

   The phrase can include special characters such as nonbreaking spaces, tabs, and carriage returns. You must enter special characters in the Change dialog box using different keystrokes than you use when typing them in the text. (These and other special characters are listed in table 6.1 in Chapter 6, in Appendix C, and in the inside front and back covers of this book.)

3. Type the phrase with which you want to replace found text in the Change To text box. In figure 7.8, zero-zero space dollar sign (00 $) is being changed to zero-zero tab dollar sign (00^T$).

4. Click the Match Case check box if you want to find only those instances in which the capitalization matches what you have typed in the Find What text box. Leave the Match Case box unchecked if you want PageMaker to search for all matches, regardless of case.

Change

Find what: `00 $`

Change to: `00^T$`

Options: ☐ Match case   ☐ Whole word

Search document: Search story:

◉ Current publication   ○ Selected text

○ All publications   ◉ Current story

                 ○ All stories

[Find]   [Change]   [Change & find]   [Change all]   [Attributes...]

Fig. 7.8

Changing a phrase.

5. Click the Whole Word check box if you want to find only those instances in which the Find What text is preceded by a space and followed by a space or a punctuation mark (such as a period). Leave the Whole Word check box unchecked if you want to find all the places where the combination of letters occurs. Leave the Whole Word check box unchecked, for example, if you want to find the words *ask*, *asking*, *asked*, *task*, and so on when you search for *ask*.

6. Under Search Document, you can opt to search the current publication only, or all open publications. This option is a new option available with PageMaker 5.0, which enables you to open more than one publication at a time.

7. Under Search Story, you can opt to search the currently selected text only (if you selected text before choosing the Change command), search the current story only, or search all stories. Note that if you chose to search all open publications in step 6, then all stories are automatically searched.

8. You can click Attributes to display the Change Attributes dialog box (see fig. 7.9). You can use this dialog box to find and change the paragraph style (if a style sheet was used in formatting the text, as described in Chapter 8) or to find and change individual font/size/style combinations.

9. Click OK to exit the Change Attributes dialog box and return to the Change dialog box. Click Find to find the next occurrence only (and go on to step 8), or click Change All to substitute all occurrences of the found text with the text you entered in the Change To box.

   If no text was entered in the Change dialog box, all occurrences of the text attributes are changed as specified in the Change Attributes dialog box. If you entered text in the Change dialog box, only text that matches both the entered phrase and the text attributes is changed. If no text attributes are entered, any text that matches the entry in the Change dialog box is changed, and the text takes on the attributes of the found text.

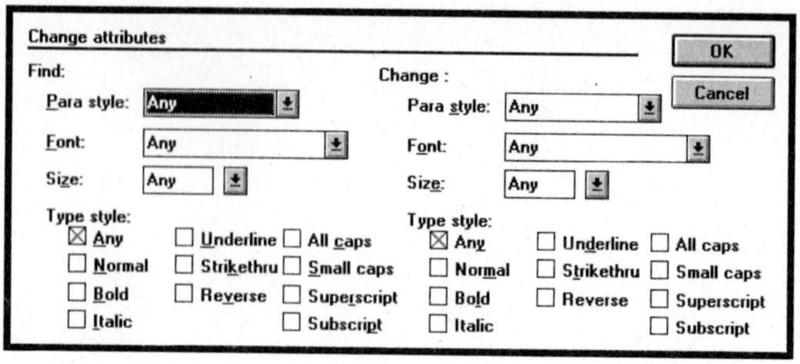

Fig. 7.9

The Change Attributes dialog box.

10. If you clicked Find (rather than Change All), you selectively can keep or change each found occurrence. When PageMaker finds the next occurrence of the Find What text or attributes, that area is highlighted in the story window. You can click Find again if you don't want to change that text, or you can click Change or Change & Find to change the text as described in step 9.

Finding Text in Story View

When you use the Find command on the Utilities menu, or the keyboard shortcut Ctrl+8, the dialog boxes displayed are similar to those displayed when you use the Change command. With the Find dialog box, however, you enter search information only—not replace information (see figs. 7.10 and 7.11).

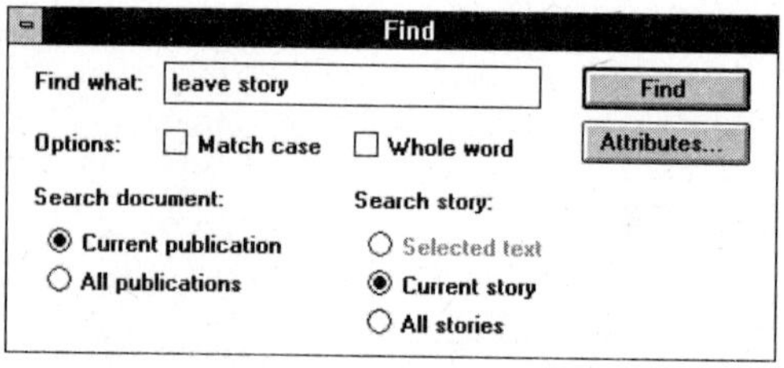

Fig. 7.10

The Find dialog box.

You can close the Find dialog box and jump quickly to the next occurrence of the text you last entered in the Find dialog box by choosing the Find Next command from the Edit menu (or by using the keyboard shortcut Shift+Ctrl+9).

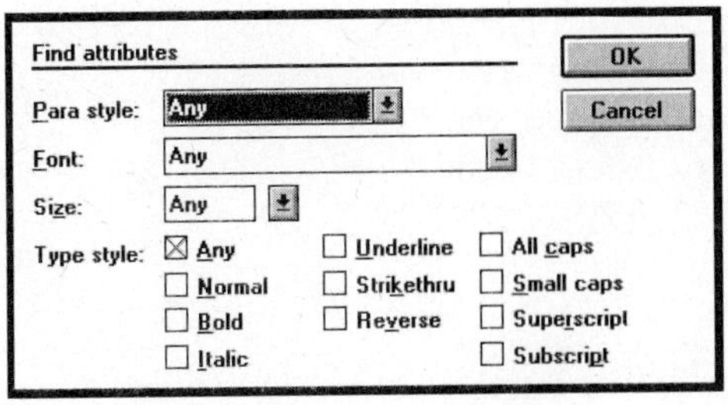

Fig. 7.11

The Find
Attributes dialog
box from the Find
dialog box.

Jumping to a Specific Spot in Layout View

If you find a word or phrase using one of the search commands in
Story view, but need to see where it is on a page before you decide to change it, you can jump to the exact spot in Layout view
that is currently selected in Story view by choosing Edit Layout
(Ctrl+E) from the Edit menu.

T I P

Chapter 17 includes several examples of using global searches in
formatting long publications such as books and manuals.

Using the Spelling Checker

The spelling checker is part of the Story Editor. With a story window
open and active, you can choose Spelling from the Utilities menu, or
use the keyboard shortcut Ctrl+L. In the Spelling dialog box, you can
choose to check the spelling in all of a publication's stories at one time,
in the current story only, or in selected text (see fig. 7.12).

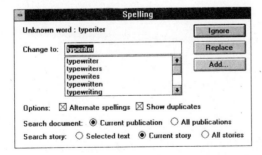

Fig. 7.12

The Spelling
dialog box.

PageMaker adds the capability to open more than one publication at a time, and the Spelling command now offers the option of searching all stories in all open publications. You can also opt to display or not display alternate spellings (suggested by the spelling checker), or to find or not find duplicates (the same word repeated—for example, "my my"). The spelling check process will go faster if you turn these last two options off.

PageMaker searches the text and checks spelling against a 120,000-word U.S. English dictionary (or a dictionary that you create or select as described below). When PageMaker finds a word that isn't in the dictionary, that word is displayed in the dialog box along with any close matches (if the Alternate Spellings option is turned on). Page-Maker also locates duplicate words (two identical words in a row, if Show Duplicates is on) and possible capitalization errors (lowercase words following a period and a space). You then can choose one of the following alternatives:

- Click Ignore to leave the word unchanged and go on with the search.

- Retype the word in the Change To text box, and then click Replace or press Enter to change the word and continue the search.

- Double-click a word in the list of close matches to replace the found word and go on with the search. The slower alternative is to click once a word in the list of close matches, and then click Replace.

- Click Add to add, edit, or remove a word in the dictionary (see fig. 7.13).

- Click the close box to close the Spelling dialog box and end the search.

Fig. 7.13

Adding a word to the dictionary dialog box.

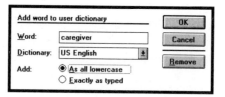

PageMaker comes with a 120,000-word dictionary in the U.S. English version or an 80,000-word dictionary in the International English version. You can also purchase other dictionaries from Aldus, including dictionaries in other languages and dictionaries for the medical and legal professions. You can use PageMaker's Dictionary Editor to create your own user dictionary (as an alternative to adding terms to the 100,000-word dictionary) or to combine two or more dictionaries.

If you have more than one dictionary in your PageMaker system, you can use the Paragraph command under the Type menu to choose the dictionary used in the spelling checker, as described in Chapter 8.

Keystrokes for typing special characters are shown in Table 6.1 in Chapter 6, and these and other useful mouse and keyboard shortcuts are repeated in Appendix C and the inside front and back covers of this book.

Chapter 17 includes several examples of using global searches in formatting long publications such as books and manuals.

For Related Information

◄◄ "Using the Edit Menu Commands," p. 216.

►► "Making Entries in the Paragraph Specifications Dialog Box," p. 314.

►► "Using Inline Graphics," p. 459.

FROM HERE...

Summary

You can type text in the Story Editor or use the text tool from the toolbox to type text directly on a page. When in Story view, you have access to PageMaker's spelling checker and global search/replace commands. You use the same text selection techniques described in this chapter—in either Story view or Layout view—when you use the commands and techniques explained in the next chapter to change the text's formatting.

Formatting Text

The capability of setting type in different fonts and formats is an essential feature of any desktop publishing system. PageMaker's formatting features enable you to position, size, and align text on a page. In Chapter 6, you learned that PageMaker can incorporate some of the formatting attributes set up in a word processing program. After importing most documents into PageMaker, however, you usually need to change the format of the text, case-by-case or globally through a style sheet. This chapter explains the basic mechanics of applying type specifications. Using PageMaker's Text tool with the Type menu and Control palette, you easily can change your publication's text format and style. Chapter 16 describes some of the thought that goes into developing type specifications, including the higher principles and informed practice of good typography and publication design.

The procedures and steps described in this chapter are part of the page-layout process presented in Chapter 5. Specific commands change the appearance of the text, such as the shape and size of the characters, the distance between characters and lines, and the alignment of the text relative to the column guides or margins. You can set up rules that run above or below a paragraph as part of the text format, which is more efficient than using PageMaker's line tools to draw rules between paragraphs. You can change the type specifications for the entire publication quickly using style sheets, or you can change small segments of text using individual commands. You can apply text formatting commands in Layout view, where you see the effects of changes immediately, or in Story view, where you do not see the formatting.

Chapter 6 offers information that can help you decide how much formatting and editing to do in advance with your word processor, and how much work to do directly in PageMaker. Although PageMaker preserves the formatting from a word processor, you occasionally need to format in PageMaker. First, a word processor may not be capable of producing the kind of formatting your design specifications demand. Second, in the division of responsibilities on your team, the author who uses a word processing application may only enter text, and the designer who uses PageMaker may do all the formatting.

As Chapter 6 stresses, do as much editing as possible (typing new text or changing the content of existing text) by using the PageMaker Story Editor or your word processor. The WYSIWYG screen in Layout view slows the program during text editing. On the other hand, you probably want to format most of the text (changing the appearance of the type) in Layout view, where you can see the effects as you make the changes. However, the same formatting can be done faster in Story view, where you cannot see the effects of the changes immediately.

 NOTE Note that all the commands described in this chapter—including commands offered through the Control palette—are available in both Layout view and Story view. In Story view, however, some formatting may not be visible.

Reviewing Default Settings

Unless you specify otherwise, text typed directly into PageMaker with the Text tool uses the default characteristics. Table 8.1 lists the normal default settings for all text in PageMaker.

Table 8.1 PageMaker's Text Default	
Specification	**Default**
Font name	Times (or similar, if available on the target printer)
Size	12 point (or next size smaller)
Leading	Auto
Style	Normal
Position	Normal
Case	Normal
Hyphenation	On, Manual plus Dictionary
Pair kerning	Above 12 points
Paragraph alignment	Left

Specification	Default
Indents	None
Spacing between paragraphs	Zero
Tab stops	Every half inch

The default specifications apply to new text typed in PageMaker and to unformatted text files imported into PageMaker. You can change the default type specifications by selecting the Pointer tool and using the Type menu commands. You also can change the defaults using the Text tool if no text is selected and the text insertion point is not positioned on the page.

If you select text with the Text tool then apply Type menu commands or use the Control palette to change type specifications, the changes apply to the selected text only. The default settings for new typed text remain the same. If you apply these commands when a publication is open but no text is selected, you change the defaults for new text typed in the current publication. If you apply these commands when no publication is open, you can change the defaults for all new publications. Chapter 16 includes more tips about changing PageMaker's default settings.

For Related Information

◀◀ "Importing Formatted Text," p. 247.

▶▶ "Planning Your Design Specifications," p. 708.

FROM HERE...

Changing Type Specifications

Type specifications determine the appearance, or font, of the text characters. You can open the Type Specifications dialog box from the Type menu and choose options for defining the type specifications of selected text (see fig. 8.1). Some of these options are repeated as commands on the Type menu and also have keyboard shortcuts. You also can change all the options in the Type Specifications dialog box through the Control palette (as shown in the next section). When you first open the Type menu or any of the associated dialog boxes or submenus, the screen displays the options that apply to the current selection.

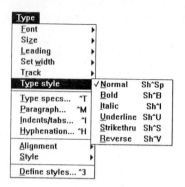

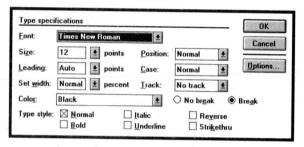

Fig. 8.1

The Type menu commands (top) and the Type Specifications dialog box (bottom).

Using the Control Palette in Character View

PageMaker 5.0 adds a *Control palette* you can use to change type specifications. If the Control palette is open on-screen, using this palette is the fastest way to change more than one type specification at a time, because you don't need to open a menu or a dialog box. The only faster way to change a single attribute is to use a keyboard shortcut (listed in Table 8.3, in Appendix C, and on the inside front and back covers of this book).

You can choose one of three different appearances for the Control palette: Layout view, Character view, or Paragraph view. These three views were introduced in the Chapter 2 section "Examining the Control Palette." Basic methods of making entries in the Control palette are described in the Chapter 5 section "General Characteristics of the Control Palette." This section describes the Control palette's Character view in detail (see fig. 8.2).

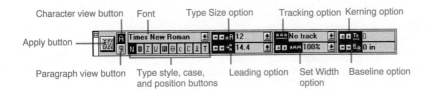

Fig. 8.2

The Control palette in Character view.

Reviewing Features of the Control Palette

You display or hide the Control palette by choosing Control palette from the Window menu or typing Ctrl+' (single quote). If you choose Control palette when no publication is open, the palette does not appear until you open a publication. If the Control palette is displayed when you close a publication, the palette reappears when you next open the publication.

To display the Control palette in Character view, choose the Text tool in the toolbox and click the A—the Character view button—at the left of the Control palette. When the Control palette is in text mode—either Character view or Paragraph view—the palette also is called the *Text palette*.

Remember that if you use the Control palette to change type specifications after selecting text with the Text tool, the changes apply to the selected text only. If you apply changes through the Control palette when a publication is open but no text is selected, you change the defaults for new text typed in the current publication. (To change defaults for all new publications, you must use commands under the Type menu when no publication is open. Chapter 16 includes more tips about changing PageMaker's default settings.)

When the Control palette is on-screen, you can activate it by simply clicking the palette or by typing Ctrl+` (accent). When you're in this palette, as in any dialog box, you can move through the controls in several ways: clicking the mouse pointer on a control, pressing the Tab key, or pressing Shift+Tab to tab in reverse order. These and other keyboard shortcuts are listed in table 8.2. (See table 5.3 in Chapter 5 for additional shortcuts that apply in Layout view.)

Table 8.2 Keyboard Shortcuts in the Text Palette

Shortcut	Task
Ctrl+' (single quote)	Display or hide the Control palette
Ctrl+` (accent)	Switch between the Control palette and the publication or story window

continues

Table 8.2 Continued

Shortcut	Task
Tab	Move to the next option
Shift+Tab	Move to the previous option
Arrow keys	In Character view, move the cursor between characters in an edit box
Esc	Display the last valid value for an option
Enter	Apply changes and move to the next option
Space bar	Turn the current button on or off
Shift+F11	Scroll through valid units of measure in the current option

You can make entries in the Control palette by clicking buttons, choosing from drop-down lists, editing the entry as text, or using scrolling arrows (*nudge buttons*) to select values. The following list describes these techniques:

■ Click a button to turn an option on or off. A change you make by clicking a button takes effect immediately.

■ Choose from a pull-down menu. Changes made through menus on the Control palette take effect immediately.

■ Type an entry in a text box, as in any dialog box. Press Shift+F11 in the text box to cycle through the units of measure available for the option. You can enter most measurements in increments as fine as .001 and font sizes from 4 to 650 points.

■ Perform arithmetic on an entry. You can add to or subtract from any existing value for an option using the symbols on the numeric keypad (+, –). If, for example, the current measure is 12 points, you can increase the value 2 points by positioning the cursor after the 12 or after the unit of measure and typing **+2**. You need not enter the unit of measure if it is the same as the current default measure.

■ Click a nudge button to increase or decrease a value by a set amount. Hold down the Ctrl key as you click a nudge button to increase the nudge amount by ten times (*power nudge*). Depending on the unit of measure, the default nudge is one of the following: .01 inch, 1 point (if picas or Ciceros are used), or 1 mm. You can adjust the nudge amounts through the Preferences command (described in Chapter 4).

Changing the Unit of Measure

TIP

The unit of measure shown in the Control palette always reflects the current unit of measure, as set with the Preferences command on the File menu. You can override this unit in the Control palette (or any dialog box) by entering a one-character abbreviation for the unit of measure you want to specify, as described in Chapter 4. In the Control palette, you can also cycle through different units of measure in the currently active control area by pressing Shift+F11. Changing the unit of measure does not affect any text or graphics already on the page.

To exit the palette and activate all changes, press the Enter key or click the mouse in any other window. Many changes made on the palette are not reflected on the page until you exit the palette or click the Apply button on the left side of the palette (refer to fig. 8.2).

Using the Control Palette To Change Character Attributes

You can use the Control palette in Character view to change the font and size (and other attributes) of text you have selected with the Text tool, such as the text shown in figure 8.3. The control areas of the Control palette in Character view are described briefly in this section, but the individual attributes are described in more detail later in this chapter under "Making Entries in the Type Specifications Dialog Box."

Text typed with Very Loose and Very Tight Tracking

Fig. 8.3

The Control palette in Character view with selected text.

When you select text with the Text tool, the Control palette in Character view includes the following control areas:

- *Apply button.* Click to display the changes made to selected text without exiting the Control palette.

- *Palette view option buttons.* Click the A to display Character view or ¶ for Paragraph view (described later in this chapter).

■ *Font.* Displays the name of the font applied to the current text selection, which you can change by choosing from the drop-down list. If no font is listed here, then the current text selection includes more than one font.

■ *Type style, case, and position buttons.* These buttons represent the following options: N = normal, B = Bold, I = Italic, U = Underscore, R = Reverse, Θ = Strikethru, c = Small caps, C = All caps, ^{S} = Superscript, and $_S$ = Subscript. Attributes applied to the current text selection are chosen. If no attributes are chosen, then the selected text includes mixed attributes. These options are spelled out more explicitly in the Type Specifications dialog box.

■ *Type Size option.* Displays the size of the font applied to the current text selection. You can change the size by typing a new number, choosing a value from the drop-down list, or clicking the nudge buttons to change the size in .1-point increments. Hold the Ctrl key as you click the nudge button to change the size in 1-point increments. If no size is listed here, then the current text selection includes more than one size.

■ *Leading option.* Displays the leading value for the current text selection, which you can change by typing a new number, choosing from the drop-down list, or clicking the nudge buttons to change the leading in .1-point increments. Hold the Ctrl key as you click the nudge button to change the leading in 1-point increments. If no value is listed here, then the current text selection includes more than one leading specification.

■ *Tracking option.* Displays or adjusts the tracking—the formula for spacing between characters—for the current text selection. You can choose a different setting from the drop-down list.

■ *Set Width option.* Displays or adjusts the horizontal width of characters in the selected text. Values greater than 100% make characters wider than the original font design; values less than 100% make characters narrower. You can change the value by typing a new number, choosing from the drop-down list, or clicking the nudge buttons to change the value in 1% increments. Hold the Ctrl key as you click the nudge button to change the value in 10% increments.

■ *Kerning option.* Displays or adjusts the space between characters in the selected text. Values can range between +1.00 em space and -1.00 em space. A value of 0 indicates normal spacing. You can change the value by typing a new number or clicking the nudge buttons to change the value in .01 em increments. Hold the Ctrl key as you click the nudge button to change the value in 0.1 em increments.

■ *Baseline option.* Displays or adjusts the position of the baseline of selected text relative to other characters in the paragraph. Values greater than 0 make characters higher than the adjacent text; values less than 0 make characters lower. You can change the value by typing a new number or clicking the nudge buttons to change the value in fixed increments.

Click the Apply button, press the Enter key, or click the document window for the new value to take effect.

Making Entries in the Type Specifications Dialog Box

When you choose the Type Specifications command (Ctrl+T) from the Type menu, the screen displays the Type Specifications dialog box. From this dialog box, you define the font name, size, leading, width, position, case, track, color, and style of the selected characters (see fig. 8.4). These specifications define a character's appearance. You also can use the Control palette to define all these options except color, break, and the additional options. You can use other commands on the Type menu to define all options except case, color, break, position, and the additional options.

Type specifications			OK
Font:	Times New Roman		Cancel
Size:	12 points	Position: Normal	Options...
Leading:	Auto points	Case: Normal	
Set width:	Normal percent	Track: No track	
Color:	Black	○ No break ⦿ Break	
Type style:	☒ Normal ☐ Italic ☐ Reverse		
	☐ Bold ☐ Underline ☐ Strikethru		

Fig. 8.4

The Type Specifications dialog box.

Specifying Font Name and Size

Traditionally, a *font* is a specific combination of typeface, size, and style. A *typeface* is the more general name. For example, 10-point Times italic is a different font from 12-point Times italic, but both are the same typeface (Times). Most desktop publishing applications reverse these traditional meanings and refer to typefaces as fonts, as the Type Specifications dialog box does.

Typefaces and sizes appear in scrolling windows in the Type Specifications dialog box. To choose a typeface, use the scrollbars to locate the name you want and click that name to choose it.

The typefaces appearing in the dialog box are determined by the printers and the typefaces you have installed through Windows. If you have installed more than one kind of printer, PageMaker displays only those typefaces that are designed for the *currently selected* printer. If you have installed more typefaces than the current printer or cartridge can handle, you should choose only typefaces for which your printer is set up. See Chapters 10 and 13 for more information about printing. See "Font Management" in Chapter 13 for more information on installing fonts.

To choose a size, scroll to any number in the size window and click that number. Or using the Size box, specify any size from 4 to 650 points in .1-point increments—you are not limited to the sizes listed on the scrolling menu. Not all printers, however, handle all sizes of every typeface. You should enter a custom font size only if the current printer accommodates scalable fonts, such as a PostScript or a PCL level 5 printer (such as the HP LaserJet IV). Choosing a custom size on other types of printers may result in font substitution or bit-mapped printing. (For a detailed discussion of printer fonts, see Chapters 13 and 16.)

Specifying Leading

Leading (rhymes with *heading*) is a measure of the distance from the base of one line of text to the base of the next line (see fig. 8.5). If you specify Auto in the Leading box, PageMaker adjusts the leading when you change the point size of the text. If you enter a specific value for the leading and you change the point size, you may need to change the leading, too. You may set leading in any value from 0 to 1300 points in .1-point increments.

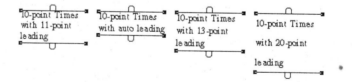

Fig. 8.5

Examples of different leading.

When you choose automatic leading, PageMaker sets leading at 120 percent of the point size to the nearest tenth of a point. For example, 10-point type gets 12-point leading. You can change the percentage value for automatic leading by choosing the Paragraph command from the Type menu then changing the Spacing option in the Paragraph Specifications dialog box.

To achieve a particular look, you may want to specify the leading precisely as part of the design specifications (see Chapter 16). Changing the leading also is a way to fit copy into a defined space. For example, you can adjust the leading to squeeze text on a tight page, expand text to fill an area, or force two columns to the same length (see Chapter 16).

Solving the Mystery of Last-Line Leading

T I P

Sometimes the last line of a paragraph appears to have more leading than the rest of the lines, even though all the text is the same size and leading is set to Auto. Check to see if the carriage return at the end of the paragraph is set to a larger size than the rest of the text or set with different leading. You can select the carriage return by dragging the I-beam over the space between the period at the end of the paragraph and the first character of the next paragraph. Use the Control palette or the Type Specifications command to specify the same font, size, and leading values as the rest of the paragraph.

Changing Character Width and Tracking

The Set Width option enables you to expand or compress the width of characters by specifying a value between 5 and 250 percent in .1-percent increments. Set Width works only if the selected printer supports scalable fonts, such as a PostScript or a PCL level 5 printer (such as the HP LaserJet IV). Choosing a custom width on other types of printers may result in font substitution or bit-mapped printing.

A drop-down list appears when you click the arrow at the right of the Track field, itemizing PageMaker's tracking options, which range from Very Loose to Very Tight (see fig. 8.6). Tracking adds or subtracts a defined amount of space between letters in the selected range of text. The amount of change relates to the font and size of the text. If you change the font or size, therefore, the tracking amounts also adjust. (For more information on kerning the spaces between two letters manually and recommended guidelines for spacing, see Chapter 16.)

Very Loose Track	C A L E N D A R
No Track	CALENDAR
Very Tight Track	CALENDAR
70% Width	CALENDAR
Normal Width	CALENDAR
130% Width	CALENDAR

Fig. 8.6

Examples of different width and track settings.

T I P   Tracking in PageMaker 5.0

Tracking in PageMaker 5.0 is looser than previous versions of PageMaker. When you convert a publication created in PageMaker 4.0 to PageMaker 5.0, text with a tracking value other than zero may change. If you have modified your old tracking information file or want to keep the original tracking, you can copy the file in which your old tracking information is stored (KERNTRAK.BIN) to the USENGLSH subdirectory in the Aldus directory, and change the name to one recognized by PageMaker 5.0 (TRAKVALS.BIN). Another alternative is to use the Edit Tracks Addition (described under "Editing Tracking Values" later in this chapter) to re-create the tracking values in PageMaker 5.0.

Specifying Color

You can apply color to text through the Color palette or through the Color option in the Type Specifications dialog box. (Color is explained in detail in Chapter 12.)

Specifying Break/No Break

PageMaker 5.0 adds a new option of specifying No Break to keep a line from breaking (that is, automatic text wrap) at any point in selected text. For example, you might select names and titles such as "Pres. William Clinton" and set No Break to prevent the words from being separated by a line break. If the phrases are very long, this works best when the text margins are wide.

Specifying Type Style

The six type styles listed in the Type Specifications dialog box also appear in a submenu from the Type Style command on the Type menu. The styles have keyboard equivalents:

F5 or Ctrl+Shift+space bar	Normal text
F6 or Ctrl+Shift+B	Boldface
F7 or Ctrl+Shift+I	Italic
F8 or Ctrl+Shift+U	Underscore
Ctrl+Shift+S	Strikethru
Ctrl+Shift+V	Reverse

Specifying Position and Case

The options for the position of text are Normal, Superscript, and Subscript. Superscripts and subscripts may affect the leading where they occur to prevent them from touching text on adjacent lines. You can manually adjust the leading of all the text to match the lines changed by PageMaker, but the better solution is to change the size and/or position of the superscripts or subscripts themselves. You can adjust your preferences for the size and position of superscripts and subscripts in the Type Options dialog box. Open this box by clicking the Options button in the Type Specifications dialog box. Some printers cannot print superscripts and subscripts in all sizes.

You can convert any text to all capital letters or small capital letters (see fig. 8.7). Small caps usually are 70 percent of the height of full caps, but you can adjust your preferences for the size of small caps in the Type Options dialog box. Open this box by clicking the Options button in the Type Specifications dialog box.

Normal Capitalization
ALL CAPS
SMALL CAPS

You can click the Options button in the Type Specifications dialog box and set your own preferences for the size of small caps, superscripts, subscripts, and for the position of superscripts and subscripts. You enter values in the Type Options dialog box as percentages of the point size (see fig. 8.8). In specifying Superscript position, a value of 0 positions the superscript on the baseline of the normal text, and a value of 100 positions the superscript at the top of normal text. A value of 0 for Subscript positions the subscript on the baseline of normal text, and a value of 100 positions the subscript ascent at the baseline of normal text. The default for subscript and superscript is 33.3 percent.

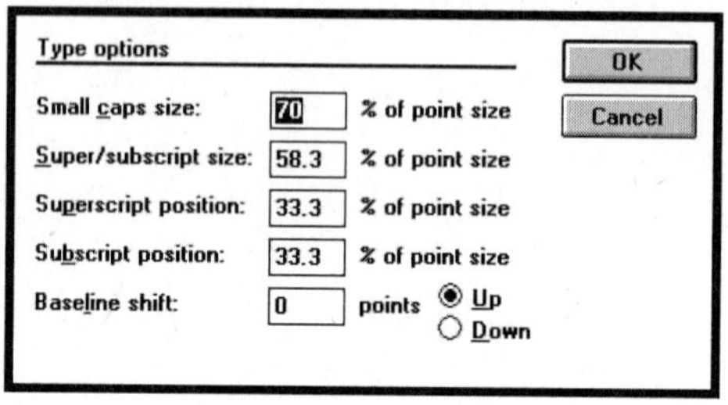

Fig. 8.8

The Type Options dialog box with default values.

PageMaker 5.0 adds the option of shifting the baseline for selected text up or down in .1-point increments. You might want to do this to force text in one column to match the baselines of text in adjacent columns, but this is better accomplished by customizing PageMaker's vertical ruler and activating the Snap to Rulers command (see "Specifying Layout Ruler Units" in Chapter 4). Chapter 11 includes examples of adjusting baselines to position inline graphics (see "Using Inline Graphics") and drop caps (see "Creating Initial Caps and Drop Caps").

Using Menu Commands To Change Type Specifications

You can change six settings from submenus of the Type menu, which is faster than opening the dialog box if you want to change only one variable (see fig. 8.9). The command names correspond to the field labels described in the previous sections: Font, Size, Leading, Set Width, Track, and Type Style.

Each command opens a submenu of choices. If you have text selected that shares the same characteristics, the current setting shows a check on the submenu. If the selected text includes a mix of attributes, nothing is checked on the submenu. If no text is selected, a check indicates the current default. The font list and size list reflect the fonts and sizes that are installed on your system and the selected printer.

For size, leading, and width attributes, you can enter a wider range of values than what appears on the submenu. Choose Other to open a dialog box, which enables you to enter any value within the range supported by PageMaker.

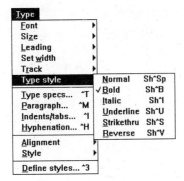

Fig. 8.9

The Type menu
with the Type
Style submenu
showing current
selection.

Commands under the Type menu duplicate some of the options available through the Control palette and the Type Specifications dialog box, as described in earlier sections of this chapter. In addition, the Edit Tracks command under PageMaker 5.0's new Aldus Additions submenu enables you to edit the tracking values that are applied through the Type menu commands or Control Palette, as described under the next heading.

Editing Tracking Formulas in PageMaker 5.0

PageMaker 5.0 includes an Aldus Addition named *Edit Tracks* that enables you to edit the font-tracking information for individual fonts. This information is the formula that is applied when you choose one of the tracking settings from the Track submenu under the Type menu, or from the Track drop-down list in the Type Specifications dialog box or in the Control palette. Changes you make through the Edit Tracks addition are stored in the TRAKVALS.BIN file in the USENGLSH subdirectory in the ALDUS directory, and they apply to all publications. (See earlier tip about opening PageMaker 4.0 publications in PageMaker 5.0, "Tracking in PageMaker 5.0.")

To change the tracking values for a font, choose Edit Tracks from the Aldus Additions submenu under the Utilities menu. The Edit Tracks dialog box displays tracking values as five lines plotted against a grid (see fig 8.10). The top line represents Very Loose tracking, and the lines below represent Loose, Normal, Tight, and Very Tight tracking, respectively. Each track is a collection of values that correlates the size of a font with a specific amount of change in the letter spacing. The steepness of the line determines how much the letter spacing is tightened or loosened as the font size changes. A flat line, for example, keeps the letter spacing proportionately the same at all sizes. A line that slopes down to the right results in proportionately tighter spacing at larger font sizes.

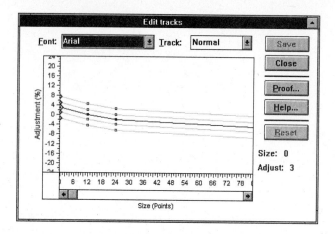

Fig. 8.10

The Edit Tracks
dialog box.

Along each line in the Edit Tracks dialog box are dots that represent
the point sizes of the font for which tracking values have been defined.
If you scale the font to a size for which no tracking value has been defined—falling on the line between dots—PageMaker calculates the
tracking value based on the curve connecting the defined values.

To edit a track, first choose the font from the Font drop-down list to
display the tracks defined for that font. Then click on a track to select
it, or choose from the Track drop-down list to select a line. The selected or active track appears as a solid line. Existing tracking values
appear as black squares along the line; these black squares also serve
as "handles" which you can move to change the tracking values.

To move a handle and thereby change the shape of the line, position
the pointer over a handle until the pointer changes to an X, then hold
down the mouse button and drag the handle to a new position. You,
instead, can select the handle by clicking on it, and then press the Up
or Down arrow to adjust the tracking value in one-tenth percent increments, or press the Right or Left arrow key to adjust the point size in
one-tenth point increments.

You can add a point by positioning the pointer over any part of a selected track where there is no handle, then hold the Alt key (the
pointer changes to a plus sign) and click to add a point. Remove a point
by positioning the pointer over any part of a selected track where there
is a handle, then hold the Alt key (the pointer changes to a minus sign)
and click to remove the point.

After making changes to the tracks for a specific font, you can choose
Reset to return the tracks to their original values and start over, choose
Cancel to close the dialog box without saving changes, or choose Save
to save the values in the TRAKVALS.BIN file and close the dialog box.

Before saving the values, or to view samples of the current saved values, you can print a proof sheet to see the effects of the tracking values.

To print a proof sheet, click the Proof button in the Edit Tracks dialog box. In the Create Proof Sheet dialog box you can specify which tracks and which sizes of the font you want to see printed on the proof sheet. You can also type the text you want to see printed—a short phrase and a longer one (see fig 8.11).

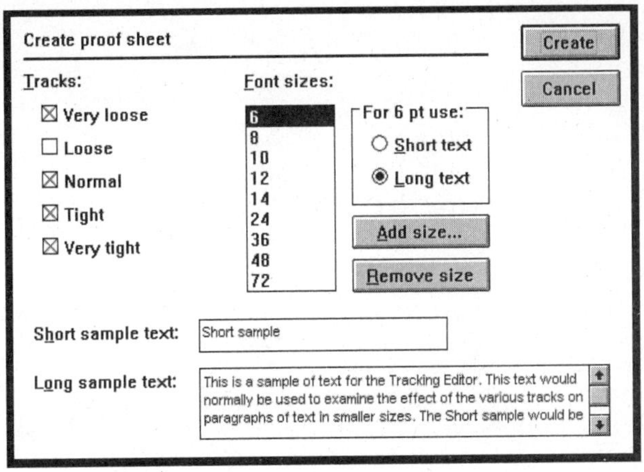

Fig. 8.11

The Create Proof Sheet dialog box.

Choose Create in the Create Proof Sheet dialog box to create a new, untitled publication with sample text for all tracks and sizes selected. If you have made no changes in the Edit Tracks dialog box, the Edit Tracks Addition closes the dialog boxes and displays the new Untitled publication with samples of tracked text, ready to be saved and/or printed. If you have made changes to the tracking values, you are prompted to save the values.

You can also copy tracking information from one font to another. In the Edit Tracks dialog box, first select the source font, then press Ctrl+C to copy the font information. Next, select the font you want to change and press Ctrl+V to paste the font-tracking values. You can then select and edit the individual font tracks, as described earlier.

Using Keyboard Shortcuts

Table 8.3 provides a list of keyboard shortcuts for changing type specifications. You turn off selected style settings using the same function key that turns on the setting (this key is called a toggle).

Table 8.3 Keyboard Shortcuts for Changing Type Specifications

Shortcut	Task
F5 or Ctrl+Shift+space bar	Return text to normal style
F6 or Ctrl+Shift+B	Boldface text
F7 or Ctrl+Shift+I	Italicize text
F8 or Ctrl+Shift+U	Underscore text
Ctrl+Shift+S	Strike through text
Ctrl+Shift+V	Reverse text
Ctrl+Shift + <	Decrease point size
Ctrl+Shift + >	Increase point size
Ctrl+Shift+L	Align text left
Ctrl+Shift+C	Align text center
Ctrl+Shift+R	Align text right
Ctrl+Shift+J	Justify text
Ctrl+Shift+F	Force justify text
Ctrl+Shift+A	Set automatic leading
Ctrl+Shift+X	Set normal character width
Ctrl+Shift+Q	Turn off tracking
Ctrl+Shift+\	Make text superscript
Ctrl+\	Make text subscript
Ctrl+Shift+K	Make text all caps

See Chapters 10 and 13 for more detailed information about printing.

FROM HERE...

For Related Information

◄◄ "Examining the Control Palette," p. 59.

◄◄ "General Characteristics of the Control Palette," p. 211.

►► "Applying Colors," p. 559.

►► "Font Management," p. 592.

Defining Paragraph Formats

Paragraph specifications determine the relationships between characters, lines, paragraphs, and the text and margins or column guides. Paragraph specifications apply to whole paragraphs, regardless of how much text is selected. In other words, when you choose one of the Type menu commands that affects whole paragraphs—Paragraph, Indents/Tabs, or Hyphenation—the options you choose apply to all the text in a paragraph where the text-insertion or selection point is positioned. Changes you make to the Control palette in Paragraph view also affect the entire paragraph.

The default paragraph specifications listed under "Reviewing Default Settings" earlier in this chapter apply to new text typed in PageMaker and to unformatted text files brought into PageMaker. Remember that you can change the default type specifications in several ways: select the Pointer tool and use the Type menu commands; use the Text tool if no text is selected and the text insertion point is not positioned on the page; or use the Styles palette to redefine all the body text in the publication, as described later in this chapter.

Some paragraph formatting options have keyboard shortcuts (mentioned throughout this section and summarized in Appendix C and the inside front and back covers of this book), and most options also can be changed through the Control palette. In addition, you can use style sheets to change paragraph formats (see "Using Style Sheets" later in this chapter). When you first open the Type menu, any of its associated dialog boxes or submenus, or the Control palette, the screen displays the options that apply to the current selection.

Using the Control Palette To Change Paragraph Attributes

PageMaker 5.0 adds a Control palette you can use to change type specifications. If the Control palette is open on-screen, using this palette is the fastest way to change more than one type specification at a time, because you do not need to open a menu or a dialog box. (The only faster way to change a single attribute is by using a keyboard shortcut.) Depending on the option chosen, the Control palette can have three different appearances: Layout view, Character view, or Paragraph view. These three views are introduced under "Examining the Control Palette" in Chapter 2. Basic methods of making entries in the Control palette are described in Chapter 5 under "General Characteristics of the Control Palette" and earlier in this chapter under "Reviewing Features of the Control Palette." This section describes Paragraph view in detail (see fig. 8.12).

The Control palette in Paragraph view.

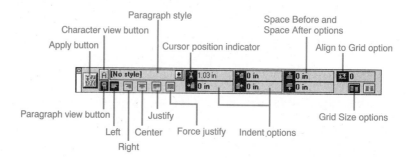

To display the Control palette in Paragraph view, choose the Text tool in the toolbox and click the ¶ (the Paragraph view button) at the left of the Control palette. When the Control palette is in text mode—either Character view or Paragraph view—the palette is also called the Text palette.

Remember that if you use the Control palette to change paragraph specifications after selecting text with the Text tool, the changes apply to the selected text only. If you apply changes through the Control palette when a publication is open but no text is selected, you change the defaults for new text typed in the current publication. To change defaults for all new publications, you must use commands under the Type menu when no publication is open. Chapter 16 includes more tips about changing PageMaker's default settings.

You can use the Control palette in Paragraph view to change the alignment and indentation (and other attributes) of text you have selected with the Text tool, such as the text shown in figure 8.13. The control areas of the Control palette in Paragraph view are described briefly in this section, but the individual attributes are described in more detail in the next section, "Making Entries in the Paragraph Specifications Dialog Box."

The Control palette in Paragraph view shows current paragraph specifications.

When you select text with the Text tool, the Control palette in Paragraph view includes these control areas:

- *Apply button.* Click to display the changes made to selected text without exiting the Control palette.

- *Palette-view option buttons.* Click the A to display Character view (described earlier in this chapter) or ¶ for Paragraph view.

- *Paragraph style.* Displays or changes the style applied to the currently selected paragraph. If no text is selected, this area displays the default style. To apply a different style, choose from the drop-down list. To create a new style, position the cursor in the paragraph whose attributes you want to use in the style and type a new style name in this area.

- *Alignment buttons.* Displays the alignment of the currently selected paragraph. Click an icon to change the alignment. Horizontal lines inside each box give visual clues to the alignment: left, right, centered, justified, and force-justified.

- *Cursor-position indicator.* This value shows the position of the cursor on the publication page relative to the left edge of the text block. This information is useful in setting indentations visually. You can position the cursor inside a paragraph where you want the indentation to be (for example, ten characters to the right of the margin), and then type the value shown in one of the indent options areas (described next).

- *Indent options.* These three areas display or adjust the left indent, first-line indent, and right indent of the currently selected text. PageMaker applies the left indent to the first line as well, unless you specify different values in the two fields. Indentation is measured from the left and right of the text block.

- *Space Before and Space After options.* Displays or adjusts the amount of blank space above and below a paragraph.

- *Align to Grid and Grid Size options.* When the unit of measure for a publication's vertical ruler is set to points (using the File Preferences command as described in Chapter 4), you can use Align to Grid to align the baselines of adjacent columns of text. Choose this option to maintain alignment in any paragraph that adds space for rules, is a different point size than other paragraphs, or uses different leading than normal body copy. Turn on this option by clicking the icon at the lower right in the Control palette. In the control area above the icon, set the Grid Size to match the leading of the body copy. (See "Aligning Text to the Horizontal Grid" later in this chapter.)

You can change the attributes of selected paragraphs by selecting the appropriate area in the Control palette and entering a new value, or adding, subtracting, multiplying, or dividing the value. You can enter most measurements in increments as fine as .001.

Click the Apply button, press the Enter key, or click the document window to activate the new value.

Making Entries in the Paragraph Specifications Dialog Box

When you choose the Paragraph command from the Type menu or press Ctrl+M, the Paragraph Specifications dialog box appears (see fig. 8.14). You can choose the options that affect paragraph indentation, alignment, breaks within and between paragraphs, rules (lines above or below paragraphs), and spacing between paragraphs, letters, and words. You also can assign different dictionaries to different paragraphs for use in hyphenating or checking spelling.

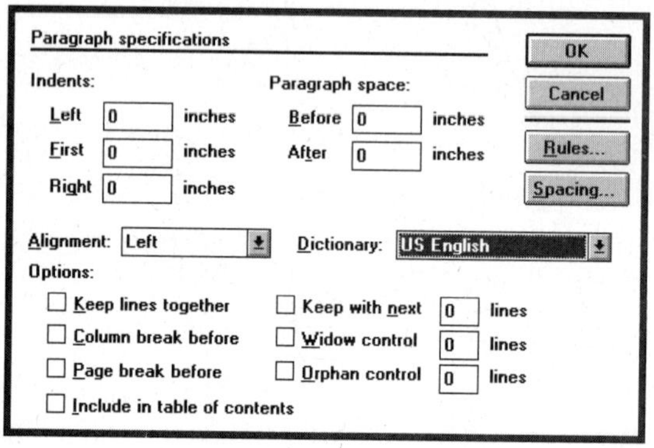

Fig. 8.14

The Paragraph Specifications dialog box.

Changes made in the Paragraph Specifications dialog box when text is selected are not reflected in the text on-screen until you close the dialog box.

Indenting Paragraphs

The Paragraph Specifications dialog box enables you to set paragraph indentations. You also can set or change indentations through the Control palette as described earlier or through the Indents/Tabs command from the Type menu, which is described later in this chapter. The difference between these two alternatives is that you can specify decimal increments for indentations with the Paragraph command or Control palette, but you are limited to fixed increments on the ruler line if you use the Indents/Tabs command. Any changes made to the Indents/Tabs ruler line or the Control palette are reflected in the Paragraph Specifications dialog box, and vice versa.

You may set three different indentation settings for any paragraph: Left indent, First line indent, and Right indent. Figure 8.15 shows how different Left and First line indentation settings affect the text and what those settings look like in the Control palette and on the Indents/Tabs ruler line. Notice that you can use these settings to create a *hanging indentation*. In the third example, the Left indent is set at 0.25 inches, and the First line indent is set at 0.25 inches. (For a description of how to change the indentation settings on the ruler line, see "Changing Indentation Settings on the Ruler Line" later in this chapter.)

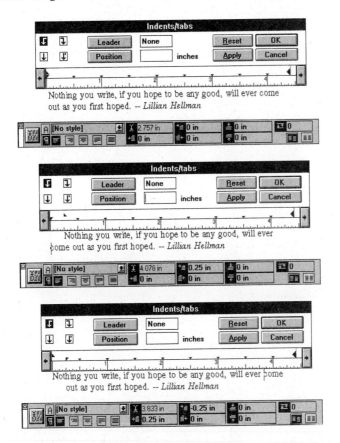

Fig. 8.15

Paragraph indentation settings made in Paragraph Specifications dialog box— none (top), first (middle), and left (bottom)—are also reflected in the Indents/Tabs dialog box and the Control palette as shown here.

The unit of measure shown in the dialog box reflects the current setting of the Preferences command on the File menu. You can use the Preferences command to work in inches, picas and points, centimeters, or ciceros (see Chapter 16), or you can enter values in any unit of measure by including the unit-of-measure abbreviation in the entry (see Chapter 4).

Aligning Paragraphs

PageMaker offers five alignment options for paragraphs: Align Left, Align Right, Align Center, Justify, or Force Justify. Forced justification justifies the last line of a paragraph, and this option also can force a single line of text to spread across a column or a text block, which sometimes is used in advertising or on stationery.

You can specify alignment in several ways: open the Paragraph Specifications dialog box and choose the alignment directly from the Alignment drop-down list; choose an option from the Alignment submenu under the Type menu; use the Control palette described earlier; or use the keyboard shortcuts (see fig. 8.16). Any changes made through the menu, keyboard, or Control palette also are reflected in the dialog box.

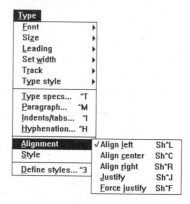

Fig. 8.16

The Alignment submenu with keyboard shortcuts for paragraph alignment.

Controlling Breaks

Six of the options at the bottom of the Paragraph Specifications dialog box control the breaks within and between paragraphs. If you click Keep Lines Together, the paragraph does not break across columns or pages. If the entire paragraph cannot fit in the column, PageMaker starts the paragraph in the next column or on the next page. The Keep Lines Together option is useful for keeping together lines of a heading or lines in a table.

You also can choose Column Break Before or Page Break Before to force the corresponding break before a paragraph. These options sometimes are applied to heading levels that start new stories or new topics. If you click Keep with Next, then the paragraph is not separated from the paragraph that follows it, and you can specify how many lines of the next paragraph must appear with the current paragraph. The Keep with Next option is useful for setting any heading level.

Setting Specifications for Subheads

T I P

You should set any heading or subheading with the Keep Lines Together and the Keep with Next options. Keep the heading with at least two lines from the next paragraph or apply Widow Control to the next paragraph (see following paragraph). If you create space below each heading by adding a carriage return rather than using the preferred method of specifying space below, then keep the heading with at least the next three lines.

You can use the Widow Control option to specify the minimum number of lines that can fall at the end of a column or page before you start a new paragraph. If you set Widow Control to 1 line, for example, PageMaker never permits one line of a paragraph to end a column. The entire paragraph moves to the next column or page unless at least two lines fit at the bottom of the column. (Most editors also define *widow* as any incidence of a single word or part of a word that falls on a line by itself at the end of a paragraph. PageMaker does not control these cases automatically. Single-word widows usually are fixed by editing the text.)

The Orphan Control option enables you to define the number of lines at the end of a paragraph that can be separated from the rest of the paragraph by a column break or a page break. If you set Orphan Control to 1 line, PageMaker never permits one line of a paragraph to fall at the top of a new column or page. The entire paragraph moves to the next column or page unless at least two lines fit at the top of the next column.

Solving Conflicting Specifications

When fitting text in a column, PageMaker considers all options for paragraph breaks. The specifications for adjacent paragraphs may conflict when PageMaker tries to fit the space allowed in the column. Suppose one paragraph, such as a heading, is set with the Keep with Next option, and the next paragraph is part of a long table set with the Keep Lines Together option. The column cannot fit both the heading and the table, so PageMaker breaks one or more of the specifications you have set.

If you find that columns and pages break in ways you did not expect or cannot control by adjusting the windowshade at the bottom of text blocks, check the break settings for the paragraphs that are part of and adjacent to the breaks.

Setting Paragraph Spacing

You specify the spacing between paragraphs in the Paragraph Specifications dialog box as shown in figure 8.17 or through the Control palette as described earlier. When you type a hard carriage return in the text, PageMaker increases the usual spacing between lines by the amounts you entered in the Before and After boxes.

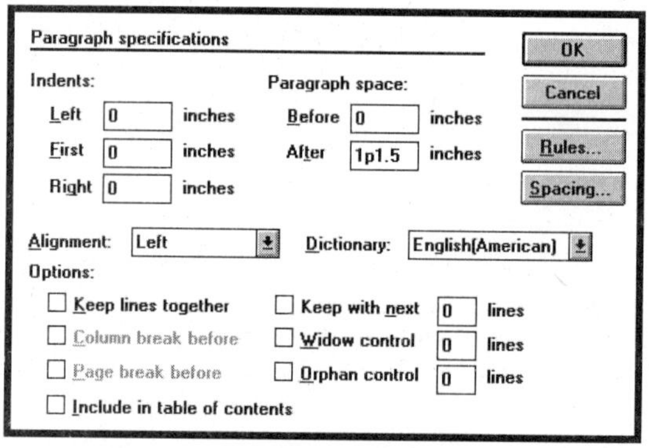

Fig. 8.17

Specifying spacing between paragraphs.

This method of defining paragraph breaks yields more flexible results than using extra carriage returns (empty lines) to add space between paragraphs. For example, PageMaker does not add the space before a paragraph if the paragraph starts at the top of a column. Also, you easily can adjust globally the space between paragraphs if you format using style sheets (see "Using Style Sheets" later in this chapter).

Eliminating Double Carriage Returns

T I P

You can use the Change command in the Story Editor to replace globally all double carriage returns with one carriage return, and instead use paragraph spacing to add space between paragraphs. If you are accustomed to double-spacing between paragraphs, however, you may want to experiment with the spacing setting on short publications before you decide to delete all double carriage returns in a long publication's text.

Choosing a Dictionary for Hyphenation and Spelling

The Dictionary pull-down menu in the Paragraph Specifications dialog box lists the installed language dictionaries that control hyphenation and check spelling. You can assign different dictionaries to different paragraphs within a publication, but using more than one dictionary slows down text composition and the spelling checker. To assign a special dictionary to a whole publication, no text should be selected when you choose the Paragraph command. To assign a special dictionary to all new publications, choose the Paragraph command when no publication is open. In either case, choose a dictionary by clicking the arrow at the right of the Dictionary field to display the list of available dictionaries. Drag the mouse to choose the dictionary you want and release the mouse button.

Including a Paragraph in the Table of Contents

You can include any paragraph in the table of contents by choosing the Include in Table of Contents option in the Paragraph Specifications dialog box (see Chapter 14).

Adding Rules and Aligning Text to Grid

You can specify rules (ruled lines) as part of the paragraph formatting. You can create lines above or below a selected paragraph through numerical specifications instead of using one of PageMaker's drawing tools. Those lines automatically move with the text when the text is reflowed due to editing changes—without using the inline graphics feature (described in Chapter 11).

Click the Rules button in the Paragraph Specifications dialog box to open the Paragraph rules dialog box (see fig. 8.18). Check the Rule Above Paragraph or Rule Below Paragraph options to add a ruled line above or below a paragraph.

A rule may be assigned a Line Style, Line Color, Line Width, and Indent. This Line Style list is the same as the style list on the Line submenu of the Element menu, except that you cannot reverse ruled lines that are part of the text. The Line Color list is the same as the color list on the Color palette (see Chapter 12).

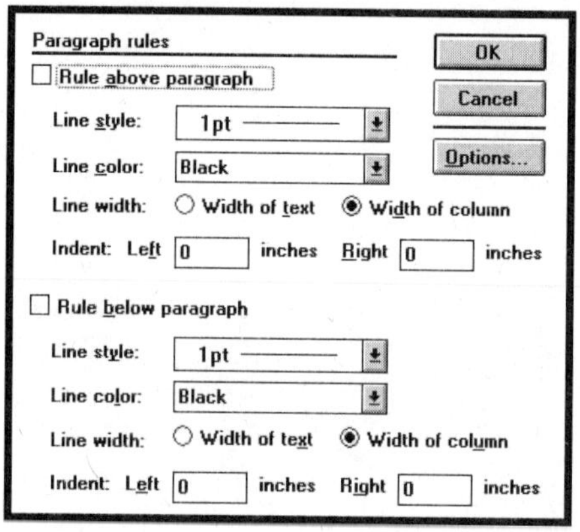

Fig. 8.18

The Paragraph
Rules dialog box.

You can specify Line Width to be the width of the column or to match the line of text nearest the rule. Note that the use of the word *width* here is analogous to its use in distinguishing text width (margin-to-margin) from text length (column inches). This definition is the opposite of the word's more common use in defining the width of a line drawn with one of PageMaker's line tools, where the width is the thickness of the line and the length is the measure from end to end.

You can adjust the line width by specifying indentations from Left or Right, relative to the text or column as specified in the Line Width setting. If you want the line to be shortened, enter a positive value; if you want the line to be extended, enter a negative value.

Another option enables you to control the distance of the lines from the text. Click the Options button in the Paragraph Rules dialog box to open the Paragraph Rule Options dialog box (see fig. 8.19). With the controls set to Auto, the lines usually run along the top and bottom of the slug of the top line of the paragraph. The *slug* is the horizontal bar that contains a line of text and the leading. The slug normally is invisible, but you see it as a black bar behind white text when you select text with the Text tool.

To increase the distance between the text and the ruled lines, enter positive values in the Top or Bottom fields in the Paragraph Rule Options dialog box. Enter these values in the unit of measure listed in the dialog box or use abbreviations for points and picas or other units of measure (see Chapter 4).

When you increase the thickness of a rule through the Style setting, the line expands toward the text from the edge of the slug. You can set wide rules above and below a one-line paragraph and reverse the type to display white type on a black background. (See Chapter 17 for more tips on using rules to set up reverse text on a black background.) Figure 8.20 shows examples of rules in text.

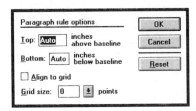

Paragraph rule options

OK

Top: **Auto** inches above baseline

Cancel

Bottom: Auto inches below baseline

Reset

☐ Align to grid

Grid size: 0 ⬍ points

Fig. 8.19

The Paragraph Rule Options dialog box.

Paragraph set with 1-point ruled line above and below, normal defaults (width of column, no special options for spacing).

Paragraph set with 1-point ruled line above and below, width of text, .25 inches above baseline at top, .25 inches below baseline at bottom.

Paragraph set with 6-point ruled line above and below, top rule .25 inch above baseline, bottom rule .25 inch below baseline.

Two 12-point Rules

Two 12-point Rules

Reverse text, top rule .1 inch above baseline, bottom rule on baseline

Fig. 8.20

Examples of rules in text.

The Align to Grid option in the Paragraph Rule Options dialog box enables you to force the rule and the text of the paragraph to align to an invisible grid. The rule and text "snap to" the nearest increment specified as the Grid size value, measured from the top margin. This feature is most useful for magazine and newspaper publishers who want the baselines of text to align horizontally across columns and pages, but the feature can be helpful in any publication. You easily can achieve horizontally aligned baselines when all the text is the same size and has the same leading. This alignment is difficult to maintain, however, when you have paragraphs with rules, different sized headings, and figures.

Choose Align to Grid to maintain alignment in any paragraph that adds space for rules, is a different point size than other paragraphs, or uses different leading than normal body copy (see fig. 8.21). Set the Grid size in the Paragraph Rule Options dialog box to match the leading of the body copy. Note that you can apply this option in the Paragraph Rule Options dialog box to align the text of any paragraph, whether or not the text has a rule above or below it, but it works only if the leading is set to a numerical value, not to auto leading. These options also can be set through the Control palette in Paragraph view as described earlier in this chapter.

NOTE If you have multiple leading values set (14/18 for headlines and 10/12 for body text), you can get odd leading values on some lines if you check Align to Grid.

Fig. 8.21

Examples of text with Align to Grid turned on (left), forcing text following a heading to align to adjacent column of body text (middle), and Align to Grid turned off (right).

Text set in 10-point Times.
Text set in 10-point Times.

Text set in 10-point Times.
Text set in 10-point Times.

Text set in 10-point Times.
Text set in 10-point Times.Text set in 10-point Times.Text set in 10-point Times. Text set in 10-point Times. Text set in 10-point Times. Text set in 10-point Times.

Text set in 10-point Times.
Text set in 10-point Times.

24-point

Text set in 10-point Times.
Text set in 10-point Times.

Controlling Spacing of Lines, Words, and Letters

In unjustified text, font and kerning tables determine the amount of space between words and letters. In justified text, PageMaker adds or deletes imperceptible amounts of space between letters and words to make the text fit between the left and right margins (see fig. 8.22). Generally, you should let PageMaker's default values control spacing, unless you have enough experience with typography that you feel comfortable changing these values and you plan to proofread the copy carefully to check the effects of your spacing adjustments. Chapter 16 includes detailed guidelines for typographical spacing.

The next sections describe how to adjust spacing values through the Spacing Attributes dialog box. If you change these values and end up with a result you don't want, you can always reset the text to have the default values by selecting the paragraph(s) and opening the Spacing Attributes dialog box and clicking Reset—a new option offered in Pagemaker 5.0.

> In the process of force-justifying this paragraph, PageMaker first adjusted the spacing between words (within the limits specified in the Spacing dialog box). After this process, words that extended past the end of each line were broken at the hyphens (if any were inserted by PageMaker's automatic hyphenation process when the text was placed). Next, to make the line exactly flush at the right margin, spacing was adjusted between the characters within the words (within the limits specified in the Spacing dialog box). Finally, if the line was still not flush at the right margin, PageMaker extended the space between the words beyond the limits specified in the Spacing dialog box.

Fig. 8.22

Force-justified text.

Adjusting Word and Letter Spacing

Click the Spacing button in the Paragraph Specifications dialog box to open the Spacing Attributes dialog box (see fig. 8.23). These options control the amount of space added or deleted between words and characters, determine the minimum size for automatic kerning, and adjust the formula for automatic leading and the leading method.

```
Spacing attributes                          [   OK   ]
Word space:          Letter space:          [ Cancel ]
  Minimum   [50]  %    Minimum   [-5] %
  Desired   [100] %    Desired   [0]  %     [ Reset  ]
  Maximum   [200] %    Maximum   [25] %
Pair kerning:  ☒ Auto above [12]  points
Leading method: ◉ Proportional  ○ Top of caps  ○ Baseline
Autoleading:  [120]  % of point size
```

Fig. 8.23

The Spacing Attributes dialog box.

You specify the word and letter spacing values as percentages. For example, 100 percent is equal to one normal space that the space bar creates, as defined for that font.

The Spacing Attributes dialog box enables you to specify the following attributes:

- *Minimum, Desired, and Maximum spacing allowed between words.* You can use values from 0 percent to 500 percent. During the justification process, PageMaker starts with the desired space between each word on the line and expands or condenses from that point within the limits specified as minimum and maximum. For unjustified text, the spacing specified in the Desired box is used throughout.

- *Minimum, Desired, and Maximum spacing allowed between letters.* You can use values from –200 percent to 200 percent. During the justification process, PageMaker adjusts the space between words first, as described in the previous paragraph, then adjusts the space between letters within words. These settings do not apply to unjustified text (0 percent is assumed).

Activating Pair Kerning

Kerning refers to the fine adjustments made to the space between certain combinations of letters to achieve a balanced look. When kerning is off, each character has a specific width determined by the font selection and the character. Every 10-point Times italic A, for example, has the same width.

When kerning is on, the spacing between two letters is adjusted slightly in accordance with the values stored in PageMaker's table of kerning pairs. PageMaker 5.0 has improved the kerning formulas. In figure 8.24, the space between the A and the V is smaller than the space between the V and the E because of the shapes of the letters. If the spacing between the different pairs is not adjusted or kerned, the A and V seem farther apart than the V and E. Kerned text generally looks better than unkerned text.

Fig. 8.24

Monospaced (top), proportionally spaced (middle), and kerned (bottom) letters.

KNAVE
KNAVE
KNAVE

The Pair kerning option in the Spacing Attributes dialog box activates automatic kerning for all text larger than 12 points. You may change the point sizes at which kerning is turned off, or you may turn off all kerning for a publication or selected paragraphs.

Using Automatic Kerning for Large Fonts Only

T I P

Large fonts, such as those used for headlines, are more attractive when kerned. But pages display and print more quickly if you turn off kerning for small point sizes. If you do not want to turn off kerning entirely, you can set kerning to a number higher than any point size you are using.

For more information on the pros and cons of kerning and ways to kern the spaces between letters manually or with the Expert Kerning addition, see "Kerning Headlines and Titles" in Chapter 16.

Changing the Leading Method or Autoleading Formula

You can change the method of leading and the formula for automatic leading in the Spacing Attributes dialog box. With normal Proportional leading, the baseline of each line of text is placed two-thirds of the way down from the top of the slug. (Recall that the slug is the text plus the leading.) The Top of Caps leading option places the baseline a distance from the top of the slug equal to the height of the tallest font ascender in the line. The Baseline option aligns the baseline of the text with the bottom of the slug.

Autoleading usually is 120 percent of the point size of the type style. You can change this percentage for selected paragraphs. Selecting individual paragraphs is a handy method for making copy fit a limited amount of available space (see "Copy Fitting" later in this chapter).

Using the Indents/Tabs Command

When you invoke the Indents/Tabs command from the Type menu (Ctrl+I), the screen displays a ruler line that you use to set or change tabs and indentation settings for selected paragraphs. You can specify settings for left text margin, first-line indent, right text margin, flush-left tab, flush-right tab, center tab, and decimal tab (see fig. 8.25). Changes made to the indentation settings on the ruler line are reflected in the Control palette in Paragraph view and in the Paragraph Specifications dialog box, as described earlier in this chapter under "Indenting Paragraphs." You define indentation by clicking and dragging icons on the ruler line of the Indents/Tabs dialog box. You also can specify indentation by entering numeric values in the Control palette or Paragraph Specifications dialog box.

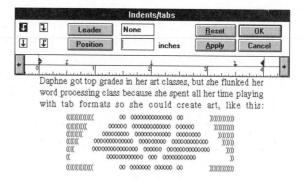

Fig. 8.25

Ruler line and icons representing tabs and indentation settings.

PageMaker sets default tabs every 0.5 inch on the ruler line. If you set tabs in the word processing program before placing the text, PageMaker's tabs change to reflect those settings.

To display the ruler line, choose the Indents/Tabs command from the Type menu. If the Pointer tool is selected when you invoke this command, or if the Text tool is selected but the cursor is not positioned within any text block, the ruler line displays the default settings for the publication. Any indents or tabs you set change the defaults and affect the new text you type. If the Text tool is selected and the cursor is positioned within a paragraph, the settings you see on the ruler and the changes you make apply only to that paragraph.

The ruler line window first appears in the center of the screen if no text is selected, or the window appears over the line of text in which the cursor is positioned (see fig. 8.26). You can move the window and use the scrollbars to put the window above the first line of the paragraph you want to format if the cursor was not positioned there.

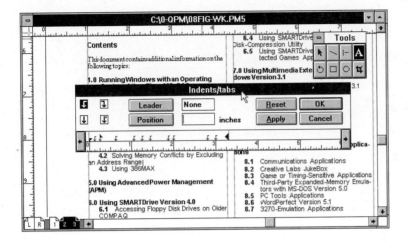

Fig. 8.26

The ruler line window positioned above the text to be formatted.

Positioning the Indents/Tabs Ruler above the Column

T I P

The Indents/Tabs dialog box is a window you can move on-screen by dragging the title bar with the pointer. You also can use the scrolling arrows at each end of the ruler to move the ruler inside the window. For convenience in setting tabs and indents, position the zero point of the Indents/Tabs ruler above the left column guide of the text.

The Indents/Tabs ruler always appears in the scale that matches the screen view. For example, the ruler shows a wider measure in the Fit in Window view than in Actual Size. When you are working in close views, you may not be able to see both the left and right margins in the Indents/Tabs dialog box. Use the scroll arrows at the ends of the ruler to see extensions of the measure.

Changes made on the ruler line are not reflected on-screen until you close the ruler line window or click the Apply button (a tremendous productivity aid added in PageMaker 5.0). Remember that changes made to the ruler line affect only the selected text. Changes made with the Pointer or Text tools without any text selected become the new default values. These changes also can be saved within a style. (See "Using Style Sheets" later in this chapter.)

T I P   **Using the Table Editor instead of Tabs**

Using PageMaker's Table Editor utility is an alternative to setting tabs directly in Layout view. You can use Table Editor to create complex tables in which each row/column entry is a cell with margins that can contain paragraphs. (The Table Editor is discussed in Chapter 11.)

Changing Indentation Settings on the Ruler Line

The three indentation variables—Left indent, First line indent, and Right indent—were described in detail earlier in "Indenting Paragraphs." You learned how to adjust these settings through the Paragraph Specifications dialog box. Three icons on the Indents/Tabs ruler line represent the three settings:

- *Left indent icon.* This icon is the bottom half of a triangle that appears at the zero point on the ruler line when all indentation is set at zero (the default). To move the Left indent icon only, hold the Shift key as you click and drag the icon. (If you don't hold the Shift key, you drag both the Left indent and the First line indent.)

- *First line indent icon.* This icon is the top half of the triangle that appears at the zero point when indentation is set at zero. To move the First line indent icon only, click and drag it. To move the Left indent and First line indent icon together, click and drag the Left indent icon.

- *Right indent icon.* This icon is the triangle that appears at the right margin on the ruler line when indentation is set at zero. To move the Right indent icon, click the icon and drag it to the left. (You cannot force the Right indent to the right beyond the width of the text block.)

Changes made to the ruler line are reflected in the text after you close the ruler window or when you click the Apply button.

Adding and Deleting Tabs on the Ruler Line

Default tabs appear as small inverted triangles on the ruler line. You can move these tabs by dragging them, or you can delete the tabs by dragging them off the ruler. The first new tab you add deletes all default tabs to the left of the new tab.

To add a tab, define the type of tab by clicking one of the icons for a left, right, center, or decimal tab (again, see fig. 8.26). If you want, choose the Leader option by clicking the Leader button to open a drop-down list of choices. A tab leader is a character that fills in the space between two tab stops. You can choose a line of periods, hyphens, or underscores from the list. You can define your own leader characters by clicking the Custom option and typing one character or two alternating characters in the box.

After defining the tab, position it by clicking just above the ruler line where you want to set the tab. The numeric value of the new tab position appears in the ruler line window. To move a tab, click the tab marker and hold down the mouse button as you drag the tab horizontally along the ruler line. As you move a tab, the ruler line window displays the current ruler measure.

You can change the tab's alignment or leader settings by first selecting the tab on the ruler line. Then click a tab icon or choose from the Leader drop-down list.

You can add, move, or repeat a tab in another way. First, select a tab icon or an existing tab on the ruler line. Then type a numeric position in the Position field and choose an option from the Position drop-down list: Add tab, Move tab, or Repeat tab. The Repeat tab option sets a series of tabs at the increment of the distance between the highlighted tab and the zero point on the ruler line.

To delete a tab, click the tab marker and hold down the mouse button as you drag the tab off the ruler line, or click the tab marker and choose Delete Tab from the Position drop-down list.

Settings are limited to the increments on the ruler line. The number of increments per unit of measure depends on the size in which you are working on-screen. For example, when you work in 200% size, you can use smaller increments than when you work in a reduced view of the page. You cannot set more than 40 tab stops on the ruler line. If you try to add a tab and PageMaker does not accept it, the ruler line may already have 40 tabs set.

After you set tab stops on the ruler line, close the ruler window or click the Apply button, and text with tab characters falls into place below each tab stop. To add tab characters to text, position the I-beam before the character you want to align and press the Tab key.

Copying the Indents/Tabs

You can copy a ruler line from one paragraph to subsequent paragraphs. Select the text you want to change, beginning with the paragraph that has the ruler you want to copy and including the subsequent paragraphs you want to match the first one. When the ruler line appears, it shows only the settings that apply to the first paragraph selected (see fig. 8.27). Make any changes to the ruler, such as adding or deleting tabs, and then close the ruler line window. The new ruler line applies to all the selected text. You must make at least one change on the ruler line to register any changes in the text. If you don't want to change the ruler line, make one change and click Apply; then reverse the change and click Apply again.

Controlling Hyphenation

Normally, PageMaker hyphenates text as you are typing or placing the text on the page. The program searches for each word in a Houghton-Mifflin dictionary containing more than 120,000 terms and a supplementary dictionary containing words you add. The process is almost instantaneous. Through the Hyphenation dialog box, you can turn off hyphenation, add terms to the dictionary, and control hyphenation at any time on a case-by-case basis.

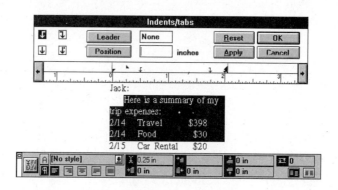

Fig. 8.27

Ruler line showing settings for first selected paragraph.

You can open the Hyphenation dialog box by choosing the Hyphenation command from the Type menu or by choosing the Hyphenation option when you are defining styles (see fig. 8.28). The basic option is to turn hyphenation on or off. If hyphenation is on, you can choose from three methods of hyphenation: Manual Only, Manual Plus Dictionary, or Manual Plus Algorithm. If hyphenation is turned off, PageMaker suppresses all hyphenation, even the discretionary hyphens that you added manually (Ctrl+hyphen).

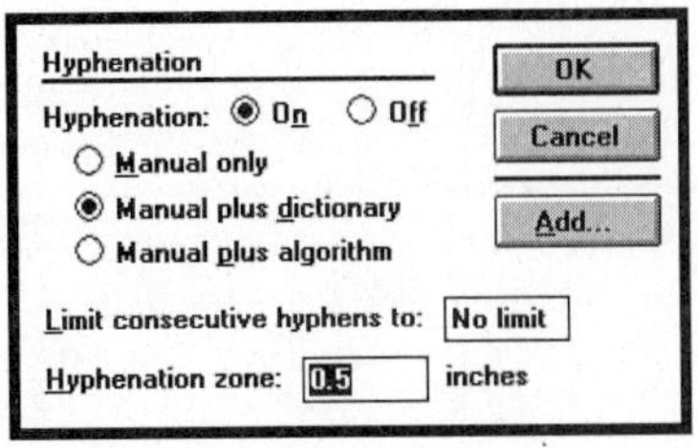

Fig. 8.28

The Hyphenation
dialog box.

The following list describes the three methods of hyphenation:

- *Manual Only*. If you choose this hyphenation method, PageMaker hyphenates words that contain discretionary hyphens. To insert discretionary hyphens manually within words, press Ctrl and the hyphen key simultaneously. You can insert these discretionary hyphens using the word processor before you place the text, or you can insert them in the Story Editor or the Layout view in PageMaker. Discretionary hyphens behave the same way as automatic hyphens: they appear on-screen and in print only when they fall at the end of a line.

- *Manual Plus Dictionary*. When this option is on, PageMaker hyphenates words containing discretionary hyphens and words found in the dictionary. If a conflict arises, the discretionary hyphens prevail.

- *Manual Plus Algorithm*. When this option is on, PageMaker may hyphenate words with discretionary hyphens, dictionary hyphens, or the dictionary algorithm. This method provides the greatest range of flexibility in hyphenating. Using Manual Plus Algorithm generally reduces the amount of white space in hyphenated text through increased hyphenation.

Deciding When To Use Manual Only

You generally choose Manual Only if you want to minimize the amount of hyphenation in a very short publication. Don't insert any discretionary hyphens until you have finished all other editing and formatting in Layout view. Insert discretionary hyphens selectively to eliminate wide right margins at the end of unjustified lines or wide rivers of white within justified text.

Choosing Manual Plus Dictionary is a more efficient method of correcting many wide ragged-right margins or wide rivers. Choose Manual Plus Dictionary, set a wide but acceptable Hyphenation Zone, and limit the number of hyphens in a row to one.

You can limit consecutive hyphens to a specified number by typing any number from 1 to 255 or typing the words *no limit*.

The Hyphenation Zone determines the width of the space you want to allow at the end lines of unjustified text before hyphenating. If you allow a 0.5-inch Hyphenation Zone, for example, then a word that starts within 0.5 inch of the right margin or right indentation setting is forced to the next line. Words that start to the left of the 0.5-inch zone are hyphenated if possible.

A narrow Hyphenation Zone results in a great deal of hyphenation. The wider the Hyphenation Zone, the more ragged the right margin is. When hyphenation is turned off, the Hyphenation Zone is the length of the longest word in the text.

T I P   **Reducing the Number of Hyphens**

Turn on hyphenation for justified text. During the justification process, PageMaker adjusts the spaces between words or letters, and if necessary, hyphenates words or expands the space between words beyond the maximum allowed. If you want fewer hyphens, turn off justification and use flush-left text, or expand the allowance for word and letter spacing in the Spacing Attributes dialog box.

Changing Hyphenation on a Case-by-Case Basis

If hyphenation is turned on, you can suppress hyphenation for individual words by typing a discretionary hyphen in front of the word. To override the dictionary hyphenation breaks for a word, you can insert a discretionary hyphen at the preferred break in the word on the page. If you want to change the way a word is hyphenated in all cases, you can add or remove words from the dictionary.

Adding Words to the Dictionary

Click the Add option in the Hyphenation dialog box if you want to add a word to the dictionary (see fig. 8.29). If you select a word in the text before choosing the Hyphenation command and choosing Add, the selected word appears in this dialog box with current hyphenation possibilities shown as tildes (~). You can edit this word, or you can type any word and enter tildes where you want to allow hyphenation.

Add word to user dictionary		OK
Word:	care~giv~~er	Cancel
Dictionary:	US English	Remove
Add:	○ As all lowercase ⦿ Exactly as typed	

Fig. 8.29

The Add Word to User Dictionary dialog box.

You can enter up to three tildes at each hyphenation point: one tilde indicates the most preferable break, two tildes indicates the next preferable, and three tildes indicates the least preferable but allowable break points. If you never want the word hyphenated, type a tilde at the beginning of the word in this dialog box.

If you have installed more than one dictionary, you can add words to other dictionaries. Choose the option you want from the Dictionary pull-down menu that appears when you click the arrow to the right of the Dictionary field in the Add Word to User Dictionary dialog box. If you add a word that is already in the dictionary, the new hyphenation replaces the old. Choose Remove to remove the word from the dictionary. You can use the Dictionary Editor to combine dictionaries from earlier versions of PageMaker or from word processors with a PageMaker 5.0 dictionary.

Repairing Corrupted Publications

T I P

You can automatically repair a corrupted publication by pressing Alt+Shift while choosing Hyphenation from the Type menu. If the computer beeps once, PageMaker has found no problems. If it beeps twice, PageMaker has found and corrected a problem. If the computer beeps three times, PageMaker found a problem but could not correct it.

For Related Information

◀◀ "Examining the Control Palette," p. 59.

◀◀ "Changing Preferences," p. 156.

▶▶ "Working with Reverse Text," p. 466.

▶▶ "Creating a Table of Contents," p. 639.

FROM HERE...

Using Style Sheets

The electronic style sheet is one of the most powerful yet (unfortunately) least used features of desktop publishing applications. A *style sheet* is a collection of shortcuts for applying type specifications—character attributes and paragraph formats—used throughout the publication. A style sheet system enables you to define the character attributes and paragraph format for each type of text element in a publication: major headings, subheadings, captions, and body text. After you design a style sheet for a publication, you can format the text by typing short keystroke commands, making menu selections, or clicking the Styles palette. This method eliminates the need to use several different commands to format each paragraph.

In designing a style sheet, you define a number of styles by name, or *tag*—one for each heading or paragraph format in your publication. For example, a book's style sheet may include styles for the chapter title, three levels of headings, body text, and figure captions. A magazine or newsletter may have several styles for text, figure captions, article titles, and bylines. Styles give publications a consistent appearance by ensuring that headlines, captions, and other similar blocks of text are the same throughout the publication.

Each style has two major elements: the style name—for example, Head—and the text attributes the style describes—for example, 24-point Helvetica, centered, bold text. A series of styles becomes a style sheet. PageMaker comes with a default style sheet that includes five styles and additional sample style sheets in templates that you can use and modify for your publications. You can copy these style sheets from documents stored in PageMaker's template subdirectory (if you opted to install the templates that come with PageMaker) using the copy option described later in this section.

For each publication, you can create a new style sheet, modify an existing style sheet, import a style sheet along with text from a word processor, or modify text without using a style sheet. The process of formatting characters and paragraphs with a style sheet can take place in PageMaker or in some word processors like Microsoft Word. Style sheets created in word processors that PageMaker supports can be imported along with the text into PageMaker if the correct import/export filter has been installed (as explained in Chapter 6).

Styles set the character and paragraph format specifications for whole paragraphs. A paragraph in PageMaker includes all the text between two hard carriage returns. If you want to modify part of a paragraph, highlight the words with the Text tool and change their attributes individually, not with a style sheet. If you want to change the attributes of entire paragraphs, the most efficient method is to use the style sheet function.

Character-specific formats include all attributes that are applied using the Font, Size, Leading, Set Width, Track, and Type Style commands from the Type menu. You also can make many of these entries using the Type Specifications command, the Control palette in Character view, or keyboard shortcuts. The quickest method of applying complex formats, however, is with a style sheet. When you create a style sheet, you can apply it through the Control palette in Paragraph view or through the Styles palette.

Paragraph-specific formatting includes all settings that are applied using the Paragraph, Indents/Tabs, Hyphenation, and Alignment commands from the Type menu. You also can make many of these entries using the Control palette in Paragraph view or keyboard shortcuts. With a style sheet, however, you can apply the character attributes and the paragraph formats in one step.

Viewing Styles

To view the styles set for your publication, choose Style from the Type menu. You also can view styles by opening the drop-down list of styles in the Control palette in Paragraph view (described earlier in this chapter) or choosing Style Palette from the Window menu (Ctrl+Y). The Styles palette, like the toolbox and Colors palette, first appears near the top right corner of the publication window (see fig. 8.30). You can drag the title bar to move the Styles palette anywhere on-screen, and you can drag the border to resize the palette.

Fig. 8.30

The Styles palette.

The Styles palette indicates the style of the selected text. A plus sign (+) follows the style name if you have further modified the format of the selected text using Type menu commands.

An asterisk (*) following a style name indicates that you have imported the style along with the text from a word processor. PageMaker removes the asterisk if you modify the style using the Define Styles command after the style is imported.

You can also view the styles that have been applied to each paragraph in Story view without opening the Styles palette. First, select the Text tool and position the insertion point anywhere in the story you want to edit. Choose Edit Story from the Edit menu (Ctrl+E) and choose Display Style Names from the Story menu. The Story window displays the names of applied styles in the column to the left of the text (see fig. 8.31).

Adding New Styles

You can add new styles any time during the layout of the publication. You can use several methods to add new styles:

- Define the new style from scratch.
- Base the new style's attributes on selected text.
- Base the new style's attributes on another style in the current publication.
- Copy a whole style sheet from another publication.
- Import the style sheet with the imported word processing document.

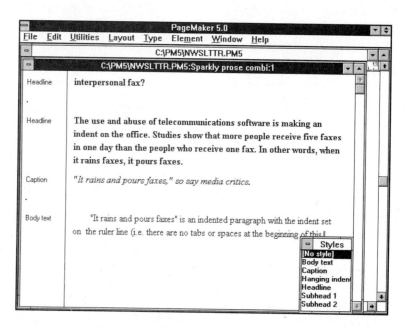

Fig. 8.31

The Story window listing style names.

To define a new style from scratch, open the Edit Style dialog box by pressing the Ctrl key and clicking No Style in the Styles palette. Or choose the Define Styles command from the Type menu (Ctrl+3) and click New in the dialog box (see fig. 8.32). PageMaker opens the Edit Style dialog box (see fig. 8.33).

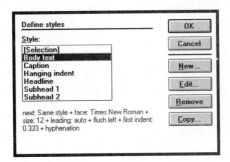

Fig. 8.32

Using the Define Styles dialog box to open the Edit Style dialog box.

In the Edit Style dialog box, type the name of the new style (see fig. 8.34). Give the style an easily recognizable name. If you are cloning the new style from an existing style, that style is listed in the Based On field. You can change the Based On style at any time by changing the name in this field or typing **No style** if you do not want this style to be related to any other. If you edit the style named in the Based On field and change any attributes that are shared by this new style, the new style also changes.

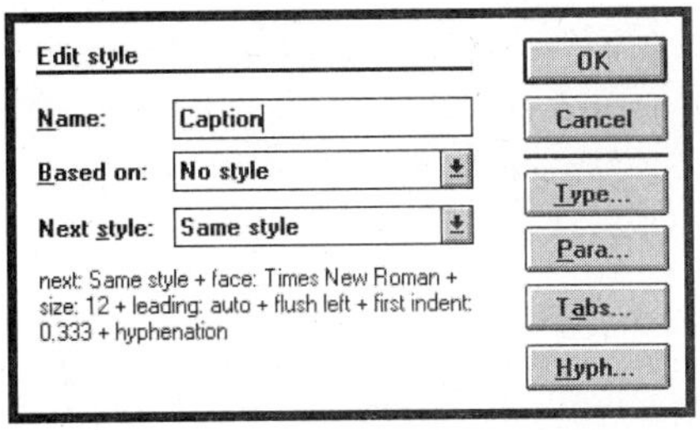

Fig. 8.33

The Edit Style dialog box.

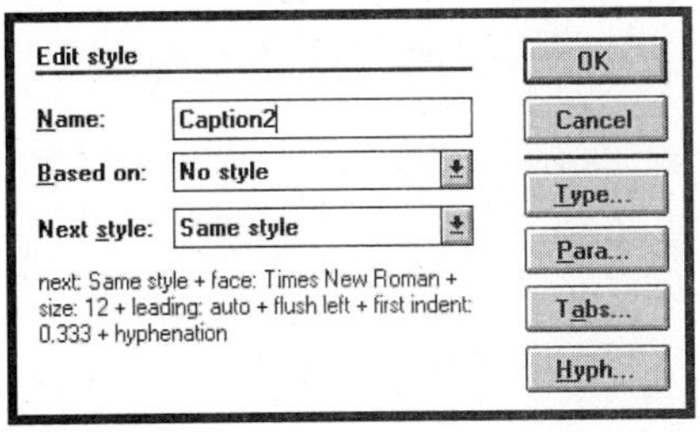

Fig. 8.34

Type specifications of an existing style used to create a new style.

T I P   Cloning an Existing Style

If you want to create a new style that is similar to an existing style, click once on the name of the style you want to copy in the Define Styles dialog box; then click New. The Edit Style dialog box shows the specifications of the cloned style, and you can modify the attributes you want to change.

T I P   Basing a Style on a Formatted Paragraph

To base a new style on the attributes of a formatted paragraph, position the insertion point in the paragraph. Then type a new style name in the style area of the Control palette in Paragraph view. PageMaker asks if you really intend to add a new style to the Styles palette, so you can confirm that you did not make an error in typing an existing style name.

If the Control palette is not open or if you want to make further modifications in creating the new style, position the insertion point in the paragraph. Then choose Define Styles from the Type menu (Ctrl+3), click Selection in the Define Styles dialog box, and click New. The Edit Style dialog box shows the specifications of the selected paragraph.

If you type a style name in the Next Style field, PageMaker formats the next paragraph with this style after you type a carriage return that ends a paragraph in the current style. The Next Style option is useful for setting the style names for headings that are always one line or one paragraph long and always followed by another style. For example, Body text style may follow Heading level 1. If you set a style for blank lines that will hold inline figures, you can set the next style for the caption. Using this feature can save time in changing from one style to another.

After you choose the Name, Based On, and Next Style names, click any of the four options to choose the new style attributes: Type, Para, Tabs, or Hyph. Choosing Type lets you change attributes in the Type Specifications dialog box (see fig. 8.35). Para changes specifications in the Paragraph Specifications dialog box (see fig. 8.36). Tabs modifies the indent and tab specifications in the Indents/Tabs dialog box (see fig. 8.37). Hyph changes the options in the Hyphenation dialog box (see fig. 8.38).

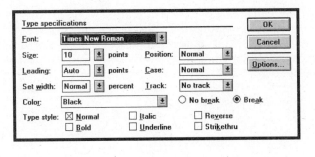

Fig. 8.35

The Type
Specifications
dialog box.

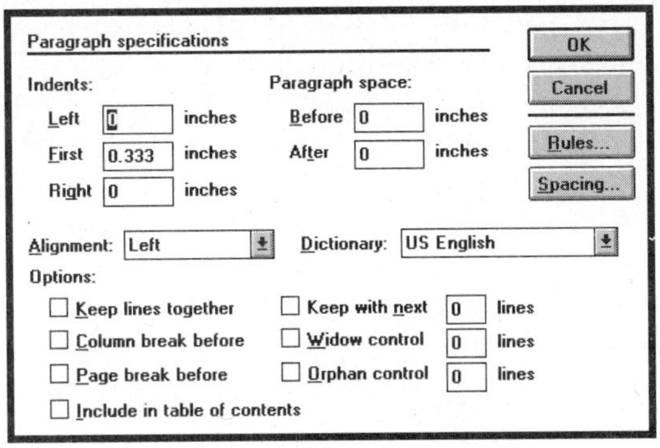

Fig. 8.36

The Paragraph
Specifications
dialog box.

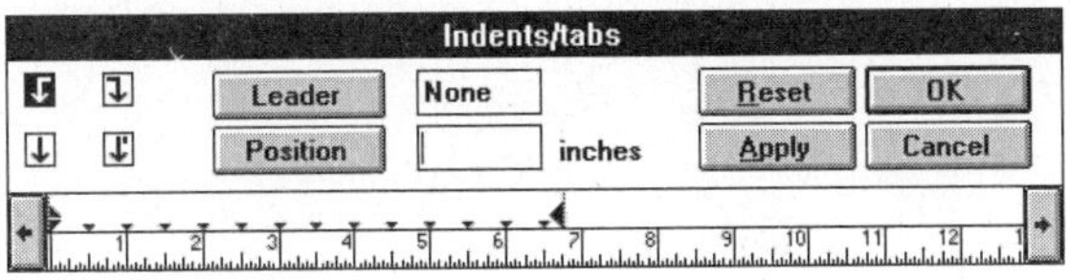

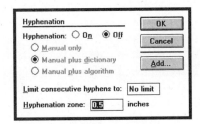

Fig. 8.37

The Indents/Tabs
dialog box.

Fig. 8.38

The Hyphenation
dialog box.

Copying Styles from Other PageMaker Publications

To copy an entire style sheet from another PageMaker publication,
choose Define Styles from the Type menu to open the Define Styles

dialog box; then click Copy. PageMaker adds style names from the copied publication to the list in the Styles palette. If the current publication includes any styles with the same name as styles in copied publications, PageMaker asks whether you want to replace the old styles with the copied ones. If you choose yes, the old styles and all text in the current publication that has been formatted with those styles change to match the copied style sheets.

Importing Styles Selectively

If you don't want to copy an entire style sheet from another publication, you can selectively import styles to PageMaker in several ways. The simplest method is to open the publication that contains text formatted using the style you want to import. Then use the Text tool to copy a paragraph of text set in that style and paste the text into the new publication. Finally, you can delete the pasted text; the style is added to the Styles palette automatically.

If you want to import several styles that all are used in the same story in another PageMaker publication, you can use the story importer. In PageMaker 5.0 you import by using the Place command from the File menu and choosing a PageMaker publication. PageMaker opens the Place PageMaker Stories dialog box as shown in figure 8.39, where you can choose the story you want to import (identified by the first words in each story). When you import the story, all the styles the story uses are added to the Styles palette. Then you can delete the story; the styles remain.

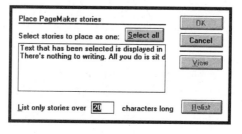

If you think you will be importing styles often, you can create a PageMaker template with all the styles that you use. Create a separate story for each style plus one story that includes all the styles. Type **All Styles** as the first words in the story that contains all styles. Type the style name as the first word(s) in each separate story that includes only one style. When you want to import a style, use the Place command and choose this template to open the Place PageMaker Stories dialog box.

You can easily create a short text block with all the styles from a larger text block by using the List Styles Used command from the Aldus Additions submenu under the Utilities menu, as described under "Listing the Styles Used" later in this chapter.

Designing Styles in Your Word Processor

Style sheets you create in Microsoft Word and other word processing applications can be imported along with the text into PageMaker if the appropriate import/export filter has been installed. When you import text set with style names, choose the Retain Format option in the Place dialog box that opens after you choose the Place command from the File menu (Ctrl+D). The imported text retains the formatting set in the word processor, and the style names from the word processor become part of the PageMaker style sheet. For more specific control over importing styles, open the Import Filter dialog box by holding the Shift key and clicking OK in the Place dialog box (see fig 8.40). Chapter 6 explains this feature in detail.

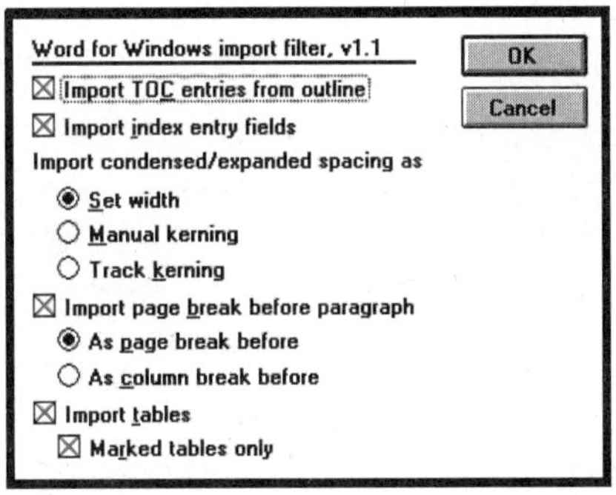

Word for Windows import filter, v1.1
[OK]
[Cancel]
☒ Import TOC entries from outline
☒ Import index entry fields
Import condensed/expanded spacing as
  ◉ Set width
  ○ Manual kerning
  ○ Track kerning
☒ Import page break before paragraph
  ◉ As page break before
  ○ As column break before
☒ Import tables
  ☒ Marked tables only

Fig. 8.40

The Import Filter dialog box.

The imported text takes on the attributes of the style in the style sheet of the PageMaker publication (if the style names are the same), or PageMaker adds the new style names to the PageMaker style sheet (if the names do not match).

Assigning Style Tags in Your Word Processor or Spreadsheet

If a style sheet has been set up in PageMaker, you can type style names, or tags, as part of the text in any word processor or spreadsheet. PageMaker can read a style tag from a word processor or spreadsheet if you enclose the name in angle brackets (< >). The brackets must appear at the beginning of the paragraph, and the style name in the brackets must match the style name in PageMaker exactly so PageMaker can modify the text to the new style (see fig. 8.41). If a paragraph does not have its own style, the paragraph takes on the attributes of the paragraph that precedes it.

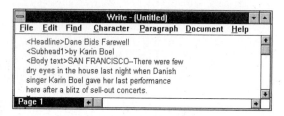

Fig. 8.41

Text as it looks in a word processor with style tags added before paragraphs.

When you import text set up with style names in brackets, choose the Retain Format option in the Place dialog box. The imported text takes on the attributes of the style in the style sheet of the PageMaker publication.

Assigning Style Names in a Spreadsheet

You can use a special trick to add style names in a spreadsheet if you want each row to break into two or more lines with different formatting in PageMaker. For example, suppose that the row in the spreadsheet contains the following words:

firstname   lastname   company   address   city   state   zip

And you want this final format in PageMaker:

firstname lastname
company
address
city, state zip

You can insert a blank column in front of the *firstname*, *company*, and *address* columns, fill each blank column with a different bracketed style tag, then export the spreadsheet data as ASCII text. Use any word processor to globally search for a right bracket (<) and change it to a carriage return followed by a right bracket. Then import the text into a PageMaker publication where the styles are set up with the same names.

If these instructions are too cryptic, see Chapter 20.

Removing a Style

To remove a style from the style sheet, choose Define Styles from the Type menu to open the Define Styles dialog box. Click the style name you want to delete and then click Remove. Paragraphs that have been formatted with the deleted style retain their formatting, but the Styles palette identifies these paragraphs as having No Style.

Editing Styles

You use the same techniques to edit a style as to create a new style. Start by choosing the Type Define Styles command, choosing the style you want to change in the dialog box, and clicking Edit. You also can jump directly to the Edit Styles dialog box by holding the Ctrl key and clicking the style's name in the Styles palette.

Seeing the Attributes of a Style

T I P

To view the specifications for a particular style, choose Define Styles from the Type menu and then choose a style. The dialog box lists all the style's attributes.

When you edit a style, all text in your publication that has been formatted with that style changes to match the new format. For example, if your style is called *bodytxt2* and you change the font of bodytxt2 from 10-point Helvetica to 14-point Times Roman, all text labeled bodytxt2 changes to 14-point Times Roman when you return to the Page Layout view.

Formatting Text Using Styles in PageMaker

To change the style of text, select the Text tool, and then click in the paragraph you want to change. You can use one of the text-selection methods to highlight a series of paragraphs. Then choose a style in one of these ways: choose from the drop-down list in the Control palette in Paragraph view; click a style in the Styles palette; or choose a style from the submenu of the Type Style command.

To display the Styles palette if it is not already shown on-screen, choose Style Palette from the Window menu (Ctrl+Y). The Styles palette contains a list of the different styles you have set up in the publication. When you select text, the style name appears in the Styles palette to show what style name formats the current text (see fig. 8.42). Search the list in the Styles palette for the style you want and click once on the name. The text reformats with the new style's attributes (see fig. 8.43).

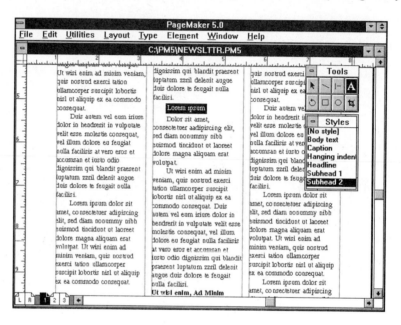

Fig. 8.42

Body text with PageMaker's default attributes.

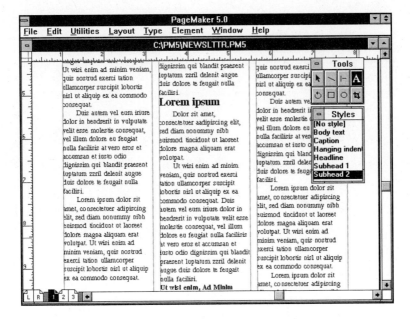

Fig. 8.43

Text modified from Body Text to Subhead2.

Listing the Styles Used

PageMaker 5.0 includes a new Aldus Addition called *List Styles Used* that lists the names of all styles used in a selected story and the number of paragraphs using each style. To list the styles, first select a text block with the Pointer tool in Layout view, and then choose List Styles Used from the Aldus Additions submenu under the Utilities menu. PageMaker creates the list as a separate text block on the layout (see fig. 8.44). You can position the text block on a blank page and print out the block if you like.

No style, 7.
    Body text, 16.
Caption, 2.
Hanging indent, 1.

Headline, 1.

Subhead 1, 2.

Subhead 2, 2.

Fig. 8.44

Example of styles listed using the List Styles Used command.

Note that this utility lists only the styles that are actually applied within the selected story (that is, the selected text block and all linked text blocks). The utility does not list all the styles used in the publication or all the styles available in the Styles palette. To get a comprehensive list of all styles used in the publication, you can use this command on each story and collect all the generated text blocks onto one page for printing.

FROM HERE...

For Related Information

◄◄ "Importing Formatted Text," p. 247.

Fitting Copy

During the page-layout process you may find that fitting copy can be a major problem. What do you do when the text for a four-page newsletter runs to four-and-a-half pages? How do you make a table of numbers fit into a defined area on the page? How can you force two columns to end at the same measure when they consist of different amounts of text?

PageMaker does not have an automatic vertical-justification feature that fits copy exactly from the top to the bottom margin. To fit copy in a column or on a defined number of pages, you can change the length of the text in a column.

The most direct method of forcing text to fit a designated number of pages or making two columns the same length is to adjust the length of text in each column by dragging the bottom windowshade handles up or down. For example, if the text of a four-page price list is two or three lines too long, you may decide to add one line of text to each column by dragging down the windowshades to extend below the bottom page margin. If an article falls a few lines short of filling a two-column page, you can drag up the bottom handle of the longer column to make the two columns end at the same measure on the page.

If you have strict standards about making text meet the bottom margins or if your extra text is too long to fit by extending the bottom margin on each page, you may need to use one of the following approaches to make text fit.

Changing the width of the text is one way to change the amount of space that the text occupies. Chapter 5 describes how to change the width of columns before filling them with text; Chapter 6 describes the steps involved in changing the size of text blocks after positioning text on a page. Another way to change the size of a text block is to change the point size. These methods work fine for copy fitting if you are designing the document as you go along or designing the text deliberately to fit the space allowed. For very long documents or documents that must match the design specifications, however, changing the width or size of the text often is not feasible.

A better approach to fitting copy is changing the leading (the space between the lines) through the Leading submenu under the Type menu or the Type Specifications dialog box (see figs. 8.45 and 8.46), or through the Control palette or the Define Styles command under the Type menu. If you use small increments, this method is the least disruptive to the basic design. PageMaker permits .1-point increments. If the text divides into many columns or text blocks throughout the document, changing the leading is much faster than changing the width of every text block. Unless you use a style sheet, you cannot globally change the width of an entire publication's text after the text has been placed. You must adjust each text block individually.

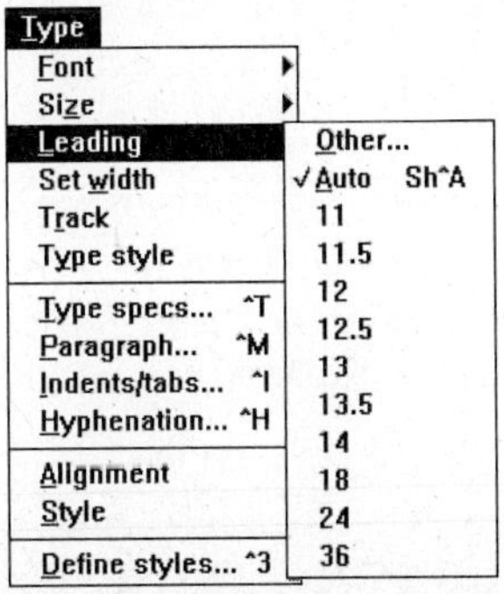

Fig. 8.45

The Leading submenu.

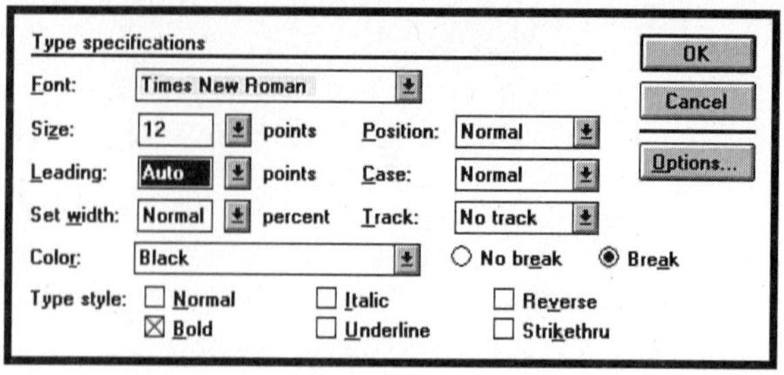

Fig. 8.46

Changing
leading using the
Type Specifica-
tions dialog box.

Changing All Leading in Copy

You can use the Define Styles command to change the leading or
any other style for all body copy. If you did not use a style sheet
to format the text, you can change the leading for whole stories by
using the Select All command with the Text tool inside the text
area. Next, move through the document and reset the leading on
individual headings where necessary.

If you used automatic leading in formatting the body text, you can
change the space between lines by choosing the Select All command with the Text tool inside the text area. Then choose the
Paragraph command. The Spacing button in the Paragraph Specifications dialog box opens the Spacing Attributes dialog box, where
you can adjust the formula for automatic leading. Autoleading
usually is 120 percent of the point size of the type. You can set
this value higher to expand the text or lower to contract the text.

Remember that PageMaker can make adjustments within the nearest tenth of a point. For 12-point type, the smallest increment you
can use to change automatic leading is 1 percent, which is fine if
you are printing to a high resolution typesetter. A 300-dpi laser
printer, however, can handle differences of only one-fourth of a
point. In this case, the smallest practical increment for changing
automatic leading on 12-point type is 2 percent.

You also can gain space by scaling tables you imported as graphics
from the Table Editor (see Chapter 11). If you are fitting a table of
tabbed text into a space of a specific width, you can change the tabs
and, if necessary, the type size. To fit a tabbed table into a space of a
set length, you can adjust the leading. You also can adjust the Spacing
attributes in the Paragraph Specifications dialog box, which appears
when you choose the Type Paragraph command. This setting controls

the amount of space between paragraphs. Each line of the table is treated as a paragraph with space Before or After (see fig. 8.47). To fit copy before the page-layout stage, see "Fitting Copy" in Chapter 16.

Table set with no spacing between lines:

2/14	Travel	$398
2/14	Food	$30
2/15	Car Rental	$20
2/15	Food	$50
2/16	Travel	$398

Table set with .025-inch spacing between lines:

2/14	Travel	$398
2/14	Food	$30
2/15	Car Rental	$20
2/15	Food	$50
2/16	Travel	$398

Fig. 8.47

Adjusting tables by changing the Spacing attributes in the Paragraph Specifications dialog box.

For Related Information

◀◀ "Moving Guides," p. 190.

◀◀ "Working with Text Blocks, " p. 257.

▶▶ "Fitting Copy," p. 722.

FROM HERE...

Summary

This chapter and Chapter 6 discuss the range of formatting options that PageMaker provides. Now you can compare PageMaker's features with the capabilities of your word processing program and decide how to approach any large publication project. Remember that you can do as much formatting in the word processing program as you like, as long as PageMaker retains that formatting when you place the text on the page.

Few word processing programs, however, have the full range of options PageMaker has for choosing typefaces and sizes and for controlling the amount of space between words, letters, and lines of text. Chapter 5 provides more tips about efficient methods of applying these specifications in the page-layout stage. Chapters 15 and 16 offer suggestions on modifying the defaults for these settings, and Chapters 17 through 21 contain examples of the settings used in specific publications. Before you move into the multifaceted design and layout steps, however, read Chapter 9 to learn about the sources of graphics for a PageMaker publication.

Working with Graphics

The capability to incorporate graphics and text on a page is one of PageMaker's characteristics as a page-composition program. In PageMaker, you have three methods of incorporating graphics: you can create new graphics with PageMaker's built-in graphics tools, use the Paste command to bring in graphics from the Windows Clipboard, and use the Place command to bring in graphics created in other programs. This chapter introduces you to the alternatives available for adding graphics to a page and demonstrates how to prepare graphics in other programs.

PageMaker contains graphics tools that enable you to draw such simple shapes as boxes, ellipses, and lines. PageMaker's Place command enables you to import graphics created in other programs, such as Windows Draw (PIC), In•A•Vision (PIC), Lotus 1-2-3 (PIC), Symphony (PIC), Windows Paint (MSP), PC Paintbrush (BMP and PCX), Publisher's Paintbrush, AutoCAD, and other applications that create HPGL plotter files (PLT). In addition, you can use the Place command to import graphics created in applications that produce Windows Metafiles (WMF), Encapsulated PostScript (EPS) formats, or TIFF formats (TIF). With the Place command, you also can import spreadsheets as text or graphics, as well as MacPaint files created on a Macintosh computer and transferred to the PC with the file extension PNT.

In this chapter you learn to use PageMaker's tools to create graphics and to import graphics created in other programs. You also learn to use the Pointer tool to select, move, and scale graphics and to use the cropping tool to trim the edges from imported graphics. This chapter explains the differences among graphics from various sources, and you learn how to manipulate imported TIFF images to adjust contrast and brightness.

Chapter 11 describes some of the special effects you can create with graphics or text using PageMaker's transformation tools. Chapter 12 describes the application of color and printing color graphics.

Using Graphics Supported by PageMaker

To meet different needs, PageMaker imports two basic kinds of graphics from other programs: *object-oriented* or *vector graphics,* and *bitmapped graphics.* All graphics you create with PageMaker's tools are object-oriented. You also can create graphics of either type using other applications and import them into PageMaker.

With these basic formats, you can create reports containing AutoCAD designs, newsletters with illustrations created through Windows Paint, magazines containing pictures scanned from photographs, and many other kinds of illustrated materials. With all of PageMaker's options for importing graphics, you have the capability of importing high-quality graphics into many types of publications.

The next sections describe the differences among these types of graphics, but on a practical basis you can determine the type of graphic you are importing in two ways. First, files created by object-oriented graphics programs usually have the file extension PIC, PLT, WMF, WMT, CGM, DRW, or EPS in the name shown in the Place command dialog box. The placement icon looks like a pencil or a box containing the letters PS (for Encapsulated *PostScript* file). File names representing bitmapped graphics usually have the file extension BMP, MSP, PCX, PNT, or TIF, and the placement icon looks like a paintbrush or a box containing a crosshair. Table 9.1, presented later in this chapter, lists the file extensions recognized by PageMaker and the applications that create them.

Object-Oriented Graphics

Object-oriented graphics consist of separate objects like boxes, lines, and ellipses. PageMaker's built-in graphics are object-oriented graphics, and you can import object-oriented graphics from other programs. Object-oriented graphics are sometimes called *vector graphics* because the lines and patterns you see are actually stored as mathematical formulas for the vectors composing the image. A *vector*, shown in figure 9.1, is a line defined by a starting point, a directional angle, and a length.

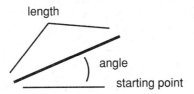

Fig. 9.1

Example of a vector.

You can create object-oriented graphics in PageMaker or with drafting, draw, and spreadsheet programs. Programs that produce object-oriented graphics that PageMaker can place include Windows Draw (see fig. 9.2), In•A•Vision, AutoCAD, Lotus 1-2-3, Excel (see fig. 9.3), Symphony; and applications that produce PIC, WMF, PLT, and Encapsulated PostScript (EPS) formats (see fig. 9.4).

Fig. 9.2

PIC-format graphics created in Windows Draw.

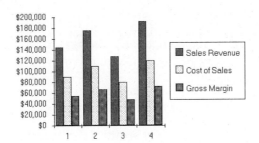

Fig. 9.3

A graph created in Microsoft Excel.

Fig. 9.4

Graphic drawn with Adobe's Illustrator program to create Encapsulated PostScript (EPS) code.

You can easily edit object-oriented graphics because you can change or move individual elements in the application that created them. (You cannot edit or move individual elements in imported graphics in PageMaker.) Because these vector graphics are defined mathematically, the program clarifies the graphic during the printing process to create crisp line art and precise fill patterns. Many users, therefore, consider vector graphics better-quality images for line art than bit-mapped graphics.

Encapsulated PostScript Format

You can create *Encapsulated PostScript format files* using draw programs or direct coding in the PostScript programming language. You also can create EPS versions of individual pages of a PageMaker publication using the Print command, as described in the section "Converting a PageMaker Page to an EPS Graphic" in Chapter 13. If you create the image directly in code, when you place the image in PageMaker, you see only a box reserving the space for the graphic. If you use a program that creates a screen image and the encapsulated code (like CorelDRAW!, Micrografx Designer, or Adobe's Illustrator), when you place the EPS file in PageMaker, you can see the graphic and scale or crop the file as you would any other graphic. Figure 9.4 shows an example of these graphics.

Using the Primary Sources of EPS Files

T I P

You can use Adobe's Illustrator or Aldus FreeHand on a Macintosh to create graphics and save them in Encapsulated PostScript format (IBM Windows version). You also can transfer any EPS file from the Macintosh to a PC and place the graphics in PageMaker.

Bit-Mapped Graphics

Bit-mapped graphics consist of a pattern of dots, or *pixels*, instead of being stored as mathematical formulas. This type of graphic comes from paint programs such as Windows Paint, PC Paintbrush, or Publisher's Paintbrush. Figure 9.5 shows bit-mapped graphics drawn with Windows Paint.

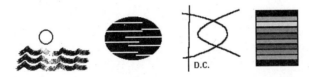

Fig. 9.5

Bit-mapped images drawn with Windows Paintbrush.

Because bit-mapped images consist of dots rather than whole objects, you cannot easily break bit-mapped images into separate elements like boxes, circles, and lines. Programs do not *layer* objects one above the other as PageMaker does. When you draw a circle on top of a square, for example, intersecting dots that compose the circle actually replace the dots that composed the square.

Bit-mapped images are not smooth like vector graphics when printed. Therefore, many users consider bit-mapped graphics inferior to vector graphics for most line art. Bit-mapped images, however, are superior for scanned images and fine art images that call for air-brush effects.

NOTE Some bit-mapped graphics may seem distorted on-screen, but they print well if the original graphic was not distorted. Graphics generally look best displayed on the same equipment used to create them. For example, a graphic created on equipment using a Hercules Graphics Card may look distorted when placed by PageMaker on equipment with a VGA or Super VGA graphics card or a different monitor.

T   I   P **Using Object-Oriented or Bit-Mapped Graphics**

Use object-oriented graphics rather than bit-mapped graphics for line art whenever possible. Bit-mapped graphics have a jagged appearance and take much longer to print.

When bit-mapped graphics are required, do not include text in the file in the paint program. Place the graphic portion in PageMaker and use PageMaker's text tools to add captions and labels.

Scanned Images

Scanned images also are bit-mapped images, but the latest scanning applications enable you to store images in your choice of graphic format. These formats can include the paint-type formats supported by PageMaker (PCX), PIC format, EPS format, or Aldus's Tagged Image File Format with the file extension TIF. The TIFF format is bit-mapped and enables higher resolutions than most paint programs.

You can edit images in a paint program or in a program that enables you to edit PCX, PIC, EPS, or TIF files before inserting the files into PageMaker. Scanners that can create and save images in one of these formats include scanners by Canon, Datacopy Corporation, DEST Corporation, Microtek Lab, Inc., and Ricoh Systems, Inc. You also can use Aldus PhotoStyler for adjusting gray and color values in TIFs and for creating special effects.

You can scan line art, such as a graphic logo, and save it in PIC format. PIC is an object-oriented format, but PageMaker does not store the scanned image as layered elements or as separate, editable objects as it would if you created the logo from scratch using a drawing application.

You can scan continuous-tone images, such as photographs or artwork created with brushes or charcoals, and save them in PIC format. However, these images are saved more commonly in a paint or TIFF format. Save continuous-tone images in paint format if you are using them *for position only* to show where a halftone will be stripped in at the print shop. Save the images in TIFF format if you plan to print the scanned image as part of the final page layout. Good-quality scanned photographs can look like halftones when printed, even though the images may look coarse on your low-resolution screen (see fig. 9.6).

Fig. 9.6

A scanned image.

Compressing TIFF Images through PageMaker   T I P

Scanned images can be very large and take up a lot of disk space.
You can use PageMaker to compress large TIFF files as you import
them by holding the Ctrl+Alt keys and clicking OK in the Place dialog
box (described in the section "Importing Graphics Created in Other
Programs" later in this chapter). You can decompress a TIFF image
that PageMaker has compressed by holding the Ctrl key and clicking
OK in the Place dialog box.

Choosing Scanning Resolution

If your scanner offers a choice of resolutions, choose the one that
is no higher than your printer's resolution. The image may seem
rough on low-resolution screens but should look better when
printed (see fig. 9.7).

You can conserve disk storage space and shorten printing time by
saving at lower resolutions. For example, an image saved at 72 dpi

continues

Choosing Scanning Resolution (continued)

can offer acceptable results when printed on a 300 dpi printer. For high-resolution imagesetters, you need to save the image at 100 dpi or more when printing at 1200 dpi, or at 300 dpi or more when printing at 2400 dpi or more. It is a good idea to test this yourself by saving a sample scan at various resolutions and printing it on the final printer before doing all the scans for a heavily illustrated publication. (DPI on a scanner refers to the number of data "samples" taken per inch, not the actual number of dots or pixels.)

Fig. 9.7

Scanned images at 72 dots per inch (left) and 300 dots per inch (right).

FROM HERE...

For Related Information

▶▶ "Importing EPS Graphics Colors," p. 559.

▶▶ "Converting a PageMaker Page to an EPS Graphic," p. 590.

Drawing with PageMaker's Tools

All of PageMaker's built-in graphics tools appear as icons in the tool-box. The toolbox, shown in figure 9.8, is actually a window. You can move the toolbox to any position by dragging its title bar, or you can hide the toolbox by using the Toolbox command from the Window menu.

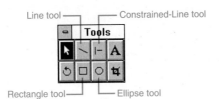

Line tool — — Constrained-Line tool

Rectangle tool — — Ellipse tool

Fig. 9.8

The toolbox.

The toolbox contains eight tools. You have seen how to use the Text tool and the Pointer tool to select, move, and size blocks of text. In this section, you learn to draw straight lines and create boxes, circles, and ovals with the toolbox's four drawing tools:

- The Line tool

- The Constrained-Line tool

- The Rectangle tool

- The Ellipse tool

All four drawing tools work the same way. When you select one of the tools, the pointer changes to a crossbar. You move the mouse to position the crossbar on the page or pasteboard and hold down the mouse button as you drag the crossbar. The object appears on-screen as you drag. As long as you keep holding down the mouse button, you can keep adjusting the size of the object. When you release the mouse button, the graphic is set. To change the size or position of a completed graphic, you must switch to the Pointer tool.

Drawing Straight Lines

You use the Line tool and the Constrained-Line tool to draw straight lines. The Line tool draws lines at any angle; the Constrained-Line tool draws only horizontal or vertical lines or lines at a 45-degree angle.

When you use the Line tool, the diagonal lines begin and end exactly at the crossbar points. A constrained line begins at the crossbar point and ends at the 45-degree increment nearest the ending crossbar location.

If you need to draw a mixture of perpendicular lines, lines angled at 45 degrees, and lines angled differently than 45 degrees, you can use the Line tool. Hold down the Shift key when you use the Line tool to draw a perpendicular line or a line angled at 45 degrees. Regardless of which tool you used to draw a line originally, you can rotate the line to any angle using PageMaker's rotating tool (described in Chapter 11).

When you draw a diagonal line, PageMaker centers the line on the crossbar, regardless of the line's thickness (see fig. 9.9). When you draw perpendicular lines, the crossbar point marks the edge of the line. You can flip a perpendicular line to the opposite side of the crossbar by dragging slightly in the direction you want the line to fall as you are drawing.

Fig. 9.9

Perpendicular lines with handles at one edge and diagonal lines with handles in the center.

After you have drawn a line, you can use the Pointer tool to select and edit it, as described in the section "Editing Graphics" later in this chapter.

Creating Boxes

You use the Rectangle tool to draw boxes in any proportion. If you hold down the Shift key while you are drawing, you draw squares. The Rectangle tool produces boxes with right-angle corners, but you can make them rounded using the Rounded Corners command on the Element menu before or after drawing the box. The Rounded Corners dialog box enables you to choose from varying degrees of roundness (see fig. 9.10).

Fig. 9.10

The Rounded Corners dialog box.

To set the degree of roundness of corners *before* you draw a box, first be certain that nothing on the page is selected (no existing box should display handles). Choose the Rounded Corners command from the Element menu and make a selection in the dialog box. All new boxes that you draw with the Rectangle tool take on the latest setting for rounded corners.

To set the degree of roundness of corners *after* you draw a box, first be certain you have selected the box you want to change with the Pointer tool (the box should display eight handles). Choose the Rounded Corners command from the Element menu and make a selection in the dialog box. Only the selected box takes on that setting for rounded corners.

All the boxes you draw in PageMaker have horizontal and vertical edges when first drawn. After you draw a rectangle, you can use the Pointer tool to select and edit the rectangle, as described in the section "Editing Graphics" later in this chapter. You can create parallelograms (skewed boxes) or rotate boxes in PageMaker 5.0 using the new transformation features described in Chapter 11. You can use the Line tools to create a polygon of any shape, composed of separate straight lines, but you cannot fill the polygon with a pattern. You can, however, use other graphics programs to create polygons and import them into PageMaker.

Using the KeyLiner Command

PageMaker 5.0 adds an Aldus Addition called KeyLiner, which automatically draws a rectangular box around a selected graphic or text block. Traditionally, *keylining* is a copy preparation technique in which a layout artist outlines certain areas of artwork on a tissue overlay, with instructions to the printer or camera operator about placement, size, and content of an illustration. You can use keylining in this way or to drop boxes over scanned photographs that will be replaced with traditional halftones. The KeyLiner feature is also a convenient alternative to using the Rectangle tool from the toolbox, because KeyLiner automatically centers the box around the selected object.

To use this command, select the text block or graphic with the Pointer tool and choose KeyLiner from the Aldus Additions submenu under the Utilities menu. PageMaker opens the KeyLiner dialog box, where you can specify the number of points away from the edges of the object you want the box to start (see fig. 9.11). You also can choose Bring Box to Front of Object or Send Box Behind Object. Click Attributes to display the Fill and Line dialog box (described later in this chapter and shown in fig. 9.26). Figure 9.12 shows a box created by using the KeyLiner Addition.

Fig. 9.11

The KeyLiner dialog box, with the text block to be keylined selected in Layout view.

Fig. 9.12

Text framed in a box by using KeyLiner Addition.

After you create a box by using the KeyLiner command, the box is just like any other rectangle drawn with the Rectangle tool. You can use the Pointer tool to select and edit the box, as described in the section "Editing Graphics" later in this chapter.

Creating Circles and Ovals

The Ellipse tool enables you to draw circles and ovals. When using this tool, you drag the crossbar diagonally to define the area where the circle or oval falls. If you hold down the Shift key while you are dragging the crossbar, you create a circle.

All ellipses drawn in PageMaker have horizontal and vertical axes. After you draw a circle or ellipse, you can use the Pointer tool to select and edit the graphic, as described in the section "Editing Graphics" later in this chapter. If you want an ellipse to have a diagonal axis, you can use PageMaker's rotating tool, described in Chapter 11. You cannot draw arcs (segments of circles, as used in pie graphs) in PageMaker, but you can draw a circle or ellipse and cover part of the graphic with a box. (Assign a line of *None* and a fill of *Paper* so the box isn't visible.) You also can import arcs drawn in other programs.

For Related Information

▸▸ "Working with Transformations," p. 504.

FROM HERE...

Importing Graphics Created in Other Programs

For many publications, PageMaker's graphics tools are sufficient— especially when you have no illustrations other than lines, boxes, and ellipses. For heavily illustrated material, however, other programs are the primary sources of graphics. You use the Place command from the File menu to import graphics created in other programs.

When you import graphics, PageMaker places the entire graphics file as a single graphics object, regardless of how large the graphic is or how many objects are in the original source file. If the graphic includes text, PageMaker retains the font settings specified in the graphics program. Chapter 12 describes how PageMaker handles color graphics.

The beginning of this chapter described the four basic types of graphic formats (object-oriented, Encapsulated PostScript, bit-mapped, and

scanned images). Table 9.1 lists the types of graphics programs that
PageMaker supports and gives the common extension for each type.
Please note that some applications can save files in a variety of formats
and not all supported applications are listed in the table. You also can
use OLE (Object Linking and Embedding) commands to import graphics from these and other programs, as described in the section "Understanding Object Linking and Embedding" later in this chapter.

Table 9.1 Graphics File Sources and File Name Extensions

Graphics Program or Format	File Extension
Encapsulated PostScript (various sources)	EPS
Scanned Images (various sources)	TIF and others
MacPaint (Macintosh computers)	PNT
PC Paintbrush, Publisher's Paintbrush, and others	PCX
Windows Paint	MSP
AutoCAD and HPGL plotter files	PLT
GDI metafiles	WMF
Windows Draw!, Windows Graph, In•A•Vision, Lotus 1-2-3, PC Paint, Symphony, Videoshow Graphics File Format, and others	PIC
HP Graphics Gallery, Dr. Halo DPE, and others	TIF
CGM Graphics File Format	CGM
Micrografx Designer	DRW

Be sure to save your graphics files with their normal (default) extensions if you want PageMaker to recognize the file format when you use
the Place command. PageMaker's graphic-importing capability is file-
extension sensitive. If the extension of the file name you are placing
(PCX, TIF, PIC, and so on) is not recognized by PageMaker, another
dialog box appears and prompts you for the type of file you are importing. File types listed include only those for which the filter has been
installed. If you do not see the type of file you want in the list, you can
use Aldus Setup to install additional filters (see "Installing PageMaker"
in Appendix A). If no filter is available for the type of file you want to
import, you can try using OLE commands, as described in the section
"Understanding Object Linking and Embedding" later in this chapter.

Viewing Your List of Installed Filters

T I P

You can view a list of all the filters you have installed by holding the Ctrl key as you choose the About PageMaker command from the Help menu.

To import graphics from other programs into PageMaker, follow these steps:

1. If you want to place the graphic as an independent element on the page, select the Pointer tool.

   If you want to place the graphic as an inline graphic (part of a text block), select the Text tool from the toolbox. Then click the insertion point in the text block where you want to insert the graphic.

2. Choose the Place command from the File menu.

   PageMaker opens the Place Document dialog box with a list of text and graphics files on your disk.

3. In the Place Document dialog box, find the name of the text file you want to place (see fig. 9.13). But don't click the file name until you read step 4.

   If the name of the file you want does not appear in the list, try one of the following techniques to check all the directories and disk drives on your system.

   ■ If the file name is not visible, drag the scrollbars to move down the list.

   ■ Click c:\ to view the list at the next higher directory level on the current drive.

   ■ Click a directory name and click OK or press Enter to view the files in the subdirectory. Or double-click the directory name to view the files in the subdirectory.

   ■ Click the arrow at the right of the Drives area to view a drop-down list of all drives, then click a:, b:, c:, or whatever other drive (if more drives exist) to view the list of files on another drive.

   Notice that you change directories and disks in the Place Document dialog box using the same techniques you learned in Chapters 2 and 4 for the Open Publication dialog box. The difference is that the Open command dialog box lists only PageMaker publications, but the Place Document dialog box lists text and graphics files.

NOTE If the file name still does not appear after checking all directories and disk drives, then your disk does not contain the graphic file or PageMaker does not recognize the file. You must install the correct filters for each file format you will be using by going through the installation procedures described in Appendix A.

4. After you find the name of the file you want to place, double-click the name if you want to import the file without changing any options in the Place dialog box. Otherwise, click once on the name to select it and choose from the following options:

- Place the file as an independent graphic (see fig. 9.13).

- Replace an entire graphic that you selected before you chose the Place command.

- Place file as an inline graphic in a text block where you positioned the text cursor before you chose the Place command (see fig. 9.14).

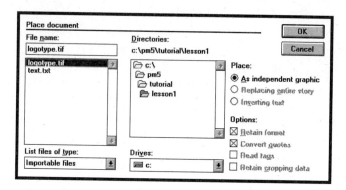

Fig. 9.13

The Place dialog box when a graphic file format is chosen and an existing graphic selected on the page.

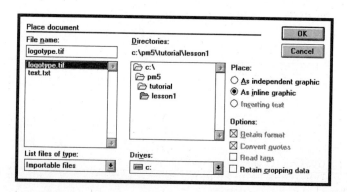

Fig. 9.14

The Place dialog box when a graphic file format is chosen and the text cursor inserted on the page.

If you are replacing an entire graphic, the Retain Cropping Data option becomes active. If you cropped the graphic that you are replacing, PageMaker applies the same cropping data to the new graphic.

The Retain Format, Convert Quotes, and Read Tags options have no effect on graphics files.

5. Click OK to close the dialog box and place the file.

If the graphic to be imported is larger than 256K (or whatever size is specified in the Auto Include Images Under value in the Other Preferences dialog box), PageMaker opens a dialog box with the following message:

> The graphic in the linked file would occupy ___ KBytes in the publication. Include complete copy in the publication anyway?

The actual size of the graphic (569KBytes, for example) appears in the dialog box (see fig. 9.15). If you choose Yes, then PageMaker imports the entire original graphic and stores it as part of the publication. The size of the PageMaker publication increases by the size of the graphic. If you choose No, PageMaker stores a low-resolution, bit-mapped, screen-display version of the graphic as part of the publication. The original graphic file is *linked* to the publication. When you print the publication, PageMaker looks on the disk for the original graphic file and prints it at high resolution. Chapter 13 describes how to manage linked graphics and text files.

Fig. 9.15

Dialog box offering link option.

If the imported graphic is smaller than 256 (or whatever size is specified in the Auto Include Images Under value in the Other Preferences dialog box), or after you make a selection in the dialog box for larger graphics, the pointer changes to a graphic placement icon.

6. If you are importing the graphic as an independent element, place the graphic placement icon where you want the top left corner of the graphic to appear; then click once. Let the snap-to column guides help you position the graphic placement icon.

   If you are importing the graphic as an in-line graphic, PageMaker imports the image automatically. PageMaker places the graphic framed in eight handles (see fig. 9.16).

Compressing TIFF Images as You Import Them

You can compress TIFF images through some graphics applications, or you can compress TIFF images through PageMaker when you use the Place command. For moderate LZW compression, press and hold Ctrl+Alt as you click OK in the Place dialog box. For maximum LZW compression, press and hold Shift+Ctrl+Alt as you click OK. Keep holding the keys for at least two seconds after clicking OK.

Compressed versions of graphics may show banding and less accurate colors on-screen. You can change the image back to a decompressed format by selecting the graphic and choosing the Place command again. Choose the Replacing Entire Graphic option and hold the Ctrl key as you click OK.

PageMaker creates a compressed version of the file and gives it a new name by adding two characters before the extension (overwriting the last two characters of the original file name if necessary). The following list shows the characters PageMaker uses:

Type of TIFF Image	Moderate Compression	Maximum Compression	Decompressed
Monochrome	_P	_L	_U
Palette Color	_P	_L	_U
Grayscale or full color	_D	_M	_U

You can discard the noncompressed version of the file if you want. PageMaker automatically decompresses the images when printing the publication.

Fig. 9.16

A graphic image placed on the page.

A graphic imported from another program usually is the same dimensions as it was in the original program, but you can change the image size or trim edges. You also can adjust the size of a graphic as you place it by using the drag-place feature (see following tip).

Placing Large Graphics in Small Areas

T I P

If the original graphic is much larger than the position reserved on the page, you can size or crop the graphic on the pasteboard before moving it onto the page. You also can use the *drag-place* feature to reduce the graphic as you place it.

To use the drag-place feature, you define the area for the graphic by holding the mouse button and dragging the loaded graphic placement icon diagonally. An outline of a box appears on the page as you hold down the mouse button and drag. When you release the mouse button, the graphic you are placing takes on the dimensions of the box.

You can scale and crop imported graphics in PageMaker, but you cannot change the line widths, fill patterns, or colors using PageMaker's menus. You must edit the graphics in their original program. To edit graphics imported with the Place command, you must open the original application through Windows (or DOS). You can open the original application through PageMaker if you import the graphic using the OLE commands, as described in the section "Differences Between OLE Commands and the Place Command" later in this chapter.

For Related Information

◀◀ "Bitmap Image Preferences," p. 161.

▶▶ "Importing EPS Graphics Colors," p. 559.

▶▶ "Managing Linked Text and Graphics Documents," p. 597.

Importing Spreadsheets as Graphics

PageMaker comes with filters for importing spreadsheet data as text (described in Chapter 6) or as graphics (described in this section). You also can import graphics created in a spreadsheet; examples are bar charts and pie charts. These file names must have the appropriate extensions so PageMaker can recognize and properly convert the files with the Place command. Table 9.2 lists the formats PageMaker supports and their normal filename extensions. You also can use OLE commands to import data from these and other programs, as described later in this chapter. (For a description of creating and importing tables from PageMaker's Table Editor, see the section "Using the Table Editor" in Chapter 11.)

Table 9.2 Spreadsheets and Databases PageMaker Can Place

Application	Extension
dBASE III+, IV versions 1.1-1.5	DBF
Excel 2.1-4.0 Spreadsheets	XLS
Excel 2.1-4.0 Charts	XLC
FoxPro	DBF
Lotus 1-2-3 Spreadsheets	WKS, WK1, or WK3
Lotus 1-2-3 Graphics	PIC
Quattro Spreadsheets	WK1, WKS
Quattro Graphics	PIC
R-Base	DBF

Application	Extension
SuperCalc Spreadsheets	WK1, WKS
SuperCalc Graphics	PIC
Symphony Spreadsheets	WRK, WR1
Symphony Graphics	PIC

When you use the Place command to import spreadsheet data, PageMaker offers two options: importing data as text or graphics, and importing the entire spreadsheet or a range of cells. For example, you can import Microsoft Excel spreadsheet data as text or a graphic. When you select an Excel spreadsheet in the Place dialog box, PageMaker opens a dialog box asking if you want to import the spreadsheet as text or a graphic (see fig. 9.17). You also can specify a range of cells or a range name. (See Chapter 6 for information about importing data as text.)

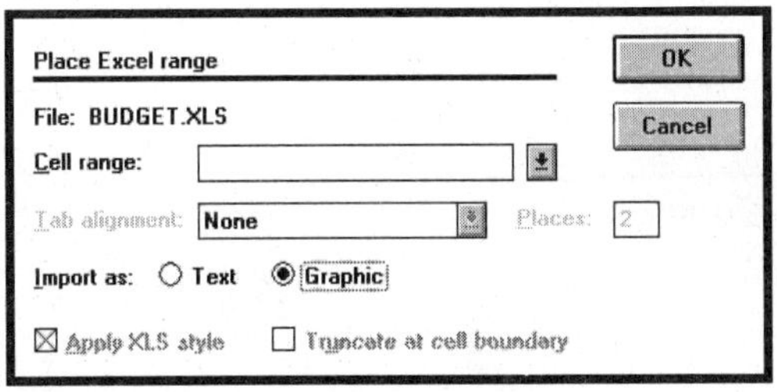

Fig. 9.17

The Place dialog box when you import a spreadsheet.

Importing Data as Text or a Graphic

When you import data as text, you can edit the text in PageMaker, but PageMaker doesn't import all the formatting done in the spreadsheet. If you import the spreadsheet as a graphic, PageMaker retains all the formatting done in the spreadsheet, but you must use the original spreadsheet application to edit the data.

Also, if you import the data as text you are limited to only 40 columns. "Hidden" columns in the spreadsheet are not counted or imported. Imported as a graphic, PageMaker supports any number of columns.

Importing an Excel Spreadsheet or Chart as a Graphic

Before you import an Excel chart as a graphic, be sure Excel is installed on your system and the directory in which Excel is installed is listed in your DOS path statement in the AUTOEXEC.BAT file (or the Excel application must be in the same directory as the imported file). Also be sure enough memory is available to run both applications at the same time, because PageMaker launches Excel when importing Excel files through OLE.

In addition, fonts used in the chart or spreadsheet should be available in PageMaker, and the same printer should be targeted in both files to avoid font substitution problems.

You can scale and crop charts and spreadsheet data imported as graphics the same as any other imported graphics, as explained in the section "Editing Graphics" later in this chapter. You can activate the original program and edit the chart or the data by double-clicking the graphic in PageMaker, provided you have enough memory to run both applications simultaneously.

FROM HERE...

For Related Information

◀◀ "Importing Unformatted Text," p. 250.

▶▶ "Using the Table Editor," p. 522.

Pasting Graphics from the Clipboard

Besides using PageMaker's graphics tools to create an object or using the Place command to import graphics, you can cut, copy, and paste objects through the Windows Clipboard. The Clipboard is a temporary storage area that contains the objects most recently cut or copied in the Windows environment. PageMaker replaces the items in the Clipboard each time you use the Cut or Copy command, and you erase any objects in the Clipboard when you close Windows.

To use the Clipboard, select one or more objects on-screen. Using the Cut or Copy command from the Edit menu, put the selected text or graphic into the Clipboard. The next time you use the Paste command, PageMaker positions the graphic from the Clipboard in the center of the screen. However, if the Text tool is active and the text cursor is positioned within a text block, the pasted graphic becomes an inline graphic, as described in the section "Using Inline Graphics" in Chapter 11.

You can cut or copy a graphic from the Clipboard of the current PageMaker publication, another PageMaker publication, or a graphics program you are running under Microsoft Windows. (See Chapter 2 for a description of running multiple programs under Windows.) In PageMaker 5.0, you also can bring graphics directly from one Page-Maker publication to another by dragging the graphic from one open publication window to another.

Maintaining Links through the Clipboard

T I P

Items copied within PageMaker, from one location in a publication to another or from one publication to another, retain all linking information. Items copied from another application into PageMaker through the Clipboard also retain linking information and become OLE-linked. Therefore, if you do not want the objects to be OLE-linked, you should use the Place command rather than Copy and Paste to get graphics from other Windows applications into PageMaker.

Using the Print Screen Key To Capture Images

T I P

You can use the Print Screen key (Prt Scr) to capture the current screen image into the Clipboard, and then use the Paste command to paste the image into PageMaker. This method is useful when you are creating manuals and books that need screen images or when you want a graphic that cannot otherwise be imported into PageMaker. Simply use the application that created the graphic to display it on-screen, and then press Prt Scr to capture the entire image into the Clipboard. Next, open the PageMaker publication into which you want to paste the graphic, and choose the Paste command (Ctrl+V). Use the Cropping tool to trim the parts of the screen that you do not want.

Understanding Object Linking and Embedding (OLE)

PageMaker 5.0 enables you to take advantage of Windows 3.1's Object Linking and Embedding (commonly known as OLE, pronounced *oh-lay*). PageMaker's OLE commands—Insert Object, Paste, Paste Special, and Paste Link—enable you to embed or link a graphic you can edit by double-clicking the graphic to launch the application in which the graphic was created (assuming the graphic application is OLE-compliant). You then can make the required edits while still in the PageMaker document.

If the object is *embedded*, the illustration remains under control of the original application so you can edit the object, but edits to the embedded file do not affect the original. When you double-click the object with the Pointer tool, you automatically open the original application so you can edit the object. You also need the original application to create the screen image and print the object; so if you move the PageMaker document to another system, that system needs to have the application that created the embedded object.

If the object is *linked*, everything that applies to embedded objects is still true, except that changes you make through PageMaker are made directly to the source file. Changes to linked graphics can therefore affect all occurrences of that graphic in other PageMaker documents. You can specify whether PageMaker should update the object automatically if you change the object using the original application when PageMaker is not active. Otherwise, PageMaker updates the object only when you request.

To list and manage linked files, use the Links command from the File menu to display the Links dialog box (see fig. 9.18), as described in the section "Managing Linked Text and Graphics Files" in Chapter 13. You can use the Links command to update, cancel, or change links from one graphic file to another. You also can update or change your link preferences through the Links command. No command is available for listing and managing embedded graphics.

To embed a graphic you have copied to the Clipboard, use the Paste command or the Paste button in the Paste Special dialog box. To link a graphic, use the Insert Object command, the Paste Link button in the Paste Special dialog box, or the Paste Link command from the Edit menu. The differences among these commands are described in the next sections.

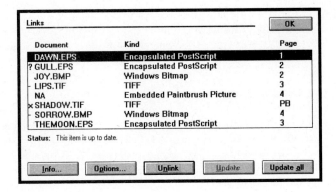

Links			OK
Document	**Kind**	**Page**	
DAWN.EPS	Encapsulated PostScript	1	
? GULL.EPS	Encapsulated PostScript	2	
JOY.BMP	Windows Bitmap	2	
- LIPS.TIF	TIFF	3	
NA	Embedded Paintbrush Picture	4	
x SHADOW.TIF	TIFF	PB	
- SORROW.BMP	Windows Bitmap	4	
THEMOON.EPS	Encapsulated PostScript	3	

Status: This item is up to date.

[Info...] [Options...] [Unlink] [Update] [Update all]

Fig. 9.18

The Links dialog box.

Differences between OLE Commands and the Place Command

Before you embed or link graphics in a PageMaker document, you must understand the difference between using OLE and using PageMaker's Place command. Embedded graphics always are stored as part of the PageMaker publication, and linked graphics always are stored as external files. The Place command offers a choice: you can import a screen image of the graphic onto the page with links to the original graphic file, or you can store the imported graphic as part of the publication.

You can manipulate placed graphics using PageMaker commands such as scaling, rotating, and skewing, and you can manipulate grayscale images using PageMaker's Image Control command. But you cannot change details of the graphic unless you go through the Windows Program Manager or File Manager to launch the original application in which the graphic was created. You can edit embedded and linked graphics by double-clicking the graphic in PageMaker to launch the original application.

Linked graphics, as well as placed graphics that are not stored as part of the publication, require the presence on disk of the original graphic file. PageMaker reads this file when the document prints to produce high-resolution output of the image.

Pasting any object—especially an OLE object—usually requires more memory (RAM) than using the Place command to import the same object.

Whether you import the graphic through OLE or through the Place command, you maintain the link between the PageMaker document and the graphic using the Links command from the File menu and the Link Info and Link Options commands from the Element menu. Chapter 13 contains more information about these commands.

The Paste Command

When you use the Paste command in PageMaker, you let PageMaker decide how to treat the graphic. If you have cut or copied the object in the Clipboard from another Windows application that supports OLE, then PageMaker embeds an OLE object. If you created the object in a program that is not an OLE source, PageMaker pastes the object into the publication with no links to the original file.

If the Clipboard stores the graphic in more than one format, PageMaker automatically chooses the most compatible format—the first format listed in the Paste Special dialog box. The Paste Special command enables you to control the graphic more directly.

Paste Special

Sometimes the Clipboard stores an object in more than one format. In this case, you can choose from the available formats by choosing the Paste Special command from the Edit menu. The Paste Special dialog box lists the available formats for the current Clipboard contents, with the richest (most like the original graphic) format listed first. If you click Paste, you embed the object. If you click Paste Link, you link the object. To link an object, you must copy it from a document that already has been saved on the hard disk—you cannot link an object to an untitled (unsaved) document.

Paste Link

You can automatically link an OLE object from the Clipboard without going through the Paste Special dialog box. Just choose the Paste Link command from the Edit menu.

Insert Object

The Insert Object command from the Edit menu creates an OLE object in another application and inserts it as an OLE-embedded object in a PageMaker publication. This quick access to other applications is handy if you have not already launched the other application under Windows and you want to embed or link an object or a package.

The Insert Object command opens the Insert Object dialog box where you can choose from the list of installed applications that support OLE (see fig. 9.19). By double-clicking an application name, you launch that application and can create or open a graphic (or whatever type of file that application creates).

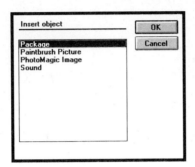

If you double-click Package in the Insert Object dialog box, the Object Packager dialog box appears and shows the icons and names of each OLE package available (see fig. 9.20). An OLE package is simply an icon that you can paste into any Windows application that supports OLE. By double-clicking the icon, you launch the application and open the associated file.

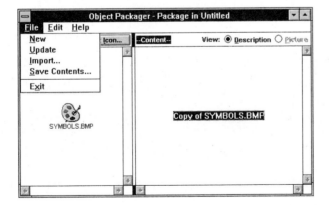

You can add a new package or object by choosing Import from the Edit menu and finding a file you want to package. (You use the same techniques you used for finding a file in the Place dialog box, as described in the section "Importing Graphics Created in Other Programs" earlier in this chapter.) Save new objects or packages by choosing the Save contents command from the File menu.

To copy a package into a PageMaker publication, click a package to select it then choose Copy Package from the Edit menu. Double-click the Control box in the upper left corner of the Object Packager window to close it. The package icon appears on the page in PageMaker (see fig. 9.21).

Fig. 9.21

A package icon
on a page in
PageMaker.

You can move, scale, and crop a package as you would any other graphic in PageMaker. When you double-click the package, you launch the application that created the packaged object and can view or edit the object from that application window.

Using Package Icons To Access Parts of a File

One innovative use for this feature in PageMaker is to paste package icons on the Pasteboard. Use the icons as buttons to open files that you frequently want to access without showing the whole file in the PageMaker publication. For example, you can create a document of graphic symbols that you frequently use, storing many symbols in one file.

Represent the file as a package icon on the Pasteboard in a PageMaker publication (again see fig. 9.21). Whenever you want to use one of the symbols, double-click the package icon to open it (see fig. 9.22). Choose the symbol you want to use, choose Copy from the File menu of the OLE application, close the application, and choose Paste in PageMaker. This method is an alternative to using PageMaker 5.0's new Library feature described in Chapter 14.

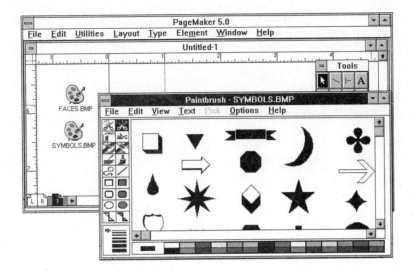

Fig. 9.22

Symbol file
window open,
ready for
selective copying
into PageMaker.

Edit Original

If you have selected an OLE-linked graphic in PageMaker, you can edit
the graphic by choosing the Edit Original command from the Edit menu
to launch the program in which the graphic was created. This method
is the alternative to simply double-clicking the object. The text of the
command changes depending on the type of object selected. If no object
is selected, the command shows as Edit Original, but it is grayed on
the menu. If an OLE object is selected, the command shows the name of
the originating application and the type of file, such as Paintbrush Picture
object or PhotoMagic Image object.

For Related Information

▶▶ "Managing Linked Text and Graphics Documents," p. 597.

FROM HERE...

Editing Graphics

The remaining sections describe how to select graphics and change
them in PageMaker. Some of these techniques apply to all types of
graphics—those created in PageMaker or those imported using the

Place command or an OLE command. Capabilities that have restricted applications are clearly noted. For example, you cannot change the line widths or fills of imported objects, and you cannot crop objects drawn with PageMaker's tools.

Selecting an Object

The first thing you need to learn about editing a graphic or any object in PageMaker is that you must *select* the object before any commands or palette entries can take effect. Failing to select the object is the single biggest stumbling block for beginners—they don't look to see if an object is selected before they try changing it.

When you first draw a graphic using one of PageMaker's tools, the graphic remains selected (until you click elsewhere) and you can change its size or position by making entries in the Control palette as described in Chapter 5. After you have deselected the graphic, you must use the Pointer tool to select the graphic again—using any of the selection techniques described in Chapter 5—before you can change anything about the graphic. The second big stumbling block for beginning PageMaker users is failing to switch back to the Pointer tool before selecting a graphic. When you have any other graphics tool selected, you can only draw new graphics or make menu and palette selections.

Small black squares called *handles* frame the graphic in several instances: when you first create a graphic with one of PageMaker's drawing tools, when you first place the graphic using the Place command, and when you select the graphic with the Pointer tool.

Chapter 5 discussed several selection methods, which are summarized in the following list:

- ■ *Selecting a single graphic.* First select the Pointer tool from the toolbox then click the Pointer tool on any part of the object. Two handles appear on a line; eight handles appear on a box or ellipse.

- ■ *Selecting two or more objects.* Select the Pointer tool, hold down the Shift key, and click each object.

- ■ *Selecting all objects within a rectangular area.* Hold down the mouse button as you drag the Pointer tool diagonally from one corner of the area to the opposite corner.

- ■ *Selecting a layered object.* If the graphic is on a layer below other graphics or text blocks, your first click with the pointer selects only the object on the top layer. Press Ctrl as you click again to select the object on the next layer down, and continue Ctrl+clicking until the graphic you want is selected.

Changing Line Widths and Fill Patterns

When you create a new object—line, box, or ellipse—with one of PageMaker's tools, the object first takes the default line (line style), line width (or weight), and fill pattern that you set, or the object takes PageMaker's defaults of hairline width and no fill pattern. You can change these settings before or after you draw the object. (You cannot change the line styles and fill patterns used in imported graphics, how-ever, except through the original program.)

You can choose line styles from the Line submenu under the Element menu to change the appearance of any line or border around any rect-angle or ellipse created with PageMaker's built-in tools (see fig. 9.23). PageMaker 5.0 offers the capability to adjust the line weight and set the background of line styles to transparent or reverse. You do this by choosing Custom from the Line menu to display the Custom Line dialog box (see fig. 9.24). You can fill boxes and ellipses with patterns from the Fill submenu (see fig. 9.25).

You can adjust the line and fill in one step by choosing the Fill and Line command to open the Fill and Line dialog box (see fig. 9.26). Then choose from the drop-down lists for Fill and Line styles as well as color. These commands affect only graphics created in PageMaker; you can-not apply the commands to graphics imported from other programs.

Element	
Line	**Custom...**
Fill	**None**
Fill _and line...	**Hairline**
	√.5pt ————
Bring to front ^F	1pt ————
Send to back ^B	2pt ————
Remove transformation	4pt ————
	6pt ━━━━
Text wrap...	8pt ━━━━
Image control...	12pt ■■■■
Rounded corners...	4pt ═══
	5pt ═══
Define colors...	5pt ═══
Restore original color	6pt ═══
	1pt – – – –
Link info...	3pt ▬ ▬ ▬
Link options...	6pt ▬ ▬ ▬
	4pt • • • • • •
	4pt • • • • • •
	√Transparent
	Reverse

Fig. 9.23

The Line
submenu.

You can change the line style and fill pattern using the Element Line and Fill commands before or after you draw a graphic. To set the line style and fill pattern *before* you draw a line, box, or ellipse, first be certain that nothing on the page is selected. If no existing element displays handles, choose the Element Line or Fill command and make a selection from the drop-down menu. All new lines, boxes, and ellipses that you draw take the latest settings for line style and fill pattern. The fill pattern setting does not affect lines.

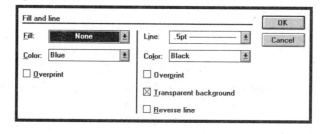

Normally, if the fill or line color is different from the color of other objects that fall below the graphic (for example, on a lower layer), the area where the fill or line will print is knocked out (that is, not printed) on the color separation for the colors that surround the graphic. Click Overprint for the Fill or Line (or both) if you do not want the surrounding colors knocked out. See the section "Overprinting Colors" in Chapter 12 for more information about the Overprint option and knockout and its effects on colors.

To set the line style and fill pattern *after* you draw a graphic, first be certain you have selected the element you want to change and it displays handles. Choose the Element Line or Fill command and make a selection from the drop-down menu. Only the selected elements take the changed settings.

Moving PageMaker Objects

After you select a graphic, you can move or scale it by using the Pointer tool or making entries in the Control palette. To move one or more selected objects with the Pointer tool, click the Pointer tool on any part of the selection except the handles. Hold down the mouse button, and the pointer becomes a four-directional arrow. Drag the object or group to the new location.

To move a graphic that has a fill pattern, you can click anywhere on the object. To move a graphic that does not have a fill pattern, place the pointer on the border. To move a selection along horizontal or vertical lines, hold down the Shift key as you drag.

As described in Chapter 5, the Control palette has two areas that control the position of a selected object on the page:

- *The X position.* The horizontal position of the element's current reference point relative to the zero point on the rulers. (Note that the current reference point is the one shown largest in the proxy icon, left of the X and Y control areas on the Control palette, which is not necessarily the top left corner of the element.) You can see these values change as you move the object or change the reference point. You can enter values to move the object or click one of the arrows left of the X to nudge the object in increments specified through the Preferences command (as described in Chapter 4).

- *The Y position.* The vertical position of the element's current reference point relative to the zero point on the rulers. This value can be changed or nudged as described for the X value.

Figure 9.27 shows the Control palette with the X and Y control areas.

Fig. 9.27

The Control palette in Layout view showing controls for moving and scaling objects.

T I P   Positioning Graphic Elements Precisely

You can use several methods to position graphic elements precisely. Use the Control palette to make entries as fine as .001 units, use the snap-to effect of the nonprinting guides, or work in 200% size so you can move objects in fine increments (see Chapter 5).

Scaling PageMaker Objects

As described in Chapter 5, the Control palette has four areas that control the size of a selected object on the page (refer to fig. 9.27):

- *W value.* The width of the element in the current unit of measure as well as the percentage of the original width (if the element has been scaled). You can change or nudge this value as described for the X value.

- *H value.* The height of the element in the current unit of measure as well as the percentage of the original height (if the element has been scaled). You can change or nudge this value as described for the X value.

- *Percentage-scaling options for width and height.* These values change if you change the width or height, or you can enter a percentage value to change the width or height. The percentage value reflects the change from the object's original size for imported graphics. For graphics drawn in PageMaker, the value reflects the object's size changes during the current editing session; if you deselect the object to work on other tasks, the percentage changes back to 100%.

- *Proportional-scaling option button.* When you turn on this button, PageMaker retains the original proportions of height to width when you resize the graphic. The values in the percentage fields change in tandem, regardless of which value you manipulate in scaling.

As an alternative to using the Control palette, you can place the pointer on a handle of a selected object and drag to *scale* (stretch or shrink) the graphic. The pointer becomes a two-directional arrow when you hold down the mouse button to scale a graphic. You also can make changes to the Control palette values that affect the size of the selected object.

When you use the Pointer tool to change the length of any line, you also can change the angle of the line. If you hold down the Shift key as you drag one of the handles, you force the line to follow a 45-degree path. You can change a diagonal line to a vertical or horizontal line by holding down the Shift key as you drag a handle. If you do not hold down the Shift key while dragging, you can stretch the line in any direction. You even can change the angle of a line that was originally drawn with the Constrained-Line tool.

You can change the shape and size of a box by using the Pointer tool to select the object and drag one of the handles. Two-dimensional objects have eight handles, one at each corner and one in the middle of each side. When you drag one of the side handles, you stretch the graphic along one axis only. In other words, you stretch the graphic out of proportion. When you drag one of the corner handles, you stretch the graphic in two directions at the same time.

If you hold down the Shift key while dragging a corner handle, you can create several effects:

- If you used PageMaker's tools to draw the graphic, lines become or remain horizontal or vertical; boxes become or remain squares; ovals become circles; and circles remain circles.

- If you have imported the graphic from another program, you size the graphic proportionally (see fig. 9.28).

Fig. 9.28

Using the Shift key to size a graphic created in another program.

Sizing versus Moving

T I P

To change a graphic's size, drag one of the handles. To move a graphic to another position, drag anywhere on the object *except* a handle.

Sizing PageMaker's Graphics

When you use one of the tools from the toolbox to draw graphics, use this method to save time. Position the crossbar carefully when you start and don't release the mouse button until you are sure the graphic is the correct size.

If you make a graphic the wrong size, you can fix it in three ways:

- Make entries in the Control palette while the graphic is still selected.

- Press Shift+Del immediately to remove the graphic then draw the object again.

- Select the Pointer tool to change the graphic's size or position.

T I P   Watching the Pointer

When drawing, moving, or scaling a graphic, always be certain the pointer's appearance reflects your intention before you make a change. A crossbar indicates you are about to draw a new object. A four-headed arrow indicates you are about to move the selected objects. A two-headed arrow indicates you are about to scale an object.

Moving and Scaling Imported Graphics

You can select, move, and scale imported graphics using the same techniques you use for selecting, moving, and scaling graphics created with PageMaker's tools, described in the previous sections. However, a few differences are worth noting.

When you move or scale graphics imported from other programs, the speed of the drag can make a difference. If you drag quickly, the graphic image disappears as it changes, and you see only the outline of the area that the graphic fills. When you finish dragging the object and release the mouse button, the graphic reappears on-screen in the new size or location. If you drag slowly, you can see the entire image changing as you work.

When you change the size of some bit-mapped images in PageMaker, you may notice that parts of the image show a Moiré pattern: a grid of perpendicular and diagonal lines. You can avoid this effect by using PageMaker's *magic stretch* feature, which jumps to fixed reduction and enlargement settings. The higher the resolution of your printer, the finer adjustments you can get in magic stretch. Select the graphic with the Pointer tool. To retain original proportions, hold down the Shift key as you are stretching the graphic. To activate magic stretch and jump to the best scales for printing, hold down the Shift and Ctrl keys as you are stretching (see fig. 9.29).

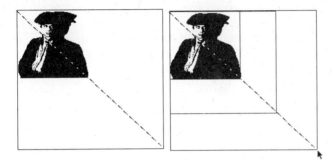

Fig. 9.29

Proportionate scaling (left) and magic stretch (right).

Imported graphics also can have picture scaling and cropping options and a printer-resolution scaling option in the Control palette. The following list describes these controls:

- *The Scaling button.* When you select an imported graphic with the Pointer tool, PageMaker highlights the Scaling button. Entries you make in the Width and Height fields or in the Percentage-scaling fields change the size of the graphic.

- *The Cropping button.* When you select an imported graphic with the Cropping tool, PageMaker highlights the Cropping button. Entries you make in the Width and Height fields crop the image.

  You can switch between cropping and scaling without going to the toolbox by clicking the Scaling or Cropping button in the Control palette.

- *The Printer-resolution-scaling option.* This option is available in the Control palette when you are scaling a bit-mapped graphic. Turn on this option to scale the image so its resolution is compatible with the printer resolution. This option has the same effect as magic stretching with the mouse.

Figure 9.30 shows the Control palette that appears with imported graphics.

Fig. 9.30

Control palette
when an
imported bit-
mapped file is
selected.

Cropping Imported Graphics

The Cropping tool trims edges from an imported graphic without
changing the size of the rest of the graphic. Cropping does not change
the size of the original graphic (whether the graphic is linked or part of
the PageMaker publication), so the amount of disk space the graphic
requires remains the same. You cannot crop graphics drawn with
PageMaker's built-in graphics tools.

You can crop an imported graphic by making entries in the Control
palette, as shown in figure 9.30. Click the Cropping option in the Control palette, select a reference point on the proxy, and change the values for X and Y or H and W. The reference point remains stationary. To
crop the right side of the graphic, for example, select a reference point
on the left side of the Proxy. To crop evenly from all sides, select the
center reference point.

To crop a graphic using the mouse, select the Cropping tool in the
toolbox then select the graphic. Click the Cropping tool on the graphic
to display the handles. Place the Cropping tool over any handle and
drag. You can trim horizontally or vertically by dragging one of the
middle handles; you can trim diagonally by dragging one of the corner
handles (see fig. 9.31).

Fig. 9.31

Graphics before
cropping (left)
and after
cropping (right).

If you hold down the Shift key while dragging one of the corner handles,
the cropped image retains the proportions of the original image. If you
crop a graphic too much, you can drag the handles to enlarge it again.

The full image is stored with or linked to the PageMaker publication,
and you always have the option of returning to the original full-size

image by using the Cropping tool to drag one of the handles. You also can move the image around inside the crop frame by placing the Cropping tool anywhere on the graphic, except on a handle, and dragging (see fig. 9.32). In the figure, the image is moved to the left but retains the same proportions.

Fig. 9.32

Image moving inside crop frame without changing the size of the frame.

Replacing Cropped Graphics

If you import a new graphic to replace a cropped graphic, you have the option in the Place dialog box of retaining cropping information, as described earlier in this chapter. You also can opt to retain cropping data when updating links, as described in the section "Managing Linked Text and Graphics Documents" in Chapter 13. In either case, if you choose to retain cropping data, PageMaker matches the cropping best if the new graphic is the exact dimensions as the old. If you change the dimensions of an imported graphic in the original file after you have cropped it in PageMaker, the cropping effect may not be what you expect when you import the new file or update the link.

Controlling Paint and TIFF Graphics Images

You can use the Image Control command from the Element menu to change the appearance of imported graphics that are stored in paint or black-and-white TIFF graphic formats. You can change lightness, contrast, screen pattern, screen angle, and lines per inch. First, select the graphic you want to change then choose Image Control from the Element menu to open the Image Control dialog box (see fig. 9.33).

The Image Control dialog box is a window you can move on-screen by dragging the title bar. Moving the box lets you set up the screen display for the best view of the graphic as you change the settings. You can try different settings then click Apply to view the settings without closing the dialog box. Or you can click Default to change to the original settings, click Cancel to close the dialog box without changing the graphic, or click OK to close the dialog box and change to the new settings.

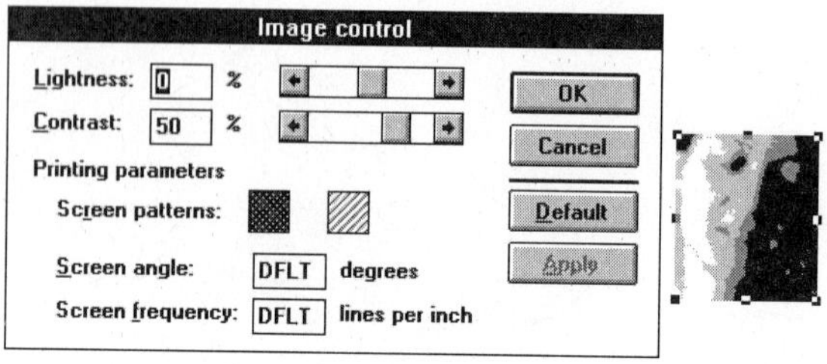

Fig. 9.33

The Image Control dialog box.

The first two options affect the appearance of individual dots within the image:

■ *Lightness.* Click the arrows beside Lightness to make the entire image darker or lighter.

■ *Contrast.* Click the arrows beside Contrast to make light areas of the image lighter or darker relative to the surrounding background.

You also can adjust the Lightness and Contrast settings by making numeric entries in the text boxes next to those fields.

The next three options affect the screen when the image prints (see fig. 9.34):

■ *Screen Patterns.* You can choose a normal Screen Pattern of dots or diagonal lines for special effects.

■ *Screen Angle.* PageMaker usually uses the default Screen Angle that is built into the printer—usually 45 degrees; however, you can change this angle.

■ *Screen Frequency.* If Screen Frequency is set to DFLT (default), then PageMaker uses the printer defaults for lines per inch (lpi). The defaults usually are 90 lpi for PostScript imagesetters and lower for laser printers. By entering a frequency here, you override all printer defaults.

Normal Grayscale

Default 45° line screen

90° line screen

Default dot screen

90 lpi dot screen

30 lpi dot screen

Fig. 9.34

Examples of different screen settings: Normal Grayscale, Default 45° line screen, 90° line screen, Default dot screen, 90 lpi dot screen, and 30 lpi dot screen.

Activating Other Applications To Edit Imported Graphics

In PageMaker 5, you can activate the program that originated a non-OLE imported graphic and edit the content by holding down the Alt key and double-clicking the imported graphic. The originating program (or one that recognizes the file name extension of the imported file) must be available on your hard disk. After you edit and save the graphic, you must use the Links command from the File menu to update the version placed in PageMaker, as explained in the section "Managing Linked Text and Graphics Documents" in Chapter 13.

As described in the section "Edit Original" earlier in this chapter, you can activate the original program and edit OLE-linked images by double-clicking on the object, or by selecting the object and choosing the Edit Original command.

FROM HERE...

For Related Information

◄◄ "Using the Control Palette in Layout View," p. 211.

►► "Overprinting Colors," p. 545.

►► "Managing Linked Text and Graphics Documents," p. 597.

Summary

Now that you know what alternatives are available for adding graphics to a page, you can make decisions about using PageMaker or another program to create graphics. Chapter 10 offers more specific advice about making design specifications for graphics from diverse sources. Chapter 6 provided tips about using PageMaker's tools during the layout process and took you through the steps involved in laying out a publication, incorporating the information you learned in Chapters 3 through 5.

Printing

Your ultimate goal in the production process is to print your publication on a high-resolution printer. Sometimes this output becomes the actual distribution copy or copies. More often, the output serves as the *camera-ready pages* from which the document is reproduced by photocopy or offset-printing equipment. In this chapter, you learn the differences among various printers' capabilities. You also learn how to install the printer driver (during the process of installing Windows or PageMaker), how to select the printer for a publication (if you use more than one printer), and how to print a publication.

This chapter covers the basic steps in printing a publication to a laser printer. Chapter 12, "Making Color Separations," includes additional information about preparing and printing color publications, including color separations. Chapter 13, "Special Considerations in Printing," discusses more advanced issues in printing, including how to add new fonts to your printer, how to create a disk file that can be printed at another location (such as a service bureau), how to set up "signatures" for printing booklets, how to manage large graphics files, and how to diagnose problems in printing.

Knowing Your Printers

Before designing publications for PageMaker, become familiar with the capabilities of your printer. Not all printers support all of PageMaker's features (reverse type and white lines, for example). Some printers produce graphics and text at higher resolution than other printers.

Some printers require certain sizes of special paper or film; others use many different sizes of lightweight stock. Available fonts also vary from printer to printer. Generally, you want to design your publications with your final-copy printer in mind.

Printers Supported by PageMaker and Windows 3.1

The printing devices available for personal computers fall into several categories: character printers, plotters, dot-matrix printers, ink-jet printers, laser printers, phototypesetters or imagesetters, color printers, and color film recorders. Normally, laser printers and photo-typesetters/imagesetters are used for the final printing of a PageMaker publication, because laser printers and phototypesetters can handle outline fonts and produce typeset-quality publications and can print at much higher resolutions than can dot-matrix printers and ink-jet print-ers. Color printers are used to produce color proofs for review before sending the final publication to an offset print shop for reproduction.

Publications created in PageMaker can be printed on all PostScript printers, such as the Apple LaserWriter II NT and NTX, the IBM Per-sonal PagePrinter, and the QMS ColorScript printer; all PostScript-language imagesetters, such as the Linotronic, the Agfa Pro Set 9400, 9600, and 9800, and the Varityper 4300 and 5300; the Hewlett-Packard (HP) LaserJet series of printers and compatible printers that use HP's Printer Control Language (PCL 4 and PCL 5); non-PCL printers, such as the Hewlett Packard InkJet and PaintJet and the Epson LQ series dot-matrix printers; color film recorders, such as the Matrix (with AGFA ChromScript RIP); and continuous-tone color printers, such as the Scitex Iris InkJet. You also can print on any other printers that are com-patible with Windows 3.1, including dot-matrix printers such as the IBM Proprinter and the Canon Color Laser copier (used with Zenographic SuperPaint). PageMaker does not support plotters.

To actually print on any supported printer, four conditions must be met: First, the *printer* must be installed (that is, physically attached to your system—although physical installation is not actually necessary to specify a printer as the target printer and thereby access its fonts and capabilities while building a publication). Second, the printer *driver* (that is, the software that runs the printer) must be installed through Windows. Third, the printer driver must be assigned to an active *port* (the location at the back of your computer to which the printer is physically attached). Finally, the printer must be selected as the *target printer*. This chapter describes how to meet these conditions.

Resolution

One difference among printers is the resolution at which they print. *Resolution* is a measure of the density in which text and graphics are printed and usually is specified in dots per inch (dpi). Laser printers, such as the Apple LaserWriter and Hewlett-Packard LaserJet, print at 300 dpi. This resolution is considered high compared to most dot-matrix printers, which print at 120 dpi, but is considered low compared to typesetting equipment, imagesetters, or film recorders which can produce as many as 5,000 dots per inch.

The higher the resolution, the smoother is the appearance of the edges of text and graphics. The lower the resolution, the greater is the jagged-ness of the edges. Some printers have a range of settings for resolution, as shown in table 10.1. Most such printers can print pages of text at the higher resolutions. Pages containing graphics, however, may overload some printers' processing capabilities unless the printers are set to lower resolution for graphics or more memory is added. (Lowering the graphics resolution usually does not impair the resolution of text.)

Table 10.1 Resolutions of Some Printers Compatible with PageMaker

Printer	Resolution Settings in DPI
Apple LaserWriter	300
HP LaserJet	300, 150, or 75
HP PaintJet XL300 (ink jet)	300
QMS ColorScript 100	300
Tektronix Phaser IIsd (color)	300
Star NX-2430 (dot matrix)	340
NewGen TurboPS/400P	400
IBM LaserPrinter 10P	600
LaserMaster Unity 1000	1000
Linotronic	100 1200, 900, 600, or 300
Linotronic	300 2400, 1200

Paper Stock, Size, and Print Area

Printers vary in the type of paper (stock) and the size of paper they can handle. The printer manufacturer's specifications tell you what types and sizes of paper can be used in the printer. Most laser printers can use any lightweight paper stock; special paper stocks with a slightly glossy coating that helps the toner print solid black areas also are available. Phototypesetters and imagesetters use photosensitive film that is developed by using a chemical process, which yields the best results for solid black areas and fine typography. The film comes in rolls (offering variable page sizes) and can be solid white or transparent. Ink-jet printers usually require special paper with a wax coating.

Regardless of paper size, the area on which a printer can print is limited: A border at the edges of the paper usually is reserved for gripping the paper as it goes through the printer. Print area is further limited by the printer's memory; the border around large paper sizes, therefore, may be larger than the border around small paper sizes.

T I P   **Determining the Print Area**

If the printer's instruction manual does not list the device's maximum print area, you can check this yourself by setting up a PageMaker publication the same size as the maximum paper size handled by the printer. Use the PageMaker Rectangle tool to draw a box that overlaps all four edges of the paper, and assign the box a shade of gray or black. As you print the page, the printer's maximum print area is revealed by blank borders at the edges of the paper.

If you plan to create designs containing elements that *bleed* (run) off the edges of the paper, you must make the page size of the publication smaller than the maximum print area of your printer.

Types of Fonts

Some printers (such as those that use a daisywheel) are limited to printing only the characters on their print elements. Dot-matrix printers and laser printers, however, can change the appearance of the characters they print by using different combinations of dots to produce a different font. Printer fonts differ in how their character shapes are defined and how the fonts are accessed by the printer. (Installing and managing fonts is discussed in detail in Chapter 13, "Special Considerations in Printing," and design considerations in choosing fonts is discussed in Chapter 16, "Typography.")

Character Definition

The shapes of characters in a font usually are defined in one of two ways: by a map of dots to represent each character or by a mathematical formula for the outline of each character. By using PageMaker, your choice of printers is greatly increased, because PageMaker uses both bit-mapped fonts and outline fonts.

Each character in a *bit-mapped font* is composed of a pattern of dots. Bit-mapped fonts generally consume more memory than outline fonts and print more slowly. The printed results, however, are typically crisp and true to the font design, especially in high-resolution printing. Bit-mapped fonts cannot be *scaled* (sized when printing)—every size of every font you intend to use must be installed on your printer. If you enter a point size that is not available, PageMaker substitutes the next smaller available size in the bit-mapped font. You also cannot rotate, expand, or condense bit-mapped fonts. You must install both portrait and landscape versions of these fonts if you intend to print publications in both page orientations. Bit-mapped fonts commonly are used in PCL 4 printers, such as the Hewlett-Packard LaserJet series. (Some PCL 4 printers, however, such as the LaserJet IID and the LaserJet IIP, enable you to use portrait fonts as landscape fonts and vice versa.)

Outline fonts are just that—font outlines that the printer interprets and prints like bit-mapped fonts. Because outline fonts print faster and can be scaled, these fonts are more flexible than bit-mapped fonts. (In PageMaker, you can scale fonts from 4 to 650 points, in one-tenth-point increments.) Outline fonts also can be expanded, condensed, and rotated by using PageMaker commands. These fonts are commonly used with PostScript printers, although many other types of printers—such as the HP LaserJet III series of printers and other PCL 5 printers—use outline fonts because of their faster printing speed. The HP LaserJet IV series prints both PostScript and PCL fonts. You also can get scalable fonts on many printers by using TrueType fonts, now supported by Windows 3.1 and later versions, or by using a type manager such as Adobe Type Manager (ATM).

Using a Type Manager

T I P

You can install a type-management program such as Adobe Type Manager on your system to increase the number and flexibility of fonts on a PCL 4 printer. A type manager can generate scalable fonts even for printers designed to print only bit-mapped fonts and can accommodate rotated, expanded, and condensed text. Type managers are discussed in Chapter 13.

Font Access

A major difference among printers is the number of built-in fonts available to each device (see table 10.2). Built-in fonts are, in effect, part of the printer's circuitry. A font built into the printer is always available for any publication.

Sometimes printer fonts are available in replaceable cartridges that can be inserted into the printer. The Hewlett-Packard LaserJet Series II has one built-in font (12-point Courier), for example, and you can add more fonts on cartridges. The choice of fonts depends on which cartridge is loaded in the printer and selected in the Target Printer dialog box (displayed after you select the Target Printer command on the File menu). Most PostScript printers feature at least four built-in typefaces (Courier, Times, Helvetica, and Symbol), each available in any size and style (normal, boldface, italic, and boldface italic).

Table 10.2 Built-In Fonts of PageMaker-Compatible Printers

Printer	Fonts
Apple LaserWriter	Times, Helvetica, Courier, Symbol (all sizes, all styles)
Apple LaserWriter Plus	Times, Helvetica, Courier, Symbol, Avant Garde, Bookman, New Century Schoolbook, Helvetica Narrow, Palatino, Zapf Chancery, Zapf Dingbats (all sizes, all styles)
LaserJet and LaserJet Plus	
Cartridge A	Helvetica 14 point Times 10-point normal Times 10-point bold Times 10-point italic Times 10-point bold italic Times 8-point normal Courier 12-point normal Line printer 8-point light
Cartridge B	Helvetica 14 point Times 10-point normal Times 10-point bold Times 10-point italic Times 10-point bold italic Times 8-point normal Courier 12-point normal Line printer 8-point medium
Linotronic	Courier, Times, Helvetica, and Symbol (all sizes, all styles)

Windows includes the *width tables* (required for printing) and *screen fonts* (required for displaying fonts on the screen) for all the fonts listed in table 10.2 and for some additional downloadable fonts as well. A width table assigns the space for each alphabetic character, number, and symbol in a given font. A screen font is a bit-mapped version of the outline font used in printing the text. Screen fonts are used to display text on-screen. Screen fonts and width calculations can be handled by the type manager instead, if you use one.

Fonts that are neither built into the printer nor included in the printer's cartridges can be transferred (or *downloaded*) to the memory of some printers. The TrueType fonts that come with Windows 3.1 are downloadable fonts. You can purchase additional downloadable fonts from the printer manufacturer or a software developer who makes compatible downloadable fonts. Adobe Systems is one of the primary sources for downloadable PostScript fonts. Bitstream is a popular source of downloadable bit-mapped fonts for either PostScript or PCL printers.

The steps involved in downloading fonts to a printer are discussed in the section "Downloading Soft Fonts," in Chapter 13.

For Related Information

▶▶ "Managing Fonts," p. 592.

▶▶ "Working with PageMaker's Font List," p. 706.

▶▶ "Planning Your Design Specifications," p. 708.

FROM HERE...

Installing the Printer

Instructions for installing a printer are provided in the manufacturer's printer manual. The first step is to use a cable to connect the printer to your computer. After you connect your printer (or printers), you must install your printer's driver through the Windows Control Panel before you can print a publication.

The Windows Control Panel displays a list of printers supported by Windows and prompts you to select the printers you are using. Select all the types of printers that you may use for your publications, whether these printers are hooked up to your computer or to another computer you intend to use for final printing.

After you have installed Windows, you can define your printer setup through the Windows Control Panel, where you can add printers to the list of those already available and change printer connections. This process is described in the next section.

After you install several printers, you can use PageMaker's Page Setup command to set up the target printer for a particular publication and change its specifications before you start printing. (Because PageMaker composes the publication for the target printer, always specify the target printer before you start the publication. If you must change the printer while working on the publication, PageMaker reformats the document to the new printer's specifications.) The PageMaker Print command (on the File menu) also enables you to choose a different printer or change the specifications for the selected printer. Both the Page Setup and Print commands are discussed later in this chapter (see the section "Using the Print Command," and see also "Choosing the Target Printer through PageMaker," later in this section).

Adding Printers through the Windows Control Panel

You can install a new printer driver or change the printer specifications by using the Windows Control Panel. To use the Control Panel, start Windows and follow these steps:

1. Open the Windows Program Manager.

   Double-click the Program Manager icon to open the Program Manager window (if not already open); or press Alt+Tab until you see the Program Manager listed in the center of the screen, and then release the Alt and Tab keys; or, from any Windows application, choose Switch To from the Control menu, and select the Program Manager from the list of active applications.

   If you accepted the normal defaults in installing Windows and have not changed your system, a program group icon named "Main" is displayed in the Program Manager (see fig. 10.1).

2. Open the Main program group window by double-clicking the Main icon.

   The Control Panel icon is displayed in the Windows main window (see fig. 10.2).

3. Double-click the Control Panel icon.

   The Control Panel window displays a number of icons, including the Printers icon (see fig. 10.3).

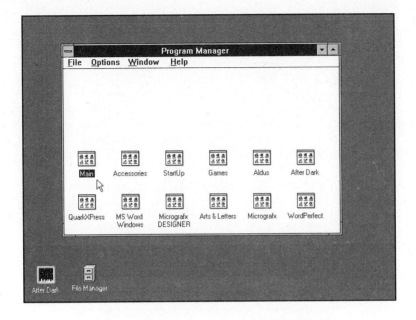

Fig. 10.1

The Microsoft Windows Program Manager window, with the Main program group icon displayed at the far left of the top row of icons.

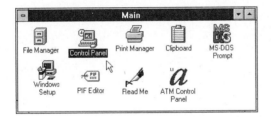

Fig. 10.2

The Control Panel icon in the Windows main program group.

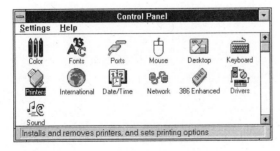

Fig. 10.3

The Control Panel window displays the Printers icon.

4. Double-click the Printers icon.

    The Printers dialog box displays the list of currently installed printers and the ports to which they are assigned (see fig. 10.4). By clicking the Add button on the right side of the dialog box, you can add a new printer driver to your system. By clicking the Connect button, you can change a currently installed printer's physical port assignment or change the Timeout Value (described in Chapter 13). The Setup button accesses a dialog box offering options specific to the type of printer selected. (This is the same dialog box displayed by the Setup button in the Print Document dialog box, described later in this chapter.) The Remove button removes the selected printer from the list. The Help button opens an on-line help window containing information about installing or changing printers.

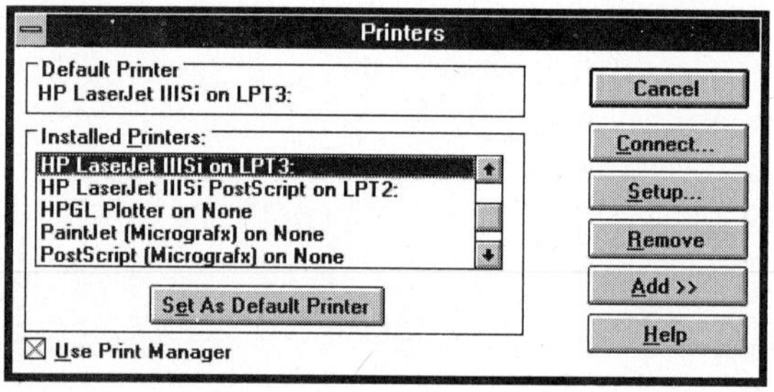

Fig. 10.4

The Printers
dialog box.

If you remove a printer from the Printers list through the Windows Control Panel and then open a PageMaker publication that was previously composed for that printer, PageMaker recomposes the publication for whatever new printer you choose. This can result in changes to the appearance of the text if the new printer does not support the same fonts as the original printer.

5. After making any entries or changes, as described in the following sections, close the Printers dialog box by double-clicking the Control box in the upper left corner of the dialog box or by pressing Alt+F4. (You can close any windows on-screen the same way.)

Adding a Printer Driver

For PageMaker's Page Setup or Print command to list a printer, you must install the printer driver for that printer through the Windows Control Panel. A *driver* is software that "translates" information sent from your computer into a form the printer can recognize. Microsoft Windows comes with many printer drivers. The printer manufacturer also may supply a driver that updates or supplements the drivers that come with Windows.

To add a printer driver to the list of printers installed on ports through the Control Panel, click the Add button in the Printers dialog box (displayed after you double-click the Printers icon). The dialog box expands to include a scrolling window that lists the types of printers supported by Windows (see fig. 10.5).

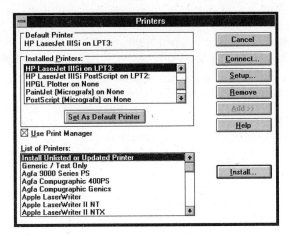

Fig. 10.5

The Printers dialog box expanded to display the List of Printers after the Add button is selected.

Use the scrollbars to scroll through the List of Printers to find the type of printer you want to install, and then double-click the printer name (or click the printer name once to select it, and then click the Install button). If the type of printer you want to install is not listed, double-click Install Unlisted or Updated Printer.

If the driver is already available in the Windows directory, it is automatically added to the list of printers installed on ports. Otherwise, Windows prompts you to insert in drive A the disk containing the driver or to specify the appropriate path to the printer driver. Change the path name if necessary and insert the disk (supplied with Windows or by the printer manufacturer). Click OK. After you insert the correct driver disk, Windows installs the driver.

Updating a Printer Driver

You also can use the Control Panel to install a newer version of a driver already installed. Treat the newer version as a completely new driver, and follow the procedure for adding a new driver, double-clicking Install Unlisted or Updated Printer in the list. Windows knows whether a printer driver for that type of printer is already on the system and prompts you to confirm that you want to replace the old driver.

Changing Printer Connections

You must connect your printer to a port. Typically, LPT1, LPT2, and LPT3 are parallel ports; COM1 and COM2 are serial ports. Usually, you connect your computer and printer before installing Windows, and you are prompted to specify to which ports any printers are connected during the Windows installation. If your system has only one communications port but you use two different printers, you can specify the same port for the two printers through the Control Panel, but you may need to change the cable connections each time you change printers.

If you change the cable connections between your computer and printer, you must use the Control Panel to tell Windows and PageMaker where to send the printed pages. Open the Control Panel window and double-click the Printers icon. Then click the printer name in the Installed Printers list to select that printer, and click the Connect button. In the Connect dialog box, click the name of the port to which the printer is now connected (see fig. 10.6).

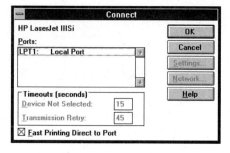

Fig. 10.6

The Connect dialog box.

This dialog box also is where you can change the Timeout length—as is sometimes necessary if printing large or complex graphics. Chapter 13 describes this feature in more detail.

Changing Printer Setup Options

In addition to selecting the type of printer and assigning a printer port, you can tell Windows the source of your paper (automatic feed, manual feed, or a paper tray), the size of the paper, and the orientation of the paper—Portrait (tall) and Landscape (wide). To set these options, open the Control Panel window and double-click the Printers icon. Click the printer name in the Installed Printers list to select that printer, and click the Setup button to display the dialog box that enables you to set your options for paper source, size, and orientation for that printer.

This dialog box is printer-specific: The options available vary depending on the printer selected. Figures 10.7 and 10.8, for example, show the dialog boxes for the Apple LaserWriter Plus and the Hewlett-Packard LaserJet III, respectively.

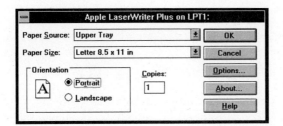

Fig. 10.7

The printer setup dialog box for the Apple LaserWriter Plus printer.

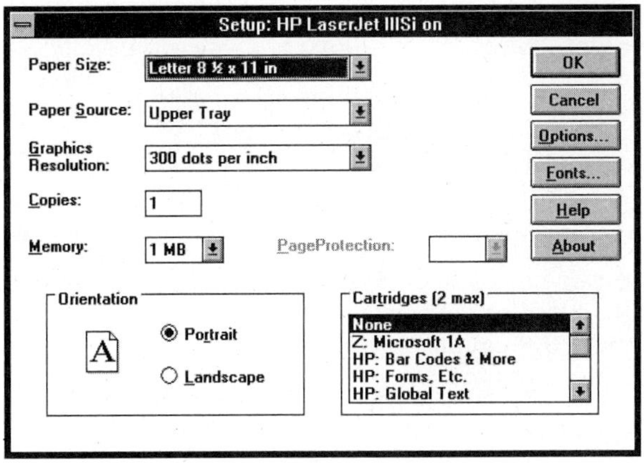

Fig. 10.8

The printer setup dialog box for the Hewlett-Packard LaserJet IIISi printer.

You can set the default values for number of copies, orientation, paper size, paper source, printer memory, graphics resolution, and font cartridge in this printer setup dialog box (refer to fig. 10.8). You can change these settings for individual printings in the Print Document dialog box (displayed after you choose the Print command on the File menu).

Click the arrow to the right of the Paper Source option to select a paper tray or to select Manual Feed from the drop-down list. Click the arrow to the right of the Paper Size option to select a paper size. The Paper Source and Paper Size drop-down lists show options specific to the type of printer you selected.

Most printers enable you to choose Portrait or Landscape orientation. (Some dialog boxes list these options as Tall and Wide.) Portrait, or

Tall, orientation is how you usually print on a piece of letter-sized paper (11 inches tall and 8 1/2 inches wide); the longer measurement is the vertical measurement. Landscape is the same as Wide orientation; the longer measurement is the horizontal measurement. If your printer supports Landscape orientation, you can choose Portrait or Landscape for any size paper.

> **CAUTION:** Some printers do not print well in Landscape orientation. For some reason, these printers must work harder, take longer, and sometimes drop information if you try to use them to print in Landscape orientation. In printers such as the LaserJet Series II, some downloadable fonts cannot be used in both Portrait and Landscape orientation on a single page. Also, some older models of PostScript cartridges do not support landscape printing or require additional memory. These restrictions do not apply if you have plenty of printer memory and use a type manager.
>
> To determine whether your printer is capable of printing this orientation, create a short sample document in Landscape orientation and try printing the sample—before you embark on a large or complex project that requires Landscape orientation.

You also can specify in this dialog box a default number of copies to be printed; this number can be overridden in the Print dialog box in PageMaker. (See "Specifying the Number of Copies" in the section "Using the Print Command," later in this chapter).

Click the About button in your printer's setup dialog box to view the version number of the current printer driver. Click the Help button for access to on-line help in setting up printers.

A printer setup dialog box also can include an Options button for changing other setup options available for the type of printer selected. You can specify a percentage for enlarging or reducing the printed page on some printers, for example, or specify a font cartridge for printers that use cartridges. PostScript printers enable you to reduce or enlarge the printed image by entering a value in the Scaling Percent box. Finally, if you print on a color printer, you can choose the Use Color option (that is, print in color).

Printer resolutions are shown in a drop-down list, and font-cartridge names are shown in scrolling windows for PCL printers. In the dialog box in figure 10.8, for example, you can choose among 21 cartridges. (See Chapter 17, "Creating Business Reports, Books, and Manuals," for examples of the different fonts on each cartridge.) You also can choose from graphics resolutions of 75, 150, or 300 dots per inch (dpi). Letters display more jagged edges at the lower resolutions, but the quality of text is not dramatically reduced, and the pages print faster. Lower resolutions are good for printing drafts during the production process. In fact, pages with complex graphics or large bit-mapped images cannot be printed at 300 dpi without overloading the printer's memory.

Changing the Default Printer

If only one printer is connected to a port at a time, that printer becomes the default printer for PageMaker and all Windows applications. If printers are connected to two or more ports, you can change the default printer by choosing from the Default Printer list in the Printers dialog box (displayed after you click the Printers icon on the Windows Control Panel). To set the Windows default printer, double-click the printer and port listed in the Printers dialog box.

If no publication is open, you also can use the Page Setup command on PageMaker's File menu to specify the default printer used by PageMaker. You also can open a publication and use this command to specify the target printer for that particular publication without changing the default printer for all other publications.

Choosing the Target Printer through PageMaker

As you design and produce any publication, one of the first questions you must ask yourself is this: What printer is to be used for the final camera-ready pages?

Often, you use the same printer throughout the entire production sequence, from early proofs to final masters. In fact, most installations probably have only one printer (or only one type of printer, if more than one printer is available). If the printer on which you intend to print the final version of your publication is different from the printer you use for drafts, you must specify the *final printer* as the target printer before you start building your publication. The target printer specified in the Page Setup dialog box determines the list of available fonts and the print area for the publication.

You specify the target printer by using the Page Setup dialog box (see fig. 10.9), which first appears after you choose the New command, and can be changed at any time by using the Page Setup command on the File menu. You choose a current draft printer—different from the target printer—by using the Print command, discussed in the section "Using the Print Command" later in this chapter.

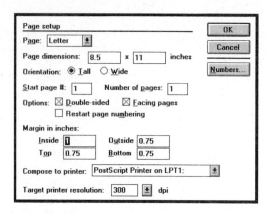

Fig. 10.9

The Page Setup
dialog box, in
which the target
printer is
specified.

Specify the target printer in the Page Setup dialog box as you first start
working on a publication, and never change it. If you change the target
printer after you start a publication, the stored publication itself
changes as PageMaker substitutes fonts as necessary, adjusts bit-
mapped images, and changes the print area. If you change only the
printer used for drafts of a publication (by using the Print command on
the File menu), however, the text is recomposed to match the new
printer's fonts as closely as possible, but PageMaker adjusts letter and
word spacing to correspond with the line breaks as they appear if the
target printer is used. Only the text in current memory is recomposed—the stored publication on disk keeps such elements as the
fonts and print area for the target printer.

If you do change the target printer for a publication, PageMaker asks
whether you want to recompose the entire publication to match the
new printer's capabilities (see fig. 10.10).

Fig. 10.10

PageMaker's
query to a
change in target
printers during
work on a
publication.

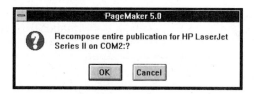

If your system has only one printer or one type of printer with only one
set of fonts, you can set the target printer once during the program
installation process and never change it. If your system has more than
one printer but the printers are all the same type—for example, all
Hewlett-Packard LaserJets with the same cartridge—you can use the
Print command on the File menu to change from one printer to another
at any time without changing the target printer specification.

CAUTION: If you switch the target printer of an existing publication, be prepared to adjust for differences in fonts, print area, and the printer's capability to handle rotated, expanded, and condensed text. Graphics also may need to be resized to match the new target printer's resolution. All these adjustments are likely to affect the spacing of your publication, including line breaks and overall text length.

A type manager reduces font substitution problems that can occur if you switch target printers and can facilitate printing transformed text to printers that do not otherwise support transformations (rotating, skewing, and reflecting). Transformations are described in Chapter 11, "Creating Special Effects and Complex Layouts." Type managers are described in Chapter 13.

If you have more than one type of printer available, use the Control Panel to specify the printer you are using before you build your publication.

The list of printers displayed in the Page Setup dialog box or the Print Document dialog box includes all printers installed during the initial Windows installation steps or through the Windows Control Panel (as described earlier). That a printer has been installed through Windows does not necessarily mean, however, that the printer is connected to your current system. You can prepare a publication for final printing on a PostScript printer that is not connected to your computer, for example, and print drafts to a non-PostScript printer.

You also can adjust the target printer's resolution in the Page Setup dialog box. This does not literally change the printer's resolution but rather changes the resolution at which PageMaker composes the publication and affects the behavior of PageMaker's "magic stretch" feature, as described in Chapter 9, "Working with Graphics." Set the target resolution, therefore, at the final target printer's value—the imagesetter's resolution, for example, even if you have no imagesetter on your system and must send the final file out to a service bureau for printing.

Printing at Lower Resolutions

T I P

Generally, work with the final printing resolution, as specified in the Page Setup dialog box, as you build the publication—especially when scaling bit-mapped graphics. Then, just before you get ready to print a draft, change the setting to use lower-resolution printing for faster printing of draft copies. If you run into memory-overload problems while printing a publication at 300 dpi, try printing at 150 or 75 dpi, or print the graphics separately.

For Related Information

◄◄ "Moving and Scaling Imported Graphics," p. 386.

▶▶ "Working with Transformations," p. 504.

▶▶ "Managing Fonts," p. 592

▶▶ "Creating Business Reports, Books, and Manuals," p. 731.

Using the Print Command

The Print command—located on the File menu and available only in Layout view—is used throughout the production process to print preliminary versions and final copies of publications. Because this command is so frequently used, it has a keyboard shortcut: Ctrl+P. Invoking the command causes PageMaker to display a dialog box in which you specify the number of copies and range of pages to be printed, as well as other special options (see fig. 10.11). Three buttons at the right side of the dialog box—Setup or Paper, Options, and Color—access additional dialog boxes or change the contents of the Print Document dialog box.

The buttons in the control area at the right of the dialog box remain available after you change the appearance of the selection area of the box by clicking a button. Click the Document button to display the Print Document printing options. Click Paper to display the Paper printing options if printing to a PostScript printer, or click Setup to display the Printer Setup dialog box if printing to a non-PostScript printer. Click Options to display the Printing Options selections. Click Color to display the Color printing options. The different appearances of the Print document dialog box and subsidiary dialog boxes are described later in this chapter, in the sections "Printing Options with PostScript Printers" and "Printing Options with PCL Printers."

Regardless of the type of printer or the appearance of the Print Document dialog box, click the Print button to print the publication, or click Cancel to end the Print command without printing and without saving any changes made to the options in the dialog box. You also can click the Reset button to reverse any changes you make in the dialog box.

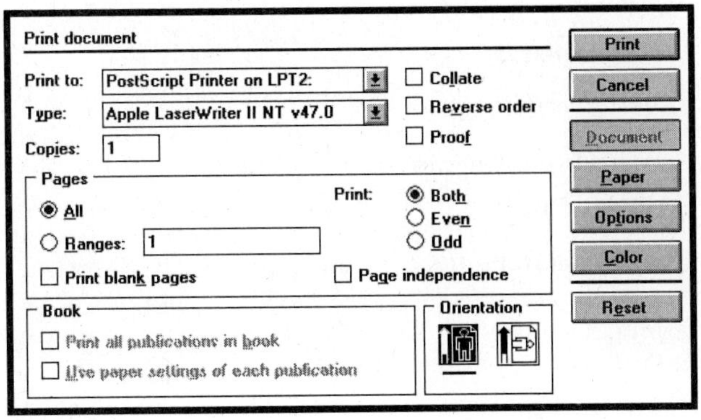

Print document

Print to: PostScript Printer on LPT2:
Type: Apple LaserWriter II NT v47.0
Copies: 1

☐ Collate
☐ Reverse order
☐ Proof

Print | ☐ All
Pages | ☐ Ranges: 1
☐ Print blank pages

Print: ● Both
○ Even
○ Odd
☐ Page independence

Book
☐ Print all publications in book
☐ Use paper settings of each publication

Orientation

Print
Cancel
Document
Paper
Options
Color
Reset

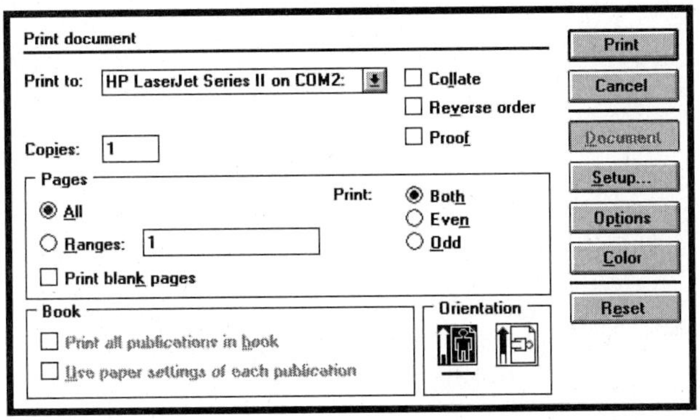

Print document

Print to: HP LaserJet Series II on COM2:
Copies: 1

☐ Collate
☐ Reverse order
☐ Proof

Pages | ● All
○ Ranges: 1
☐ Print blank pages

Print: ● Both
○ Even
○ Odd

Book
☐ Print all publications in book
☐ Use paper settings of each publication

Orientation

Print
Cancel
Document
Setup...
Options
Color
Reset

Fig. 10.11

The Print
Document dialog
box after a
PostScript printer
is selected
(above) and after
a non-PostScript
printer is selected
(below).

Saving Your Publication before Printing

T I P

Immediately before issuing the Print command, save your publication. Complex pages (those with large bit-mapped images, for example) sometimes can cause a printer to malfunction and force you to reboot your computer. If you reboot, you lose some data—which takes time to replace, even if you lose only one page of changes. You can save yourself a significant amount of time and exasperation by saving your publication before you begin to print. You also can use the Save As command to make the file smaller so that it will print faster.

Entering Document Printing Options

After the Document button in the Print Document dialog box is selected, it becomes dimmed, and the dialog box displays the information most likely to vary between one printing of a publication and the next. You may choose one printer for draft copies, for example, and another for the final printing. You may want multiple copies of the drafts for distribution to editorial readers, but only one copy of the final pages. The range of pages you print can often be what changes most in this dialog box from printing to printing. These and other options are described in the following sections.

Selecting the Current Printer

Two methods of selecting a printer for a publication are available. The target printer is set up by choosing the Page Setup command (see "Choosing the Target Printer through PageMaker," in the "Installing the Printer" section, earlier in this chapter). The current printer—which may or may not be the same as the target printer—is selected in the Print Document dialog box. The target printer is the printer intended for the final printing of your publication, whereas the current printer specified in the Print Document dialog box can be either the target printer or a draft printer.

After the Document button in the Print Document dialog box is selected, it becomes dimmed, and the dialog box displays the currently selected printer. You can click the arrow at the right of the printer name to display a drop-down list of any other printers installed on your system (see fig. 10.12). This list shows the printers that are currently installed through the Control Panel (see the section "Installing the Printer," earlier in this chapter). If other names appear on this list, you can change the current printer selection by selecting another printer name.

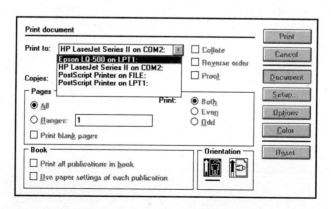

Fig. 10.12

The Print Document dialog box, with a drop-down list of available printers displayed.

If you change the type of printer for a publication, the text is adjusted to use fonts supported by the draft printer that match the new printer's fonts as closely as possible; based on information taken from the target printer driver, PageMaker also adjusts letter and word spacing to correspond with the line breaks as they appear if the target printer is used. The printed draft, therefore, looks similar to—but may not exactly match—the final publication. The stored publication remains unchanged, and the Layout view continues to show how the publication is to look after it is finally printed on the target printer specified in the Page Setup dialog box.

Selecting PPD Files for PostScript and TrueType Printers

If you intend to print to a PostScript printer, the PPD files for your printer model should be in the PPD directory, which is in the USENGLSH directory, which is in turn in the Aldus directory. PPD (PostScript printer description) files provide information to PageMaker about your printer and help ensure accurate color printing.

You select a PPD file by choosing from the Type option drop-down list, which lists different models (if any are available) of the current printer selected in the Print Document dialog box (refer to fig. 10.11).

The README.TXT file, which is copied to the PM5 directory as you install the program, contains a list of PPD file names and corresponding printers. If a PPD is not available for your printer brand or model, you can request these files from your printer manufacturer, dealer, or service bureau. If you cannot obtain a PPD file for your particular printer, use the PPD file for another printer with similar capabilities (fonts, paper sizes, and memory).

You can customize a PPD file to calibrate color screen densities, add page sizes, and add font names, as described under in Chapter 13. PageMaker 5.0 eliminates PDX (printer description extension) files.

Specifying the Number and Sequence of Copies

You specify how many copies you want to print of each page in the Print Document dialog box (as many as 32,000 copies), and you can indicate whether the pages are to be printed in reverse order and/or collated. If you are printing only one copy of a publication, PageMaker normally prints from the beginning to the end of the publication. If your printer outputs pages face down, the pages come out in the correct order. If your printer outputs pages face up, however, the printed stack of pages comes out in reverse order. In this case, you can select the Reverse Order check box to force the final stack of pages to be output in the correct order.

If you print more than one copy and select the Collate check box, PageMaker prints one complete copy of the entire publication before printing the next copy. This option is useful if you want to review the first copy while the other copies are printing or if you are printing final copies for distribution.

T I P   Collating Multiple Copies Adds Printing Time

Collating saves you the time you would spend sorting the copies manually, but the process often involves significantly longer printing time. If copies are not collated, the printer processes each page only once and prints multiple copies immediately from the same drum image. During collation, the printer must process each page for each copy—that is, the device reprocesses the drum image for each sheet of paper printed. You can speed up printing by setting the printer to make multiple, uncollated copies.

Printing Proofs

Select the Proof check box for faster printing. Graphics print only as rectangles if you enable this option; you cannot see the actual graphic or image on the printed page.

Printing a Range of Pages

PageMaker's default setting is to print all pages of the publication. But if you need to make changes that affect only a few pages, or you want to print the finished parts of a publication still in progress, you can print a specific range of pages instead of the entire publication. Enter the beginning and ending page numbers in the Ranges text box of the Print Document dialog box. PageMaker 5.0 enables you to enter a series of pages or ranges, separated by commas. To print pages 1 though 3 and 5 through 9, for example, enter 1-3, 5-9. You can enter up to 64 characters in the page range area. Page Range entries are remembered after you save the publication, so always check to make sure that you are printing the pages you want now—not a previous session's page selection.

> **CAUTION:** If you use the Book command to assemble a series of publications (described in Chapter 14), PageMaker can automatically number all pages sequentially from one publication to the next, but it does not renumber pages in a publication for which you set the page range option.

Printing Blank Pages

Usually, PageMaker does not print the blank pages in a publication (pages that contain only master page elements). You can select Print Blank Pages, however, to force all pages of the publication to print. Usually, you leave this option unselected if printing drafts for editing or proofing, but select the option for the final printing so that every page of the publication is represented by a numbered, printed page. If you are printing color separations, turn this feature off to prevent imagesetting four pieces of blank film for each blank page.

Printing Double-Sided Copies

Usually, you print all pages of a publication (both even- and odd-numbered) in succession, each on a single side of a piece of paper. For a double-sided publication, these single-sided master pages are then printed back to back by photocopying or offset printing.

If you want to print double-sided pages directly through a laser printer, however, but the printer does not have duplexing capabilities, use the Odd option in the Print area to print only odd-numbered pages first. Then select the Reverse Order check box, flip the stack over, feed it back into the printer, and print only even-numbered pages on the back of the odd-numbered pages.

> **CAUTION:** The orientation of the paper tray and the position of output pages vary from printer to printer, and you may need to add an extra (even-numbered) blank page to the end of a publication with an odd number of pages before you print the publication. Experiment with a short (three- to five-page) double-sided publication before trying to print a large publication double-sided through a laser printer. Make sure that you select the Print Blank Pages check box (see "Printing Blank Pages" in this section).
>
> Some printers cannot pass the same sheets of paper through a second time. Refer to the documentation that came with your printer to determine its capabilities in this area.

The Even/Odd Print options are not available if you are printing spot-color overlays, thumbnails, or tiles (described later in this chapter).

These options also are unavailable if your printer has duplexing capabilities. (See the section "Printing with a Duplex Printer," later in this chapter.)

Setting Page Independence

Select the Page Independence check box if you want PageMaker to download font information for each page and then clear the font information from the printer's memory before printing the next page. Otherwise, PageMaker downloads and clears fonts as necessary. Select this option if you are printing to a file that you plan to open in a post-processing program (for further processing after PageMaker, such as a page-imposition program) that handles font downloading differently than PageMaker does (and in which the pages in your publication may be moved around). Then the font information is stored correctly with each page. If you print directly to a printer, however, leave this option unselected so that your publication prints faster.

Printing Books

Select the Print All Publications in Book check box, under Book, if the current publication includes a book list of related PageMaker publications and you want to print all the publications. Do not select this option to print the current publication only. This option is dimmed if the current publication does not include a book list. The Book command is discussed in Chapter 14.

Normally, as you print from a book list, the print specifications of the current publication temporarily override—but do not change—the print specifications stored with each publication in the book list. The one exception is Orientation, which always prints as set up in the individual publications. If you select Print All Publications in Book, you also can choose to use all the other paper settings set up for each separate publication in the book (paper sizes, printer bins, manual feed, and so on) by selecting the Use Paper Settings of Each Publication check box. Selecting this option, however, adds to your printing time.

Setting Orientation

If you click the Tall icon for Orientation, PageMaker prints the short edge of your pages at the top of the paper. Click the Wide icon to print the longer edge of each page at the top of the paper. This setting should be the same as that for Orientation in the Page Setup dialog box.

Printing the Publication

After you complete your entries in the Print Document dialog box, you can make additional entries specific to your printer by selecting the Setup, Paper, Options, or Color buttons described later in this chapter, or you can simply click the Print button to print the publication. PageMaker prepares each page for printing and either prints it directly or sends it to the Print Manager—a *print spooler* that is part of the Microsoft Windows 3.1 operating environment, described later in this chapter under "Printing through the Windows Print Manager."

As PageMaker prepares each page for printing, the program displays a dialog box showing a changing message about the current status of the printing process, as well as a sliding bar to indicate the percentage of completion (see fig. 10.13). As each page is printed or prepared for the Print Manager, PageMaker highlights the icon for that page in the lower left corner of the Publication window. After PageMaker finishes its part of the printing process, you can resume working on the publication or run any other Windows program. (If you close the Windows environment itself, however, you terminate the printing process.)

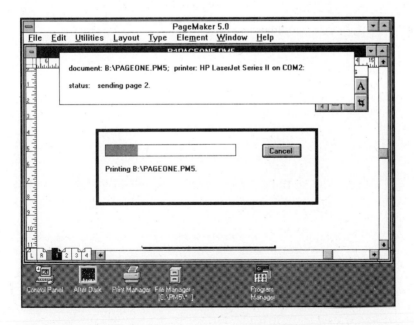

Fig. 10.13

Dialog boxes showing the status of the printing process.

Printing through the Windows Print Manager

The Print Manager enables any program running under Windows to perform all its print processing quickly and to store the results on the computer's hard disk. You can resume working with the program while printing is in progress.

If you send more than one file to the printer, the Print Manager lines up the files and feeds them to the printer in the order in which you sent them. You can view the list of files in the print queue, temporarily stop the active printing process, and reorder the priority of jobs in the queue by displaying the Windows main window and double-clicking the Print Manager icon. The resulting window shows the list of jobs in the print queue (see fig. 10.14). Click the Pause button to stop printing temporarily; click the Resume button to resume printing. Select a job by clicking it to highlight it, and click Delete to remove it from the print queue.

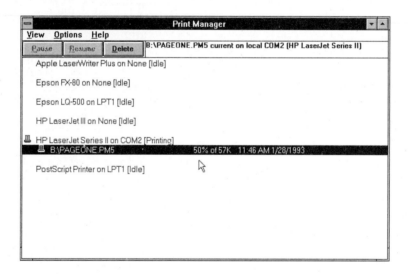

Fig. 10.14

The Print Manager window.

The window in figure 10.14 shows that the publication, PAGEONE.PM5, is being printed on an HP LaserJet Series II printer attached to the COM2 port. Nothing else is printing or waiting to be printed.

Open the Options menu on the Print Manager menu bar to set a selected job to Low Priority, Medium Priority, or High Priority. Within each category, jobs are printed in the order submitted.

Printing Directly to the Printer

To print through the Print Manager, Windows needs enough free space on the disk and in memory to store the pages while they are waiting to be printed. If you don't have enough available disk space, you may need to turn off the Print Manager and print the publication directly to the printer from PageMaker. This procedure requires less disk space but ties your system up in the printing process so that you cannot continue working while the printing is in progress.

To turn off the Print Manager, follow these steps *before* choosing the Print command. These same steps are described in greater detail, along with figures illustrating the various windows, in the section "Installing the Printer," earlier in this chapter (refer to figs. 10.1, 10.2, and 10.3).

1. Open the Windows Program Manager.

   Remember that you can double-click the Program Manager icon to open that window (if not already open); or press Alt+Tab until the Program Manager is listed in the center of the screen; then release the Alt key; or, from any Windows application, choose Switch To from the Control menu, and select the Program Manager from the list of active applications.

2. Open the Main program group window by double-clicking the Main icon.

3. Double-click the Control Panel icon.

4. Double-click the Printers icon.

5. Deselect the Use Print Manager check box at the bottom left of the Printers dialog box.

   The Print Manager is used if the Use Print Manager check box is selected (displays an X); it is not used if that box is blank (see fig. 10.15).

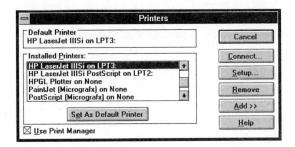

Fig. 10.15

The Use Print Manager check box appears in the bottom left corner of the Printers dialog box.

6. Double-click the Control box in the upper left corner of the Print-ers dialog box, or press Alt+F4, to close the dialog box. Close additional windows on the screen the same way as necessary.

7. Return to PageMaker, and print the publication.

Hold the Alt key and press Tab one or more times until you see PageMaker listed in the center of the screen, and then release the Alt key. Alternatively, from any Windows application, choose Switch To from the Control menu, and select PageMaker from the list of active applications (provided PageMaker was still active as you began these steps).

Stopping the Printing Process

You can stop the printing process by clicking Cancel in the dialog box that PageMaker displays while pages are being formatted for the print spooler (refer to fig. 10.13). The dialog box disappears after PageMaker completes its portion of the printing process. You still can cancel printing by opening the Print Manager window and clicking the name of the publication or print job to select it, and then clicking the Delete button (refer to fig. 10.14). If more than one publication is in the print queue, you can use the Delete button to remove selected publications from the queue even before they start printing. Remember that, if the Print Manager is active, you can open it by holding the Alt key and pressing Tab one or more times until you see PageMaker listed in the center of the screen and then releasing the Alt key.

FROM HERE...

For Related Information

▶▶ "Customizing PPD Files," p. 607.

▶▶ "Using the Book Command," p. 637.

Setting Additional Printing Options for PostScript Printers

The names of the buttons at the right side of the Print Document dialog box—and the dialog boxes these buttons access—change depending on the type of printer selected. If a PostScript printer is selected, the buttons include Paper and Options (refer to fig. 10.11). These buttons and their dialog boxes are described in the following sections.

Entering Paper Printing Options for PostScript Printers

After the Paper button in the Print Document dialog box is selected, it becomes dimmed, and the Paper dialog box appears and displays information relating to paper size and print scaling (see fig. 10.16). These and other options are described in the five subsections that follow. (Some of these options also are available after the Setup button in the Print Document dialog box is selected. The Paper button is displayed only if a PostScript printer is selected and physically installed on the system; the Setup button is displayed if a non-PostScript printer is selected.)

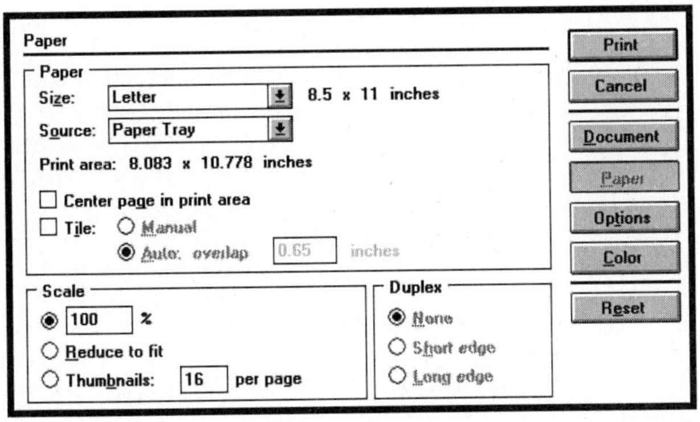

Fig. 10.16

The Paper dialog box that appears after the Paper button is selected in the Print Document dialog box.

Determining Paper Size, Source, and Print Area

After you select the arrow to the right of the Size drop-down list box, PageMaker displays a drop-down list of the paper sizes listed in the PPD file for the current printer. Some printers also offer a Custom paper size option; if you choose Custom, you can enter the exact width and height of the paper you want to use. The Custom option also enables a Transverse option, whereby the publication page prints across the width of the imagesetter film or paper roll. This option saves paper or film.

If you enter custom paper sizes often, you can edit the PPD file for the printer to include the custom sizes in the drop-down list (see Chapter 13 for more details).

Notice that paper size is not the same as page size. Paper size is literally the size of the sheets of paper or rolls that you feed into your printer. The paper size must be larger than the page size for printer's marks (such as crop marks) to be printed, if that option is selected, as described later in this chapter under "The Print Options Dialog Box for PostScript Printers" and "Printer Options for PCL Printers."

PageMaker enables you to specify custom page sizes up to 42 inches square. Unfortunately, few printers can handle paper this large. (The Versatec printer, to name one example, can print rasterized versions of PageMaker pages that have been saved as EPS files and handles pages up to 42 inches wide and of any length.) To print publications of page sizes larger than your printer's maximum paper size, you can print reductions of the pages or use the tiling option. These options are described in the sections "Additional Printing Options for PostScript Printers" and "Additional Printing Options for PCL Printouts," later in this chapter.

By selecting the arrow to the right of the Source drop-down list box, you can select different paper sources (bins or trays) as offered in the Source drop-down list. These sources also are derived from the PPD file for the selected printer.

PageMaker also displays the printable area size (Print Area) of the selected paper size, as determined by information in the PPD file. You cannot change this information. The print area must be larger than the page size for printer's marks (such as crop marks) to be printed, if that option is selected, as described later in this chapter.

Normally, PageMaker prints pages in the center of the paper if the page size is smaller than the paper size. If your printer's print area also is centered on the paper, the Center Page in Print Area option makes no difference. If the printer's print area is off center from the paper area, however, selecting the check box for this option affects the position of the printed page on the paper. This option has no affect on tiled printing (described in the following section).

Printing Parts of Pages by Using Tiling

By using the Tile option, you can print pieces of large pages on smaller paper. A common application of the Tile option is to print tabloid-sized, 11-by-17-inch pages on 8 1/2-by-11-inch paper, as shown in figure 10.17. You can assemble the "tiled" sheets into one piece for reproduction, or you can use them as proof sheets only. (You can print the final version of a tabloid page on a Linotronic typesetter's 12-inch wide roll of photosensitive paper without using the Tile option.)

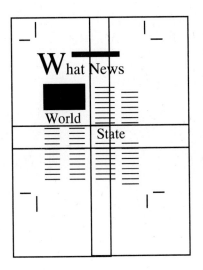

Fig. 10.17

A tabloid-sized page printed on 8 1/2-by-11-inch paper by using the Tile option (left) and a full page printed with crop marks on a Linotronic typesetter (right).

If you "tile" pages, you can select the Auto option and specify in inches how much you want the images on each tile to overlap. (You set the minimum amount for tiling overlap, but PageMaker tries to give you as much overlap as possible and may exceed the amount that you specify.) As you set your minimum overlap, remember that most printers cannot print closer to the edge of the paper than approximately 1/4 inch, and some printers cannot print closer than 1/2 inch. After you choose the Auto option and start printing, an indicator tells you how many tiles will print and how much of the job has been printed.

You also can manually force parts of the printed tiles to overlap. If you select Manual tiling, you control the placement of the upper left corner of each tile by relocating the zero point on the ruler, as described in Chapter 5. First you define the limits of each tile piece by moving the zero point on the ruler line, and then you choose the Print command and select the Manual tiling option. You print one tile with the zero point at the top left corner of the page, for example, and then move the zero point to mark the top left corner of the next tile in order to overlap with the adjacent tile; print again. If you are printing a large page size in tiles onto 8 1/2-by-11-inch paper, for instance, the zero point might first be at the top left corner of the page and then moved to the 10-inch mark below the top corner, causing a one-inch overlap between two tiles.

Manual tiling is also useful if you want to reprint one tile after you have printed all the tiles on Auto, or for printing the last few tiles of a page interrupted during printing. Because moving the zero point on one page effectively moves it for all pages, you can print the currently specified tile for all pages in the document at once.

Whether you select Auto or Manual tiling, you generally need some overlap to achieve precise alignment between adjacent tiles after you print and paste them together. At minimum, the overlap must account for the nonprinting edges of the paper (that is, at least .25 inches on a laser printer).

T I P   **Avoiding Manual Tiling of Facing Pages**

If you use PageMaker's Manual tiling feature, make sure that the Facing Pages option in the Page Setup dialog box is turned off. Because facing pages have a single zero point, you must move the zero point twice as many times to tile a facing-page publication.

Reducing and Enlarging Pages

Some printers—such as PostScript printers—can print percentage reductions or enlargements from 5 to 1,600 percent. If you use this type of printer, you can enter a percentage reduction or enlargement, in increments as small as one-tenth of one percent (**.1**), in the % text box in the Scale area of the Paper dialog box (refer to fig. 10.16). Some standard reductions for printing on 8 1/2-by-11-inch paper are shown in table 10.3.

Table 10.3 Reduction Percentages Required To Fit Oversize Proofs on an 8 1/2" x 11" Page	
Original Size (in inches)	**Percentage Reduction Needed To Fit on 8 1/2" x 11" Paper**
8 1/2" x 11" (letter)	100%
11" x 14" (legal)	77%
11" x 17" (tabloid)	64%
15 1/2" x 22 1/2" (newspaper)	48%
34" x 44"	25%

PageMaker 5.0 enables you to instruct PageMaker to scale the printed pages to fit the specified paper size. Select the Reduce To Fit radio button in the Scale area of the Paper dialog box to set this option (refer to fig. 10.16). If you print printer's marks or page information, PageMaker also scales the pages to fit these items into the print area.

The top left corner of each page, as shown on-screen, always corresponds to the top left corner of the printed page; all enlarging or reducing is done to the right and downward. The results of printing enlargements, therefore, are predictable: If you scale a page to be larger than the printer paper, you lose part of the right and bottom edges of the page. You can print these missing portions of the page, however, by using the Tile option (see "Printing Parts of Pages by Using Tiling," earlier in this section).

The results of printing reductions, on the other hand, may not be what you expect. Only the graphics and text blocks that actually touch the page on-screen appear on the printout. Graphics and text blocks that overlap the page and pasteboard are printed, but elements that fall totally onto the pasteboard are not printed in a reduction.

Working in Large Scales

If you use very small point sizes for text throughout a publication or need more columns than can fit on an 8 1/2-inch-wide page, try working in larger point sizes on a tabloid-sized page on-screen. Then print the publication at a 50 percent reduction to fit on an 8 1/2-by-11-inch page.

Notice that the Scale specification in the Paper dialog box overrides the scaling specification in the printer-specific dialog box that is accessed through the Windows Control Panel or by selecting the Setup button in PageMaker's Print Document dialog box. (See the section "Installing the Printer," earlier in this chapter.)

Enlarging To Reduce for Higher Resolution

If you want high-resolution final pages but don't have access to a high-resolution imagesetter, print the pages enlarged—at 400 percent, for example—on a 300 dpi laser printer, and then use a photocopier or Photostat service to reduce the pages—by, say, 25 percent. The result is a 1,200 dpi master.

You can use a similar trick to get high-quality color output on a short run of color images. Print the color pages enlarged on a color printer, and then reduce them on a good-quality color copier. The effect may be improved by printing the enlarged copy at a low resolution, such as at 65 dpi.

Printing Thumbnails

The Thumbnails option enables you to print miniature versions of up to 100 publication pages per printed page, with facing pages paired, as shown in figure 10.18. Not all printers support this option. Dot-matrix printers, for example, do not print thumbnails, but PostScript and PCL printers do. If the currently selected printer does not have thumbnail capabilities, this option appears dimmed in the dialog box. Thumbnails can serve as useful reminders of the contents of a publication and can be used as planning tools during the design and production process, as discussed in Chapter 16.

Fig. 10.18

Example of a publication printed by using the Thumbnails option.

If you specify separate page ranges (in the Print Document dialog box) in printing thumbnails, each new range starts a new printed page.

Printing on a Duplex Printer

If your printer has duplexing capabilities—as do such printers as the Hewlett-Packard LaserJet IID and the LaserJet IIISi—you can select the Duplex option of the Paper dialog box to print on both sides of the paper (refer to fig. 10.16). (You access this option by selecting the Paper button in the Print Document dialog box for PostScript printers or the Options button if you are printing to a non-PostScript printer.)

The specification you select for Duplex printing depends on the page's orientation and its binding edge. If your page orientation is Tall and the publication is to be bound along the left vertical edge, select Long Edge. If your page orientation is Tall and the publication is to be bound along the top edge, select Short Edge. Conversely, if the page orientation is Wide, select Long Edge if the publication is to be bound along the top and Short Edge if the publication is to be bound along the left side.

Notice that the Duplex specification in the Paper dialog box overrides the duplex specification in the printer-specific dialog box that is accessed through the Windows Control Panel. (See the section "Installing the Printer," earlier in this chapter.)

Understanding the Print Options Dialog Box for PostScript Printers

After a PostScript printer is selected and the Options button in the Print Document dialog box is selected, it becomes dimmed, and the Options dialog box appears and displays the information that relates to printing PostScript files (see fig. 10.19). These options are described in the three sections that follow.

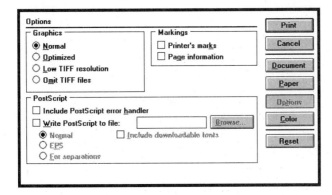

Setting Graphics Printing Options

The Normal option in the Graphics area of the Options dialog box sends all the image data contained in the graphic to the printer. Select the Optimized radio button to eliminate any data that the printer cannot handle, and PageMaker removes this extraneous data, speeding up the printing time on the job.

CAUTION: Optimized versions of scanned halftones or gray scale images print as nicely as do nonoptimized versions, but scanned line art may blur slightly if you choose this option.

Select the Low TIFF Resolution radio button to print imported bit-mapped images at 25-72 dpi rather than at the resolution at which the images were scanned or saved. Using this option also can accelerate printing, but offers a better idea as to how graphics actually look when printed than does using the Proof option of the Print Document dialog box, as described earlier in this chapter.

Select the Omit TIFF Files radio button to exclude imported TIFF images whenever printing separation files to disk so that you can link the PageMaker publication to high-resolution versions of the images by using a separation program such as Aldus Preprint.

Including Printer's Marks and Other Page Information

Select the Printer's Marks check box in the Markings area to generate the crop marks traditionally used to indicate where pages are cut when trimmed to final size (see fig. 10.20). This option also produces registration marks for aligning color separations if you print color overlays or separations (see Chapter 12, "Making Color Separations").

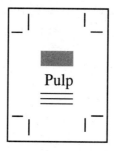

Select the Page Information check box to include the file name, current date, and the spot- or process-color separation names in 8-point Helvetica type in the lower left corner of each page, beyond the page edges and crop marks.

These two options are available only if you print on a paper size with a print area that is at least 1/2 inch longer and wider than the page size specified for the publication. You need at least a .875 inches beyond the page size on all sides to print both options on a page. You also can use the Printer's Marks option if you print a reduced page size by using the Scale option discussed in "Reducing and Enlarging Pages," earlier in this section.

Setting PostScript Options

Select the Include PostScript Error Handler check box to copy PageMaker's PostScript error handler to your printer (or to a PostScript file). If this option is enabled and a PostScript error occurs as you print your publication, the error handler prints an error message on the page on which the error occurred. This option is described in Chapter 13.

Select the Write PostScript to File check box to create a printable version of the publication on disk. This option is useful if you want to take the file to another system (such as that of a service bureau) for printing, if you want to create an EPS version of a page so it can be handled like a graphic, or if you want to create OPI-compatible color separations. You assign a name to the newly created PostScript file by typing the name in the text box to the right of the option. Selecting the Browse button to the right of the text box accesses a dialog box that enables you to locate an existing file name on your system. You also can use the Browse dialog box to save the named file in a directory other than the PageMaker program directory. The Browse button is enabled after you select Write PostScript to File.

Selecting Write PostScript to File enables the Normal, EPS, and For Separations option buttons. Selecting Normal creates a printable file that you can print from another system, as discussed in the preceding paragraph. (Normal is the default selection.) Selecting EPS creates an Encapsulated PostScript version of a page that you can treat like any graphic (as described in Chapter 13). Selecting For Separations creates OPI-compatible separation files that you can open and print from Aldus Preprint or other post-processing programs (as described in Chapter 12).

Click Include Downloadable Fonts if you want all fonts used in the publication to be included in the disk file. This option is useful if the fonts are not installed on the system from which the file will be printed, but it makes the file very large. Do not include the fonts if you don't have to.

For Related Information
◄◄ "Changing the Zero Point," p. 191.

►► "Printers Marks and Page Information," p. 574.

►► "Converting a PageMaker Page to an EPS Graphic," p. 590.

►► "Creating Design Alternatives," p. 669.

FROM HERE...

Setting Additional Printing Options for PCL Printers

As mentioned earlier in this chapter under "Using the Print Command," the names of the buttons at the right side of the Print Document dialog box—and the dialog boxes these buttons access—change depending on the type of printer selected. If a PCL printer such as a Hewlett Packard LaserJet is selected, the buttons include Setup and Options. These buttons and their dialog boxes are described in the sections that follow.

Understanding the Printer Setup Dialog Boxes

When you install a PCL printer through the Control Panel, as described in the section "Installing a Printer" earlier in this chapter, you set up certain defaults for the printer. These default settings include those for printer resolution, paper size, paper source, printer memory, paper orientation, and cartridges. You can change these and other settings for the current publication by clicking the Setup button in the Print Document dialog box. PageMaker displays the same dialog box you access for PCL printers by clicking the Printers icon in the Windows Control Panel (as described earlier in this chapter). Figure 10.21 shows the printer setup dialog box for a Hewlett-Packard LaserJet Series II printer.

Changes made in this dialog box through the Print command in PageMaker do not affect default settings made through the Windows Control Panel or the settings made by using PageMaker's Page Setup command. (See the sections "Choosing the Target Printer through PageMaker" and "Installing the Printer," earlier in this chapter.)

CAUTION: Usually, publications set up in the Page Setup dialog box as having Portrait *page* orientation are output on printers set up in the Print Document dialog box for Portrait *paper* orientation as well. Similarly, Landscape pages are usually printed on Landscape paper. If the orientation of the page differs from the orientation of the paper, PageMaker displays a warning message before printing the page. Choosing different orientations for pages and paper has the effect of rotating the entire page image on the paper by 90 degrees (see fig. 10.22).

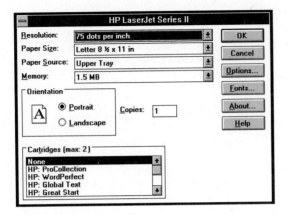

Fig. 10.21

The printer setup
dialog box for
the HP LaserJet
Series II printer.

Model Airplane Contest

Top 3 Win a Trip to Palm Beach
in the cockpit of a Cessna!
1st place also wins $5,000
2nd place $2,000, 3rd $500

Rules

1. Models must be constructed of paper and balsa wood and glue only.
2. Model must be between 8 and 12
inches long and wide.
3. Entries must be received by mid-
night, August 30.
4. Send for official entry form and
more details.

Fig. 10.22

A Portrait page
(left) printed on
paper set up for
Landscape
orientation
(right).

Setting Graphics Options for PCL Printers

Select the Options button in the Printer Setup dialog box for PCL printers to access additional options that affect graphics (see fig. 10.23).
The Dithering options affect how bit-map graphics are printed. None,
Coarse, and Fine represent a scale from lower to higher print quality,
with higher quality adding to the printing time. The Intensity Control
enables you to make one adjustment that causes all graphics to be
printed darker or lighter. Select the Print TrueType as Graphics check
box if you want text set in TrueType fonts to be handled like graphics.

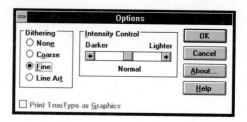

Fig. 10.23

The printer setup Options dialog box for PCL printers.

Graphics Resolution Affects Fonts

The graphics resolution of the printer affects the appearance of text if you click the Print TrueType as Graphics check box in the Options dialog box or if you print PostScript fonts to a non-PostScript printer by using a type manager. For best resolution in printing text as graphics, set the graphics resolution to 300 dpi in the Resolution drop-down list box of the printer-specific Setup dialog box. (See also the tip about fixing this problem in Chapter 13, in the section "Diagnosing Problems in Printing Fonts.")

If you can't get a page containing a graphic to print at 300 dpi (because of memory problems), but you want the text to print at 300 dpi, you can print the page at 75 or 150 dpi to print the graphic, delete the graphic from the page, and print the page again at 300 dpi. You must then resort to traditional tools, such as an X-ACTO knife and wax or glue, to cut the graphic out of the low-resolution printout and paste it into the higher-resolution printout.

Setting Font Options for PCL Printers

Select the Fonts button in the printer setup dialog box for a PCL printer to add, delete, or download fonts (see fig. 10.24). This dialog box lists only bit-mapped, downloadable fonts. ATM or TrueType fonts are not be listed here.

Setting Printer Options for PCL Printers

Select the Options button in the Print Document dialog box for a PCL printer to access several of the same options described for PostScript printers (see fig. 10.25). These options, described in detail earlier in this chapter, are summarized in the sections that follow.

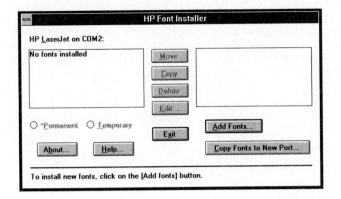

Fig. 10.24

The printer setup
Fonts dialog box
for PCL printers.

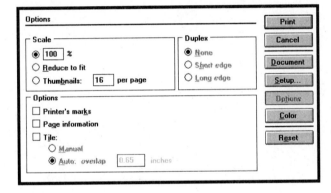

Fig. 10.25

The printer
Options dialog
box for a PCL
printer.

Reducing and Enlarging Pages

You can enter a percentage reduction or enlargement, from 5 to 1,600 percent, in increments as small as one-tenth of one percent (.1) in the % text box in the Scale area of the Options dialog box (refer to fig. 10.25). The top left corner of each page on-screen corresponds to the top left corner of the printed page; all enlarging or reducing is done to the right and downward. See "Reducing and Enlarging Pages" in the section "Additional Options for PostScript Printers," earlier in this chapter, for more information about how this option works and to view some common reduction formulas.

PageMaker 5.0 enables you to instruct PageMaker to scale the size of the printed pages to fit the specified paper size. Select the Reduce To Fit radio button in the Scale area to set this option. If you print printer's marks or page information, PageMaker also scales the pages to fit these items into the print area.

Printing Thumbnails

The Thumbnails option enables you to print miniature versions of up to 100 publication pages per printed page, with facing pages paired, as shown in figure 10.18, earlier in this chapter. PCL printers support this option in PageMaker 5.0. If the currently selected printer does not have thumbnails capability, this option is dimmed in the dialog box. Thumbnails can serve as useful reminders of the contents of a publication and can be used as planning tools during the design and production process, as discussed in Chapter 16.

If you specify separate page ranges (in the Print Document dialog box) when printing thumbnails, each new range starts a new printed page.

Including Printer's Marks and Other Page Information

Select the Printer's Marks check box in the Options area to generate the crop marks used to indicate where pages are cut when trimmed to final size (refer to fig. 10.20). This option also produces registration marks for aligning color separation if you print color overlays or separations (see Chapter 12).

Select the Page Information check box to include the file name, current date, and the spot- or process-color separation names in 8-point Helvetica in the lower left corner of each page, beyond the page edges and the crop marks.

These two options are available only if you print on a paper size with a print area at least 1/2 inch longer and wider than the page size specified for the publication. You need at least a .875 inches on all sides to print both options on a page. You also can use the Printer's Marks option if you print a reduced page size by using the Scale option discussed in "Reducing and Enlarging Pages," earlier in this section.

Printing Parts of Pages by Using Tiling

By selecting the Tile check box, you can print section of large pages on smaller paper. A common application of the Tile option is to print tabloid-sized, 11-by-17-inch pages on 8 1/2-by-11-inch paper, as shown in figure 10.17, earlier in this chapter. You can assemble these "tiled" sheets into one piece for reproduction, or you can use them as proof sheets only. (You can print the final version of a tabloid page on a Linotronic typesetter's 12-inch wide roll of photosensitive paper without using the Tile option.) This option is explained in detail in "Printing

Parts of Pages by Using Tiling" in the section "Setting Additional
Options for PostScript Printers," earlier in this chapter.

Printing on a Duplex Printer

If your printer has duplexing capabilities—as do such printers as the
Hewlett-Packard LaserJet IID and the LaserJet IIISi—you can select the
Duplex option to print on both sides of the paper.

The specification you select for Duplex printing depends on the page's
orientation and its binding edge. If your page orientation is Tall and the
publication is to be bound along the left vertical edge, select Long
Edge. If your page orientation is Tall and the publication is to be bound
along the top edge, select Short Edge. Conversely, if the page orientation is Wide, select Long Edge if the publication is to be bound along
the top and Short Edge if the publication is to be bound along the left
side.

Notice that the Duplex specification in the Paper dialog box overrides
the duplex specification in the printer-specific dialog box that is accessed through the Windows Control Panel. (See the section "Installing
the Printer" earlier in this chapter.)

For Related Information

▶▶ "Printers Marks and Page Information," p. 574.

▶▶ "Creating Design Alternatives," p. 669.

FROM HERE...

Printing in Color

PageMaker enables you to add color to your publications and to print
spot- or process-color separations of imported color images. These
images can be printed on a color or a black-and-white printer, or they
can be prepared for commercial color printing by printing color separations (separate page printouts for each color). PageMaker offers built-in
support for color printers; images are automatically printed in color
unless you specify otherwise. If the printer does not have color capability, the images are printed in black-and-white.

Figure 10.26 shows the Color dialog box accessed through the Color
button of the Print Document dialog box; Chapter 12 discusses the

options available in this dialog box in detail and shows you how to prepare your publications for spot-color overlays and for offset printing.

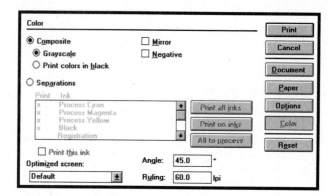

Fig. 10.26

The Color dialog box for PostScript printers.

For Related Information

▶▶ "Creating Color Publications," p. 531.

FROM HERE...

Summary

If you have only one printer in your office, workshop, or studio and use only the fonts hard-coded into your printer, the process of printing a publication is straightforward: You select the Print command on the File menu. If you have more than one printer from which to choose, you can use the Target Printer command to select the final printer for a particular publication. Use the Control Panel to add or remove printer and font names from the lists shown in dialog boxes. You also can use the Control Panel to switch printer connections or to change the option settings for a particular printer.

This chapter concludes Part II of the book, which presents a description of PageMaker's basic features and describes all of the steps and options in producing a simple, one-color publication. The next section describes some of PageMaker's more advanced features and offers tips and suggestions for handling more complicated page layouts. In particular, Chapter 12 presents additional information about preparing and printing color publications, including color separations. Chapter 13 expands on many of the topics introduced in this chapter and offers trouble-shooting procedures for solving printing problems.

P A R T

III

Advanced Techniques

OUTLINE

Part III describes advanced techniques that are not essential for simple publications but offer tremendous design and productivity aids for professional publishers. You learn efficient production techniques for creating special effects or unusual page layouts. You also learn how to produce camera-ready color separations for spot or process color printing.

Finally, you learn about some of the complex problems you may need to solve in the production process, such as how to print a publication to disk, how to manage fonts in order to minimize printing problems, how to work with large picture files, how to prepare publications for printing at a service bureau, and how to diagnose problems in printing. You also learn how to manage large projects and large documents.

Creating Special Effects and Complex Layouts

This chapter describes some of PageMaker's advanced features for creating special effects and solving tricky layout problems. In this chapter you learn how to work with objects in layers, including two methods for dropping shading behind reverse text. You also learn how to anchor graphics within the text as part of the text flow, how to wrap text around graphics, and several methods for creating drop caps and initial caps.

This chapter also describes PageMaker 5.0's new Multiple Paste command (for pasting multiple copies of the same object at specified intervals on a page) and how it is useful in creating forms as well as any design with repeated elements. You learn how to use PageMaker's new transformation features (rotating, skewing, or mirroring text or graphics at any angle), with special tips on creating common elements like polygons and stars.

This chapter includes a description of PageMaker's Table Editor and the process of importing tables. The Table Editor enables you to create tables of rows and columns of text, including rules between rows and columns and shaded cells, and to save them in a graphics format for importing into PageMaker.

None of the techniques described in this chapter are essential for creating a publication in PageMaker, but you will find this chapter a handy reference when you are ready to try some of these techniques as your experience with PageMaker grows and your designs become more complicated.

Arranging Elements in Layers

One feature of PageMaker that is also a characteristic of drawing applications, and that distinguishes PageMaker from any word processing program, is that elements can be arranged on top of each other in *layers*, as shown in figure 11.1. Normally, the first element you position on a page establishes the bottom layer, and each element added occupies another layer on top of the last.

You can change the order of the layers by using the Send to Back and Bring to Front commands on the Element menu. You also can work through the stack by Ctrl+clicking to select objects below another object. These techniques are described in the next sections.

Clicking through Layers

An element can become concealed when it falls on a layer below any imported graphic or a rectangle or ellipse created in PageMaker with a Fill assigned through the Element menu. Any time an element is hidden under another, you can select the hidden element easily by holding the Ctrl key and clicking on the location of the hidden element. Repeated clicks will select elements on successive layers. If there are more than two layers, keep clicking until the element you seek is selected. This feature is useful when multiple layers are stacked on top of one another.

Usually an object comes to the top layer automatically when you move it or scale it. If this happens, you can return it to its original layer using the Send to Back command, described next.

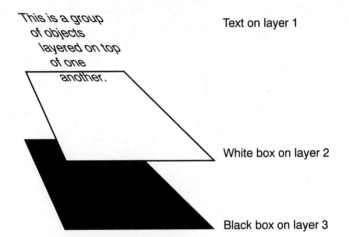

This is a group of objects layered on top of one another.

This is a group of objects layered on top of one another.

Text on layer 1

White box on layer 2

Black box on layer 3

Fig. 11.1

Examples of layered objects.

Using the Send to Back/Bring to Front Commands

To change the layering sequence of elements, you can select an element and use the Send to Back command on the Element menu (Ctrl+B) to move it to the lowest layer, or the Bring to Front command on the Element menu (Ctrl+F) to move it to the top layer.

When only two objects are layered, the Send to Back command is a useful alternative to clicking through the layers with the mouse. You can select the top one by clicking it with the pointer, and then using the Send to Back command to uncover the object below.

The Bring to Front command especially is useful when you are dealing with more than two layers of objects. Ctrl+click to click through the layers until the desired object is selected; then use the Bring to Front command to bring the selection to the top layer. After editing or moving the object, use the Send to Back command if necessary.

T I P   **Reordering Multiple Layers**

When working with three or more objects that have gotten out of order in layers, you can reorder them using the Send to Back command. First select the object that you want to end up on top, and choose Send to Back. Then select the object you want on the next layer down, and choose Send to Back again. Continue selecting objects in the order you want them layered and choosing Send to Back. Stop when the first object you selected appears on the top layer.

The Send to Back command is available only if the active element is layered above another element on the page, and the Bring to Front command is available only if the active element is behind another element. Otherwise, the commands will be gray on the menu.

Creating Drop Shadows

Making duplicates of a graphic and using these duplicates to create drop shadows is a common use of the Send to Back command.

1. Draw the top layer of the graphic by using one of PageMaker's tools.

2. Use the Fill command under the Element menu to create a fill pattern.

3. Use the Copy command to create a duplicate graphic, and then use the Paste command to bring the duplicate back onto the same PageMaker page.

   This positions a copy on top of the object, offset slightly down and to the right. You can keep this default setting, or move the graphic to the position where you want the drop shadow (see left side of fig. 11.2).

4. Use the Fill command again to select the shadow pattern.

5. Select the Send to Back command on the Element menu.

The right side of figure 11.2 shows the finished figure with the drop shadow in place.

Fig. 11.2

The drop shadow moved to the desired position (left) and the final graphic with the drop shadow in place.

Wrapping Text around Graphics

You can wrap text around graphics with PageMaker's Text Wrap command on the Element menu. This is more efficient than manually wrapping text by adding carriage returns or tabs within the text, or creating separate text blocks. The Text Wrap dialog box enables you to choose different options for wrapping text. Under Wrap Option, you decide whether the text should overlap the graphic, wrap around the rectangular space occupied by the graphic, or wrap around the irregular-nonrectangular-shape created by the graphic. You can set the Text Flow to wrap to the next column, wrap below the graphic, or wrap on both sides of the graphic, if it is narrower than the column. You also specify the Standoff, the distance between the graphic and the text.

By setting the Text Wrap option without a graphic selected, you set the default, which applies to all subsequently placed graphics.

The following sections describe different methods of wrapping text around a graphic, including two methods for forcing text to flow inside a graphic boundary.

Jumping Text over a Graphic

The first text-wrapping method forces the text to jump over the graphic. Follow these steps for this text-wrapping method:

1. First position and size the graphic on the page (see fig. 11.3). Use the Pointer tool to select the graphic.

2. Choose Text Wrap from the Element menu.

3. Select the icon for a rectangular graphic boundary, the middle icon in the top row (see fig. 11.4). Set the Text Flow icon for text jumping over the graphic, the middle icon in the second row. In the Standoff in inches text boxes, type the amount of space that you want between the graphic and the text, the graphic boundary.

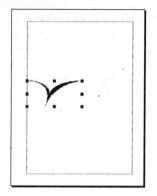

Fig. 11.3

The graphic
positioned and
sized on the
page.

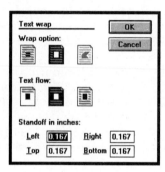

Fig. 11.4

The Text Wrap
dialog box with
the icon for a
rectangular
graphic bound-
ary and the
Standoff in
inches.

4. Click OK to close the dialog box and view the effects (see fig. 11.5).

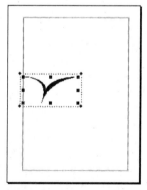

Fig. 11.5

Graphic is
framed in eight
sizing handles
plus a dotted
boundary box
with four
handles.

5. Using the Place command dialog box from the File menu, select a text file in the Place dialog box (as described in Chapter 6) and flow your text on the page. The text continues after the graphic (see fig. 11.6).

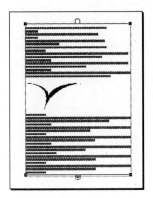

Fig. 11.6

The text jumping over the graphic.

Remember that there are many different approaches to building a page. You need not wait until after you have set up a text wrap option before placing text around a graphic, as implied by step 5. You can place the text first, and then position the graphic and set up the text wrap.

Notice, however, that text wrap added after the text is placed can result in overflow text in the last text block of the story. You can check this quickly by using PageMaker 5.0's Find Overset Text command on the Aldus Additions submenu under the Utilities menu, as described in Chapter 6.

Wrapping Text around the Sides of a Graphic

The second text-wrapping method wraps text around both sides of a graphic—or one side if the graphic is positioned against the text margin. Follow these steps for this method:

1. Place and size the graphic in the column. Use the Pointer tool to select the graphic (see fig. 11.7).

2. Choose Text Wrap from the Element menu.

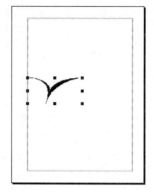

Fig. 11.7

The graphic
positioned and
sized on the
page.

3. Select the icon for a rectangular graphic boundary—the second
   icon in the top row.

4. In the Standoff in inches text boxes, type the amount of space
   between the graphic and the text.

5. Set the Text Flow icon to wrap around the text—the third icon in
   the second row (see fig. 11.8).

Fig. 11.8

The Text Wrap
dialog box with
the icon selected
for a rectangular
graphic bound-
ary, Standoff in
Inches set, and
Text Wrap set for
wrapping around
the graphic.

6. Place the text (see fig. 11.9).

Creating a Custom-Shaped Graphic Boundary

All graphics in PageMaker have rectangular boundaries unless you customize the boundary around the graphic. A custom boundary can take
any shape you want and can create interesting design options on the
page.

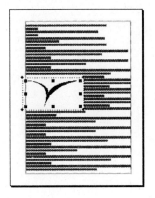

Fig. 11.9

The text wrapped around the graphic.

To create a custom boundary, follow these steps:

1. Click on the graphic and choose the Text Wrap command in the Element menu.

2. Select the second Wrap Option and the third Text Flow option, which forces the text to wrap on all sides of the graphic (see fig. 11.10).

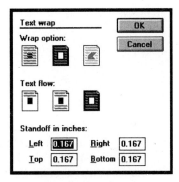

Fig. 11.10

The initial Text Wrap options for the custom-shaped graphic.

3. Click OK. Diamond-shaped handles appear around the graphic boundary (see fig. 11.11).

4. To change the shape of the boundary, drag the diamond-shaped handles to form a new shape (see fig. 11.12). You can add more diamond-shaped handles by clicking on the graphic boundary where you want the new handle to appear. To erase a handle, drag it on top of another handle.

Fig. 11.11

Diamond-shaped
handles around
selected graphic.

Fig. 11.12

Forming a new
graphic shape.

5. After the custom boundary is in place (see fig. 11.13), if you
   choose the Text Wrap command again you will see that the third
   Wrap option is now selected in the Text Wrap dialog box, the irregular boundary (see fig. 11.14). You can still change the Text
   Flow option to choose whether you want the text to flow around
   part or all of the graphic.

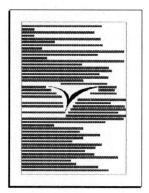

Fig. 11.13

Text wrapped
around a custom-
shaped graphic.

Fig. 11.14

The Text Wrap
options for the
custom-shaped
graphic.

Regulating Text Flow   T I P

When changing the shape of the graphic boundary, hold down the
space bar to stop text from flowing until all the boundaries have
been readjusted.

Flowing Text Inside an Irregular Shape

There are several ways of forcing text to flow inside a graphic boundary
rather than around the outside. We describe three methods here. In
all three cases, you have to start with rectangle or ellipse drawn in
PageMaker in order to get to the Text Wrap dialog box, but we end up
making it small and invisible, so only the text is apparent in the shape
of the text wrap boundary.

Reversing Text Wrap Boundary Points

By this method, you simply reverse the corners of the text wrap boundary on a rectangle. In these steps, you add the text last, but you can
also go through these steps by drawing the rectangle on top of the text.

1. Use the Rectangle tool to draw a rectangle the size of the shape
    you want to fill (see fig. 11.15).

Fig. 11.15

A box
created with
PageMaker's
Rectangle tool.

2. Choose Text Wrap from the Element menu. Select the icon for a
    rectangular graphic boundary as the Wrap option—the second
    icon in the top row—and select the third icon in the second row
    (see fig. 11.16). Then click OK to close the dialog box. (Standoff
    values do not matter here.)

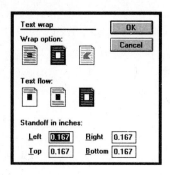

Fig. 11.16

The Text Wrap
dialog box with
Text Wrap
selected.

3. With the rectangle still selected and the boundary visible, drag
   the left side of the boundary box across to the right side of the
   box.

   You can drag a side of a text wrap boundary box by holding the
   pointer on the dotted line of the boundary box and holding the
   mouse button until the pointer becomes a four-pointed arrow, and
   then dragging (see fig. 11.17).

Fig. 11.17

Boundary box
before (left) and
after (right) left
edge of bound-
ary box dragged
to right edge of
box.

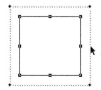

4. Drag the top left handle of the boundary box across to the right
   side of the box (see fig. 11.18).

   You cannot drag a whole side of a boundary box beyond its opposite side, but you can have the same effect by dragging individual
   handles.

5. Drag the bottom left handle of the boundary box across to the
   right side of the box (see fig. 11.19).

   By these three steps, you have effectively "flipped" the boundary
   box: the two handles that were originally on the left of the box are
   now on the right, and vice versa.

6. Drag the rectangle to position the top left corner of the boundary
   box beyond the left margin of the text block (see fig. 11.20).

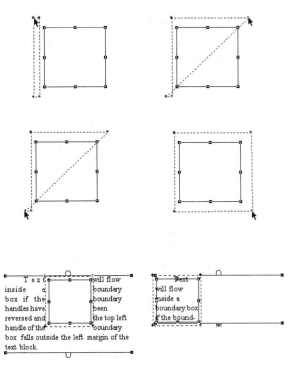

Fig. 11.18

Top left handle before (left) and after (right) being dragged.

Fig. 11.19

Bottom left handle before (left) and after (right) being dragged.

Fig. 11.20

Text flows around box (left) unless top left corner of boundary box is beyond left margin of text block (right).

The text should now fall inside the graphic boundary (see fig. 11.20). You can continue to adjust the handles of the text wrap boundary as much as you want—so long as the top left corner of the boundary box remains outside the left text margin.

Note that if the top corner of the boundary box falls inside the text block, text will wrap outside the box. When you position the boundary box corner beyond the left margin, PageMaker changes the size of the text block to force it to be the depth of the boundary box. Text can be flowed above and below this text in separate text blocks, but you might have to create the separate text block yourself (using techniques described in Chapter 6) (see fig. 11.21).

The graphic rectangle is still visible. You can keep the border visible if you want and manipulate the rectangle and boundary further to frame the text—the boundary box can even be inside the rectangle (see fig. 11.22). You can add a fill to the rectangle and set the text in reverse if you like.

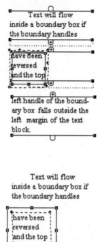

Fig. 11.21

Text flowed above and below in separate text blocks.

Fig. 11.22

Boundary box inside rectangle.

If you do not want the rectangle to be visible, follow the next steps.

7. With the rectangle still selected and the boundary visible, choose "None" from the Line submenu under the Element menu, and choose "Paper" from the Fill submenu.

If you want to adjust the boundary box later, remember that the boundary box will be visible only when the rectangle is selected, and that you can move individual points or sides of the boundary box independently, but to move the whole boundary box you must move the rectangle. For this reason, we give the rectangle a "Paper" fill so it can be selected by clicking it (see fig. 11.23). (If the rectangle had no line and no fill, it could only be selected by dragging the mouse and capturing it using the selection marquee described in Chapter 5.)

You can instead assign a fill to match whatever background you want, if another graphic falls below the text layer.

Since the white rectangle now conceals part of the text, there's one more step to completion.

8. With the rectangle still selected and the boundary visible, choose Send to Back from the Element menu (see fig. 11.24).

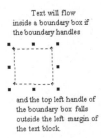

Fig. 11.23

White-filled rectangle conceals the text.

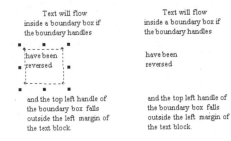

Fig. 11.24

White rectangle is sent to back layer (left) then deselected (right).

You can select the rectangle by holding the Ctrl key as you click the pointer on the text, to click through layers.

You can add new points to the edges of the boundary box by clicking on it, and drag the added points to create unusual effects (see fig. 11.25).

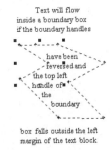

Fig. 11.25

Text wrapped inside irregular borders.

Text in a Circle

With a lot of patience, you can force text to flow inside a circle or ellipse. This is the first of two methods.

1. Use the Ellipse tool to draw a circle or ellipse the shape you want the text to wrap into, preferably on the pasteboard or an empty area of the page (see fig. 11.26).

Fig. 11.26

An ellipse drawn
to the shape of
the text to be
wrapped.

2. Choose Text Wrap from the Element menu. Select the icon for a rectangular graphic boundary as the Wrap option—the second icon in the top row—and select the third icon in the second row (see fig. 11.27). Then click OK to close the dialog box. (Standoff values do not matter here.)

   The standoff measurements entered here can be approximate—you can adjust the final size of the boundary later by dragging its handles in layout view. In this case, we're creating a boundary box that will be 3 inches square (see fig. 11.27).

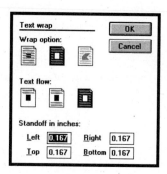

Fig. 11.27

The Text Wrap
dialog box with
Text Wrap
selected.

3. With the ellipse still selected and the boundary visible, drag the left side of the boundary box across to the right side of the box (two right circles in fig. 11.28). Drag the top right boundary handle and then the bottom right boundary handle across to the left side of the ellipse.

   By these steps, you have effectively "flipped" the boundary box: the two handles that were originally on the left of the ellipse are now on the right, and vice versa.

4. This next step is time-consuming. Click on the boundary box to create many additional points, and drag each one to match the edges of the circle—or a little inside if you want to inset the text from the visible ellipse border (see fig. 11.29).

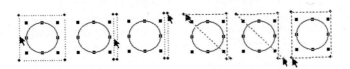

Fig. 11.28

Reversing left and right sides of the boundary box.

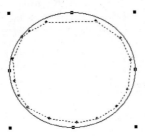

Fig. 11.29

Boundary box conforms to ellipse edges.

5. Drag the ellipse to position it over the text block you wish to "capture" (see fig. 11.30).

As for my next book, I am going to hold myself from writing it till I have it ... im- pend- ing i ... m ... g... hea...

Fig. 11.30

Ellipse positioned over the text.

6. Position the ellipse such that one of the sizing handles that frames the ellipse's rectangular limit extends beyond the left edge of the text block (see fig. 11.31).

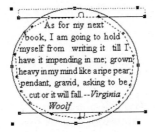

As for my next book, I am going to hold myself from writing it till I have it impending in me; grown heavy in my mind like a ripe pear; pendant, gravid, asking to be cut or it will fall. --*Virginia Woolf*

Fig. 11.31

The ellipse's left sizing handles extend beyond left margin of text block.

The text should now fall inside the graphic boundary. You can continue to adjust the handles of the text wrap boundary as much as you want—so long as the top left corner of the sizing box remains outside the left text margin.

When you position the ellipse beyond the left margin, PageMaker changes the size of the text block to force it to be the depth of the boundary box. Text can be flowed above and below this text in separate text blocks, but you might have to create the separate text block yourself (using techniques described in Chapter 6).

The graphic ellipse is still visible. You can keep the border visible if you want and manipulate the rectangle and boundary further to frame the text—the boundary box can even be inside the ellipse. You can add a fill to the ellipse and set the text in reverse if you like.

If you do not want the ellipse to be visible, follow steps 7 and 8 in the previous series.

Text in a Circle: The Pan Handle Method

The second method described here is called the "pan handle" method because the final boundary box looks like a circular pan with one point extended out to beyond the left edge of the text block.

1-5. Follow the first 5 steps of the previous method.

6. Drag one point from the boundary box to position it beyond the left margin of the text block (see fig. 11.32).

Fig. 11.32

Extended corner or "pan handle" of boundary box is beyond left margin of text block.

When you position the "pan handle" of the boundary box beyond the left margin, PageMaker changes the size of the text block to force it to be the depth of the boundary box. Text can be flowed above and below this text in separate text blocks, but you might have to create the separate text block yourself (using techniques described in Chapter 6).

Using Text Wrap To Create Unequal Gutter Widths

When you set up columns on a page using PageMaker's Column Guides command, PageMaker forces gutters of equal width between all the columns. If your design calls for unequal gutter widths on just one page, you can easily change the text width by dragging a handle of the text block. If you want the same unequal columns on every page, you can draw a line on the master page and use the Text Wrap feature to force this condition.

For example, to create the wider gutter before the first column in the publication shown in figure 11.35, follow these steps.

1. First use the Column Guides command from the Layout menu to set the gutter width to the narrowest gutter you want on the page.

2. Place the text in columns now, or at the end of these steps.

3. Use the Constrained-line tool to draw a line between the first and second column (see fig. 11.33).

Fig. 11.33

Line drawn between first and second column.

4. With the line selected, use the Text Wrap command to set text Wrap on and specify the standoff (see fig. 11.34). Click OK to close the dialog box.

   If you want the gutter to force text in both columns off by the same amount, position the line in the center of the gutter and specify a left and right standoff equal to half the apparent gutter width you wish to achieve. If you want the gutter to force the text in the left column farther left, draw the line on the left edge of the gutter and specify a left standoff equal to the distance you want to force the text left. Right standoff can be zero (see fig. 11.34).

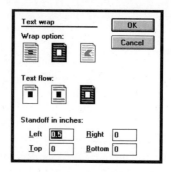

5. With the line still selected, use the Line submenu under the
Element menu to set the line to "None" so it is invisible (see
fig. 11.35).

See Chapter 5 for more information on using the Column Guides
command.

For Related Information

◀◀ "Setting Column Guides," p. 185.

◀◀ "Selecting with the Pointer Tool and Text Tool," p. 204.

◀◀ "Importing Text by Using the Place Command," p. 232.

◀◀ "Working with Text Blocks," p. 257.

◀◀ "Importing Graphics Created in Other Programs," p. 363.

Using Inline Graphics

PageMaker lets you position *inline graphics*, graphics that are part of the text and move with the text. This capability is useful for incorporating symbols as part of a sentence, as shown in figure 11.36, and for positioning figures next to captions when you want them to move with the text flow, as shown in figure 11.37.

Fig. 11.36

Inline graphics can be symbols incorporated within a sentence.

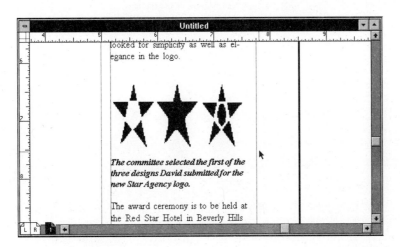

Fig. 11.37

Inline graphics can be figures above a caption and part of the text flow.

Adding an Inline Graphic Using the Paste Command

You can use two methods to create an inline graphic. Both methods can be used in Layout view or in Story view and work with any graphic created using PageMaker's tools or a graphic that has been imported. The only difference is that in Layout view you see the graphic on-screen exactly as it will print, and on Story view you see inline graphics as small gray box icons within the text.

Follow these steps to use the first method:

1. Select a graphic that is already part of the PageMaker publication and choose Cut or Copy from the Edit menu (see fig. 11.38, left).

2. Select the Text tool and position the text insertion point in the text where you want the inline graphic to appear (see fig. 11.38, middle).

3. Choose Paste from the Edit menu (see fig. 11.38, right).

Fig. 11.38

The rectangle selected and copied (left), text cursor positioned at end of paragraph (middle), and graphic pasted into text (right).

and any one of us would be lucky to come to the same end.

and any one of us would be lucky to come to the same end.

You can scale it with the Pointer tool as described next, under "Editing Inline Graphics."

T I P   **Forcing Screen Redraw**

If part or all of the inline graphic seems to disappear, select the current view from the View submenu under the Layout menu—this forces the screen to redraw. You can instead change to a different view of the screen, or click the secondary mouse button twice to toggle between Actual Size and Fit in Window views.

Adding an Inline Graphic Using the Place Command

The second method of creating an inline graphic is applicable to graphics that are imported into PageMaker.

Follow these steps to use this method:

1. Select the Text tool and position the text insertion point in the text where you want the inline graphic to appear (see fig. 11.39).

and any one of us
would be lucky to
come to the same
end.|

Text cursor positioned within text block.

2. Choose Place from the File menu. Select the graphic you want to import as an inline graphic from the Place dialog box (see fig. 11.40).

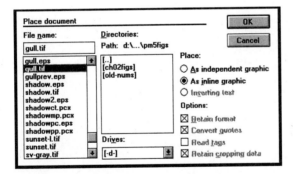

Fig. 11.40

The Place dialog box with Inline graphics selected.

3. Click OK to close the dialog box and view the effect (see fig. 11.41).

If part or all of the inline graphic seems to disappear, select the current view from the View submenu under the Layout menu—this forces the screen to redraw.

You can scale the graphic with the Pointer tool or adjust the baseline as described next.

Fig. 11.41

The graphic
appears within
the text.

and any one of us
would be lucky to
come to the same
end.

Editing Inline Graphics

Inline graphics display handles when selected, and they can be scaled
and cropped like any other graphic in Layout view. You can apply color
to inline graphics and manipulate them through the Image Control command if they are paint or TIFF images. Story view is represented by a
graphic symbol only and cannot be manipulated as a graphic unless
you return to Layout view (see Chapters 5 and 9).

Inline graphics can be formatted like any text. You can use commands
under the Type menu to set indents, leading, tracking, and kerning, as
described in Chapter 8. You can adjust the baseline by dragging the
graphic up or down with the Pointer tool in Layout view, or changing
the Baseline Shift value in the Control palette or in the Type Options
dialog box (see fig. 8.3 and fig. 8.8, in Chapter 8), but you cannot drag
an inline graphic from one line of text to another. To move an inline
graphic, you must select it with the Text tool, choose the Cut command, and then position the text insertion point at the new location,
and choose Paste.

When you select an inline graphic with the Text tool and choose the
Type Specs command from the Type menu, PageMaker displays the
Inline specifications dialog box (see fig. 11.42). You can adjust the leading (distance above or below the baseline) and tracking (distance between the inline graphic and adjacent characters). Chapter 8 describes
both these options in more detail as they apply to ordinary text, and
they work the same way for graphics.

Fig. 11.42

Inline Specifica-
tions dialog box.

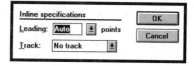

If part or all of the inline graphic seems to disappear, select the current
view from the View submenu under the Layout menu—this forces the
screen to redraw.

Creating Boxed Text as an Inline Graphic

You can insert a box as an inline graphic and make it frame the text that follows it. This is a good alternative to using PageMaker's text rules to create lines above and below paragraphs of text (but not boxes), or to creating the boxed text as a separate story that is not part of the main story (since you cannot include two elements—a text block and a rectangle—as a single inline graphic).

1. Use PageMaker's Rectangle tool to draw a box the size you want—column width, for example (see fig. 11.43).

2. With the rectangle selected, choose Copy or Cut from the Edit menu.

3. Select the Text tool, and position the cursor at the beginning of the text you want boxed. Press Enter once to create a new line.

4. Use the arrow key to move back up to the new blank line, and choose Paste from the Edit menu to bring the rectangle into the text as an inline graphic (see fig. 11.44).

We know you will be
happy with this product if
you follow these simple
guidelines.

Instructions:
1. Wear latex gloves

**Caution: Do not let the
liquid come in contact
with skin.**

2. Wipe all surfaces.

We know you will be
happy with this product if
you follow these simple
guidelines.

Instructions:
1. Wear latex gloves

**Caution: Do not let the
liquid come in contact
with skin.**

2. Wipe all surfaces.

5. Triple-click on the box with the Text tool (I-beam) to select the entire paragraph, including the carriage return.

6. Choose Leading from the Type menu and set the leading value to 0.1 point, or set leading through the Control palette (see fig. 11.45).

Fig. 11.45

Box shifts with
leading change.

If part or all of the inline graphic seems to disappear, select the
current view from the View submenu under the Layout menu—
this forces the screen to redraw.

7. Select the box with the Pointer tool and drag it as low as possible—so the top of the box meets the baseline of its paragraph
(see fig. 11.46).

8. Drag the lower right corner to make the box column width (or
whatever width you choose) and the depth of the text you wish to
box (see fig. 11.46).

Fig. 11.46

Box dragged as
low as possible
and scaled to
encompass the
desired lines of
text with Pointer
tool.

We know you will be
happy with this product if
you follow these simple
guidelines.

Instructions:
1. Wear latex gloves

**Caution: Do not let the
liquid come in contact
with skin.**

2. Wipe all surfaces.

9. Use the Text tool to select the boxed lines of text; then use the
Indents/Tabs command or the Control palette to set left and right
indents for the boxed text (see fig. 11.47).

You might need to readjust the depth of the box after this step if
changing the indents adds a line of text.

10. If you want to select the box again with the Text tool, to delete it
or change the line and fill settings, it will be easier to select it in
Story view, where it is an icon on a line of its own.

We know you will be
happy with this product if
you follow these simple
guidelines.

Instructions:
1. Wear latex gloves

**Caution: Do not let
the liquid come in
contact with skin.**

2. Wipe all surfaces.

Fig. 11.47

Text indented
within the box.

Handling Figures and Figure Captions

In most cases, you want text blocks to be linked continuously throughout a publication, article, or story. If you place figures as inline graphics
and keep the figure captions as part of the main story, they flow with
the text. You can place illustrations as inline graphics on lines of their
own above each caption. Select the figure with the Text tool (or simply
position the text cursor on the line with the figure) and use the Paragraphs command from the Type menu, or the Control palette in Paragraph view, to specify the space above and below the figure. It's also
a good idea to set the leading to Auto and click the Spacing button in
the Paragraph dialog box to set the Autoleading percent to 100% for
the graphic. The most efficient way to make this spacing consistent
throughout the publication is to set up a style (as described in Chapter 8) and apply it to each line that contains an inline figure.

If you do *not* want PageMaker to move figures and captions when you
edit the text preceding the caption, the following three methods of
separating captions from text are available:

■ You can type each caption individually in PageMaker.

■ You can use a word processor and type all the captions in a
separate caption file. You then place that file as a stream separate from the rest of the text. This procedure is useful if you do
not know exactly where you will put each figure in the final
publication.

■ You can type the captions into the main text file. When you place
the text, use the Cut and Paste commands to separate the captions from the body of the text and make them individual unlinked
blocks.

In any case, the illustrations can be placed as independent graphics,
or as inline graphics within the figure caption text block—to take advantage of the paragraph spacing features mentioned above for inline
figures.

Including Symbols in Text

Special symbols commonly are embedded within text. Many software manuals, for example, use symbols to represent special keys outlined in boxes, such as the function keys and the Ctrl and Alt keys. Page-Maker lets you insert inline graphics as part of the text flow so that they move when the text moves. This insertion is an alternative to creating the symbols as a font, and each method offers its own unique benefits.

If you want to insert the symbols as a graphic, use a graphics application to create them, or use PageMaker's built-in graphics tools if the symbols are simple lines, rectangles, or ellipses. Scale the symbols to the desired sizes in the graphics application before importing them into PageMaker. You can scale graphics in the page layout application. If you scale graphics in the graphics application, however, graphics will be the same size every time you import, and you eliminate the inconvenience of repeatedly scaling the graphic.

To create a symbol or set of symbols as a font, you must use a font-generating application, such as Publisher's Type Foundry (Z-Soft). After the font is created and loaded into the system, you can insert the symbols in the text by typing the keyboard characters you assigned for each symbol and using the Font command from the Type menu to select the symbol font.

The advantage of creating the symbols as a font is that you can input them while typing in the word processor or the page layout program. You also can easily and consistently scale them through the type-scaling commands. You can also search and replace characters and fonts. If you set the symbol to the letter E, you can quickly type the text using the letter E as the symbol, and then search for the whole word E and replace it with the letter E in the symbol font.

Working with Reverse Text

When you set text in the Reverse style—available through the Type Style submenu under the Type menu or through the Type Specs command and dialog box—it takes on the color of the background or paper. In order to see reverse text, you can position the reverse type over a black or shaded background by adding a graphic element on the layer below. If the reverse text is part of a larger text block, it's a good idea to anchor the graphic. If the type is 20 points or smaller, you can create reverse type backed by paragraph rules. Both these methods are explained in the next sections.

Layering Reverse Type over a Graphic Element

The most common practice is to use a graphic element as backdrop to reverse type. When working with reverse type larger than 20 points, this is the only way to show the type. (If the type is less than 20 points, you can use a paragraph rule as described next.)

As a production aid, put a nonreverse character at the end of the text (see fig. 11.48). If the reverse text falls on a white (Paper) background, you still can see where the reverse text is in relation to other text and graphics.

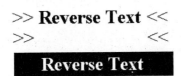

Fig. 11.48

A nonreverse character placed at the end of reverse text.

Anchoring the Background Graphic with a Text Block

You can use the exact same steps described earlier under "Creating Boxed Text as an Inline Graphic" to create a box with a fill as background for reverse text. Go through all the steps described there; then select the box with the Pointer tool and use the Fill and Line command under the Element menu to define the box border and fill. Select the text with the Text tool and choose Reverse from the Type Style submenu under the Type menu. Figure 11.49 shows an example of text handled this way.

Fig. 11.49

Reverse text over an inline black rectangle.

Working with Reverse Type Smaller than 20 Points

When working with reverse type smaller than 20 points, you can use the paragraph rules feature of PageMaker rather than use a graphic element as backdrop to the type. This technique works only if you want whole one-line paragraphs to be reversed.

1. Select the paragraph to be made reverse on a black background.

2. Choose the Paragraph command from the Type menu and click the Rules option in the Paragraph Specifications dialog box. In the Paragraph Rules dialog box, set 12-point rules (the largest available, or smaller if the text is smaller) above and below the line of text (see fig. 11.50).

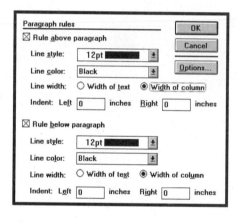

Fig. 11.50

Paragraph Rules dialog box with 12-point rules set above and below the paragraph.

3. Click OK to close the dialog boxes and view the effect.

    If you selected the whole paragraph, it will be shown in reverse video and you have to click away from the text to deselect it and see the effect. Figure 11.51 shows the effect of the same settings— 12-point rules—on text sizes from 24 down to 6. Point sizes over 20 result in a gap between the rules unless you make additional adjustments as described in the next step.

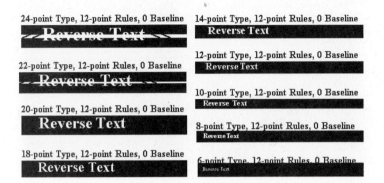

24-point Type, 12-point Rules, 0 Baseline
Reverse Text

22-point Type, 12-point Rules, 0 Baseline
Reverse Text

20-point Type, 12-point Rules, 0 Baseline
Reverse Text

18-point Type, 12-point Rules, 0 Baseline
Reverse Text

14-point Type, 12-point Rules, 0 Baseline
Reverse Text

12-point Type, 12-point Rules, 0 Baseline
Reverse Text

10-point Type, 12-point Rules, 0 Baseline
Reverse Text

8-point Type, 12-point Rules, 0 Baseline
Reverse Text

6-point Type, 12-point Rules, 0 Baseline
Reverse Text

Fig. 11.51

12-point rules set above and below reverse text, from 6- to 24-point sizes.

Notice that the apparent width of the two 12-point rules gets smaller as the point size of the type gets smaller. You can force the two rules to stay wider apart by making adjustments to the leading of the paragraph and to the baseline shift of the rules as described in the next step.

4. If you want to adjust the thickness of the lines, you can try different rule widths, or click the Options button in the Paragraph Rules dialog box to get the Paragraph Rule Options dialog box, and specify the distance of the top rule above the baseline, and a distance for the bottom rule to be below the baseline.

These distances depend on the size of the type, the thickness of the rules, and the amount of black you want above and below the type. Figure 11.52 shows the effect with 24-point type set up with 12-point rules, the top rule positioned .25-inch above the baseline and the bottom rule .05-inch below the baseline. This closes up the gap that occurs with type sizes larger than 20 points when no baseline adjustment is made.

24-point Type,12-point Rules set .25 above and .05 below baseline
Reverse Text

Fig. 11.52

24-point type with 12-point rules shifted above and below baseline.

Creating Zoom Text

Technically speaking, "zoom text" is a term invented by designers to describe text that appears to zoom out from the page, creating a three-dimensional illusion. This is a feature that is built into a command in some illustration programs like CorelDraw and Aldus FreeHand. The term is also applied to the special effect that you get when you layer the same characters on top of each other and offset each one slightly, as described here.

Follow these steps to create the zoom text in figure 11.56.

1. In a new, empty text block, type the word or words you want to zoom, and use the Control palette or the Font and Size submenus from the Type menu to set it the way you want.

   You need not make the text a separate text block, but there are two good reasons for doing this as we recommend. One is that, after step 4, it will be hard to use the Text tool to select all the lines that compose the zoom text in layout view unless you can use the Select All command as used in these steps. Another good reason is that when it is a separate text block you can rotate and skew and mirror it to create the special effects shown in figure 11.59 at the end of this section.

   Also, you can choose or change the font and size later if you want, but you need to be sure that the words fit on one line (see fig. 11.53).

Fig. 11.53

Word fits on one line when set in desired font and size.

2. Press Enter at the end of the text to add one carriage return; then triple-click on the text with the Text tool to select the entire line, including the carriage return, and press Ctrl+C (Copy) as many times as you like—the more copies the deeper the zoom.

   In this case, you make 11 copies (see fig. 11.54).

Fig. 11.54

Eleven copies of the same text, all in the same text block.

SAVE!
SAVE!
SAVE!
SAVE!
SAVE!
SAVE!
SAVE!
SAVE!
SAVE!
SAVE!
SAVE!

3. Beginning at the bottom line and leaving the bottom line black, one by one, select every other line of text and type Ctrl+Shift+V.

   Ctrl+Shift+V is the keyboard shortcut for setting reverse type. You can instead select [Paper] as the color through the Color palette or click the reverse type button in the Control palette in character view. Every other line becomes white or invisible (see fig. 11.55).

SAVE!

SAVE!

SAVE!

SAVE!

SAVE!

SAVE!

Every other line becomes white or invisible.

4. With the text cursor positioned in the text block, choose Select All from the Edit menu (Ctrl+A).

5. With all the words selected, use the Control palette or the Leading submenu under the Type menu to change the leading to a small value.

   If part or all of the text seems to disappear, select the current view from the View submenu under the Layout menu—this forces the screen to redraw.

6. Click away from the text to deselect/select it and view the effect. The zoom affect varies depending on the value you choose here. Smaller values make a tighter zoom (see fig. 11.56).

7. If you want to change the font, size, or leading, click the Text tool on the text and choose Select All from the menu; then use the Control palette or commands under the Type menu to change all the type at once.

   In selecting the text with the Text tool, click the baseline marker of the I-beam (the line that crosses it about one-third the way up from the bottom) as close as possible to the baseline of the text. If you have trouble selecting the text this way, you can open the text in Story view to make changes as described in the next step.

Fig. 11.56

Zoom effects
created with
1-point, 2-point,
and 3-point
leading.

If you have trouble inserting the text cursor in the text block so you can open it in story view, you can choose Edit Story from the Edit menu, and then choose the Find command from the Utilities menu. Type the zoom word, click All Stories, and click Find. The Story view of the zoom text will open.

8. If you want to change each line separately, select individual lines in Story view.

This is the technique you use to create the effects shown in figure 11.57.

Fig. 11.57

Zoom effect
when each line
of text is made
a different shade
of black, from
100 percent to
10 percent in
10-percent
increments (left)
and then a
different size
(right).

Note that to set text in different shades, you can create different shades of black, as described in Chapter 12, and add them to the Color palette.

9. Use the transformation features described later in this chapter to create special effects like those shown in figure 11.58.

FROM HERE...

For Related Information

▸▸ "Creating Color Publications," p. 531.

▸▸ "Applying Colors," p. 559.

Fig. 11.58

Zoom text
rotated, skewed,
and mirrored.

Creating Initial Caps and Drop Caps

The practice of starting a paragraph with a large capital letter is as old as hand-written, illuminated manuscripts, where the initial caps could be detailed illustrations with nymphs picking flowers from ascenders and resting in the bowls of capital B's. The challenge in using initial caps (large letters that sit on the same baseline as the first line of a paragraph) lies primarily in keeping the spacing between lines even. Drop caps (large letters that nestle beside several lines of a paragraph) offer some additional challenges, some of which are solved by PageMaker 5.0's new Drop Cap command. This and other solutions are presented in the next sections.

Creating Large Initial Caps

The leading for any line is determined by the largest characters in that line. If you want to create large initial caps that sit on the same baseline as the first line of a paragraph, you must adjust the leading for the large letter. The first example in figure 11.59 shows a 24-point initial cap with automatic leading in a line of text that is otherwise 8-point type. In the second example, the leading on the 24-point letter has been changed to zero. (You can use a leading measure smaller than the type size when the text has no letters with descenders or is all uppercase.)

Fig. 11.59

Adjusting leading
to create 24-
point initial cap.

Initial caps are large letters at the beginning of a paragraph, on the same baseline as the first line.

Initial caps are large letters at the beginning of a paragraph, on the same baseline as the first line.

If part or all of the text seems to disappear, select the current view from the View submenu under the Layout menu—this forces the screen to redraw.

Using the Drop Cap Utility

PageMaker 5.0 introduces an Aldus Addition named Drop Cap that creates a drop cap at the beginning of a paragraph automatically. This saves the considerable amount of trouble it takes to create one on your own (as explained in the next sections).

To use the Drop Cap feature, follow these steps:

1. Select the Text tool and position the cursor in the paragraph that will have the drop cap; choose Drop Cap from the Aldus Additions submenu under the Utility menu.

2. Enter the number of lines deep that you want the drop cap to extend in the Drop Cap dialog box (see fig. 11.60). Before finalizing the change, you can click Apply to view it. You can also click Remove to remove a drop cap from a paragraph.

   Note that you can move through a series of paragraphs by clicking the Prev or Next paragraph button, selectively applying or removing drop caps, and then clicking OK to apply changes to many paragraphs at once.

3. Click OK. PageMaker automatically creates a large drop cap that sits beside several lines of text, on the baseline of the last line that it affects (see fig. 11.61). PageMaker simply automates the keystrokes and commands that you can go through yourself in creating a drop cap—explained in the next section—adding soft carriage returns and tabs. You can see the results more clearly in the Story Editor.

4. If you want to align the first line of text with the other lines, you can use the Text tool to position the text cursor between the first and second characters in the paragraph and then press the Tab key.

   You may find that the Drop Cap feature works fine without this last step.

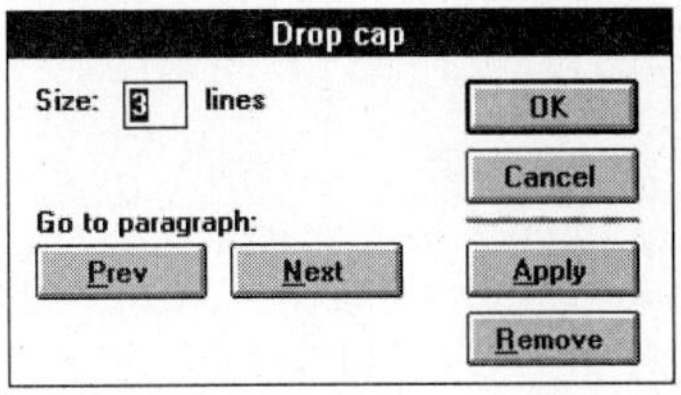

Fig. 11.60

Drop Cap dialog box.

Fig. 11.61

Drop cap in paragraph before and after using the Drop Cap command.

The Drop Cap takes on the same indentation as set for the paragraph. Usually the first-line indentation should be zero—or the same as the left indentation—in paragraphs with drop caps.

5. Check the hyphenation of the first few lines.

When the Drop Cap utility wraps text, it breaks words by inserting soft returns which strip out hyphens. The words are still broken, but you will have to add the hyphens through the keyboard.

6. Avoid editing the first lines of the paragraph (other than hyphens).

Avoid changing the size of the type or making changes to the first line of text. These changes can cause different line breaks. If you change the line breaks, you will have to manually strip out and move the soft carriage returns that the Drop Cap utility inserted.

You cannot undo drop caps or change the number of lines for the drop cap once it is set, unless you first manually undo the process—reverse the steps described in the next section.

Save the Publication before Using the Drop Cap Command

T I P

If you think you will want to undo the drop cap and experiment with different settings, save the publication before using the Drop Cap command. If the results are not what you want, use the Revert command to cancel the drop cap and try a different setting.

Creating Custom Drop Caps as Subscripts

You can create your own custom drop caps by going through the same steps that the Drop Cap utility automates: setting them as subscripts and adjusting their size and position. You can also edit the drop cap created by the Drop Cap utility—change the size or position—if you understand how these steps work.

The following steps show how PageMaker created the custom drop cap shown in figure 11.61. You can also go through these same steps to customize a drop cap created with the Drop Cap utility.

1. Type the paragraph. In this example, the text is set in 12-point Times (see fig. 11.62).

2. Select the first letter (D).

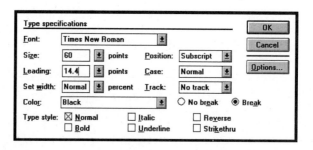

Drop caps are large capital letters at the beginning of para-graphs.

If the paragraph already has a drop cap, this step will be easier in Story view than in Layout view.

3. Use the Type Specs command on the Type menu to display the Type Specifications dialog box. Set the letter larger than the rest (in this case, 60 points), set the leading to match the rest of the text in the paragraph (12-point type with auto leading would have 14.4-point leading), and position the letter as a subscript (see fig. 11.63).

Type specifications		
Font: **Times New Roman**		**OK**
Size: **60** points	Position: **Subscript**	**Cancel**
Leading: **14.4** points	Case: **Normal**	**Options...**
Set width: **Normal** percent	Track: **No track**	
Color: **Black**	○ No break ◉ Break	
Type style: ☒ Normal ☐ Bold	☐ Italic ☐ Underline	☐ Reverse ☐ Strikethru

4. Click the Options button in the Type Specifications dialog box and set the Subscript size to 100% of point size and the Subscript posi-tion to 50% of point size (see fig. 11.64).

Fig. 11.64

Type Options dialog box shows custom settings for subscript size and position.

5. Click OK on the open dialog boxes to close them and view the effects (see fig. 11.65).

   Lines of text overlap the drop cap. If part of the text disappears on the screen, select the current view from the View submenu under the Layout menu to redraw the screen.

Fig. 11.65

The drop cap is overlapped by text.

6. With the text cursor still positioned in the paragraph, use the Indents/Tabs command on the Type menu to display the Indents/Tabs ruler. Set a left tab into position to the right of the drop cap (in this case, 0.656 inches, see fig. 11.66). Then click OK to close the dialog box.

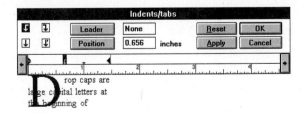

Fig. 11.66

Indents/Tab dialog box shows new tab set to right of drop cap.

7. Press Shift+Enter (soft return or line break) and Tab after each
   line next to the drop cap (see fig. 11.67).

Fig. 11.67

A drop cap
created as a
subscript.

D rop caps are
large capital
letters at
the beginning of
paragraphs.

If the baseline of the drop cap doesn't match exactly the baseline of the
text, you can adjust it through the Control palette (by entering values
or using the nudge buttons) or through the Type Options dialog box.
The Control palette is the better choice because you can see incremental changes by clicking the Apply button as you work.

You can apply your own variations of this technique to create other
drop caps.

Creating Custom Drop Caps as Inline Graphics

There is yet another way to create a custom drop cap, and that is by
placing it as an inline graphic. You can use this technique to place ornate drop caps like the S in figure 11.73, or you can use this technique
to add any symbol or graphic at the beginning of a paragraph—not
necessarily a text character. (If you do want to create a text character
as a graphic, you can use the trick described in the next section.)

1. Create the graphic that you want to position as the drop cap.

   In this example, we will use an ornate "S" scanned from an old
   manuscript. You can also use the trick described in the next section to turn any text character into a graphic. You might simply
   use PageMaker's Rectangle tool to draw a box the size you want to
   create a custom look for your document—in which case you
   would cut or copy it and use the Paste command instead of the
   Place command in the step 3.

2. Select the Text tool, and position the cursor at the beginning of
   the paragraph.

3. Choose Place from the File menu, and click once on the name of
   the graphic you are importing in the Place dialog box, and be sure
   the option to place as an inline graphic is selected (see fig. 11.68).

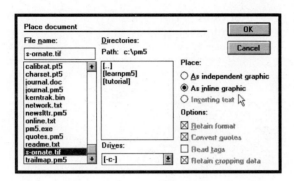

Fig. 11.68

Find the graphic drop cap in the Place dialog box.

4. Click OK to close the dialog box and place the graphic.

   The graphic appears at the cursor position in the paragraph. If it is very small, you might not be able to see it until the next step.

5. Select the graphic with the Pointer tool and drag the lower right corner to make the graphic as large or small as you wish (see fig. 11.69). You can also use the Cropping tool to trim it if you need to.

Fig. 11.69

Use the Pointer tool to scale the graphic to the size you wish.

6. Select the graphic with the Pointer tool and drag it down so the top of the graphic aligns with the ascent height of the first line of the paragraph (see fig. 11.70).

Fig. 11.70

Graphic dragged down so the top of the graphic aligns with the ascent height of the first line of the paragraph.

7. Select the graphic with the Text tool by dragging across it to high-light it (see fig. 11.71).

Fig. 11.71

Graphic high-
lighted with the
Text tool.

8. Choose Leading from the Type menu and set the leading value to
   1 point, or set leading through the Control palette (see fig. 11.72).

   If part or all of the box seems to disappear, select the current view
   from the View submenu under the Layout menu—this forces the
   screen to redraw.

Fig. 11.72

Text around
graphic shifts
with leading
change.

9. With the text cursor still positioned anywhere in the paragraph,
   use the Indents/Tabs command on the Type menu to display the
   Indents/Tabs ruler. Set a left tab into position right of the drop
   cap.

10. One by one, position the text cursor at the end of each line that
    falls next to the drop cap, and press Shift+Enter and Tab to get the
    effect shown in figure 11.73.

Fig. 11.73

A drop cap
created as an
inline graphic.

11. If you want to select the graphic again with the Text tool, to delete
    it or change the line and fill settings, it will be easier to select it in
    Story view, where it is an icon at the beginning of the paragraph
    (see fig. 11.74).

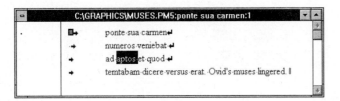

Fig. 11.74

Inline graphic
shows as an icon
in Story view.

Creating Text as a Graphic

If you want to create a drop cap as an inline graphic as described
above, but you want the graphic to simply be text (with no border or
lines added), you can use the trick described here. You add these steps
as extensions of step 3 from the previous sequence, and you can drop
these steps there and go on with the rest of the steps to add the finishing touches to the drop cap shown in figure 11.78.

You can also use the steps described here to create any text as a
graphic, and place it as an inline graphic or as a stand-alone graphic.
(See "Embedding Transformed Text within a Text Block," later in this
chapter.)

3a. Choose Place from the File menu, and click once on the name of
the graphic you are importing in the Place dialog box, and be sure
the option to place as an inline graphic is selected (see fig. 11.75).

In this case, you want to choose the file named DATETIME.TYM.
This is a date/time stamp that comes with PageMaker and is normally found in the ALDUS\USENGLSH\FILTERS directory.

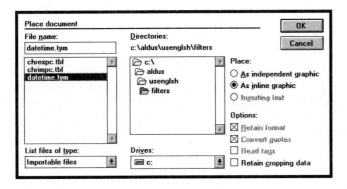

Fig. 11.75

Find the file
named
DATETIME.TYM
in the Place
dialog box.

3b. Click OK to place the DATETIME.TYM file.

PageMaker displays the Time Stamp import filter dialog box (see
fig. 11.76).

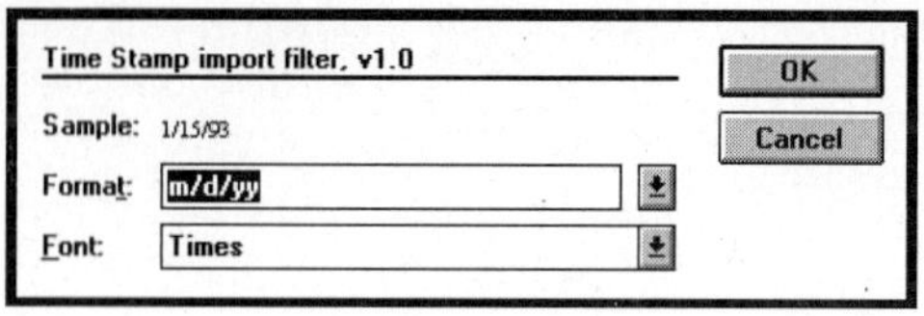

Fig. 11.76

The Time Stamp
import filter
dialog box.

Normally, you enter a date/time format in this dialog box, but you
can also enter any letter of the alphabet in the Format area and
that character will be placed in the publication as a graphic, as
you will see in the next steps.

3c. Type the letter or character that you want to use as the drop cap,
and choose a font (see fig. 11.77).

If you are creating a drop cap using S, H, D, M, or Y, you must precede the character with a backslash (\ ). Otherwise, these characters are interpreted as indicating seconds, hours, day, month or
minutes, or year.

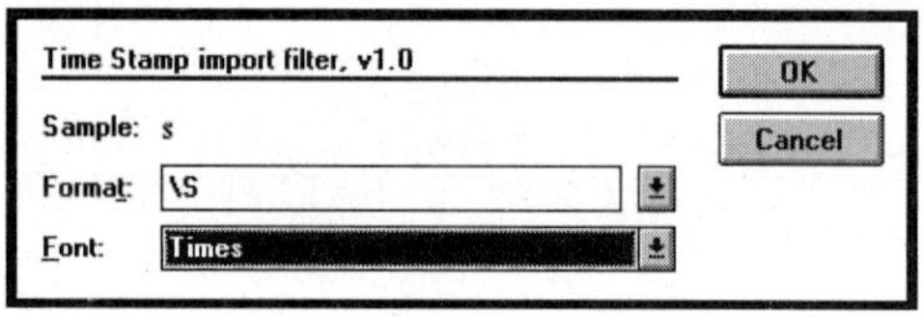

Fig. 11.77

Type any text
character, but
precede S, H, D,
M, or Y with a
backslash.

Since you can choose from any available font, including symbol
fonts like Wingdings or Zapf Dingbats, you can create symbols as
graphics if you like.

You can also type up to 47 characters in this dialog box, to create
graphics out of whole words or phrases.

4. Click OK to close the dialog box.

In this case the text cursor was positioned in text, so the graphic
is placed as an inline graphic. If you are placing it as an independent graphic, you will get a loaded graphic placement icon that
you can click to place the graphic anywhere on the screen. This
technique is used later in this chapter (see "Embedding Transformed Text within a Text Block").

5. Select the graphic with the Pointer tool and drag the lower right
corner to make the graphic as large or small as you wish (see fig.
11.78).

You can also use the Cropping tool to trim it if you need to, and if the graphic seems invisible when you first place it you can make it visible by clicking on it with the Cropping tool.

S ponte sua carmen

numeros veniebat ad aptos et quod temtabam dicere versus erat. Ovid's muses lingered.

Fig. 11.78

Use the Pointer tool to scale the graphic to the size you wish.

6. Go on with steps 6 through 11 in the previous section.

For Related Information

◀◀ "Overriding the Unit of Measure," p. 142.

FROM HERE...

Using the Multiple Paste Command

PageMaker 5.0 adds a new Multiple Paste command that lets you paste multiple copies of the clipboard contents at specified intervals on the page in Layout view. This replaces a little-known technique that was possible with earlier versions of PageMaker, called "power paste," which still works in PageMaker 5.0 and is explained after Multiple Paste here. After explaining the Multiple Paste command and the power paste feature, this section demonstrates how these commands are useful in creating special formats such as bar charts and forms.

Using the Multiple Paste Command

Follow these steps to use the Multiple Paste command.

1. Position the object you wish to copy where you want it on the page before going through the next steps. This will set the first location relative to where the copies will be pasted.

2. Use the Pointer tool in Layout view to select the object or group of objects on the page.

In this example, we simply select a box drawn with PageMaker's Rectangle tool (see fig. 11.79).

Fig. 11.79

A box is
selected.

3. Choose Copy from the Edit menu (Ctrl+C).

4. Choose Multiple Paste from the Edit menu.

5. Enter the number of copies and the horizontal and vertical offset in the Multiple Paste dialog box.

   A positive number in the horizontal offset positions the copies to the right of the copied object(s), or you can enter negative values to position copies to the left. Positive values in the vertical offset area position copies below the copied object(s), negative values put copies above it.

T I P

Determining the Distances for the Multiple Paste Command

Have you ever tried mentally converting the "analog" representation of inches on the ruler lines to decimal values like 1.875 in a dialog box? In PageMaker 5.0, you don't have to guess the distances you want between copies. If you like to work visually at first, make one copy of the object and place it where you want the first multiple-pasted copy to appear. Check the X and Y coordinates of the two objects in the Control palette, and subtract the values from each other. The differences are the values you want to enter in the Multiple Paste dialog box. Don't forget to delete the copy you made for this tip before selecting the original object and using the Multiple Paste command.

The unit of measure shown in the dialog box corresponds to the unit of measure specified in the Preferences dialog box, but you can override the unit by entering abbreviations as explained in Chapter 4: enter **i** after the number for inches, **m** for millimeters, **p** for picas, or **c** for Ciceros.

In this case, we enter 3 copies and a horizontal measure of 1.25 inches (see fig. 11.80).

6. Click OK to close the dialog box and make the copies (see fig. 11.81).

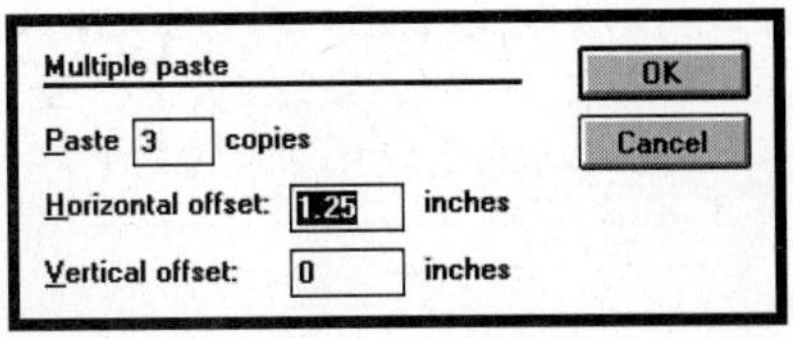

Fig. 11.80

Entries in
Multiple Paste
dialog box.

Fig. 11.81

Copies of the
box are posi-
tioned 1.5 inches
apart.

If the copies did not end up exactly where you expected, you can reposition them individually, but it will usually be more efficient to delete
the copies and go back to step 2 again, making fine adjustments to your
entries in the Multiple Paste dialog box.

Values in the Multiple Paste dialog box remain the same throughout
your work session until you change them. You can make copies of an
object on one page, for example, and then set up any other object in
any other location or on any page (as in steps 1 and 2, above) and use
the Multiple Paste command again to position copies at the same
intervals.

Using Multiple Paste within Text

If the Text tool is selected and the text cursor is inserted within text,
you can paste multiple copies of the text or graphics that are currently
in the clipboard, and they become part of the text or inline graphics. In
either case, you can specify a number of copies but not an offset value.
See "Inline Graphics" earlier in this chapter.

> **CAUTION:** Using the Multiple Paste command in Story view
> (Ctrl+E) does not yield the results you might expect. When you
> select a portion of text in the story in Story view and use the Cut
> (Ctrl+X) or Copy (Ctrl+C) command, using the Multiple Paste com-
> mand creates multiple copies of a new text block that contains the
> Clipboard contents (the Cut or Copied text), and each text block
> is a separate story. The text blocks appear in Layout view; you
> don't see any immediate changes in the Story view windows.

Using the Power Paste Feature

The "power paste" feature described here was the only equivalent to the Multiple Paste command in earlier versions of PageMaker, and you can still use it as an alternative. This might be the preferred method of pasting when you want to position objects visually on the screen rather than numerically through a dialog box. Follow these steps.

1. Position the object you wish to copy where you want it on the page before going through the next steps. This will set the first location relative to where the copies will be pasted.

2. Use the Pointer tool in Layout view to select the object or group of objects on the page.

   In this example, as before, we simply select a box drawn with PageMaker's Rectangle tool (see fig. 11.82).

Fig. 11.82

A box is selected.

3. Choose Copy from the Edit menu (Ctrl+C).

4. Press Ctrl+Shift+P to "power paste" the first copy.

   This puts a copy of the object exactly on top of it. On-screen it might look like nothing happened—it looks like the object you first selected is still selected.

5. Use the Pointer tool to drag the selected copy to the position you wish for the first of the multiple copies. Don't release the mouse button until the copy is exactly where you want it (see fig. 11.83).

Fig. 11.83

Drag the copy to the first position.

6. Hold Ctrl+Shift, and press P as many times as the number of additional copies you want.

   Each time you press Ctrl+Shift+P another copy is created and positioned at the same relative distance from the last copy as you set up in step 5. In this case, we pressed Ctrl+Shift+P three more times (see fig. 11.84).

Fig. 11.84

Three more
copies of the box
appear next to
the first two.

You can use this technique or the Multiple Paste command to create
the common examples described in the next sections—bar charts and
forms—or any other use of multiple copies.

Creating Bar Charts

Bar charts, like the one shown in figure 11.91, are probably the single
most common form of business graphics. Here is a technique for
quickly producing a series of bars in PageMaker, scaled to accurate
dimensions. In this case, we create the bars side-by-side. You can use
similar steps to create bars one above the other.

1. Decide how wide you want to make your bars. Using the Rectangle
   tool, draw a rectangle the width of one bar, and the height of one
   unit on the vertical scale, or a decimal multiple of one unit (that
   is, ten units, one hundred units, one thousand units, and so on).

   For this example we declare the height of the basic bar (the bar
   we will scale in the next step) to be equivalent to $1,000. You can
   draw this rectangle visually on the screen, or specify precise dimensions in the Control palette (see fig. 11.85).

Fig. 11.85

The first rectangle
is the width of all
bars. The height
is equivalent to 1
(or 10 or 100 or
1000, and so
on) unit.

It doesn't matter exactly what size your basic unit is in points or
inches, so long as you know it represents 1, 10, 100, or 1,000 chart
units and it matches the scale you have set up on the axes. You
can make it any height, or you can make it exactly 1.000 inches
tall—you will see how to work with these two alternatives in the
next steps.

2. Select the Text tool, and drag an outline below the bar to create a small text block the width of a bar label. Type a label (in this case, 1990) and choose Align Center from the Alignment submenu under the Type menu.

The results are shown in figure 11.86.

1990

3. Use the Pointer tool to select both the rectangle and the text label (see fig. 11.87); then choose Copy from the Edit menu (Ctrl+C).

1990

In the next steps, we will use the Multiple Paste command, but you can instead use the power paste feature described earlier. Remember to hold the Shift key when dragging the first copy to keep it to precise horizontal movement.

4. Choose Multiple Paste from the Edit menu.

5. Enter the number of bars minus one as the number of copies and the offset in the Multiple Paste dialog box.

In this case, we enter 3 copies and a horizontal measure of 1.25 inches (see fig. 11.88).

6. Click OK to close the dialog box and make the copies (see fig. 11.89).

Multiple paste

OK

Paste 3 copies

Cancel

Horizontal offset: 1.25 inches

Vertical offset: 0 inches

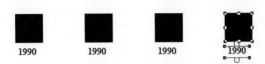

Fig. 11.89

Copies of the box are positioned 1.5 inches apart.

7. Choose Control palette from the Window menu (if that palette is not already displayed).

8. One by one, select each bar, and then click the bottom center reference point on the Proxy and make an entry in the percentage-scaling option next to the Height area in the Control palette.

   The table below shows the values to use in scaling for this example. The results are shown in figure 11.90.

Bar #	Desired value	Vertical Scale
1	$550	55%
2	$800	80%
3	$1,000	100%
4	$1,200	120%

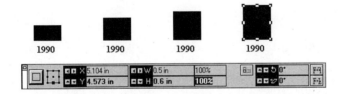

Fig. 11.90

Bars of different heights.

Changing Scaling Percentages

T I P

You will notice that after you have changed a scaling percentage on a graphic drawn with one of PageMaker's tools, then moved on to another object, the scale shows 100% again when you return to the object. The scaling percentage doesn't change for imported graphics—it shows 100% only if the graphic is the same size as when imported.

9. Finish the chart by editing the text labels below each bar and add-ing a title, legend, and caption, if appropriate (see fig. 11.91).

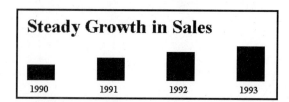

Fig. 11.91

The finished chart.

You can use PageMaker's Line tool to add axes if you like. You can also use the Line tool and the Multiple Paste command or power paste to add tick marks on the vertical axis.

Creating Forms

You can use the Multiple Paste command or power paste feature to create forms composed of repeated lines drawn with PageMaker's Line tool, or you can use paragraph rules as part of the text to get a similar effect. These two alternatives are described next.

Using Paragraph Rules

The most efficient way of creating evenly-spaced horizontal ruled lines is to set them up as rules in a text block. This feature is described in detail in Chapter 8, but here we show some specific examples of using rules to create forms. Remember that you set up paragraph rules by inserting the cursor in a paragraph, choosing Paragraph from the Type menu and clicking the Rules button in the Paragraph Specifications dialog box to get the Rules dialog box (see fig. 11.92).

Figure 11.93 shows text set in 12-point Times with 24-point leading and one-point rules above each paragraph. Instead for formatting the "City State Zip" line differently—adding a rule below the paragraph as well—an extra carriage return is added after "Zip" to create a blank line with the same 1-point rule above the paragraph that effectively adds a rule below "City State Zip."

```
Paragraph rules                    [    OK    ]
☒ Rule above paragraph             [  Cancel  ]
   Line style:    [ 1pt ————  ⬍ ]
   Line color:    [ Black      ⬍ ]  [ Options... ]
   Line width:    ○ Width of text  ◉ Width of column
   Indent:  Left [0]  inches  Right [0]  inches

☐ Rule below paragraph
   Line style:    [ 1pt ————  ⬍ ]
   Line color:    [ Black      ⬍ ]
   Line width:    ○ Width of text  ◉ Width of column
   Indent:  Left [0]  inches  Right [0]  inches
```

Fig. 11.92

Paragraph Rules dialog box.

Name

Company

Address

City   State   Zip

Fig. 11.93

Text set in 12-point Times with 24-point leading and 1-point rules above each paragraph.

You can adjust the distance between the rule and the baseline through the Paragraph Rule Options dialog box (see fig. 11.94), accessed by clicking the Options button in the Paragraph Rules dialog box (refer to fig. 11.92).

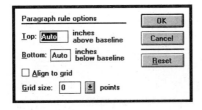

```
Paragraph rule options              [    OK    ]
Top: [Auto]  inches above baseline  [  Cancel  ]
Bottom: [Auto] inches below baseline [  Reset  ]
☐ Align to grid
Grid size: [0]  ⬍ points
```

Fig. 11.94

Paragraph Rule Options dialog box.

As long as the ruler settings are the same for every line in the text, and the text is set in one size with one leading value, the distance between the ruled lines will be equal to the leading value plus the space above and below paragraph (set in the Paragraph Specifications dialog box).

T I P — **Using Leading To Control the Distance between Lines in a Series**

You can adjust the space above and below paragraphs to change the distance between the rules, or you can adjust the leading, as we did in this example. This is the best way to control the distance between the lines precisely—the distance between the lines will always be equal to the leading so long as the space above and below each paragraph is set to zero. Otherwise, you will have to calculate the distance between lines as the sum of the leading (usually in points) plus the space above and below paragraphs (usually in inches, or in picas and points).

One of the great advantages of using paragraph rules rather than lines drawn with PageMaker's Line tool in creating forms is that you can quickly change the distance between the lines by changing the leading or paragraph spacing.

Because you can rotate and skew text in PageMaker, you can even use paragraph rules to create vertical lines and slanted headings, like those shown in figure 11.95.

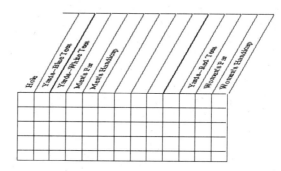

Fig. 11.95

Vertical lines and slanted text labels created using paragraph rules and the rotate and skew features.

You can set paragraph rules to a color that is different from the text by selecting Line Color in the Paragraph Rules dialog box. You can also use the Define Colors command to set up tints as new colors, such as the 30 percent gray used in figure 11.96.

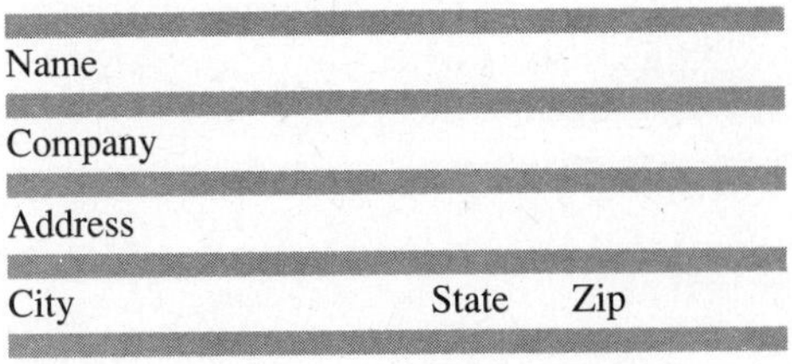

Name		
Company		
Address		
City	State	Zip

Fig. 11.96

Paragraphs with 30%-gray rules.

The primary limitation to using paragraph rules to create evenly spaced ruled lines is that they can only have two line lengths—width of text or width of column. You can get around this limitation by using underscores in the text or PageMaker's Line tool to create lines, as described next.

Using Underscores in the Text

You can type a series of underscores to create ruled lines in text. This enables you to create forms with entry areas of variable length (not just text width or column width, as for paragraph rules). The one caution is that in some fonts a series of underscores prints like a dashed line— with tiny gaps between each character. Test the font you intend to use before creating a complex form this way.

You can type the underscores using the keyboard, or, if the entry areas fall at regular intervals on each line, set up tabs with underscores as the tab leader character in the Indents/Tabs dialog box. Tabs are explained in detail in Chapter 8. Figure 11.97 shows two forms that were created using underscores.

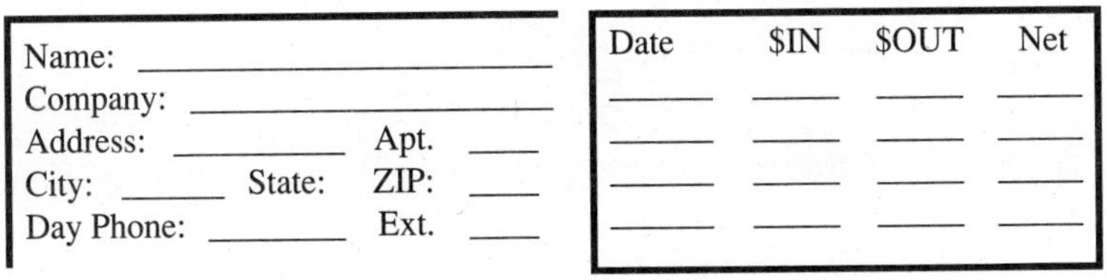

Fig. 11.97

Forms created by setting up tabs with underscore as the tab leader (left) and by typing underscores (right).

Name: _____
Company: _____
Address: _____ Apt. ____
City: ____ State: ZIP: ____
Day Phone: _____ Ext. ____

| Date | $IN | $OUT | Net |

In general, it's less efficient (more time consuming) to set up underscores than to use paragraph rules, if you have a choice. Another drawback of using underscores in designing a form is that you have little control over the thickness or style of the lines. Paragraph rules (described earlier) and lines drawn with the Line tool (described next) offer a wide assortment of line styles.

Using PageMaker's Line Tool

PageMaker's Line tool can be used in combination with the Multiple Paste command to create ruled lines on forms easily. The Multiple Paste command—and the power paste alternative—were described earlier in this chapter. Here we offer a few examples of forms created using ruled lines that would have been more difficult or impossible using paragraph rules or underscores—the otherwise preferred methods of putting lines on forms.

Overlapping Lines

PageMaker offers a variety of line styles through the Line submenu of Fill and line command under the Element menu, but you can create your own custom effects by layering one style of line on top of another and by assigning custom line weights through the Line or Fill and Line commands under the Element menu. Figure 11.98 shows a few varieties of lines created by overlapping two styles.

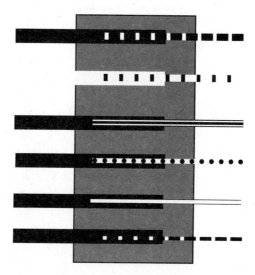

Fig. 11.98

Different line styles layered on top of one another create new styles.

Form Composed of Alternating White and Gray Bars

The first example, figure 11.102, shows a form composed of lines of text over a series of gray rectangles with a line of None and a gray fill. If your text is less than 12 points, you can create the same effect by drawing lines and assigning them a gray color.

1. Type the text first, and set up the desired the font, size, leading, and paragraph spacing.

2. Draw the first line (or rectangle) to frame the first line of text below the heading (see fig. 11.99).

   Size and position the first rectangle carefully over the text.

Item	Aisle
Frozen Foods	6
Fruits (Canned)	7
Fruits (Fresh)	12
Fruits (Frozen)	6
Paper Products	4
Vegetables (Canned)	8
Vegetables (Fresh)	12
Vegetables (Frozen)	6

Fig. 11.99

First line of text framed in a rectangle.

3. Select the rectangle with the Pointer tool and choose Copy from the Edit menu (Ctrl+C).

   In the next step, using the power-paste method of copying is recommended, as described earlier in this chapter. If you want to use the Multiple Paste command, you should enter a vertical offset equivalent to twice the sum of the text leading plus paragraph spacing values. Remember that this will be a complicated calculation if the leading is specified in points and the paragraph spacing is set in inches or picas. It will be easier if the text has zero space above and below the paragraphs; then you can specify the vertical distance using the abbreviation for points and picas. For example, if the text has 24-point leading and you want one gray box behind every other line, you enter a 48-point vertical offset by typing 0p48 in the Multiple Paste dialog box. If all this planning and calculating seems too left-brained for you, use the power-paste method described in the next steps.

4. Before going through the next steps, you can zoom in to a 200% or 400% view of the left edge of the text and the rectangle for maximum precision in positioning the first copy of the line.

5. Press Ctrl+Shift+P to power paste a copy of the rectangle exactly on top of the first one.

6. Use the Pointer tool to drag the copy over the third line of text after the heading, skipping one line of text and holding the Shift key as you drag to keep the movement vertical. Position the rectangle carefully before releasing the mouse button (see fig. 11.100).

Size and position the second rectangle carefully over the third line of text.

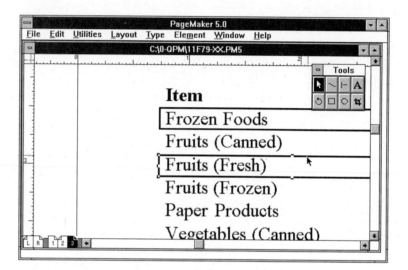

Fig. 11.100

Third line of text framed in a second rectangle.

7. Zoom back out to Actual Size or Fit In Window view for the next step.

8. Press Ctrl+Shift+P as many times as necessary to place more copies of the rectangle over subsequent lines of text (see fig. 11.101).

9. Use the Pointer tool to drag a marquee around all the rectangles. Shift+click on the text block to deselect/select it and any other element that is not one of the rectangles you just created.

10. Choose Fill and Line from the Element menu and set the Fill to 30% and Line to None.

11. Choose Send to Back from the Element menu.

The final result is lines of text backed by alternating stripes of white (or paper color) and gray (see fig. 11.102).

Item	Aisle
Frozen Foods	6
Fruits (Canned)	7
Fruits (Fresh)	12
Fruits (Frozen)	6
Paper Products	4
Vegetables (Canned)	8
Vegetables (Fresh)	12
Vegetables (Frozen)	6

Fig. 11.101

Rectangles frame every other line of text.

Item	Aisle
Frozen Foods	6
Fruits (Canned)	7
Fruits (Fresh)	12
Fruits (Frozen)	6
Paper Products	4
Vegetables (Canned)	8
Vegetables (Fresh)	12
Vegetables (Frozen)	6

Fig. 11.102

Form composed of lines of text backed by wide lines set in light gray.

If the rectangle around the last line of text does not frame the text with the same relative positioning as the rectangle around the first line of text, or if you decide to change the font or size of the text and this shifts the text away from the rectangles, select all the text with the Text tool and make incremental changes to the leading.

Changing the Space between Lines

T I P

Once you have created a series of lines using the Line tool and the Multiple Paste command, there is no easy way to change the spacing between them. The best method might be to delete all but the first line and use the Multiple Paste command again to space them differently.

One of the great advantages of using paragraph rules rather than lines drawn with PageMaker's Line tool in creating forms is that you can quickly change the distance between the lines by changing the leading or paragraph spacing.

Creating a Calendar

The monthly calendar format is ideal for using PageMaker's drawing tools instead of paragraph rules for three reasons. First, the basic grid of lines will be the same on 12 pages—so you can set it up on the master page once using PageMaker's lines and rectangles—but the text will be different on every page so no text appears on the master page as part of the lines. Second, PageMaker's drawing tools offer a wider variety of choices in widths (as seen in the last example). Finally, although you can use paragraph rules to set up the grid of lines—even on the master page—it is probably quicker to design using drawn elements.

We offer this example here not because you are likely to want to create a calendar—although you can see how easy it would be—but because similar steps can be used to create any publication that uses the same underlying grid of lines on every page. See the next section, "Creating On-Screen Forms."(You can also create a calendar using the template named CALENDAR.PT5 that comes with PageMaker, and place dates that have already been created as tabbed text for each month and stored in the CALENDAR directory.) Follow these steps:

1. Start a new PageMaker publication with 12 pages.

    You would actually use 14 pages if you add a front and back cover, or 28 if you plan to print on the back of each month's page something other than the next month as well as a front and back cover.

2. Turn to the master page to create the grid of lines.

    If you are printing something other than another month on the back of each page, you will be working on a 24- or 28-page double-sided, facing-page publication, and the grid of lines for the month will be added to only one of the master pages.

3. Draw the rectangle that will frame the days of the month (see fig. 11.103).

    Since you will be dividing this area into exactly 7 columns and five or six rows, it's a good idea to scale this rectangle to a horizontal measure that is easily divisible by 7, and a vertical measure that is easily divisible by 5 or 6. This is easy if the Control palette is open as you draw, so you can see the width and height change as you draw or scale the rectangle.

    This doesn't mean you have to make the calendar exactly 7-by-5 inches. Let's say you planned a calendar in which the grid is about 7.5 inches wide and 4.5 inches deep. Why not change the specs slightly to 7.7 inches wide? Keep the 4.5 inch measure if you will be allowing 5 weeks, but change it to 4.2 or 4.8 if you want 6 weeks in each month. These adjustments will make the next steps easier to calculate, but this convenience isn't necessary since you can enter dimensions as fine as .001-inch in the Control palette.

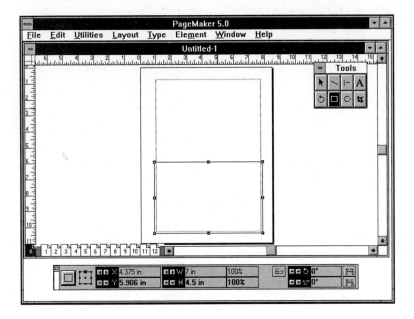

Fig. 11.103

Rectangle frames calendar area.

4. Use the Constrained-line tool to draw a vertical line that exactly overlaps the left edge of the rectangle.

5. With the line selected, choose Copy from the Edit menu (Ctrl+C).

6. Choose Multiple Paste from the Edit menu, and type **6** as the number of copies, with a vertical offset of zero and a horizontal offset equal to the width of the rectangle divided by 7.

In this case, we created a 7-inch wide rectangle, so we enter a horizontal offset of 1 inch (see fig. 11.104).

```
Multiple paste                    [  OK  ]

Paste [6]  copies                 [ Cancel ]

Horizontal offset: [1]    inches

Vertical offset:   [0]    inches
```

Fig. 11.104

Multiple Paste dialog box shows 6 copies and a 1-inch horizontal offset.

7. Click OK to make the copies (see fig. 11.105).

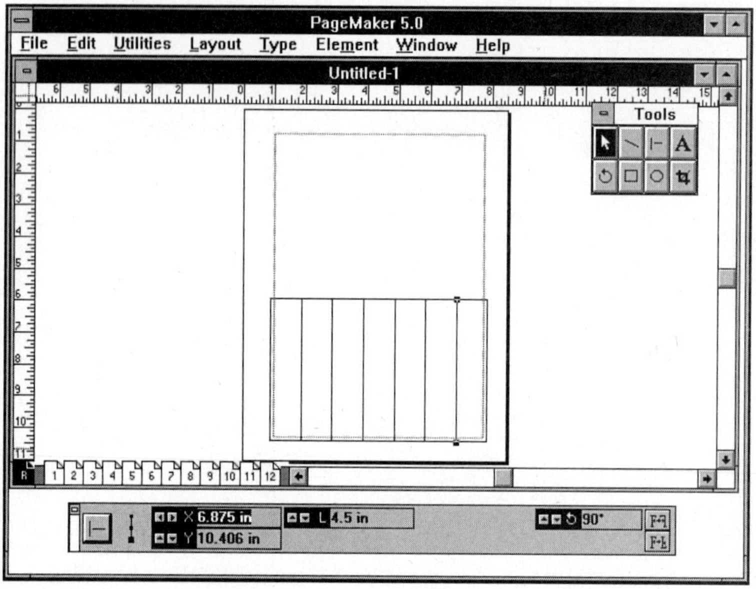

PageMaker 5.0

Fig. 11.105

Six lines divide the rectangle into 7 columns.

8. Delete the first line that overlaps the left edge of the rectangle.

Follow similar steps to create the rows for weeks:

1. Use the Constrained-line tool to draw a horizontal line that exactly overlaps the top edge of the rectangle.

2. With the line selected, choose Copy from the Edit menu (Ctrl+C).

3. Choose Multiple Paste from the Edit menu, and type **4** as the number of copies to make a 5-week grid (or **5** to make a 6-week grid), with a horizontal offset of zero and a vertical offset equal to the height of the rectangle divided by 5 (or 6).

   In this case, you create a 4.5-inch high rectangle and you want a 5-week grid, so you enter a horizontal offset of .9 inches (see fig. 11.106).

4. Click OK to make the copies (see fig. 11.107).

5. Delete the first line that overlaps the top edge of the rectangle.

Fig. 11.106

Multiple Paste
dialog box
shows 4 copies
and a .9-inch
vertical offset.

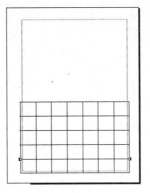

Fig. 11.107

4 lines divide
the rectangle into
5 rows.

6. Add other graphic elements to fit your design. Set the line widths
   and colors as you wish.

   In this case you changed all the lines to 4-point width and added a
   gray rectangle above the grid, where the name of the month will
   appear. You added thinner horizontal lines to divide each day into
   morning and afternoon, and you added a thin column of text to
   put "AM" and "PM" at the left of the grid (see fig. 11.108). If you
   had planned ahead, you could have added the thinner horizontal
   lines by doubling the number of lines and halving the offset distance in the Multiple Paste dialog box. Then you could select the
   lines by Shift+clicking on them and changing the width.

7. Turn to the first page and set up text blocks as shown in figure
   11.109.

   The text block that includes dates is set up with right-align tabs,
   and the dates are typed as number 1 through 31 separated by
   tabs, with two tabs at the end of each week (or a carriage return
   and a tab). Then the leading is adjusted until the text fits consistently within each week. By setting up the date text this way, you
   can easily adjust the dates for each month.

   Alternatively, you can omit the dates in this step and, in step 11,
   place the dates provided with the PageMaker templates; then
   adjust each placed set of dates to match your design.

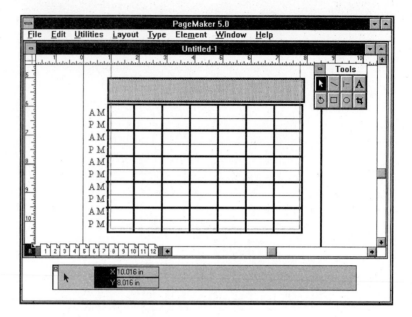

Master page
calendar
graphics.

Dummy text block
set up on first
page.

8. Use the Pointer tool to drag a selection marquee around all the text blocks to select them.

The grid will not be selected because it is on the master page.

9. Choose Copy from the Edit menu (Ctrl+C).

10. Turn to each page and choose Paste from the Edit menu (Ctrl+P).

    PageMaker positions the text blocks in the same relative spot on each new page.

11. Return to page 1 and edit the text for the month (see fig. 11.110).

    You can edit the month by selecting the dummy text and typing the new month name. You can edit the text for the dates the same way, but if the dates are set as described in step 10, you can move the position of the first date by positioning the cursor in front of the number 1 and pressing the Tab key to move it across the week. Adjust the other dates by adding a tab at the end of each week and removing the extra tab or carriage return between dates that separated weeks in the dummy text. Delete dates at the end of each month as appropriate.

    If you are placing dates for each month from the files supplied by Aldus with the PageMaker templates, you have to adjust the tab settings, leading, and point size of the dates for each month to match your design. (You don't need to place the dates for the exact month you are creating; you can place the dates for any month that begins on the same day of the week as the month you are formatting. Delete dates at the end of each month as appropriate.)

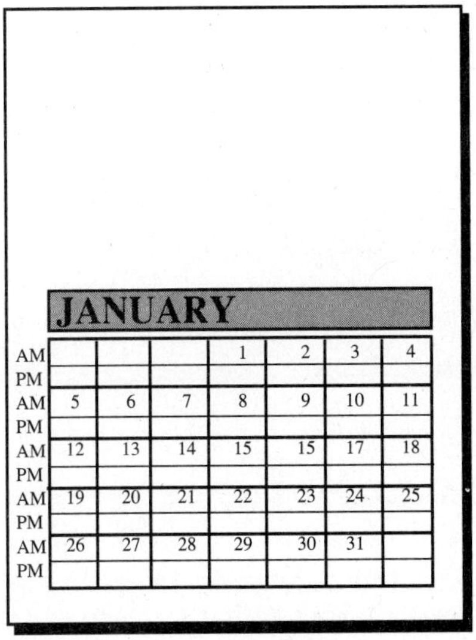

Fig. 11.110

Edit the text for each month.

12. Repeat step 11 on each page of the calendar.

You can use similar steps as these to create any publication that uses the same underlying grid of lines on every page, such as the on-screen forms described in the next section.

Creating On-Screen Forms

You can use a combination of the steps under the last few headings to create on-screen forms. Build the basic form—including ruled lines and text—on the master page. Then create dummy "fill-in" text on page 1. To fill in the form, select all the text on page 1, copy it, and paste it on to a new page. Then edit the text to fill in the variable information. Figure 11.111 shows examples of the master page, page 1, and page 2 of such a form.

Fig. 11.111

The master page, page 1, and page 2 of an on-screen form.

BACW Member Value!

Present this coupon and your membership card to receive this value.

BACW Member Value!

Company
Address
City   ST ZIP
Phone
Description
Coupon Value: xxx
Expires: xxx

Present this coupon and your membership card to receive this value.

BACW Member Value!

TechArt San Francisco
400 Pacific Avenue
San Francisco   CA 94110
(415)362-1110
Graphic Design, Full Page Layout, Linotronic Output, Color Separations
Coupon Value: 20% off one job
Expires: 12/31/94

Present this coupon and your membership card to receive this value.

For Related Information

◀◀ "Adding Rules and Aligning Text to Grid," p. 319.

◀◀ "Using the Indents/Tabs Command," p. 326.

Working with Transformations

PageMaker 5.0 provides three *transformation* functions—rotating, reflecting, and skewing (see fig. 11.112). They are called transformation functions because they transform—that is, change the form or shape of—objects. These features are useful in creating special page designs in newsletters, magazines, fliers, or ads. You also can use the rotating feature to rotate a whole page of text, thereby mixing Tall and Wide page orientations in a single publication. The rotation function is available through a tool in the Tool palette and as an option in the Control palette; the other two functions are available through the Control palette only (see fig. 11.113).

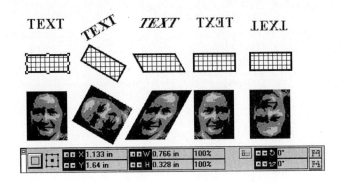

Fig. 11.112

Examples of rotating, skewing, and reflecting an object.

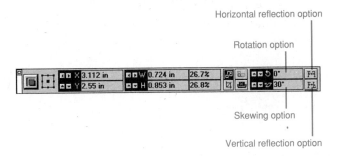

Horizontal reflection option

Rotation option

Skewing option

Vertical reflection option

Fig. 11.113

Control palette in layout view shows rotating, skewing, and reflecting control areas.

You can rotate, skew, and/or reflect any object—text or graphic—that is selected with the Pointer tool in layout view. You can transform whole, unlinked text blocks, but not individual words or paragraphs within a text block, and not text blocks that are threaded or linked to other text blocks in the story. Also, you cannot transform a text block if it is also open in a story window (that is, if the story is listed under the Window menu). You can transform inline graphics if you select them with the Pointer tool.

You can edit transformed text directly in layout view or in story view.

If your printer does not support transformed text, PageMaker will still print it using a low-resolution screen font. You can avoid this problem by using TrueType fonts or a type management utility such as Adobe Type Manager (see the section "Using a Type Manager" in Chapter 13). All PostScript printers support transformed text.

Rotating Text and Graphics

The rotating function lets you rotate selected objects on a page at any angle in increments as fine as .01 degree. Degrees are measured counterclockwise; you increase the angle by rotating counterclockwise or decrease the angle by rotating clockwise. Zero degrees is at the 3 o'clock position. You can rotate objects visually on-screen, using the Rotating tool, or by an amount you specify in the Control palette.

Rotating Visually On-Screen

To rotate an object visually on-screen, follow these steps:

1. Select the Rotating tool from the Tool palette, and select the object(s) by clicking on it with the Rotating tool—just as you might with the Pointer tool, except that you can't drag the Rotating tool to select objects.

   The mouse pointer changes to a starburst pointer in layout view.

2. Position the starburst pointer at a focal point—the point you want to be the origin for the rotation—and hold down the mouse button (see fig. 11.114).

3. To make the object rotate, keep holding down the mouse button, and drag in the direction of the desired rotation. Shift+dragging the starburst pointer (pressing the Shift key as you drag the mouse) constrains the rotation to multiples of 45-degree angles.

   A cross (+) on-screen indicates the focal point around which the rotation occurs—the first position of the starburst pointer. A dotted line called the *rotation lever* extends from the focal point (+) to the starburst as you drag it, indicating the angle of rotation (see fig. 11.115). You can also see the angle of rotation change in the Control palette as you drag, if the Control palette is open, and the Proxy on the Control palette rotates (in 45-degree increments) to approximate the new position.

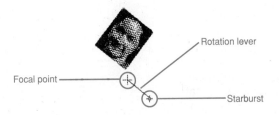

Fig. 11.115

A rotation lever follows the starburst as you drag it around the focal point.

4. Release the mouse button when you have rotated the object(s) as much as you want (see fig. 11.116).

Fig. 11.116

Rotated graphic.

Rotating through the Control Palette

Instead of using the Rotating tool, you can rotate entirely through the Control palette, following the steps described here.

1. Choose Control palette from the Window menu (or press Ctrl+') if it is not already displayed.

2. Use the Pointer tool to select the object(s) to be rotated.

3. Click on the point in the Proxy around which you want to rotate.

   The point you click on the proxy will remain fixed while the rest of the points rotate around it. If you want the object to rotate around a point that is away from it, you can use the rotating tool as described earlier, or rotate through the Control Palette (see fig. 11.117) and then drag the object to another position.

Fig. 11.117

Control palette in
layout view
shows rotating
control areas.

Rotation value

4. Press the Tab key or use the mouse to activate the rotate control
area in the Control palette, and type the angle of rotation (in
degrees).

Remember that degrees are measured counterclockwise—you
increase the angle by rotating counterclockwise, or decrease the
angle by rotating clockwise. Zero degrees is at the 3 o'clock
position.

You can reverse a transformation as soon as you have applied it
by choosing Undo apply from the Edit menu, and you can reverse
all transformations for a selected object by choosing Remove
Transformations from the Element menu. This command cannot
be undone, so it's a good idea to Save your publication before
using it, so you can Revert to the saved version if you change your
mind.

5. Click the Apply button or press Enter to view the effects of the
rotation (see fig. 11.118).

Fig. 11.118

Angle of rotation
entered in
Control palette.

Rotation value

See later in this chapter for examples of using the Rotating tool to create symmetrical objects such as polygons and 3-dimensional objects
such as package designs.

Skewing Text and Graphics

You can use the skewing function to change the angle between the axes
of selected objects. (Normally the x and y axes are set at 90-degree

angles.) You can skew any object horizontally up to 85 degrees in increments as fine as .01 degrees. Skewing can be visualized as the action of
the blades of scissors, as shown in figure 11.119 below.

In skewing, the
change of the
angle between
the axes is
similar to the
movement of
the blades on
scissors.

1. Choose Control palette from the Window menu (or press Ctrl+') if
   it is not already displayed.

2. Use the Pointer tool to select the object to be skewed.

   Note that you can rotate or reflect a group of objects, but you can
   skew only one object at a time.

3. Click or double-click the point in the Proxy from which you want
   to skew.

   If you click on the reference point, it appears as a small rectangle
   on the Proxy, and the equivalent point on the selected object remains stationary as you skew.

   If you double-click on the reference point, it appears as a two-way
   or four-way arrow, and the equivalent location on the selected
   object moves as you skew the object.

4. Press the Tab key or use the mouse to activate the skewing control area in the Control palette, and type the angle of the skew (in
   degrees).

   Positive numbers move the top edge of the object to the right, and
   negative values move the top edge to the left, regardless of the
   selected reference point.

5. Click the Apply button or press Enter to view the effects of the
   skew (see fig. 11.120).

Fig. 11.120

Skewed object
and correspond-
ing Control
palette entry.

Skew Value

Remember that you can reverse a transformation as soon as you have applied it by choosing Undo apply from the Edit menu, and you can reverse all transformations for a selected object by choosing Remove Transformations from the Element menu. This command cannot be undone, so it's a good idea to Save your publication before using it, so you can Revert to the saved version if you change your mind.

See later in this chapter for examples of using the skewing option to create 3-dimensional objects such as package designs. See also the rotated and skewed text in figure 11.126, later in this chapter.

Reflecting Text and Graphics

The reflecting function transforms an object into a mirror image of itself.

1. Choose Control palette from the Window menu (or press Ctrl+') if it is not already displayed.

2. Use the Pointer tool to select the object(s) to be reflected.

3. Click on the point in the Proxy across which you want to reflect.

   You can imagine that a horizontal axis and a vertical axis cross at this point, and that when you click on the reflecting option the object will pivot around the axis. If you are reflecting a rectangle horizontally, for example, there is no difference between selecting the top left, middle left, or bottom left reference point on the Proxy—they all lie on the same axis.

4. Click the Horizontal-reflecting button or the Vertical-reflecting button in the Control palette (see fig. 11.121).

When you reflect an object horizontally, PageMaker adds 180 degrees to the rotation value in the Control palette, because reflecting an object horizontally is equivalent to reflecting it vertically and then rotating it 180 degrees.

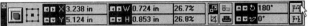

Fig. 11.121

An image
reflected
horizontally.

Remember that you can reverse a transformation as soon as you have
applied it by choosing Undo apply from the Edit menu, and you can
reverse all transformations for a selected object by choosing Remove
Transformations from the Element menu. This command cannot be
undone, so it's a good idea to Save your publication before using it, so
you can Revert to the saved version if you change your mind.

Embedding Transformed Text within a Text Block

You cannot transform individual characters, words, or paragraphs
within a text block, nor can you paste a transformed text block into
another text block, but there is a handy way of turning any text into a
graphic—provided it is all on one line and under 48 characters long.
This method involves placing the DATETIME stamp that comes with
PageMaker as a graphic—a process described earlier for creating
custom drop caps, but the steps are repeated here to show
transformation.

1. Choose Place from the File menu, and click once on the name of
   the graphic you are importing in the Place Document dialog box
   (see fig. 11.122).

   In this case, you want to choose the file named DATETIME.TYM.
   This is a date/time stamp that comes with PageMaker and is normally found in the ALDUS\USENGLSH\FILTERS directory.

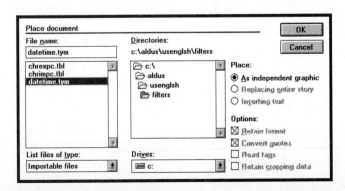

Fig. 11.122

Find the file
named
DATETIME.TYM
in the Place
Document dialog
box.

2. Choose the option to place the file as an independent graphic; then click OK to place the DATETIME.TYM file.

   You can place the graphic as an inline graphic—if the Text tool is selected and the text cursor is positioned in the text block where you want the graphic when you choose the Place command—but we recommend working with the text as an independent graphic first and then using the Cut and Paste commands to position it with text.

   PageMaker displays the Time Stamp Import Filter dialog box (see fig. 11.123).

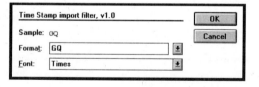

Normally, you enter a date/time format in this dialog box, but you can also enter any letter of the alphabet in the Format area and that character will be placed in the publication as a graphic, as you will see in the next steps.

3. Type the letter, character, word, or phrase that you want to transform—up to 47 characters—and choose a font (see fig. 11.124).

   If you are creating text that includes S, H, D, M, or Y, you must precede the character with a backslash (\). Otherwise, these characters are interpreted as indicating seconds, hours, day, month, or year.

Since you can choose from any available font, including symbol fonts like Wingdings or Zapf Dingbats, you can create symbols as graphics if you like.

You can also type up to 47 characters in this dialog box, to create graphics out of whole words or phrases.

4. Click OK to close the dialog box and get the graphic placement icon (see fig. 11.125).

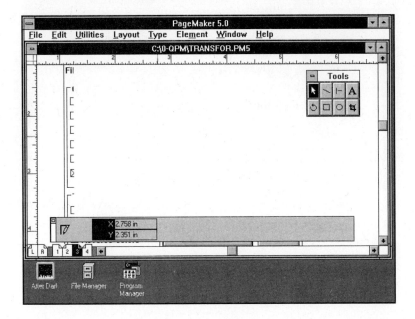

Fig. 11.125

The graphic placement icon represents a PIC file.

5. Click the graphic placement icon on the page to place the graphic (see fig. 11.126), and then go on with steps described earlier to rotate, skew, and/or reflect the graphic text, and scale it to the size you want.

   You can also use the Cropping tool to trim it if you need to, and if the graphic seems invisible when you first place it you can make it visible by clicking on it with the Cropping tool.

6. With the graphic text selected, choose Copy from the Edit menu (Ctrl+C).

7. Select the Text tool from the Tool palette and click to position the text cursor within the text block at the point where you want the graphic text to appear.

8. Choose Paste from the Edit menu (see fig. 11.127).

If the graphic seems invisible when you first place it you can make it visible by clicking on it with the Cropping tool, and you can also use the Cropping tool to trim it if you need to.

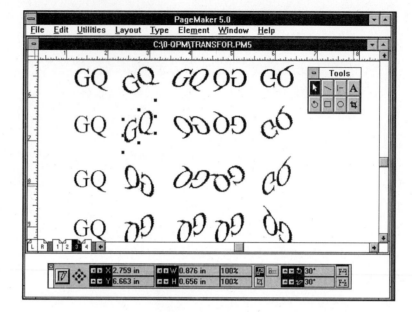

Fig. 11.126

The letters "GQ" placed as a graphic and then scaled, rotated, skewed, and reflected to try various combinations of transformations.

Fig. 11.127

Transformed graphic text becomes an inline graphic within a text block.

For more information

about GQ Herbal Products,

please write to:

GQ Herbal Products

400 Pacific Avenue
Paradise, California 94133

The graphic text can also be scaled or transformed just like any other inline graphic—by first selecting it with the Pointer tool—or shifted on the baseline by dragging it with the pointer or by selecting it with the Text tool and using commands from the Type menu. See the section "Using Inline Graphics" earlier in this chapter.

Using the Rotation Tool To Create Polygons

You can use the technique described here to draw any polygon shape with equal-length sides all around—equilateral triangles, pentagons, hexagons, or polygons with seven or more sides. (You can use the Rectangle tool instead of this technique to draw perfect squares.) A five-sided polygon (pentagon) is created in this example.

1. Use the Constrained-line tool, or the Line tool with the Shift key, to draw a straight horizontal line like the one shown in figure 11.128.

2. With the line still selected, choose Copy from the Edit menu (Ctrl+C).

3. Press Ctrl+Shift+P as many times as appropriate to make duplicates of the line—one for each additional side of the polygon—layered on top of the first.

   If you are making a triangle, you press Ctrl+Shift+P twice to make two more copies—for a total of three lines or sides. Here we press these keys four times, to make four more sides for our 5-sided pentagon.

4. Press Ctrl+' to open the Control palette if it is not already open, and, with the top line selected, click on the center point of the Proxy to select it.

5. Press the Tab key or use the mouse to activate the rotate control area in the Control palette, and type the angle of rotation yielded by the following formula:

   360° (number of sides to the polygon).

   For example, 72 degrees for a five-sided polygon, 60 degrees for a six-sided polygon, and so on.

6. Select the next horizontal line in the stack.

Fig. 11.128

Effects of steps 1-8 in creating a 5-sided polygon.

7. Repeat steps 4 and 5, this time entering twice the number of degrees yielded by the formula—144 for our 5-sided polygon.

8. Repeat steps 6 and 7, entering three times the number of degrees for the fourth horizontal line, four times the degrees for the fifth line, and so on.

   In our example we are creating a five-sided figure, so we repeat steps 6 and 7 two more times, entering 216 and 288 degrees for the next two lines. Table 11.1 shows the successive number of degrees that you enter for various polygons.

Table 11.1 Degrees of Rotation for Each Side of a Polygon

Line #	Triangle	Pentagon	Hexagon	Octagon	Nonagon
1	120	72	60	45	40
2	240	144	120	90	80
3	0	216	180	135	120
4	-	288	240	180	160
5	-	0	300	225	200
6	-	-	0	270	240
7	-	-	-	315	280
8	-	-	-	0	320
9	-	-	-	-	0

9. Use the Pointer tool to rearrange the lines into a polygon shape (see fig. 11.129).

Fig. 11.129

Five lines after rotating (left) and after rearranging to create a pentagon (middle) or a star (right).

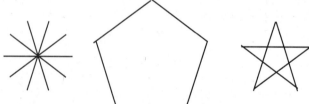

By giving the same lines a different arrangement, you can create star shapes.

You can change the line style, but you cannot fill this type of polygon since it is not a closed shape. If you want a filled polygon, and you don't have a drawing program that you can use to create one, you can try a variation on the steps outlined above. First, draw a rectangle instead of a line. then go through all the same steps to rotate copies and arrange them corner to corner as in figure 11.130.

Next, use PageMaker's Ellipse tool to draw a circle that encompasses the opening between the rectangles but does not extend beyond their outer edges; it should touch each corner when the rectangles meet. Choose None from the Line submenu, and a fill from the Fill submenu under the Element menu. Use the Send to Back command from the Element menu to put it on the bottom layer, below the rectangles (see fig. 11.130, middle).

Finally, select all the rectangles and assign a Line and Fill of Paper (see fig. 11.130, right).

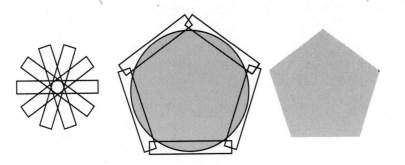

Fig. 11.130

White rectangles cover the filled circle leaving a filled polygon shape.

Creating Radial Symmetry

Radial symmetry describes any object composed of a single shape that is repeated in a pattern around a central point. An example of radial symmetry is a flower, such as the one shown in figure 11.131. In this technique the Rotating tool is used to create simple patterns in which the shapes do not need to meet precisely at the edges—that is, they can overlap, or there can be gaps between them.

You can use this technique to create any radially symmetrical design that allows some gap or overlap between the units of the design.

1. Create or import an object that will become the basic unit of the radial design, using whatever tool is appropriate. In this example, use the Ellipse tool to create a long ellipse (see fig. 11.131).

2. With the object selected, choose Copy from the Edit menu (Ctrl+C).

3. Press Ctrl+Shift+P as many times as appropriate to make duplicates of the object.

4. Press Ctrl+' to open the Control palette if it is not already open, and with the top line selected, click on the point of the Proxy around which you want the rotation to occur to select it.

5. With the top copy that you made in step 3 still selected, press the Tab key or use the mouse to activate the rotate control area in the Control palette, and type the angle of rotation yielded by the following formula:

    360° (number of repeated units).

For example, if you want ten units, type **36** as the number of degrees (360 divided by 10). Some other common values are shown in the following table.

Number of repeated units in Circle	Degrees
2	180
3	120
4	90
5	72
6	60
7	51.43
8	45
9	40
10	36

6. Select the next object in the stack and repeat step 5, this time entering twice the number of degrees yielded by the formula—144 for our 5-sided polygon.

7. Repeat steps 5 and 6, entering three times the number of degrees for the fourth object, four times the degrees for the fifth object, an so on.

Figure 11.131 shows the results of these steps if the center point is selected on the Proxy (left) or if an end point is selected (right).

Fig. 11.131

The results of these steps if the center point is selected on the Proxy (left) or if an end point is selected (right).

Creating Three-Dimensional Effects

Packaging design often calls for accurate 3-dimensional perspective views of rectangular-sided objects such as boxes. The technique described here shows you how to use PageMaker's transformation functions to create relatively accurate 3-D perspectives for several common engineering views by creating the sides of the box as rectangular objects, and then scaling, skewing, and rotating them into place around a common point.

If you will be adding text to the package, transform the text blocks using the same formulas given here for the sides of the package, which in this example are imported rectangular graphics. One advantage of adding the text in PageMaker (rather than making it a part of a scanned image, for instance) is that it remains editable, although it has been transformed, so you can create designs before the text has been finalized, and then edit the text as necessary.

1. Create the side, front, and bottom faces of the package as rectangular objects using a graphics application.

   Here we are going to work with each side as a single object. If you construct the sides in PageMaker, using rectangles and text, you will have to perform any scaling or skewing in the next steps on one element at a time, but you can rotate a multiple-object selection.

2. Place them in PageMaker and, if the graphics are not already in a common scale, you should scale them as necessary.

   You want to be sure that the top and front of the box are the same width, and the side of the box is the width of the top and the height of the side (see fig. 11.132). This is easy with the Control palette open, so you can view and change the width and height of each element in numerical values.

Fig. 11.132

Side, Top, and Front of a package design, each element placed as a separate object in PageMaker.

3. Arrange the three sides with their long sides touching, as if the package were flattened (see fig. 11.133).

4. Select the side of the package; then in the Control palette click on the top right reference point, change the scale percentage for the height to 87 percent (or 87 percent of the current scale value, if it is not 100 percent), enter a rotation value of –30° and a skew value of –30° (see fig. 11.134).

Three graphics
arranged as if
package were
flattened.

Side of package
is transformed
with scaling,
skewing, and
rotating.

5. Select the top of the package; then, in the Control palette, click on the lower left reference point, change the scale percentage for the height to 87 percent (or 87 percent of the current scale value, if it is not 100 percent), enter a rotation value of 30° and a skew value of –30° (see fig. 11.135).

Top of package
is transformed
with scaling,
skewing, and
rotating.

6. Select the front of the package; then, in the Control palette, click on the top right reference point, change the scale percentage for the height to 87 percent (or 87 percent of the current scale value, if it is not 100 percent), enter a rotation value of 30° and a skew value of 30° (see fig. 11.136).

7. Use the Pointer tool to align the sides if they fell out of alignment after the transformations.

The transformation values given here produce what is called an isometric view. The values for some other common views are listed in Table 11.2. Note that, while an isometric view uses the same vertical scaling percentage for each face, some of the other views require different scaling percentages for the different faces, so they must be scaled separately.

Fig. 11.136
Front of package is transformed with scaling, skewing, and rotating.

Table 11.2 Values for Some Common 3-Dimensional Views

View	Face	Vertical Scale	Skew Degrees	Rotate
Axonometric	Side	70.711%	-45	90
	Front	100%	0	45
	Bottom	70.711%	-45	45
Isometric	Side	86.602%	-30	90
	Front	86.602%	30	30
	Bottom	86.602%	-30	30
Dimetric	Side	96.592%	-15	90
	Front	96.592%	15	60
	Bottom	50%	-60	60
Trimetric	Side	96.592%	-15	90
	Front	86.602%	30	45
	Bottom	70.711%	-45	45
Trimetric	Side	96.592%	-15	90
	Front	70.711%	45	30
	Bottom	86.602%	-30	30

Fig. 11.137
Axonometric, Isometric, Dimetric, and two Trimetric views of a package.

For Related Information

◄◄ "Knowing Your Printers," p. 393.

▶▶ "Managing Fonts," p. 592.

Using the Table Editor

The Table Editor is a stand-alone utility for creating and editing *tables*—text arranged in rows and columns. The Table Editor provides several benefits as an alternative to setting tabs with the Indents/Tabs command. The Table Editor offers you the flexibility of making the width and depth of each column or row easy to adjust, letting text wrap within each *cell*, shading rows or columns, and creating rules between columns and rows. Chapters 17, 18, and 19 provide examples of tables created using the Table Editor.

Using the Table Editor is easy. You create a table using the Table Editor, export the table as a Windows Metafile graphic, and then place the table as a graphic in PageMaker. These steps are described in the following sections. The commands used in the Table Editor are similar to those used in other PageMaker modes. The following sections describe in detail only those commands that are unique to the Table Editor.

Creating a Table

To create a table, start the Table Editor by double-clicking the Table Editor icon in the Aldus program group window within the Windows Program Manager. Choose New from the File menu. The Table Setup dialog box prompts you to enter the basic characteristics of the table—each of which can be changed at any time through the Table Setup command (see fig. 11.138). The table characteristics include number of columns, number of rows, table size, and the gutters between rows and columns.

When you click OK in the Table Setup dialog box, the screen displays a blank table that has numbers down the left side of the window to indicate rows and letters along the top of the window to indicate columns following the conventions of most spreadsheet applications (see fig. 11.139).

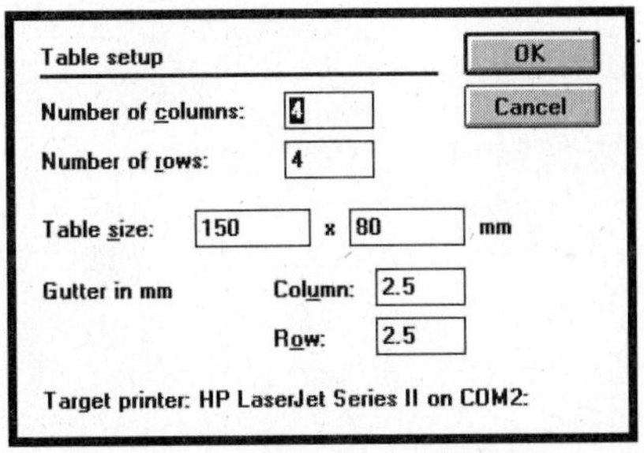

Fig. 11.138

The Table Setup
dialog box.

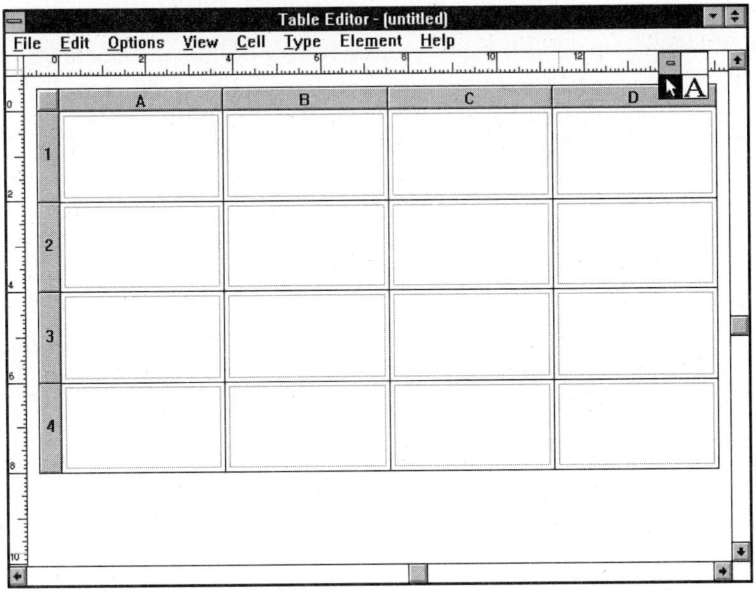

Fig. 11.139

A blank table.

You can hide or display the nonprinting grid labels and grid lines using
the Grid Labels and Grid Lines commands on the Options menu.

Typing and Editing Text in Cells

To enter text in a cell (the intersection of a row and a column), select
the Text tool from the Tool palette, click the cursor in a cell, and type.
As you type, text wraps within the cell if the text line is wider than the
column. You move to a new cell by moving the pointer to another cell
and clicking, or by pressing Enter (to move down one cell) or Tab (to
move right). If you want to force a new line within the current cell,
press Shift+Enter.

You can select an entire row by clicking on the row label to the left of the window. Similarly, you can select an entire column by clicking on the column label at the top of the window. To select a group of rows or columns, drag along the labels at the left or top. You can select a group of cells—not necessarily entire rows or columns—by clicking in one cell and dragging to another. To select the entire table, click in the top left corner of the label bars.

You can select and edit text using the techniques described in Chapters 5 and 7 for selecting and editing text in PageMaker. You can format the text in a selected cell by using Type menu commands, which are the same as the corresponding commands on the Type menu in PageMaker (as described in Chapter 8). All text in a cell, however, must have the same format. You cannot format individual words or paragraphs.

If you select cell text with the Text tool and choose the Cut or Copy command, only the text is cut or copied. If you select a cell with the Pointer tool and choose the Cut or Copy command, the text, borders, and shade of the cell also are cut or copied (see "Changing the Cell Borders and Shades" in this chapter). When you paste the selection into another cell, the pasted text retains its format attributes if the new cell is empty. The pasted text takes on the new cell's attributes if that cell is not empty.

If a cell contains only numbers (plus the period, comma, or hyphen), you can use the Number Format command from the Cell menu to choose among nine number formats (see fig. 11.140).

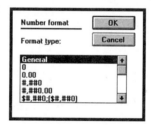

Fig. 11.140

The Number Format dialog box.

You also can calculate the sum of numbers contained in a row or column. To calculate a sum, drag the mouse pointer over a series of cells in one column or one row and choose Sum from the Cells menu. Next, click in the cell where you want the sum to appear. This action replaces the cell's previous contents. Numbers preceded by a minus sign are subtracted from positive numbers in calculating the sum.

Sizing the Table

You can resize a row or column by dragging a boundary in the band at the top or left of the table that shows row and column headings. Alternatively (or to size more than one row or column at a time), you can select a series of rows or columns and then choose the Row Height or Column Width commands from the Cell menu. In either case, when you change the size of a row or column, the adjacent row or column is adjusted automatically to preserve the width and height of the overall table. If you want to change the width or height of the table and preserve the width or height the adjacent columns or rows, hold down the Alt key as you drag the boundary.

The amount of text in the largest cell determines the minimum height of a row. You can decrease the height of a row only to the point that all text still fits in all cells. You can work around this limitation by decreasing the point size of the text, increasing the width of the column with the limiting cell, or decreasing the size of the gutters.

You can create a cell that crosses several rows or columns by selecting a range of cells and choosing Group from the Cell menu. The Table Editor considers the group of cells to be one cell, which the Table Editor identifies by the cell in the upper left corner. You can reverse this process at any time by selecting the cell and choosing Ungroup from the Cell menu. The text format, line style, and shade of the upper left corner cell of the range determines the format of the group.

You can add rows or columns by selecting a cell and choosing Insert from the Cell menu to display the Insert dialog box (see fig. 11.141). Type the number of rows or columns you want to insert, and then click Row or Column. When you click OK, new rows are added above or new columns are added to the left of the selected cell. The width of all columns or the height of all rows is adjusted to accommodate the new additions without changing the size of the table.

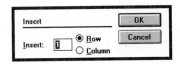

Fig. 11.141

The Insert dialog box.

You can add rows to the bottom or columns to the right side of a table with the File menu's Table Setup dialog box, as described earlier in this section.

You can delete a row or column by selecting the row or column (or a cell in the row or column) and choosing the Delete command from the Cell menu. In the Delete dialog box, you can specify whether you want to delete the row or the column of the current cell. The table shortens when you delete a row, but when you delete a column, the other columns adjust automatically to maintain the same table width. You cannot undo this delete operation.

Changing the Cell Borders and Shades

The Table Editor usually creates one-point rules between rows and columns. You can specify different borders by selecting any cell (or range of cells) and choosing Borders from the Element menu. In the Borders dialog box (see fig. 11.142), you can specify that the style you choose from the Line drop-down list be applied to one or more of the four sides of the selection's perimeter (the horizontal and vertical borders of all cells in the selection) or to all the interior cells in the selection.

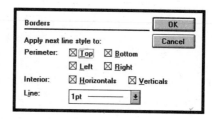

Fig. 11.142

The Borders dialog box.

After setting the borders, choose a style for the border lines from the Line drop-down list. You can also set the border for selected cells by choosing from the Line submenu on the Element menu (see fig. 11.143).

T I P **Setting the Same Lines Styles Repeatedly**

The options you set in the Borders dialog box are saved until you change them. For example, if you want to make thick horizontal lines above two different, nonadjacent rows, you can select the first row, use the Borders command to specify the top perimeter; then choose a style from the Line drop-down list. Next, select the second row above which you want a thick line and go directly to the Line menu. You need not use the Borders command again until you want to change the last selection.

You can define a shade for one or more cells by selecting the cells and choosing a shade from the Fill submenu on the Element menu (see fig. 11.143). If you select a range of rows, you can choose Alternate Rows from the Fill submenu and then choose the Fill you want—the Table Editor applies the selected Fill to every other row in the selection, beginning with the top row in the selection.

You can cut, copy, and paste line styles and fills from one cell to another. If you select a cell with the Pointer tool and choose the Cut or Copy command from the Edit menu, the text, line styles, and fills are cut or copied from the selected cell. When you then use the Paste command, all cut or copied attributes are pasted into the new cell if the cell is empty. If the cell is not empty, the pasted text takes on the attributes of the new cell.

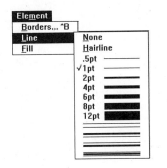 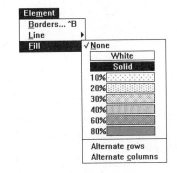

Fig. 11.143

The Line submenu (left) and Fill submenu (right).

Importing Data into the Table Editor

You can use the File menu's Import command to import tab-delimited or comma-delimited ASCII text into the Table Editor. The text formats can be imported from a word processor, a spreadsheet, or a database, as long as the file has been saved in ASCII text format. The delimiters (tabs or commas) determine the breaks between columns, while hard carriage returns determine the breaks between rows.

In the Import File dialog box, you can choose to replace the entire table with the imported data or to import the data into a preselected range of cells only. If the data to be imported represents more cells than are selected, the Table Editor displays an alert box. The alert box enables you to cancel the import or to import only the data that fits in the selected cells.

528

You can transpose rows and columns automatically as you import data. Before you select the Import command, choose the Define Flow option from the Edit menu. (The Define Flow option also determines how rows and columns behave when pasted with the Paste command.) In the Define Flow dialog box, you can choose the usual Left to Right, then Down flow, or the transposing Top to Bottom, then Right flow (see fig. 11.144).

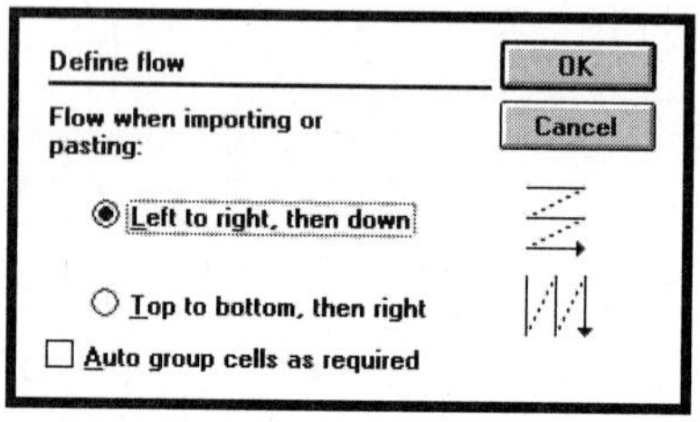

Fig. 11.144

The Define Flow
dialog box.

To group cells automatically when you import or paste text that spans two or more cells in the original source, check Auto Group Cells as Required. For example, if you type a long title such as *Import/Export Figures between 1980 and 1990* in a spreadsheet cell, that text overflows across adjacent cells (if the cells are empty). In the Table Editor, however, the same title in a long cell text wraps to fit within the cell's width and makes the cell deeper to accommodate the text, unless you check Auto Group Cells as Required.

Exporting from the Table Editor

You should use the File menu's Save command often while building a table. This process saves the table in a format that can be edited by the Table Editor. To import a table from the Table Editor into PageMaker, you must use the Table Editor's Export command. The Export to File dialog box enables you to choose between two formats and to export the entire table or the selected range of cells only (see fig. 11.145).

If you export the table as text, the export file name receives the extension TXT, and the file retains none of its text formats, line styles, or shades. After you import the text into PageMaker, however, you can edit the text. If you export the table in Windows Metafile format (that is, as a graphic), the export file receives the WMT extension, and the table is exported to PageMaker as a graphic. The table then can be scaled and cropped like any other graphic. If, however, you want to edit the table in PageMaker, you must use the techniques described later in this chapter.

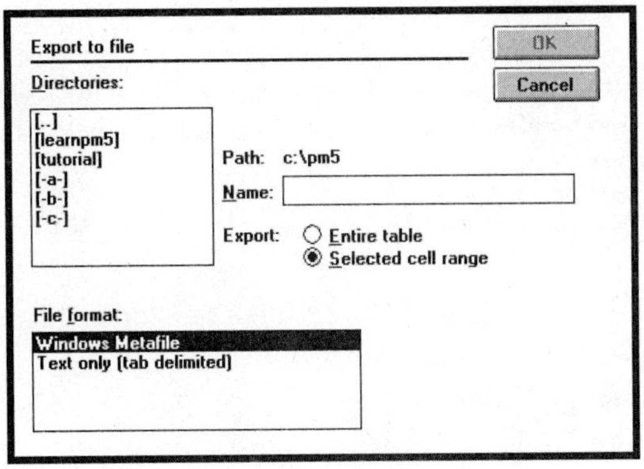

Fig. 11.145

The Export to File
dialog box.

Importing a Table into PageMaker

You can use the following three methods to import into PageMaker a table or selection of cells from the Table Editor:

- You can select cells in the Table Editor, choose the Copy command from the Edit menu, and then open the PageMaker publication and use the Paste command from the Edit menu.

- You can use the Place command while in Layout view in PageMaker to import the entire table.

- You can use the Import command while in Story view in PageMaker to import the entire table.

The Copy, Paste, Place, and Import commands are described in Chapters 5, 6, and 9.

The imported table is linked to the PageMaker publication as described in Chapters 6 and 9. If you exported the table from the Table Editor in text format, the imported table is text and can be edited like any text in PageMaker. If you exported the table as a graphic, the imported table can be scaled or cropped, but you can edit the table only as described in the following section.

Editing a Table in PageMaker

To edit a table that has been created using the Table Editor and imported into PageMaker in Windows Metafile format (as a graphic), hold down the Ctrl key and triple-click anywhere inside the table. This process starts the Table Editor and opens the original table file with the TBL extension.

You can use the same methods to edit the table as you used to create the table. When you save the changes, the exported WMT file is updated automatically. The table in the PageMaker publication is updated automatically in the PageMaker publication if the following occur:

■ The link between the PageMaker publication and the WMT file is up to date, as shown in the Links dialog box (described in Chapter 13).

■ The Update Automatically option is checked in the table's Link Options dialog box (described in Chapter 13).

■ You opened the table directly through PageMaker and not through the Table Editor as a separate program running under Windows.

If you update a table directly through the Table Editor, you must export the table in WMT format again to replace the older table in PageMaker. You must use the same name that was identified in the link with the PageMaker publication or use PageMaker's Place command to replace the older table.

FROM HERE...

For Related Information

◀◀ "Using the Edit Menu Commands," p. 216.

◀◀ "Using Object Linking and Embedding with Text," p. 256.

◀◀ "Inserting and Selecting Text," p. 275.

◀◀ "Formatting Text," p. 293.

◀◀ "Importing Spreadsheets as Graphics," p. 370.

▶▶ "Managing Linked Text and Graphics Documents," p. 597.

Summary

In this chapter you have learned some of PageMaker's more advanced features—features that enable you to create limitless design possibilities. This is the first chapter in Part III of the book, chapters that take you beyond the essential functions in creating a publication with PageMaker. The next chapters continue these advanced topics, including using color in publications (Chapter 12), special considerations in printing (Chapter 13), and managing large documents, large projects, or large publication departments (Chapter 14).

Creating Color Publications

O ne of the most exciting aspects of desktop publishing today is the capability to create high-quality color documents with your personal computer. Over the last several years, desktop publishing applications have made significant inroads into the world of color prepress, the process of preparing pages for printing on an offset press. This has been possible due to a variety of technological advances, including the color capabilities offered by PageMaker.

Color can be reproduced on press in two basic ways: spot color or process color. Some printing presses can print one publication using a combination of both spot and process color. Spot-color printing uses special premixed inks. In *process color separation*, color pages are broken down into four pieces of film representing the primary press inks (cyan, magenta, yellow, and black) necessary for full color reproduction. Since the release of PageMaker 3.0, PageMaker users have had the option of producing spot-color overlays. PageMaker 5.0 introduces the capability to print four-color process separations of pages, including those containing Encapsulated PostScript (EPS) illustrations. With the help of other programs, you can also print pages containing continuous-tone color images (color photographs).

PageMaker enables you to assign colors to text and graphics and to preview the colors on a color monitor, to print color separations in black and white on any laser printer or PostScript typesetter, and to print color pages on a color printer. PageMaker's color feature is useful for several purposes:

- Designing color publications and previewing the colors on a color monitor

- Creating color comps (examples) of design ideas

- Creating color separations for offset printing

- Printing color pages and overhead transparencies on a color printer

This chapter discusses how to create and apply colors in PageMaker and how to create color separations. It also explains how offset printers produce color, when to use color printers, and how to prepare mechanicals for color printing.

General Considerations

To take advantage of PageMaker 5.0's excellent capabilities for printing color separations, it's important to understand some of the basics of color printing. With desktop publishing, designers and production staff now have the technology to control the entire prepress process. If you decide to take advantage of these capabilities, be aware that four-color process separation is an art, a science, and a craft that merits considerable study and practice. This section is a brief introduction to color. Other sections describe how color is created, applied, and printed with PageMaker.

The computer can be part of the production of final film for printing at various levels. For example, many times pages are created in PageMaker and output to film, with traditional process color separations stripped in manually. It is becoming more practical, however, to bring together all elements, including high-resolution images, on a page and output them directly from PageMaker to a PostScript imagesetter.

No matter which alternative you choose, you must talk to your printer before preparing any job that involves printing in color. The best method is often dictated by the time required for the job or its cost.

Spot Color versus Process Color

Generally, you can prepare film for color printing jobs in two ways. One way is to create separate plates for printing with spot colors; the other way is to create separate plates for each of the four process colors—cyan, magenta, yellow, and black. Figure 12.1 illustrates the difference between spot and process color.

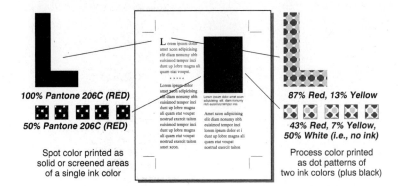

100% Pantone 206C (RED)

50% Pantone 206C (RED)

Spot color printed as
solid or screened areas
of a single ink color

87% Red, 13% Yellow

43% Red, 7% Yellow,
50% White (i.e., no ink)

Process color printed
as dot patterns of
two ink colors (plus black)

Fig. 12.1

A close-up of
the same color
produced as spot
color and as
process match.

Spot-color separations involve preparing film that will be used by a printer who loads the printing press with premixed ink colors. PANTONE colors are one of the most common systems for premixing inks, and PageMaker incorporates color libraries for PANTONE colors as well as other color systems such as TRUMATCH, Focoltone, DaiNippon, and TOYO. A publication prepared for a spot-color printing job results in one sheet of film for each premixed ink.

Process color is usually used for publications that require more than a few colors or use continuous-tone images, such as photographs. Process color is made up of four inks—black and the three subtractive primaries: yellow, cyan, and magenta—printed one on top of the other in a pattern of halftone dots. If you stand back and look at the page normally, your eye is tricked into seeing the solid colors that result from mixing the primaries. If you magnify a color image from any newspaper or magazine, you can see the patterns of nonoverlapping dots in the three colors (plus black).

Both spot color and process color require separation of color elements, and PageMaker lets you specify either type of separations for any color you create.

Spot Color

To understand spot color, think of a pen plotter. The plotter can print with up to four colors of ink, but if you superimpose an area of one color on another, the resulting color is muddy. Offset-printing presses produce spot color in much the same way. The printer mixes several colors of ink to match each color indicated by the design. The ink colors are usually mixed according to formulas given in swatchbooks for PANTONE Matching System (PMS) colors. Each press ink well is then filled with one custom-mixed color.

Because the spot colors don't usually overlap on the final page, you can print a single camera-ready version of the page, and on a tissue overlay mark instructions that tell the printer which parts are to be printed in each color. The printer then creates several negatives of the page and blocks out different sections of each negative to make several plates, each plate containing the parts of the page image to be printed in a particular color. However, because PageMaker can print spot-color separations automatically, with PageMaker you can save the time it takes the printer to block out different color elements on the negatives.

If the press has only one ink well, the job is run through once with one color, then the pages are allowed to dry, the press is cleaned and filled with a second color, and the dry pages are run through a second time for the second color. Many print shops have presses that can print two or more colors in one run, but each color requires a separate plate, or color separation.

The procedure for printing spot color is labor-intensive and time-consuming; drying time alone can add days to a multiple-color print run performed on a one-color press. When you use a press that can print two or more colors in one run (industrial-strength dryers can help set one color before the sheet reaches the next set of rollers), waiting time is shortened, but you still pay extra for each color the printer has to mix and load on the press. This method is often used to print a publication with just one, two, or three colors.

Process Color

To understand process color, think about a pointillist painting. The painting consists of many minute dots of paint, but the eye blends the dots into solid tones. Similarly, in four-color process printing, adjacent dots of ink printed in different colors—usually cyan, magenta, yellow, and black—are interpreted as a single color by the eye. For example, in areas where yellow and cyan are printed together, the eye perceives green. With this technique you can produce an infinite number of colors by printing a fine pattern of dots with the three subtractive primary colors plus black.

If you are producing a publication that uses more than a few spot colors, you may choose to use the four-color process in the final printing. Because four-color presses are designed to print all the colors in one run, the printer does not need to change the colors in the press. For this reason, you may choose to print spot color as process color—that is, set up the colors using one of the color matching systems (so you can see what the final color should look like in a swatchbook) but specify in the Edit Color dialog box that each color be printed as a process color. (This procedure is described later in this chapter.)

You can create a PageMaker publication to be printed with a few spot colors or entirely by the four-color process. You can also mix these methods—printing four-color separations of most of the color elements and adding a few spot colors—but limiting the number of spot colors to one or two is a good idea. This is usually how brochures that have silver or gold ink are handled; the silver or gold is a spot color mixed by the printer. If you want the printer to mix a spot color (to match your corporate logo color, for instance), you generally want to find a printing company with a five- or six-color press. This type of equipment is more expensive than the normal four-color press, and the printing is, therefore, more expensive. Large print runs can help lower the per-piece price.

Color Swatchbooks

For spot-color printing, you must specify the precise color you want the offset print shop to use. You can do so in a number of different ways. For example, you can give the printer a sample of the color, such as a piece of paper or a piece of material, and indicate that it be duplicated as closely as possible.

A more precise way of specifying color is to use a color matching system, such as the PANTONE Matching System (PMS). PageMaker comes with several color libraries of standard color matching systems, including DaiNippon, Focoltone, PANTONE®, PANTONE® Process Color System, TOYO, and TRUMATCH. Ink swatchbooks for these systems can be purchased at any graphic arts supply store. Printers can usually get most of these types of inks, or they will mix the inks they have to match your swatch. Check with your print shop to see which color systems they can match before choosing a system for your publication. You can specify a swatchbook color number in the Edit Color dialog box to create a color (as described later in this section).

Although you can use PageMaker's libraries and the on-screen view of colors to specify colors for your publications, having a swatchbook for reference is a good idea. Color monitors only approximate the final printed color, and you can also use the specifications in the swatchbook to create colors using a monochrome monitor. The swatchbook is also a good reference when specifying spot colors at the print shop.

Swatchbooks usually present inks grouped according to hue (place in the color spectrum, as in red versus blue), *saturation* (amount of color, as in red versus pink), and *luminance* (amount of brightness, as in dull red versus fire-engine red). You often see two colors side-by-side with the same hue but different saturations. Each color sample is usually accompanied by information on the primary colors and their proportion that make up the color (see fig. 12.2). By taking time to understand and use a swatchbook, you can learn a great deal about color. For example, you may be surprised to find that the difference between two apparently dissimilar colors can be as little as 10 percent cyan and 5 percent black.

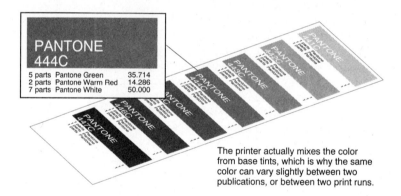

Fig. 12.2

Close-up of PMS swatch with ink density information.

The printer actually mixes the color from base tints, which is why the same color can vary slightly between two publications, or between two print runs.

CAUTION: Be careful when specifying colors for type or for thin graphic elements such as rules. Swatches usually are printed in one-inch strips or squares, but the colors look different when printed as a thin headline or rule. In a thin line, bright colors look duller, dark colors (such as a deep blue) may look black, and light colors (such as pastels) may nearly disappear. To visualize how your printed color will look, use a piece of white paper to cover up all but a small piece of the swatch. Try to use a piece of paper that matches your printing stock, because even white paper comes in a range of hues.

Ink swatchbooks generally give you a sample of a wide range of different inks, printed on both coated and uncoated paper. Paper type is very important; the appearance of the ink varies a great deal depending on the type of paper on which it is printed. In general, inks appear more brilliant on coated papers, and softer and duller on uncoated papers.

The Cost of Color

In the past, one of the biggest obstacles to using color in offset-printed communications was cost. But each color adds only 10 percent to offset printing costs—the prepress costs are the greater expense in most color productions. Traditionally, the term *prepress* described the steps that the print shop goes through to prepare a page for printing, from the time the mechanical is delivered until the printing plate is made from a negative. More recently, prepress describes the higher-end electronic color processing systems such as Hell Systems and Scitex—systems you can run your PageMaker publication through for the highest-quality preparation of full-color images (usually originating as color photographs or slides). For most publications, however, you don't have to go to a higher level of color preparation, and PageMaker can handle many of the tasks that were previously part of prepress processing costs.

If the page is to be printed in one color and is comprised solely of text and line art, the traditional prepress steps are simple: photograph the page and develop the negative. If the page is to be printed in more than one color, the print shop must make color separations of the page and prepare one negative for each color to be printed, selectively concealing (masking) other colors and trimming areas where colors overlap (traps) and edges where colors meet (butts). These traditional methods take a great deal of time, use sophisticated cameras and other equipment, and require considerable skill; they are therefore costly. PageMaker has built-in functions that automatically perform many of these steps, so the prepress process takes less time, uses less expensive equipment, and requires less specialized skills.

Following are a few guidelines in choosing color and the type of color processing:

- Use spot color when you

    Have a limited budget and cannot afford process color

    Need three or fewer colors

    Need special inks, such as fluorescent, metallic, or pearlescent

    Want to match a logo color exactly

■ Use process colors when you

Have an adequate budget and large print run

Are using four or more colors in the design

Need to include scanned color photographs in your publication

■ Use spot and process color when you

Have the budget to print in five or more inks

Need a lot of colors, but one or two must match a color precisely

Need a lot of colors plus a special ink, such as fluorescent, metallic, or pearlescent

Regardless of whether you are using spot or process colors, the cost of color printing increases if you have large areas of solid color coverage, if you supply the camera-ready artwork as positive images on paper rather than as negative film, if your design calls for bleeding color off a cut edge, and if you use the print shop or a prepress service to prepare color photographs for printing.

FROM HERE...

For Related Information

▶▶ "Working with Color," p. 674.

Defining Colors in PageMaker

PageMaker enables you to define spot colors, process colors, and lighter versions of either, called *tints*. You can also select predefined spot and process colors from six color-matching systems included with PageMaker. You assign colors to text or graphics in PageMaker by first defining the color and then applying it. This section describes the ways you can define colors in PageMaker.

Colors appear as black, white, and shades of gray on a monochrome monitor and in color on a color monitor. The accuracy with which the printed colors match the displayed colors depends on the number of colors your hardware supports and the differences between electronic display technology and printing technology. In general, do not select a color based on how it looks on your screen. To specify a color, always use the values printed in the process-color charts or the inks printed in the spot-color swatchbooks, as described earlier in this chapter in the section "Color Swatchbooks."

When you create colors in PageMaker, you set up a color sheet that applies to all the colors in a publication, just as a style sheet applies to all the text. As with style sheets, you can edit and remove colors from a color sheet and copy colors from one publication's color sheet to another.

PageMaker can print *color separations,* which means that it can print an object or objects (text or graphics) on separate sheets for each color—one sheet for each spot color or four sheets for process colors. The objects on these sheets are *registered* (aligned) on the final composite page (see fig. 12.3 and the four-color insert). This capability makes it easy to prepare camera-ready film for most color printing jobs.

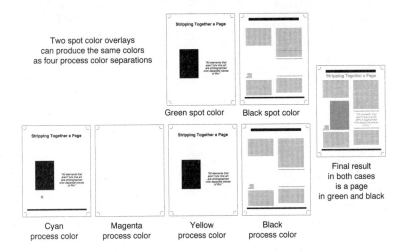

Two spot color overlays can produce the same colors as four process color separations

Green spot color   Black spot color

Cyan process color   Magenta process color   Yellow process color   Black process color

Final result in both cases is a page in green and black

Fig. 12.3

Spot-color overlays and four-color process separations printed from PageMaker.

PageMaker provides a basic default color palette that includes three colors you can change or delete (Blue, Green, and Red), plus three colors that are always available: [Paper], [Black], and [Registration] (see fig. 12.4 and four-color insert). [Paper] indicates opaque, which is white (or a color of your choice). [Black] is the initial default color for all text and graphics, and the color definition for [Black] cannot be changed. [Registration] is the color you assign to elements you want PageMaker to print on every spot-color overlay, such as registration marks that you add manually (see "Crop Marks and Registration Marks" in the "Printing in Color with Offset Printing" section of this chapter).

Use the buttons in the Define Colors dialog box (displayed when you select the Define Colors command on the Element menu, as described next) to change or add color definitions. From this dialog box, you can create a new color, edit an existing color definition (change how a color looks), copy a color sheet from one publication to another, or remove a color from the color sheet. When you click a color name to select it, the color is displayed in the Color box at the top of the dialog box. You can edit the existing colors in the default color palette, including the [Paper] color but excluding [Registration] and [Black]. You can remove or rename any color that does not appear in brackets in the dialog box.

Fig. 12.4

The Colors palette shows the default colors.

Editing Existing Colors

To edit colors, first choose Define Colors from the Element menu. This action displays the Define Colors dialog box, which lists the colors already defined (see fig. 12.5).

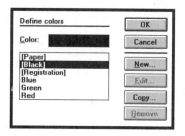

Fig. 12.5

The Define Colors dialog box with the default color names.

You edit a color either by double-clicking the color in the Define Colors dialog box or by clicking the color once to select it and then clicking the Edit button to display the Edit Color dialog box (see fig. 12.6 and the four-color insert). You can also display the Edit Color dialog box by holding down the Ctrl key and clicking a color name in the Colors palette. In the Edit Color dialog box, you can change the name of a color by replacing the name shown in the Name field.

You can choose whether the color will be separated as a spot color (on a sheet of its own), as a process color (on four sheets when process color separations are printed), or as a tint (a percentage lighter than 100% of a spot or process color). You can also change the color model and the color percentages used to define the color by using one of three color models: RGB (red, green, and blue), HLS (hue, lightness, and saturation), or CMYK (cyan, magenta, yellow, and black). You can create a color from scratch, base the color on an existing color and change it, or choose a color from a color library. All these features are described in the following sections.

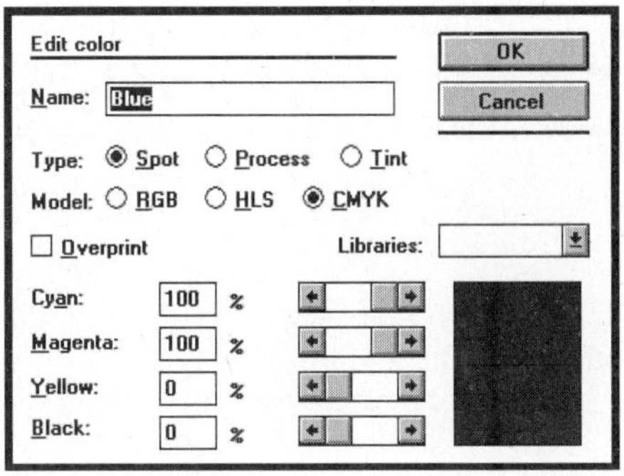

Fig. 12.6

The Edit Color
dialog box.

The number of scrollbars and scrollbar labels changes to reflect the
color model you choose (described later in this section). You mix colors by varying the percentages of their defining values: You either type
numbers in the text boxes near each scale name or scroll the scrollbars (located to the right of the text box). Percentages range from 0 to
100 percent for all values except hue, which ranges from 0 to 359 degrees. You can use a color reference guide from an art supply store to
help determine the percentages, or you can mix colors on-screen and
preview the results of various percentage settings if you have a color
monitor. The rectangle in the lower right corner of the Edit Color dialog
box displays the original color in its lower half and the new mixed color
in its upper half. Choose OK to accept the new color, or choose Cancel
if you decide to keep the original color.

Choosing a Color Model

The choice of a color model to work with in the Edit Color dialog
box depends on your preference; the color model does not affect
how the color is displayed on-screen or printed. You can match
most colors using any color model.

The RGB color model is the one used to display colors on computer monitors, and it is used in mixing colors for printing in some
countries (but not the United States). Traditional graphic artists
are accustomed to working with the HLS system when they create
new colors. If you are not familiar with the HLS system, you probably should stick with the CMYK color model when creating new
colors, or use one of the color libraries that come with Page-
Maker. Using a color library such as the PANTONE system—with
the aid of a color swatchbook—is the most efficient method of
assigning colors when you have a monochrome monitor.

continues

Choosing a Color Model (continued)

Use the CMYK color model if you plan to print process color separations. If you use the other models, PageMaker converts the values to CMYK values for you. You can have more control, however, by entering the values in the CMYK model directly.

If you think you might convert your spot colors to process colors for the final publication, use the CMYK color model in defining the color. This way, you can choose Process in the Edit Color dialog box later to convert the colors from spot to process color.

If you plan to print your publication on slide film, use the RGB color model, the model used by most color slide recorders.

Spot, Process, and Tint Colors

If you click the Spot option in the Edit Color dialog box, PageMaker prints anything the color is applied to on a separate sheet when you print separations through the Print command. You can always change a spot color to a process color. If you do so, PageMaker calculates the CMYK percentages for you, regardless of the color model you used to define the color in the first place.

If you click the Process option in the Edit Color dialog box, PageMaker prints anything the color is applied to on one or more of the four process color separations: cyan, magenta, yellow, and black. If you change a process color to a spot color, PageMaker prints anything the color is applied to on a separate sheet when you print separations.

If you click the Tint option, the dialog box changes to show a base color drop-down list and only one percentage scale (see fig. 12.7). You can change the name to whatever you want, but the best idea is to simply add the percentage value as part of the base color name. Any color identified as a tint is also identified with a special tint symbol in the Colors palette.

If you're working with only a limited number of colors, such as black and one accent color, you can create additional visual interest and the feeling of a multicolor piece by using tints. You can combine different tints of one color on a page to get more variety when printing with only one or two ink colors. Color tints can be attractive when printed in large blocks or across a whole page. In addition, with a light tint you can overprint type in black or most other colors. Be careful when overprinting type, however, because color tints such as gray may not provide enough character definition.

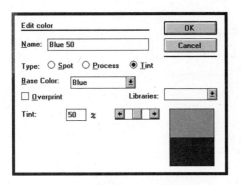

Fig. 12.7

The Edit Color
dialog box when
Tint is selected
(left), and tints
listed in the
Colors palette
(right).

Creating Tinted Fills, Lines, Borders, or Text   T I P

You don't have to create tints as fills for rectangles and ellipses
drawn with PageMaker's tools. Instead, you can use PageMaker's
Rectangle and Ellipse tools and the Fill submenu of the Element
menu to apply percentage screens. For example, a 30% red fill
produces a pink tint. To make a line or text gray or tinted, however, you must create a tint in the Colors palette.

Using Tints To Get a Variety of Effects from the Same Color   T I P

You can make the same color overprint in some cases and not in
others by creating two versions of it and calling one a 100% tint.
Choose Overprint for only one of the versions. Apply one version
of the color to elements when you want to overprint, that is, when
you want to mix both the new color and the background color.
Apply the other version to elements that you want to knock out
(not overlap) background colors.

RGB Color Model

Red, green, and blue (RGB) are used to display color on computer
monitors, and this is a good model to use if you plan to use PageMaker
for on-screen presentations. To create a color, enter a percentage value
in the fields for Red, Green, and Blue in the Edit Color dialog box, or use
the scrollbars adjacent to each to indicate values (see fig. 12.8 and the

four-color insert). The color created is displayed in the dialog box. This color is only a simulation. You can expect some variation between the color displayed on the monitor and the final printed color.

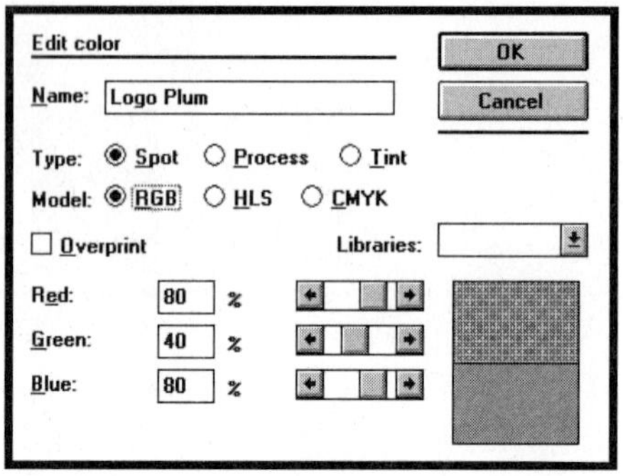

Fig. 12.8

The Edit Color dialog box with RGB selected as the color model.

HLS Color Model

HLS (hue, lightness, and saturation) is the common system for identifying the way in which artists' paints are mixed. *Hue* is the quality that gives a color its name, such as red, orange, yellow, green, blue, and violet. *Lightness* is a measure of the amount of light reflected from a color; black reflects almost no light and white reflects almost all light. *Saturation* is a measure of the tint, or purity, of a color.

To create a color, enter a percentage value in the fields for Hue, Lightness, and Saturation in the Edit Color dialog box, or use the scrollbars adjacent to each to indicate values (see fig. 12.9 and the four-color insert). The color created is displayed in the dialog box. This color is a simulation only; you can expect some variation from the color displayed on the monitor and the final printed color.

CMYK Color Model

The CMKY (cyan, magenta, yellow, and black) color model is the best model to use when specifying colors for process separation. This way, you can be sure to specify whole numbers as percentages for each screen. Normally, screens are specified in 5% increments.

To create a color, first type a name in the Edit Color dialog box. Then specify the percentages of CMYK desired by typing a value in the field adjacent to each color or by using the scrollbars (see fig. 12.10 and the four-color insert). The color you specify is displayed in the dialog box. This is only a simulation. The color displayed on the monitor will vary from the final printed color. You can specify CMYK colors to print spot color or process color separations.

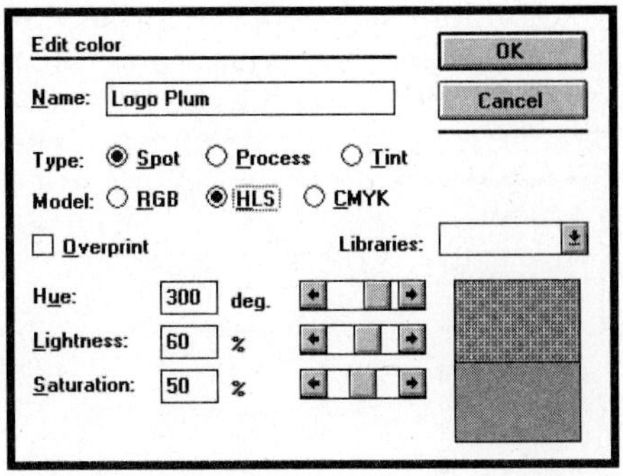

Fig. 12.9

The Edit Color dialog box with HLS selected as the color model.

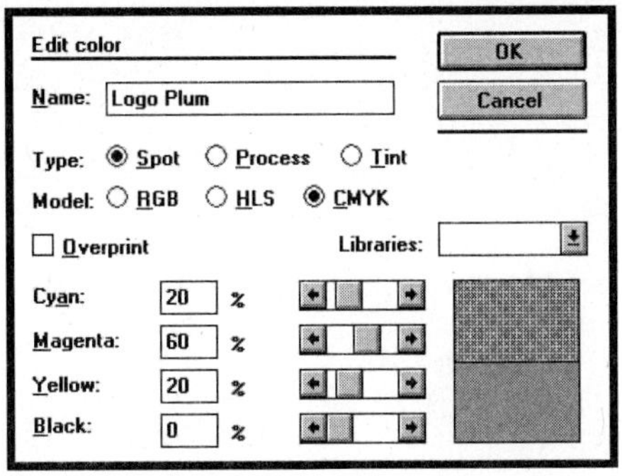

Fig. 12.10

The Edit Color dialog box with CMYK selected as the color model.

Overprinting Colors

By default, colors *knock out* other colors positioned behind them. This means that the top color prints, and colors that the top color overlaps do not print. Sometimes, however, you want a color (usually a dark color or black) to print on top of other colors without knocking them out. This is one way to prevent gaps when the registration is slightly off in printing. You can use overprinting also to create a new color in spot-color printing. Choose Overprint in the Edit Color dialog box when you want a color to print over other colors on the page.

You can override this setting for individual elements on a page by activating or deactivating Overprint in the Fill and Line dialog box, as described in Chapter 9.

A Word about Knockouts (Traps and Butts)

Printing is fairly simple if you're using more than one color but the elements of different colors don't touch. Colors must meet precisely in the separated overlays, however, if elements touch (for example, purple type in the middle of an otherwise solid red circle, called a *trap*). If the colors are even a hairline out of register, you see the mistake in the printed piece, either as a dark line where the colors overlap or as a gap between the colors (see fig. 12.11 and the four-color insert). You usually want the two colors to overlap at the adjoining edge (the *butt*) by only a point or so (about the width of an X-ACTO blade).

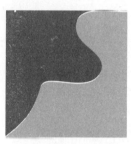 

With perfect registration colors meet but do not overlap (except black, which usually overprints all other colors).

When registration is off slightly, gaps show as white lines and overlapping colors yield a darker, muddy line.

PageMaker enables you to print two overlapping colors with the Overprint option in the Edit Color dialog box. When this option is *not* selected, each element is printed in its color with the space required by the overlapping element cut out (see fig. 12.12 and the four-color insert). These knockouts butt each other exactly (without any overlap), however, so this technique may not yield the most accurate results. You may end up with poor registration between the two colors. You may prefer to deliver color separations without knockouts (with Overprint selected), as shown in figure 12.13 and the four-color insert.

If you don't want to be responsible for registration, you can use the Overprint option but tell the print shop to prepare the knockout. Another method is to use the Overprint option but prepare your mechanical as a *keyline*, which is an unseparated single-page printout. Using the circle example shown in figures 12.12 and 12.13, you place the circle (as an outline) and the type on one mechanical, and write instructions for color specifications on an overlay. These instructions might read "Circle prints PMS 282. Type prints PMS 141 and traps in circle." See figure 12.14.

Circle with knockout
in Spot Color 1

Text in
Spot Color 2
with Overprint off

Composite
makes text slightly darker
where it overlaps at edges

Fig. 12.12

Overlapping
colors printed
with knockout
(no overprint).

Circle with no knockout
in Spot Color 1

Text in
Spot Color 2
with Overprint on

Composite
makes text slightly darker
all over

Fig. 12.13

Overlapping
colors printed
with the overprint
option.

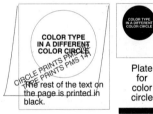
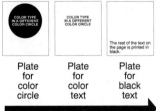

Artwork delivered to printer as
one black-and-white image marked:
"CIRCLE PRINTS PMS 282
TYPE PRINTS PMS 141"

Printer makes three
plates with
different elements
blocked out.

Final result prints
text in one color,
circle in another,
with no overlap.

Fig. 12.14

A keyline marked
for color trap.

Using Color Libraries

You also can define a color by selecting a color library or color matching system in the Edit Color dialog box. PageMaker comes with several color libraries, including Crayon, DIC Color Guide, Focoltone, Greys, PANTONE®, PANTONE® Process Color System, TOYOPC, and

TRUMATCH 4-Color, and you can create custom libraries of your own by using the Create Color Library Addition. This section describes how to use a color library or create one of your own. Before selecting colors from a color library, be sure that your print shop supports the system you want to use.

If one or more of these color systems is not listed in the drop-down list of the Edit Color dialog box, the library information file is not in the correct location on your hard drive. You can install libraries through Aldus Setup, which is an icon in the Aldus program group under the Windows Program Manager.

Each library works the same way. For example, if you choose PANTONE®, PageMaker displays the PANTONE® (PMS) library (see fig. 12.15 and the four-color insert).

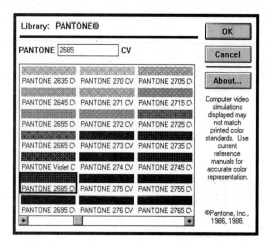

Fig. 12.15

The PANTONE® Library dialog box.

You select a PMS color either by using the scrollbar to locate the color and clicking the color name or by typing the PMS color number in the box at the top of the dialog box. You can also use the arrow keys to move from one color swatch to adjacent ones in the scrolling display of colors. You can select several colors at once by holding the Shift key and clicking each color you want to add to the Colors palette. Because the colors in the dialog box show numbers that correspond to catalog numbers—and catalogs or swatchbooks are available for each of these color systems—you can choose an exact color easily, even with a monochrome monitor.

Click OK to close the Library dialog box and return to the Edit Color dialog box, where you can either choose OK to add the PMS color to your color palette or edit the color.

Changing the Names of Colors from a Library

T I P

You can change the name of the color chosen from a library by entering a different name in the Edit Colors dialog box after you choose the color. For example, you might want to name a color according to the type of element you apply it to, such as Logo Color. This is fine if you will be printing process color separations of the color, or if you will be printing a series of the same publication each with a different spot color for "logo color" elements. But if you will be using the library color as a spot color and you want the print shop to recognize the name, it's a good idea to keep the name that is assigned in the library.

CAUTION: If you choose the Crop Marks option in the Print command dialog box when you print color separations, PageMaker prints the color names you have assigned for each spot color. PANTONE color names and numbers have specific meanings to commercial printers. Therefore, if you edit a color that is based on a PANTONE color, it is a good idea to change the new color's name to avoid confusing the staff at your print shop.

When you close the Edit Color dialog box, the Define Colors dialog box remains open. Click Close to close the box and record all changes, or click Cancel if you decide not to record any changes or additions.

Crayon Color Library

The Crayon color library includes the 64 basic crayon colors developed by Crayola. These colors are familiar to anyone raised in the United States, but this is not a system traditionally used in printing. Nevertheless, you can choose colors from this library and set them to print as spot or process colors.

To select a color from the Crayon system, choose the Define Colors command from the Element menu. Then choose New to display the Edit Colors dialog box, and choose Crayon from the Library drop-down list to display the Crayon Library dialog box. Either type the full name in the Crayon Color area or click a color in the scrolling display of colors.

DIC Color Guide (DaiNippon Spot Color System)

The DIC Color Guide, or DaiNippon library, is a system for identifying spot ink colors. DaiNippon colors are cataloged in a swatchbook; choosing a color from this system ensures accurate color reproduction on a press.

To select a color from the DaiNippon system, choose the Define Colors command from the Element menu. Then choose New to display the Edit Colors dialog box, and choose DaiNippon from the Library drop-down list to display the DaiNippon Library dialog box. Either type the full identification number in the DIC Color area, or click a color in the scrolling display of colors (see fig. 12.16).

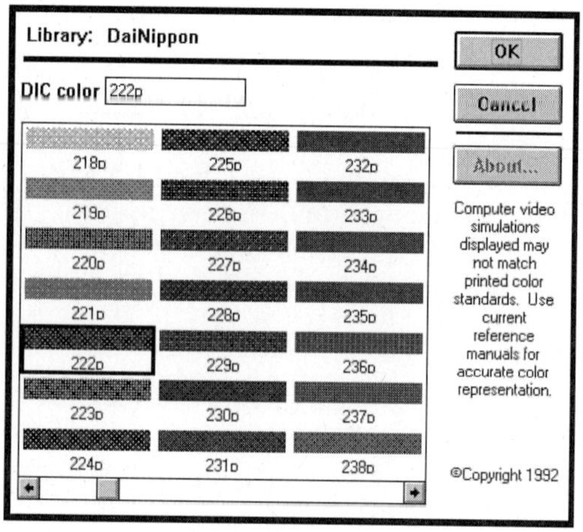

Fig. 12.16

The DaiNippon Library dialog box.

Like CMYK colors, DaiNippon colors can be printed as spot colors or process colors. Greatest accuracy will be achieved if you choose a spot-color separation and let your printer mix the ink according to the color shown in the DaiNippon swatchbook. PageMaker separates the DaiNippon color to its process color equivalent, but some colors may vary from the original DaiNippon color when finally printed by this method.

Focoltone Process Color System

The Focoltone system was created to facilitate the selection of accurate process colors. The basic 763 Focoltone colors consist of combinations of cyan, magenta, yellow, and black in varying percentages from 5 to 85 percent, in 5 percent increments. Additionally, 13 variations on each color are created by eliminating one, two, or three of the process colors. For example, color #1000, a light brown, contains 15 percent cyan, 30 percent magenta, 50 percent yellow, and 25 percent black. Variation number 1, color #1001, contains 15 percent cyan, 30 percent magenta, 50 percent yellow, and 0 percent black.

To select a color from the Focoltone system, choose the Define Colors command from the Element menu. Then choose New to display the Edit Colors dialog box, and choose Focoltone from the Library drop-down list to display the Focoltone Library dialog box. Enter a number in the FCS area above the display of colors (see fig. 12.17). You can also scroll through the display of colors and click a color. The Focoltone colors were designed for process colors, so keep the Process color option that is automatically selected in the Edit Color dialog box when you choose a Focoltone color, and turn on Process Separation in the Print command dialog box for best results.

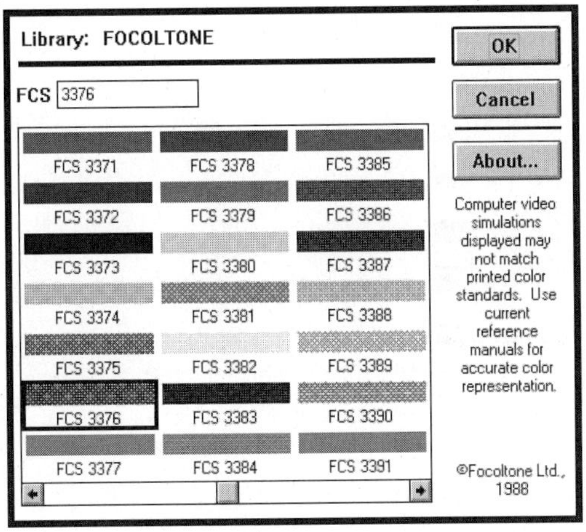

Fig. 12.17

The Focoltone Library dialog box.

Greys Library

The Greys library contains shades of grey (tints of black) from 1% to 100% in 1% increments. Each shade is available as either spot or process color.

To select a color from the Greys system, choose the Define Colors command from the Element menu. Then choose New to display the Edit Colors dialog box, and choose Greys from the Library drop-down list to display the Greys Library dialog box. Either type the full name in the Greys Color area, or click a color in the scrolling display of colors.

PANTONE and PANTONE Euro Spot Color Matching System

The PANTONE Matching System (PMS) is a standard used by designers and commercial printers for specifying colors and mixing spot-color inks. The system is based on nine basic PANTONE colors plus black and white. When mixed in various percentages, these colors yield the more than 700 colors in the system. The colors in the PANTONE® Library dialog box are listed in the same order as in the *PANTONE Color Formula Guide 747XR*, a color swatchbook available from most art supply stores. Choosing a color from this system ensures accurate color reproduction on a press.

This system is the most widely used color matching system in the United States. The PANTONE Euro Library is also available to match colors from the slightly different PANTONE swatchbooks used in Europe.

To select a color from the PANTONE system, choose the Define Colors command from the Element menu. Then choose New to display the Edit Colors dialog box, and choose PANTONE® from the Library drop-down list to display the PANTONE® Library dialog box. Enter a number in the PANTONE area above the display of colors (see fig. 12.18 and the four-color insert). You can also scroll through the display of colors and click a color. The color you specify is displayed in the dialog box.

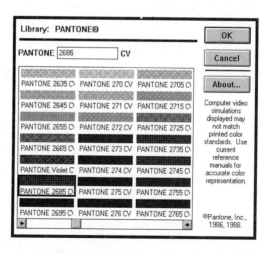

Fig. 12.18

The PANTONE® Library dialog box.

This color is a simulation of the PANTONE color; the CV after each color name indicates the color is a computer video simulation of the actual PANTONE color. Like CMYK colors, PANTONE colors can be printed as spot colors or process colors. Greatest accuracy is achieved if you choose a spot-color separation and let your printer mix the ink according to the color in the PANTONE swatchbook. PageMaker separates the PANTONE color to its process color equivalent, but some colors may vary from the original PANTONE color when finally printed by this method. For better results in printing process color separations, use the PANTONE Process Color System, described next.

PANTONE® Process Color System

The PANTONE® Process Color System was developed for achieving optimum results in printing PANTONE colors as process color separations using PostScript output devices. To select a color from the PANTONE® Process Color System, choose the Define Colors command from the Element menu. Then choose New to display the Edit Colors dialog box, and choose PANTONE® Process Color System from the Library drop-down list to display the PANTONE® Process Color System Library dialog box. Enter a number in the PANTONE area above the display of colors (see fig. 12.19). You can also scroll through the display of colors and click a color.

The PANTONE Process Color System colors were designed for process colors, so keep the Process color option that is automatically selected in the Edit Color dialog box when you choose a PANTONE Process Color, and turn on Process Separation in the Print command dialog box for best results.

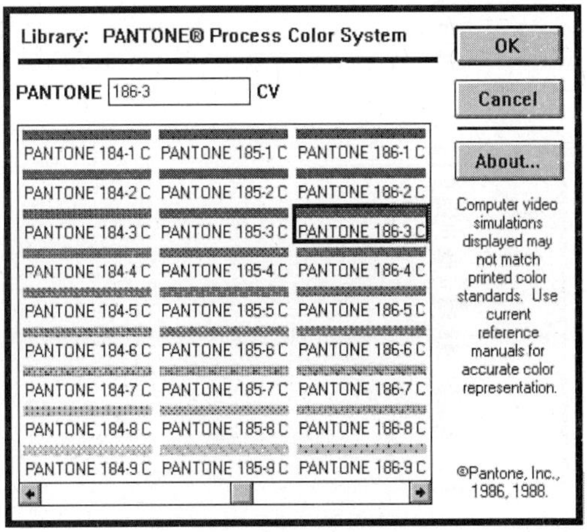

Fig. 12.19

The PANTONE® Process Color System Library dialog box.

TOYOPC Color System

The TOYOPC (Process Color) library is a system for identifying process colors that are cataloged in the TOYO 88 Color Finder swatchbook; choosing a color from this system ensures accurate color reproduction on a press.

To select a color from the TOYO system, choose the Define Colors command from the Element menu. Then choose New to display the Edit Colors dialog box, and choose TOYOPC from the Library drop-down list to display the TOYO Library dialog box. Type the full identification number in the TOYO Color area or click a color in the scrolling display of colors.

TRUMATCH Process Color System

Like the Focoltone color system, the TRUMATCH system was developed for achieving optimum results in printing process color separations using PostScript output devices. The TRUMATCH system is based on 50 hues, with value graduations or tints of each color totaling about 2000 colors. You must use the TRUMATCH Colorfinder swatchbook when creating colors using this system, because your monitor can only approximate the color on-screen.

To select a color from the TRUMATCH system, choose the Define Colors command from the Element menu. Then choose New to display the Edit Colors dialog box, and choose TRUMATCH from the Library drop-down list to display the TRUMATCH Library dialog box. Enter a number in the TRUMATCH area above the display of colors (see fig. 12.20 and the four-color insert).

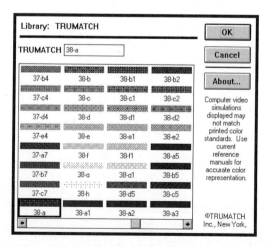

Fig. 12.20

The TRUMATCH Library dialog box.

You can also scroll through the display of colors and click a color. The TRUMATCH colors were designed for process colors, so keep the Process color option that is automatically selected in the Edit Color dialog box when you choose a TRUMATCH color, and turn on Process Separation in the Print command dialog box for best results.

Creating Custom Color Libraries

PageMaker 5.0 introduces an Aldus Addition called Create Color Library, which quickly creates a custom color library that includes all the editable colors currently on your Colors palette (excluding [Paper], [Black], and [Registration]).

You simply set up the Colors palette for a publication to include the set you want in your custom color library, and then choose Create Color Library from the Aldus Additions submenu on the Utilities menu. In the Create Color Library dialog box, shown in figure 12.21, type the name of the new library, ending with the extension BCF. You can enter a number of Rows and Columns sufficient for displaying the number of colors in your current palette. In the Notes area, type information that can be viewed when the library is opened through the Edit Colors dialog box. Click Browse if you want to determine where the library will be saved; however, saving all libraries in the default C:\ALDUS\USENGLSH\COLORS directory is a good idea. Finally, click Save to save the custom library.

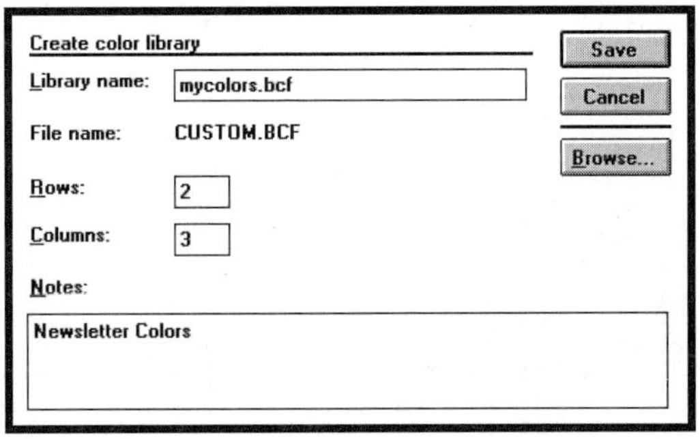

Fig. 12.21

The Create Color Library dialog box.

When you next choose the define Colors command and click New or Edit to create a new color, your custom library will be available in the drop-down list of libraries. Whatever Notes you typed will be displayed when you click the About button when the library is open (see fig. 12.22).

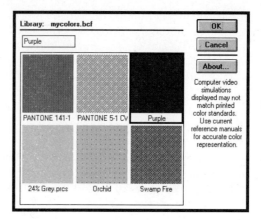

Fig. 12.22

A custom color library accessed through the Edit Colors dialog box.

Creating a custom library is a handy way of collecting the colors you use into one library and then deleting the other color libraries from your hard disk to save space. Creating a custom library also saves you time scrolling through a library to find the color you want—assuming that your custom library is smaller than the libraries that come with PageMaker.

Creating New Colors

To create a new color, choose Define Colors from the Element menu. PageMaker displays the Define Colors dialog box (see fig. 12.23).

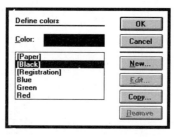

Fig. 12.23

The Define Colors dialog box with the default color names.

To create a new color, double-click the [Black] or [Registration] color name, or select any other color and click New. PageMaker then displays the Edit Color dialog box (see fig. 12.24). You can display the Edit Color dialog box for a new color also by holding down the Ctrl key and clicking the [Black] or [Registration] color name in the Colors palette. (See "Applying Colors" in this chapter.)

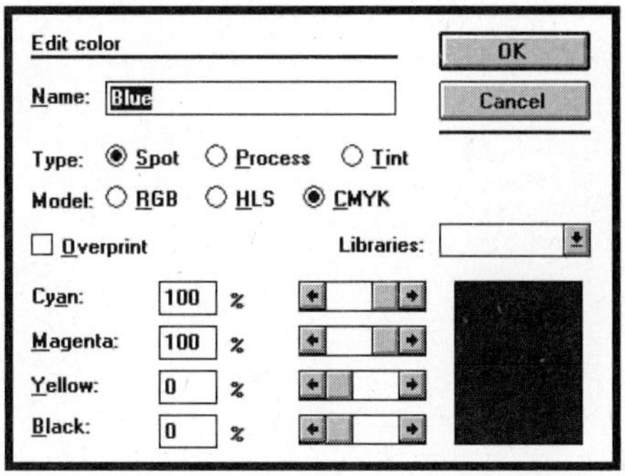

Fig. 12.24

The Edit Color
dialog box.

Type the name of the new color in the Name field, where the blinking
cursor appears. If the name you type is not on the palette, PageMaker
adds the new name to the color sheet but does not delete or change
any existing names. If you type a name already on the palette,
PageMaker prompts you to use a different name. (You must click the
Edit button in the Define Colors dialog box if you want to change an
existing color definition.) If you type a reserved PANTONE color name
(Process Black, Process Yellow, Process Magenta, or Process Cyan),
PageMaker prompts you to use a different name. PANTONE colors must
be selected through the PANTONE Library dialog box (as described
previously in this chapter).

Removing Colors

You can remove a color from the color sheet by choosing Define Colors
from the Element menu, choosing a color, then clicking Remove in the
Define Colors dialog box. Text and graphics that the removed color has
been assigned to become black, and tints of the color become a shade
of gray. You cannot remove the three basic colors defined by Page-
Maker: [Paper], [Black], and [Registration]. Removing a color from the
current publication's color sheet does not affect the color sheets of
other publications. If you want all the objects that have the color to
change to another color besides [Black], see the section "Replacing a
Color" later in this chapter.

Copying Colors from Other Publications

You can copy the color sheet from another publication to the current
one by choosing Define Colors from the Element menu and clicking
Copy in the dialog box. The Copy Colors dialog box displays a list of
other publications whose color sheet you can copy (see fig. 12.25).
Scroll through the list to find the name of the publication you want.

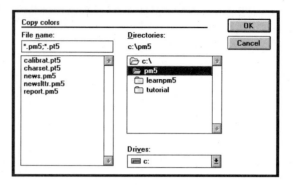

Fig. 12.25

The Copy Colors
dialog box.

You can select a disk drive and directory path as you do in similar dialog boxes, such as the Open, Place, Save As, and Export dialog boxes. Double-click the c:\ to change to the next higher directory on the current drive. Double-click a directory name in brackets to open it. To change drives, select the drive from the Drives drop-down list. Type a path name in the File Name text box and click OK to display the publications in the specified directory. Type ***.*** in the File Name text box to list publications with extensions other than PM5 or PT5.

Choose the publication whose color sheet you want to copy by double-clicking the publication name or by selecting the publication name and clicking OK. When you click Close in the Copy Colors dialog box, all the colors defined in the selected publication are copied into the current publication. If an existing color shares the same name as a color you are copying, PageMaker asks whether you want to replace the existing color with the copied color definition.

T I P   **Importing Colors Selectively**

If you don't want to copy an entire color palette from another publication, you can import styles selectively in PageMaker. The simplest method is to open the publication that contains elements that use the colors you want to import, use the Pointer tool to select and copy those elements, then paste them into the new publication.

If you think you will be doing this often and you want to be really organized, you can create a PageMaker template for each different set of colors you use, then open the template or Copy the template through the Edit Color dialog box when you start a new publication.

Importing EPS Graphics Colors

If you import an EPS graphic containing spot or process colors, those colors are added to the Colors palette in PageMaker for the publication. An EPS sign in a bracket appears at the beginning of the color name to indicate that it is an imported EPS color. You can apply these imported colors to objects, convert spot colors to process colors, and affect whether the colors print (through the Print command). However, you cannot edit the color values to create different colors.

For Related Information

◄◄ "Importing Graphics Created in Other Programs," p. 363.

FROM HERE...

Applying Colors

You can apply color to text or graphic elements created in PageMaker, or to black-and-white graphics imported from other applications. You cannot change the colors in imported color graphics through PageMaker directly; you must change the colors using the program that originally created the graphics.

You can apply colors to any selected object through the Colors palette. You also can apply colors to graphics created using PageMaker's tools through the Fill and Line command. You can apply colors to text through the Type Specifications dialog box (accessed through the Type menu's Type Specs command or Define Styles command, as described in Chapter 8.

To apply a color, first display the Colors palette by either choosing Color Palette from the Window menu or using the keyboard shortcut, Ctrl+K. The Colors palette lists all the colors you have defined with the Define Colors command (see fig. 12.26).

You can resize the palette window in the same way you size any window: Position the cursor along the edge of the palette until the cursor changes to a double-headed arrow, and drag the edge of the palette until it is the size you want. You can make the palette large enough to display the full list of all colors you have created, or you can keep the palette small (to allow more room on-screen for the page layout and pasteboard) and use the scrollbars to move through the list of colors. You close the Colors palette by double-clicking the palette's Control menu icon (in the top left corner), by choosing the Color Palette command from the Window menu whenever it has a check mark next to it, or by pressing Ctrl+K.

The Colors palette.

When the Colors palette is displayed, you assign a color to an object (text or graphic) by selecting that object and then clicking a name in the Colors palette. The following sections describe this procedure for text, PageMaker graphics, and imported graphics.

Applying Color to Text

You apply color to text by first selecting the text with the Text tool and then selecting a color from the Colors palette. (You can assign color to text also with the Type menu's Type Specs command, as discussed in Chapter 8. Text color can be included in a style sheet definition. You can assign colors to text and anchored graphics while in Story view, but the color is not displayed until you return to Layout view.

T I P   Creating Gray Lines, Borders, or Text

Remember that you can assign a percentage of shading to the fill of a rectangle or ellipse drawn in PageMaker through the Element menu's Fill submenu. But to make a line or text gray or tinted, you must create a tint in the Colors palette, as described previously in this chapter.

Applying Color to PageMaker Graphics

You can apply color to lines, rectangles, and ellipses created with PageMaker's drawing tools. In choosing colors for lines, remember that color in thin lines appears lighter than the same color applied to a larger, solid area.

You can assign a Fill color to any two-dimensional object, such as a box or an ellipse, created with PageMaker's graphics tools. To display the fill color, however, you must choose a fill other than None or Paper from the list displayed in the Fill submenu of the Element menu or in the Fill and Line dialog box. You can apply a tinted fill—such as 30% red—by applying a fill color of Red (that is, 100% Red) and then choosing the 30% fill pattern. (To create the same effect for a line or for text, you must define 30% Red as a new color.) The Fill submenu is shown in figure 12.27.

Element	
Line	▶
Fill	√ None
Fill and line...	Paper
	Solid
Bring to front ^F	10%
Send to back ^B	20%
Remove transformation	30%
	40%
Text wrap...	60%
Image control...	80%
Rounded corners...	
Define colors...	
Restore original color	
Link info...	
Link options...	

Fig. 12.27

The Fill submenu.

You also can make the object's border stand out by selecting different fill patterns to get solid borders around lighter-colored interiors or by setting the border and the fill to different colors.

PageMaker 5.0 enables you to assign different colors to the Line and Fill of rectangles and ellipses drawn using PageMaker's drawing tools. You click the rectangle icon at the top of the Colors palette to select the Fill color, and click the diagonal line icon to select the Line color. You can also click the down-pointing arrow to choose Line, Fill, or Both from a drop-down list. You quickly assign a color to a border of a filled object by holding the Shift key as you click the Color name in the palette.

PageMaker 5.0 adds a Fill and Line command that enables you to assign separate colors for the fill and border of an object created in PageMaker, as well as make the same selections from the Fill or Line submenu below the Element menu (see fig. 12.28). The Fill and Line dialog box enables you to set selected objects to Overprint objects below them. By doing so, you override the Overprint attribute assigned through the Edit Color dialog box, which was described previously. See also "A Word about Knockouts (Traps and Butts)" earlier in this chapter.

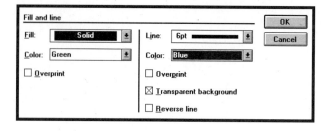

Fig. 12.28

The Fill and Line
dialog box.

You can select more than one object at a time and then assign one
color to the whole group. If all the selected objects are already assigned the same color, that color is highlighted in the Colors palette.
If the selected objects are assigned different colors, no color is highlighted in the Colors palette.

Applying Color to Imported Graphics

You can assign one color to black-and-white graphics imported from
other graphics applications with the Place command. You cannot, however, assign colors to only parts of such graphics. Multicolor graphics
created in other applications and imported into PageMaker may be
displayed in color, and will be separated into spot or process colors as
specified in the original application—unless you switch spot colors to
process colors through the Edit Colors command. Colors assigned to
EPS graphics are added to the Colors palette in PageMaker when the
graphic is imported, and PageMaker adds EPS to the color name.

Replacing a Color

You can change all the elements assigned the same color to another
color. Choose Define Colors from the Element menu, click the name of
the color you want to replace, then click Edit. Change the name of the
original color to the name of the color you want to replace it with, and
click OK. PageMaker displays an alert box asking if you want to change
all elements that have the original color to the new color name. If you
agree, PageMaker deletes the original color name from the palette and
changes the color of all objects that were assigned that color. Objects
that were a tint of the original color become a tint of the replacement
color. See also "Removing Colors," earlier in this chapter.

Restoring Original Colors

Use the Restore Original Color command from the Element menu to remove PageMaker-applied color from an imported color graphic (that is, colors applied to the graphic in the original program, but modified through PageMaker's define Colors command). This allows PageMaker to print or color-separate the graphic according to the color information imported with the graphic. The appearance of the graphic on-screen does not change.

This command is dimmed when no graphic is selected, when you select a graphic to which no PageMaker color has been applied, or when you select a graphic imported in a file format that cannot include color information, such as monochrome or grayscale TIFF. Remember, however, that you can apply a single color to a monochrome or grayscale TIFF in PageMaker, and you "remove" the color simply by selecting the graphic and choosing Black from the Colors palette.

For Related Information

◀◀ "Specifying Color," p. 304.

◀◀ "Editing Styles," p. 343.

◀◀ "Changing Line Widths and Fill Patterns," p. 381.

FROM HERE...

Proofing Colors On-Screen

On-screen color proofing, or *soft proofing*, is a method currently being used only for preliminary and position proofing. Soft proofing is not reliable as a final proofing technique because using the color on a monitor to simulate the color of ink on paper is extremely difficult.

Most monitors are based on a cathode ray tube (CRT) that displays colors by electrically stimulating phosphors on the surface of the tube. The transmitted color is made up of dots of the additive primaries (red, green, and blue) that make up white light. These dots, or *screen pixels*, are fixed in size and position. CRT displays create different colors by varying the intensity of pixels. If red and green pixels are stimulated at the same intensity, for example, the result is yellow. If the intensity of green is reduced, the result is orange.

Printed color, on the other hand, is reflected; it is made up of dots of the subtractive primary colors—yellow, cyan, and magenta—plus black. Different colors are created by varying the size of the dots (the density of the printed ink).

When you proof color pages on your monitor, be sure that all color images are correctly linked to your publication (discussed in Chapter 13), that detailed graphics are set to display at high resolution by means of the Preferences command (on the File menu, discussed in Chapter 4), and that your monitor is set to display as many colors as your graphics card allows.

T   I   P   Displaying a Single Image at High Resolution

To display a single image at high resolution when the Preferences resolution is set to Normal or Gray Out, press the Ctrl key as the image starts to appear on-screen. This procedure works when PageMaker displays or redisplays the page—that is, when you move to a different page or change the view of the page.

Calibrating Color Monitors

If you have created color separations with a personal computer, you know that many variables come into play in getting the results you want. One key challenge is calibrating the color definition on display and output devices. This enables you to achieve the most predictable results possible.

There are a variety of solutions for monitor calibration on the Macintosh, ranging from simple, no-cost solutions to hardware and software solutions that cost thousands of dollars. On the PC platform, however, only simple solutions are currently available: some common-sense steps can help ensure consistency in the colors that appear on your monitor. For example, keep the lighting conditions stable in the room where you're working. To do so, use artificial light that has the same brightness at all times of day, or use a color swatchbook to select colors. It's reasonable to expect that solutions for color calibration for both Windows and PageMaker will be developed someday.

COMPUADD LEASING
BUGLE

YOU JUST WON'T BELIEVE
THE RAVES FOR COMPUADD LEASING

Our special leasing correspondent, Patsy Miller, has been beating the bushes and has found early good response to the new CompuAdd Leasing program.

"They're Grrrrreat!"

DANTE COMINOTTO from HQ had this to say about the program: "CompuAdd Leasing is *really* good. They're quick and easy to deal with. One phone call is all it took. They'll do all the work for you!"

Boldly stepping out and giving the new leasing program a try, Dante was especially pleased with CompuAdd Leasing's thorough credit process. His customer, West Alabama Home Health Care, was an interesting test case because they don't like to guarantee their leases. Dante called his CompuAdd Leasing Marketing Rep with the deal and she promised to call the customer within 10 minutes.

Not only did Paula, the Marketing Rep, call the customer right away but... "Within 90 minutes," says Dante, "she called me back with an approval." (The BUGLE talked to Paula later to find out how CompuAdd Leasing was able to do the deal without a personal guarantee—she told us that the customer's credit was so clean that it was a "no brainer".)

OK, OK. So Dante got paid for this Endorsement. Big Deal.

We admit it...Dante said these great things and he got paid for it. Actually, CompuAdd pays everybody an extra 1% commission for every leasing transaction! And this was a big deal. A nice big $10,000 transaction— a nice extra $100 in Dante's pocket.

But Really, He Did it for the Shoes.

"Sure," you're thinking, "he came up with all these praises about CompuAdd Leasing for the money". But you're wrong. We've learned that Dante was actually motivated by our special get-acquainted promotion. You know, the one: do a deal with CompuAdd Leasing before May 1st and we'll send you a **$50 gift certificate from the FOOT LOCKER**, America's

most complete athletic footwear store. Haven't heard about the promo? Call your CompuAdd Leasing Marketing Representative at 800/537-0088 for details.

After all, with approvals like Dante's running in the 90 minute range, you'll need to be as fast on your feet as possible.

We gave **DANTE COMINOTTO** a $50 gift certificate from the Foot Locker... we'll give you one too. Call your CompuAdd Marketing Rep at 800/537-0088 for details.

ASK THE LEASING GUY
He's in Sales Too

Dear Leasing Guy: I'm afraid. Afraid to offer leasing to my customers. I just don't know much about it and I might not appear totally buttoned down. *But I'm also afraid that my extra 1% commission is just slipping away.*

Dear Afraid: Fear not. You don't have to know a lot about leasing. That's what we're here for. Call us. Explain the transaction you're working on. Together we'll come up with a way of buttoning down the deal. LG

Dear Leasing Guy: I'm worried. Worried because I had a bad experience with leasing once. How can I be sure CompuAdd Leasing will be better than those other companies? But I'm also worried that if I don't use leasing I'll lose out on that terrific extra commission.

Dear Worried: Is our name CompuAdd Leasing or what? We want every sale as badly as you do. We price, we fuss, we worry over every transaction. Just like you do. Call us. Let's worry together. LG

The only thing you really have to know about leasing is our phone number: 800/537-0088

CompuAdd
LEASING

SEPTEMBER/OCTOBER 1991

COMPILATIONS

The newsletter for the Micro Focus COBOL Community

MICRO FOCUS

Micro Focus Acquires Stingray Software

Micro Focus has acquired Stingray Software Company, Inc., a Wisconsin-based corporation, in exchange for 600,000 shares of Micro Focus, representing a value of $16 million at current share prices.

With this acquisition, Micro Focus is now directly supplying the Stingray IMS emulation package for the PC

The merger with Stingray strengthens a successful relationship that has existed since 1987. Stingray developed an IMS environment for IBM personal computers and Personal System/2® computers which has been marketed by Micro Focus as the IMS Option™ to Micro Focus COBOL/2 Workbench™. IMS is a database/data communications system (IMS DB/ DC®) sold by IBM for mainframes and used by many companies worldwide.

The merger brings Stingray's IMS technology under the control of Micro Focus. The staff of Stingray will continue with Micro Focus to ensure the continued maintenance and development of the technology.

"Stingray's mainframe expertise and wealth of technology strengthens Micro Focus' commitment and capability to provide the most complete and robust tools for the mainframe development marketplace," said Paul O'Grady, Chairman of Micro Focus Group Plc.

Stingray will play a key role in Micro Focus' initiatives to develop additional mainframe emulation

continued on page 15

FIPS 21-3 Certification for Micro Focus COBOL

Micro Focus COBOL/2 compilers for DOS, OS/2 and UNIX environments were among the first COBOL products to receive Federal Information Processing Standard (FIPS) 21-3 certification.

After July of this year, all computer hardware and software must meet the FIPS 21-3 standard before it can be purchased by any branch of the federal government. Micro Focus COBOL/2 V2.5 (DOS-OS/2), Micro Focus COBOL/2 for UNIX V1.3 and Microsoft COBOL V4.5 were tested by the National Institute of Standards and Technology (NIST) with the COBOL Compiler Validation Standard 85 (CCVS85) Version 2.1 test suite and were validated at High Level with no errors. In addition, Microsoft COBOL 4.5, a COBOL compiler based on Micro Focus COBOL/2 also passed the FIPS 21-3 tests.

One of the future requirements for FIPS 21-3 certification was the inclusion of Intrinsic Functions. Intrinsic Functions are macros that allow programmers to code whole procedures in a single statement. In 1989, 42 intrinsic functions were added to the ANSI'85 COBOL standard to make the COBOL language more efficient.

Version 2.5 of Micro Focus COBOL/2 for DOS and OS/2 includes ANSI'85 intrinsic functions. These functions automate many routine programming tasks dealing with calendar arithmetic, financial functions, numerical analysis, and mathematical/statistical and trigometric functions.

The Micro Focus COBOL product line also supports FIPS FLAGGING, the other major addition to the federal standard.

continued on page 3

This four-color newsletter includes a color scan and a graphic at the bottom of the page. The graphic was created in Aldus FreeHand and framed in a custom, text wrap border. The front page contains process colors and a spot PANTONE color.

Reprinted by permission of Micro Focus USA, Palo Alto, California.

IMAGE AS ART

LET US PUT YOUR IDEAS TO WORK
A CREATIVE COLLABORATION

*Bring us your word
processor files and
let us put together a
layout for any pro-
ject that suits your
style as well as
your budget.*

TECHART
SAN FRANCISCO

**400 PACIFIC
SAN FRANCISCO
PHONE: 362-1110
FAX: 362-2811**

This four-color
page layout
includes a
scanned color
photograph.

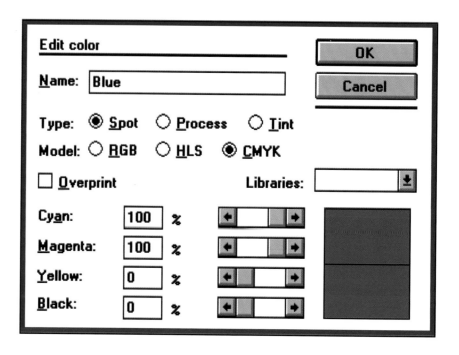

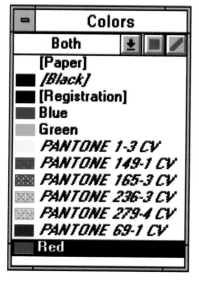

The Edit Color dialog box shows the four color components when CMYK is selected (top); the Color Palette shows spot, process, and PANTONE identified colors (bottom).

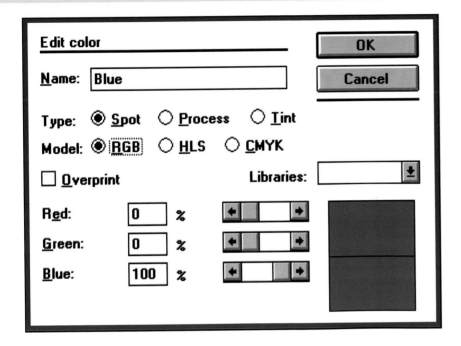

Edit color

Name: Blue	OK
	Cancel

Type: ● **S**pot ○ **P**rocess ○ **T**int

Model: ● RGB ○ **H**LS ○ **C**MYK

☐ **O**verprint   **L**ibraries:

R**e**d: 0   %

Green: 0   %

Blue: 100 %

Edit color

Name: Blue	OK
	Cancel

Type: ● **S**pot ○ **P**rocess ○ **T**int

Model: ○ **R**GB ● HLS ○ **C**MYK

☐ **O**verprint   **L**ibraries:

H**u**e: 240 deg.

Lightness: 50 %

Saturation: 100 %

The Edit Color
dialog box
shows three color
components when
RGB (top) or HLS
(bottom) is selected.

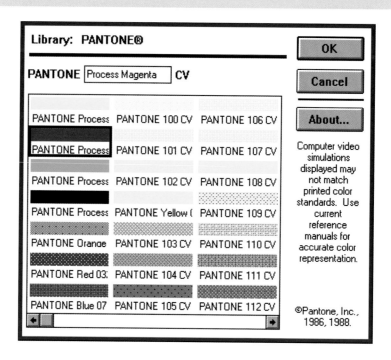

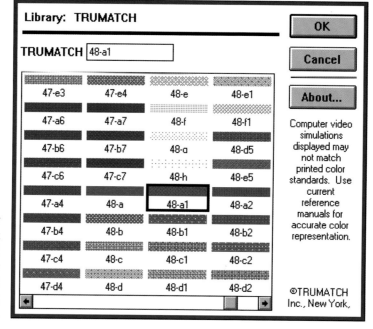

The Edit Color dialog box when PANTONE library (top) or TRUMATCH library (bottom) is selected.

Color versions of three figures from Chapter 12.

With perfect registration, colors meet but do not overlap (except black, which usually overprints all other colors).

When registration is off slightly, gaps show as white lines, and overlapping colors yield a dark, muddy line.

Adjacent spot colors must meet exactly, without gaps or overlap between them (top).

TEXT DARKER THAN CIRCLE

TEXT DARKER THAN CIRCLE

TEXT DARKER THAN CIRCLE

Circle with knockout in Spot Color 1.

Text in Spot Color 2 with Overprint off.

Composite makes text slightly darker where it overlaps at edges.

Overlapping colors printed with overprint off (middle).

TEXT DARKER THAN CIRCLE

TEXT DARKER THAN CIRCLE

Circle with no knockout in Spot Color 1.

Text in Spot Color 2 with Overprint off.

Composite makes text slightly darker all over.

Overlapping colors printed with overprint on (bottom).

Screens for cyan, magenta, yellow, and black are normally rotated relative to each other (right) to prevent Moiré patterns in printing process colors.

Magnified versions of spot (left square in each pair) and process versions of black, blue, green, and red (right).

Black

Blue

Green

Red

Spot color overlays (right) and four-color process separations (below) yield the same colors in the final printing (far right).

Green

Black

Final result in both cases is a page in green and black.

Cyan

Magenta

Yellow

Black

For Related Information

◄◄ "Displaying Graphics," p. 158.

►► "Managing Linked Text and Graphics Documents," p. 597.

FROM HERE...

Printing in Color with Color Printers

Regardless of how carefully you calibrate your monitor or imagesetter, it's important to obtain a quality color proof of your work. In the simplest case, this might be a printout on a 300-dpi color printer. In the case of pages containing color photographs, a proof made from the actual film, such as a proof created on a Matchprint or Chromalin system, is necessary.

You can print color pages with PageMaker directly on color dot-matrix printers, thermal-transfer printers, ink-jet printers, and film recorders supported by Microsoft Windows and PageMaker. For example, the QMS ColorScript 100 color printer is a 300-dpi PostScript thermal printer that can serve for color proofing or for short-run color productions. Most high-resolution color printers use an ink-jet technology, creating images by spraying minute droplets of ink. Printing a color publication is no different from printing a black-and-white publication. If the printer you select in the Print dialog box (displayed when you select the Print command on the File menu or press Ctrl+P) has color capabilities, PageMaker prints the publication in color. If you print a color publication on a black-and-white printer, PageMaker converts the page image to monochrome black and shades of gray.

If you intend to print a publication on a color printer as the final output, you need to know what colors the printer is capable of reproducing, then define colors that match the printer's colors. If you are using a high-resolution PostScript color printer, you should be able to print any color you want. If you are printing on a low-resolution dot-matrix printer, however, your choice of colors is more limited.

Inexpensive dot-matrix color printers can cost less than $1000. The trade-offs for the low cost can include low resolution, slow printing speed, a limited color palette, poor color quality, and banding (streaks across the printed image that result from a moving carriage). Nevertheless, a dot-matrix color printer can be a worthwhile investment for in-house presentations and for printing proofs of color images that might later be output on a printer of greater capability. Dot-matrix color printers are available from Epson, Canon, Brother, Toshiba, and others.

The next step up is color ink-jet printers, which offer higher resolution and better color than dot-matrix printers. Ink-jet printers can cost less than $800 (the Hewlett-Packard DeskJet 500C, for example) to $3,000 or more (the Hewlett-Packard PaintJet XL300, for example). The wide price range in this group reflects the variation in color quality and other features such as installed memory, speed, and paper handling.

At the high end, PostScript color printers can cost as little as $5000 (the Tektronix Phaser IIPXe, for example) or as much as $80,000 (DuPont Imaging Systems 4Cast). In this category are thermal printers that use heat to seal color pigments in a wax or plastic coating onto Mylar, laser printers that use color toner cartridges, and printers that use thermal dye technology to produce output approaching the quality of photographs. Thermal printers are made by Kodak, Mitsubishi, QMS, Tektronix, and Versatec, among others. These printers offer the best output, but the high investment must be justified by a high volume of color printing. For this reason, most people take disk files to a service bureau for color output of this quality.

Besides compatibility and the cost of the printer itself, you need to figure the cost of supplies into your decision to buy a color printer. For best results, most ink-jet or thermal color printers require either special coated paper or special transparent film if the printer accommodates overhead transparencies. In addition, you need to stock a good supply of color ribbons, ink cartridges, or toner cartridges. You will be surprised at how quickly the color supply dwindles when you are printing full-page color images with solid color backgrounds.

Many color print jobs, especially large-volume runs, are best handled by an offset print shop (discussed in "Printing in Color with Offset Printing," later in this chapter). Some color publications, however, can be printed on a color printer. The following sections explain some of the jobs you probably can handle easily rather than take to an offset print shop.

Comps and Proofs

Color printers are often used to print *comps* (to give a client an idea of how a design looks in color) or *position proofs* (to show the position and general color of elements on a page). You can print full-color images on a single page, or you can print separated spot-color images on separate sheets of acetate. Printing color on acetate is a good way to check the registration of separated colors. These proofs often look similar to the screen display of some color monitors, and some people object to using position proofs as final proofs because they do not predict color press results accurately enough.

Short-Run Color Publications

Color printers also can be used for short-run color publications. If you need more than a few color copies, the slow printing speed and cost of color cartridges or inks make it more economical to print only one color master and then reproduce that master on a color copier. For very large quantities, you will want to use offset lithography—the traditional printing press. Offset printing has its own set of considerations and specialized vocabulary, discussed in "Printing in Color with Offset Printing," later in this chapter.

Presentation Materials

Presentation materials, such as slides and overhead transparencies, are rarely offset printed because they are needed in such low quantities. Four methods of creating color images for presentations are commonly used: printing on a color printer, printing on a film recorder, coloring a black-and-white image by hand, and overlaying adhesive color acetates.

You also can print the images on paper and reproduce them with color photocopiers or color photoprocessors; or you can photograph the images on paper or on-screen to make slides. Some color printers offer the option of printing on clear acetate, which is useful for color overlays to check registration and for multicolor overhead transparencies. Conversely, you can use a high-end Matchprint system to produce good quality color images on acetate (usually used for color proofing), then use them as overheads.

If you do not have a color printer, you can use PageMaker to design on-screen color images, then convert the color areas to paper color, print them in black and white on acetate, and color the images yourself. You can color a black-and-white image by hand with a brush and color inks or with color pens. Make sure that the inks you are using will adhere to the transparent film and will not bleed across boundaries on paper. Coloring by hand this way requires skill and patience to ensure even coverage and to avoid streaking.

You can add color to printed images also by using traditional paste-up techniques. Unless you are skilled with pens or brushes, you get the best results by overlaying printed images with adhesive color acetates, which are available at art supply shops. You can lay a sheet of color over the printed image, trace over the area to be colored by using a cutting edge, and pull the color away from those parts of the image not to be colored (see fig. 12.29).

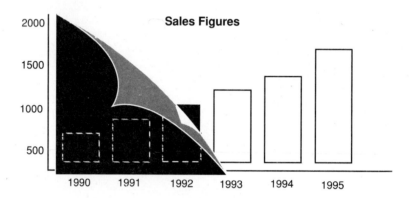

Fig. 12.29

Use a cutting edge to trace over an area to be colored.

Printing in Color with Offset Printing

When you need a color publication printed, especially in large quantities, usually you first print it in black and white on a PostScript printer or typesetter and then send it to an offset print shop to be printed in color. Even if a color printer is available, the offset print shop needs black-and-white mechanicals, also called *camera-ready masters*.

Printing a publication in only one color is the same as printing in black and white. You provide one camera-ready master for each page, and the print shop applies a color ink to the press. For multicolor printing, on the other hand, each page element to be printed in a particular color must be separated from elements to be printed in other colors because each color requires a different printing plate.

Offset printing offers two ways of producing colors on a page: *spot color* and *process color*. Both methods require you to separate colors, but the separations are different, depending on which method you use. For spot color, each color is printed on a separate overlay and made into a separate printing plate. Ink is mixed to match precisely each color used on the page, and each ink well on the press is loaded with a different mixed color. For process color, each color is split into its primary components (cyan, magenta, yellow, and black), and each ink well on the press is loaded with one of these colors.

Making good color separations traditionally is a difficult, exacting process. Many highly trained artisans have specialized in color separation all their lives. They work like surgeons to meticulously cut the edges around artwork where two colors meet on a page (traps and butts). If the trim is off by as much as the width of the knife edge, the two colors will overlap or have a gap between them.

PageMaker can print separated spot colors or four-color process separations; each color is printed on a separate sheet of paper or transparency with crop marks and registration marks to show how the overlays are to be aligned.

Printing Color Separations

Color publications can be printed as composites, whereby all the colors are printed on one sheet (usually for proofing) or as color separations, whereby each color is printed on a separate sheet. Color separations are usually printed on a high-resolution imagesetter as negatives on film. This procedure saves several steps at the print shop and makes the job easier for the print shop to handle, especially for process color printing or if screens (tints) of spot colors are involved.

In printing from PageMaker, you can specify whether to print all colors or specific colors, whether each ink should overprint or knock out the elements under it, and the screen angles of the process color separations.

To print color separations, choose Print from the File menu, then click the Color button in the Print dialog box to display the Color dialog box (see fig. 12.30). If you click Composite, which is the normal setting used in printing proofs, all colors are printed on one page. When Composite is selected, the normal default is to print Color/Grayscale versions of the page. This means that the pages print in color on a color printer, or as grayscale on a black-and-white printer—20% black appears darker than 20% yellow, for instance. If you click Print Colors in Black, the pages print in black and white (even on a color printer); with this option, 20% black looks the same as 20% yellow, for instance.

If you click Separations, all page elements assigned a particular color are printed together on a sheet, and each color is printed on a different sheet. Click Negative to print the pages reversed—usually on transparent film in an imagesetter. Click Mirror to print a mirror image of the page on film. This changes the right-reading/wrong-reading aspect of the result, and reverses the side of the film on which the emulsion sits relative to the page image. Set Mirror to on for right reading, emulsion side down and for wrong reading, emulsion side up. Set Mirror to off for right reading, emulsion side up and for wrong reading, emulsion side down. (*Right-reading* refers to pages printed with the text in a normal, readable sequence; *wrong-reading*, on the other hand, refers to what some people call "mirror writing," in which the text is readable when you hold the page up to a mirror.) It's best to check with the commercial print shop for what they prefer for these settings.

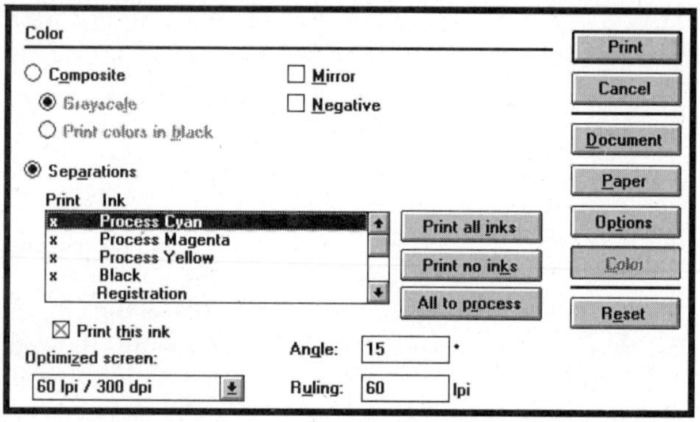

Fig. 12.30

The Print dialog box when the Color button is clicked or grayed and a PostScript printer is selected.

If you do not want to print all colors, double-click the color names in the scrolling list of colors to display or remove the X. (Colors with an X are printed.) As an alternative to double-clicking, you can click a color once and then click Print This Ink to add or remove an X.

You can also click Print All Inks to automatically add an X next to every color and be sure that all colors are printed. Or click Print No Inks to erase all Xs from the left of each color, and then choose the inks to print by highlighting them as described earlier.

Click All to Process to convert all colors to process colors for this printing. This does not affect how colors are defined in the Edit Color dialog box.

In many cases, you will simply make the selections described here and press Print. You usually will apply the Printers Marks and Page Information options, and you might need to prepare additional notes on the pages for the print shop. You can also print the separations to disk, for handling through Aldus Preprint or for a prepress OPI service. In printing process color separations to a PostScript imagesetter, you can also specify the screen angle and ruling (lines per inch) at which each color is printed, and adjust the screen densities for your type of printer. All these topics are covered in the next section.

Adjusting Screen Angles

As mentioned earlier, the film that must be generated to produce plates for four-color process printing consists of a pattern of halftone dots for each color (cyan, magenta, yellow, and black). Traditional halftone screens are generated by photographing an image through a screen that contains dots of various sizes (see fig. 12.31). Lighter areas of an image are made up of smaller dots; darker areas are created by larger dots. The spacing of the lines of dots is called the screen frequency, or screen lines per inch (lpi).

Fig. 12.31

A traditional halftone screen enlarged.

If cyan, magenta, yellow, and black were printed directly on top of each other, the result would be muddy and inexact colors. So in traditional color printing, each color is printed at an angle; the combined angles, when printed together, form tiny rosettes of color, which simulate a particular hue. (This is *not* the same as the screen angle specified for imported grayscale images in the Image Control dialog box, described in Chapter 9.)

The traditional screen angles rotate cyan at 105° or 15°, magenta at 75°, yellow at 0° or 90°, and black at 45°. Spot colors are always printed at 45° unless you specify otherwise. Because Postscript rounds 72 points per inch, the traditional screen angles cannot be produced accurately using imagesetters. The algorithms for the angle of rotation necessary, called *irrational* angles, were developed by Dr. -Ing. Rudolph Hell GmbH., the parent company of Hell Graphics Systems, now Linotype-Hell Company. All prepress systems have licensed these screen angles for use on their equipment.

The preceding angle values are the default values normally assigned by PageMaker, or PageMaker assigns the screen angles it finds in the PPD file for the selected printer. You can change the angles of rotation—and the screen frequency or ruling—through the Print Color dialog box. This is not something you should try without considerable knowledge. If you accidentally change the screen settings, you can get back to the defaults by choosing Default from the Optimized Screen drop-down list. Be sure that the settings on the imagesetter match those you specify here, or you might not get the results you want. If you do want to change the screen angles, you're probably familiar with some of the arcane knowledge that follows.

To understand some of the potential problems of printing color separations to PostScript imagesetters, it's important to understand how PostScript devices simulate halftone screens. Imagesetters cannot physically create dots of various sizes; a pixel is either on or off. To create halftone dots, an imagesetter prints pixels grouped in cells, with each cell corresponding to a halftone dot, thus simulating the traditional halftone dot. On an imagesetter, the only line frequencies possible are those that divide evenly into the resolution of the imagesetter, because it cannot print half a pixel. As a result, color separations printed on PostScript imagesetters cannot always accurately reproduce irrational screens. Sometimes they produce Moiré patterns in color images.

Producing irrational screens requires tremendous computational power, so Adobe has licensed Linotype-Hell's *rational tangent* screening (RT screening) algorithm, which approximates the ideal values. RT screening, however, limits the variety of screen angles and frequencies that can be achieved and varies the screen frequency from plate to plate, producing unsatisfactory results (especially Moiré patterns) with some images. Most PostScript imagesetters manufactured before 1991 use RT screening. Newer imagesetters, however, use improved screening methods.

High Quality Screening (HQS)

The merger of Hell Graphics and the Linotype Company has led to the incorporation of some of Hell's irrational screen technology in Linotype's PostScript RIP 30 and RIP 40. High quality screening (HQS) algorithms approximate traditional screen angles by modifying the traditional angles only slightly (see table 12.1). For an image set to print with a line frequency of 133 lpi, each plate printed using HQS angles varies from the traditional angles somewhat, but the variance from plate to plate is much less than RT angles.

Table 12.1 Screening Methods

Process Color	Traditional Angle/Screen	RT Screening Angle/Screen	HQS Screening Angle/Screen
Cyan	15°/133 lpi	18.435°/133.871 lpi	15.0037°/138.142 lpi
Magenta	75°/133 lpi	71.565°/133.871 lpi	74.9987°/138.142 lpi
Yellow	0°/133 lpi	0°/127 lpi	0°/138.545 lpi
Black	45°/133 lpi	45°/119.737 lpi	45°/138.158 lpi

Adobe Accurate Screens

Accurate Screens is a technology for optimizing the results of process printing developed by Adobe Systems Incorporated. Accurate Screening uses a rational algorithm that attempts to eliminate the need for the heavy computational power required by irrational screening algorithms.

Accurate Screen first examines the difference between the desired screen and the achievable screen. When the program determines that the optimum screen and angle would require printing half a pixel, it builds a "supercell" and distributes the error over that supercell. For example, if a cell measuring 14.5 pixels is required, Accurate Screens builds a supercell of 29 pixels that represents the same dot size as 14.5 pixels. By using memory more efficiently, more cells are possible.

Calibrating the Imagesetter

An important calibration that needs to be made for working with color separations is the adjustment of the imagesetter used to output film. It's important to adjust the gray screens printed on the imagesetter to match those used by a software program so that a 10 percent screen, for example, prints as 10 percent rather than 12.5 percent. A key piece of equipment called a densitometer is often used by service bureaus to measure the screen percentages printed by an imagesetter.

Choose Use PPD Transfer Function in the Print Color dialog box to adjust the screen densities for your type of printer. For critical color printing, you can calibrate these screen densities by running tests and then editing the transfer function in the PPD file.

Printers Marks and Page Information

If the page size specified in the Page Setup dialog box (displayed when you select the Page Setup command on the File menu) is smaller than the paper size, you should select the Printers Marks option in the Print Options dialog box as described in Chapter 10. When this option is selected, PageMaker prints crop marks and registration marks on each sheet (see fig. 12.32). *Crop marks* indicate where to trim a page to create the final page size. *Registration marks* help the printer check and align the plates used in printing different colors.

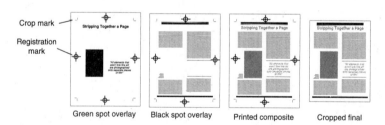

Printed page showing crop marks and registration marks.

Crop mark —
Registration mark —

Green spot overlay   Black spot overlay   Printed composite   Cropped final

If the page size is smaller than the paper size and you choose the Page Information option in the Print Options dialog box (as described in Chapter 10), PageMaker prints the name of each color in the area beyond the page margins. Otherwise, you need to label each overlay with the color you want the offset printer to use (see "Marking Mechanicals for Solid Spot Color" in this section).

If the page size is the same as the paper size, the Printers Marks and Page Information options are not available. However, you should add registration marks manually to help the printer align the overlays. To add the registration marks manually, on the master page draw one registration mark like the one shown in figure 12.33.

Registration mark composed of a circle and two straight lines.

Use PageMaker's Ellipse tool and Straight-line tool with Hairline option for line width. Select the entire graphic and choose [Registration] from the Colors palette (the Color Palette command on the Window menu or its keyboard shortcut, Ctrl+K) or from the Define Colors dialog box (displayed when you select the Define Colors command on the Element menu). Copy and paste the registration marks around the four sides of the master page in the margins. The registration marks, and any elements assigned the [Registration] color name in the Colors palette, are included on all separations printed with the Separations option.

When you deliver the separations to the print shop, be sure to instruct the printer to delete the registration marks on the final plates.

Marking Mechanicals for Solid Spot Color

In addition to indicating which page elements should be in color—or physically separating them yourself—you must specify on your mechanical what spot colors you want. If you used standard color names or numbers from a color matching system supported by your print shop, and you printed the pages on paper large enough to accommodate the Printers Marks and Page Information options described previously, the name of each color is printed on each separation beyond the crop marks.

If you used names that are not standard or are unknown to the print shop, you can give the print shop a sample of the color you want (a piece of paper, a company logo, and so on) and ask them to duplicate the color as closely as possible.

If you decide not to use PageMaker to print spot-color overlays, but to let the print shop separate the spot colors, you can print the page without the Separation option and mark your black-and-white mechanical with instructions about which page elements should be in which colors. You can write these instructions directly on the mechanical (keyline mechanical) using a nonreproducible blue ink pen or pencil, or you can write them on a tissue overlay. The printer photographs the mechanical once for each color and masks any unwanted images from each set of films.

Preparing a PageMaker Publication for OPI

Four-color process printing is the only method used to print continuous-tone color images (such as color photographs). If your publication includes continuous-tone color images, you can print the separations directly to any imagesetter, or you can create higher-quality color separations using PageMaker's Open Prepress Interface (OPI), which links PageMaker to sophisticated color prepress systems such as Scitex, Crosfield, or Hell. You can use the procedures described here to prepare disk files for a prepress service bureau or to create files to be handled through Aldus PrePrint or another separation utility such as Publisher's Prism. (This step is required with PageMaker 5.0, however, only if you want to separate imported RGB TIFF files, because you can print color separations for all other elements directly from the program.)

You can use a low-resolution color scanner on your PC to create a full-page layout to show the prepress house or the print shop how to position and crop the image. Then you can take your disk files to a prepress service to transfer your full-page layout into its system for the final color processing and output the color separations for the layout—exactly as you planned it. These services scan your original color photograph with a highly sensitive scanner and replace your low-resolution image. This way, you have saved some of the prepress costs by going as far as you can on your own.

These prepress services can serve as a liaison to printers and color trade shops. Although prepress services may themselves have the equipment to do appropriate desktop-color page makeup for many jobs, most also work closely with traditional suppliers. They are knowledgeable about the most effective ways of combining the capabilities of desktop systems and other equipment, and they can help you work within your budget to achieve the best results.

To create the OPI files, you select a PostScript printer in the Print dialog box, then click Options to display the Print Options dialog box. Next, click Write PostScript to File to create a printable version of the publication on disk (see fig. 12.34). You assign a name to the file by typing in the text box to the right of the check box; or click Browse to open a dialog box that enables you to find an existing file name on your system or save the named file in a directory other than PageMaker's default, which is the PageMaker program directory. Click For Separations to create OPI-compatible separations files that you can open and print from Aldus PrePrint or other post-processing programs.

```
Options
┌─ Graphics ─────────────────┐   ┌─ Markings ──────────────┐      [ Save ]
│ ● Normal                    │   │ ☐ Printer's marks        │
│ ○ Optimized                 │   │ ☐ Page information       │      [ Cancel ]
│ ○ Low TIFF resolution       │   └─────────────────────────┘
│ ○ Omit TIFF files           │                                   [ Document ]
└─────────────────────────────┘
┌─ PostScript ──────────────────────────────────────────┐           [ Paper ]
│ ☐ Include PostScript error handler                      │
│ ☒ Write PostScript to file:  [            ] [ Browse... ]│         [ Options ]
│   ○ Normal          ☐ Include downloadable fonts         │
│   ○ EPS                                                  │         [ Color ]
│   ● For separations                                      │
└──────────────────────────────────────────────────────── ┘        [ Reset ]
```

Fig. 12.34

Print Options dialog box with Write PostScript to File and For Separations selected.

For more information about the use of PageMaker with OPI, as well as the availability of OPI-compatible prepress systems in your area, check with your local prepress house.

For Related Information

◄◄ "Setting Additional Printing Options for PostScript Printers," p. 420.

FROM HERE...

Summary

The future of printing is color. Color printing, however, is expensive— even if you can avoid the cost of making color overlays, the masters used in making plates to print each color.

Under the impact of electronic technology, the publishing process is changing across the entire spectrum of production. To understand and adapt to the changes in methods, roles, and relationships, you need to understand the entire process. If you have never worked with color, you should find out more about how offset printers produce color. If you are familiar with color printing, you should see how the separations produced by PageMaker—color separations, color comps, and final printed publications—compare with traditional color productions.

Special Considerations in Printing

C hapter 10 covered the basic steps in printing, and Chapter 12 showed how to print color publications and color separations. This chapter discusses some of the special considerations or challenges that can arise in printing documents. You learn how to create a disk file that includes all the printer-language instructions needed for printing the publication—including linked graphics. You also learn how to prepare your publications to be moved from one system to another or printed at another location, such as a service bureau. This chapter describes how to convert a page in a publication to a graphic file, how to manage fonts and linked graphics, and how to diagnose problems in printing. The first section describes a new feature of PageMaker 5.0 that enables you to create signatures for folded booklets.

Building Booklets

PageMaker 5.0 includes an Aldus Addition called Build Booklet that enables you to print pages as *spreads*, that is, side-by-side pairs for creating signatures or facing-page layouts. For example, if you are creating a four-page, 8.5-by-11-inch newsletter to be printed on

11-by-17-inch sheets of paper and folded, you can use the Build Booklet Addition to print pages one and four on one side of an 11-by-17-inch sheet and pages two and three on another 11-by-17-inch sheet. This procedure creates only two camera-ready sheets for final back-to-back reproduction. The Build Booklet command creates a new, untitled publication that positions the contents of two pages on one spread. Figure 13.1 shows the four different page spreads that Build Booklet can create for an eight-page publication. You can also create signatures for longer documents that will be perfectly bound (wherein folded signatures are glued to the spine).

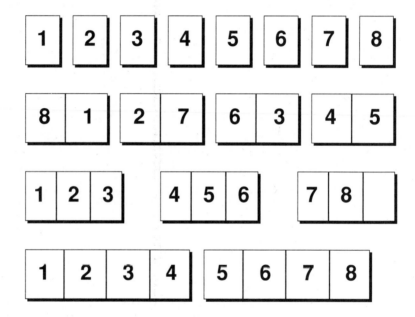

Spreads for an 8-page newsletter using different layout options: None (top row), 2-up spreads (second row), 3-up spreads (third row), and 4-up spreads (last row).

The Build Booklet Addition gives you several options to determine how the final publication will look. You can insert additional blank pages, revise the order of the pages, or delete pages. The Addition also can automatically adjust the placement of page items to account for paper thickness, increase the space between publication pages, and invert the pages for printing. Any change you make affects the publication copy created by the Addition, not the original publication.

> **CAUTION:** The Build Booklet procedure requires working disk space on your hard drive equal to about two-and-a-half times the size of the finished publication.
>
> Also, you should go through all edit cycles and finalize the pages of the original publication before using the Build Booklet command. You can make changes to the spreads created by the Build Booklet command, but changes that affect the text flow from one page to another will be difficult to manage. If extensive changes are required, a better idea is to enter them in the original publication and then use the Build Booklet command again.

To create page spreads for a booklet, first create the publication and save it. The publication should start on an odd-numbered page—you can insert a blank first page and/or adjust the starting page number, if necessary, in the original publication; or you can add a blank page through the Build Booklet Addition, as described here. Usually, the publication is a fixed number of pages (2, 4, 8, 12, 16, and so on) that will be printed and stapled or bound as a folded booklet or signature. The Build Booklet command can handle up to 500 pages per publication. (The Build Booklet addition creates spreads from the active publication only—it does not assemble pages from a series of publications that have been linked through the Book command.)

Next, choose Build Booklet from the Aldus Additions submenu under the Utilities menu. The Build Booklet dialog box is displayed (see fig. 13.2).

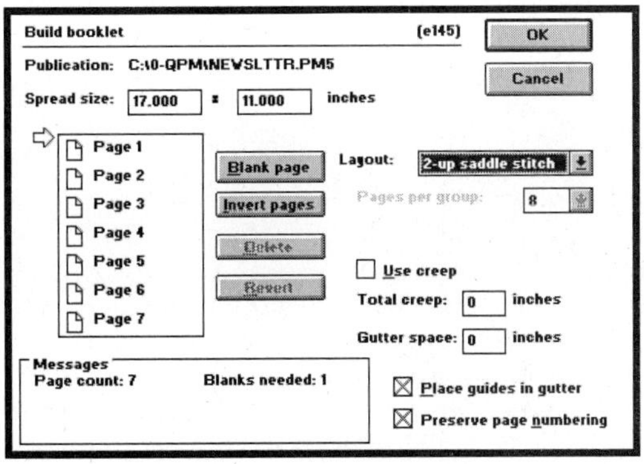

Fig. 13.2

The Build Booklet dialog box.

The Layout drop-down list offers six layout options: None, 2-up Saddle, 2-up Perfect Bound, 2-up Consecutive, 3-up Consecutive, and 4-up Consecutive. (Refer to figure 13.1 to see the results of each of these options.) Select the layout you want:

■ Choose None if you want to create a new publication with the same content as the original publication, but with increased page size or with rearranged pages. This method is handy for changing the page size of a publication when you want all the elements to remain centered within the new page edges instead of aligned to the left page edge, as happens when you simply enlarge the pages through the Page Setup dialog box (as described in Chapter 4). This method also serves as an alternative to the Sort Pages addition (described in Chapter 5).

■ 2-up saddle stitch is for standard booklet printing, where the entire publication will be produced as one folded and stapled booklet. Usually, saddle-stitched (or stapled) booklets are no more than 32 pages if you are using very thin paper stock (such as newsprint) and much smaller if you are using thicker paper. For longer publications, choose the next option.

■ Select 2-up perfect bound if you want to create a series of folded booklets (signatures) that will be bound with adhesive to a spine. With this option, you can specify the number of pages per signature in the Pages per Group area. The number entered here should be an even number, usually divisible by 4 (4, 8, 12, 16, and so on).

For example, if you have a 64-page publication that you will bind by gluing four 16-page signatures together, enter **16** in the Pages per Group area. The offset printer assembles pages in 16-page groups (four sheets printed on both sides and folded in half) and staples or stitches each group. Then the four page groups are pressed together and glued at the spine. Finally, a cover page (not included in the pages handled through the Build Booklet command) is wrapped and glued around the glued spine.

■ Select 2-, 3-, or 4-up consecutive to create multipage spreads (wherein the sets of 2, 3, or 4 pages in the original publication are combined side by side into a single page, in order to save paper or film when printing or imagesetting) or to create 2-, 3-, or 4-panel brochures, centerfolds, and so on.

PageMaker initially calculates the Spread Size as twice the size of the original publication pages if you choose one of the 2-up layout options, or three or four times the original page size for the 3-up or 4-up option, respectively. PageMaker also adds the gutter size, if you enter one. You can make this area larger by entering numbers manually if you want to accommodate printers marks or registration marks, as described in Chapter 10.

The area at the left in the dialog box shows the page numbers, and the Message area at the bottom of the dialog box tells you whether you need to adjust your settings or page count to get the results you want. To add a blank page, click the left side of the box to position an arrow between the two page numbers; then click Blank Page (see fig. 13.3). If you don't add enough pages to fill the signature, the Build Booklet Addition automatically leaves blank pages at the end of the signature in the new publication it creates.

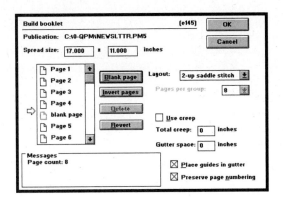

Fig. 13.3

The arrow shows where a blank page is inserted if you choose Blank Page.

To move pages, first select them by clicking the page icons in the Build Booklet dialog box. Shift+click to select a range of pages, or Ctrl+click to select nonconsecutive pages or deselect pages in a range. Then hold down the Alt key as you drag the selected pages to a new location in the sequence. Nonconsecutive selections appear consecutively after you reposition them. You can delete pages by selecting them and clicking the Delete button. Click the Invert Pages button to reverse the pages from ascending to descending order (or vice versa).

Select the Use Creep option if you want the Addition to adjust page placement to account for paper thickness. This option is desirable if you are printing signatures with many pages (usually 16 or more), because without creep, the pages that fall in the middle of the folded booklet or signature will appear to have wider inside margins, and narrower outside margins, than pages that fall at the front and back of the folded signature. To correct this problem, select Use Creep and specify the Total Creep amount that you expect to result from the paper thickness and number of pages.

T I P   **Estimating Creep Value**

Talking with your commercial printer before entering a creep value
is a good idea, but you can estimate that value yourself by creating a
mockup of one signature on the same paper stock that you will use
in the final production. Draw an outline of the page margins on the
top and bottom pages of a sample stack of paper that represents one
signature, and then fold the stack and staple it at the fold. Trim the
outside edges so that they meet evenly. Then open the signature,
and measure the difference in the page width between the top
and bottom pages of the unfolded signature to estimate the creep
amount. (You also can estimate the creep amount by measuring the
width of the widest strip trimmed from the folded signature.)

You can add space uniformly between pages by entering a Gutter Space
value. PageMaker automatically changes the spread size to accommodate the value that you enter.

Select Place Guides in Gutter if you want the Build Booklet Addition to
add nonprinting ruler guides in the gutter of the new publication.

If you select Preserve Page Numbering in the Build Booklet dialog box,
the Build Booklet Addition positions page numbers on pages in the new
publication if page-number markers are included on the master pages
of the original publication. The page numbers of the new publication
will reflect the arrangement in the Build Booklet dialog box. The Build
Booklet Addition adds page numbers to any blank pages that you inserted, renumbers subsequent pages, and changes the numbers on
rearranged pages as necessary. If you deselect Preserve Page Numbering, the Build Booklet Addition deletes page numbers in the new publication—as might be desirable for brochures printed with the 3-up
consecutive layout.

When you finish making your entries in the Build Booklet dialog box,
click OK. PageMaker closes the current publication and opens a new,
untitled publication with a page size equal to the spread size specified
in the Build Booklet dialog box. It then copies the contents of each page
of the source publication to part of a new page. Each old page takes up
all of a new page if you chose None as the Layout option, or half a new
page if you chose one of the 2-up options, or one third of a new page if
you chose 3-up, or one fourth of a page if you chose 4-up.

When PageMaker has finished building the booklet, choose Save from
the File menu to save the new publication. You can make edits to the
new publication, subject to the caution mentioned earlier about making
changes that affect the flow of text from one page to the next. Notice

that the master pages of the new publication are blank—master-page information is transferred to individual pages, including the original page numbers. Choose Print from the File menu to print the publication.

Remember that to print the full spreads, your printer must accommodate the new page size. Otherwise, if the paper size is smaller than the spread size, you can print reductions or print the document using the tiling feature (described in Chapter 10), but this nearly cancels the advantages of having created the spreads!

For Related Information

◀◀ "Setting Additional Printing Options for PostScript Printers," p. 420.

◀◀ "Setting Additional Printing Options for PCL Printers," p. 430.

FROM HERE...

Changing Systems and Using Service Bureaus

If you take your PageMaker document from one system to another, you need to take the following files also:

■ All linked graphics files used in the publication

■ Printer and screen fonts used in the document (or a list of fonts, so you can check that they are installed in the other system)

■ If you have customized the kerning tables used in the publication, you need to take kerntrak.bin, the file that contains custom kerning information.

When you copy the publication to the new system, it's a good idea to use the same directory structure and directory names for storing the linked graphics files as you used in creating the publication. When you open a publication, PageMaker looks in the following places for the linked files: the original location or the last location for which the link was identified, the root directory or the startup drive, and the same directory as the publication. If the files aren't found in one of these locations, PageMaker asks you to relink all the files. Managing linked graphics is described later in this chapter.

T I P   **Copying Linked Graphics**

One way to ensure that all the linked files are included is to create a new directory at the root level on the hard disk, and then open the PageMaker publication and choose Save As from the File menu. In the Save As dialog box, change to the new directory, and click Copy Files Required for Remote Printing (which also copies special files such as the track-kerning resource file needed in printing) or Copy All Linked Files (to include all linked graphics whether or not they are included as part of the publication). Then copy the new folder to a disk for transport. You can use a compression utility such as PKZIP if the files cannot fit on one disk.

T I P   **Relinking Moved Files Quickly**

If all the linked graphics have been moved to one directory, it's easy to add this directory to the list of places PageMaker looks for subsequently "found missing" files. When you locate one file in the Cannot Find dialog box, hold the Ctrl key as you click OK, and PageMaker looks in this directory for any other linked files and updates them automatically.

If you will only be printing (not editing) the document on the other system, you might prefer to send the document as a single printable disk file, as described in the next section. Whether you send all the files related to the publication or one printable disk file, always keep a backup.

Working with Your Service Bureau

Before preparing a publication to be printed at a service bureau, check with the staff to find out whether they have the fonts you need and how they prefer to receive the files. If they have all the fonts and are using the same version of Windows and PageMaker as you are, they might prefer to print the file directly from PageMaker. Otherwise, they might prefer a printable disk file.

Also, be sure you are using the PPD file that corresponds to their imagesetter. Ask them for a copy of their PPD file if necessary.

In delivering the disk files to be printed, it's a good idea to include the latest draft printout from your laser printer, a list of the settings you used for printing, and a list of the fonts and types of graphics used.

For Related Information

◀◀ "Using the Print Command," p. 410.

◀◀ "Setting Additional Printing Options for PostScript Printers," p. 420.

◀◀ "Setting Additional Printing Options for PCL Printers," p. 430.

FROM HERE...

Printing a Publication to a Disk

Instead of printing a publication directly to a printer, you can "print" the publication to a disk file. This creates a single, printable disk file of the publication, including all linked graphics and downloadable fonts. You then can print the file using the COPY command under DOS (you do not need Windows or PageMaker), or you can use the Print command under Windows (you do not need PageMaker).

When you want to transfer a publication to another system, printing to disk is especially useful in the following circumstances:

■ The other system does not have PageMaker or the same version of PageMaker.

■ The other system does not have the same version of Windows.

■ The other system does not have the same fonts installed. Storing fonts as part of the printable disk file is an option that you can turn on or off. The file is much larger when you include fonts, so it's a good idea to find out what fonts the other system has before including them in your printable file.

■ You do not want to worry about having all the linked files or providing instruction about how the files are linked.

■ The PageMaker publication is too large to fit on a floppy disk. You can create several printable files by printing a few pages at a time to disk.

■ You want to transmit the publication by modem.

> **CAUTION:** When a file is printed to disk, an ASCII file that contains PostScript code is created. You cannot edit the file using PageMaker. However, you can use a text editor to modify the ASCII file if you know the PostScript language.

> **CAUTION:** When you use downloadable fonts in a publication and want to include them in your print file, the fonts must be listed under the FILE port—that is, [PostScript, FILE]—in the WIN.INI file. (See the discussion on updating the WIN.INI file in "Installing Soft Fonts" in Appendix A.)
>
> If the fonts in the publication are not permanently downloaded to the printer used for the final version, you must download the soft fonts as temporary fonts when you print the file. (See "Downloading Soft Fonts" in Appendix A.)

Creating a Printable Disk File

To create a printable disk file of a PageMaker publication, follow these steps:

1. Choose the Print command from the File menu.

2. In the Print dialog box that appears, choose a PostScript printer.

   Remember that you can choose any driver that has been installed through Windows, even if that printer is not hooked up to your system. If no PostScript driver is installed on your system, see Chapter 10 for information about adding printer drivers. The following steps are based on the use of the PostScript driver that comes with PageMaker 5.0. These steps may vary if you are using a different printer driver version.

3. Choose the Options button.

   Figure 13.4 shows the dialog box for the Aldus PostScript driver.

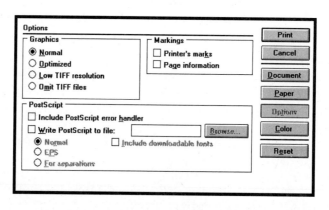

Fig. 13.4

The Print Options dialog box.

4. In the PostScript area, choose Write PostScript to File, Normal, and Include Downloadable Fonts (if you need to). Type the name of the file you want to create.

5. Choose Print to close the dialog box and print.

PageMaker displays a dialog box showing its progress as it creates a printable PostScript file and saves it on disk. You can then print this file as described in the next section.

Printing the Disk File from DOS

To print from DOS the disk file created in the preceding section, at the DOS prompt type the COPY command followed by the name of the file to be printed (including the path to the file) and the name of the port to which a PostScript printer is attached. For example:

```
COPY C:\BOOK1\CH01.PRN COM1:
```

prints the CH01.PRN file, which is stored in the BOOK1 directory on drive C, to the printer attached to the COM1 port.

Printing a Disk File from Windows 3.0

T I P

The Windows Print command prints a listing of the Encapsulated PostScript code, not the page image. To print the PostScript code disk file from Windows, start Windows and choose Main from the Window menu. Double-click the File Manager icon in the Windows main window, double-click the name of the directory where the disk file is stored, and click the name of the disk file to select it. Choose Print from the File menu, confirm the name of the file to be printed in the dialog box, and click OK to start printing.

For Related Information

◄◄ "Installing the Printer," p. 399.

▶▶ "Installing and Using Fonts," p. 902.

FROM HERE...

Converting a PageMaker Page to an EPS Graphic

Besides printing a printable version of the entire publication to disk, you can use the print command to create an EPS graphic version of individual pages of the publication. These EPS versions of pages can be placed like graphics in a PageMaker publication.

Creating the EPS File

The steps for creating an EPS version of a page are similar to those for creating a printable disk file of a PageMaker publication, described previously.

1. Choose the Print command from the File menu.

2. In the Print dialog box, specify one page to be printed, and choose a PostScript printer. (You can print only one page at a time to an EPS graphic file.)

   Remember that you can choose any driver that has been installed through Windows, even if that printer is not hooked up to your system. If no PostScript driver is installed on your system, see Chapter 10 for information about adding printer drivers. The following steps are based on the use of the PostScript driver that comes with PageMaker 5.0. These steps may vary if you are using a different printer driver version.

3. Choose the Options button to display the Options dialog box (refer to fig. 13.4).

4. In the PostScript area, choose Write PostScript to File, EPS, and Include Downloadable Fonts (if you need to). (Refer to figure 13.4.) Type the name of the file you want to create.

5. Choose Print to close the dialog box and print.

PageMaker displays a dialog box showing its progress as it creates a printable PostScript file and saves it on disk. You can then place this file in a PageMaker publication as described in the next section.

Placing the EPS File in PageMaker

After PageMaker has created the EPS version of the page, you can use the Place command to import it to PageMaker as a graphic. The graphic can be scaled, cropped, rotated, skewed, or mirrored like any other graphic. Remember, however, that this is a PostScript graphic and must be printed to a PostScript printer.

Note that when you create the EPS file, you can opt to include the downloadable fonts. Otherwise, you need to be sure that those fonts are installed on the system when you place the file in PageMaker and print it.

Creating EPS Pages: Windows versus Macintosh

EPS pages created under Windows, as described here, result in graphics files that display as gray boxes on the screen when placed in PageMaker but print as exact page images, including fonts and graphics. The gray box is the size of the page as specified in the Page Setup dialog box of the document from which the graphic was created.

When EPS pages are created on Macintosh systems with the Include Screen Version option selected and then placed in PageMaker on the Macintosh, they display as visible images (not gray boxes).

Creating Logos and Other EPS Graphics in PageMaker

You can use the techniques just described under "Converting a PageMaker Page to an EPS Graphic" to create graphics or logos that can be imported to PageMaker. This can be convenient if you don't have a suitable graphics application and you want to use PageMaker to create the graphic. Printing it to disk as an EPS graphic solves the dilemma: a logo or graphic composed of more than one element in PageMaker cannot be scaled or cropped as easily as an imported graphic that is a single object.

The real trick here is to create the logo or graphic in a PageMaker publication of its own and set the page size as small as possible to still include all the elements of the graphic. Ideally, the edges of the graphic meet the edges of the page exactly, with no extra margin. Remember that placed EPS graphics created in PageMaker display as gray boxes on the screen. By making the page size match the graphic size, you will know that the graphic fills the gray box and does not need to be cropped.

For Related Information

◄◄ "Installing the Printer," p. 399.

Managing Fonts

Up to this point, we have assumed that the fonts you use are already installed on your system as screen fonts and printer fonts. How did they get there? What do you have to do to add a font? What if you have trouble printing a font? These questions might never concern you if yours is already set up, and you always produce the same documents or use the same formats with the same tried-and-true fonts every time. However, if you get adventurous with a new document design by adding new fonts or trying new combinations of fonts, and you run into problems in printing the document, the answers to these questions might help.

Appendix A describes in detail how to install new fonts and download fonts to the printer. Such juicy topics are relegated to Appendix A because they are not things that you do *with* PageMaker; they are performed through Windows or the font installation program that comes with the fonts you buy. This section summarizes some basics of font management as they relate to printing from PageMaker.

Installing Fonts

The first step in using a font is to install the screen font on your system. The second step is to install the printer font files on your hard disk or a hard disk attached to your printer. These steps might be handled for you automatically when you install a new font or a new printer, or when you install a new application that comes with fonts, such as Adobe Type Manager or Windows.

After installing the screen and printer fonts, you can select the fonts through PageMaker when the appropriate printer is selected in the Page Setup dialog box. When you print the document, PageMaker automatically sends (downloads) the fonts to the printer as needed by each page during the printing process. If you have installed the screen font, but do not have the equivalent printer font installed on your printer and you are not using a font manager, you can choose the font from the PageMaker menus. But when you print the document, either the font will print as low-resolution bitmap characters (based on the screen font) or another font will be substituted.

Some service bureaus will give you their screen fonts on disk so you can use them in your documents. But the document will have to be printed by a service bureau that has the printer fonts, which are licensed only to the purchaser.

Limiting the Number of Fonts

If you are following the rules of good design, your pages probably use a limited number of different typefaces, styles, and sizes. There are at least two reasons other than good design for limiting the number of fonts you use in a document: time and space. The more fonts you use, the more space they require in your printer's memory (if they are downloaded fonts) and the more time it takes to print each page.

As you learned in Chapter 8, a font is a combination of typeface and style. To use the entire "family" in the Palatino typeface, for example, you need to download four fonts: normal, bold, italic, and bold italic. Different typefaces and styles take up different amounts of memory, and different types of graphics make different demands on memory as well.

Each font requires 50K to 90K of memory in printing. Bold, italic, and condensed versions of an outline font (a PostScript or TrueType type-face, for example) are three separate fonts; each one takes up printer memory. If you are using bitmap fonts (such as those commonly used on Hewlett-Packard PCL printers), each *size* is also a separate font file that takes up printer memory. If you are having trouble printing a docu-ment that uses many fonts, and you do not have a font disk attached to your printer, try to reduce the number of fonts used in the document, or follow some of the other suggestions in this section for downloading fonts.

Experiment a little with downloadable fonts before you design a large document that calls for them, and before you decide whether to download the fonts before you start printing or as part of the printing process. Try printing one or two sample pages with representative graphics as well as text that uses all the fonts called for in the design.

Opening a Publication with Missing Fonts

When you open a publication that uses fonts not currently installed on the system, PageMaker displays the PANOSE Font Matching dialog box, which was described in Chapter 4. You use this dialog box to choose which fonts will be substituted, and whether to substitute them temporarily or permanently. By making temporary substitutions, you can work on a publication on any system, and the publication retains all the original font assignments when you print it from the original system.

If some fonts have a question mark next to them in the font list (in the Font submenu under the Type menu, or in the drop-down list in the Type Specifications dialog box, or in the drop-down list in the Control palette in character view), it means the font is used somewhere in the publication but that font is not currently available on the system. The most common causes for this are opening a publication that was created on another system (and having PANOSE Font Matching turned off when you use the Open command), or changing the target printer through the Page Setup dialog box. (The font list is determined by the current printer selection.)

If you don't believe that you have used the font in the publication, it could be assigned to a nonprinting character, such as a carriage return or a tab, and this will not affect the printing. If you have used the font and don't want to change it, try changing the target printer in the Page Setup dialog box. This is the printer that affects the list of fonts in the menus and dialog boxes. You can still print to a draft printer by choosing another printer through the Print dialog box.

If you have used the font but want to change to one of the available fonts, you can change the style sheet definitions (if you used styles to format the text, as described in Chapter 8) or use the Change command in the Story Editor (described in Chapter 7).

Using a Type Manager

As mentioned in Chapters 8 and 10, fonts are commonly differentiated as being either *scalable outline fonts* (such as PostScript and TrueType fonts) or *nonscalable bitmap fonts* (such as those commonly used on Hewlett-Packard PCL printers). Outline fonts can be stored as mathematical formulas for each character, or as miniature software programs that draw the outline of each character when executed. This means that the formula or program for the characters in the font can be stored in one file and used to generate characters of any size. Nonscalable bitmap fonts, on the other hand, must be stored as complete character sets for each size installed. They can take up a tremendous amount of disk space and memory.

To eliminate the need to install every size of a bitmap font, you can use a type manager (such as Adobe Type Manager) along with scalable fonts to generate the bitmap versions used by the printer as you print, rather than store them on the disk. With a type manager, you can scale a font to virtually any size you want, and you can also rotate text in .001° increments. Using a type manager with scalable fonts also reduces the amount of memory PageMaker needs to display and print fonts in large point sizes. Table 13.1 summarizes how different fonts are handled on different printers, with or without a type manager installed.

Table 13.1 Font Formats and Printers

Font Format	Printer	Prints as
PostScript	PostScript	PostScript, downloaded as needed
PostScript with ATM bitmaps	Non-PostScript	High-resolution
PostScript	TrueType	PostScript, downloaded as needed
TrueType	TrueType	TrueType, downloaded as needed
TrueType	PostScript	PostScript Type 3 bitmaps, or a combination of Type 1 outlines (type sizes 16 points and larger) and Type 3 bitmaps (type smaller than 16 points); equivalent printer-resident fonts substitute by default (see note)
Other type manager	PostScript or TrueType	PostScript fonts print as PostScript; others as high-resolution bitmaps
Other type manager bitmaps	Non-PostScript or non-TrueType	High-resolution
Non-PostScript or non-TrueType with no type manager	Any	Installed printer fonts

Note: You can change the defaults mentioned in printing TrueType fonts to PostScript printers through the Advanced Options dialog box. This dialog box is accessed through PageMaker's Print command or Window's Control Panel, as described in Chapter 10.

> **CAUTION:** The graphics resolution of the printer affects the appearance of text if you are printing PostScript fonts to a non-PostScript printer by using a type manager. For best resolution in printing text as graphics, set the graphics resolution to 300. (See the tip on correcting this problem later in this chapter, under "Diagnosing Problems in Printing Fonts.")

Temporarily Downloading Fonts

When using fonts that are not built in your printer, the fonts must be sent, or downloaded, to the printer before printing the page or document. Windows does this automatically when printing, as long as the printer fonts have been installed and listed in the WIN.INI file.

The WIN.INI file is automatically updated when new fonts are added through the Fonts icon in the Windows Control Panel or through Adobe Type Manager. These procedures, as well as instructions for updating WIN.INI manually, are explained in Appendix A.

Permanently Downloading Fonts

Each temporarily downloaded font takes up space in the printer's memory, and it is flushed out when the page or document is printed. As an alternative, you can download fonts to the printer before you print, using such programs as Adobe's Font Downloader, which is included with every font you buy from Adobe.

Permanently downloaded fonts do not have to be downloaded for each print job. Instead, they remain in the printer's memory as each page is printed and until the printer is turned off. You can print publications more quickly this way, but the number of fonts downloaded limits the amount of memory remaining for processing each page.

If you have predownloaded any fonts at the beginning of the day, and you run into memory problems when printing pages with graphics that do not use those fonts, you can flush the fonts out of the printer's memory by turning it off. When you turn the printer back on, print the pages with graphics first, before you permanently download the fonts again.

Appendix A describes how to download fonts and the difference between downloading temporarily and permanently.

For Related Information

◄◄ "PANOSE Font Matching," p. 163.

◄◄ "Changing Type Specifications," p. 295.

►► "Typography," p. 699.

►► "Installing and Using Fonts," p. 902.

FROM HERE...

Managing Linked Text and Graphics Documents

PageMaker offers the option of linking external sources of text and graphics to the publication. In this way, changes in the external file are incorporated in the PageMaker version of the graphic or text when the publication is opened or updated through the Links command under the File menu. PageMaker 5.0 also supports the Windows 3.1 OLE (object linking and embedding).

With the linking feature, you also can control the size of a PageMaker publication. Scanned-image files are often stored at 300-dpi resolution and can be quite large, sometimes larger than 256K. Rather than include the full images in the publication, you can show low-resolution versions of these images in the publication, and then link the larger, external graphics file for use in printing.

When you print the publication, linked files must be available to print them at the specified resolution. You can print a publication without having the linked files present, but the graphics will print as the low-resolution screen version stored in PageMaker.

Linking Graphic Files

When you use the Place command from the File menu to import a graphic to a publication, PageMaker checks the size of the graphic file. If the file is smaller than 256K, the entire graphic is imported and stored as part of the PageMaker document. If the file is larger than 257K, PageMaker displays a dialog box like the one in figure 13.5.

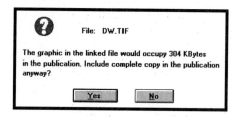

Fig. 13.5

The dialog box
offering the Link
option.

If you choose Yes, the entire graphic is imported and stored as part of
the PageMaker publication. The size of the PageMaker publication is
increased by the size of the graphic. If you choose No, PageMaker
stores a low-resolution, bit-mapped, screen-display version of the
graphic as part of the publication. The original graphic file is *linked* to
the publication. When you print the publication, PageMaker looks on
the disk for the original graphic file and prints it at high resolution. If
PageMaker cannot find the linked file when you print the publication,
it displays the message shown in figure 13.6.

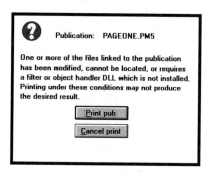

Fig. 13.6

PageMaker looks
for the scan file
when printing
the PageMaker
publication.

If you choose to print, PageMaker prints the publication using the low-
resolution versions of the graphics files stored as part of the publication. If you want to be sure that the original, high-resolution versions
of the graphics files are used, click Cancel and relink the large files, as
described later in the section "Managing Linked Text and Graphics
Documents."

T   I   P   **Storing Linked Graphics Files**

Store scanned-image files and other large graphic files in the same
directory as your publication. If you copy the publication to another
disk, copy the graphics files, too. Without the linked graphics files,
the images print at low resolution, even on high-resolution printers.

Setting Default Link Options

You can set up the default for link options before importing graphics or text into a publication. If you choose the Link Options command from the Element menu when no publication is open, you can set the defaults for all new publications. If you choose the Link Options command when a publication is open and no graphics or text are selected, you can set the defaults for all new graphics placed in that publication (but this does not change the link options set up for graphics already placed in the publication). In either case, the Link Options dialog box is displayed (see fig. 13.7). (If you choose the Link Options command when a graphic or text is selected, you can set the linking options for that element only, as described in the section "Managing Linked Text and Graphics Documents" later in this chapter.)

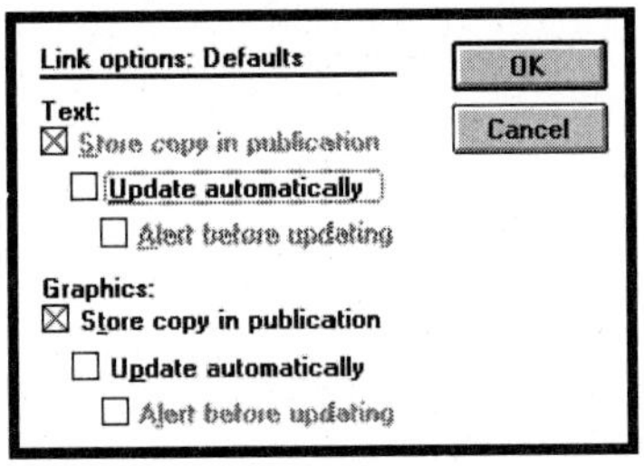

Fig. 13.7

The Link Options dialog box.

The Store Copy in Publication option is grayed out in the Link Options dialog box for text and EPS graphics because all imported text and EPS files are stored in full as part of the publication. You always can print the publication without access to the external files.

If you select Store Copy in Publication for graphics (and no graphics were selected when you opened the Link Options dialog box), all graphics that are subsequently imported are stored in full as part of the publication, and you can print the publication without accessing the original graphics files. The PageMaker publication file size, however, will be larger if you store graphics as part of the publication rather than link imported graphics.

You can opt to update the text or graphics when you open a publication if the original file has been modified since you placed or updated the imported document. If Update Automatically is not checked in the Link Options dialog box, changes to the original file are not reflected in the PageMaker publication. If you select Update Automatically, you also may choose Alert Before Updating to have PageMaker display an alert box before updating a changed file. With the alert box, you can choose on a case-by-case basis whether to update each changed graphic or story.

Changes made through the Link Options dialog box when no text or graphics are selected do not affect the link options of text and graphics already imported and linked. Only new imports take on the new defaults.

If you choose the Link Options command when an imported graphic or story is selected, the options you choose apply to that graphic or story only. This process is the same as clicking the Options button in the Links dialog box, described later in this chapter in the section "Managing Linked Text and Graphics Documents."

Checking or Changing Link Settings

Use the File menu's Links command to view and manage the linkages in a publication. The Links dialog box (see fig. 13.8) lists all documents—text and graphic files—imported to the PageMaker publication, giving their name, file type, and the page number on which they appear.

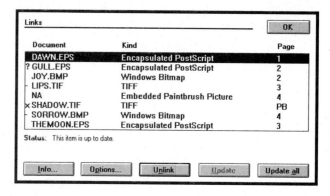

Fig. 13.8

The Links dialog box shows several status indicators.

The link status indicators are displayed before each file name as appropriate. If no symbol appears before the document name, the element is updated; it has not been changed since last updated or imported. Table 13.2 lists the link status indicators and their meanings.

Table 13.2 Link Status Indicators

Indicator	Meaning
?	The file is missing. It has been moved, deleted, or updated, and PageMaker cannot find it. If you click the file and then click the Info button at the bottom of the Links dialog box, you can redirect PageMaker to the moved or renamed file, as described later in the section "Updating Linked Files."

Indicator	Meaning
+	The external file has been modified since it was placed or updated in the PageMaker publication. If you select the file and click Update in the Links dialog box, or if you click Update All, the modified version of the file is brought into or linked to the PageMaker publication.
[_]	The external file has been modified since it was placed or updated in the PageMaker publication, but you have instructed PageMaker not to update this element. Select the file and click the Options button in the Links dialog box to change to automatic updating, or select the element and choose Update to update the selected element.
!	The internal and external versions of the file have been updated since being placed or updated in the PageMaker publication. If you select the file and click Update in the Links dialog box, the external version of the file replaces the internal version, and changes made to the internal copy are discarded.
x	The publication is not storing a complete copy of the external file. The publication is storing a low-resolution version of a high-resolution external document that must be available when printing.
*	The file needs a filter to be printed, and PageMaker cannot locate the filter. (The * indicator is in the Kind column.) Run SETUP.EXE in the PM5 directory (as described in Appendix A) to copy the appropriate filters from the original set of PageMaker installation disks.
NA	The object was pasted without links or is an OLE-embedded object. Because all information about a pasted or embedded object is stored in the publication, there is no source document.
◊	The internal copy of the object has been modified.

The Page column lists the page numbers on which the imported element appears or one of the following indicators:

Page #?	The linked inline graphic is in a story that has not been placed on a page yet. In other words, the story is in the Story Editor (described in Chapter 7). Inline graphics are described in Chapter 11.
LM	The linked element is on the left master page.
RM	The linked element is on the right master page.

PB	The linked element is on the pasteboard.
OV	The linked inline graphic is part of the text over-flow in a text block that has not been fully flowed.
UP	The linked text element is an open story that has not yet been placed.

The Link Info dialog box (see fig. 13.9) details information about the selected file. To display this dialog box, you can select a file and click the Link Info button, or simply double-click a file name in the Links dialog box. You also can display this dialog box for a selected object by choosing the Link Info command from the Element menu.

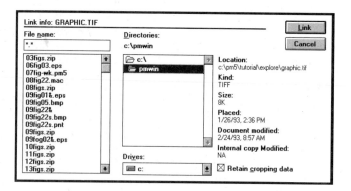

The left side of the Link Info dialog box lists the files on the system that can be linked to a PageMaker publication. You can rejoin or change the link to the currently selected element by double-clicking a different file name, clicking a file name and then clicking Link, or typing a different file name in the Name text box on the right side of the dialog box. (You must type the full path if the file's drive and directory do not appear in the Path space above the Name text box.) The file you select becomes the new link to replace the element selected when you open this dialog box.

Other information in the dialog box follows:

Location	Drive, directory, and name of the file
Kind	Type of file
Size	Size of the file, or NA if not known
Placed	Date and time the file was last placed in the publication

Original modified	Date and time the external file was last modified
Internal copy modified	Date and time the element was last modified in the publication

Changing Link Options for Individual Files

When you click the Options button in the Links dialog box, you get a dialog box that enables you to change the link options for the currently selected graphic (see fig. 13.10) or text file (see fig. 13.11) only. You get this same dialog box if you choose the Link Options command from the Element menu when a text block or imported graphic is selected. This dialog box is an abbreviated version of the dialog box displayed after you choose the Link Options command from the Element menu to change the defaults when no text or graphic files are selected.

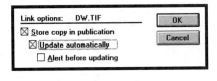

Fig. 13.10

The Link Options dialog box when a graphic is selected.

Fig. 13.11

The Link Options dialog box when text is selected.

The entries in these dialog boxes were described in detail previously in this chapter.

Click a graphic to highlight it in the Links dialog box, and click Unlink to sever the link between the selected document and the PageMaker publication. The graphic remains in the PageMaker publication, but no links are stored and PageMaker will no longer check or update the status of the file. If you unlink a linked OLE object, it becomes an embedded OLE object.

Updating Linked Files

If you click Update in the Links dialog box, you replace the current internal version of a file with the latest external version. This option is dimmed if the two versions are already up-to-date. If the internal and the external versions are modified, PageMaker displays a warning asking you to confirm that you want to discard the changed internal version.

Clicking Update All updates the internal version of all elements that are not up-to-date *and* for which Update Automatically has been checked in the Link Options dialog box. (Links for which Update Automatically has been turned off must still be updated individually.)

> **CAUTION:** If you crop an imported graphic and later update a link to the original graphic, select the Retain Cropping Data option in the Place Document dialog box or in the Link Info dialog box. Otherwise, PageMaker imports or updates the entire graphic to fit in the cropped frame, possibly distorting the graphic.
>
> This option applies only to objects you replace or relink using PageMaker's linking options. PageMaker automatically retains cropping information for hotlinked files, for OLE-linked or OLE-embedded graphics, and when you relink to a file that PageMaker could not find while opening or printing the publication.

> **CAUTION:** If you link a text file and then add inline graphics to the file in PageMaker, you lose the graphics if you update the text file with a changed external file. If you expect to be updating external text files, don't import inline graphics until you update the internal text file through the Links command for the last time. Inline graphics are described in detail in Chapter 11.

Remember that you are also given an opportunity to update links when you open a PageMaker publication that has links to external files that PageMaker cannot find.

FROM HERE...

For Related Information
▶▶ "Selecting Filters, Additions, and Other Options," p. 900.

Printing Small Paper Sizes on a Laser Printer

You can run small paper sizes through the manual feed slot of most laser printers. If the printer supports the paper size you are using, you will have no problem printing from a PageMaker publication with a small page size specified in the Page Setup dialog box. PageMaker centers the dimensions of the page on whatever paper size is selected in the Print dialog box. If the printer does not support the paper size you are using, you can use one of the two tricks described here to get the results you want.

The easiest solution is to set up the publication using one of the standard paper sizes supported by your printer, but set up the margins to frame an area smaller than your final paper size. If the manual feed slot in your printer includes an adjustable feeding mechanism that forces the small paper to be centered through the printer, the margins should be centered horizontally but positioned near the top of the paper (for Portrait or tall orientations), or centered vertically but positioned near the left edge of the paper (for Landscape or wide orientations). Figure 13.12 shows how the margins for a postcard would be positioned when the page size is Letter size (8.5-by-11 inches).

Fig. 13.12

Postcard set up on letter-size page for Portrait (left) or Landscape (right) printing when centered in a manual feed slot.

If the manual feed slot in your printer recommends that small paper be aligned to the right edge of the feed tray, the margins should be aligned to the top right corner of the paper for Portrait or tall orientations, or to the top left edge of the paper for Landscape or wide orientations. Figure 13.13 shows the margins for a postcard when the page size is Letter size (8.5-by-11 inches), but the paper must be aligned right and face down in a manual feed slot (as required by older printers such as the Apple LaserWriter and LaserWriter Plus).

Postcard set up
on letter-size
page for Portrait
(left) or Land-
scape (right)
printing when
paper must be
aligned right and
face down in a
manual feed slot.

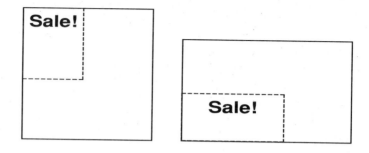

If the publication has already been set up with the smaller page size specified in the Page Setup dialog box, you have two choices. If it's a very short publication and you will always be printing directly to the smaller paper (never to larger paper with crop marks, for example), you can change the page size to match one of the standard sizes supported by the printer, set the margins as recommended previously, and move all the elements on each page to the new margins.

Otherwise, if you want to keep the page size small in the Page Setup dialog box, you can print the publication to nonstandard paper in the laser printer by tiling. If the manual feed slot in your printer includes an adjustable feeding mechanism that forces the small paper to be centered through the printer, calculate half the difference between your page width and the printer's paper width; then drag the zero point that distance to the left of the page. If the manual feed slot in your printer recommends that small paper be aligned to the right edge of the feed tray, calculate the total difference between your page width and the printer's paper width; then drag the zero point that distance to the left of the page.

Then choose the Print command and click the Paper button (for PostScript printers) or the Options button (for non-PostScript printers) and select manual tiling, as described in Chapter 10.

Regardless of which method you use, it's a good idea to test printing one page on the normal paper size first, by feeding the paper through the manual feed slot. Verify that the page will print in the location you expect when you use the smaller paper size.

FROM HERE...

For Related Information

◄◄ "Using the Print Command," p. 410.

◄◄ "Setting Additional Printing Options for PostScript Printers," p. 420

◄◄ "Setting Additional Printing Options for PCL Printers," p. 430.

Customizing PPD Files

PPD (PostScript Printer Description) files provide information to PageMaker about your printer and help ensure accurate color printing. They describe the features available with the printer, including the amount of printer memory, predefined paper sizes, resident fonts, and optimized screens in printing color separations. If you print to a PostScript printer, the PPD files for your printer model should be in the C:\ALDUS\USENGLSH\PPD directory. PageMaker uses this information to determine what PostScript information to send to the printer when you print your publication.

As explained under "Selecting PPD Files for PostScript and TrueType Printers" in Chapter 10, you select a PPD file by choosing from the Type option drop-down list, which lists different models (if any are available) of the current printer selected in the Print Document dialog box. The README.TXT file, which is copied to the PM5 directory as you install the program, contains a list of PPD file names and corresponding printers.

PageMaker 5.0 eliminates PDX (Printer Description Extension) files, which provided a way of customizing printer descriptions in earlier versions. With PageMaker 5.0, you can now customize a PPD file to calibrate color screen densities, add page sizes, and add font names, as described here. For example, if you install additional resident fonts or memory in your printer, you must create a custom printer file that supplements your printer's PPD file. Some of the lines from the PPD file for a Linotronic 300 imagesetter are listed at the end of this section.

To create a custom printer file, follow these steps:

1. Use any text editing program or the Windows Notepad to open the file named SAMPLE+.PPD that comes on the PageMaker disks.

2. Save the file as text-only (an option available with any text editor or word processor) under a new name. The name you choose will be displayed by PageMaker in the Type list box in the Print Document dialog box, if you check Display PPD Name in the Preferences dialog box as described in step 8. (Otherwise, the nickname you enter in the next step will be displayed in the Type list.)

3. Find the line that reads

```
*NickName: "MyPrinterFile"
```

and change it to a nickname that you choose. The nickname might be a way of giving you a clue about the PPD customization, such as

```
*NickName: "MoreFonts"
```

4. Find the line that reads

```
*Include: Printer.PPD
```

and change it to include the name of the original PPD file for the printer. For example, the PPD file for the Linotronic 300 would be

```
*Include: L300_493.PPD
```

This tells PageMaker to read both the original PPD file and the custom PPD file when you choose the custom PPD file in the Print Document dialog box (in step 9).

5. To add or change font information, find the line that reads

```
*% Font Information
```

On the lines below the Font Information comment line, list the new resident fonts you have added to your printer. Note that this step does not physically add the fonts—it merely lists the fonts that you should have already added by following the instructions that came with the new fonts or with your printer.

The fonts must be listed in the standard format used in PPD files, such as

```
*Font Helvetica: Standard "(001.002)" Standard ROM
*Font Helvetica-Bold: Standard "(001.002)" Standard ROM
*Font Helvetica-BoldOblique: Standard "(001.002)" Standard ROM
*Font Helvetica-Oblique: Standard "(001.002)" Standard ROM
```

You can get a complete list of the printer-resident fonts, preformatted for inclusion in the custom PPD file, by downloading the PPDShell.ps file (that you can find in C:\ALDUS\USENGLSH\UTILITIES\PS_TOOLS) to the printer port. To do this, choose Run from the File menu in the Windows Program Manager and type the following (if the printer port is LPT1):

```
COPY C:\ALDUS\USENGLSH\UTILITIES\PS_TOOLS\PPDSHELL.PS LPT1:
```

This prints the font names out in the format you need to type them in the custom PPD file.

6. To add custom paper sizes (if your printer supports them), first convert your custom paper size to points (72 points = 1 inch). Then find the lines in the custom PPD file that read

```
PageSize MyPaper: "statusdict begin 684 864 0 1
setpageparams end"
```

```
ImageableArea MyPaper: "0 1 684 864"
```

```
PaperDimension MyPaper: "684 864"
```

Replace MyPaper with your own name for the custom paper size. Replace the width and height values (in points) with your custom numbers. In the examples shown above, the width is 684 points (9.5 inches) and the height is 864 points (12 inches). To add a new custom paper named `TintedFilm` that is 10 inches (720 points) wide and 15 inches (1080 points) tall, you would change the preceding lines to look like this:

```
PageSize TintedFilm: "statusdict begin 720 1080 0 1 setpageparams end"

ImageableArea TintedFilm: "0 1 720 1080"

PaperDimension TintedFilm: "720 1080"
```

You can verify that your printer supports custom paper sizes by opening the original PPD file and finding the line

```
VariablePaperSize: True
```

or

```
CustomPaper: True
```

7. After making any changes to the file, save it as text only and store it in the C:\ALDUS\USENGLSH\PPD folder with the other PPD files.

8. Open PageMaker, and choose Preferences from the File menu. Choose Other in the Preferences dialog box, and choose Display PPD Name in the Other Preferences dialog box. Then close the Preferences dialog boxes.

9. When you next choose Print from the File menu, you should see the new custom PPD filename (assigned in step 2) or the nickname (assigned in step 3) in the Type list in the Print Document dialog box.

Following are some lines from the PPD file for the Linotronic 300:

```
*PPD-Adobe: "4.0"
*% Adobe Systems PostScript(R) Printer Description File
*% Copyright 1987-1992 Adobe Systems Incorporated.
*% All Rights Reserved.
*% Permission is granted for redistribution of this file as
*% long as this copyright notice is intact and the contents
*% of the file is not altered in any way from its original form.
*% End of Copyright statement
*FormatVersion: "4.0"
```

```
*FileVersion: "2.3"
*PCFileName: "L300_493.PPD"
*LanguageVersion: English
*Product: "(Linotype)"
*PSVersion: "(49.3) 106"
*ModelName: "Linotronic 300 v49.3"
*NickName: "Linotronic 300 v49.3"

*% General Information and Defaults ===============
*FreeVM: "992406"
*LanguageLevel: "1"
*Extensions: FileSystem CMYK
*ColorDevice: False
*DefaultColorSpace: Gray
*VariablePaperSize: True
*FileSystem: True
*?FileSystem: "
...(lines not shown)
*DefaultResolution: 1270dpi
*SetResolution 635dpi: "
...(lines not shown)
*SetResolution 1270dpi: "
...(lines not shown)
*% Halftone Information ===============
*ScreenFreq: "150.0"
*ScreenAngle: "45.0"
*DefaultScreenProc: Dot
*ScreenProc Dot: "
...(lines not shown)
*% Paper Handling ===================
*% Use these entries to set paper size most of the time,
unless there is
*% specific reason to use PageRegion.
*OpenUI *PageSize: PickOne
*OrderDependency: 30 AnySetup *PageSize
*DefaultPageSize: Letter.Transverse
*PageSize Letter.Transverse: "Letter"
*PageSize Ledger: "ledger"
*PageSize A4.Transverse: "A4"
*PageSize A5.Transverse: "A5"
*PageSize ISOB5.Transverse: "B5"
*PageSize Letter: "letter"
*PageSize Legal: "legal"
*PageSize Tabloid: "11x17"
*PageSize A3: "a3"
*PageSize A4: "a4"
```

```
*PageSize A5: "a5"
*PageSize ISOB5: "b5"
*?PageSize: "
...(lines not shown)
*% The following entries provide information about specific
paper keywords.
*DefaultImageableArea: Letter.Transverse
*ImageableArea Letter.Transverse: "0 1 612 792 "
*ImageableArea Ledger: "1 0 1224 792 "
*ImageableArea A4.Transverse: "0 1 595 841 "
*ImageableArea A5.Transverse: "0 1 419 595 "
*ImageableArea ISOB5.Transverse: "0 1 498 709 "
*ImageableArea Letter: "1 0 612 792 "
*ImageableArea Legal: "0 1 612 1008 "
*ImageableArea Tabloid: "0 1 792 1224 "
*ImageableArea A3: "0 1 842 1191 "
*ImageableArea A4: "1 0 596 840 "
*ImageableArea A5: "1 0 420 595 "
*ImageableArea ISOB5: "1 0 498 709 "
*?ImageableArea: "
...(lines not shown)
*% These provide the physical dimensions of the paper (by
keyword)
*DefaultPaperDimension: Letter.Transverse
*PaperDimension Letter.Transverse: "612 792"
*PaperDimension Ledger: "1224 792"
*PaperDimension A4.Transverse: "595 842"
*PaperDimension A5.Transverse: "420 595"
*PaperDimension ISOB5.Transverse: "499 709"
*PaperDimension Letter: "612 792"
*PaperDimension Legal: "612 1008"
*PaperDimension Tabloid: "792 1224"
*PaperDimension A3: "842 1191"
*PaperDimension A4: "596 840"
*PaperDimension A5: "420 595"
*PaperDimension ISOB5: "499 709"
```

Troubleshooting Problems in Printing

The most common problem you are likely to encounter in printing is
that the document (or selected pages) will not print. Specific problems
might be indicated by an error message on the screen, or the printing

process might literally take forever with no results. The root of the problem may be mechanical, or it may be related to the construction of the document pages. This section describes how to diagnose and solve some of the most common problems in printing.

Troubleshooting Mechanical Problems

The most obvious diagnostic steps may sound silly, but they are the most common causes of printing problems. Besides, these problems are equipment-based and are usually easier to solve than problems that arise from the document's construction. The symptom of the problem might simply be that the file will not print, or you might get a clue from an error message such as Can't Print to LPT. In either case, go through the checks suggested here first.

Examine the front panel of the printer to determine if the "On-Line Busy" light is flashing, which indicates that the printer is processing your document. Other lights on the front panel may flash to indicate a particular problem, such as low toner or jammed paper.

Check to see that the printer is turned on. Make sure that paper is in the paper trays and that the paper trays are firmly inserted in their slots. Verify that the printer cable is firmly connected to both printer and computer.

Open the Control Panel and double-click the Printers icon. Examine the settings for your printer driver to verify that the printer driver is active and properly configured for your printer and port.

If you are printing under Windows 3.0, examine the printer settings in PageMaker (Page Setup and Print in the File menu), and be sure they match the Control Panel settings for the active printer. (Remember that under Windows 3.0, you must change printers only through the Control Panel. Under Windows 3.1, you can change printers also through the PageMaker Page Setup and Print commands.)

If you are using a serial printer, examine your COM port settings. Open the Windows Control Panel and double-click the Ports icon. Click the icon for the COM port to which your printer is connected and click Settings. Consult the documentation that came with your printer to determine the correct settings for Baud Rate, Data Bits, Parity, Stop Bits, and Flow Control. Verify that your printer is configured using these settings. If all settings are correct, lower the baud rate until the printer prints. Baud rates should be configured identically for both the printer and Windows COM port. (If you are using a parallel printer, no port configuration is required.)

If your printer is responding to the print command issued from PageMaker (that is, the proper light is flashing to indicate that the printer is processing your print job), the print job might be exceeding the memory capacity of your printer. This situation is more common with PostScript devices than with non-PostScript printers such as PCL, dot-matrix, and ink-jet printers. This problem is addressed in several of the next sections.

Solving the Problem of Limited Disk Space

If the Print Manager is on and you get an I/O error saying that the computer is out of disk space, you have insufficient space on your hard drive for Print Manager to write the file to disk. When you print a file to the Print Spooler in Windows, a temporary print file that requires space on the hard disk is created. If the publication is very large, and you do not have enough free space on your hard disk, you can try one of the solutions listed here.

The long-term solutions are to add more disk space (that is, buy a bigger drive), delete unnecessary files from your current hard drive, or use a file compression utility to free more disk space. Another alternative is to print the publication to the Print Spooler one page at a time. The simplest and most immediate solution, however, is to turn the Print Manager off.

Print Manager is essentially a spooling device. When Print Manager is on, you can send your job to the printer and get back to work. Printing may take a little longer, but meanwhile you have access to your computer. When Print Manager is turned off, your computer is tied up until your job has finished printing; it is not available for other tasks.

To turn Print Manager off, open the Windows Control Panel and double-click the Printers icon. Uncheck Use Print Manager in the lower left corner of the Printers dialog box. Click OK. Unchecking this box increases the amount of time it takes before you can use your computer again during printing. This procedure is described in more detail in Chapter 10.

Troubleshooting Problems in Printing Fonts

If pages fail to print at all, the fonts may require more memory or disk space than what is available. (These two problems were addressed in previous sections.) This section addresses the problem that the pages print, but the fonts do not print the way you intended.

An Unrecoverable Application Error Message

If you get the `Unrecoverable Application Error` message when printing to an HP LaserJet III, it could be a result of using version 3.7 of the LaserJet III printer driver with Adobe Type Manager and the Use Prebuilt or Resident Bitmap Fonts option. The best solution is to obtain a newer version of the driver from Hewlett-Packard (by calling 303-353-7650). Another solution is to turn off Use Prebuilt or Resident Bitmap Fonts through Adobe Type Manager. A third solution is to remove the bitmap fonts that cause this problem.

To remove fonts, open the Control Panel through the Windows Program Manager and double-click the Printers icon (these steps are described in detail in Chapter 10). Choose the HP LaserJet III in the Printers-Configure dialog box, and then click Fonts. Hold down the Ctrl key and click the following font names to select them: GillSans 10, GillSans 12, NewTimes RomanPS2 10, and TimesNewRomanPS 12. Click Remove. Click OK to close the dialog boxes.

The Fonts Print Smaller than Expected

If you are printing to a PCL printer and the fonts print smaller than specified, you have probably chosen a bitmap font in a size that you have not installed. Bitmap fonts are defined by their typeface, style, and size. If you are printing to a PCL printer and have not installed the size you specified and are not using a type manager, the font will be printed at the nearest smaller size.

If fonts print extremely small on a PostScript printer, you are probably using an old PostScript printer driver. The best solution is to use the PostScript driver that comes with PageMaker 5.0, as described in Chapter 10.

Some Characters Do Not Print Correctly on a PCL Printer

Some fonts do not include special characters such as a dagger, typesetter's apostrophe, and quotation marks. If the font does include a special character that is not printing, you may have configured your Windows printer driver incorrectly. Open the Windows Control Panel and double-click the Printers icon. Verify that you have specified the correct settings for your printer. Verify that you have chosen the correct printer brand and type. If you have a printer that is not listed, consult the documentation that came with your printer or contact the printer manufacturer to determine which printer brand and type you should choose.

If you are printing using a serial cable, your COM port settings may be incorrect. To adjust the COM port settings, open the Windows Control Panel and double-click the Ports icon. Click the icon for the COM port to which your printer is connected, and then click Settings. Consult the documentation that came with your printer to determine the correct settings for Baud Rate, Data Bits, Parity, Stop Bits, and Flow Control. If all the settings are correct, lower the baud rate until the printer prints correctly. Baud rates should be configured identically for both the printer and the computer.

Justified Text Prints Ragged Right

When you print to an HP DeskJet 500C using the version 2.0 driver, justified text may print ragged right instead. You can correct the problem by getting a newer driver from Hewlett-Packard (by calling 303-533-7650).

The Fonts Print Smashed Together

Another problem is fonts that looked "smashed." This problem may occur on a PostScript printer if you have printer font metrics (PFM) files but not the printer font (PFB) file for the font you want to print. When this happens, PageMaker substitutes another font's characters but uses the metrics for the font you specified to keep the correct line and page breaks. Install the correct printer font for the font you have chosen. (Consult the documentation that came with your fonts for information about installing printer font files. If you are using Adobe Type Manager, you may need to update your softfonts list. See Appendix A or your ATM documentation for more information.)

This problem can also occur when the printer font you want to use is not listed in the WIN.INI entry for the printer you are using. Edit your WIN.INI to include the location of printer fonts, as described in Appendix A.

Finally, your font files might be damaged. Replace your PostScript printer font files and printer font metrics files. Consult the documentation that came with your fonts for information about installing these files.

The Fonts Look Good On-Screen but Print Incorrectly

Sometimes PostScript fonts look fine on the screen, but they will not print to the PostScript printer. They print as Courier or as jagged bitmaps, or they are incorrectly sized or placed.

The graphics resolution of the printer affects the appearance of text if you click Print TrueType as Graphics in the Printer Setup Options dialog box (described in Chapter 10), or if you are printing PostScript fonts to a non-PostScript printer (such as the HP LaserJet II or III) using a type manager. PCL printers treat Adobe Type Manager fonts as graphics. Check the resolution specified through the Print command by clicking the Setup button in the Print Document dialog box when the PCL printer is selected. For the best resolution in printing text as graphics, set the graphics resolution to 300.

> **CAUTION:** If you cannot get a page with a graphic to print at 300 dpi (due to memory problems), but you want the text to print at 300 dpi, you can print the page at 75 or 150 dpi to print the graphic and then delete the graphic from the page and print it again at 300 dpi. You will have to resort to traditional tools like an X-ACTO knife and wax or glue to cut the graphic from the low-resolution printout and paste it into the higher-resolution printout.

T I P   Editing the WIN.INI File

You can use the Windows System Configuration Editor to edit SYSTEM.INI, WIN.INI, CONFIG.SYS, and AUTOEXEC.BAT. Open the Windows System Configuration Editor by choosing Run from the File menu of the Program Manager and typing **SYSEDIT.EXE**. The System Configuration Editor displays windows with SYSTEM.INI, WIN.INI, CONFIG.SYS, and AUTOEXEC.BAT as editable text files that can be searched, printed, and saved using commands on the System Configuration Editor menu bar. Click the WIN.INI menu bar to activate that window, edit the file, and then choose Save from the File menu.

After editing WIN.INI—by this or any means—you must restart Windows for the change to take effect.

If none of the above explains the problem—that the fonts look good on the screen but print incorrectly—the fonts you are using probably are not downloading to the printer. (See "Downloading Fonts" in Appendix A.)

If you are running ATM and the PostScript fonts that print are not the same as the fonts on the screen, your fonts may have been remapped in the ATM.INI file, which tells ATM which printer font metrics (PFM) files and which printer font (PFB) files to use for a specified font.

Although you can reassign font files for any font name you choose, it's not recommended as a general practice. You may want to remap your ATM.INI file occasionally. (For example, Futura Bold prints bolder from the PC than from the Macintosh. To print the same weight of Futura Bold on the PC as on the Macintosh, you can remap your Futura Bold font in your ATM.INI to Futura Medium Bold.) Other times, you may want to undo some remapping and restore the original mapping.

Before changing the ATM.INI file, make a backup and store it in a safe place. If Windows or ATM cannot launch using the edited ATM.INI, you can copy your original ATM.INI back to your Windows directory.

Here are some font mappings in the Fonts section of the ATM.INI file:

```
[Fonts]

Futura=c:\psfonts\pfm\fuw_____.pfm,c:\psfonts\fuw_____.pfb

Futura,BOLD=c:\psfonts\pfm\fuh_____.pfm,c:\psfonts\fuh_____.pfb

Futura,BOLDITALIC=c:\psfonts\pfm\fuho____.pfm,c:\psfonts\fuho____.pfb

FuturaMedium,BOLD=c:\psfonts\pfm\fuh_____.pfm,c:\psfonts\fuh_____.pfb
```

In this example, Futura Bold prints as Futura Medium Bold. Note that the PFM and PFB files for Futura Medium Bold have the file names fuh_____, and that these files have been assigned to both Futura Medium Bold and Futura Bold. By assigning these files to the Futura, BOLD entry, you force ATM to display and print Futura Medium Bold when you specify Futura Bold. To change this, you must remap the Futura, BOLD entry to reference the Futura Bold metric and printer files. The modified entry appears as

```
Futura,BOLD=c:\psfonts\pfm\fub_____.pfm,c:\psfonts\fub_____.pfb
```

Your fonts may also have been remapped in the Alias section of ATM.INI. Scroll through ATM.INI until you locate the Alias section. Beneath the [Alias] header, you might find

```
Futura,BOLD=FuturaMedium,BOLD
```

Like the previous example, this one shows Futura Medium Bold substituted when Futura Bold is specified. Delete this line if you do not want the substitution.

You must quit Windows and restart it for ATM to recognize any changes you make to ATM.INI. Additional information about special mapping of fonts is in the README.TXT files on the disk of fonts you purchased. For more information about PostScript fonts and font mapping with ATM, consult your *ATM User's Guide* or contact Adobe Systems, Inc.

Troubleshooting Problems with Graphics in the Document

If none of the steps suggested so far solves the printing problem, or if some pages do not print or do not print completely, or if the pages print but the graphics resolution is poor, try the following tests to determine the nature of the problem.

The Pages Will Not Print

If several pages print successfully but then the document stops printing, first try turning the printer off and on again to flush the printer memory; then set Pagemaker to resume printing where it left off. If the next page still will not print, try printing pages in reverse order. Or start the printing process from the page after the page that failed to print. For instance, if pages 1 through 9 print but printing stops on page 10, try printing from page 11. This way, you might be able to isolate the problem to one page.

If the pages that fail to print contain graphics, you can verify that the graphics are the source of the problem by clicking Proof in the PageMaker Print dialog box when you print. When you click Proof, PageMaker prints rectangles in place of the graphics in your document. If the document prints when Proof is selected, one of the following is probably true: one or more graphics files are corrupt, the combination of graphics and PageMaker elements exceeds the capacity of the printer memory, or the page is taking longer to compose than allowed by the printer Timeout value.

Before you go to the trouble of simplifying your pages or graphics, try increasing the time Windows allows for processing printer information. Two updates must be made to do this. First, open the Windows Control Panel and double-click the Printers icon (these steps are described in detail in Chapter 10). Select your printer in the Printers-Configure dialog box; then click Connect. In the next dialog box, enter a Transmission Retry value of 600 or more; then click OK to close the dialog boxes.

Next, edit the WIN.INI file using Windows Notepad or Sysedit (using techniques mentioned previously in this chapter and described in detail in Appendix A). Find the line that reads

```
TransmissionRetry/Timeout=45
```

and change the value to the same one you specified in the Printers-Configure dialog box. Do not add or delete spaces or change the file in any other way. Choose Save from the File menu; then close Notepad or Sysedit.

If the page still fails to print, you can simplify the page by removing PageMaker elements that are not part of the page design. Often, documents that cannot be printed have elements obscured by other objects. The more layers you have in a document, the more time and memory will be required to print the document.

Because of the way information is stored for grayscale TIFF images, the amount of memory required to process the image increases as the resolution becomes higher. For this reason, printing images takes longer at higher resolutions. This is another good reason to scan images at a lower dpi than what your printer can support. You might run into memory overload or printing time-out errors when printing pages with grayscale TIFF images at high resolutions, especially the high resolutions offered by imagesetters such as the Linotronic models. If the document contains TIFF pictures, reduce the resolution of the printer and the line screen (the number of halftone lines per inch). If the document prints at the lower resolution and line screen, your printer requires additional memory to print the job at the resolution and line screen you specified.

If you are printing to a PostScript printer and have complex EPS files, simplify them. Remove any elements in your graphics file that are obscured by other elements. Adjust the flatness of curves in your drawing. Flattening a curve (that is, reducing the number of points used to define the curve) can yield memory savings, but making drastic changes may compromise the quality of the output. If you have blends in EPS picture files, reduce the number of steps in the blends. If you have graduated fills, consult the documentation for the program that you used to create the fills for information about simplifying them. Consult the documentation that came with your illustration package for more information about simplifying drawings without compromising design.

Resolution and line screen are generally much higher on imagesetters and, therefore, imagesetters require significantly more memory to print a document. As a result, documents that print successfully at low resolutions or to a PCL printer may fail to print to a PostScript imagesetter.

Graphics Print at Low Resolution

If you are outputting proofs to a PCL printer (such as a printer in the Hewlett-Packard LaserJet series) and plan to send the document to a PostScript imagesetter for final output, be aware that EPS files are not processed by PCL devices. PageMaker sends the low-resolution bitmaps incorporated in the document to the PCL printer, but sends the actual EPS files to the high-resolution imagesetter.

If you are printing to a PostScript printer and the graphics seem to print at a low resolution, the link between the EPS or TIFF file and the PageMaker document is probably severed (that is, the picture is missing). Reestablish the link to print the high-resolution picture files. Choose Links from the File menu, click the missing picture, and then click Update. A directory dialog box is displayed. Locate the missing picture and click OK. PageMaker reestablishes the path between the picture and the document. Updating the links between a picture file and a PageMaker document was described previously in this chapter in the section "Managing Linked Text and Graphics Doucments."

If all the graphics are properly linked and they still print at low resolution, the resolution of the printer might be set lower than 300 dpi. Check the specified resolution through the Print command by clicking the Setup button in the Print Document dialog box when the PCL printer is selected. For the best resolution in printing text as graphics, set the graphics resolution to 300.

If you are using an old version of a driver for a LaserJet III printer, see "The Fonts Look Good On-Screen but Print Incorrectly" section in this chapter for tips on correcting this problem.

Troubleshooting Problems in Printing Colors

Color issues are discussed in Chapter 12. This section describes a few color considerations that relate directly to printing.

The Color Will Not Print on a Color Printer

PageMaker documents that contain imported color graphics or are set up with different colors through the PageMaker menus should print in color on any color printer supported by Windows (but not plotters). If the color does not print on your printer, be sure that you specified Use Color for your printer driver. To do this, open the Windows Control

Panel and double-click the Printers icon. Click the Configure and Setup buttons in successive dialog boxes to access the Printer on Port dialog box. Make sure you have selected a printer brand and model that supports color output from Windows.

The Color Separation Plates Will Not Print

You can print color separations of a PageMaker document to any PostScript printer or imagesetter by checking the Separations option in the Color dialog box accessed through the Print command.

If you have imported TIFF and EPS pictures, make sure the picture files are linked to the document. Use the File menu's Links command to check and establish the links as described previously in this chapter in the section "Managing Linked Text and Graphics Documents."

If the picture files are linked to the document but you do not get separation plates, make sure that TIFF picture files are in CMYK format and that EPS files contain color plate information. Not all illustration and photo retouching software can save picture files with color separation information.

If some but not all color plates print, you have not selected All Inks in the Print Color dialog box, or you have not created all the colors in PageMaker.

Using the Windows Error Handler

As an aid to troubleshooting, you can download the PostScript error handler built into Windows. To do so, choose the Print command, select a PostScript printer, and then click the Options button. Click the check box next to Include PostScript Error Handler.

Remembering To Turn Off the Error Handler

T I P

Settings you make through the Print dialog boxes are stored as part of the publication. Remember to turn off the error handler after the problems are solved or before sending the publication to a service bureau.

You can also set the error handler to print for all publications through Windows. First double-click the Printers icon in the Windows Control Panel.

Under Windows 3.1, click the Setup, Options, and Advanced buttons in successive dialog boxes. Then check Print PostScript Error Information in the Advanced Options dialog box.

If there is a printing problem, the error handler will print out a page with the error and the offending command. Look up the error and command in a PostScript manual, or call a technician at Aldus to determine what you should do next.

If All Else Fails

If the document did not print and the Windows error handler didn't reveal the problem, the PageMaker document may be damaged. In this case, create a new document with the same page dimensions as the existing document. View both documents in Fit in Window, and position them side-by-side by choosing Tile from the Windows menu. Drag-copy the elements on each page from the existing document to the corresponding pages in the new document (by opening a new publication in a window next to the current publication window and dragging the elements from the original publication to the new publication). Print the new document.

FROM HERE...

For Related Information

◄◄ "Installing the Printer," p. 399.

◄◄ "Using the Print Command," p. 410.

◄◄ "Printing in Color with Color Printers," p. 565.

◄◄ "Printing Color Separations," p. 569.

▶▶ "Installing and Using Fonts," p. 902.

Summary

This chapter offered some useful tips on building booklets, printing your publications to disk files, and managing fonts and graphics to minimize printing problems. This chapter also covered many problems you might encounter in printing PageMaker publications. The next chapter offers additional suggestions for managing large projects or producing large publications.

Managing Large Documents

N ot all documents produced with PageMaker are short fliers and brochures. PageMaker is well-suited for producing long publications, and can be a workhorse in a large production department facing a continuous stream of serious deadlines. This chapter offers productivity aids that can be useful in any publication department which handles document production under tight deadlines. The chapter also describes some management strategies and advanced features to simplify the production of long documents and complex documents that involve many files and can require the organization of a workgroup, such as the following:

- If your publications are so large that the system slows down when you are working, you can follow the procedures suggested here for managing system memory.

- You should organize your disk files and establish naming conventions early in the project. Special strategies for managing files in a workgroup are given here.

- PageMaker 5.0 adds a command for displaying publication information. You can also import a date/time stamp into a publication for project control.

■ The Book command enables you to join a series of separate PageMaker publications as a single document, so that you can print the whole series in one step and opt to have PageMaker number all pages sequentially from one publication to another.

■ You can generate a table of contents and an index for a single PageMaker file or for a series of publications linked through the Book command.

■ PageMaker 5.0 adds a Library feature in which you can store and easily access common elements—both text and graphics.

■ You can create scripted sequences of steps to automate PageMaker procedures that you use often in your organization or over the life of a large project.

Memory and System Resource Management

Normally, the memory usage in your computer is automatically controlled by DOS, Windows, your memory manager, and the applications you are running. Information stored in memory is always available immediately, but because memory space is limited, bits of information are constantly being put into memory then replaced by new information as needed. The process of getting new information from the hard disk and moving it to memory takes milliseconds, made up primarily of disk access time. When the milliseconds add up to noticeable delays while you are working, you will probably want to add more memory to the system.

If you have already installed as much memory as your system can handle, or if you don't want to spend the time and money to add more memory, you can participate in the memory management process by knowing what takes up memory and how to make the best use of it.

Exactly 128K of memory is used for Windows *system resources*. Sometimes you might have a problem starting a new application because the part of memory reserved for Windows system resources is all used, even though there is plenty of free memory left for running the application. The first sections of this chapter offer tips on how to make the most of memory and system resources.

You can see how much free space is available for memory and for system resources by choosing the About Program Manager command from the Help menu of the Program Manager.

You can get access to virtual memory—and have access to even more RAM than you have installed on your system—by setting up a permanent swap file on your hard disk. See the Windows documentation for more information about this option and for other Windows Optimization procedures.

The Program Manager at Startup

Each open application under Windows uses up some part of the system resources, as well as part of the larger memory area. When you close an application, the parts of the system resources the application was using are usually freed up. The one exception is the Program Manager. Because the Program Manager is always running (when you close it you exit Windows), it never frees or recycles system resources after they are allocated.

Each open window uses some system resources, and each icon in each open window uses some resources. If, when you start Windows, the Program Manager opens with only the Program Manager application window open, you start out using fewer resources. The Program Manager window also requires more system resources for each icon it shows. Similarly, each window opened under the Program Manager requires more or fewer system resources depending on the number of icons in the window.

Closing the windows under Program Manager once they have been opened does not free system resources. The best way to minimize the initial allocation of system resources is to choose Save Settings on Exit in the Options menu of the Program Manager window (if that option is not already checked), close all the windows under Program Manager and exit Windows 3.1. When you restart Windows, you will be using the least possible amount of system resources. Thereafter, when you exit Windows, be sure that Save Settings on Exit is not checked.

You can have icons for the same application stored in more than one program group. Windows provides several program groups arranged by type of application, and a program group called Aldus can be created during the installation process. You can keep or delete these groups and create your own. For example, you can create a different program group for each project. The Newsletter program group might include the icon for the template that starts PageMaker and opens the template in a double-click. The same program group might include an icon for a graphics application and for a mailing list of all newsletter subscribers.

Delete icons for applications that you never use. Remember that you can start any application using the Run command from the File menu under the Program Manager, or by finding and double-clicking the application under the File Manager. You delete an icon by clicking it once to select it, and then choosing Delete from the File menu.

If you are always using the same application(s) under Windows, such as the File Manager, PageMaker, and one graphics application, put the icons for those applications in one group window and start Windows with only that window open, using the procedure described two paragraphs earlier for saving changes to the Program Manager for future startups. You can create a new group icon by choosing New from the Program Manager File menu and clicking Program Group. With a group window open, you can add an application icon by choosing New from the Program Manager's File menu and clicking Program Item.

If you always use the same application(s), in Windows 3.1 you can add icons to the Startup program group under the Program manager. The icons in that folder automatically start when you start Windows. In Windows 3.0, you had to add lines to the WIN.INI file to automatically launch the application when you start Windows; this still works in Windows 3.1. To launch PageMaker, for example, you type a line in WIN.INI with Run= or Load= followed by the directory path to the program. For example:

```
Run=C:\PM5\PM5.EXE
```

In either case, you do not need to open a window under the Program Manager to start the most common application.

There is no right or wrong way to set up the Program Manager, but there are an infinite number of possibilities. A few have been mentioned here. Whatever approach works for you, simply remember that one goal is to make the best use of precious space for system resources.

Open Applications

One of the great things about working under Windows is that you can have several applications running at once and even several document windows open under each application. For example, under PageMaker 5 you can open more than one publication at a time and view the publications in different windows on-screen. The problem is that memory is used by each open window on the screen. This includes windows that show documents and palettes, such as the Control palette and the Colors palette.

Remember that you can free system resources by closing applications, but you do not free resources by simply closing windows and palettes that are not in use. After you open a palette or a document window in PageMaker, the system resources used by that window remain allocated until you close PageMaker. When you have two or more applications running at the same time, make sure it's because you routinely go back and forth between the two, not just because Windows enables you to run multiple applications.

If you use several applications at the same time and keep your system running all day or even all week, the system might get slower and slower as the day or week progresses. You might regain some of the speed by quitting all applications and Windows and then restarting Windows.

Reboot To Recover Memory

In spite of all the tricks you might use to conserve or release memory, you still can run into problems that cannot be controlled. The most common problem is that even when you quit an application, not all of the memory or resources it was using will be released. This can be due to the application itself not releasing memory. Other times, after running many different applications, memory contains a lot of small (and therefore unusable) fragments.

You can rebuild Windows system resources space by closing and restarting Windows. To clear the larger memory area, you must reboot your system. The portion of memory allocated for system resources is more likely to become filled if you leave your computer on 24 hours a day, but it can happen to anyone who uses a lot of different applications. Remember that rebooting the system is a possible solution whenever you run into the `Insufficient memory` message.

Of course, you can ignore all the suggestions in these sections if you have no problems with memory, system resources, or system speed!

Organizing Your Disk Files

Organizing your disk files before you start building a document in PageMaker is a good idea, especially if the document you are building is very large or uses many source files. This section offers a few guidelines that can save you trouble in the long run. Part V of this book offers specific examples of disk organization systems for large projects.

Decide on Naming Conventions

No matter how you organize your files, developing logical naming conventions is a good idea. Decide on the conventions to use for all new files created during the project. The first goal is to be able to find documents easily and know what they contain. One helpful guideline is to name the different parts of the document so that they appear sequentially when you view them alphabetically. For example, a chapter document may be named CHAP1 or CH1 or 1, but you don't want a set of documents related to one book to use different naming standards, such as CHAP1, CH2, 3, and 04.

If two or more people are involved in the production process, the disk organization and file-naming conventions should be determined by the production manager and recommended to the production crew. File organization and naming conventions may be incorporated into the project's list of standards and review items that cover other topics such as editorial conventions. You can also develop guidelines for moving or renaming files as they progress through the production process.

Copy All Project Files to One Hard Disk

If possible, assemble all source files—the text and picture files as well as the PageMaker templates and publication files—on one primary hard disk. This disk can be your internal hard disk if your computer is the primary workstation for page layout activities, or it can be the file server If you are on a network and several people are involved in the final document production. This hard disk can be a separate hard disk or a removable hard disk if you need to carry the files from one station to another.

Set Up Project-Specific Directories

Try to set up a single directory on the hard disk for each document or publication, and move all the text and graphic files into that directory. If many files are involved, divide the main document directory into subdirectories. Some publishers like to keep text sources in one directory and graphic elements in another. Another way of dividing the files is to put the text and graphics files related to a single chapter together in a directory, so that you end up with one directory per chapter.

The publication-specific directory also can include a directory of the fonts used in the publication. Copies of these fonts can be stored in the

Windows or PageMaker directory. If you keep a set in the publication directory, however, you can easily remember to take copies when you move the publication to another system to be printed.

Changing the Default Directory for Saving PageMaker Publications

As long as the PM5 directory is in the PATH statement in the AUTOEXEC.BAT file, you can change the default directory that PageMaker saves files to by changing the path statement in the Program Items Properties dialog box accessed through the Windows Program Manager.

Suppose you want to save most of your files in the C:\BIGBOOK directory. Open the Program Manager Window; then open the Aldus program group window (or whatever group you store the PageMaker program icon in). Click the PageMaker program icon to select it; then choose Properties from the File menu.

Change the path statement in the Command Line box from C:\PM5\PM5.EXE to C:\BIGBOOK\PM5.EXE. Click the Change Icon button and enter C:\PM5\PM5.EXE so Windows will display the PageMaker 5.0 icon instead of a generic Windows icon in the Program Manager. Click OK to close the dialog boxes. Click OK when you get the message The specified path is invalid. Even though PM5.EXE is not in the BIGBOOK directory, Windows will find it as long as the PM5 directory is listed in the PATH statement of AUTOEXEC.BAT.

Back Up All Files Regularly

Keep all files related to one document in a single directory. One tip that was offered in Chapter 13 is worth repeating here.

Copying Linked Graphics   T I P

When you are copying publications, one way to ensure that all linked files are included is to create a new directory at the root level on the hard disk; then open the PageMaker publication and choose Save As from the File menu. In the Save As dialog box, change to the new

continues

Copying Linked Graphics (continued)

directory, and click Copy Files Required for Remote Printing (which also copies special files such as the track-kerning resource file needed for printing) or Copy All Linked Files (to include all linked graphics whether or not they are already included as part of the publication). Then copy the new folder to a disk for transport. You can use a compression utility such as PKZIP to compress the files if they cannot fit on one disk.

These few steps are worth taking before you begin assembling text and graphics on a page. Taking time with these preliminaries can save you hours over the life of a large project. Applying these simple steps to small projects is easy.

Managing a Workgroup

Until now, you have learned some general rules and guidelines for organizing disk files in a large project. This section presents a scenario of how these ideas can be applied in workgroups.

A *workgroup* is any group of people with different computers working on the same projects, whether or not the workstations are actually wired together. A workgroup can also be networked through a LAN and share files through a file server. More recently, products like Novell's NetWare, Banyan's Vines, and Windows for Workgroups offer peer-to-peer networks that let you access files stored on other workstations' hard drives without going through a file server. In any case, some planning and coordination is required to manage the flow of files through the system.

Networked Workgroup Scenario

A networked workgroup is a group of computers, each with a local hard disk, hooked up to a common file server through which the computers can share files. The first scenario describes how you might organize a publication project in a networked environment.

The File Server

The *file server* in a network is a computer with a hard disk. Depending on the size of the hard disk, the file server stores the following types of files:

■ The files for the project. These files include linked files, publication files, imported text files, and templates. Some projects may be so large that the file server's entire hard disk is devoted to the project files.

■ Other files shared among workstations, such as clip art.

■ Printer fonts, which must be stored on the file server if printing is spooled through the server. Let local workstations copy only the fonts in use on active projects.

Individual Workstations

Individual workstations store the following types of files on their local hard disks:

■ The project files in progress on the workstation. These files are often copied from the file server, used at the local workstation, then copied back to the file server. (See the following section, "Backup Procedures.")

■ Printer fonts in use on active projects

■ Applications and utilities that are commonly used, including PageMaker

If your workgroup shares one room, or if the project is well-managed and the group has good communication between members, you may not need to take extra precautions so that two people do not start working on copies of the same file at the same time. PageMaker displays a sharing violation error message if two different workstations try to open the same file on a file server, but this doesn't work if you use the file server for backups only and keep the works-in-progress on local workstations' hard drives. If procedures are followed correctly and a project coordinator monitors the status of each file as work progresses, you can prevent someone from working on an outdated version of a file.

Remember: If the group is widely dispersed in a building, if recommended procedures aren't followed, if the project is too large, if the pace is too fast, or if chaos reigns, accidents can happen.

The most efficient method of tracking the master copy of a document is through the attention of a project coordinator. The coordinator should maintain and post a log of each document's status. In figure 14.1, notice that the log tracks change to externally linked graphics files as well as to PageMaker documents.

Disk File Name	Master File Start date	WIP Station ID	Date	Back to Master Date	WIP Station	Date
CH01	4/1	SV	4/3	4/5	#ID	4/8
CH02	4/1	SV	4/3	4/8	DB	
CH03	4/1					
Linked Graphic A	4/1					

Fig. 14.1

A log of disk files.

Backup Procedures

The master files or the most recently updated versions of files that are still works-in-progress are stored on the file server. When a file must be modified, copy it to a local workstation. Under this system, the file server is the backup for the files in use at local workstations. When the work is finished, copy the file from the local workstation back to the file server.

It's a good idea to consider the most recently printed version of the documents as the current master—especially if the printed copy is to be marked with edits or other changes. Make a copy of the master version of the file when you begin entering the edits from the marked copy, and consider the copied file a work-in-progress until the edits are complete. If the work-in-progress on a workstation requires more than a day to complete on an individual file, you may want the workstation user to copy the current work-in-progress back to the file server at the end of the day to serve as an interim backup. Do not copy the work-in-progress file over the most recently printed master file on the file server. Instead, copy the interim version to a separate directory, or add a clue such as -M (for master) and -W (for work-in-progress) to the file name. Save the master file and the marked printed pages until you have successfully printed the next version; then replace the master with the work-in-progress file. This way, if a disaster happens—the work-in-progress file becomes "corrupted" or you find that you inadvertently deleted pages in the saved work-in-progress—you can always go back to the disk file that matches the last printed version and reenter the edits from scratch.

When the project is finished, copy all files from the file server to floppy disks or removable hard disks for storage. You should keep copies of all disk files at least until the final document has been mass-produced and distributed. You can erase the disk files later if storage space is limited. (If you are producing a newsletter or a magazine, for example, you can erase the disk files after each issue is printed.) At the end of each project, you can also collect parts of the document that can be reused and store them as part of a template.

Offline Workgroup Scenario

If your group does not share files through a file server, or if some members of the group are not on the network, you can use the following procedures to manage large projects. These methods also apply if you are using a peer-to-peer network such as Novell's NetWare, Banyan's Vines, and Windows for Workgroups; the only difference is that you don't need to use floppy disks or removable hard disks to move files from one station to another.

The Master Files

If your workgroup does not share files through a network, the master files for a project can be stored on one of the workstation's hard disks and individuals can go to the master workstation to get copies of files as needed. In this case, the master workstation can be set up as described in the previous section. If the files are too large to fit on floppy disks, you can use one of the following methods to copy files from the master workstation to other workstations:

- Instead of using a workstation's hard disk as the master, put all master files on an extra, external hard disk. Move this external hard disk to each workstation and copy files as needed.

- If each workstation has a removable hard disk drive, the master files can be stored on one or more removable hard disk cartridges that can be moved from station to station.

- If each workstation has a modem, or if your group has at least two modems and two phone lines, you can transfer large files directly from one workstation to another through the phone lines.

Individual Workstations

To set up individual workstations, follow the procedures described in the previous section, "Networked Workgroup Scenario."

Backup Procedures

The master files and the most recently updated files that are still works-in-progress are stored on the designated master disks. When a file must be modified, copy it to a local workstation. Under this system, the master disks are the backup for the files in use at local workstations. When the work is finished, copy the file from the local workstation back to the master disk.

For Related Information

◀◀ "PageMaker and the Publishing Cycle," p. 27.

Displaying Publication Information

PageMaker 5.0 introduced an Aldus Addition called Display Pub Info, which displays a list of all fonts, links, and styles used in a publication. The information can be saved as a text file and printed.

To use this feature, choose Display Pub Info from the Aldus Additions submenu under the Utilities menu. PageMaker displays a window listing the publication name, the list of fonts in the publication and on the system, a list of all linked files, and a list of style names (see fig. 14.2). You can suppress the display of any of these categories of information by checking the boxes at the bottom of the window. Click the Save button to save the information as a text file that you can place in PageMaker and print.

Fig. 14.2

The Pub Info window displays fonts, links, and styles used in the publication.

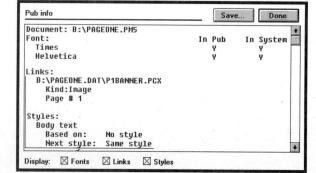

Adding a Date/Time Stamp

You can add a date/time stamp quickly to any publication by following the steps described here. This is handy for control in printing drafts; by looking at a printout, you can see easily when it was printed. You can use the steps described here also to create any text as a graphic, and place it as an inline graphic or as a stand-alone graphic.

1. Choose Place from the File menu.

2. Find the file named DATETIME.TYM (see fig. 14.3). This is a date/time stamp that comes with PageMaker and is normally found in the ALDUS\USENGLSH\FILTERS directory. Click OK to place the DATETIME.TYM file.

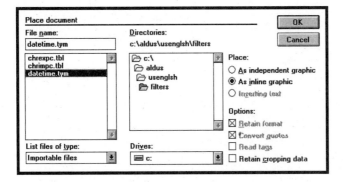

Fig. 14.3

Find the file named DATETIME.TYM in the Place Document dialog box.

3. PageMaker displays the Time Stamp Import Filter dialog box (see fig. 14.4). Normally, you would enter a date/time format in this dialog box, but you can also enter any letter in the Format area and that character will be placed in the publication as a graphic.

    Type the date and time in whatever format you like (see fig. 14.5). Use the letters D, H, M, S, and Y for days, hours, minutes, months, seconds, and year, respectively. For example, DD/MM/YY prints the day, month, and year and HH:MM::SS prints the hour, minute, and second.

    You can type up to 47 characters in this dialog box, adding more words or phrases. If the added words include D, H, M, S, or Y, you must precede the character with a backslash (\) to avoid misinterpretation. For example, to add the project name *Shadow*, you would type \S\ha\dow in the dialog box.

4. Choose a font.

5. Click OK to close the dialog box.

Fig. 14.4

The Time Stamp
Import Filter
dialog box.

Time Stamp import filter, v1.0 —————— OK   Cancel
Sample: 1/15/93
Format: m/d/yy
Font: Times

Fig. 14.5

Type any text
character, but
precede D, H, M,
S, or Y with a
backslash.

Time Stamp import filter, v1.0 —————— OK   Cancel
Sample: 01/28/93 04:05:54 Shadow Inc.
Format: m/dd/yy hh:mm:ss \S\ha\dow Inc.
Font: Times

If you are placing the date/time stamp as an independent graphic, you will get a loaded graphic placement icon that you can click to place the graphic anywhere on the screen. If the Text tool was selected and the text cursor was positioned in text when you chose the Place command, you can place the graphic as an inline graphic. Place it on the master page if you want it to appear on all printed pages, or place it on a document page to show the version of that page.

If part or all of the inline graphic seems to disappear, select the current view from the View submenu under the Layout menu; this forces the screen to redraw. Alternatively, you can change to a different view of the screen or simply click the secondary mouse button twice to toggle between Actual Size and Fit in Window views. You also can make the graphic visible by clicking it with the Cropping tool.

When you change page views or otherwise redraw the screen, the date and time update automatically.

You can select the graphic with the Pointer tool and drag the lower right corner to make the graphic larger or smaller (see fig. 14.6). You can also use the Cropping tool to trim the graphic.

For Related Information

◄◄ "Creating Text as a Graphic," p. 481.

◄◄ "Embedding Transformed Text within a Text Block," p. 511.

FROM HERE...

⸱01/28/93 04:11:0⸱5 Shadow Inc. ⸱ ⸱
⸱

Fig. 14.6

Use the Pointer
tool to scale the
graphic.

Using the Book Command

The Book command enables you to associate a number of separate
PageMaker files as a single, long publication. PageMaker uses this book
list to assemble all parts of the publication in printing, in numbering
pages, and in generating an index or a table of contents.

To create a book list, open the first publication in the series. This publication should be the table of contents, the front matter, or the cover
page of the publication. Choose Book from the File menu. The Book
Publication List dialog box lists the books on the right and all directories and PageMaker publications on the left (see fig. 14.7). To add a
PageMaker publication to the book list, double-click the publication
name in the left window, or click the name and then click Insert.

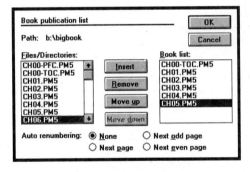

Fig. 14.7

The Book Pub-
lication List
dialog box.

Newly selected publications are added at the end of the book list. You
can rearrange the order of the publications by clicking individual file
names and then clicking Move Up or Move Down. You can remove a
publication from the book list by selecting the name and clicking Remove. (This maneuver does not delete the file from the disk; it removes
only the file name from the list.)

The Auto Renumbering option at the bottom of the Book Publication
List dialog box offers four options:

■ Click None if you want each publication printed from the book list
to start with page 1 or whatever number you specify in the Page
Setup dialog box for each publication.

- Click Next Page if you want PageMaker to number the pages sequentially through all publications in the book. If Chapter 1 ends on page 22, for example, Chapter 2 will begin with page 23.

- Click Next Odd Page if you want each new chapter (or publication in the book list) to begin on an odd-numbered page.

- Click Next Even Page if you want each chapter to begin on an even-numbered page.

Note that the Book feature changes page numbers if you do not check Restart Page Numbering in the Page Setup dialog box, as described in Chapter 4. Check the Restart Page Numbering option in a particular publication if you want the page numbering of each section of the publication always to begin with the page number specified in the Start Page # dialog box for that section. (The dialog box is displayed when you use the New command from the File menu to begin a new publication, or when you choose the Page Setup command from the File menu.) For example, you might turn Restart Page Numbering on for the Preface and Chapter 1, but turn it off for other chapters.

The Book feature handles page numbering, but it does not insert pages to fill gaps between sections. You must insert blank pages at the end of chapters that end on odd-numbered pages, for example, if the next chapter starts on an odd-numbered page and you want to print a sheet for each page number, including blank pages. Chapter 5 describes how to insert blank pages.

When you choose Utilities, Create Index, or Create TOC (described later in this chapter) when a publication that includes a book list is open, PageMaker creates the index or generates the table of contents for the entire book—including all publications in the book list—and numbers the pages according to the sequence of the list. When the book list is associated with only the first publication in the book, the entire book is assembled only when the first publication is open and you use one of the book-related commands. You can generate an index or table of contents for individual chapters by opening any part of the book except the first file.

FROM HERE...

For Related Information

◄◄ "Assigning a Starting Page Number," p. 147.

◄◄ "Inserting and Removing Pages," p. 176.

Creating a Table of Contents

PageMaker can generate a table of contents, including page numbers. You first use the Paragraph command or the Define Styles command to identify lines or paragraphs in the text to be included in the table of contents, and then use the Create TOC command to generate the list. You can generate a table of contents for a single publication or for a series of publications associated through the Book command. The table of contents becomes a new story that you can place and edit in your publication.

You can select lines to be included in the table of contents after you finish building a publication, but the process of planning an outline usually precedes the writing (even if the outline itself changes during the writing process). If you know the outline before you start building the PageMaker publication, you can determine how many outline heading levels you want to include in the table of contents and set them up for inclusion through the style sheet specifications (as described in Chapter 8).

Identifying Table of Contents Entries

To include a line or paragraph in the table of contents, select the Text tool from the Tools palette and position the text insertion point in the paragraph. Choose the Paragraph command from the Type menu, and check Include in Table of Contents in the Paragraph Specifications dialog box (see fig. 14.8).

Alternatively, you can make the table of contents attribute a part of a style by using the Define Styles command to create or select a style and click Para in the Edit Style dialog box to open the Paragraph Specifications dialog box, as described in Chapter 8.

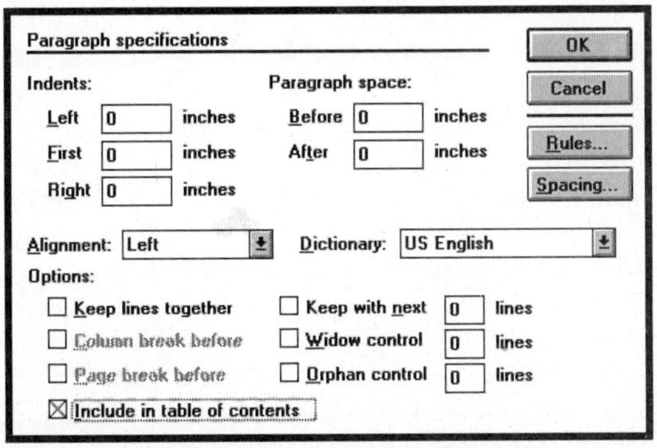

Fig. 14.8

The Paragraph Specifications dialog box.

640

If you want to remove an entry from the table of contents, you can uncheck the Include in Table of Contents box for selected paragraphs or styles. Other entries in this dialog box are described in Chapter 8.

Including Production Notes in a Table of Contents

You can use the table of contents feature to log production notes for a work-in-progress. This method is especially useful when working in a team, because you can distribute the printed list of missing or unfinished parts and make sure that each person knows what holes he or she must fill.

Production notes that are appropriate for printing in the table of contents of a work-in-progress include general comments about missing or unfinished elements, such as:

```
Figure 2.3 to be created

More text to come from author
```

Create a special style (as described in Chapter 8) for production notes and set it up to be included in the table of contents. Type the production notes at points throughout the text where elements are missing or unfinished. When you generate the table of contents, the production notes and their page numbers are printed below each section heading. Delete the production notes when you add the missing elements, before printing the final document.

Generating a Table of Contents

If you know how many pages the table of contents requires, insert the appropriate number of blank pages at the beginning of the document before generating the table of contents. You also can put the table of contents in a separate publication linked to the rest of the document through the Book command (described earlier in this chapter), and number the table of contents pages with roman numerals (through the New or Page Setup commands described in Chapter 4). You also may generate the table of contents twice: once to place it and determine how many pages it requires, and a second time to generate the correct page numbering. Plan on generating a printed version of the table of contents at least twice: once for proofing, followed by editing before the second and (possibly) final generation.

If you want the table of contents to be a separate PageMaker publication, use the New command from the File menu before you generate the table of contents. Save the new publication as the table of contents, and use the Book command (described earlier in this chapter) to select all the publications to be included in the table of contents. Generate the table of contents with this new publication open.

To generate the table of contents, open the publication and choose Create TOC from the Utilities menu. If the table of contents is to cover a series of publications, the open publication should be the one that associates all related publications through the Book command, as described earlier in this chapter.

When the Create Table of Contents dialog box is first displayed (see fig. 14.9), PageMaker assigns the title *Contents* at the top of the table of contents text, but you can change this title to any title you want (up to 30 characters long) or delete the title. You also can opt to replace the existing table of contents (if you have generated one previously), or generate the new table of contents without replacing the old one. (This capability is helpful if you want to compare the two tables of contents.)

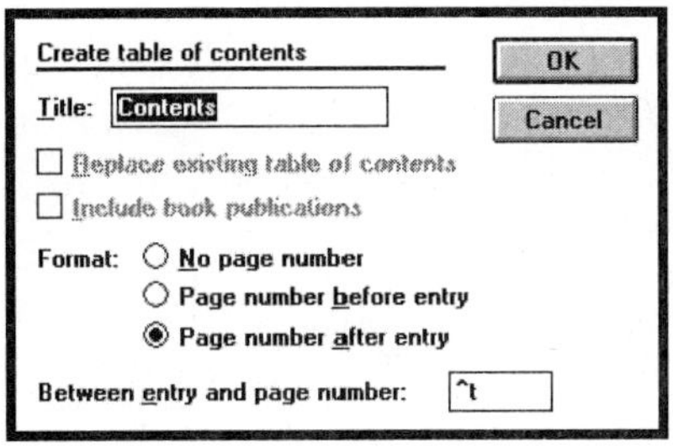

Fig. 14.9

The Create Table of Contents dia-log box.

If your publication is part of a book list (as described earlier in this chapter), you can opt to generate the table of contents for only the current publication or for all the publications in the book list.

You can format the table of contents by choosing to print page numbers before or after each entry, or by choosing not to print page numbers. In the dialog box, you also can set the character to appear between the entry and the page number. This character is usually a tab, which is typed as a caret and a lowercase letter *t* (^t).

Click OK to generate the table of contents. PageMaker then searches the publications for table of contents entries, collects them, and formats them. Depending on the publication's size and the number of table of contents entries, this process can take several minutes.

If you replace the existing table of contents, that text is replaced in the current publication. If you don't replace the current table of contents or this is the first time you are generating the table, PageMaker generates the table and the mouse pointer changes to a loaded text icon if you are in Layout view. You can place the table of contents in the publication just as you place imported text, as described in Chapter 6. If you are in Story view when you generate the table of contents, PageMaker opens a new story window for the table of contents. Choose Place from the File menu to return to Layout view and place the table of contents as a new story.

When generating a table of contents, PageMaker creates special styles to use if the paragraphs to be included in the table of contents are formatted using a style sheet. With generated style names, PageMaker precedes the original paragraph style name with TOC. The default font for table of contents is Times Roman, with the size and type style (bold, italic, or normal) matching the original paragraph. The tab stops for each heading level are copied from the original paragraphs in the text.

After generating the table of contents, you can revise the table's style by using the Define Styles command as described in Chapter 8. If you change the name of the generated styles (or import TOC styles from another publication), however, PageMaker reverts to generating the standard styles when you regenerate the table of contents.

Generating Different Lists of Contents for the Same Publication

You can generate different lists of contents for the same publication. One list might be a standard table of contents, a second list might include only illustrations, another might include only tables, and another might include only chapter titles. To do this, use a different style name to format each element you want included in one of the lists. Then, before generating each list, go through the style sheet names using the Define Styles command, click Edit to change each style, click Para(graph) to edit the style, and check or uncheck Include in Table of Contents as appropriate. Then generate the table of contents.

If you think you will go through these steps more than once, save the publication under a different name each time you change the styles. For example, you might save the document with ordinary table of contents definitions under the name FINAL.PM5, and then save the version that generates the list of figures as FIGURES.PM5 and the version that generates the list of tables as TABLES.PM5. Later, if you edit the publication and need to regenerate the lists, simply copy the style sheets from FINAL.PM5, FIGURES.PM5, and TABLES.PM5 to change the style sheets before you print.

Editing a Generated Table of Contents

You can edit the text of a generated table of contents the same way you edit any text in PageMaker. The better method, however, is to make any changes to the table of contents by editing the headings in the publication and through the Paragraph or Define Styles commands, and then regenerate the table of contents.

The table of contents shows page numbers in the format set up through the Numbers option in the Page Setup dialog box (displayed with the New command or the Page Setup command from the File menu, as described in Chapter 4).

For Related Information

◄◄ "Selecting a Format for Page Numbers," p. 148.

◄◄ "Including a Paragraph in the Table of Contents," p. 319.

FROM HERE...

Creating an Index

PageMaker's index feature automates indexing to the greatest extent possible. If you have created an index manually—by finding the words in the final manuscript, typing the words and the page numbers, and then sorting them—you can appreciate PageMaker's capability to sort the entries and assign page numbers.

The process of creating the index entries in the first place, however, is no trivial task. Creating a good index requires time as well as forethought. Some rules to good indexing follow:

■ *Be consistent.* If you are going to make entries under *soups*, for example, don't refer to *broths* separately. Instead, if you want to list the word *broths* in the index, refer the reader to the listings under *soups*. Also, be consistent in spelling and capitalization of entries. If you index some entries as *soups* and others as *Soups*, they appear as two entries in the final index.

■ *Be concise.* If you want to list ten different references to *soups*, don't repeat the same ten listings under synonyms such as *broths*. Refer the reader to only one listing.

■ *Be comprehensive.* Make sure that the index refers to all the topics a reader may want to look up.

The following sections describe the mechanics of indexing in PageMaker.

Identifying Index Entries

You can create index entries in Layout view or Story view, but Story view offers the advantage of the Edit menu's Find command, which you can use to search for words to index. You also can see index markers in Story view, to see which words have been indexed.

To identify an index entry, select a word or phrase to be indexed, or position the text insertion point next to the topic in the text and choose Index Entry from the Utilities menu. If a word or phrase is selected, the Add Index Entry dialog box (see fig. 14.10) displays the selected phrase in the level 1 Topic field. If the text insertion point is positioned in the text but no text is selected, the level 1 field is empty. If the text insertion point is not positioned, the Page Reference option is dimmed.

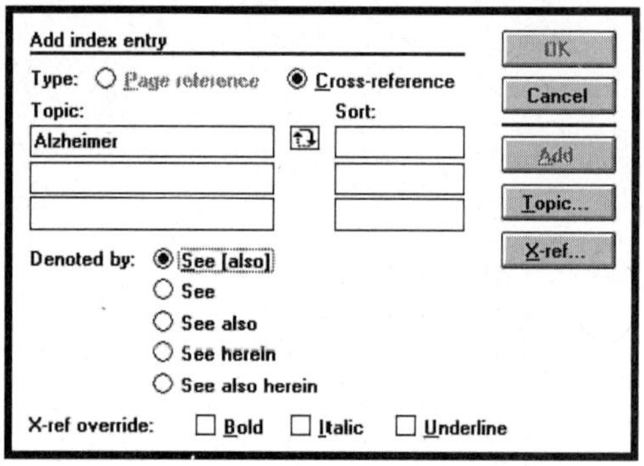

Fig. 14.10

The Add Index Entry dialog box with Cross-Reference selected.

The two Type options give you a choice between adding a topic with a page number reference or a cross-reference. The rest of the options, except the Topic and Sort fields, change depending on which option is selected. (These options are described in the following section.)

The Topic option includes three fields to accommodate three heading levels. The topic you type or display in the first heading level field will be indexed in alphabetical sequence with all other level 1 headings in the index. There must be an entry in the first heading level if you want to type a topic in the second heading level field. Level 2 headings will be indexed in alphabetical sequence below the level 1 headings with which they are associated. Similarly, there must be level 1 and level 2 entries if you want to make a level 3 entry, and level 3 headings will be indexed below the level 2 headings with which they are associated.

You can edit or type text in any of the three fields, or you can position the cursor in a field and click the Topic button to choose from a list of topics already set up for this publication. (The Topic button is discussed later in this chapter.)

Creating an Index Entry Quickly

To create an index entry without going through the Add Index Entry dialog box, select the text you want as the level 1 index entry (in Layout view or Story view) and press Ctrl+Shift+; (semicolon). PageMaker creates an index entry with the default indexing options, shown when you open the Add Index Entry dialog box.

If you want to index every instance of the same word or phrase in one or more publications, use the Change command. First choose Edit Story from the Edit menu to activate Story view. Then choose Change from the Utilities menu to open the Change dialog box. In the Find What box, type the word or phrase you want to index. In the Change To box, type a caret and semi-colon (^;), followed by the word or phrase you want to index. Click Selected Text, Current Story, All Stories, and Click Current Publication or All (Open) Publications to specify the extent of text you want changed; then click Change All.

Indexing a Person's Name

T I P

To create an index entry of a person's name as a level 1 index entry, select the name (typed as first name followed by last name) and press Ctrl+Shift+Z. PageMaker bypasses the Add Index Entry dialog box, using the default index entry options, and adds the name in Last name, First name sequence. Hyphenated last names are recognized as single last names. To index under the last name, but include a person's middle name or initial, put a nonbreaking space between the first name and middle name or initial.

You can click the looped arrow icon at the right of the level 1 Topic field to move topics from one level to another.

You can make entries in the Sort fields to specify sorting that is different from the spelling shown in the topic list. For example, if a topic starts with a number, such as *2 megabytes*, it is sorted as a symbol and appears at the beginning of any alphabetical list. You can force the *2 megabytes* entry to sort under *T* by typing **two** in the Sort box next to the heading. You should use the Sort boxes also to set initial-cap entries to sort with lowercase entries as appropriate. (Otherwise, *soups* and *Soups* appear as two entries.)

You also can use the Sort fields to force words with accents to sort in the same order as words without accents. Normally, PageMaker sorts words with accent marks to follow the same word without accents. For example, *elan* sorts in front of and separate from *élan*. To force *elan* and *élan* to sort as the same word, you can type **elan** in the sort box next to the *élan* index entry.

Whether you are creating a page reference or a cross-reference, you can click OK to close the dialog box and record the changes to the index, click Cancel to close the dialog box without recording any changes to the index, or click Add to record the current entry without closing the dialog box. You also can select from a list of index topics by clicking the Topic button, as described later in the chapter in the section "Selecting Topics from a List."

Selecting Page Reference Options

If you select the Page Reference option in the Add Index Entry dialog box, the dialog box displays five options for identifying the range of pages that cover the topic, plus the option of setting these particular page numbers in bold, italic, or underline (to differentiate them from other page numbers listed under the same topic). Figure 14.11 shows the Add Index Entry dialog box with the Page Range options listed.

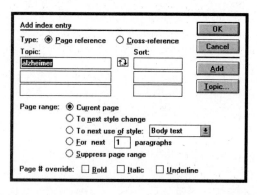

Fig. 14.11

The Page Range options after selecting Page Reference.

The Page Range options make it easy for PageMaker to determine the page range and adjust the range when page breaks change. These options follow:

Click Current Page if the topic is mentioned on only one page.

Click To Next Style Change option if the topic ends when the paragraph style changes. This option is useful if the next style change indicates a new heading, but you need to be cautious in using this option if the next style is a figure caption, for example, or some other style that does not end the topic. In the latter case, use To Next Use of Style instead.

Click To Next Use of Style and then select from the drop-down list the style name that marks a change of topic.

Click For Next __ Paragraphs and enter the number of paragraphs that mention the topic. This option is less reliable than the previous two options because you must update the number of paragraphs in this dialog box if editing adds or deletes paragraphs in the text.

Click Suppress Page Range when you want to create a major topic that prints on a line of its own without page references, above a series of level 2 headings that do have page references, or cross-references.

You can select any number of Page # Override options to differentiate the current page numbers from other page numbers that reference the same topic. If the style for the index is normal, clicking Italic makes these page numbers print in italic. If the style for the index is italic, however, clicking Italic makes these page numbers print normal.

Setting Topics and Page Numbers Differently

T I P

If you want the topic to print as normal text and *all* the page numbers to print in italic, click Italic once when you make the first index entry. This setting becomes the default for all subsequent entries unless you change it. You should make this decision before starting the indexing process. Otherwise, you must edit each index entry individually if you change your mind.

Selecting Cross-Reference Options

If you select the Cross-Reference option in the Add Index Entry dialog box, the dialog box displays five options to denote the phrasing of the cross-reference and the option of setting this particular cross-reference in bold, italic, or underline (refer to fig. 14.10). The five options for denoting phrasing follow.

See Also is the default setting that enables PageMaker to choose the phrasing. PageMaker then uses See if no page number references are under this topic, or See Also to refer readers to the current entries and the entries in the cross-reference.

See Herein refers the reader to the other level 2 or level 3 entries under the current topic. See Also Herein refers the reader to the page references in the main entry as well as the other level 2 or level 3 entries under this topic.

As with page number references, you can select any number of the X-ref Override options to differentiate the current page numbers from other page numbers that reference the same topic. For example, if the style for the index is normal, clicking Italic makes these reference topics print in italic. If the style for the index is italic, however, clicking Italic makes these topics print normal.

Selecting the Topic button enables you to choose from a list of topics under which this cross-reference will be indexed, and the X-ref button enables you to choose from a list of topics to be referred to in the cross-reference.

Selecting Topics from a List

When you click the Topic button in the Add Index Entry dialog box, you see the Select Topic dialog box (see fig. 14.12). You get a similar dialog box (see fig. 14.13) when you click the X-ref button in the Add Index Entry dialog box when Cross-Reference is selected. Use these dialog boxes to select a topic from a list of existing topics rather than type one. This way, you ensure that the spelling, case, and phrasing are identical to other entries.

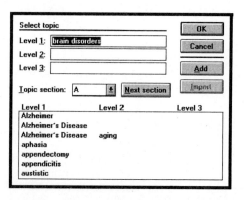

Fig. 14.12

The Select Topic
dialog box.

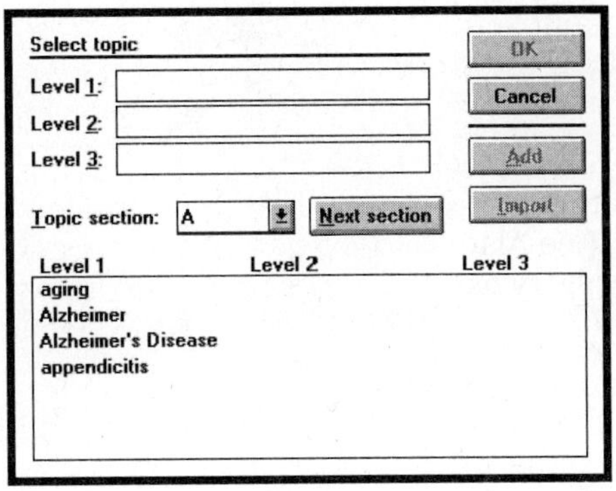

Fig. 14.13

The Select Cross-
Reference Topic
dialog box.

You can use the scrollbars to scroll through the list of topics. You also can select the section of the alphabet you want to view by clicking the arrow at the right of the current section and choosing from the drop-down Topic Section list, or clicking Next Section to view the next alphabetical section that contains topic entries.

Topics you choose here are assigned the page number of the current text insertion point if Page Reference is selected in the Add Index Entry dialog box. The topics are cross-referenced if Cross-Reference is selected and you click the Topic button in the Add Index Entry dialog box. The topics become the topics being referred to (that is, *See* or *See also* topics) if Cross-Reference is selected and you click the X-ref button in the Add Index Entry dialog box.

To choose a topic from the Select Topic dialog box, highlight the desired topic and click OK. PageMaker returns you to the Add Index Entry dialog box and inserts the selected topic in the Topic edit boxes. If you choose a topic and click Add, PageMaker adds the topic as an index entry at the current text insertion point (for page references) or as a cross-reference entry, and keeps the Select Topic dialog box open so that you can add more topic references at the same insertion point in the text.

Click Import in the Select Topic dialog box to import the topic list from the indexes of every other publication in the book list associated with the current publication. This feature helps ensure consistency. Only topics you select (and press Add or OK) appear in the index of the current publication.

T   I   P
Adding Level 2 or 3 Entries

You can type level 2 and level 3 entries in the Add Index Entry dialog box, and then click the Topic button to display the Select Topic dialog box. Select the level 1 topic and hold the Ctrl key when you click OK. Even if the level 1 topic in the Topic list showed level 2 entries, only the level 1 topic is entered in the Add Index Entry dialog box, retaining the level 2 and level 3 entries you typed.

Editing the Index

If you are new to indexing, plan to generate the index more than once to refine the entries until the final index is as consistent, concise, and comprehensive as you can make it. You can add, change, delete, and reorganize entries through the Show Index command or by working directly in Story view.

Using the Show Index Command

You always can generate and print the index, as described in the following section, but you can save time in the first round of edits by using the Show Index command from the Utilities menu, which lists all topics and page references or cross-references (see fig. 14.14). The Index includes entries for all publications in the book list. To view the index entries for only the current publication, press the Ctrl key as you choose Show Index from the menu.

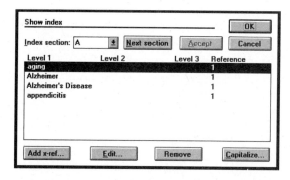

Fig. 14.14

The Show Index dialog box.

The Show Index dialog box shows three levels of index entries and their page numbers. The page number column, labeled Reference, may also list one of five codes for text not placed on numbered pages:

PB   Text is on the pasteboard

LM   Text is on the left master page

RM   Text is on the right master page

OV   Text flows beyond the margins in Layout view

UN   Text is in an unplaced story in Story view

?   Text is in a page range that may have changed

You can use the scrollbars to scroll through the index. To choose the section of the alphabet you want to view, select from the drop-down Index Section menu. To view the next alphabetical section that contains index entries, click Next Section.

When you click the Add X-ref button in the Show Index dialog box, PageMaker displays the Add Index Entry dialog box. This dialog box is the same as the Add Index Entry dialog box described earlier, but the Page Reference option is grayed. With the Show Index command, you can add only cross-references, not page references.

When you select an index entry in the Show Index dialog box and then click the Edit button, PageMaker displays the Edit Index Entry dialog box. This dialog box is the same as the Add Index Entry dialog box described earlier.

When you select an index entry in the Show Index dialog box and then click the Remove button, the page reference entry is removed from the index but *the topic remains* in the index. You can remove unreferenced entries when you generate the index using the Create Index command, described later in this chapter in the section "Generating an Index."

Click the Capitalize button to get a dialog box that lets you capitalize the selected entry, all Level 1 entries, or all entries. The Capitalize button is available only when you generate an index from a single publication. You must click OK in the Show Index dialog box to finalize the changes and close the dialog box, or click Accept to save the changes to the index without closing the dialog box.

Working in Story View

PageMaker stores an index marker before each entry, and these markers are displayed in Story view as small white diamonds in black squares (see fig. 14.15). You can cut, copy, paste, or delete index entries as you would any text by selecting the index marker in Story view and using the commands for cutting, copying, pasting, or clearing under the Edit menu (or their keyboard shortcuts), as described in Chapters 5 and 7.

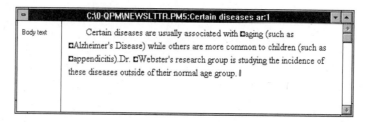

Fig. 14.15

Story view shows index markers as black-and-white diamonds.

You can change an individual entry by selecting the index marker in Story view and choosing the Index Entry command. You can change entries in the dialog box as described in the preceding section.

You can search for index markers in Story view by using the Find command and entering for a caret and a semicolon (^;) for the search criterion.

Generating an Index

After you create, review, and edit your index entries, use the Create Index command from the Utilities menu. Using this command generates the index as text that you can place on pages in the PageMaker publication and print. No matter how much you edit the index using the methods described in the preceding sections, plan on generating a printed version of the index at least twice: once for proofing, followed by more editing before the second and (possibly) final generation.

If you want the index to be a separate PageMaker publication, use the New command from the File menu before generating the index. Save the new publication as the index, and use the Book command (described earlier in this chapter) to select all the publications to be included in the index. Generate the index with this new publication open.

When the Create Index dialog box is first displayed (see fig. 14.16), PageMaker assigns the title *Index*, which appears at the top of the index text. You can change this title to any title you want (up to 30 characters) or delete the title. You also can opt to replace the existing index. (If you are generating a second index without replacing the old one, include a version number as part of the title so that you know which one is the most recent.)

Create index	
Title: Index	OK
☐ Replace existing index	Cancel
☐ Include book publications	Format...
☒ Remove unreferenced topics	

If your publication is part of a book list (as described earlier in this chapter), you can generate the index for only the current publication or check Include Book Publications to generate the index for all the publications in the book list.

Check Remove Unreferenced Topics to remove topics without page numbers or cross-references. Unreferenced topics can develop when you import topics from another index but do not use them, or when you delete page references through the Story Editor or the Show Index command. Checking this option does not remove the entries in which you elect to Suppress Page Reference.

You can format the index by clicking the Format button in the Create Index dialog box. The Index Format dialog box (see fig. 14.17) is displayed, enabling you to include or exclude section headings and determine the paragraph format of index entries. (The Index Entry command, described earlier, enables you to set the *character* formats for the index entries.)

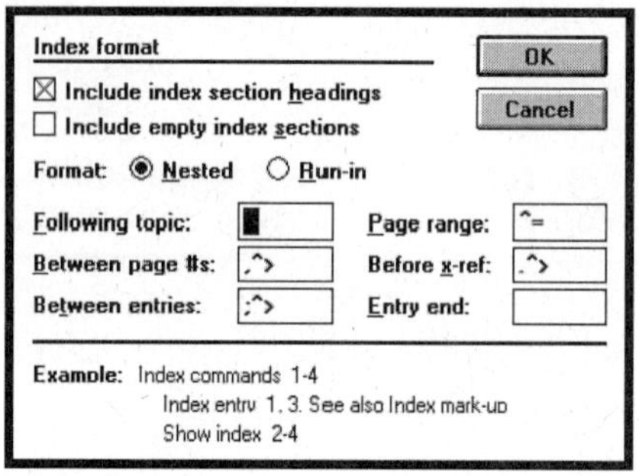

Index format		OK
☒ Include index section headings		Cancel
☐ Include empty index sections		

Format: ⦿ Nested   ○ Run-in

Following topic:	▮	Page range:	^=
Between page #s:	,^>	Before x-ref:	.^>
Between entries:	;^>	Entry end:	

Example: Index commands 1-4
Index entry 1, 3. See also Index mark-up
Show index 2-4

Fig. 14.17

The Index Format
dialog box.

Check Include Index Section Headings to include headings that mark the beginning of each alphabetical section of the index (that is, A, B, C, and so on). If this option is not checked, the headings do not appear, but more spacing appears between alphabetical sections. Click Include Empty Index Sections if you want headings for alphabetical sections under which no entries exist. The phrase *No entries* is added to empty sections.

The Format option enables you to choose between two paragraph formats: Nested (in which each entry is a separate paragraph, with progressive indentation for different levels) or Run-In (in which all levels fall into one paragraph per entry). An example of the current selection is displayed at the bottom of the dialog box.

The last six options in the dialog box enable you to specify characters to appear following a topic, between page numbers, between entries, between a page range, before a cross-reference, and at the end of an entry. Commonly used separators include

semicolon (;)

en-space, which is represented by a caret and a greater than symbol (^>)

en-dash, which is represented by a caret and a hyphen (^-)

Click OK in the Index Format dialog box to return to the Create Index dialog box; then click OK to generate the index. PageMaker searches the publications for index entries and then collects, sorts, and formats them. The process may take several minutes.

If you opted to replace the existing index, that text is replaced in the current publication. If you opt not to replace the current index, or if this is the first time you are generating the index, PageMaker generates the index and the mouse pointer changes to a loaded text icon if you are in Layout view. You can place the index in the publication just as you place imported text, as described earlier in this chapter. If you are in Story view when you generate the index, PageMaker opens a new story window for the index. Choose Place from the File menu to return to Layout view, and place the index as a new story.

After you generate the index, PageMaker applies the specified styles to the title, section headings, index entries, and topic references. If these styles do not already exist in the style sheet for the publication, PageMaker creates them when it creates the index. Generated style names include Index Title, Index Section, Index Level 1, Index Level 2, Index Level 3, and Index Run-In.

After you generate the index, you can revise index styles by using the Define Styles command, as described in Chapter 8. If you change the name of the generated styles, however, PageMaker reverts to generating the standard styles again if you regenerate the index.

Editing a Generated Index

T I P

You can edit the text of a generated index the same way you edit any text in PageMaker. A better idea, however, is to make any changes to the index through the Create Index or Show Index command and then regenerate the index.

The index shows page numbers in the format set up through the Numbers option in the Page Setup dialog box (displayed with the New command or the Page Setup command from the File menu).

Including Production Notes in a Draft Index

You can use automatic indexing to flag and list missing information in paragraphs in a work-in-progress. For example, you may insert dummy text to hold a place for missing words or phrases, such as:

```
Giuseppe Verdi was born on date? in city?

See page ?? for more information about Giuseppe Verdi.

Continued on page ??
```

continues

Including Production Notes in a Draft Index (continued)

You can index only the missing element (such as *date?*) or, better yet, enough of the phrase so that you know which date is missing. The automatic index lists the phrase you index and the page number.

If you are using the index feature only for production notes, you can set all entries to level 1. Otherwise, precede every production entry in the index with a special character (such as a question mark), or create a level 1 entry called *000 Production Notes* and set all production notes as level 2 entries under this heading. (By putting a symbol or 000 at the beginning of the level 1 index entry, you print all these entries at the beginning of the index. Use ZZZ instead if you want all notes to appear at the end of the index.) Delete the index entries when the questions are resolved.

Creating and Using a Library

A library is a very useful feature that PageMaker 5.0 offers in a convenient palette form. A library is a file that can store any page element you can create or import into PageMaker. You can store, organize, search for, and retrieve items using the Library palette. An entry can be a single element or multiple-selected items. After elements are stored in a library, they can be dragged to any document page.

Libraries can be useful for storing commonly used document elements. For example, you might create one library to use for all your projects, or you might create one library for each long document.

You open or close the Library palette by choosing Library Palette from the Window menu (see fig. 14.18); Library Palette is a toggle command that shows a check mark when the palette is displayed. If a library is already associated with the publication (because the Library palette was open when you last saved the publication), the Library palette opens immediately when you choose Library Palette from the Window menu. If no library is associated with the current publication, then a dialog box is displayed, prompting you to select an existing library or create a new one (see fig. 14.19 in the following section).

When the Library palette is open, you can add elements to the library by selecting them in the document window in PageMaker and then clicking the Add button (the plus sign) in the palette, or by using the Copy command to copy selected objects in PageMaker or any Windows application and then clicking the Add button. You copy an element from the Library onto a page or onto the Pasteboard by dragging it from the palette. These procedures are described in detail under the next headings.

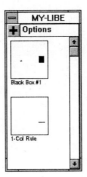

Fig. 14.18

The Library palette.

Like the Colors palette and Styles palette and many other windows, the Library palette can be moved on the screen by dragging the title bar, and sized by dragging the lower right corner. If the library includes more elements than those which will fit in the palette window, scroll bars are displayed on the right.

You can close the palette by double-clicking the Control box at the top-left corner or by choosing the Library palette command from the Windows menu. Single-click on the Control box to open the menu and use commands to Move, Size, or Close the palette.

Opening a New or Existing Library

To create a new library when the Library palette is open, choose the New Library command from the Options menu on the Library palette. To open an existing library, choose Open Library from the Options menu. In either case, PageMaker displays the same Open dialog box that is displayed when you choose the Library palette command from the Windows menu when no library has been associated with the publication (see fig. 14.19).

To create a new library, type a new library name with the extension .ZDB and click OK. You can use standard Windows procedures to determine the directory and disk onto which the library will be stored. PageMaker displays a dialog box confirming that the file does not already exist, and asking if you want to create it. If you click Yes in this second dialog box, an empty Library palette is displayed with the new name you assigned.

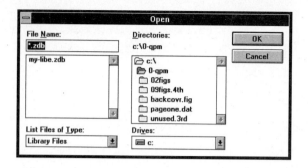

Fig. 14.19

The Open dialog box for opening a new or existing library.

To open an existing library, use standard Windows procedures to locate the library and then double-click on the name to open it. PageMaker displays the Library palette containing elements from the named library.

In either case—whether you are creating a new library or opening an existing one—the newly opened library replaces any previously opened library in the palette. You cannot have two libraries open at the same time. All elements in a library are automatically saved when the Library palette closes.

Adding and Removing Library Elements

When the Library palette is open, you can add elements to the library simply by selecting them in the document window in PageMaker and then clicking the Add button (the plus sign) in the palette. You can also add elements from the Clipboard by using the Copy command to copy selected objects in PageMaker or any Windows application, and then clicking the Add button in the Library palette. A library element can be a single item or a group of items that were multiple-selected.

If Edit Item After Adding is checked (on the Library palette's Options menu) when you click the Add button, PageMaker displays the Item Information dialog box (see fig. 14.20) where you can enter a Title for the element, an Author, and a Date (or accept the current date as the default). You can also enter one or more keywords and a description of the element. You can list elements in the palette by Title (as described later under "Displaying Library Elements"), or search for them by Keyword (as described later under "Searching for Library Elements").

Deselect Edit Item After Adding on the Options menu in the Library palette if you want to add elements to the library without naming them or assigning keywords right away. You can access the Item Information dialog box at any time, and add or change the information by double-clicking the element in the Library palette.

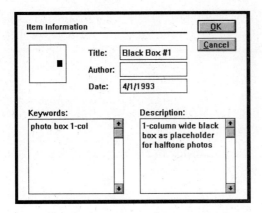

Fig. 14.20

The Item Informa-
tion dialog box.

All elements in a library are automatically saved when the Library palette closes. The library also stores all linked information about each
element, and that information is included in the publication when an
element is copied from the library.

You can remove an element from an open library by selecting it (clicking on it) in the Library palette and then choosing Remove Item from
the Options menu on the palette.

Copying Elements from a Library

You copy an element from the Library onto a page or the Pasteboard
by dragging it from the palette. A selected object in the palette is surrounded by a thick line, and a drag-and-drop cursor icon follows your
mouse cursor as you drag the element onto the page, indicating the
approximate placement of the object.

To include an element from a library as an inline graphic, you must first
drag it onto the page or the pasteboard. Next, select the element with
the Pointer tool, and use the Cut command from the File menu (Ctrl+X).
Then select the Text tool and click the I-beam to position the text cursor within a text block, at the position where you want the element to
appear. Finally, choose Paste from the File menu (Ctrl+V).

Cataloging and Searching for Library Elements

If a library includes many elements, searching for each element by
scrolling through a visual display in the palette may become inefficient.
There are several ways to make locating an element easier. One way is
by searching for an element or group of elements, as described here.

Another way is to display the elements by name, as described under the next heading. In either case, you can only search or sort by information that you typed in the Item Information dialog box (refer to fig. 14.20).

The Search feature is not only useful for finding a particular object, but you can also use it to find a category of objects and display only those objects in the palette—without actually removing the other objects from the library itself.

To search for objects, choose the Search Library command from the Options menu on the Library palette. This command displays the Library Catalog dialog box (see fig. 14.21).

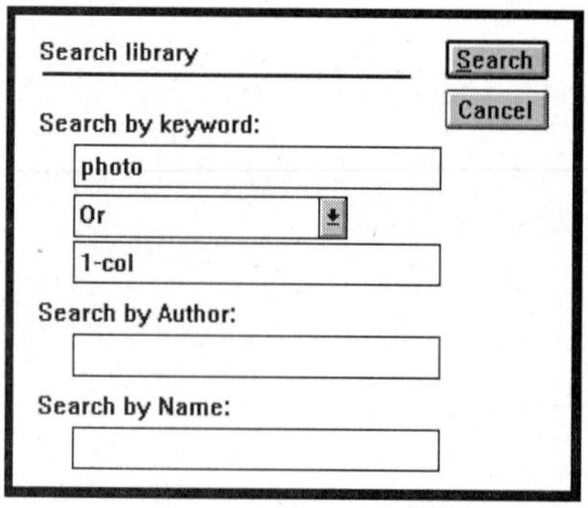

Fig. 14.21

The Library Cata-
log dialog box.

You can search by keyword, by author, and/or by name. If you enter a combination of these options—typing both a name and an author, for instance—then the search process locates only those items that have the exact name and author that you entered. When searching by keyword, you can choose from the drop-down list to search for One Keyword Only or to include two keywords separated by *and, or,* or *but not.*

Once you have used the Search Library command to display only a subset of all the elements in the library, you can return to a full display by choosing Show All Items from the Options menu in the palette.

Displaying Library Elements

Whether the Library palette currently displays all elements in the library or a subset of elements found by the search techniques described in the previous section, you can choose between three different displays in the palette. Choose Display Images from the Options menu on the Library palette to display each element visually in the palette.

Choose Display Names from the Options menu to display only the names you assigned in the Item Information dialog box. Choose Display Both if you want to see a visual image along with the name.

Running Scripted Sequences of Steps

PageMaker 5.0 introduces an Aldus Addition called Run Script. A *script*, called a macro in some applications, is a series of instructions that automates a sequence of steps that you would otherwise perform using the mouse and the keyboard. For example, you could write a script that will automatically lay out the next issue of a monthly newsletter. Starting with either a template or a new, blank publication, the script could place the text and artwork, size them to fit the columns, then save and print the new publication. All this could be accomplished with one command.

Writing a Script

Scripting requires no programming knowledge. In order to write a script, you should have a good working knowledge of how PageMaker works, and you should have the *Aldus PageMaker Script Language Guide* from Aldus to learn how. You can get the guide from Aldus Customer Services at (206) 628-2320.

The entire scripting guide is not reproduced here, but the command language is similar to the actual menu commands in PageMaker. For example, the following instructions would close the currently open publication, open a publication called "mypub.pm5," select the first drawn object in the publication and delete it, remove pages 2 and 3, and then save the publication:

```
close
open "mypub"
select 1
delete
removepages 2 3
save
```

The following instructions would save the currently open publication, close it, and then open a new five-page publication:

```
save

close

new 5
```

You can write scripts directly in PageMaker and run them from an open publication. You can also export scripts as text-only files so they can be run from any publication, or type them using any word processing application that lets you save files in text-only (ASCII) format. To export the text from PageMaker, you need to install the ASCII text export filter that comes with PageMaker. This filter is normally installed automatically when you install PageMaker, unless you do a custom installation and opt not to install all filters. You can install the filter using the same Setup program that you used to install PageMaker. See "Selecting Filters" in Appendix A.

Running a Script

To run a script, you need PageMaker 5.0 (or later) and the Aldus Addition called Run Script. This Addition is installed automatically when you install PageMaker, unless you do a custom installation and opt not to install all Additions. To run a script from within PageMaker, select the text of the script with the Text tool, and then choose the Run Script command from the Aldus Additions submenu under the Utilities menu. To run a script that has been saved as an external ASCII file, choose the Run Script command. In either case, the Run Script dialog box is displayed.

If you have selected the text of the script using the Text tool in PageMaker, you can click Run Selection to run the script. To run a script that has been saved as an external ASCII file, locate the text file name using the same techniques you use to locate a file in the Open or Place dialog box; then double-click the file name to run the script.

Summary

You can create a publication in PageMaker without using any of the features or suggestions presented in this chapter. These features are indispensable, however, if you produce many documents or very large documents.

This chapter ends the part of the book that describes advanced production techniques, and completes the presentation of PageMaker's
features and commands. You now understand the basics of using
PageMaker throughout the production process. The next part of this
book unites these techniques by presenting finished publications as
case studies and explaining how these publications were designed
and created using PageMaker. Summaries of basic design principles
and production tricks that can be applied to any publication are also
discussed.

Publication Design

PART

IV

OUTLINE

PageMaker as a Design Tool

Typography

Part IV focuses on how you can apply to your PageMaker publications the principles of good design and the discipline of efficient procedures used by professional typesetters and text designers. You learn how to design a PageMaker publication, how to use master pages and template systems, and how to prepare pages for an offset printer. You also learn how to select fonts for a publication, how to create special effects such as drop caps, and how to use leading and kerning to adjust the spacing of text.

PageMaker as a Design Tool

Besides being a workhorse in laying out publication pages, PageMaker is a wonderful design tool. The following lists four of PageMaker's most helpful features:

- Use PageMaker to sketch out rough ideas for designs to be reviewed with the rest of your team or your client. (The term *client* can include managing editors, publication department managers, or end-user groups—anyone with whom the designer must share decisions.)

- Use the structure PageMaker provides for organizing specifications for the production team.

- Create template systems and style sheets to ensure that all parts of a publication follow the same specifications.

- Select from 17 different line styles (in black or white), 16 different shade patterns, and a full spectrum of colors to add designer touches to any publication. PageMaker 5.0 introduces custom line widths and the capability to set borders in different colors from the fill of rectangles and ellipses. You can see how these options are used in some of the examples in Part V.

This chapter discusses considerations for any publication design and offers tips about how you can use PageMaker as a design tool. The chapter presents design considerations in the sequence you follow in

PageMaker when you build a publication from scratch. You first see how you use PageMaker to develop a series of different design ideas for a project. Next, you learn what goes into a template system so that you can create a series of publications with the same design. Finally, you learn how the designer can work ahead of the production team, sketching the layout of each page of the publication before the text and graphics from other programs are placed on the pages. Desktop publishers often play all these roles. If you are the designer, production team, author, and editor, you can learn how to follow the steps of all these professionals.

In practice, some of these steps may be done first on paper rather than at the computer; in fact, the designers on some teams may never touch the mouse. Whether you—as the designer—are simply writing out the design specifications or actually setting up the master template, you should know how PageMaker works before making your specifications. For example (as described in Chapter 16), you cannot enter column widths directly. PageMaker defines a page in terms of the margins, the number of columns, and the space between columns. Your specifications, therefore, should be in terms of the number of columns and the space between them, rather than the width of the column itself. (You can move column guides to get an exact width, but you miss the advantages of PageMaker's automatic column guides.)

Traditionally, a designer becomes involved in a production only after the writing is complete or well under way. If the project team is small, however, and the authors are willing, some design specifications can be incorporated into the text during the writing stage. If you plan the design ahead of time, for example, you can let the authors know whether they should type two carriage returns between paragraphs and indent the first line of each paragraph. Other design details, such as the page size and margins, can be decided later—after the writing but before the text is placed in PageMaker. In other words, you can wait to develop some design specifications until after you learn what text and graphics are required for the publication.

This chapter shows you how to prepare your design specifications in terms of PageMaker's commands and capabilities.

Using Packaged Templates

A template is a PageMaker document that has been saved using the Template option in the Save dialog box. PageMaker automatically adds the extension PT5 to template files, and they open as untitled publications, to prevent the original template from being altered. Usually, a template file includes the basic elements that will be included in any publication started from the template, including a style sheet and master page elements. Templates can be extremely helpful productivity tools—significantly reducing the number of steps required to start new publications that are similar to other publications—and can serve as "design police" to ensure that the same design specifications are applied consistently to a series of publications.

PageMaker comes with 16 templates that can give you a quick start in building new publications. These templates offer the advantage of doing a lot of the work for you, plus the benefits of cloning (reproducing) a professional design. The templates include the following: Avery label grids, two brochures, a calendar template (with placeable date files for the month and year you specify), cassette labels and liner notes, CD label and liner notes, disk labels, an envelope, a FAX cover sheet, an invoice, a manual, a newsletter, a purchase order, and videocassette labels. You open each of these templates by using the new PageMaker 5.0 Aldus Addition named *Open Template*.

You work with these templates the same way as templates you create yourself (as described under "Building a Template," later in this chapter). When you choose the Open Template command from the Utilities menu and locate a template you want to use, PageMaker opens it as an untitled publication. You are in no danger of changing the template itself—these files are saved with a special "ATG" extension in C:\ALDUS\USENGLISH\ADDITION\TEMPLATE. You can quickly create custom templates by starting with one of PageMaker's templates, modifying it to your specifications, and then saving it with a new name ending in PT5.

Creating Design Alternatives

You can use PageMaker to create a series of quick "comps" of different designs for a publication before you decide on the final design. A designer's *comp* is a comprehensive layout of a design idea, usually drawn by hand with pencils, rulers, and colored pens. The advantages of sketching out your ideas with PageMaker rather than using pencil and ruler are threefold:

- Copying and moving elements on a page is easy if you are working on a single design.

- Making copies of the first design and modifying it to create alternative designs is an efficient design practice.

- Showing clients crisp text and graphic elements printed on a high-resolution printer makes an effective presentation.

Identifying the Essential Elements

One step in the design process is identifying the essential elements of the publication to be created. Suppose, for example, that you are creating a newsletter. Although the production manager views the elements in terms of articles that must be written by various authors, the designer uses another perspective to view the newsletter. The designer may list the newsletter's design elements as the following:

- Page size and margins
- Underlying grid structure
- A style sheet for the text elements
- Running headers and running footers
- Two different page formats (right and left)
- Three heading levels
- Four types of graphics
- Color

This particular publication may also include one or more of the following special considerations or constraints that affect the design:

- Feature articles requiring special placement
- Sidebars or pull quotes distinct from the rest of the text on a page
- Custom graphics requiring special placement

For this proposed publication, you can make rough sketches of your design ideas by hand, using pencils or pens and other traditional tools, or you can take advantage of PageMaker as a design tool and use the program's built-in text and graphics features to create representations of your basic design elements. For example, you can use shaded boxes to show where graphics will be placed and crop marks to show the page size. To enhance the design, you can use ruled lines. Figure 15.1 shows how PageMaker illustrates design ideas for the chapters of a book. You can also use "greek" text to show the position and size of text on a page. *Greek text* refers to any text used to represent the font, but not the content, to be used on a page. Typesetters use standard block paragraphs that are called greek, but the text looks more like Latin ("Lorem ipsum dolor sit..."). This use of the term *greek* differs from that used to describe the appearance or display of text in the Fit in Window view, where text in small point sizes appears as gray bars on-screen.

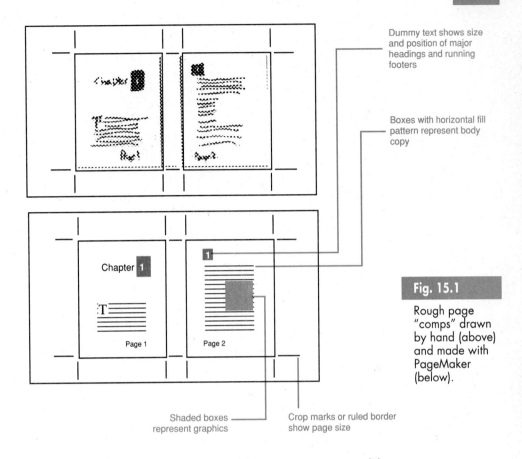

Dummy text shows size and position of major headings and running footers

Boxes with horizontal fill pattern represent body copy

Shaded boxes represent graphics

Crop marks or ruled border show page size

Fig. 15.1

Rough page "comps" drawn by hand (above) and made with PageMaker (below).

After you create the basic elements of your publication, you can modify the design or rearrange the elements on the page to develop variations. Rather than create a different PageMaker publication to represent each design idea, you use one design publication to create and show many pages of design variations (see fig. 15.2).

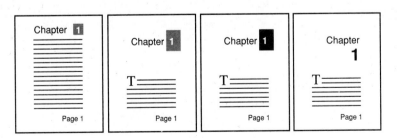

Fig. 15.2

Example of a design publication with variations.

PageMaker enables you to perform the following tasks:

- Create representations of all the basic design elements once and store them on the pasteboard.

- Use the Copy and Paste commands to place individual design elements on each page layout. Use PageMaker's tools to resize, crop, and transform elements as needed.

- Change type specifications (specs) or style tags of selected text as needed to represent each new design.

- Add a new page for each new design idea.

- Use greek text as a marker to develop design ideas, and then re-place the greek text with imported text while maintaining the form of the original design.

T   I   P   **Making Duplicates of the Basic Design Elements**

Store all the basic design elements on one side of the pasteboard (see fig. 15.3). When starting a new design idea, use the Copy and Paste commands to move all the basic elements from one side of the pasteboard to the other, and move the duplicated elements onto the new page to create a new design. After completing one design, insert a new page and repeat the copy and paste operation to begin build-ing a second design (see fig. 15.4).

Looking At Unique Design Features

The master-page elements for the initial design publication should in-clude only specifications that are known and unchangeable. If all the elements of the design are open to change, you may leave the master pages blank in a design publication. (See Chapter 5 for a discussion of master pages.)

Many elements to be positioned on the master pages of finished publi-cations are considered variable elements during the design phase. For example, the page number will appear in the same place on each page in a finished publication, but it might appear in different locations in different designs. You enter these variable elements directly on the *numbered pages* of the design publication but on the *master pages* of the final publication or template.

Although you place the actual text and graphics in final publications, you can create representations of the basic elements in your design publication. You need not know the exact text or contents of the publication to rough out a design idea. You can use dummy text for headlines or headings, sample text for body copy, and black or gray boxes for figures. When using the Place command to place text in a PageMaker publication, you can select whether the new text will be replacing an entire story or placed as a new item. You can also replace graphics by the same method. In this way, you can place sample text and, when your design is complete, quickly replace it with the correct copy for your publication. (See Chapters 5, 6, and 9 for discussions of the Place command.)

If the trim size of the publication will be smaller than 8 1/2 by 11 inches (or the size of the paper on which you print the design ideas), you can use a solid border in the design publication to represent the edges of the pages. This border enables you to see how the final pages will look when trimmed. In the final publication, however, you should use crop marks rather than solid lines to indicate the edges of the paper (see fig. 15.5). Otherwise, the solid lines may show in the final publication—especially if the pages will be folded into signatures before being trimmed. (A *signature* is a single sheet of paper on which an even number of pages is printed—usually 16 or 32. The pages are arranged so that the signature can be folded and trimmed to create a booklet or a small section of a larger publication.)

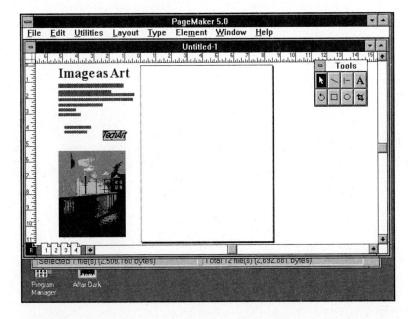

Fig. 15.3

Basic elements shown on the pasteboard.

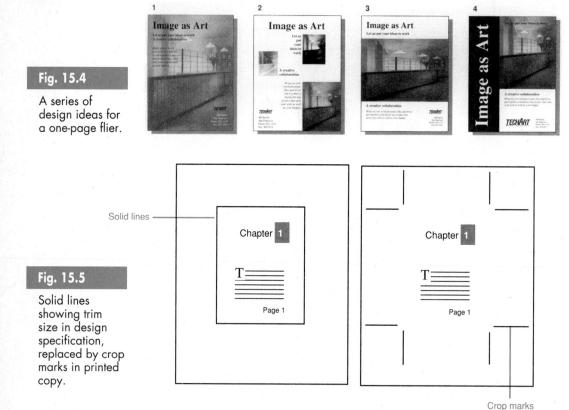

Fig. 15.4

A series of
design ideas for
a one-page flier.

Fig. 15.5

Solid lines
showing trim
size in design
specification,
replaced by crop
marks in printed
copy.

After you choose one design idea, you translate this idea into the specifications for PageMaker and the other programs used to construct the
parts of the publication. Ideally, you then sit down at the computer
with PageMaker and build the basic template system for the final
publication.

Working with Color

PageMaker 5.0 adds the capability to print process color separations—
a quantum leap from PageMaker 4.0's spot color capabilities. In working with color, however, most users will be constrained by the cost of
color printing. Generally, color printing requires a much higher minimum quantity run in order to be cost-effective compared to one-color
or spot-color printing. Following are a few tips on how to keep printing
costs down while making the best use of color in your designs.

If your budget is tight, consider printing on colored paper, or use one of the new patterned papers that have become available through most well-stocked paper suppliers and mail-order houses. Consider printing the entire publication in one color ink or a tint of black to get a custom look.

If you are printing a series of publications with the same basic design— newsletters, for instance, or brochures for a series of lectures or different products—consider printing only some of the common elements in color, and have these color elements printed all at once in one large print run. Then, when you print each newsletter or brochure, supply the offset print shop with as many preprinted sheets as needed, and let it print the current publication's text and graphics in black (or only one color).

If you are using one spot color, consider using different tints of the color in the publication to get a variety of tones. Print the graphics in a tint of the color. Try printing a light tint of the spot color in a fine pattern over the entire page. Be flexible about your second color and ask the printer what inks might already be on the press from a previous client's job—this might save you the extra charges for cleaning and re-inking the press. (See Chapter 12 for descriptions of how to create, apply, and print colors in PageMaker.)

For Related Information

◀◀ "Adding Master-Page Elements," p. 183.

◀◀ "Importing Text by Using the Place Command," p. 232.

◀◀ "Importing Graphics Created in Other Programs," p. 363.

◀◀ "Creating Color Publications," p. 531.

FROM HERE...

Building a Template

When you start a new publication, you must go through a certain series of steps and commands to set up the pages before you begin placing text and graphics from other programs. In traditional terms, you *define* the design specifications for the publication. In PageMaker, you make selections in the Page Setup dialog box and add gridlines and other elements on the master pages.

A template is a PageMaker publication that embodies the basic design specifications (see fig. 15.6). The basic grid system for each page appears on the template. The template also includes common elements that will appear within the publication in specific locations or at repeated intervals. For example, a newsletter template might include a style sheet, a basic grid structure on the master pages, parts of page one (such as the newsletter banner), and parts of other pages (such as the masthead), or an area for a mailing label. A template is set up with all the defaults tailored to match the design specifications for the publication.

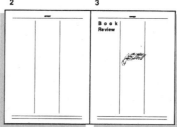

Fig. 15.6

Thumbnails of a template for a four-page newsletter.

To create a template, first create a publication with standard, shared elements. When you use the Save command the first time, or any time you use the Save As command, you have the option of saving the document as a Publication or as a Template. PageMaker automatically assigns the extension PM5 to publications, and assigns the extension PT5 to templates.

To use a template, choose Open from the File menu, select the template for your publication, and click OK. A template opens as a new, untitled publication that you can continue building without affecting the original template.

After you create a template, you can clone it to create a series of publication files that follow the same design specifications. A long document, for example, may have one template that is cloned to create a series of sections or chapters that follow the same design specifications. A short document produced on a regular basis, such as a newsletter, may have one template from which every issue is cloned. Some documents may be composed of sections that follow different design specifications, requiring a series of templates—one for each different section layout.

The benefit of using templates is that the activities described in the following sections are executed only once during the production cycle instead of once for every new file in the full document. As you follow the design steps for publications, you soon see how much time you can save by using a series of templates for large publications.

Using PageMaker's Templates

PageMaker comes with a collection of templates created by professional designers for Aldus. Instead of making your own templates from scratch, you can use these templates for Avery labels, brochures, calendars, cassette labels and liner notes, CD labels and liner notes, diskette labels, envelopes, FAX cover sheets, invoices, manuals, newsletters, purchase orders, and videocassette labels. Each of these templates is opened by using the new Aldus Addition that comes with Pagemaker 5.0, called Open Template.

To modify a template, choose Open Template from the Aldus Additions submenu under the Utilities menu, and choose a template name from the dialog box to open the template as an untitled publication. Adapt it to your publication, and then save the copy as a new template for current and future use.

The next sections describe the process and benefits of creating templates—publications that already are set up with a standard design that can be shared by many publications.

Defining the Standards

Before you lay out your page grid, you should define the basic defaults and standards you will use throughout the publication. These defaults and standards include the page size and orientation, the margins, the target printer, and the unit of measure. After a publication has been opened, these specifications are stored with the publication.

In the following sections, these standards are discussed in the sequence in which they appear as you build a template in PageMaker. For example, you specify page size, orientation, margins, and target printer in the Page Setup dialog box before you set the unit of measure for a publication. Remember that most of the commands mentioned in this chapter already have been described in detail in Chapters 4 through 10, and they are mentioned here strictly as they apply to creating templates.

Defining the Page Setup

You define the paper size and orientation through the Page Setup dialog box when you open a new publication (see fig. 15.7). By setting these standards in a template, you ensure that all other templates cloned from that template will have the same page size and orientation.

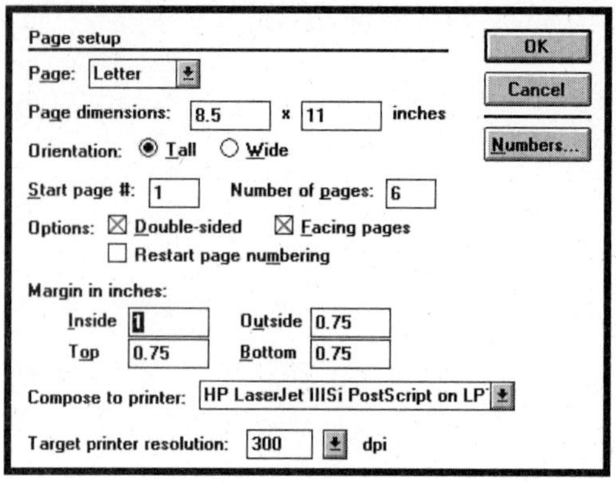

Page setup

Page: Letter

Page dimensions: 8.5 x 11 inches

Orientation: ● Tall ○ Wide

Start page #: 1   Number of pages: 6

Options: ☒ Double-sided   ☒ Facing pages
☐ Restart page numbering

Margin in inches:
Inside 0   Outside 0.75
Top 0.75   Bottom 0.75

Compose to printer: HP LaserJet IIISi PostScript on LPT

Target printer resolution: 300 dpi

OK
Cancel
Numbers...

Fig. 15.7

Using the Page Setup dialog box to choose page size and orientation for a new publication.

Most publications have the same page size for all sections, but the orientation of the pages, which can be Tall or Wide, may vary from section to section. For instance, you may have a set of appendixes with financial reports that must be printed wide to accommodate many columns of numbers. In this case, you can set up two templates—one for all tall pages and one for all wide pages—or you can rotate the text blocks and graphics on the wide pages.

T I P   Alternating Tall and Wide Pages from Two Templates

If your publication alternates between tall and wide pages, you can rotate all the text blocks and graphics as needed to give the page a wide orientation, or you can set up tall and wide pages using two different template files. In this case, you might want to rotate the text of the running headers and footers in the wide publication so that they match the position of the headers and footers in the tall publication. (Chapter 11 describes how to rotate text.) You also need to insert blank pages as necessary where the pages alternate between tall and wide, to maintain correct page numbering.

Although the page size is usually the same as the final publication after it is mass produced, bound, and trimmed, you can deliberately specify larger page sizes for special layouts. You may specify, for example, that you are printing on 8 1/2-by-11-inch paper (refer to fig. 15.7) and use that setting as the board size for designing a 6-by-9-inch booklet, as shown in figure 15.8. You can use nonprinting guides, margins, and columns to define the 6-by-9-inch layout area and use the area beyond

that to print project-control information, registration marks, and instructions to the printer. The printed pages also can show crop marks
that you draw on the master pages, because the automatic crop marks
feature does not accurately show the page size in this case.

Fig. 15.8

6-by-9-inch
booklet defined
as 8 1/2 by 11
in Page Setup
dialog box, with
crop marks and
project-control
information
added on the
master pages.

The margins defined in the Page Setup dialog box apply throughout
a publication. Each section of the publication that requires different
margins should have a separate template (see fig. 15.9).

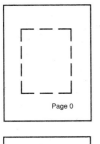

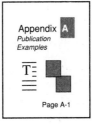
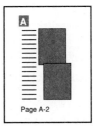

Fig. 15.9

Separate
templates for
sections of the
publication
requiring
different margins.

If the margins remain the same throughout pages or sections but the
column guides differ between them, you can work from one master
template and use PageMaker's Column Guides command from the Layout menu to change column settings. Part V shows you examples of
publications with changing column settings.

The margins are not necessarily the same as the limits of the text and graphics that appear on a page. PageMaker enables you to position text and graphics beyond the margins. The side margins determine the width of the column guides. The bottom margin determines where text stops flowing when placed in a column. Elements that can fall outside your margins include ruled lines around pages, vertical and horizontal rules that are part of the design, and running headers and footers (see fig. 15.10). You must ensure, however, that your printer can print these areas (as explained in Chapter 8).

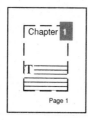

Fig. 15.10

Margins do not limit all text and graphics.

If you are accustomed to defining page layouts by width of text rather than width of margins, you must convert your specifications to the terms used by PageMaker. If, for example, you want the text to be 6 inches wide on an 8 1/2-inch-wide page, the total amount of space available for both the inside and the outside margins is 2 1/2 inches. In other words, if you know what the margins are and what the page size is, as specified in the Page Setup dialog box, you can calculate the width of the text with the following formula:

text width = (page width) – (inside margin measure + outside margin measure)

If you know the page size and the text width, you can calculate the margin allowance with this formula:

total space available for inside and outside margins = page width – text width

You can use variations of these formulas to determine the top and bottom margins or to calculate the measured depth allowed for text on each page.

You can use the following formula to calculate the widths PageMaker will set up for columns when you use the Column Guides command:

column width = [page width – (inside + outside margin measures) –

$$\frac{(\text{space between columns} \times (\text{number of columns} - 1))]}{\text{number of columns}}$$

Identifying the Target Printer

As you begin to build your template, you should first decide which printer you will use. If you have more than one printer or cartridge available on your system, you make this selection once by defining the target printer in the template in the Page Setup dialog box. From this point, all publication files cloned from this template will have the same target printer specifications. The target printer selection can affect font selections for the rest of the design. (See Chapters 10, 13, and 16 for information about font management.)

Selecting a Unit of Measure

If you give all your design specifications in the same unit of measure, you can set your preferences in the template so that the same unit of measure applies to all files made from the template. Use the Preferences command on the File menu. If you give your specifications in two or more different measures (inches for margins but points for type, for instance), select the unit of measure in which you prefer to view the ruler line. You can also set different units of measure for the vertical and horizontal rule. The Preferences dialog box is shown in figure 15.11.

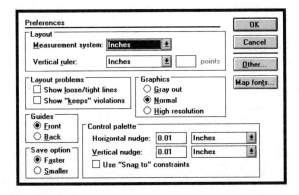

Fig. 15.11

Using the Preferences dialog box to set the unit of measure in the template.

Displaying Rulers

During the design phase, you must turn on the rulers (using the Rulers command from the Guides and Rulers submenu on the Layout menu) to lay out your grid precisely. If you leave the rulers on in the template, they are displayed automatically in all publications made from the template. During the production phase, the automatic ruler lines are convenient for scaling or cropping graphics.

Whenever possible, state your design specifications as a measure from the zero point on the ruler line. Usually, this reference point is the top left corner of the page or the tops of the inside edges of double-sided publications created with the Facing Pages option (see fig. 15.12). If your design specifications require a different zero point, you should make the position of the zero point on the page a part of the design specifications, and change the zero point in the template.

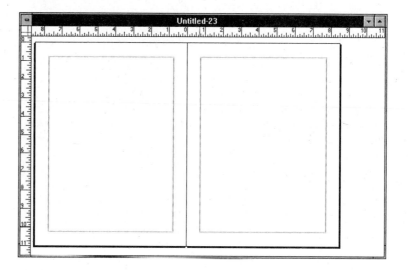

Fig. 15.12

Design specifications in reference to zero point.

Setting Defaults on the Type Menu

Although some text formatting might occur in your word processing program, you can set the defaults for the body copy by having the body text take on the default settings as you import the text. From then on, all publications cloned from the template retain the default settings you have set. Any new text typed in PageMaker and any placed text files (with a TXT extension) automatically take on the template's default settings.

To change the defaults for an entire publication, make selections on the Type menu after selecting the pointer tool rather than the text tool. These settings are discussed more comprehensively in Chapter 16.

Setting Defaults on Style Sheets

After you create a style sheet, all text takes on the characteristics you set for the body text, including the attributes for the Tabs, Type, Paragraph, and Indents. The style sheet enables you to work with many different elements at once, not just the type specification. (See Chapter 8 for more information on style sheets.)

Creating a Style Dummy

If you create a text block that uses every style at least once, you can use PageMaker 5.0's List Styles Used command under Aldus Additions in the Utilities menu (described in Chapter 8) to create a single new text block that lists each style by name and shows it in the font and format specified for that style. You can position this text block on a page of its own and print it out as a reference sheet for everyone in the production group, or as a way of checking that all the styles have been set up correctly.

You also can create a full-page dummy layout of a publication page that uses each of the styles at least once, and position the list of styles generated by the List Styles Used command in an empty area of the page to show the style names. Use Page-Maker's line tool to draw lines from each style name to a paragraph of the dummy text that uses that style.

Creating a Grid System

The best publication designs are based on underlying grids that position elements throughout publications. Using PageMaker, you can define the grid and other printing elements, such as ruled lines and folios, on master pages. Nonprinting grid lines in PageMaker include page margins, column guides (up to 20 columns per page), and up to 40 nonprinting ruler guides per page or pair of facing pages. Simple grid structures that involve one, two, or three columns are relatively easy to work with, but complex grids usually offer more design possibilities (see fig. 15.13). For example, the variety in a one-column grid structure can be achieved only by varying the type specifications and paragraph indentations. A two-column grid structure offers the added possibility of graphics and text expanding to full-page width on selected pages. A three-column grid offers at least three page variations. A four-column grid accommodates at least six variations.

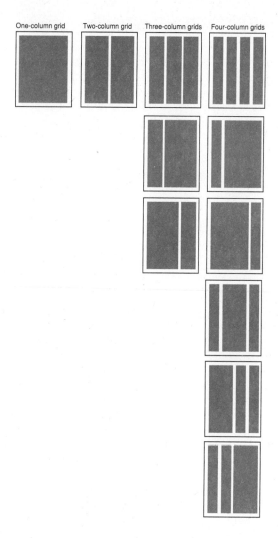

One-column grid   Two-column grid   Three-column grids   Four-column grids

Fig. 15.13

Grid structures
showing design
possibilities.

For even spacing, you can set up a grid structure with PageMaker's Column Guides command. You do not have to leave the column guides fixed to follow the grid. To set up the grids shown in figure 15.14, for example, you first set up three column guides to divide the page in thirds. You then move ruler guides to divide the page into thirds. Next, set up two columns and drag the center column guides to the first or second marker, as in the first column of figure 15.14. The second and third columns of figure 15.14 show the same technique applied to a four-column grid.

The spacing between the columns usually is set to a default width of 0.167 inch, or one pica. You can make this space wider if you plan to insert hairline rules between columns, but in general, keeping the space between columns less than 2 picas is good design practice.

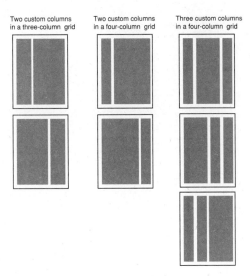

Two custom columns in a three-column grid

Two custom columns in a four-column grid

Three custom columns in a four-column grid

Fig. 15.14

Moving column guides to create custom grid settings.

Using Columns as Grid Markers

T I P

You can set the space between columns to zero and use the Column Guides command to help divide the page into equal parts. Pull ruler guides into position over the column edges to hold the divisions, and then reset the space between columns to create the guides you want to use to define the text.

Publications with the same grid on every page are much easier to produce than publications that switch between variations in the grid. A common variation, the mirror-image page layout, is particularly hard to handle. Individual page layout is not difficult, but chaos can ensue if you have to insert or delete a page after the publication is laid out, or if text edits cause text in the main column to flow away from related figures and captions in the narrow columns (see fig. 15.15). When you work with mirror-image designs, your best option is to keep text edits to a minimum and always insert or delete an even number of pages to keep all the subsequent page layouts intact.

If you must create mirror-image grid designs, specify all measures starting from the inside edges of the paper. Remember that in double-sided, facing-page publications, PageMaker sets the zero point on the ruler lines at the inside margin. On the left master page, the zero point is set at the upper right corner; on the right master page, the zero point is set at the upper left corner.

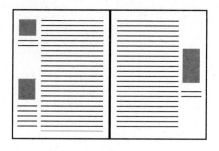

Fig. 15.15

Mirror-image
page design.

Identifying Common Text and Graphic Elements

Most of your text and graphics will vary in each publication cloned from the template. Some elements, however, are repeated throughout the publication. In a template, these repeated elements can appear on the master pages, on the pasteboard, and on some numbered pages.

Elements that appear in the same position on every page belong on the master pages. Every page holds running headers and running footers, as well as the graphic elements of the basic page design. The master-page running header and footer of a template, however, are only place holders (see fig. 15.16). Although you position these elements with the correct type specifications and alignment, the text of each publication created from the template probably will change. When you clone the template, one of your first steps is to change the text of the running header and running footer.

In addition to the elements that belong on the master pages, other elements may be repeated irregularly throughout the publication. You create these elements once and then store them on the pasteboard. Whenever you need the repeated elements, you can duplicate them with the Copy and Paste commands from the File menu (see fig. 15.17).

You can use the pasteboard, for example, to store a graphic symbol that appears at the end of every article in a newsletter or magazine. When you reach the end of an article, you simply copy the symbol from the pasteboard. Just as you create text place holders for the running header and running footer, you create standard dummy text blocks for headlines or captions within the publication and store them on the pasteboard. If your publication includes display ads in predetermined sizes, you can store the correct size boxes on the pasteboard. You then use the Copy and Paste commands from the File menu to duplicate and position the blocks as you lay out the pages.

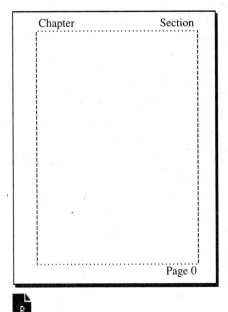

Fig. 15.16

The running
headers and
footers on the
template.

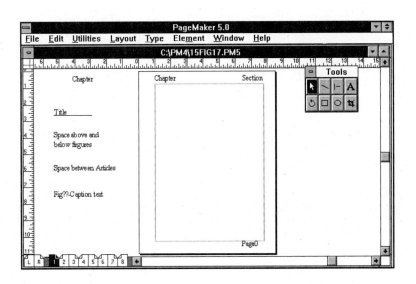

Fig. 15.17

Commonly used
elements on
master pages
and pasteboard.

Adding Standard Elements to Numbered Pages

Besides the elements positioned on the master pages or stored on the pasteboard, your publication may contain elements that appear predictably on certain numbered pages. For example, the template for a newsletter should include the banner from the first page (see fig. 15.18). If all issues of the newsletter are always the same length, you may be able to predict the positions of the subscription information and other permanent features. You also can add place holders for the headline text for feature articles that start on the first page.

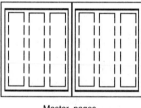

Master pages

Fig. 15.18

Newsletter templates with standing elements on fixed numbered pages.

The Red Line

Page 1

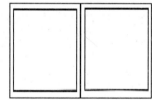

Page 2   Page 3

TheRedLine
123 Main
They City

Page 4

T I P   **Storing Dummy Headlines on the Pasteboard**

On the pasteboard, store templates for headlines. Use templates that include dummy text and are one, two, or three columns wide.

Determining the Number of Templates Required

You already have seen that a separate template file is required for each unique page size, orientation, and margin setting. In addition, you can use templates to handle any other essential differences among sections of your publication. For example, if the basic format of running headers and footers changes between major sections of a publication, you need more than one template (see fig. 15.19). On the other hand, if the only difference between sections is the number of columns, one template may suffice.

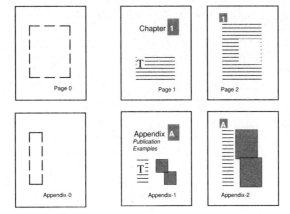

Fig. 15.19

A multiple-template system.

Create separate templates if any of the following conditions occur:

- Page size varies
- Page orientation changes (and you do not want to rotate text and graphics)
- Master-page elements change (except the text of running headers and footers)
- Basic grid changes

Adding Instructions for Working with the Template

If the person designing the template is not the same person who uses it in production, the designer should list the steps necessary for working with the template. The steps can be simple, serving primarily as reminders of each step. For example, a designer may list the following instructions:

1. Open the template and immediately save it under a new name.
2. Change the running headers and footers on the master pages to reflect a new chapter number or volume/issue and date.

3. Change the volume and date information on the first page, below the newsletter banner.

4. Place the table of contents on the first page before placing the feature article.

5. Delete these instructions.

6. Continue placing text and graphics as specified for the current issue.

To catch the attention of the production staff, you can type instructions directly on the template's pasteboard, the right master page, or the first page (see fig. 15.20). The production person can move the instructions or delete them after reading.

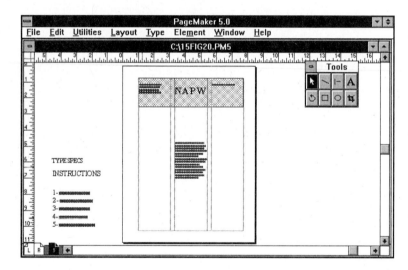

Fig. 15.20

Type specifications and instructions for using the template.

FROM HERE...

For Related Information

◀◀ "Using Style Sheets," p. 334.

◀◀ "Rotating Text and Graphics," p. 506.

◀◀ "Managing Fonts," p. 592.

▶▶ "Typography," p. 699.

▶▶ "Installing and Using Fonts," p. 902.

Creating Specifications for Other Programs

Chapter 16 presents most of the necessary considerations for selecting fonts for different text elements. You can put some specifications, such as those for the position and format of running headers and footers, directly into your PageMaker template. You can implement other specifications, such as type specifications or style sheet tag names, with your word processing program. You can set up line widths and fill patterns as default values in the PageMaker template. You can also store these objects as defined elements on the pasteboard or apply them in the graphics programs you use to create the content of the publication.

A designer should have a good idea of the number and sources of graphic elements that go into the publication. Knowing the capabilities and limitations of the available programs, the designer must specify how each illustration should be treated. For example: What are the size limitations or preferences for the figures? If you are following a grid system, each figure's width must match the increments allowed by the grid. For instance, a two-column grid allows only two figure widths (one column wide or full-page width); a three-column grid allows three figure widths; a four-column grid allows four widths; and so on.

The designer must answer other questions. What fonts, styles, and sizes will be used in illustrations and their captions? Will the figures be enlarged or reduced during page composition? Will photographs and other special illustrations be pasted up by hand or scanned into the computer? You can write out these specifications, or you can use the programs that create illustrations to create figure templates just as you use PageMaker to create publication templates.

Your design specifications for body copy, captions, and figure titles should include directions for paragraph alignment (left, right, justified, or centered) and spacing between paragraphs. The designer must consider convenience and speed of production. Some formats can be handled by menu selections in PageMaker and most word processors. Other formats require special treatment and may slow down the production process.

Designing Page Layouts before Entering Content

Publications with complex grid systems require the designer's attention throughout the production cycle. That attention is especially important for magazines and newsletters that incorporate various sizes of display ads throughout the publication. The designer can work ahead of the production team to specify where ads are to be placed and how articles should jump from one page to another.

Traditionally, a designer would draw pencil roughs of each page, or *thumbnail sketches*. This term originally meant that the sketches could be literally as small as a person's thumbnail because the sketches were intended to be quick to produce. PageMaker's Thumbnails option on the Print Options dialog box creates miniature versions of the pages of the publication. (This option is available on PostScript, PCL, and DDL printers, but not on dot-matrix printers.) For example, you can make rough page layouts with shaded boxes and article titles for every page of a magazine or newsletter and print the thumbnails as a guide for building the publication (see fig. 15.21). This same rough file can be used as the starting point in placing the finished text and graphics files on each page. Another set of thumbnails may be printed to check the final layouts (see fig. 15.22).

 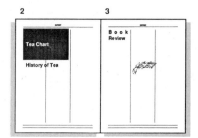 

Fig. 15.21

Thumbnail
printouts of rough
page layouts.

Building a Page Layout as a Painting

A publication does not have to be built from front to back, page by page. You can construct a publication in layers, just as painters work on canvas. The painter first pencils the rough outline on the canvas and then gradually adds layers of paint.

In PageMaker, the basic grid system is the painter's penciled sketch. You can use shaded boxes to reserve certain areas for planned graphics and particular articles. The text and graphics that you bring in from other programs to replace these place holders are like the painter's gradually added layers of paint.

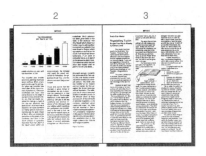

Fig. 15.22

Thumbnail printouts of finished page layouts.

During both the design and production phases, you can work on views of facing pages for double-sided publications. Working on both pages can be an advantage when you want to consider the overall impact of the open publication or you want to create graphic images that bleed across from one page to the other.

Be careful when you design page layouts that bleed off the edges of the paper or across facing pages. The top of figure 15.23 shows how part of an image that bleeds across two pages can be lost in the edges of the paper, depending on the type of printer you use. To solve this problem, specify a page size that is smaller than the paper size (see the bottom of fig. 15.23). You can determine the margin limits by printing a page covered by a solid black or shaded box.

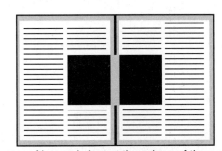

Center of image is lost at the edges of the pages
in a bleed across 8.5x11 pages

Full image is printed to edges of crop marks when the
page size is smaller than 8.5x11

Fig. 15.23

Handling bleeds.

The designer may be called in again after the PageMaker publication goes to production. (Refer to Chapters 4 through 14 for the production process following the design step.) The final design activities are described in the following paragraphs.

Going beyond PageMaker

For some publications, the final pages for distribution are printed on a laser printer. In most cases, however, you will print one set of "camera-ready" pages—either on a laser printer or on a high-resolution image-setter—and make multiple copies with a photocopier or an offset printer.

After the final pages of the publication are printed on a high-resolution printer, some final preparation may still be required before the pages are ready for reproduction. This preparation can include manual paste-up of figures that could not be produced on the computer, photograph mark-up for halftone processing, and color overlays to specify multiple-color printing.

Some artwork may be impossible to render using the computer: for example, photographs or original artwork that feature fine charcoal or airbrush techniques. In this case, you leave space for the special artwork on the PageMaker page and paste in the artwork by hand on the final version before you make multiple copies of the publication.

If you plan to paste up many elements, you may want to lay all the pages down on *boards*—heavy white paper that keeps the pages flat and prevents pasted-down elements from peeling or curling.

If you are using photographs, you can scan them into the computer and then place them on the PageMaker page (see Chapter 9), or the print shop can use a camera to create *halftones*. A halftone is composed of dots, like a scanned image; however, most scanned images are saved at low resolutions (between 72 and 300 dpi), whereas halftones have many more dots per inch.

To save time, you can use solid black boxes to reserve space for photographs on the PageMaker pages (refer to fig. 15.23). You can place a scanned image on the page for draft printings, then use the KeyLiner Addition in PageMaker 5.0 to drop a box around the placed graphic and give the box a solid fill (see "Using the KeyLiner Command" in Chapter 9). Otherwise, you can keep the scanned image of the photograph on the copy you deliver to the printer, to indicate the exact size and cropping required. You need to check with your print shop before you set up pages for halftones to see whether they prefer to receive your pages with black boxes or with the for-position-only scanned images in place.

Scanned Images versus Photographs

If the final publication will be printed on a porous paper like newsprint, a 75-dpi scanned image printed at 300-dpi can look as good as a photographic halftone.

If the final publication will be produced on glossy paper, 300-dpi scanned images may be too coarse for the final product. Still, you can scan, place, scale, and crop your PageMaker image to show the camera operator how to handle the original photograph (see fig. 15.24).

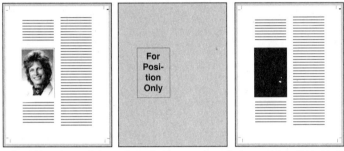

PageMaker printout with image plus marked tissue overlay, or final page printed with black box

Photo with tissue overlay indicating crop area, photo halftone will be stripped into negative

Fig. 15.24

Using a scanned image to hold the place of a halftone in the final production.

If you plan to have color in your publication, PageMaker can help you prepare the publication for commercial color printing. PageMaker 5.0's Color Separation feature in the Print Color dialog box prepares the publication by printing separate sheets for each spot or process color used in order to simplify the process of making printing plates for each color. For example, if your headlines and footers are magenta, your text is black, and your graphic is light blue, PageMaker prints three copies of that one page for spot color printing, or four copies for process color printing. The headlines and footers print on one page, the text on an-other, and the graphic spotted for color on a third. You can instead print a composite master page and label your color choices for the commercial printer, as shown in figure 15.25.

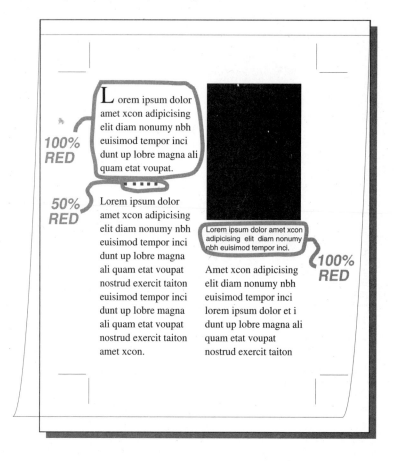

Fig. 15.25

Sample publica-tion for the commercial printer.

When commercial printers make plates for the publication, they look on each printed page for registration marks, or symbols that line up the images. If your publication size is smaller than the page size, registra-tion marks automatically print on every page when you select Separa-tions in the Color options dialog box, accessed from the Print dialog box. If your publication's page size is the same as the paper size, leav-ing no room for printing automatic registration marks beyond the crop marks, you can use PageMaker's drawing tools to create your own reg-istration marks on the master page. Use the Line and Fill command on the Element menu or the Color Palette to assign the color Registration to the graphic (see fig. 15.26). The registration marks will appear on each page—including the spot color overlays.

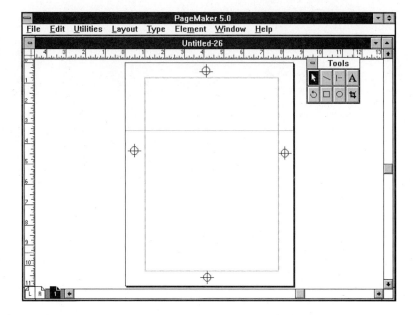

Fig. 15.26

Setting up master pages with registration marks.

For Related Information

◄◄ "Importing Text by Using the Place Command," p. 232.

◄◄ "Importing Graphics Created in Other Programs," p. 363.

►► "Typography," p. 699.

FROM HERE...

Summary

Chapters 2 through 10 describe all the basic steps in producing a publication, and Chapters 11 through 14 offer some more advanced tips and techniques. This chapter gives you more tips on the overall design of a publication, including the development of an underlying grid structure and the creation of template files, which enable you to complete large projects more efficiently. The next chapter completes your education in PageMaker and design by providing information about fonts and copy fitting to further help you design your publications for PageMaker.

Typography

D esigners and typographers have a unique set of terms for identifying the text in a publication: fonts, drop caps, leading, kerning,
and many others. In this chapter, you learn how to view a PageMaker
publication in these terms. You learn what fonts are and how fonts
used by various printers differ. You see the importance of knowing
what typefaces, sizes, and styles are available to your printer before
you start the design process. You learn how to set up your design
specifications—including special effects such as drop caps—using
PageMaker's menus. You learn to estimate the amount of text that fits
on each page and to make fine adjustments in spacing to fit copy into a
defined space.

Regardless of whether you, as a designer or typographer, are writing
the design specifications for a publication or using PageMaker to set up
the master template, you need to know how PageMaker works before
you plan your publication. In this chapter, you learn something about
how professional typesetters and designers determine what fonts to
use in a publication, and you learn how to specify them for a production team that uses PageMaker.

This chapter discusses fonts and type specifications from a design
perspective. Chapter 8 describes how to actually change the type
specifications for selected type in PageMaker. Chapter 10 describes
how different printers handle fonts. Chapter 13 discusses some of the
issues involved in managing fonts and diagnosing problems in printing
fonts. Appendix A describes how to install fonts on the system and
download them to a printer.

Understanding Fonts

The word *font* is related to the French verb *fondre*, which means "to melt or cast." The term once referred literally to the trays of cast metal letters that printers used to compose a publication. Each tray, or font, included all letters of the alphabet that were of a specific size and appearance (see fig. 16.1). One tray, for example, held only 10-point Times italic letters, another tray held only 10-point Times bold, and so on. A font, then, was a particular combination of size, typeface, and style.

More recently, however, the word font has come to mean only the name of a typeface, such as Times or Helvetica. The word has this meaning in PageMaker's Type Specifications dialog box (displayed when you select the Type Specs command on the Type menu). This definition makes sense for the new computer fonts based on formulas, such as PostScript and TrueType fonts. In these fonts, each letter of the alphabet is cast, or designed, only once to define the shape of the letter. This information is stored as a complex curve-fitting equation. A printer that uses a programming language such as PostScript to create text can produce any size of a typeface for which the printer "knows" the shape of each letter.

If you are told that a printer is limited to a certain number of fonts per page or per publication, you must know which meaning of the word *font* applies. Some printers are limited to four fonts in the more traditional sense: for example, 10-point Times Roman, 10-point Times italic,

10-point Times boldface, and 10-point Times boldface italic. For other printers, a limit of four fonts means four typefaces: Times, Helvetica, Courier, and Palatino.

When you create the design specifications for the type in a PageMaker publication, you need to be specific about which printer and which fonts (typefaces, sizes, and styles) you are using. This chapter's section on "Working with PageMaker's Font List" provides tips for selecting fonts.

Typeface

In the traditional sense, a *typeface* is a set of characters with the same basic shape for each letter. The Times typeface, for example, includes all sizes and styles of type that are variations of the same basic designs for each letter of the alphabet. Typefaces are broadly grouped into two kinds: serif and sans serif, examples of which are shown in figure 16.2. A *serif* is a fine cross-stroke that projects across the end of the main stroke of a letter (the tiny marks across the top and bottom of the lower-case *i*, for example). *Sans serif* means "without serif."

Times is a serif typeface.
Helvetica is a sans serif typeface.

Fig. 16.2

Serif and sans serif typefaces.

Typefaces also are often classified as *body-copy typefaces* or *display typefaces*. Body-copy typefaces (Times, for example) are commonly used for most text and are legible in small sizes (measured in units called points). Display typefaces (Zapf Chancery, for example) are used in display ads and logos, headings in publications, and headlines in newsletters. Display typefaces can be ornate and usually are set larger than 12 points (see fig. 16.3).

Body type can be as small as 9 points.
Body type can be as large as 12 points.

Display typefaces

are usually designed for larger sizes.

Fig. 16.3

Body-copy type and display type.

When used on computers and laser printers, typefaces are often divided into two other categories: bit-mapped fonts and outline (curve-fitting) fonts (see fig. 16.4). *Bit-mapped fonts*, which are printed as patterns of dots, may appear jagged at the edges when printed (in the same way that screen fonts appear jagged on-screen). Some bit-mapped fonts are designed to be printed at higher resolutions, and these fonts can look as good as outline fonts when produced on most laser printers. Because bit-mapped fonts are hard to scale to different sizes, the font designer must develop a different set of designs for each size. Stored as a pattern of dots, these fonts usually take up a great deal of space in the printer's memory while a page is being printed.

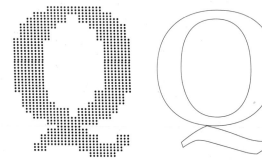

Fig. 16.4

Bit-mapped and outline (curve-fitting) fonts.

Outline fonts (also called *curve-fitting fonts*) are defined by curve-fitting mathematical formulas. These typefaces can be scaled to any size or made boldface or italic by the changing of a few variables in the formulas that define the shapes of the letters. *PostScript*, for example, is a curve-fitting language; choosing PostScript fonts when printing with a PostScript printer or typesetter ensures a smooth finished product. Because fonts stored as formulas take up less space in the printer's memory than do bit-mapped fonts, you can download more of these outline fonts at one time.

The list of typefaces, or fonts, in PageMaker's Control palette in character view, in the Font submenu under the Type menu, or in the Type Specifications dialog box (displayed when you select the Type Specs command on the Type menu) varies depending on which printer drivers you have installed, which printer you have selected as the target printer, and which fonts you have added (or deleted). PageMaker supports a wide range of typefaces, sizes, and styles that not all printers can handle. By clicking the Fonts icon in the Windows Control Panel window, you can add a new screen font to the menus (see "Adding and Deleting Screen Fonts" in Appendix A.) You cannot, however, print the publication in that font unless you also install it on the printer (see Chapter 10 and Appendix A).

In your publications, you can use fonts that your printer does not support. For example, you can specify a PostScript printer as your target printer in the Page Setup dialog box, take the finished publication to a service bureau for printing on a Linotronic typesetter, but print drafts on a non-PostScript printer specified through the Print dialog box. Although you can use your own dot-matrix printer for drafts, note that the printer converts the fonts to supported fonts or prints them as bit-mapped fonts. This substitution may be acceptable for printing draft copies, but the appearance of the publication may change significantly when you switch from one printer to another. If you plan to use your own printer throughout the entire production cycle, be sure that your design specifications call for fonts that are supported by your printer.

Size

Typesetters measure the size of type in points. The word *point* is related to the French verb *poindre*, "to prick." A point was the smallest possible mark that a printer could make on a page—about 1/72 of an inch. An inch, therefore, contains approximately 72 points.

Originating during the same time period in which the words *font* and *serif* were introduced, the term *leading* (rhymes with "heading") once referred to thin strips of metal (lead) that were inserted between lines of type to add vertical space in a column or tray of set type. For example, a type specification of 10/12 Times Roman (10 on 12 Times Roman) calls for 10-point Times Roman letters with 2 points of leading between lines.

This system of measure is the same as the picas and points listed in the Preferences dialog box (displayed when you select the Preferences command on the File menu) and used on the ruler lines (see Chapter 4 and Chapter 5). The larger 12-point unit, the *pica*, is used to measure distances on the page but is not usually used in defining type size. A 1.5-inch distance on the page is measured as 9 picas, for example, but a 1.5-inch-high character is measured as 108 points.

Originally, the size of type was measured as the full height of the cast letter or type block. This measurement included some space above and below the letter so that two lines of type would not touch each other. Because the width and exact position of the type on the block is determined by the original designer of each typeface, the apparent sizes of the letters may vary greatly among different typefaces. Figure 16.5 shows 30-point letters from an assortment of typefaces.

Note the differences between the letters in each font. Descenders (like the bottom part of the *y*) fall to different depths. Cap heights (the height of the capital letters) and x-heights (height of lowercase letters) vary. The height of ascenders (the tops of lowercase letters like *b*, *d*, and so forth—not shown in figure 16.5) also can vary between fonts.

Fig. 16.5

Letters with the same nominal size that look larger or smaller in different typefaces.

AyAyAyAyAyAyAy

The size drop-down list in the Control palette in Character view, the Size submenu under the Type menu, and the drop-down list in the Type Specifications dialog box (accessed by choosing Type Specs from the Type menu) displays the sizes available for the currently selected type-face (see fig. 16.6). With PageMaker, you can specify any size between 4 and 650 points, in one-tenth-point increments. Usually, however, you want to use the sizes supported by your printer, which may not include the full range supported by PageMaker. PostScript printers can handle any size, including sizes larger than 650 points. You also can import graphics that use larger fonts.

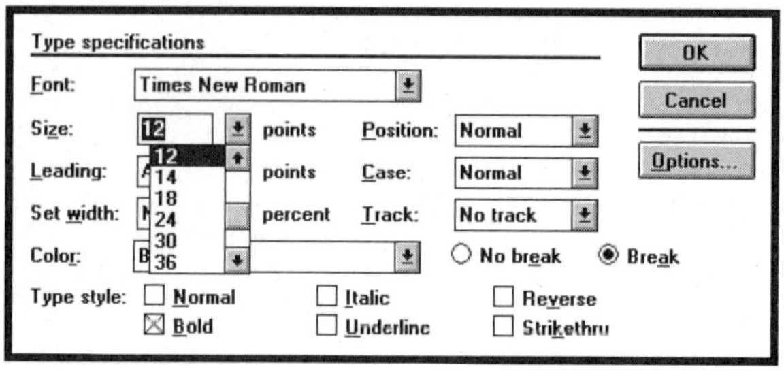

Fig. 16.6

The Type Specifications dialog box.

Type specifications		
Font:	Times New Roman	OK
Size:	12 points Position: Normal	Cancel
Leading:	12 / 14 points Case: Normal	Options...
Set width:	18 / 24 percent Track: No track	
Color:	30 / 36 No break ● Break	
Type style:	☐ Normal ☐ Italic ☐ Reverse	
	☒ Bold ☐ Underline ☐ Strikethru	

Generally, body copy is set between 9 and 12 points; headlines are usually larger. Business cards and classified ads can be smaller, using 7- or 8-point type. Text smaller than 6 points is difficult to read in most typefaces and is rarely used.

Style

The third basic element of the traditional font is *style*. Styles listed on the Type Style submenu of the Type menu and in the Type Specifications dialog box include Normal, Bold, Italic, Underline, Reverse, and Strikethru. You also can set the case to Normal, All Caps, or Small Caps. Figure 16.7 provides some examples. Any of these variables can be part of the design specifications.

Black type:
Normal
Bold
Italic
Bold Italic
SMALL CAPS

Reverse type:
Normal
Bold
Italic
Bold Italic
SMALL CAPS

Fig. 16.7

Examples of type styles available on a PostScript printer and on most printers when a type manager is used.

As is true of size, not all styles shown on PageMaker menus are supported by all printers. You want to use the styles that your printer supports. You need to become thoroughly familiar with the capabilities and limitations of your printer by testing your design ideas in short (one- or two-page) publications before building long documents.

Testing Your Printer's Range of Capabilities

Create a series of test publications with every combination of the typefaces, styles, and sizes you plan to use in your publications. Avoid being shocked by last-minute discoveries of what your printer cannot do.

Some downloadable typefaces are available in *families*, each style of which you must install separately. For instance, you install the boldface style of a typeface separately from the italic set. Even without having separate styles, you can force some roman (nonitalic) outline fonts to be bold or italic by choosing those styles from the Control palette or Type menu.

For instance, if you use a type manager such as Adobe Type Manager (ATM) and have a font that does not have actual oblique or italic versions, you can still apply the Italic attribute to it. On-screen you see the text slant. If you print to a non-PostScript printer, the printed text is also slanted because type managers generally send their fonts as graphics to non-PostScript printers. If you print to a PostScript printer, however, PageMaker does not send a graphic of the font, but the actual PostScript printer font. If you don't have the oblique or italic counterpart, your text prints in its upright position, regardless of how it looks on-screen.

Italic versus Oblique Fonts

A true italic font is composed of letterforms that are specifically designed to be different from those of its roman (nonitalic) counterpart. Italic characters are almost always slanted letters compared to their roman counterparts, but they don't have to be.

An oblique font is simply a slanting of the roman letterforms, not a complete redesign of each character. The oblique version sometimes comes with the roman version. If you have an oblique version of a font, you can access it by selecting the roman version from the Font submenu or drop-down list and then applying an Italic attribute to it.

FROM HERE...

For Related Information

◀◀ "Formatting Text Using Styles in PageMaker," p. 343.

◀◀ "Types of Fonts," p. 396.

◀◀ "Managing Fonts," p. 592.

▶▶ "Installing and Using Fonts," p. 902.

Working with PageMaker's Font List

Chapter 8 explains how to use PageMaker's Type Specs command (on the Type menu) to change type specifications. This chapter examines the Type Specifications dialog box in terms of the typefaces and fonts listed there. You learn how to change the default font and some of the advantages of using a type manager. Chapter 13 describes the use of a type manager in more detail, and Appendix A describes how to add typefaces and fonts to or delete them from the list in the dialog box.

Changing the Default Font

The default font is usually 12-point Times Roman or the closest equivalent available for the target printer. If 12-point type is not available, PageMaker uses the next smaller available size. The default font determines the appearance of new text typed directly into PageMaker and of unformatted text (with the file extension TXT) placed in PageMaker from another program.

If during a work session you want to change the default font for the current publication, select the pointer tool in the toolbox before you make a new selection with the Type Specs command. To change the default font for this session and all future PageMaker sessions, choose the Type Specs command when all publications are closed. This change is saved in the file PM5.CNF.

Using a Type Manager

A *type manager* is a program that uses outline-font technology to generate characters of virtually any size for both your screen and printer. A type manager represents your final, printed publication on-screen more accurately than is possible without using a type manager. Several page-design options (such as manual kerning, rotating text, expanding text, and condensing text) become much easier when you can see the fonts accurately on-screen. Screen fonts generated by a type manager require less hard disk space than do other screen fonts.

A type manager also increases the number of fonts available on your printer. The effect on your publication depends on the type manager you are using, the fonts you have installed, and the printer you are using. Refer to your type manager's instruction manual for information on how the type manager can expand the font capabilities of your printer.

Note that although a type manager usually increases the font capabilities of your printer, it also can slow down the printing process. If you're using a type manager that is designed to work with your printer (for example, if both your printer and type manager use bit-mapped fonts), you have the increased flexibility of outline fonts with little difference in printing time. If, however, you are using a type manager designed to work with a different printer standard (for example, if you have a PCL-language printer, like the Hewlett-Packard printers, and your type manager uses PostScript fonts), each character generated by the type manager is treated as a graphic. In this case, printing takes longer using the type manager's fonts than if you use the printer's original fonts.

T I P   **Using a Type Manager Economically**

If your type manager uses a different font standard than your printer usually works with, use the regular printer's fonts for body text and the type manager's fonts only for large text, such as headings.

FROM HERE...

For Related Information

◄◄ "Changing Type Specifications," p. 295.

◄◄ "Using a Type Manager," p. 594.

▶▶ "Installing and Using Fonts," p. 902.

Planning Your Design Specifications

Planning the design specifications of your publication involves many steps. You must determine how many fonts are available with your printer, which typefaces and how much leading to use, whether headlines and titles need to be kerned, and how to handle captions. You also should plan for special text elements such as symbols and mathematical formulas.

Choosing the Fonts

The first step in the design process is to list all the built-in fonts in the printer you plan to use for the publication's final production. You also must know which cartridge fonts and downloadable fonts you can access. With this information, you can list in your design specifications all the different fonts available for use.

T I P   **Shortening Printing Time**

Downloaded fonts can take a long time to print. If time is a concern, stick to the built-in fonts.

The second step in the design process is to list the number of fonts you plan to use in a particular publication. One reason for limiting the number of fonts involves design considerations. The best designs use only a few fonts on each page. Another reason for limiting the number of fonts is a practical one: Some printers cannot handle more than a few fonts per page. A third factor in determining the number of fonts is the number of different text elements in the publication. Such elements can include:

- Chapter openings, section openings, or feature article headlines
- Different levels of headings or headlines
- Body copy
- Figure captions
- Labels within figures
- Footnotes
- Special sections, such as sidebars, summaries, and tables

Now match the items on the two lists—the list of the fonts available (or fonts you want to use) and the list of the different elements within the publication (see fig. 16.8).

Available fonts:	Document elements:
8-point Times Roman	Figure labels
10-point Times Roman	Body copy
10-point Times Bold	Subhead
10-point Times Italic	Figure captions
14-point Helvetica	Headlines

Fig. 16.8

Beginning the type-specification process.

Printing a Type Sample Sheet   T I P

If you are not familiar with the different typefaces in the Type Specifications dialog box, or if you do not know which ones your printer supports, make and print a "dummy copy" using each option on the menu. Figure 16.9 shows some type samples.

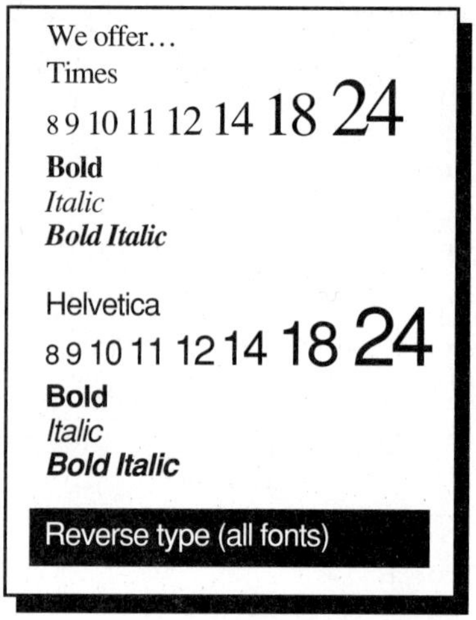

We offer...
Times
8 9 10 11 12 14 18 24
Bold
Italic
Bold Italic

Helvetica
8 9 10 11 12 14 18 24
Bold
Italic
Bold Italic

Reverse type (all fonts)

Fig. 16.9

A type sample
sheet.

If you're accustomed to having all your publications printed on a dot-matrix printer or a single-font printer that produces letter-quality output, you may find a comparatively wide range of fonts rather confusing. If so, you can approach the type specifications for a publication in two ways.

The fastest way to acquire a sense of design and develop good design specifications is to study and imitate published works similar in structure to your publication. Match your design specifications as closely as possible to those of the published document. Select fonts similar to those used for headings, body copy, and captions in the published document. You don't have to match the typefaces exactly, but try to substitute typefaces in the same category (serif or sans serif, roman, italic, boldface, and so on). Examples of publications with different type specifications are shown in Part V of this book.

A second approach to creating type specifications is to study the underlying principles that designers and typographers follow. Some guidelines are listed here:

- Don't use more than two typefaces in a publication. Usually, one typeface is serif; the other, sans serif. Use variations in size and style to distinguish among different text elements.

- Use variations in size rather than boldface type to distinguish the different heading levels. One common exception to this rule is the lowest heading level, which may be boldface in the same size and typeface as the body copy.

- Use italicized rather than underscored text in body copy. (Under-scored text is a convention developed for use in publications printed on letter-quality printers that cannot print italic.)

- Use all caps as a deliberate design strategy rather than as a way to show emphasis or to differentiate heading levels. Use variations in size instead of all-caps text to differentiate headings. One common exception to this rule occurs when the list of available fonts is too limited to accommodate all heading levels. In this case, you can use all caps to distinguish between two heading levels in the same font.

Few publications can follow all these guidelines without making some exceptions. Some of the most common exceptions have been men-tioned. One mark of a good designer is knowing when and how to break the rules.

Mixing Typefaces

As stressed in the design guidelines, you should stick to one or two different typefaces—usually a serif and a sans serif typeface—and use variations in size and style to differentiate elements.

You will find that using only one typeface whenever possible makes the production process more efficient. One convenience of using only one typeface (with different sizes and styles) is that you can globally change to any other typeface without affecting the different sizes and styles set up in the text. For example, you can select a whole story or article and change its typeface from Times to Helvetica. In PageMaker, you can search for and change text attributes through the Story Editor (discussed in Chapter 7), so you can globally change Times to Helvetica in a block of text that mixes typefaces.

Starting with one typeface can be handy if you want to quickly generate several variations on a basic design without using a style sheet; or if you use one printer for all drafts and switch to a different printer or downloadable font for the final printing. Another pragmatic reason for using one typeface is that you can save formatting time in PageMaker or your word processing program.

The number of typefaces you choose can be affected by a printer that uses permanently downloaded fonts. Because these downloaded fonts are not stored in the printer's permanent memory (ROM—read-only memory) or in the printer cartridge, they take up space in the printer's temporary memory (RAM—random-access memory). You usually can-not download more than a few fonts at a time. On some printers, you also may not be able to print high-resolution graphics when the downloaded typeface is required. Appendix A describes how typefaces can be downloaded to a printer.

At the other extreme, you may have good reasons for using more than two typefaces. For example, you may have to use all the fonts on an eight-font cartridge to achieve the required differentiation of text elements. Publications such as magazines and newsletters, which use different formats in different sections, may employ more than four typefaces throughout the publication, even though each page, feature, or advertisement uses only one or two typefaces.

Choosing Automatic or Forced Leading

If you have training in traditional typesetting, you probably are accustomed to specifying the exact leading (the space between lines) and the type size. PageMaker, however, has an automatic leading feature. If you don't specify otherwise, the program determines the leading based on the point size of the type. The default formula for automatic leading is roughly 120 percent of the point size (rounded to the nearest half-point). See figure 16.10 for examples. You can change this formula by choosing the Paragraph command from the Type menu and changing the Spacing option in the Paragraph Specifications dialog box, as described in the section "Controlling Spacing" in Chapter 8.

Automatic leading for 10-point Times is 12 points, or 10/12.

Automatic leading for 12-point Times is 14.4 points, or 12/14.5.

Automatic leading for 14-point Times is 16.8 points, or 14/17.

Fig. 16.10

Examples of automatic base-to-base leading.

The use of automatic leading is a production convenience rather than a design principle. If you change the point size of all or part of the text, the leading changes to match the new size. You can, however, override the automatic leading. You can manipulate the leading to achieve a custom look or to make copy fit a column or a certain number of pages (see "Fitting Copy within a Defined Space" in this chapter).

Aligning Text to a Grid

As described in Chapter 4, the Preferences command under the Edit menu lets you specify a unit of measure for the vertical ruler. This setting determines the look of the vertical ruler when rulers are displayed and can be used as a guide or "grid" which you can align the baselines of text on each page. To set up a grid, first determine the size and leading of most of the text in your publication—usually set in the body text style if you are using a style sheet. Then set up a vertical grid to match. Next, make sure that each text block aligns with the tick marks on the ruler. Finally, set the Align to Grid option in the Paragraph Rule Options dialog box for paragraphs that do not conform to body text leading.

For example, suppose that your body text is set in 12/14 Times—12-point Times with 14-point leading. Choose Preferences from the File menu and set the Vertical ruler to Custom by choosing from the drop-down list of options. Type **14** in the Points box next to the Vertical ruler specification in the Preferences dialog box (see fig. 16.11).

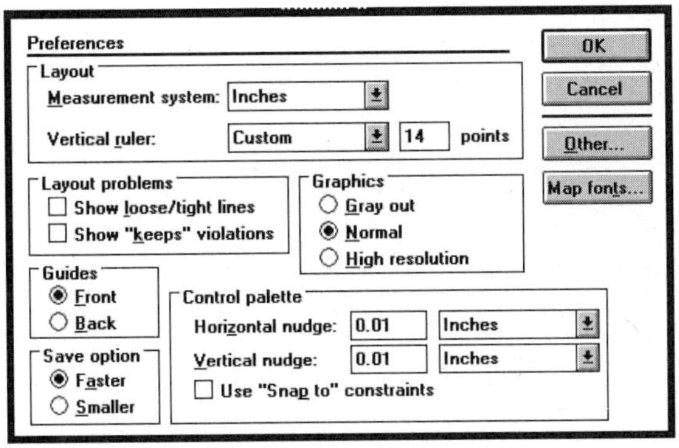

Fig. 16.11

Preferences dialog box.

Now the vertical ruler shows major divisions equivalent to 14-point "slugs" of type, and minor divisions at 1/3 of a slug. When you select a text block with the pointer tool, dotted lines appear on the ruler marking the position of the top and bottom of the text block. As long as the type has 14-point leading, you can align those dotted lines with the major tick marks on the ruler to make all your type fall onto the grid (see fig. 16.12). This process is even easier when Snap to Rulers is active on the Guides and Rulers submenu under the Layout menu (Shift+Ctrl+Y).

Finally, set the Align to Grid option in the Paragraph Rule Options dialog box or in the Control palette for paragraphs that do not conform to body text leading, such as headings and figure captions. (Refer to fig. 8.17 in Chapter 8.)

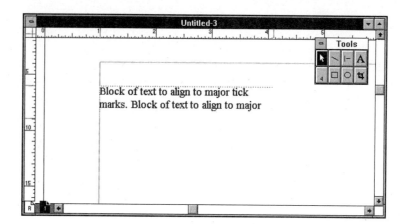

Fig. 16.12

Align text block to major tick marks on vertical ruler.

Changing Word and Letter Spacing

You can change the word and letter spacing through the Spacing Attributes dialog box, accessed through the Paragraph Specifications dialog box as described in Chapter 8 (see fig. 16.13). It's a good idea to leave these values unchanged from the default values unless you're having a serious problem with fitting a given amount of text to a fixed number of columns (see "Copy Fitting" later in this chapter). If you must change these values, follow these general guidelines:

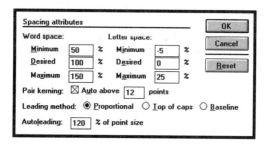

Fig. 16.13

The Spacing Attributes dialog box.

- Always look at the text carefully after making changes to the spacing attributes to be sure that the text retains an even texture (with no wide gaps between letters or dark clusters of text).

- The space between words should be smaller than the visual space between lines. The visual space between lines isn't the same as the leading; it's the space from the baseline of one line to the x-height (lower than the ascent height) of the line below.

- Tight letter spacing and loose word spacing create one extreme of unevenness, while the reverse makes word divisions hard to see.

- The narrower the columns, the more likely justified text will result in lines with wide word or letter spacing. If this becomes a problem, you may need to add more discretionary hyphens, change the design of the publication to allow wider columns, or align the text flush left rather than justify it.

- You can set light-weight typefaces looser than heavy-weight versions of the same typeface, and you can space all-cap or small-cap text more loosely than normal case.

- For ragged-right text that ends up with uneven line endings, add discretionary hyphens or edit the text to eliminate the worst cases.

Never Double-Space after Periods

T I P

If you double-space after periods, justified text can take on even wider rivers of white space when space is added between words. Unjustified text will even have an appearance not intended by the typographers who designed the type. If your text was originally prepared with double-spacing after periods, use the Story Editor to globally search for period-space-space and change it to period-space.

Kerning Headlines and Titles

Headlines and titles—such as figure titles, newsletter banners, and advertising copy—should stand out from the body copy of the publication. Because design principles suggest that you use size rather than boldface to differentiate and emphasize these elements, your headlines and titles probably will be large and may need to be kerned to tighten the space between letters for a more professional look. *Kerning* is the fine adjustment made to the spacing between certain pairs of letters to give the overall text an even appearance.

Print the publication and examine the headlines for pairs of letters with unwanted space between them. As explained in Chapter 8, the space is caused by the widths and the angles of the two adjacent letters. For example, the opposite edges of the capital *A* and the capital *V* have similar slopes. Without kerning, when the letters *A* and *V* are adjacent in a word, as in KNAVE, the space between the *A* and the *V* appears to be much wider than the spaces between any of the other letters.

Using Automatic Kerning

As noted in Chapter 8, PageMaker applies the basic kerning formulas to any text larger than 12 points in size. This process is demonstrated in the Spacing Attributes dialog box, which appears when you select the Paragraph Specifications command on the Type menu (refer to fig. 16.13). If you want to kern smaller headings and titles, you can change the minimum point size indicated in that dialog box. Suppose, for example, that you're producing a brochure in which the body copy is 9 points and the headings are 12 points. If the design specifications for the publication require kerned headings, you can use the Spacing option in the Paragraph Specifications dialog box to change the minimum nonkerning point size to 10.

Using Manual Kerning

With PageMaker's manual kerning option, you can adjust the space between any two letters. Use this procedure on a case-by-case basis—not as a global type specification.

To change the space between two letters manually, select the text tool from the toolbox. Place the text-insertion point between the two letters you want to kern. To decrease space between letters, hold down the Ctrl key as you press Backspace. To increase space between letters, hold down the Ctrl and Shift keys and press Backspace. With each press of the Backspace key, you change the space between the letters by 1/24th the usual space assigned to that font (see fig. 16.14).

AV — Automatic kerning

A|V — Ctrl+Backspace to decrease space

A|V — Ctrl+Shift+Backspace to increase space

Using Expert Kerning

PageMaker 5.0 introduces an Aldus Addition called Expert Kerning, which can be used on any text set in PostScript Type 1 fonts for which the printer fonts are available. Use this Addition as an alternative to manual kerning—on small ranges of selected text. For larger ranges of text, simply activate Pair Kerning above the size specified in the Spacing Attributes dialog box, accessed through the Paragraph Specifications dialog box, as described under "Activating Pair Kerning" in Chapter 8.

Expert Kerning removes all manual kerning in the selected text, but you can still add manual kerning to tighten or loosen the space between characters after using Expert Kerning.

To apply Expert Kerning, first use the text tool in Layout view to select the text to be kerned. Choose Expert Kerning from the Aldus Additions submenu under the Utilities menu. In the Expert Kerning dialog box, type a Kern Strength value between 0.0 and 2.0, with higher values yielding tighter spacing (see fig. 16.15).

Fig. 16.15

The Expert
Kerning
dialog box.

Specify the size of the original master design for the font, if you know it, by choosing Text, Display, or Poster in the Design Class area at the bottom of the dialog box, or by typing a size. The original size best embodies the designer's intention of how the font was to be spaced. If you don't know the original size, choose Text as the default.

When you choose OK, the Expert Kerning Addition evaluates every character pair in the selected range of text, removes any prior manual kerning, and inserts new manual kerning using expert kern-pair values.

Handling Captions

In any publication, you want to be sure to treat like elements consistently, including captions, figure titles, and labels within figures. Consistency can be difficult to achieve when you bring figures into PageMaker from other programs. Will the graphing program be able to match the fonts used in figures from other drawing packages? Will the figure be scaled larger or smaller after it is in PageMaker? As the designer, you need to specify how captions, figure titles, and figure labels are to be handled in each program serving as a source of illustrations for the publication.

To ensure consistency, you may decide to enter all figure titles and captions directly in PageMaker. But you still have to specify the font you want to use for labels within the figures. Furthermore, you may need to account for changes in type size that result when you shrink or enlarge a figure in PageMaker. As explained in Chapter 9, when you change the size of a graphic imported from another program, you also change the size of the type used in that graphic. If you know that you will be shrinking a figure by 50 percent, for example, the illustrator may need to make the type in the drawing program twice as large as the type in the final publication.

Inserting Symbols in Text

It's not uncommon to see special symbols embedded within text. For instance, many software manuals use symbols to represent special keys outlined in boxes, such as the function keys and the Ctrl and Alt keys. Some magazine publishers use a symbol to indicate the end of an article.

PageMaker enables you to insert "inline graphics" as part of the text flow, as described in Chapter 11; the graphics move when the text moves. Using graphic symbols is an alternative to creating the symbols as a separate font, and each method offers its own unique benefits.

If you want to insert a symbol as a graphic, use a graphics application to create it. You can use PageMaker's built-in graphics tools if the symbol is made up simply of lines, rectangles, or ellipses. Scale the symbol to the desired size in the graphics application before importing it or anchoring it in PageMaker, as described in Chapter 11. (Even though you can scale a graphic in PageMaker, you can be sure that the graphic is the same size every time you import it—and thus eliminate the inconvenience of repeatedly scaling the graphic—if you scale it in the graphics application instead of PageMaker.)

The advantage of creating a symbol as a graphic is that you probably already have a graphics application if you do much desktop publishing. As an alternative, you can use a scanner to input the symbol if it already exists on paper.

To create a symbol or set of symbols as a font, you must use a font-generating application such as Publisher's Type Foundry (from Z-Soft of Marietta, Georgia). After the font is created and loaded into the system, you can insert the symbols in the text: Use the Font command under the Type menu to select the symbol font and then type the keyboard characters you have assigned for each symbol.

The advantage of creating symbols as a font is that you can input the symbols while typing in the word processor or in PageMaker. You also can easily and consistently scale them with the type-scaling commands. You also can search for and replace characters and fonts (see Chapter 7). If you assign a symbol to the letter *E* on the keyboard, for example, you can type the text using the letter *E* in place of the symbol; you then can search for the whole word *E* and replace it with the letter *E* in the symbol font.

Creating Fractions in PageMaker

PageMaker has no built-in functions for creating mathematical formulas, but this section describes two techniques you can use to create mathematical formulas without resorting to a font-generating application.

Creating a Fraction within a Sentence

If you want to create a simple fraction within a sentence, you can compose it of superscripted and subscripted characters that are kerned manually to print one above the other.

To create a fraction composed of one single-digit number over another single-digit number, for example, first type the two numbers (such as a 1 and a 2, as shown in the first example in fig. 16.16). Select the first number (the numerator) and use the Type Specs command from the Type menu to set the number as an underscored superscript; then select the second number (the denominator) and use the Type Specs command to set the number as a subscript (step 2 in each example in figure 16.16).

	Step 1	Step 2	Step 3	Step 4
Example 1	12	$\frac{1}{2}$	$\frac{1}{2}$	$\frac{1}{2}$
Example 2	212	$\frac{1}{2}\,2$	$\frac{1}{22}$	$\frac{1}{22}$
Example 3	2112	$\frac{11}{2}\,2$	$\frac{11}{22}$	$\frac{11}{22}$

Steps in creating fractions within a sentence.

Finally, position the cursor between the two numbers and manually kern the two characters by holding the Ctrl key as you press the Backspace key to tighten the space between them until they are aligned with each other (step 3 of each example in figure 16.16).

To make the fraction meet the baseline of the rest of the text, select both numbers, choose the Type Specs command from the Type menu, and click the Options button to display the Type Options dialog box.

Set the Super/Subscript size to 45 percent of point size, the Superscript position to 40 percent of point size, and the Subscript position to 0 percent of point size. The results appear in step 4 of each example in figure 16.16.

To create a fraction composed of a single-digit numerator over a double-digit denominator, type the numerator between the other two digits, set as an underscored superscript. Set the two digits of the denominator as subscripts, and kern the spaces between each pair of numbers manually to create the effect shown in example 2 of figure 16.16.

To create a fraction composed of a double-digit numerator over a double-digit denominator, type the two digits of the numerator (set as an underscored superscript) between the other two digits. Set the two digits of the denominator as subscripts and kern the spaces between the end pairs of numbers manually to create the effect shown in example 3 of figure 16.16.

Creating Stand-Alone Mathematical Formulas

You can use PageMaker's "paragraph rules" feature (described in Chapter 8) to create mathematical formulas on lines of their own (for example, not embedded in a paragraph of normal text). Figure 16.17 shows a complex formula.

$$\Sigma \quad {}^{x^2}_{y^2+z^2}$$

$$\sum {}^{x^2}_{y^2+z^2}$$

$$\sum \frac{x^2}{y^2+z^2}$$

Fig. 16.17

Evolution of a complex formula.

For example, to create the formula shown in figure 16.17, follow these steps:

1. Type the characters **Sx2** on one line, then press Enter and type **y2+z2** on the second line. In this example, these characters are set in 24-point Times.

2. Select the first letter (S) and use the Type Specs command on the Type menu to set the *S* larger than the rest of the characters (in this case, 72 points). Position the letter as a subscript: Click the Options button in the Type Specifications dialog box and set the Subscript size to 100% of point size and the Subscript position to 50% of point size. In this example, set the *S* in symbol font to get the large sigma shown in figure 16.17.

3. Use the Type Specs command to set each 2 as a normal superscript.

4. Position the cursor on the second line, and use the Paragraph command on the Type menu to display the Paragraph Specifications dialog box. Specify a Left Indent wide enough to force the second line into position right of the large subscripted first letter in the formula (in this case, 0.656 inches), then click the Rules button to display the Paragraph Rules dialog box. Set up a 4-point rule (in this example) above the paragraph, set to the width of the text. (Paragraph indentation and paragraph rules are described in Chapter 8.)

5. To center the top line over the bottom line in the formula, insert a tab or spaces between the first letter in the formula (the sigma) and the rest of the characters on the first line.

You can apply your own variations of this technique to create other formulas. Note that the sigma in the formula will appear as an *S* in some views on-screen, but it prints as a sigma.

For Related Information

◀◀ "Specifying Layout Ruler Units," p. 157.

◀◀ "Changing Text in Story View," p. 285.

◀◀ "Controlling Spacing of Lines, Words, and Letters," p. 322.

◀◀ "Scaling PageMaker Objects," p. 384.

◀◀ "Using Inline Graphics," p. 459.

FROM HERE...

Fitting Copy

Copy fitting is the process of making text fit into a predefined area: a column, a page, or a specific number of pages. *Copy casting* is the process of predicting how much space a given amount of copy will require or how much copy will fit a given space. In this section, you learn how a designer estimates how copy will fit *before* it's placed in PageMaker, and you learn several methods of fitting copy after the copy has been written and edited.

Copy Casting

Traditionally, professional designers have approached the problems of copy casting from two angles. First, based on the design specifications, you can estimate how many words (or characters) can fill the allotted space. Magazine editors use this method when they ask authors to write articles of a specified word length. Second, you can take the text from the author and estimate how much space the text will fill or make up design specifications that force the text to fit a specified area.

Before placing a whole text file in PageMaker, you should estimate the amount of text that will fit and compare this figure with the text provided by the authors. If the amount of text provided differs significantly from the amount required, you can force the copy to fit by adjusting the margins in PageMaker before you place the text. Alternatively, you can use the word processing program to edit the copy until it is the desired length.

Casting from a Typecasting Reference Book

One traditional method used in copy casting is to refer to a typecasting reference book. This book, available at most bookstores, shows examples of text in various sizes and with different leadings. From these examples, you can choose the look you want for your body copy. Also provided is the average number of characters per pica for each font. Your word processing program may be able to give you a character count for your text, or you can count the number of characters per page or per line of printed copy yourself. You also may use a type gauge to measure the type against a specific column width and length to estimate the number of lines of final copy. You use another measuring guide or gauge to determine the number of lines per inch at various leadings. The sequence of calculations goes something like this:

1. Select a font to be used for the text.

2. In the typecasting reference book, look up the average number of characters per pica.

3. Determine the number of characters in the word processing file by using the word processing software or a word-counting utility.

4. Divide the total number of characters by the average number of characters per pica to estimate the total number of picas required by the text.

5. Divide the total number of picas by the column width in picas to estimate the total number of lines of final copy.

6. Look up the number of lines per column inch for the leading you will be using.

7. Divide the total number of lines by the number of lines per column inch to estimate the number of column inches of final copy.

8. Divide the number of column inches of final copy by the number of column inches per page to estimate the total number of pages.

Because this method of casting copy or estimating length is tedious and has a wide margin of error, many typesetters use a second method.

Casting Sample Pages

In this second method of casting copy, you lay out one or two sample pages in PageMaker, using the font that will be used for normal body copy, and estimate the number of characters that fit on a page. This character count is often converted to an estimated number of words to be assigned to the author. The steps for this method are as follows:

1. Type one paragraph exactly 100 characters (or words) long.

2. Set the type in the specified font.

3. Duplicate the paragraph as many times as necessary to fill the column or page.

4. Count the number of paragraphs required to fill the column or page and multiply that number by 100 to get an estimated character (or word) count per column or page.

5. Multiply the estimated count per column or page by the number of columns or pages to determine the maximum character (or word) count.

6. Use the word processing program or utility to count the number of characters in the publication.

7. Divide that number by the number of characters per final column or page to estimate the number of columns or pages that will be filled.

Using a Formula

A third method of fitting copy is to take a 100-character paragraph of text and set it in the exact width used throughout the publication. Set copies of the same paragraph in different sizes or with different leadings and measure the depth of each variation. You can estimate roughly the total number of column inches for the publication by using the following formula:

Total number of column inches for the publication =

Column inches required per 100 characters $\times$

$$\frac{(\text{Total number of characters in text files})}{100}$$

None of these copy-casting techniques absolutely guarantees that copy will fit the space allowed. You, therefore, still need to do final copy fitting directly in PageMaker by adjusting one or more of the following variables: column width, leading, hyphenation zone, and word and letter spacing (for justified text).

Adjusting the Column Width

If you are accustomed to traditional typesetting techniques, you probably have specified text in terms of the width of each column. PageMaker, however, defines a page in terms of the number of columns and the space between columns. Because you cannot enter the column widths directly, you should establish your design specifications in terms of the number of columns and the space between them rather than the width of the text column.

T I P   Determining the Best Text Width

Following is one rule of thumb for determining the best width of text: The best line width (column width) is equivalent to 60 characters of the specified typeface, size, and style. Columns that are too narrow (much shorter than 60 characters in line length) have awkward line breaks and hyphenation. Lines that are too long are hard for the reader to follow.

You should determine the final column width before you create a new publication, and stick with that column width throughout the production. You cannot automatically change all column widths throughout a PageMaker publication after the text has been placed on the pages. To change existing text, you have to adjust the width of each text block manually, or export the text and then import it onto new pages that have the changed column specifications.

Adjusting the Leading

After the design specifications are established, the most common and preferred method of fitting copy is to change the leading rather than the specifications for typeface, size, or style.

Whether you use PageMaker's automatic leading feature or specify the exact leading yourself, you always can make fine adjustments in the leading to fit copy into a defined space. Figure 16.18 provides examples. You can specify leading in half-point increments in the Type Specifications dialog box (displayed when you select the Type Specs command on the Type menu). To make copy fit, you can change the leading for the entire publication, for selected text elements, for style tags, or for selected pages. Leading is described in detail in Chapter 8.

When you adjust leading, be consistent. Change the leading on all the body copy rather than on individual paragraphs. If you cannot change or do not want to change the leading for an entire article or publication, change the leading for whole pages and keep it the same across columns on a single page.

This paragraph is exactly 100 characters long. This paragraph is exactly 100 characters long.

This paragraph is exactly 100 characters long. This paragraph is exactly 100 characters long.

This paragraph is exactly 100 characters long. This paragraph is exactly 100 characters long.

This paragraph is exactly 100 characters long. This paragraph is exactly 100 characters long.

10/10 Times

10/11 Times

10/auto Times

10/14 Times

Fig. 16.18

10-point Times with different leading specifications.

Using Hyphenation and Justification

PageMaker hyphenates text automatically, unless you use the Hyphenation command on the Type menu to turn hyphenation off for selected publications or individual paragraphs (see Chapter 8). Hyphenated text takes up less space than unhyphenated text.

You also can change the amount of space the text requires by changing the alignment: Justified text tends to take up less space than unjustified text, because the justification process can reduce the space between words and between characters within words; unjustified text has standard spacing between words and letters.

Besides using the hyphenation and justification settings to fit copy to a page, you can achieve unusual effects by changing the hyphenation zone on unjustified text. Make this adjustment with the Spacing command and dialog box. You can use a large hyphenation zone to exaggerate the ragged right margin or to minimize hyphenation without turning it off entirely. (See Chapter 8 for more information on the hyphenation zone.)

Justified text usually calls for hyphenation, especially when the columns are narrow. Unhyphenated justified text tends to have more *rivers*—wide areas of blank space running down through several lines of type, caused by forced spacing between words.

Controlling Word and Letter Spacing

Unless you have some special effects in mind, you should keep PageMaker's defaults for word and letter spacing and tracking. Most publishers are likely to accept PageMaker's defaults for these settings. Changing word and letter spacing should be the last resort in copy fitting. You may, however, want to change these settings as a deliberate design strategy for special publications, such as advertisements and brochures.

You can help fit justified text into a specific space by adjusting the spacing between words and letters. With the Spacing option in the Paragraph Specifications dialog box (displayed when you select the Paragraph command on the Type menu), you can specify the acceptable size ranges for the spaces inserted between words and letters during the justification process. These ranges are given as percentages of "normal" space for the font.

If you think that you can improve your publication's appearance by reducing the spacing between words, you should first consider the tradeoffs. With a wide allowance for spacing between words and letters, justified text may be flooded with wide rivers of blank space, but fewer words are hyphenated. Justified text with a narrow spacing allowance is likely to be highly hyphenated.

Changing the Track setting in the Type Specifications dialog box (displayed when you select the Type Specs command on the Type menu) also adjusts the amount of space required by text. This technique can be used to expand or condense all the text (in a newsletter, for example), but it is most useful in condensing selected lines (such as headings) just enough to pull up short widow lines. Note that if you plan to kern the space between characters manually—in a headline, for example—you should always set the tracking value first, then kern the letters.

Chapter 8 describes leading, and how to turn hyphenation on or off and how to adjust the hyphenation zone.

Summary

This chapter provided information about fonts and copy fitting to help you design your publications for PageMaker. You have weighed some of the considerations involved in choosing fonts for a publication and in working with built-in, cartridge, and downloadable fonts. You also have learned how to fit copy into a defined space and how to estimate the amount of space required before you place the text on the page in PageMaker.

In Chapters 2 through 16, you learn all the steps needed to produce a PageMaker publication. The next part of this book provides examples of more than 30 publications that were produced by using PageMaker. You can find notes about how the principles given in Chapters 2 through 16 were applied in each publication.

Examples of Publications Created Using PageMaker

Part V presents case studies of publications created with PageMaker. These documents illustrate specific applications of the procedures and principles covered throughout the book, and demonstrate the wide range of designs possible with PageMaker. You can develop your own designs with the help of the sample pages, sample templates, and Page Setup dialog boxes provided with many of the examples. Whether you need to create a business report or a brochure, the examples in Part V help get you started.

Creating Business Reports, Books, and Manuals

I n this chapter, you learn some specific design and production ideas that apply to reports, manuals, and books. Whether you are producing a 300-page textbook, a 30-page business proposal, or a 10-page list of illustrated steps for a procedures manual, these publications share many characteristics (see fig. 17.1). These publications are usually longer than documents like the newsletters, handouts, fliers, and other types presented in the following chapters. The full publication often is composed of several PageMaker files, so these types of documents are good candidates for template systems and the Book and Link features of PageMaker. Even if your document has fewer than 999 pages (the maximum allowed in PageMaker), dividing the material into several files still makes good sense in many cases. In this chapter, you will find tips on when and why to divide a document into several files.

V — EXAMPLES OF PUBLICATIONS CREATED USING PAGEMAKER

Example 17.1

Example 17.2

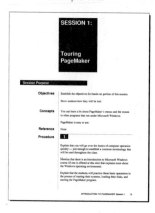

Example 17.3

Example 17.4

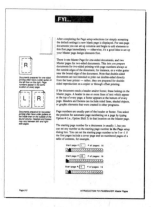

Example 17.5

Fig. 17.1

Examples of the publications in this chapter.

Another common characteristic among publications is size. Most business reports and many manuals are published in 8 1/2-by-11-inch format. Books frequently have smaller dimensions, and this chapter shows you how to prepare a document for smaller finished-page sizes.

The publications in this category have similar formats. These documents usually have a one-column format, although some have a second column for headings, captions, and figures. Traditionally, most business reports are single-sided documents, whereas manuals and books are usually double-sided documents. In this chapter, you learn how and when to use PageMaker's single-sided, double-sided, and facing-pages options.

This chapter focuses on the specific design and production ideas that apply to the types of documents just described. You can apply the same design principles and production tips to any publication in this general category: long publications composed of several sections or chapters. This chapter applies the general design principles and production tips to several examples.

Design Principles

The design principles developed by book designers can be applied to business reports and manuals. For example, because reports and manuals are longer publications, the use of white space and running headers makes the documents more attractive and easier to use. The design principles presented in the following examples range from tips for creating the design, to page layout, to choice of typefaces. By applying these principles, you can produce publications with a professional appearance; they are uncluttered and unified in design.

Many of these principles apply to all types of publications, not just those in this chapter. These principles' applications to reports, books, and manuals are described generally in this section, and then the same principles are repeated and applied specifically to the appropriate examples.

Don't be afraid of white space.

White space is any area of a page that doesn't contain text or graphics. The principle of allowing white space in the basic design applies to any document but is worth special mention in this chapter, because this principle hasn't been applied to many publications of the types presented. Traditionally, business reports have been produced with the same margin settings as those used for letters, memos, minutes, and agendas rather than designed specifically to allow white space on the pages. Books usually have minimal white space, leaving only enough room at the edges for the reader's thumbs to hold the book open without covering the text.

Perhaps in the interest of cutting printing costs, contemporary books tend to have smaller margins (less white space) than the classic proportions shown in figure 17.2. More white space in the design usually means more pages. Depending on the content of the book and how it will be used, however, you can increase the apparent white space without increasing the total number of pages by using a smaller size type, a different typeface, or tighter leading. Figure 17.3 shows the relative amount of space required if you lay out the same text in different grids and fonts.

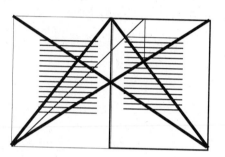

Fig. 17.2

Determining the classic proportions for book design.

The same amount of copy can look very different in different grids and fonts. The same amount of copy can look very different in different grids and fonts. The same amount of copy can look very different in different grids and fonts.

Small font,
flush left

The same amount of copy can look very different in different grids and fonts. The same amount of copy can look very different in different grids and fonts. The same amount of copy can look very different in different grids and fonts.

Same font,
justified

The same amount of copy can look very different in different grids and fonts. The same amount of copy can look very different in different grids and fonts. The same amount of copy can look very different in different grids and fonts.

Wider column

Fig. 17.3

The same amount of copy in different grids and fonts.

The same amount of copy can look very different in different grids and fonts. The same amount of copy can look very different in different grids and fonts. The same amount of copy can look very different in different grids and fonts.

Two points larger

The same amount of copy can look very different in different grids and fonts. The same amount of copy can look very different in different grids and fonts. The same amount of copy can look very different in different grids and fonts.

Change typeface

The same amount of copy can look very different in different grids and fonts. The same amount of copy can look very different in different grids and fonts. The same amount of copy

can look very different in different grids and fonts.

Large body copy,
small captions

Use a grid system.

The traditions of book design and production are older than any of the other principles discussed in this book. Gutenberg's Bible, for instance, shows traces of the grid system he used to lay out his pages. A few decades later a book named *De Divina Proportione*, written by Fra Luca Pacioli and illustrated by Leonardo da Vinci, applied the rules of classic proportion to book design. Contemporary designers still study this master work and apply the same principles in new book designs. Later, Renaissance designers used basic geometry and rules of proportion to design books (as well as buildings, rooms, and paintings). One classic method of defining the margins of a book is shown in figure 17.2. As you can see, the facing pages are crossed with a pattern of straight lines to determine the margins.

Many methods of deriving grids are based on classic proportions. You also can develop the grids for your publications by imitating similar documents that you admire. Whichever method you choose, the underlying grid for your publication merits some forethought. Chapter 15 and the examples in this chapter show how PageMaker's master-page feature enables you to lay out a grid system for a publication.

Use only one or two different typefaces in a document.

As explained in Chapter 15 and Chapter 16, the type-specification process involves listing each different element of the document that requires type specifications. For reports, books, and manuals, the list may include the following:

Body copy

Running headers

Running footers

Chapter or section titles

One or more subhead levels

Figure captions

Figure labels

Table headings

Table data

Each element may be subdivided into several other elements that require more type specifications. In the running footers, for example, you may want the page number in boldface type and the section name in italic. A common tendency is to use a different font for each element, a good idea within limits. The majority of book designers, however, follow the guiding principle of simplicity in design. If you study other published works, you see that most books use only one or two different typefaces, with variations in size and style used sparingly.

Apart from the design principle of simplicity, one reason for having few type changes in a PageMaker publication is that some laser printers are limited to 8 fonts per page or per publication. Some of the examples in later chapters show how as many as 14 different elements can be distinguished by 8 or fewer fonts.

On the other hand, most current published works use a greater variety of fonts than the traditional business report, which may feature one size of plain Courier and Courier boldface. When you switch your business reports from a letter-quality printer to a laser printer, the wide selection of fonts may seem confusing at first. The best approach in designing your first reports is to imitate the type specifications used in professionally designed documents that are similar to yours, such as the examples shown in this chapter. After you become familiar with the underlying design principles, you can easily design your own long documents.

Table 17.1 lists some of the typefaces commonly used in these types of documents. You can see that the more decorative typefaces such as Zapf Chancery are not recommended for the publications in this chapter and that the list of typefaces commonly used for books and manuals is much more limited than the list for business reports.

Table 17.1 Typefaces Commonly Used in Reports, Books, and Manuals

Typeface	Reports	Books	Manuals
Arial**	Y	Y	Y
ITC American Typewriter	Y	N	N
ITC Avant Garde*	Y	N	Y
ITC Benguiat	Y	N	N
ITC Bookman*	Y	N	Y
Courier* or Courier New**	N	N	N
ITC Friz Quadrata	Y	N	Y
ITC Galliard	Y	Y	Y
ITC Garamond	Y	Y	Y
Glypha	N	N	Y
Goudy Old Style	Y	Y	Y
Helvetica*	Y	Y	Y
ITC Korinna	Y	N	Y

Typeface	Reports	Books	Manuals
ITC Lubalin Graph	Y	Y	Y
ITC Machine	N	N	N
ITC New Baskerville	Y	Y	N
New Century Schoolbook*	Y	Y	Y
Optima	Y	Y	Y
Palatino*	Y	Y	Y
ITC Souvenir	Y	Y	Y
Times* or Times New Roman**	Y	Y	Y
Trump Mediaeval	Y	Y	Y
ITC Zapf Chancery*	N	N	N

(Y = used, N = not used, * = Standard LaserWriter font, ** = TrueType font packaged with Windows 3.1)

Use all capitals (uppercase text) as a deliberate design strategy rather than as a method for emphasizing text or indicating a heading.

If you use a letter-quality printer, you probably use uppercase type to add emphasis or to distinguish headings. Uppercase letters still can be part of your deliberate design strategy when other size or style variations aren't possible. Don't use uppercase letters, however, just because the author used uppercase letters in the rough copy. Long headings can be difficult to read when the text is all uppercase. Consider changing all-uppercase headings to upper- and lowercase letters and setting them in boldface or italic.

Only one example in this chapter uses uppercase text as a deliberate design strategy. In Example 17.4 (a manual that uses one template to switch between two grids), the most common header is "FYI" (to indicate "For Your Information"). All the other headers are short phrases ("OVERVIEW," "TRY IT," "NOTES," and "SUMMARY"); they are set in all capitals to carry the same weight visually as the FYI headers.

Use running headers and running footers to help readers find topics.

This principle is applicable to any long document—including magazines—but the rule is a mandate in reference books and manuals. Besides the page number, you should include the section or chapter name in the running headers or running footers. Place the names near the outer edges of the pages for easy reference. This principle is applied in all but one of the examples in this chapter.

Treat all figures consistently in the fonts, line weights, and fill patterns you use.

In the past, business-report figures came from a single source: one spreadsheet program on a letter-quality printer, or a team of one illustrator and one typesetter. Consistency becomes a more important issue when you start using PageMaker to assemble graphics from many different sources, such as a spreadsheet program, a drawing program, and PageMaker's built-in graphics tools. Some figures may be used full-sized in the final document, but others may need reducing or enlarging in PageMaker. To keep line weights consistent throughout the publication, you may want to use heavier lines in the drawing program if the figure will be scaled smaller in PageMaker, or use lighter lines if the figure will be scaled larger. If possible, choose fill patterns that are common to all the graphics programs you will use.

Be sure that your final figures have consistent type specifications. You can standardize captions by making them a part of the word processing text files instead of the graphics files. You can set up a style tag for the captions in your word processor if you use a style sheet. For labels within your figures, you may need to establish standards for the fonts to be used in your drawing program. For example, if your report includes many graphs and your spreadsheet program has fewer available fonts than PageMaker, you may want to match the fonts in all your images to the spreadsheet graphics. This principle is included here even though its application is not demonstrated by the examples selected for this chapter. For specific applications, see the examples in Chapter 19.

Be sure that the space between text and graphics is the same for all figures, and the space between adjacent text blocks is uniform.

You should know and declare your ideal standards for positioning graphics and text and for positioning adjacent text blocks. Your specification may be as simple as "roughly center the graphic between the adjacent text blocks," but even this simple guideline is worth stating explicitly. Don't assume that graphics will fall naturally into place. For graphics, use the Text Wrap command to create standoff between text and graphics. (See Chapter 11 for information on wrapping text around graphics.) To position graphics between text blocks that aren't wrapped around the graphic—such as two separate stories—or to position two text blocks relative to each other, you can use the technique described next.

Creating Spacing Guides on the Pasteboard

As an alternative to using text wrap and type specifications to control the spacing between figures and text, or between text blocks (such as between articles in a newsletter), you can help the production process by setting up text blocks as spacing guides and storing them on the pasteboard of the template.

Use PageMaker's Text tool and Type Specs command to create a text block with handles that are separated by the distance called for in the specifications. For example, type the words **Space between articles** and set the text in a point size that makes the vertical distance between the text block's handles a measure of the distance you want between articles. You need to type and format a separate text block for each spacing specification (see fig. 17.4).

When you need to check the spacing between two objects on the page, use the Copy and Paste commands to copy the spacing guide from the pasteboard to the page. You then can use the spacing guide to position the objects, as shown in figure 17.5. When the two objects are aligned correctly, delete the duplicate guide on the page.

This type of spacing guide is applied in Examples 17.4 and 17.5.

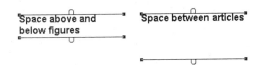

Space above and below figures

Space between articles

Fig. 17.4

Use a spacing guide to position graphics and text.

Be sure that text on each page meets the bottom margin.

Book designers traditionally have followed the principle that the text on every page should end at exactly the same point. This goal is easy to accomplish for books that are primarily body copy without graphics or subheadings, such as the traditional Victorian novel. The principle becomes increasingly difficult to apply the more your document incorporates complicating factors, such as the following:

Subheadings within each chapter or section

Figures

Footnotes

Tables that cannot be broken across pages

Limitations for widows and orphans

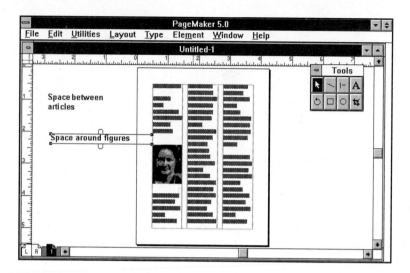

Fig. 17.5

Copying the spacing guide to the page to align separate text blocks.

You can alter the leading (line spacing) around subheadings and the space around figures to make small adjustments in the length of the text on a page. In many documents, however, you will find that ending all pages at the same point is impossible. Alignment can be especially tricky if you follow the common conventions regarding widows and orphans. These terms are used to describe the situation in which one line of a paragraph is separated from the rest of the paragraph by a page break or a column break (see "Controlling Breaks" in Chapter 8 and "Copy Fitting" in Chapter 16).

In some documents, you may plan ragged bottom margins as a deliberate design strategy. In general, however, let PageMaker's bottom margin define the maximum length of the text. As shown in the following examples, PageMaker's bottom margin isn't always the same as the limits of text on the page layout. In these examples, the running headers and footers always fall outside the page margins that are defined in the Page Setup dialog box.

Let the same graphic elements carry the theme throughout the document.

As explained in Chapter 15, PageMaker's master pages can include graphic elements that appear on every page, such as shaded boxes and ruled lines. You also can use graphics to set off headings in the text and to highlight important points. You can see how common graphic elements (black boxes, ruled lines) are applied in Examples 17.2 and 17.4. In many published books, the cover design has no relation to the inside page layouts; but a common graphic theme is often used on the cover and the inside pages of business reports, catalogs, directories, annual reports, and other documents. This technique is applied in Example 17.1.

For Related Information

◄◄ "Wrapping Text around Graphics," p. 443.

◄◄ "Creating a Grid System," p. 683.

◄◄ "Typography," p. 699.

◄◄ "Fitting Copy," p. 722.

FROM HERE...

Production Tips

The production tips in this chapter can be applied to any long document composed of several sections or chapters. The tips help you produce your publications more quickly and efficiently than you might be able to without following these suggestions. The tips range from creating separate templates for different sections to preparing text in a word processor before you start PageMaker.

Many of these tips apply to other types of publications, such as the magazines and newsletters described in Chapter 18 and the brochures described in Chapter 20. The application to reports, books, and manuals is described generally in this section; then, with the examples, the same tips are repeated along with explanations of their specific application to that example.

Make each section or chapter a separate PageMaker publication.

Several good reasons exist for breaking a long document into smaller parts and saving each as a separate file, even if your document has fewer than 999 pages (PageMaker's limit for one file):

■ Small files are faster to save and to print.

■ You must make separate files of any sections requiring a different page orientation because you cannot mix tall and wide pages in one publication file. An appendix with tables of figures may require a wide format, for example, but the rest of the document appears in tall format.

■ You may want to start with a different master-page grid for different sections of the book (see the following tip).

■ When the document is divided into several PageMaker publication files, you can set different running headers or footers for each section, making an easy reference for readers.

■ If your document is long or includes many graphics, you may need to break the document into sections to keep file sizes small enough to fit a backup on one floppy disk.

■ If different sections of the document will be completed at different times but not necessarily in sequence, you can begin each new section when it is ready. This way, you can have different sections of the publication in different stages of the production process at the same time.

■ You can divide the PageMaker production tasks among several people on the production team.

■ If a file is damaged, you lose only part of the work you have done. The production practice of dividing a document into parts is especially pertinent to the long publications in this chapter and is more rarely applied to the shorter publications described in Chapters 18 through 21.

■ PageMaker enables you to link related PageMaker publications through the Book command.

Build a master template for all sections.

If the final document will be composed of several files, build a master-template file from which all the other files are cloned. Chapter 15 offers suggestions for building template systems. You can see how those ideas are applied in each template used in the examples in this chapter.

If you expect to update sections of the document periodically without reprinting the entire book, create each section as a separate publication, include section numbers in the page-numbering system, and start each section with page 1.

This useful production trick may conflict with design ideas and the offset printer's preferences, but using section numbers as part of the page numbering system (1-1, 1-2, 1-3,...2-1, 2-2, A-1, A-2, A-3, and so on) is the best way to handle frequently changed *living* reference documents, such as procedures manuals. Within one section you can number all pages sequentially by using a compound page number that includes a fixed section number and a changing suffix (23.1, 23.2, 23.3). You enter the prefix in the Page Setup dialog box if you want it to appear in the Table of Contents and Index generated by PageMaker, and on the master pages if you want it to print on each page.

This practice is a production convenience that should be applied only to manuals that are updated frequently. Otherwise, the best practice is to number consecutively all pages in a document. You can specify the starting page number for each section in the Page Setup dialog box. None of the examples in this chapter use compound page numbers.

For longer documents, set up a style sheet and format the text by typing the tags in the word processing program.

Consistency in formatting is an important key to good design. Style sheets are especially helpful in ensuring consistency from one document to another, because you can use the same style sheet for different publications. After a style sheet has been set up for a newsletter, for example, you can use the same style sheet for all subsequent issues simply by loading that style sheet into each new issue's file; you need not re-create the style sheet for each document. This technique ensures consistency between chapters of a book or any series of documents that share the same design.

Prepare all character and paragraph formatting in Story view rather than Layout view.

Ideally, to simplify PageMaker production, you perform all editing and formatting in the Story Editor. This method is faster than working in Layout view, and fast formatting is especially appropriate for long documents that consist primarily of text. Besides the type specifications, formatting can include using hanging indents to create flush-left headers over indented copy—a format that is often misinterpreted or poorly designed as a two-column format (see fig. 17.6). A hanging indent is a format in which the first line of the paragraph is set flush left and all subsequent lines are indented.

To create the format shown in the top of figure 17.6, set up a hanging indent with a tab set at the indentation point; then enter a tab at the beginning of each paragraph to indent it. Subsequent lines of the paragraph are indented automatically as the text wraps.

Testing Your Specifications in PageMaker

T I P

Before going too far into the production of a long document, test your specifications and plans by placing text formatted in the word processor into PageMaker so that you can see what formatting elements are preserved. This procedure saves you from spending extra time formatting in the word processor, only to discover that most of the formatting is lost in PageMaker. (When you tag text for your style sheet in your word processor, you can choose Retain Format under the Place command to force the text to retain much of its formatting.) If the authors use more than one word processor, test each program's text before completing your strategy for formatting text.

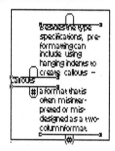

Format callouts using hanging indents when you DO want the callouts to flow with the rest of the text.

Break text into unlinked blocks when you do NOT want the callouts (or figure captions) to flow with the rest of the text.

Fig. 17.6

Preformatting that includes hanging indents.

Globally Changing Strikethru and Underline

If you use the convention of using underscores to indicate added or changed text and strikethru to indicate deleted text during review cycles, you can use PageMaker's Change command to globally strip out all underscores and delete all strikethru text to prepare the final copy.

To convert all underscores to normal text, choose Change from the Utilities menu in Story view. In the Change dialog box, click the Attributes button. Under Find in the Attributes dialog box, select the Underline type style, and under Change select Normal type style. Click OK; then click Change All. This process converts all underlined text to normal.

To delete all strikethru text, type ^? in the Find What area in the Change dialog box; then click the Attributes button. Under Find in the Attributes dialog box, select the Strikethru type style, and under Change select Any type style. Click OK; then click Change All. This process deletes all strikethru text.

For Related Information

◄◄ "Creating a Grid System," p. 683.

FROM HERE...

Examples

The examples in this chapter have been selected to demonstrate a variety of formats and to illustrate various applications of the design principles and production tips that are described in the preceding sections. As noted in those sections, not all the principles and tips that apply to books can be demonstrated in these few examples, but the design principles that are not specifically applied in these examples are illustrated in some of the examples in the chapters that follow. The following lists the five examples presented in this chapter:

- *Example 17.1.* A One-Column Format with Graphic Section Openings

- *Example 17.2.* A One-Column Format with Flush-Left Headers

- *Example 17.3.* A Two-Column Tabular Format with Small Type

- *Example 17.4.* One Template Used To Switch between Two Grids

- *Example 17.5.* Section Cover Pages

Example 17.1. A One-Column Format with Graphic Section Openings

The report used in this example is designed to accommodate relatively simple text formatting in a one-column grid that maximizes white space by using wide margins. The text also is more readable because of the narrow column that results from the wide margin settings. This same design can be applied to any business report; the generous running headers (16-point Times with a graphic background) make this design especially applicable to relatively short reports that are composed of many short sections.

This design probably isn't good for a reference manual or training guide, however, without considerable expansion of the type specifications table to accommodate a wider variety of subheads and other visual aids. Books and long reports probably wouldn't use running headers as large as the ones in this report, but a similar design could be used on chapter or section opening pages, with a narrower top margin on subsequent pages.

Description

This limited-distribution report is reproduced in 8 1/2-by-11-inch format with a tall orientation. The grid and graphic elements on the inside pages of this report are designed to carry out a theme that originates with the report cover's design (see fig. 17.7). The final document—one in a series of documents that will be published over time—contains fewer than 999 pages and is stored as one publication file. The text is made up of one source file for each section, a mailing list of names and addresses, and a text file of captions for full-page figures. The figures, not shown here, are reprints of articles from other sources and are pasted in manually.

Fig. 17.7

Final printout with a cover-page design that sets the page theme throughout the document.

> **CAUTION: Always Obtain Written Permission To Reprint.** When you include information or excerpts from other published works, as in Example 17.1, be sure to obtain written permission from the original publisher. Also, cite in your document the origin of the material.

Design Principles

All the design principles described at the beginning of this chapter are present in this report. The two principles that are especially well illustrated by this example are repeated and described here.

Don't be afraid of white space. In this report, the left and right margins are more than 2 inches each, and the top margin is 3.5 inches. The running headers and running footers extend beyond these margins to give each page the feel of a full-page grid with a great deal of white space. The relatively short length of each line of text makes the copy easy to read.

Let the same graphic elements carry the theme throughout the document. A gray rectangle crossed with white (reverse) lines is used on the cover, and a smaller gray box with white lines is repeated in the top right corner of every page as a background for the running headers.

Production Tips

In final form, this document is double-sided. Because the margins, headers, and footers are identical on every page of the report, it requires only one master page; the publication is set up in PageMaker as a one-sided document.

Although the final number of pages was not known in advance, the plan was not to exceed 32 pages. An initial setup of 32 pages was specified in the Page Setup dialog box on the template to save repeated use of the Insert Pages command.

The wide margins define the limits of the text placed from word processing files. Figure 17.8 shows how these specifications are set up in the Page Setup dialog box.

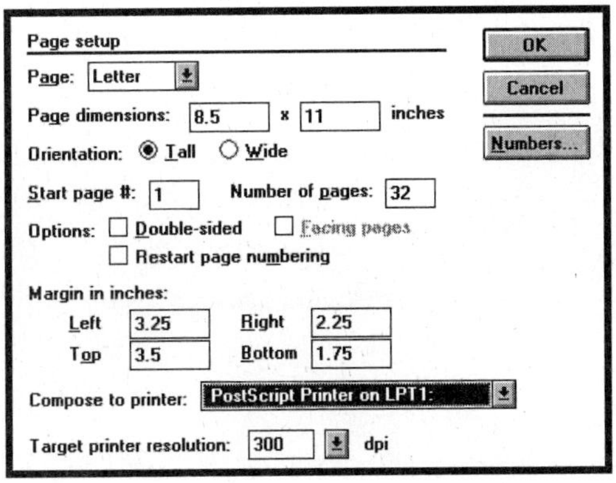

Fig. 17.8

Page Setup dialog box for one-column format with graphics.

The Template

The master page of the template includes the graphic that appears in the upper right corner of every page (see fig. 17.9). The normal default for type specifications—flush left, 12-point Times—holds for this publication. A style sheet also is set up for the document. The body copy tag uses the same default type setting. The first line of a body copy paragraph is indented 0.25 inch as set up in the Paragraph command. By using the style tag, you don't have to press the Tab key for each paragraph. Because the author originally had inserted a blank line between paragraphs, the designer decided to let this convention stand, rather than use the Paragraph command to set the space between paragraphs. Figure 17.10 shows that only four different style tags are used throughout this publication: titles, headings, bylines, and body copy.

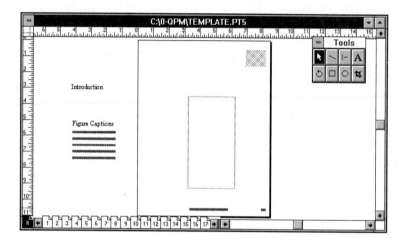

Fig. 17.9

The template with the graphic used in the upper right corner of every page.

Fig. 17.10

Type specifications table for one-column format with graphics.

Style name	Type specifications
Chapter Titles	16-point Times Bold Italic, Flush right (all other elements will be flush left)
Level 1 Headings	18-point Times Bold
Bylines	12-point Times Italic
Body copy	12-point Times, first-line indent of .25 inches, extra carriage return between paragraphs
	Auto leading used throughout

Production Steps

Use the following steps to produce this publication after the master template is set up as shown in figures 17.8 and 17.9.

1. Type and format text files in the word processing program. Type the appropriate tag for each paragraph while you are in the word processing program. Double-space between paragraphs. Store the files in the subdirectory for this report (see Chapter 6).

2. Open the PageMaker template document for this series of reports and modify the master pages and cover page to reflect the new report name. Save the modified template under the new report name (for more information, see Chapter 4).

3. Working in Fit in Window view, place text with the Autoflow command in the Layout menu (see "Typing and Bringing Text into PageMaker" in Chapter 6).

4. Return to the beginning of the document and, working in 50% Size, correct the format where necessary and open spaces for figures. Cut the flush-right chapter titles from the text block and paste them over the graphic in the upper-right corner of each page. Keep a duplicate of the section title on the pasteboard to use on subsequent pages of the same section. During this step, place the captions on the pasteboard and use the Cut and Paste commands as needed to copy the captions to the pages (see fig. 17.11). See Chapters 5 and 7 for full details about this procedure.

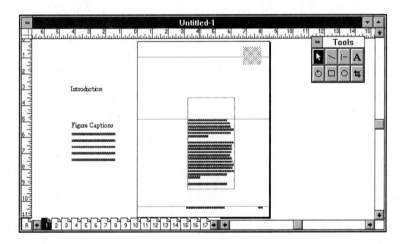

Fig. 17.11

Using the pasteboard to hold section titles and figure captions.

Preparation for Reproduction

All graphics are pasted by hand into page areas reserved for the graphics. All figures are enlarged or reduced photographically to fit the space before pasting. These limited-run reports are reproduced on photocopying equipment at a light setting so that the cut edges of the pasted figures don't show.

The starting point for any new report consists of the two master template files designed for this series: one PageMaker template (TEMPLATE.PT5) and one template for the word processor used to type the text (TEMPLATE.DOC). (The times estimated for each step in the production cycle and the actual times spent on each step can be entered into a text file named CONTROL.DOC for invoicing or project management.) If you have more than one workstation in your production environment, store the template on a floppy disk designated as the authorized source for any new reports. In this way, enhancements made to the template from any station can be saved on the floppy (as well as the hard disk) for use by the entire production staff.

Each time a new report is produced, open the word processing template and type and format the text files that compose the report. Open the master PageMaker template and save it under the new report name, then flow the text into that publication. Figure 17.12 shows the disk-file organization for this report.

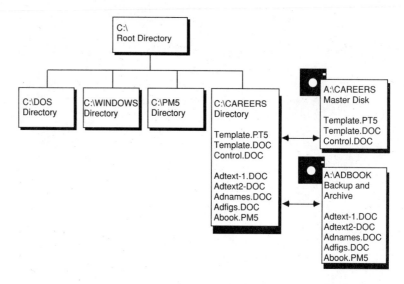

Fig. 17.12

Disk-file organization for one-column format with graphics.

Each report's text files and PageMaker file fit on one floppy disk when the document is complete. This floppy serves as a backup throughout the production cycle, and the same floppy disk becomes the final archived version of the report. If the report is very large or includes many graphics, you can use the Link command to manage the imported graphics as external files, rather than store them as part of the PageMaker publication. If you divide the report into several PageMaker publications and you want to number all pages sequentially or generate an index or table of contents, use the Book command to link the publications.

Example 17.2. A One-Column Format with Flush-Left Headers

Designed for easy reference, this manual consists of sections with many subheads. As in Example 17.1, the text is more readable because of the narrow column. In this case, the narrow right column of text is achieved by using a hanging indent. This same design can be applied to manuals, textbooks, and business reports that use many subheads in the text. This design, however, probably wouldn't be ideal for a publication with few subheads.

The production process could be simplified significantly by changing the design slightly to eliminate the use of reverse type. In this particular case, the black boxes with reverse type are printed in a second color of ink, giving the finished pages a lighter feeling than is produced by the black images shown here. (For more information on printing in color, see Chapter 12.)

Description

This procedures manual identifies subsections with reverse-type headers that appear flush to the left margin. The numbers of the steps in each procedure are printed in boxed reverse type. One text file is created for each procedure. Each new procedure starts on a new right-hand page in this double-sided document. Figure 17.13 shows the final printouts of two pages.

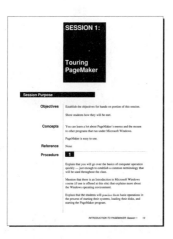

Fig. 17.13

Final printout of pages in one-column format with flush-left headers.

Design Principles

All the design principles described at the beginning of this chapter are present in this report. Four principles that are especially well illustrated by this example are repeated and described here.

Use only one or two different typefaces in a document. This manual uses Helvetica and Times, the two typefaces that are built into the Apple LaserWriter. The full type specifications table is shown in figure 17.14. Only five different fonts are used from these two typefaces. As a result, the final publication looks clean and simple, without distractions from the content.

Style name	Type specifications

Running Header	24-point Helvetica Bold (reverse)
Section Title	14-point Helvetica Bold (reverse) with 50-point leading
Step numbers	18-point Helvetica Bold (reverse)
Subheadings	14-point Helvetica, flush right tab
Body copy	12-point Times

Fig. 17.14

Type specifications table for one-column format with flush-left headers.

Don't be afraid of white space. The white space is achieved by reserving the left third of the page for section headings. Extra space also is allowed below headings and between rules and type for each step.

Use running headers and footers to help readers find topics. The running headers give the session number; the running footers show the page number at the outside margin along with the document title and session number. The use of the session number in both running headers and running footers means that each session is a separate PageMaker publication, so the running headers and footers can be entered on the master pages.

Let the same graphic elements carry the theme throughout the document. The graphic theme used is white type on black boxes. These black boxes are printed in a second color when the document is mass produced, giving the final book an attractive and unified appearance. Working with white type can be a production headache, however, because you can lose type on the page when it is not on a black box. (See the tip "Working with Reverse Type," following the production steps for this example.)

Production Tips

In this case, the text was first formatted in the word processing program, and all body copy is formatted with a hanging indent. All the text in this manual uses the same ruler line; the left margin of the section titles is the same as the left margin in PageMaker (see fig. 17.15). From the margin, the first tab is the flush-right tab set at 2.25 inches from the left margin and used by section subheads. The second tab positions the first line of all body copy at 2.5 inches from the left margin—the position of the hanging indent. A third tab is set up for tabs after bullets in short lists.

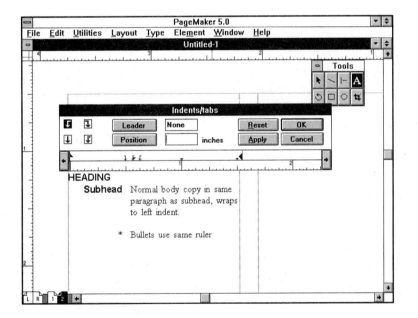

Fig. 17.15

The ruler line used for all text in one-column format with flush-left headers.

The reverse type is set up as normal (black) type in the word processing program because the word processor doesn't support reverse type. The specification is changed to reverse type after the document is placed in PageMaker.

The Template

Figure 17.16 shows the template's margin settings in the Page Setup
dialog box. The master pages of the template for this manual are set up
with one column. The master pages show horizontal and vertical ruler
guides for positioning the running header and footer and vertical rule.
The printed elements on the master page include a vertical rule and the
running headers and footers (see fig. 17.17). The running header appears in reverse type on a black backdrop. The pasteboard holds black
boxes and the ruled lines used throughout the document.

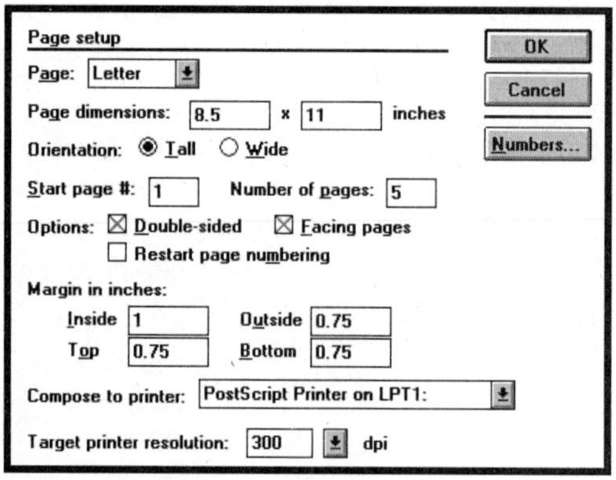

Fig. 17.16

Page Setup
dialog box for
one-column
format with flush-
left headers.

Fig. 17.17

The template,
including
repeated graphic
elements on the
pasteboard and
on the master
pages.

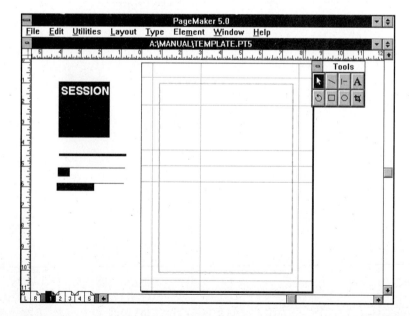

Production Steps

Complete the following steps to produce this publication:

1. Type and format the text files in the word processing program and store them in this manual's subdirectory on the hard disk. Format the text with a hanging indent and the three tab settings shown in figure 17.15.

2. Build one PageMaker template document for this manual, as shown in figures 17.16 and 17.17. Store the template in the manual's subdirectory, and clone the template to continue the manual for each new section when one section fills more than 999 pages, or when one section reaches the maximum number of bytes that will fit on your backup disks.

3. Working in Fit in Window view and using the Autoflow command in the Layout menu, place text on consecutive pages.

4. Return to the beginning of the document and, working with the text tool in Actual Size view, make the necessary formatting corrections.

5. Return to the beginning of the document and work in Actual Size view with the pointer tool selected. At the beginning of this sweep, copy the predesigned black box and ruled line (for step numbers) from the pasteboard of the template (as shown in fig. 17.18) into the Windows Clipboard. Avoid using the Copy and Cut commands for other objects (so as not to replace the Clipboard contents). At each new step number, perform the following tasks:

    ■ Paste the black box and ruled lines from the Clipboard.

    ■ Position the black box over the step number.

    ■ Use the Send to Back command.

    If you opted not to use automatic widow control, available through the Paragraph command, adjust for widows and orphans on each page (by dragging the bottom windowshade handle of the text) before placing the black boxes on subsequent pages.

6. Return to the beginning of the document and scroll through with the text tool selected, while performing the following tasks:

    ■ Select each step number.

    ■ Choose Reverse from the Type menu.

    ■ Check the alignment of the black box.

To move the black box, you need to select the pointer tool. You select the box *under* the text block by clicking the box. If the box doesn't highlight, select the Bring to Front option on the Edit menu. Repeated switching from the pointer to the text tool can be time-consuming, and this factor is one of the inconveniences of working with layered designs. If you select the incorrect text to reverse, highlight the text again, and select Reverse; the text reverts to black type.

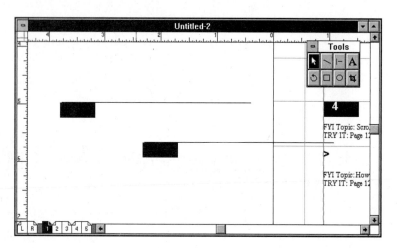

Black boxes
ready to be
pasted into the
Clipboard and
then pasted in
place on the
pages.

This example created reverse type on a black background by backing the reverse type with a graphic element, but you can create reverse type backed by paragraph rules if the text is 20 points or smaller (see Chapter 11 for tips on both methods).

All text and PageMaker files for this document are stored in one subdirectory on the hard disk (see fig. 17.19). If the publication is very large or uses many graphics, you use the Link command from the File menu to manage the graphics as external files, rather than store the graphics as part of the PageMaker publication. If you divide the document into several PageMaker publications and you want to number all pages sequentially or generate an index or table of contents, use the Book command from the File menu to link the publications.

When making backups and archiving the final files, copy all the text files on one floppy disk and all PageMaker files on another floppy disk; the text and publication files together are too large to fit on a single floppy disk.

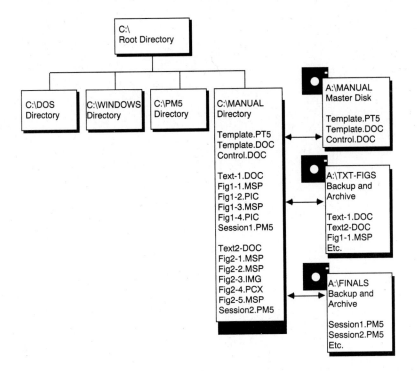

Fig. 17.19

Disk-file organization for one-column format with flush-left headers.

Example 17.3. A Two-Column Tabular Format with Small Type

The questionnaire in this example is designed to fit the greatest number of questions on a page by using narrow margins and a relatively small point size for the body copy (9-point Helvetica). This same design can be applied to many list formats (see Chapter 20). This design wouldn't be good for a book or reference manual without considerable revision of the type specifications to make the text larger. Books and reports would probably not use a different head at the top of each column, as this questionnaire does. This example is presented primarily for its demonstration of working with tabs and small point sizes.

Description

This questionnaire is set up to be exactly 32 pages long, set in 2 columns of 9-point type. All tabs are set in the word processing program, where all the text is prepared. Figure 17.20 shows the final printouts of two pages.

Fig. 17.20

Printout of pages
of questionnaire
in two-column
tabular format.

Design Principles

Many of the design principles described at the beginning of this chapter are applied in this report. For example, although the goal is to put a great deal of material on each page, the use of two columns and varying tabs creates white space. The heads are consistent and set in all capital letters to give emphasis and unify the document. One principle does merit special note.

Text on each page should bottom out to the margin. In this case, the overriding rule is to keep the full set of answer choices with its respective question, rather than break a series of answers across columns or pages. If the two columns are unequal on a page, leading is added above subhead titles, or the longer column is shortened by moving the last question into the next column.

Production Tips

Work in large type through the initial text-editing rounds so that the production staff and proofreaders can read the text easily (see fig. 17.21). Convert to a smaller typeface for the last editing rounds. By using style sheets to tag the text, you have the advantage of changing the typeface in one easy step. Set tags and tabs in the word processing program before starting the page-layout process.

Change the default type specification to 9-point Helvetica by editing the tag. This font is used in the questionnaire (except for the column headings and other exceptions noted). After all the text is placed, adjust the leading to make sure that the text fits the prescribed number of pages.

For first edit rounds:

## Work with larger text	12-point Helvetica.
Before placing in PageMaker, change all text to match the body copy specs:	9-point Helvetica with 10-point leading.
Then sweep through to set:	
## Main headings	12-point Helvetica Bold (centered)
Subheads	10-point Helvetica on 18-point leading

Fig. 17.21

Type specifica-
tions table for
two-column
tabular format.

The Template

The template file includes dummy text to be used for the column headings for each page and horizontal guides to mark the positions of the
column heads. The first page of the template suppresses the master-
page elements and begins with a lower guide for placing text. Figures
12.22 and 12.23 show the Page Setup dialog box and master pages for
the template.

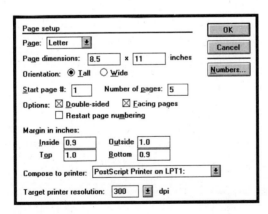

Fig. 17.22

Page Setup
dialog box for
two-column
tabular format.

Production Steps

To create this design, complete the following steps:

1. Prepare text in a word processing file. Work in 12-point type
   through the initial editing rounds. Set tabs far enough apart to
   show columns correctly in the draft printouts from the word
   processing program.

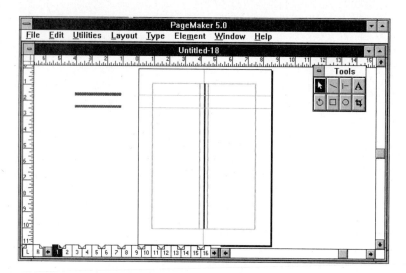

Fig. 17.23

The template for two-column tabular format.

2. Start a new PageMaker publication and set the margins and column guides on the master pages as shown in figures 17.22 and 17.23. Check the definitions you set for the style sheet. Modify the tags if necessary to automatically change the imported text to 9-point type and to change the tabs on the ruler lines.

3. Working in Fit in Window view and using the Autoflow command, place all text on all pages.

4. If the final text doesn't fit in the 32 pages allowed, edit the body copy tag to change the leading to shrink or stretch the text. Be sure to leave enough room at the end of the document to accommodate the adjustments to be made in step 6.

5. If the text still doesn't fit the number of pages allowed, scroll through the file in Actual Size and selectively change the spacing around each heading or between questions.

6. Return to the beginning of the document and scroll down each column in Actual Size view. You must force subheads and orphaned or widowed lines into the preceding or next column.

   Use the Copy and Paste commands for headings at the tops of consecutive columns. Tag the text as headline 1 to set the typeface and space around the head. Copy and Paste the word *continued* from the pasteboard to follow headings that repeat (see fig. 17.24).

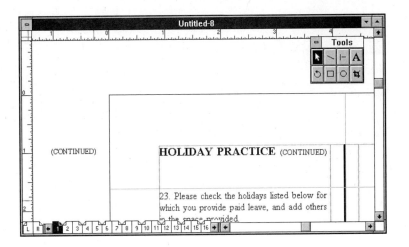

Fig. 17.24

Text for the word *continued* is copied from the pasteboard of the template when needed.

Because this document is composed of one text file (QUESTION.DOC) and one PageMaker file (QUESTION.PM5), both files can be stored in the main directory and backed up on one floppy disk with one command:

```
COPY QUESTION.* a:
```

Example 17.4. One Template Used To Switch between Two Grids

The training manual in this example has a format that alternates between two different page designs: one with a narrow left column and a wide right column, and the other with three columns. These two layouts are used throughout the publication. This design is rather tricky to work with, and it can be a production headache if you don't set up procedures like those described in this section.

You can modify the production tips in this section as appropriate and apply them to any publication that uses two or more page layouts within each file. In this case, the two-column pages usually have few graphics compared to the amount of text. The three-column pages are heavily illustrated with graphics. If these pages were laid out as two-column pages with the graphics in the first column and the text in a wide second column, the final book would be at least 30 percent longer.

Description

The design for this manual calls for page formats that alternate between two and three columns. Because different page formats aren't confined to alternating pages or separate sections, the trick is to devise master pages that can serve both formats. Figure 17.25 shows examples of printed pages from this document.

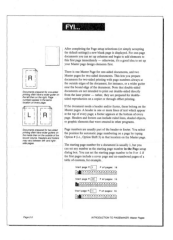
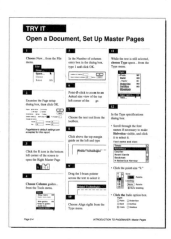

Fig. 17.25

Printout of manual using two grids.

Design Principles

Many of the design principles described at the beginning of this chapter are applied in this training manual. The use and spacing of graphic elements is especially important in this publication, as well as the inclusion of ample white space. Note how the following principles particularly enhance the final publication.

Let the same graphic elements carry the theme throughout the document. The common graphic themes are reverse type on black boxes, hairline rules between columns, and horizontal rules between steps. These elements make finding information easy and allow emphasis of the steps.

Don't be afraid of white space. White space occurs primarily on the two-column page layouts where wide spaces are allowed between paragraphs in order to accommodate figures in the narrow column. On three-column pages, the columns are allowed to be ragged at the bottom margin so that a step isn't broken across columns. This publication deliberately violates the principle that text on each page should bottom out to the margin.

Use running headers and footers to help readers find topics. The running footers on left-hand pages show the session number; the footers on right-hand pages show specific subtopics. This manual is the only example in this chapter that uses uppercase text as a deliberate design strategy. Because the most common header is "FYI" (For Your Information) and all the other headers are short phrases—"TRY IT" (shown), "OVERVIEW," "NOTES," and "SUMMARY," (not shown)—all headers are set in uppercase so that they carry the same visual weight.

Be sure that the space between text and graphics is the same for all figures. Spacing guides are used to position all graphics and captions and to separate one step from the next. Careful spacing gives the page a clean, balanced appearance.

Production Tips

All text is formatted in the word processing file as flush left with no indents. One tab is set at 0.3 inches for bulleted lists and commands. Figure 17.26 shows the six fonts from two typeface families that are used throughout the document.

Style name	Type specifications
Opening headings	24-point Helvetica Bold (reverse)
FYI	14-point Helvetica Bold (reverse)
TRY IT	24-point Helvetica Bold (reverse)
Step numbers	18-point Helvetica Bold (reverse)
Opening paragraphs	12-point Times Bold Italic
Body copy	12-point Times

Fig. 17.26

Type specifications table for manual using two grids.

The Template

The Page Setup margins define the limits of the text for both formats (see fig. 17.27). Vertical rules on the master pages fall outside these limits (see fig. 17.28). Two-column guides on the master pages are customized. The default line style is changed to hairline rule.

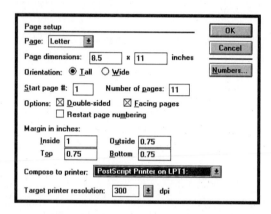

Fig. 17.27

Page Setup dialog box for manual using two grids.

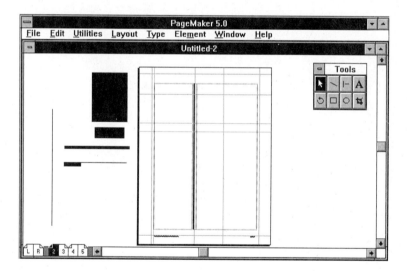

Fig. 17.28

The template for manual using two grids.

Using Thumbnail Printouts for Production Notes   T I P

When the template for the publication is complex, print thumbnails of the template and mark them up with instructions to the production team (see fig. 17.29).

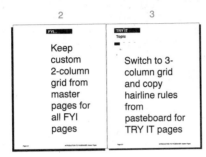

1 2 3 4

Keep custom 2-column grid from master pages for all FYI pages

Switch to 3-column grid and copy hairline rules from pasteboard for TRY IT pages

Use page 4 of template for end of TRY IT that does not fill 3 columns

Fig. 17.29

Thumbnails of the template for manual using two grids.

Production Steps

To create the publication, complete the following steps:

1. Prepare all text files flush left, with one tab for bulleted lists.

2. Set up the template with a customized two-column format on the master pages (see fig. 17.30 for this procedure).

3. As you go through the document, note the following:

   ◼ When you need a page in format 1—two columns—keep the master-page elements.

   ◼ When you need a page in three-column format, use the Column Guides command from the Layout menu to set up three columns, and use the Copy and Paste commands to copy the vertical rule from the pasteboard into the space between columns 2 and 3.

The trick to this alteration is that the column width set up automatically by the Column Guides command is exactly like the first column width of the customized format.

All text files and PageMaker documents for this manual are stored in the same subdirectory (see fig. 17.31). If the publication is very large or uses many graphics, you can use the Link command to manage the graphics as external files, rather than store them as part of the Page-Maker publication. If you divide the report into several PageMaker publications and you want to number all pages sequentially or generate an index or table of contents, use the Book command to link them.

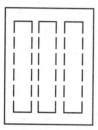 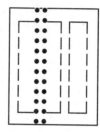 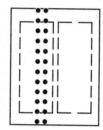

1. Use the Column guides command to set up three columns.

2. Use the Rulers command to display rulers, and move vertical guides to overlap the guides between columns one and two.

3. Use the Column Guides command to select two columns.

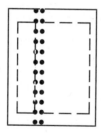 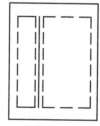 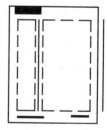

4. Move the middle column guides to match the vertical ruler guides you just created.

5. Draw a vertical hairline between columns one and two.

6. Copy/Paste the hairline and move the copy to the Pasteboard, for duplication throughout the production process. Set up headers and footers.

Fig. 17.30

Setting up the template with a customized two-column format on the master pages.

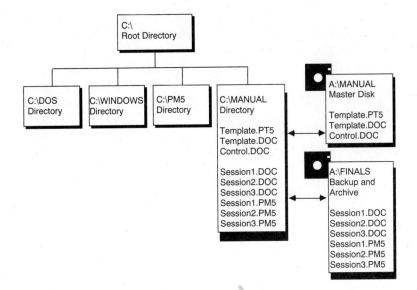

Fig. 17.31

Disk-file organization for manual using two grids.

Example 17.5. Section Cover Pages

The section or chapter cover pages in this example are created as a single-sided publication with a repeated graphic on the master page. Each numbered page of the publication contains only the new section or chapter name. The cover pages are printed without page numbers and inserted between the sections of the final document. This example is provided to show a simple technique for producing a series of cover pages that use the same basic design. You can apply this technique to any publication that uses graphic cover pages for each section.

Description

Each cover page shows the product logo on a gray background. Examples of pages from this publication are shown in figure 17.32. Because these pages contain no text, the design principles aren't applicable.

Production Tips

These cover pages are prepared for printing on 8 1/2-by-11-inch paper, but they are to be part of a document trimmed to 6 by 9 inches. The pages, therefore, can accommodate the bleed from the larger paper and show crop marks as well. If the final pages were to be 8 1/2 by 11 inches, the page size selected in this dialog box would be even larger in order to accommodate the bleed. (As explained in Chapter 15, *bleed* is the term used in offset printing to describe pages on which the inked area runs to the trimmed edges of the final document.)

This document is set up as single-sided because all the pages are right-hand pages, even though the larger document into which they are inserted is double-sided. The margin settings reflect the limits of the text, not the bleed or the trim. The Page Setup dialog box settings used for the template are shown in figure 17.33.

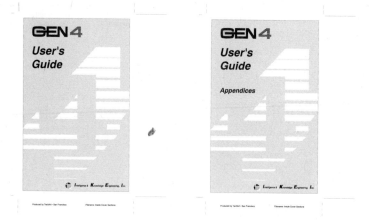

Fig. 17.32

Final printout of section cover pages.

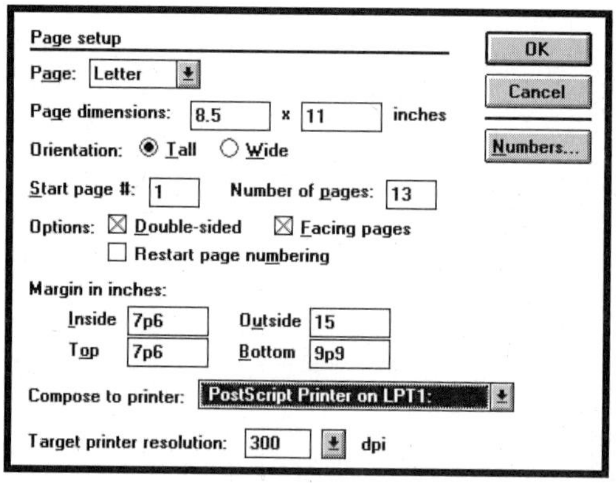

Fig. 17.33

The Page Setup dialog box for section cover pages.

The Template

The master page of the template includes the logo and the gray background, with guides to show the position of the section name (see fig. 17.34). Crop marks on the master page show the printer where to trim the printed covers. The pasteboard includes a skeletal text block that can be moved with the Copy and Paste commands and modified for each section.

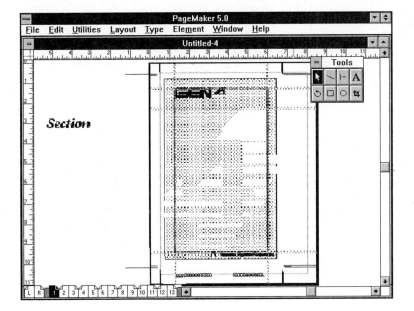

Fig. 17.34

The template for section cover pages.

Production Steps

The design steps are easy, as follows:

1. Set up the background design on the master page of the template and type dummy text on the pasteboard according to the type specifications to be used for all section titles.

2. Go through each cover page, and use the Copy and Paste commands to move the text from the pasteboard to the cover page background. Change the text to reflect the new section names.

Preparation for Reproduction

All the pages call for a bleed at the edges (see fig. 17.35). Usually, this design means that the color must be printed beyond the trim area. The pages with bleeds, therefore, should be delivered to the offset printer as a set separate from the rest of the document. Include a note stating that the pages call for a bleed. Pages like these often are handled separately because larger paper and more cuts are required than for other pages. Page numbers outside the bleed area indicate where each page will be inserted into the finished document.

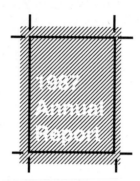

Fig. 17.35

Cover page designed for a bleed at the edges.

FROM HERE...

For Related Information

◄◄ "Saving a Document or Template," p. 165.

◄◄ "Specifying Text Flow," p. 240.

◄◄ "Editing Text in Layout View," p. 279.

◄◄ "Working with Reverse Text," p. 466.

◄◄ "Creating Color Publications," p. 531.

◄◄ "Organizing Your Disk Files," p. 627.

◄◄ "Designing Page Layouts before Entering Content," p. 692.

Summary

This chapter presented general descriptions and specific applications of the design principles and production tips that apply to long documents such as books, manuals, and reports. After studying the examples in this chapter, you should be better equipped to design your own long documents, set up the templates, and implement efficient production procedures. If you are new to PageMaker and long document production, remember to take a small portion of the text through the entire production cycle before you finalize the full cycle of production steps in your project plan.

Finally, try to avoid setting tight production deadlines—or even trying to predict the completion date—for your first large production project with PageMaker.

Creating Newsletters and Similar Publications

Magazines, newsletters, and newspapers have become so much a part of our daily lives that many readers take these publications for granted. Readers expect the design and layout to be inviting and the information precise. Publishers of these documents often create special touches that complicate the production process. These activities include kerning headlines, wrapping text around graphics, and varying page layouts. At the same time, producers of magazines, newsletters, and newspapers face more pressure to meet the deadline than any other publishers. The demand for efficiency in production techniques, therefore, is especially important.

The following four characteristics distinguish these publications from other types:

- The publications use at least two columns—and usually more—in the underlying grid. The number of columns can change from page to page.

- The flow of text for a single article or story can jump from one page to a point several pages later.

- The documents are usually produced as a series. A document of the same basic format and length is produced at regular intervals.

- The documents often call for special layouts that may involve kerning headlines, wrapping text around graphics, or pasting display ads from one PageMaker document into another.

The two newsletters described in this chapter and shown in figure 18.1 demonstrate these characteristics. These two examples represent relatively simple designs—similar to those most users are likely to tackle—rather than unusual, tricky, or otherwise award-winning designs that may present even more challenges in production than these.

Example 18.1
8 ½ x 11 Page

Example 18.2
11 x 17 Page

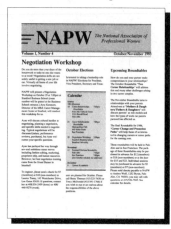

Fig. 18.1

Examples of the documents described in this chapter.

These features and other characteristics shared by newsletters, newspapers, and magazines involve their own special design and production problems and practices. These concerns are explained and illustrated in this chapter. After you understand the underlying principles behind these publications, you can apply the suggestions in this chapter to other types of documents.

PageMaker offers many features that can help you with specific production challenges in producing newsletters and similar publications. You can use PageMaker to plan your designs and therefore save yourself time. After you develop a good design for a newsletter, for example, you can use the master pages for every issue; you do not need to create formats again. PageMaker also eases such typesetting chores as kerning, wrapping text, and using different typefaces.

PageMaker 5.0 adds several Aldus Additions that are especially useful in working with these types of publications: Continuation (for adding continuation page references, described in Chapter 6); Traverse Textblocks, for jumping from one page to another on which the story continues (described under "Traversing Textblocks" in Chapter 7); Find Overset Text (also described under "Finding and Placing Overset Text" in Chapter 7); Drop Cap (described under "Using the Drop Cap Utility" in Chapter 11); and Build Booklet, for creating "signatures" (described under "Building Booklets" in Chapter 13).

Design Principles

The design principles that apply to newsletters are derived from the long traditions of newspaper and magazine publishing. Because newsletters are relatively short, design is particularly important. You must convey information in a limited space and in an uncluttered, attractive format. The principles stressed in this chapter address these needs and range from the number of typefaces and the use of ruled lines in a publication to margin considerations and the provision of ample white space.

Some of these principles apply to all types of publications, not only those discussed in this chapter. This section describes the general application of these principles to newsletters, magazines, and newspapers. Along with each example provided, the general principles are repeated and accompanied by descriptions of their specific application to that example.

Use only one or two different typefaces in a document.

Magazines and newsletters often use many more typefaces than do the business reports, books, and manuals shown in the preceding chapter, particularly if the magazine or newsletter includes display ads. The basic principle of simplicity, however, remains the best guide. Table 18.1 lists some of the typefaces commonly used in magazines and newsletters. In these publications, display ads often contain a wide variety of typefaces, but headlines and body copy use only one or two.

Table 18.1 Typefaces Used in Magazines and Newsletters		
Typefaces	Newsletters	Magazines
Arial**	Y	Y
ITC American Typewriter	Y	N
ITC Avant Garde*	Y	N
ITC Benguiat	Y	Y
ITC Bookman*	Y	Y
Courier* or Courier New**	N	N
ITC Friz Quadrata	Y	Y
ITC Galliard	Y	Y
ITC Garamond	Y	Y
Glypha	Y	Y
Helvetica*	Y	Y
ITC Korinna	Y	N
ITC Lubalin Graph	Y	Y
ITC Machine	N	N
ITC New Baskerville	Y	Y
New Century Schoolbook*	Y	Y
Optima	Y	Y
Palatino*	Y	Y
ITC Souvenir	Y	Y
Times* or Times New Roman**	Y	Y
Trump Mediaeval	Y	Y
ITC Zapf Chancery*	N	N

*(Y = used; N = not used, * = Standard LaserWriter font, ** = TrueType font packaged with Windows 3.1)*

Use variations in the grid to help distinguish different sections of the magazine.

You probably have seen how some newsletters and magazines distinguish sections by giving them different grid structures. Figure 18.2 shows an example of a publication with two different grids. The main feature begins on a facing-page spread. A graphic, the story title, and one column of text fill the left-hand page. The feature continues on the right-hand page, which contains three columns of text. Another variation may be to have letters to the editor occupying three columns and the articles, two columns.

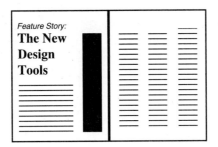

Fig. 18.2

Varying the grid structure to distinguish sections.

Use ruled lines to set off the grid of the pages.

In addition to using nonprinting guides to design your pages, you can use PageMaker's ruled lines to enhance the appearance of the pages. Designers often drop hairline rules, for example, between columns of text. This technique is demonstrated in the second example shown in this chapter: the tabloid newspaper. You also can set ruled lines as part of the paragraph specifications for text (see Chapter 8).

All columns on all pages should bottom out at the same point.

This rule is more strictly applied in magazines and newspapers than in most newsletters or any other type of document described in this book. The problems associated with making each column meet the bottom margin—and with aligning baselines—are compounded if you add subheadings in an article, have strict rules about the spacing around graphics and between paragraphs, and do not allow widows and orphans. You may need to adjust the space around headings and figures to force columns to meet the bottom margin. PageMaker's Align to Grid option, described in Chapter 8, helps automate this process, but you still must review the overall page layouts carefully to make sure that none of your other design specifications are violated in following this rule.

T I P

Using the Balance Columns Addition

PageMaker 5.0 introduces an Aldus Addition called Balance Columns that automates the process of making all the columns on a page or a facing-page spread end at the same point. For example, you place all the text in a three-column newsletter, but the last column on the last page is only half filled. You can make all three columns end at the same point—a few inches above the bottom margin—by first selecting the three columns with the pointer tool, then choosing Balance Columns from the Aldus Addition submenu under the Utilities menu. Click one of the Alignment icons in the Balance Columns dialog box to specify whether you want the columns adjusted from the bottom or the top, and click one of the Add Leftover Lines icons to specify whether the extra line of text (if any) should be added to the first or last column(s). Chapter 6 describes this Addition in more detail.

On the other hand, a ragged bottom margin, as illustrated in figure 18.3, gives you more flexibility in copy fitting. A ragged margin is better than an even margin that stops well above the bottom of the grid. This strategy is used deliberately in Example 18.1 (see figure 18.7 later in the chapter). Other examples in this chapter also illustrate bottom alignment and provide production tips for copy fitting.

Fig. 18.3

Deliberately leaving a bottom margin ragged (left) is usually preferred over ending all columns short of the bottom margin (right).

Don't be afraid of white space.

Applications of this principle vary greatly. Some magazines—*The New Yorker*, for example—fill every column completely with small type. This kind of design can be attractive as well as functional; it fits the greatest number of words into the fewest number of pages. Good designers can make designs such as this work, but if you are just beginning to learn the ins and outs of page layout, you should follow the rule of leaving some white space on the pages. As the examples in this chapter show, white space occurs primarily around article titles and subheads. This practice is common to newsletters and newspapers.

Provide estimates of the number of characters per column for contributors and editors.

Providing character-count estimates is something that most professional editors do as a matter of course when they make an assignment. These estimates help eliminate many problems that arise as you begin to lay out the pages. You must estimate the amount of space allocated for the text of each article, and the type specifications for the article determine the number of words that fit in the space. Chapter 16 describes methods of counting characters and copy casting before placing text in PageMaker.

For Related Information

◀◀ "Adding Rules and Aligning Text to Grid," p. 319.

◀◀ "Fitting Copy," p. 346.

◀◀ "Copy Casting," p. 722.

FROM HERE...

Production Tips

This chapter discusses documents that are laid out in several columns and that use figures of varying widths. The production tips offered are applicable at all stages in creating these kinds of publications—from building the publication to taking the final version to a printer. You learn, for example, when to use a drawing program to create banners and when and where to place a table of contents. You learn how to handle documents containing many illustrations and how to scale figures and pictures to column widths. Other tips tell you how to adjust spacing in multiple-column publications and how to ready your publication for printing. Many tips in this chapter apply to other types of publications, such as the booklets described in Chapter 20. This section describes how these tips apply generally to newsletters, magazines, and newspapers. In the examples, the pertinent tips are repeated, with explanations of their specific applications.

If your laser printer cannot handle large type sizes, use a scanned image or a paint figure for the banner.

If you don't have the printer font for a large display type, you can create a banner by scanning large type created on another system. You also can create the banner by using large type in a paint file. The scanned image provides the best quality on the printout if the image is saved as a high-resolution image. In either case, you probably need to clean up the image pixel-by-pixel to get smooth edges. The results always are of lower quality than if you use type in PageMaker up to 650 points. (For examples of scanned and paint-type graphics, see Chapter 9; for examples of bit-mapped characters, see Chapter 16.)

If your publication includes a list of contents or a similar element that can vary in length, place or type that element before filling the rest of the page.

Instead of placing long articles on the pages first, type or place elements that cannot be jumped to later pages. A list of the publication's contents is only one example of this type of element. You do not need to know the exact page numbers on which articles begin as you first type the table of contents, but you do need to know the number of articles to appear in the issue and the lengths of the titles (to ascertain whether any title needs two lines in the list of contents).

The calendar of events displayed on page 1 in figure 18.7, for example, must be placed before the rest of the page is laid out. Similarly, the list of contents at the top right corner of page 1 in figure 18.12 must be placed before the rest of the page can be completed.

Use a spacing guide to position text and graphics and to adjust the spaces between articles.

Precise spacing is especially important in newsletters and magazines. Set the text's offset specifications in the Text Wrap dialog box to control the distance of text wrapped around graphics. Use the Paragraph Specifications dialog box to specify space between sections within stories. See figure 17.5 in Chapter 17 for an example of using dummy text blocks as spacing guides to adjust the space between adjacent stories and between graphics and adjacent text blocks. Such spacing guides also appear on the pasteboard of the template for Example 18.2 in this chapter (see fig. 18.18, later in this chapter).

Scale pictures and figures to precise column widths.

A picture can span more than one column, but all pictures should conform to the grid lines. A picture can be one column, two columns, or three columns wide in a three-column grid design, for example, but should not be 1.5 columns wide unless your grid is designed to accommodate this variation. Figure 18.20 (later in this chapter), for example, shows the layout for a page of figures that violates this principle, but it works because the entire page is composed of figures; there are no columns of text.

Pages containing several figures look best if the figures are aligned with other pictures or headlines.

Figure 18.4 displays examples of various layouts that follow or violate this guideline. The two pages on the left in the example align one edge of each figure horizontally or vertically with the edge of another figure on the page. The pages on the right do not follow this rule. As a result, the pages on the right lack balance and appear haphazard.

Use black boxes to reserve space for photographs that need halftones dropped in by the printer.

As offset printers prepare plates for pages that require photographic halftones that are not included as part of the PageMaker publication, the printers usually black out the space left for the halftones on the camera-ready mechanicals so that the camera creates a clear *window* in the negative. You can save the printer this extra step by using PageMaker's black boxes to reserve space for halftones. The camera-ready master pages can be printed directly from PageMaker as black images on white paper, or as a negative image on film. The offset printer creates and strips in the negative halftones of the photographs that you supply as prints, negatives, or slides.

You can place a scanned image on the page for draft printings, then use the KeyLiner Addition in PageMaker 5.0 to drop a box around the placed graphic and give the box a solid fill (see "Using the KeyLiner Command" in Chapter 9). You should check with your print shop before you set up pages for halftones to see whether they prefer to receive your pages with black boxes or with the for-position-only scanned images in place.

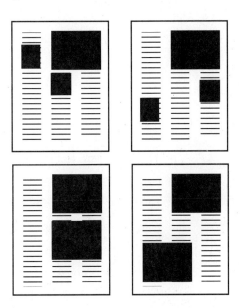

Fig. 18.4

Aligning figures with other figures (left) is preferred to scattering figures randomly on the page (right).

T I P   Talking to Your Printer before Preparing Final Camera-Ready Pages

If you have not used the offset-printing process before, make sure that you ask what form of camera-ready pages your printing service prefers. Ask, too, how the printing charges may change if you do more or less of the preparation yourself.

The offset printer must lay the halftones on transparent windows in the negative (created by black boxes on the camera-ready page), but for line art that you paste up before going to the offset printer, the paste-up artist usually wants to paste figures down on a white background. Figure 18.5 shows how you can type the name or number of the figure in the space reserved for each figure if you plan to paste the figure in. (Almost any illustration can be placed directly in PageMaker, however, so that paste-up is not even necessary, except in special cases.) To draw the white box to size, use PageMaker's Rectangle tool. To type the figure number in the box, use PageMaker's drag-place feature: Select the Text tool, and drag the I-beam inside the figure area to define the text's width before you start typing.

Use a template for all issues.

The template systems for newsletters and magazines may be elaborate compared to those for most other documents. In some of the examples that follow, you see how comprehensive a template can be. Figure 18.18 (later in this chapter) shows a tabloid template that includes 13 different place holders for type specifications, several spacing guides, and three different page layouts. Chapter 15 offers a complete discussion of template systems.

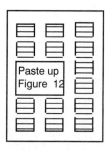

Fig. 18.5

Identifying the figure to be pasted into a white box on the camera-ready copy.

Use a style sheet for all issues.

A style sheet's *tags* enable you to apply the format specifications for a particular paragraph of text. Style sheets give your publication a consistent appearance by ensuring that minor headlines, captions, and other text in the publication are consistent throughout the document.

You can set font specifications and paragraph formats for a document by defining attributes once for each style name, or tag, in the style sheet.

Do all character formatting in advance (by using a word processor) or in Story view in PageMaker.

This suggestion carries extra weight for magazines and newsletters. If you are working under the pressure of a regular deadline, you must use the best tools available for each function. As explained in Chapter 6, working in your word processor or in PageMaker's Story Editor to edit and format text is more efficient than doing so in Layout view in PageMaker. Word processors and the Story Editor are faster because they do not need to perform all the additional screen-imaging functions required for the Layout view display.

Use pull-out quotes to extend copy that falls far short of filling the space allotted.

Pull-out quotes are short sentences excerpted from the text, printed in larger type, and set off from the rest of the page by boxes or lines. Magazines and newsletters frequently use pull-out quotes to fill space and to emphasize points from the article. A pull-out quote usually is set four to six points larger than the body copy (see fig. 18.6).

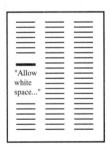

Fig. 18.6

Using a pull-out quote to fill space or emphasize specific text.

You can use a style tag for pull-out quotes, or you can create them manually. To help estimate the number of lines you need, you use formulas based on your type specifications. The following are examples of formulas based on pull-out quotes of 16-point type with 18-point leading and a 0.25-inch margin for a ruled line above the pull-out quote:

Number of Lines in Quote	Number of Inches Added
1	.5
2	.75
3	1.00
4	1.25
5	1.5

Use leading changes to make fine adjustments in copy fitting.

If the final text does not fit into the space allotted, change the leading of the body copy for selected columns, pages, or articles. As mentioned in Chapter 16, leading changes should be made consistently in adjacent columns and on facing pages. The quickest way to make text fit into a specific space is to select an entire article and change the leading globally to shrink or stretch the text. By using style sheets (described in Chapter 8), you can change leading by editing the tags for body text and other tags in the publication. The alternative is to scroll manually through pages and adjust the leading for segments of text. This technique, however, is slower and involves more work in various dialog boxes.

Avoid spanning articles across separate PageMaker publications if you divide a single issue into small pieces.

The 999-page limit enforced by PageMaker is unlikely to present a problem for magazines and newsletters, but you may want to divide a single issue into several PageMaker publications for other reasons. This is especially true if the pages contain many graphics, and you do not want to build a single publication file too large to be backed up on one floppy disk. Dividing a longer publication into separate files also is a good idea if more than one production person is to work on the publication at the same time.

Confine each text file or story to a single PageMaker file, if possible. Otherwise, the text blocks cannot be linked between documents; if the blocks are not linked, problems can arise when the text is edited. An edit that forces text overflow from the last page will not automatically flow the text into the next PageMaker file, for example, but you can add a page at the end of the current chapter and flow the text onto it. Similarly, edits that shorten the text will not automatically pull in text from the next file in the book, so it's a good idea to start any new file with text that should remain at the start of a new page.

See figure 17.5 in Chapter 17 for an illustration of how to use dummy text blocks as spacing guides to adjust the space between adjacent stories and between graphics and adjacent text blocks.

Try using the Aldus Additions that are especially useful in working with these types of publications: Continuation, for adding continuation page references (described under "Adding Continuation Page References" in Chapter 6); Traverse Textblocks, for jumping from one page to another on which the story continues (described under "Traversing Textblocks" in Chapter 7); Find Overset Text (also described under "Finding and Placing Overset Text" in Chapter 7); Drop Cap (described under "Using the Drop Cap Utility " in Chapter 11); and Build Booklet, for creating "signatures" (described under "Building Booklets" in Chapter 13).

For Related Information

◀◀ "Finding and Placing Overset Text," p. 265

◀◀ "Traversing Textblocks," p. 267.

◀◀ "Typing and Editing Text in the Story Editor," p. 280.

◀◀ "Using Style Sheets," p. 334.

◀◀ "Using Graphics Supported by PageMaker," p. 352.

◀◀ "Using the Drop Cap Utility," p. 474.

◀◀ "Building Booklets," p. 579.

◀◀ "PageMaker as a Design Tool," p. 667.

◀◀ "Understanding Fonts," p. 700.

FROM HERE...

Examples

This section contains two sample newsletters as examples of the types of publications discussed in this chapter. The first example is a two-page newsletter, every issue of which contains the same basic elements. The second example is a tabloid newsletter prepared for two-color printing.

- ■ *Example 18.1.* A Two-Page Newsletter with Repeated Basic Elements

- ■ *Example 18.2.* A Tabloid Newsletter Prepared for Two-Color Printing

These two examples represent relatively simple designs, similar to those most users are likely to attempt when first beginning to design these types of PageMaker publications. The first example is especially simple to produce, because it is designed to be assembled by a volunteer staff that changes every year. The second example is the type of publication that is often produced for several years by outside services using traditional methods—until an in-house publications group gets computers and decides to produce the publication themselves. (In this particular example, the publications group wanted to keep the same design so that readers wouldn't notice any difference. You discover how long they took to produce the newsletter themselves—before and after they became experienced in desktop publishing.)

Example 18.1. A Two-Page Newsletter with Repeated Basic Elements

The two-page newsletter in this example is designed for ease of production by a group of volunteers who are not professional publishers and who have many other, perhaps more pressing, responsibilities. One trick to help production go smoothly is that the newsletter always contains the same set of features, each of which always is the same size and occupies the same position on the pages. A collection of extra copy and artwork—house ads, helpful tips, and interesting quotations—is available for use in a month when a feature is short or missing.

The techniques used here can be applied to any publication produced regularly by a group whose primary function is not publishing. Such publications include newsletters produced by a volunteer staff, in-house periodicals produced by the administrative staff, and event calendars containing descriptions of the offerings produced by educational institutions and seminar agencies.

Description

This two-page newsletter uses a three-column format that routinely presents the calendar of events for a seminar agency. The contents always follow the same basic formula:

- A calendar of events of varying length, always on page 1.

- A feature article about the main event (300-400 words), always on page 1.

- An article about secondary events (300-400 words), always on page 1.

- An (optional) article about a person or agency, usually one of the event leaders or sponsors (200-250 words), which can start on page 1.

- An (optional) article that offers information on a topic of general interest to the readers (300-400 words), usually written by one of the seminar leaders, on page 2.

- No more than three miscellaneous fillers, such as house ads, special announcements, short tips, and notable quotations.

Figure 18.7 shows how these basic elements are laid out in one issue.

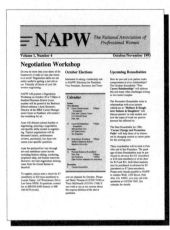

Fig. 18.7

The printout of
a two-page
newsletter.

Using the same basic design elements enables each contributor to know exactly how many words to write. And if one contributor fails to meet the deadline for copy, the editor can fill the space with one of the canned house ads, tips, or quotations. A spacing guide is included in the template as a standard for the minimum space between articles, but this space can be increased as needed to make the articles fill the pages. Such flexible standards make this publication easy to lay out.

Design Principles

The design principles listed at the beginning of this chapter generally have been applied in this newsletter. Four of those principles have been applied in a way that intentionally simplifies the production process. Because the producers of the newsletter are not professional publishers, following these principles is especially important.

Use only one or two different typefaces in a document. Only one typeface, Times, is used in several sizes and styles, as shown in the type specifications table in figure 18.8. This relatively short list of elements helps simplify the production of the newsletter.

Use ruled lines to set off the grid of the pages. Horizontal rules are used to set off standing elements, such as the calendar on page 1 and the masthead information on page 2. All rules but one—the line below the volume and date, below the banner—use the *double-line option*, also called an *Oxford rule*, from the Lines submenu. Figure 18.10 (later in the chapter) shows that the column-wide double ruled lines that frame the text on pages 1 and 2 are stored on those pages as part of the template.

Logo

	127-point Times
Banner Tag	18-point Times Italic
Volume/Issue ID	14-point Times Bold
Feature Title	24-point Times Bold
All Other Titles	14-point Times Bold, 24-point leading
Body Copy	10-point Times, auto leading
Calendar text	8-point Times
Masthead	7-point Times

Provide estimates of the number of characters per column for contributors and editors. The length of each feature is standard. The total newsletter is 7,500 characters long—about 1,500 words. Before beginning an assignment, a writer knows approximately how long it must be. The editor's primary concern is that the assignment not exceed the expected word count. If an article is too short, the extra space can be filled with a house ad, tip, or short quotation.

All columns on all pages should bottom out at the same point. This general rule is not rigidly applied in this case. If a contributor writes too much or too little, columns are left uneven; the text is not edited to change the length, and the leading is not changed.

Production Tips

The production tips offered here can be applied to any publication for which the primary goal is simplicity in the production process. These tips include ways of dealing with material that comes in varied formats and suggestions for setting up the template. You also are led through all the steps of the production process for this kind of publication.

Sources of Data

You usually can expect a wide range of sources for the text in any publication that consists of articles by a number of different authors, unless you produce an in-house newsletter for which all contributors use the same computer system. Because this newsletter is only two pages long, the editor can type short articles directly into PageMaker if they are not supplied on disk. All text formatting is done in PageMaker.

The Template

Figure 18.9 shows the Page Setup dialog box for the newsletter. The template is set up for two pages, and the relatively wide margins provide white space to help balance the wide spacing between articles.

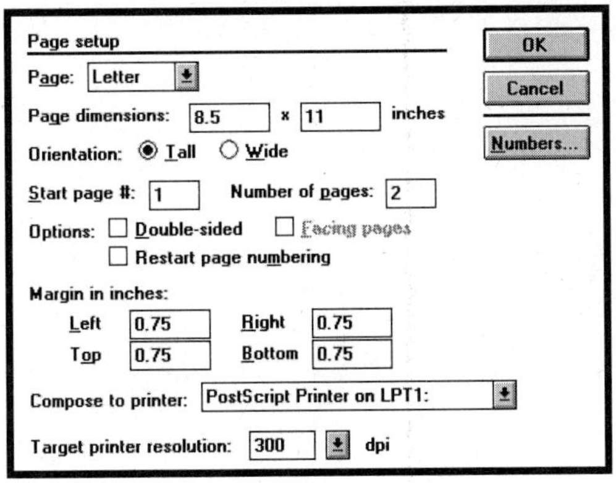

Fig. 18.9

The Page Setup dialog box for a two-page newsletter.

The template, shown in figure 18.10, uses a simple three-column format. The first page contains a standing banner and two ruled lines positioned around the calendar. Page 2 contains the masthead information and mailing label area. A list of production steps is stored on the pasteboard for easy reference.

Production Steps

To aid the volunteers who produce this quarterly newsletter, the following steps appear on the pasteboard of the template. These steps apply to this specific newsletter, but you can easily apply them to any publication of this type.

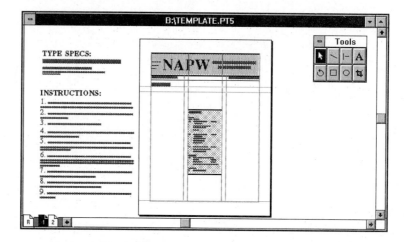

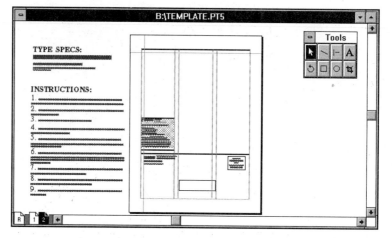

Fig. 18.10

The template for
a two-page
newsletter.

1. Collect all text files, either on disk or paper. The target character
   count is 7,500 for the entire newsletter—about 1,500 words including the calendar but excluding the standing items on the template.

2. Open the template for this newsletter. Save the template under a
   new name that includes the issue number, such as VOL1-04.PT5.
   All files for the newsletter begin with the same letters or numbers,
   such as 04-ART1.TXT and 04-ART2.TXT.

3. On page 1, change the issue identification below the banner.
   (See "Design Principles," earlier in this section, for suggestions
   on creating banners.)

4. Working in Actual Size or 70% Size, type or place each article in the space allotted and format the text as you go. (Refer to fig. 18.8 for the fonts and tags used.)

5. If the final text is too long to fit within the two pages allotted, change the leading in the body text to shrink the text. You may need to scroll down each column to check for widows and orphans and to make fine adjustments to the space between articles.

6. If the text is too short to fill the number of pages allotted, add a house ad or a famous quotation from the files. Fill empty space with items from the text files named HOUSEADS.DOC or QUOTES.DOC or from one of the graphics files, named HOUSEAD1.PIC or HOUSEAD2.PIC. (The names of your files may differ; you may choose to rename the quotations by the dates they are used, such as Q-DEC93.DOC.)

   You also can increase the spacing between articles.

7. Before printing the final master copy, print the newsletter on a laser printer for proofing. Be sure that the event coordinator or other director sees a copy before it is sent to the print shop.

8. Print the newsletter on a laser printer, and send the camera-ready pages to the printing company. Specify type, color, and weight of the paper and the number of copies.

9. Copy the PageMaker file for this issue to the archive disk named NEWS, and delete all text files from the hard disk.

Changing Tracking Instead of Leading   T I P

In step 5, the producers of this newsletter change the leading to make the copy fit the space. Instead, you can change the tracking values to tighten or expand the text slightly, but if that doesn't solve the problem you might still need to change the leading. Only one of these solutions is suggested here in order to keep the production steps simple for the volunteers who produce this newsletter. These and other methods of forcing a given amount of text into a fixed space are described in the section "Copy Fitting" in Chapter 8.

Adding Space around Article Titles

If changing the spacing between sections throughout a document, copy a blank line of the desired spacing into the Clipboard; sweep through the document; and at each break, do the following:

1. Triple-click to select the blank line.

2. Press Ctrl+V to replace the selected line with the blank line stored in the Clipboard.

For all issues of this newsletter, all work is done in one directory (see fig. 18.11). Only the PageMaker version of each issue, along with the template, is saved on the archive disk. If the imported graphics are very large, you can use the Link command to manage the graphics as external files instead of storing them as part of the PageMaker publication.

FROM HERE...

For Related Information

◄◄ "Fitting Copy," p. 346.

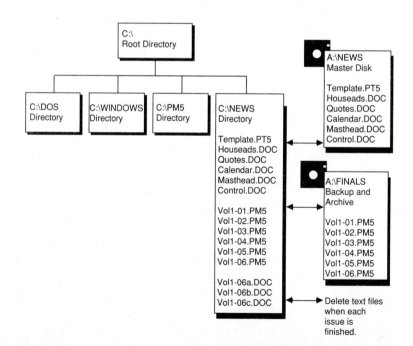

Fig. 18.11

The disk-file organization for a two-page newsletter.

Example 18.2. A Tabloid Newsletter Prepared for Two-Color Printing

The newsletter used in this example is more similar in design and format to a newspaper than to most newsletters. The tabloid-sized 11-by-17-inch pages are printed in tiled pieces on 8 1/2-by-11-inch paper for the editing reviews, and the final camera-ready pages are printed full sized on a Linotronic 300 typesetter.

The design and production tips provided here can be applied to any newsletter or newspaper publication, particularly publications consisting of many different articles, figures, and photographs. The tips that specifically address two-color printing can be applied to any two-color publication; these tips also can be adapted for three- and four-color jobs.

Description

The tabloid-sized newsletter shown in figure 18.12 is assembled from text contributed in various forms by many different authors. The production process involves a considerable amount of coordination among contributors, editors, and the production staff. Because the people involved are scattered across a wide geographic area, files are telecommunicated through a modem. The files usually can be telecommunicated as ASCII text or directly from the word processing programs used by the project.

Fig. 18.12

The printouts of a tabloid newsletter.

The final telecommunication occurs as the production group sends the finished PageMaker files to the editorial group for final review. The editors make changes directly to the files and send the revised files back to the production group. The files then are printed on a Linotronic typesetter by using the Separations option in the Color dialog box to create spot-color separations. The separations are used for two-color black-and-red commercial printing.

Design Principles

All the design principles described at the beginning of this chapter are applied in this report. Some principles, however, are particularly well illustrated. The tabloid makes effective use of ruled lines, white space, and variations in the grid. Estimates of character counts are essential for this kind of production.

Use variations in the grid to distinguish different sections of the newsletter. The three pages shown in figure 18.12 provide good examples of grid variations: The basic grid is four columns; the Corporate Technology Directory heading is two columns wide; and a page of graphs and tables includes tables and graphs that vary from one-half column to two columns wide. These grid variations help differentiate sections and maintain the reader's interest, as well as accommodate a variety of formats.

Use ruled lines to help set off the grid of the pages. This design uses hairline rules between columns and horizontal rules above article titles (refer to fig. 18.12 and see fig. 18.13). These rules set off different types of material and highlight the variations in the grid.

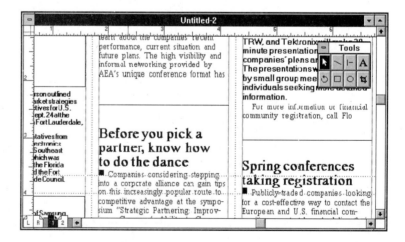

Fig. 18.13

White space and hairline rules above headlines.

Provide estimates of the number of characters per column for contributors and editors. The character counts for each article are assigned to the writers initially, but the final count may change after figures are added. The editors expect to do a great deal of editing after receiving the text from various sources.

All columns on all pages should bottom out to same point. This rule is strictly followed in this newsletter, as in most newspapers, which are the models from which this design is derived. As figure 18.12 shows, the pages are carefully aligned at the bottom margin of the grid. This alignment produces a neat, clean tabloid newspaper.

Don't be afraid of white space. White space is achieved primarily by leaving a great deal of space above headlines (refer to fig. 18.13). Otherwise, the page layouts are very dense. Again, this design strategy deliberately imitates most newspaper designs.

Production Tips

To produce a tabloid of this size and complexity every month, the production team and editors must use every trick available to make production as smooth and efficient as possible. The following anecdote illustrates this process.

A tabloid produced by conventional methods required 200 person-hours for the full production. Expecting to save a great deal of time, the production team switched to desktop publishing. The team members took a one-day class in PageMaker and engaged a designer experienced in PageMaker to build the first template, which took four days.

The first issue took more than 400 hours to produce. Much of that time was spent learning how to use PageMaker efficiently and adapting the tabloid's specifications to PageMaker's options. By the time the team had produced the sixth issue, however, the total production time was reduced to less than 40 hours—less than a quarter of the time previously required.

The tips and tricks provided here are not complete *cookbook recipes* for producing this newsletter. Many details are excluded because they are specific to this team's word processing programs, graphics programs, and editorial standards. The suggestions, however, do provide a good overview of what this type of production entails, and the ideas can be adapted to any large or complex publication project.

Sources of Data

The authors' manuscripts come in all forms. If authors and editors use the same network, files are immediately accessible to the editors. Authors working in the same building with the editors and the production crew deliver their files on disk. Other authors telecommunicate their text through modems. Occasionally, an author submits a manuscript on paper only. The editors work on the files in any word processor available and type up the stories received on paper. The editors then give the files to the production group along with marked-up thumbnails of the template, which indicate where each story is to be placed (see fig. 18.14).

If the disk files and telecommunicated files for the text have not been formatted, the production staff converts the files to the in-house word processing program and then does the formatting. If the files have been formatted in one of the word processing programs that PageMaker supports, production places the files directly in PageMaker. Most word processors cannot handle the wide variety of fonts used in this newsletter (see fig. 18.15); much of the formatting, therefore, is done in PageMaker. The large initial drop cap used in the opening paragraphs of certain articles must be positioned in PageMaker rather than in the word processing program.

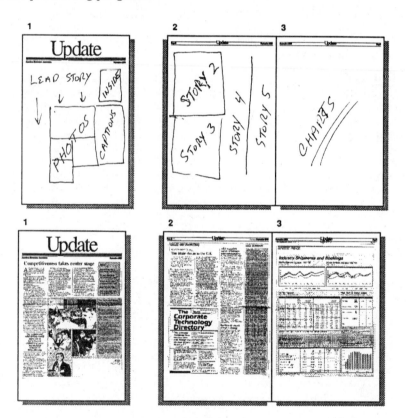

Fig. 18.14

Marked-up thumbnails of the template, showing where text is to be placed (top), and the printed pages corresponding to the thumbnails (bottom).

Style name	Type specifications
Logo/Banner	Created in Windows Draw and imported
Volume/Issue ID	14-point Times
Title 1	36-point Times Bold, 25-point leading
Title 2	27-point Times Bold, 24-point leading
Title 3	18-point Times Bold, autoleading
SUBHEAD	24-point Helvetica, all caps
Body copy body copy body copy body copy body copy	11-point Times, 12 point leading, 3-line initial drop cap paragraphs indented 1 pica
Photo Captions	8-point Helvetica Bold, 9-point leading

Fig. 18.15

The type specifications table for a tabloid newsletter.

Tagging Text in the Word Processing Program　　T I P

To save production time, provide the writers with a list of tags that matches the style names in the PageMaker style sheet, so that they can tag text in their word processing program whenever possible. PageMaker recognizes tag names put at the beginning of the paragraph and surrounded by <> brackets: <Title> before the article title, <Body copy> before the body text, and <Subtitle> before the subheading. Each paragraph without a tag name at the beginning takes on the attributes of the preceding paragraph.

T I P **Requesting ASCII Text Files**

For the best and most efficient results, authors should use the same word processing program that the production team uses. If this is impossible, ask the authors to save their files as text-only (ASCII) files, and have the production team format the text by using a word processor that PageMaker supports.

The Template

The Page Setup dialog box, as shown in figure 18.16, indicates that this newsletter has a tabloid format. Not all laser printers can handle the narrow inside and outside margins entered here (0.33 inches); some printers force a minimum margin of 0.5 inches. The template initially is set up as three pages: the first page, the second page, and a special page of graphs. Additional pages are added as needed. As shown in the following production steps, this 12-page newsletter can be developed as several PageMaker publications so that the production team can distribute the work more equally.

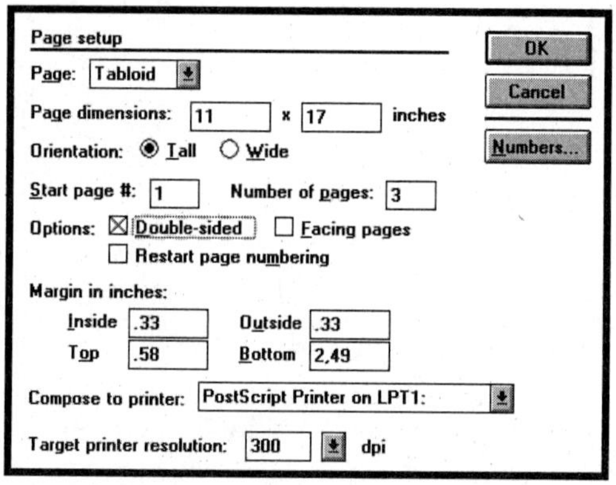

Fig. 18.16

The Page Setup dialog box for a tabloid newsletter.

T I P **Dividing a 12-Page Tabloid into Several PageMaker Files**

The template is set up as a three-page document. Each page or series of consecutive pages is started from this template, but a single issue is stored as three or more different PageMaker files (see fig. 18.17). By using this arrangement, a group of people can share the production and editing tasks. After editing and formatting is completed, you can use the Book command to link the several files.

The template for this complex document is an essential production aid for each issue (see fig. 18.18). The master pages are set in four-column format with running heads. Standard elements, including three ruled lines, five different text place holders, and one spacing guide, are stored on the pasteboard. Page 1 of the template includes the banner, and a ruler guide for starting articles on this page. Page 3 (see figs. 18.19 and 18.20) contains drop-shadow boxes where graphs and tables will be placed.

Building the template requires more than 40 hours. The design is based on specifications that match previous issues created by using traditional typesetting and paste-up methods. Forty hours includes time to build one page, to print the page by using PageMaker's Tile feature, and to write specifications for the production staff and the authors and editors, who previously did not participate in typesetting and formatting.

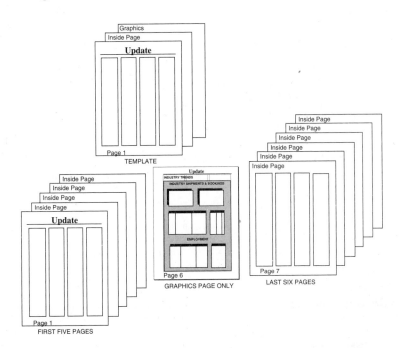

Fig. 18.17

Developing the tabloid news-letter in three separate files.

The editors use thumbnails to mark the locations of articles. To create thumbnails, the editors open the template document and use the Insert Pages command to create a 12-page empty document. They then print the empty document by using the Print command's Thumbnails option (see fig. 18.19).

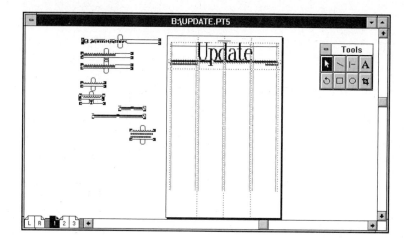

Fig. 18.18

The template
for a tabloid
newsletter.

T   I   P   **Printing Reductions of Each Page Instead of Using Thumbnails**

Because the newsletter itself is assembled as several different files and because the tabloid pages are so complex, thumbnails are not practical for viewing finished pages. Using a percentage reduction to print quick miniatures of each finished page produces more helpful results. By using a PostScript printer and the Print command's Scale option, for example, you can print the pages at a 45 percent reduction so that each page fits on one sheet of 8 1/2-by-11-inch paper. These reductions can be used for control and review purposes but not for detailed proofreading or final production.

Production Steps

If the production group uses more than one PageMaker file to build the publication, each file or partial publication must include all sequential pages, or each file can contain the full page count but handle exclusive pages. For example, one file might include the front and back pages only, another the graphics page only, and so on. The stories must be self-contained within each file—that is, you cannot jump a story that starts in one file into a different file; it must continue on one of the pages within the file. At any point during the production cycle, these pages or groups of pages may be at different stages in the following sequence of steps:

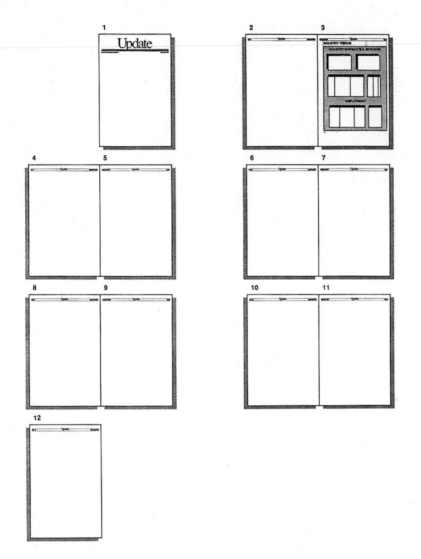

Fig. 18.19

Printed
PageMaker
thumbnails for
a tabloid
newsletter.

1. The staff collects the text files from the contributors.

2. The editorial staff edits each article before passing that article to the production group. The editors mark the dummy thumbnails for positioning articles and graphics.

3. The production staff formats the text as necessary.

4. The production staff positions each article and places black boxes where photographs are to be printed or white boxes where pictures or line art are to appear.

5. A senior editor reviews the first printouts of the composed pages. These pages are printed in pieces on 8 1/2-by-11-inch paper by using the Print command's Tile option. If the copy is too short, the editor adds copy or pull-out quotes to fill space. If the copy is too long, the editor actually removes text to make it fit the space allowed. The editor also makes notes to the production staff if any headlines need to be kerned manually.

6. After each page is laid out and edited so that all columns are aligned, a member of the production group scrolls through each column, measures all spaces around headings and figures against the spacing guide, and adds ruled lines around article titles and pull-out quotes. The standard ruled lines are stored on the pasteboard and placed on the pages by using the Copy and Paste commands. Headlines are kerned manually.

7. The final pages are printed full sized on a Linotronic 300 typesetter.

Pages containing graphs require special handling, as described in the following steps:

1. Graphs are created by using a spreadsheet graphing program to create the bars or lines.

2. The graphs are then opened in Freelance Plus (in this case—other applications could also be used), where additional formatting is performed.

3. The graphs are placed in PageMaker, where drop-shadow borders mark their positions, as shown in figure 18.20.

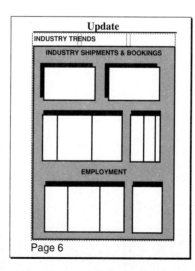

Preparation for Reproduction

The final full-sized typeset pages are marked for the printer. Color separations for pages that have color are printed by using the Spot Color Overlay option in the Print menu. Tissue overlays show where halftones must be stripped in (see fig. 18.21). The photographs supplied to the printer may need to be marked for sizing and cropping.

Along with the template, a careful organization of disk files helps make each issue's production run smoothly (see fig. 18.22). The team must be able to use the file names to distinguish one article from another within an issue. The team also must be able to distinguish between the latest version of an article and earlier versions that may have been left on disk or archived.

Fig. 18.21

A tissue overlay used to show the printer how to separate the image for color printing.

If the imported graphics are very large or numerous, you can use the Link command to manage the graphics as external files instead of storing them as part of the PageMaker publication.

In naming files, the team is guided by certain conventions, including the following:

- All names begin with the issue number and are located in a subdirectory for that issue. The volume number is not necessary, because it can be deduced from the date of the file.

- Signed articles are identified by the author's initials; three letters work best.

■ Text and graphics files are distinguished by suffix only. (See Chapter 9 for a list of graphics file suffixes and their meanings.) The PageMaker file names include issue number and page numbers.

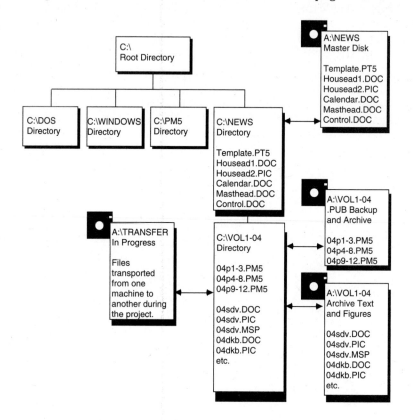

Fig. 18.22

The disk-file organization for a tabloid newsletter.

The members of the production team keep current versions of their files on their hard disks in separate subdirectories set up for each issue. The staff members remove files from their hard disks after they send the files to another computer for further changes. Each team member has a floppy disk reserved for each issue and backs up each file before sending it. The members also keep current the date and time stored in their systems so that questions about the most recent version of a file can be resolved by looking at the date of the file.

After the issue is printed, all current files are copied from all hard disks to one or more floppy disks and stored with other archived data away from the office.

See the color plates in this book for other examples of spot color printing, and the plates created for spot color versus four-color process printing.

Summary

The two newsletter examples presented in this chapter illustrate two extremes of production. The short newsletter has a relatively simple format and relaxed standards; this newsletter is easy to produce by a team whose primary function is *not* publishing. The tabloid-sized newsletter, on the other hand, involves complex grid variations and strict production standards, which are applied by a team of professionals. The design and production tips provided at the beginning of the chapter and illustrated by the examples give you a good overview of the factors involved in producing a newsletter, magazine, or newspaper. You can apply these ideas to your own production of newsletters and other publications.

Creating Overhead Transparencies, Slides, and Handouts

Desktop publishing usually is associated with books, reports, newsletters, and magazines, but PageMaker is also an excellent tool for creating presentation materials. You can develop tables and graphs in other programs, place them in PageMaker, and then use PageMaker's Text tool to add captions and topic summaries.

To produce overhead transparencies, you can use a color printer, a laser printer, or a typesetter to print the images on clear acetate. If you want 35mm slides for a presentation, you can print the pages directly to a film recorder or print the images on a color printer and then photograph the printed sheets.

Examples 19.1 and 19.3 in this chapter are designed specifically as overhead transparencies or slides. Examples 19.2 and 19.4 are designed as printed handouts. Each of these examples appears in figure 19.1.

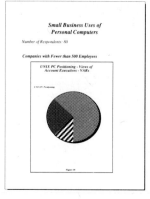

Example 19.1

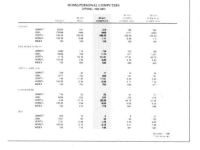

Example 19.2

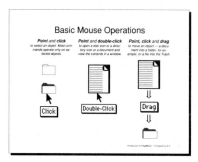

Example 19.3

Example 19.4

Fig. 19.1

Examples of presentation materials described in this chapter.

The examples in this chapter share the following characteristics:

- Presentation materials consist of a series of similar parts.

- The elements primarily are graphics, and words usually appear in a large type font.

- Each element requires some extra touches in PageMaker that are not possible in the graphics programs that create the graphs and diagrams.

T I P

Using Thumbnails To Help Prepare Your Presentation

Use the Thumbnails option in the Print Command dialog box to print a capsule summary of the topics for reference during the presentation (see fig. 19.2). Make notes on the thumbnails about the points that you want to emphasize.

1

2
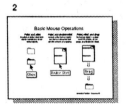

3
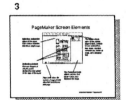

Fig. 19.2

Thumbnails used to help prepare presentation notes.

Design Principles

The design principles for presentation materials are derived from a mixture of basic design traditions, advertising guidelines, good training practices, and the technology of projecting images for an audience. The principles emphasized in this chapter concern the selection of typefaces and type sizes, the amount and content of text, and the sizes of images.

Several guidelines are dictated by the dimensions of the final product; slides, for example, usually are 35mm by 24mm. Other guidelines are borrowed from the advertising industry because the best presentation materials are similar to billboards and display ads. These principles are described in general terms in this section and then applied to specific examples later in the chapter.

Select only one or two typefaces. Keep headings of the same level the same size. Keep similar text on all images in the same typeface.

The last guideline is difficult to follow when graphic images come from different programs that use different fonts. The number of fonts available in your spreadsheet graphing program, for example, probably is smaller than the number of fonts available in your drawing program, and PageMaker probably has more fonts than either your spreadsheet or your drawing program. Before you make the final specifications for a set of presentation materials, you should know all the font options of the programs you are using, as well as which fonts your printer can handle. (Refer to Chapter 16 for additional suggestions on controlling type specifications when images are drawn from several sources.)

Table 19.1 lists the typefaces that commonly are used in presentation materials.

Table 19.1 Typefaces Used in Tables, Graphs, and Overhead Transparencies			
Typefaces	**Tables**	**Graphs**	**Overheads/Slides**
Arial**	Y	Y	Y
ITC American Typewriter	Y	Y	Y
ITC Avant Garde*	Y	Y	Y
ITC Benguiat	N	N	N
ITC Bookman*	N	Y	Y
Courier* or Courier New**	Y	N	N
ITC Friz Quadrata	N	N	Y
ITC Galliard	Y	Y	Y
ITC Garamond	Y	Y	Y
Glypha	Y	Y	N
Goudy Old Style	N	N	Y
Helvetica*	Y	Y	Y
ITC Korinna	Y	Y	N
ITC Lubalin Graph	Y	Y	Y
ITC Machine	Y	Y	Y
ITC New Baskerville	N	N	N
New Century Schoolbook*	Y	Y	Y
Optima	Y	Y	Y
Palatino*	Y	Y	Y
ITC Souvenir	N	N	Y
Times* or Times New Roman**	Y	Y	Y
Trump Mediaeval	Y	Y	Y
ITC Zapf Chancery*	N	N	Y

*(Y = used; N = not used, * = Standard LaserWriter font, ** = TrueType font packaged with Windows 3.1)*

Try to limit the text on each overhead transparency or slide to 25 or fewer words, 5 or fewer bullet points, and 8 or fewer lines.

These numbers are somewhat arbitrary; you can set different limits for different purposes, but brevity usually increases effectiveness. Billboard designers do not exceed seven words of text, if possible, and billboards have a strong impact. Viewers also may have difficulty reading and understanding slides and overhead transparencies that contain too many words in small type. If a slide seems to be growing beyond these limits, consider breaking it into two slides, dividing the main topic logically into two subtopics.

You may set your limit at 50 words per page or more, however, especially if the text is designed for a handout rather than for projection on a screen. The important point is that word count and point size require special attention when you are creating materials that will be projected as slides or transparencies.

Use parallel construction in bullet items.

All bullet items within one slide should have the same construction. All of the items might begin with a verb or an adjective, for example, or all of the items might be nouns. Parallelism is easy on the listener's eye and enhances understanding.

Give graphs short but descriptive titles.

Your graph and table titles should include enough information to be meaningful. The graph title "1987 Income," for example, conveys little information. Use more descriptive titles, such as those used in newspapers and magazines. The title "Widget Sales Increase Relative to Other Categories," for example, tells viewers the purpose of the graph.

Use a large point size for the text in images that will be projected on slides or overhead transparencies.

One rule of thumb for overhead transparencies is that the image on the paper (not the projected image) should be easy to read from approximately 10 feet away (see fig. 19.3). For most audiences, this rule means that titles should be no smaller than 36 or 24 points, and that labels and bullets should be no smaller than 18 points.

For slides, an image on 8 1/2-by-11-inch paper should be easy to read from 7 feet away (see fig. 19.4). This rule means that the text should be 18 or 24 points—slightly smaller than text for overhead transparencies.

For overhead transparencies, use black type on a white or light background; for slides, use white or light type on a dark background.

Overhead transparencies can be shown in partly lighted rooms, so dark text will stand out not only against the slide background but also against white or light walls. Slides generally are shown in dark rooms, so light text stands out better when projected on a white screen against the dark slide background and the darkened walls.

Fig. 19.3

Printout for an overhead transparency, legible at a distance of 10 feet.

10 feet

Sales Training

Fig. 19.4

Printout for a slide, legible at a distance of 7 feet.

7 feet

Sales Training

T I P   Creating Unusual Backgrounds with Special Paper

If you plan to make slides by taking photographs of the printed pages, you can create unusual backgrounds by printing on special paper—for example, colored paper, colored paper that fades from light to dark, or paper with a marble or granite pattern.

T I P   Creating Reverse Text During Film Processing

If you plan to make slides by taking photographs of the printed pages, you can print the text as black on white and then use slide film to photograph the page. Ask the film-processing lab to process the roll as color *print* film (C-41), rather than color *slide* film (E-6). What you get back essentially will be a color negative of the slide, with white type on a black background.

For variety, shoot the images with a color filter over the lens. An orange or yellow filter, for example, yields a medium-blue background rather than solid black.

For overhead transparencies, fit all images into a 7-by-9-inch area.

This rule applies particularly to framed overhead transparencies because a transparency frame usually has a 7 1/2-by-9 1/2-inch window
(see fig. 19.5). You can specify a page size of 7 by 9 inches in the Page
Setup dialog box, or you can set the margins of an 8 1/2-by-11-inch page
to confine the text and graphics to a 7-by-9-inch area.

The 7-by-9-inch ratio is a good guide to follow even when the images
are not framed. Viewing conditions may restrict some people in the
audience from seeing the edges of the overhead, but the center of the
image should be visible to everyone in the room. If you want to use the
same material for slides and transparencies, the image-area measurement limitations used for overheads also are appropriate for use with
24mm-by-35mm slides. Another advantage of these presentation sizes
is that your graphic images benefit from being surrounded by white
space.

**For materials to be made into slides, set all images within an area of
approximately 3:2 proportions.**

Frames for 35mm slides usually have a 35mm-by-24mm clear window.
You should design your graphics—especially slide images with a ruled
border—within this 3:2 proportion. If you are not using 35mm film for
your slides, calculate the proper proportions based on the final size of
your slide window. Use the following formula:

$$\frac{\text{slide width}}{\text{slide height}} = \frac{\text{PageMaker image width}}{\text{PageMaker image height}}$$

If you decide to use a width of seven inches for your images, for example, you can calculate the proportional height using this formula:

$$\text{PageMaker image height} = \text{PageMaker image width} \times \frac{\text{slide height}}{\text{slide width}}$$

If possible, design all the images in a series with the same page orientation.

Consistent page orientation makes the presentation as well as the production easier than it would be if you mixed tall and wide pages in a series. If the material you plan to present is not consistent in orientation, you can rotate text and graphics as needed or develop the presentation materials in two or more PageMaker publications.

FROM HERE...

For Related Information

◄◄ "Creating a Grid System," p. 683.

◄◄ "Planning Your Design Specifications," p. 708.

Production Tips

The production tips in this chapter apply specifically to presentation materials that are to be projected on a screen. The tips explain ways to produce high-quality material easily. By following these tips, you frequently can eliminate one or more production steps, thereby increasing efficiency.

The reasons for applying the following tips are described in general terms in this section. Some of the same tips are repeated with the examples, accompanied by explanations of their specific applications to that example.

Use automatic page numbering to number the set in sequence.

You can use PageMaker's automatic page-numbering feature to number the images used in a presentation. This feature enables you to find the images in a PageMaker document easily when you want to update selected materials. If you do not want the numbers to show when you are projecting the images, use a small point size for the page number (12 points or smaller) and place the page numbers at the bottom of the image area (see fig. 19.6). This trick is used in all the examples in this chapter.

If the page sequence changes for particular presentations or if presentations are shortened by omitting images, you still can use the automatic page-numbering feature to number the master set and print alternate numbers on each page in the same small font.

Fig. 19.6

Automatic page numbering for a set of presentation materials.

If you use a laser printer for the final output, use a gray screen rather than solid black areas for the best projection image.

If your laser printer's toner cartridge is at peak performance, you can get solid black areas to print evenly on special laser paper. Even with a good cartridge, however, black areas may print unevenly on acetate sheets for transparencies. This unevenness is exaggerated when the image is projected. You can reduce the effects of uneven toner by using gray fill patterns instead of solid black (see fig. 19.7).

Fig. 19.7

Grays print and project better than black areas that wash out with some laser printers.

Counteract the Curls

The heat that is applied to acetate sheets when they run through a laser printer tends to make them curl up toward the toner side. If you use PageMaker's Mirror option when you print acetates, they still curl toward the toner, but the text will be readable on the nontoner side. When you place them on the overhead projector, the acetates will tend to curl down, but this effect will be counteracted to some extent by the weight of the acetate.

To set the Mirror option, choose the Print command from the File menu; then click the Color button in the Print dialog box. The Mirror option is available in the Print-Color dialog box only if you are printing to a PostScript printer (see "Printing Color Separations" in Chapter 12).

To create overlays, copy the complete image on several pages and then delete portions of the image from each page.

To create a set of overhead transparencies with overlays, first create the whole image on one page in the PageMaker publication. Copy the complete image to subsequent pages, one for each overlay. Go back to the first page and delete the parts of the image that appear on the subsequent overlays. On each following page, delete all parts of the image except what should appear on that single overlay.

Figure 19.8 shows an example of a set of overlays.

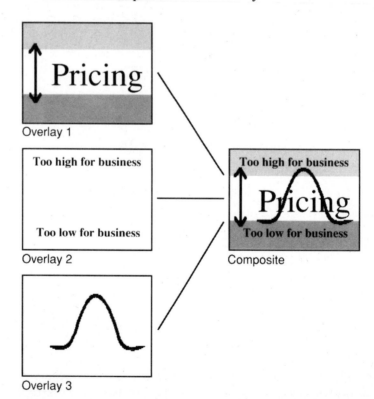

Overlay 1

Overlay 2

Composite

Overlay 3

Fig. 19.8

A series of overheads, where pages 2 and 3 add elements to page 1.

You can achieve a similar effect when you prepare slides. Build the full image first and then copy the complete image to subsequent pages. Keep the full version on the last page in the series, and delete selected elements from each page preceding the full image (see fig. 19.9).

Slide 1

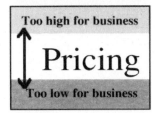

Slide 2

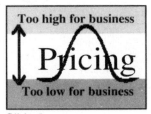

Slide 3

Fig. 19.9

A series of slides where common elements appear on each page.

Pages in a series for overlays of overhead transparencies do not repeat the same elements, but each page in a series of slides maintains elements from the previous pages and adds new elements.

For Related Information

◄◄ "Creating a Grid System," p. 683.

FROM HERE...

Examples

The following examples demonstrate a variety of formats and illustrate various applications of the design principles and production tips discussed in the preceding sections. The four examples are the following:

- *Example 19.1.* A Series of Transparencies of Graphs in the Same Format

- *Example 19.2.* A Handout Showing Tabular Figures and Graphs

- *Example 19.3.* A Series of Transparencies with Varied Formats

- *Example 19.4.* A Handout Showing a Table with Shaded Columns

Example 19.1. A Series of Transparencies of Graphs in the Same Format

The series of pie graphs in this example is designed to report the results of a survey or questionnaire. Each pie graph represents a different question and the responses of a specific set of respondents. The production tips for this example apply to many situations, such as a series of sales reports on the same list of products (in which each pie represents a different geographical region or purchasing group), a series of stock reports (in which each graph represents a different stock), or a series of profit-and-loss projections for a new company or a new product (in which each graph represents a different set of assumptions about advertising expenses, pricing, and market penetration).

Description

This overhead presentation consists of a series of pie graphs generated in a spreadsheet graphing program (see fig. 19.10). The percentage labels and part of the legend were retained from the graphing program, but the graph title and legend tags were cropped off when the image was placed in PageMaker. The legend text, graph titles, and captions then were added with PageMaker's Text tool. Notice that the titles are consistent in terms of font and point size and that the organization of each graph is similar.

  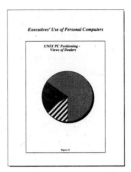

Fig. 19.10

Printout of a series of graphs in the same format.

Design Principles

Many of the design principles described at the beginning of this chapter are repeated here (in bold italic) and then applied to this series of graphs. Choices of typeface and type size are especially important.

Select only one or two typefaces. Keep headings of the same level the same size. Use the same typeface for similar text that appears in all images. In this example, the choice of fonts in the spreadsheet graphing program is the limiting factor. The percentage labels around each pie graph were preserved from the graphing program because typing and positioning the labels in PageMaker would be too time-consuming. The legend text and graph titles were typed in PageMaker in larger type sizes than are available in the graphing program.

Use a large point size for text in slides or overhead transparencies. As already mentioned, the graphing program's titles are not large enough for effective presentation material. PageMaker's tools were used to add text in the larger type sizes required for presentations.

Production Tips

Producing transparencies is easy in PageMaker because the process is the same as that for producing any publication. Usually, you use only one template. For best results, you need to be especially careful about printer settings.

If you use a laser printer for the final output, use a gray screen rather than solid black areas for the projection image. The drop shadow around each pie is filled with a 40 percent screen. This arrangement eliminates the risk of uneven toner effects that could occur if the drop shadow were solid black (see figs. 19.10 and 19.13).

The Template

The Page Setup dialog box is used to set the image area on each page (see fig. 19.11). The margin settings force an image area of 6 by 8 inches—well within the 7-by-9-inch limit recommended for transparencies.

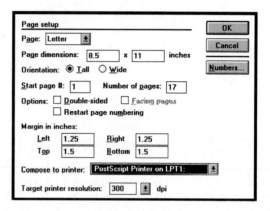

Fig. 19.11

Page Setup dialog box for a series of graphs in the same format.

The master page for this series includes the text of the legend, positioned to match the legend from the graphing program (see fig. 19.12). The graph title on each page was copied from a text block stored on the pasteboard of the template. The drop-shadow circles were created in PageMaker, stored on the pasteboard, and copied to each page.

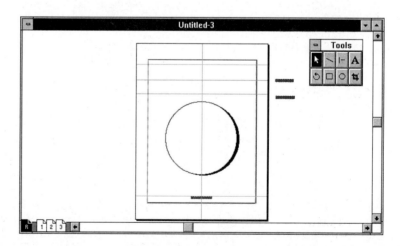

Fig. 19.12

Template for a series of graphs in the same format.

Production Steps

Creating the series of graphs in this example is not difficult. If you take particular care with the first page, developing the other pages is simple. To produce this series of graphs, follow these steps:

1. Determine the content of the presentation.

2. Create a sample graph with the graphing program, and then use the Place command (File menu) to place the sample in PageMaker so that you can check the size and position of the image. Based on this test, refine the specifications in the graph program (if your graph program enables you to adjust final graph size or font sizes).

3. Begin to build the template for the series by typing the legend text and page numbers on the master page. Draw a border around the image area, and then set guidelines for positioning the graphs. Type text in the size to be used for each graph title, and place the text on the pasteboard.

4. Create the drop shadow, using PageMaker's Circle tool, and then place the drop shadow on the page.

5. Place the sample graph (refer to step 2) on the page, and then check the position of the legend text and the size of the drop shadows (see fig. 19.13). Make sure that the longest graph title fits on the page.

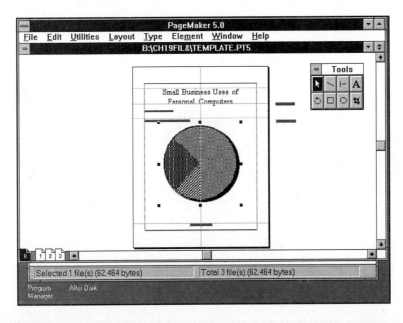

Fig. 19.13

Checking one sample graph against the template.

6. Create all the graphs in a graphing program that is compatible with PageMaker.

7. Place each graph in PageMaker, using the Place command. Copy the title text block from the pasteboard, and type the current graph title before cropping out the graph title and legend text from the graphing program.

8. Save the file each time you complete a page.

All the graphs in this example were saved under the file names that are shown in the alphabetical listing in the Place Document dialog box. This order means using 01, 02, 10, and so on, instead of 1, 2, 10, and so on (see fig. 19.14). Otherwise, the file GRAPH11 would precede GRAPH2 in the list of figures in the Place Document dialog box. If the presentation is large, you can use the Link command to manage the graphs as external files, rather than store them as part of the PageMaker publication.

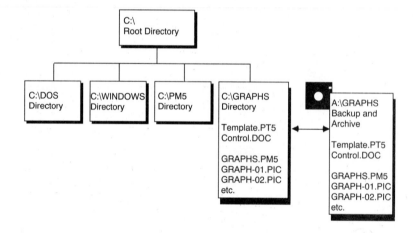

Fig. 19.14

Disk-file organization for a series of graphs.

Example 19.2. A Handout Showing Tabular Figures and Graphs

Instead of making a single presentation before a group, you sometimes want to give each person information to keep. This practice is particularly good for presenting detailed or technical information that an audience probably cannot absorb in a single viewing.

Description

The images in this example are handouts rather than overhead transparencies or slides. The goal is to show a table of statistics on the same page as a graph of those values (see fig. 19.15)—a combination that is not easy to achieve with a spreadsheet program alone. In fact, most spreadsheet programs do not support this feature.

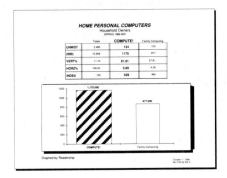

Fig. 19.15

Printout of page containing a table and graphs.

Design Principles

All but one of the design principles discussed at the beginning of this chapter apply to this set of handouts. The exception is that you do not need to limit the text to 25 words if you count the figures in the table of numbers. These figures were set in a small point size to leave white space on the pages. The small sizes are acceptable because these materials are handouts rather than slides or transparencies.

Production Tips

The production tips used for these handouts are different from those used for producing transparencies. The descriptions of the template and the production steps, however, provide valuable instructions and shortcuts.

The Template

The template for the image in this example includes a ruled grid on the master page (for the tabbed text) and a drop-shadow border for the graphs. The numbers themselves were set up as tabbed dummy text stored on the pasteboard, along with dummy text for the graph titles (see fig. 19.16). Ruler guides on the master page mark the positions of the title and table.

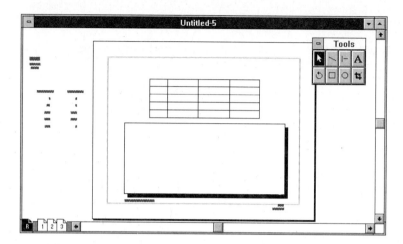

Fig. 19.16

The template for
combined table
and graphs.

Production Steps

Some of the production steps for a series of transparencies also apply
to these handouts. Combining tabular material with graphs, however,
requires additional steps.

To create the handout, follow these steps:

1. Determine the content of the presentation.

2. Begin building the template for the series. Create the drop-
    shadowed grid using PageMaker's Square-Corner and
    Constrained-Line tools. Place the grid on the master page.

3. Type the tabbed numbers as a text block, using dummy numbers,
    and set the tabs to match the grid. Place the tabbed dummy num-
    bers on the pasteboard. (You could use the Table Editor to create
    the data, but typing the data directly into PageMaker is just as fast
    when you have many small, simple tables to produce.)

4. Create one sample graph in a drawing or charting program, and
    then place the sample in PageMaker to check the size and position
    of the image. Based on this test, refine the specifications for the
    drawing program. Make sure that the longest graph title fits in the
    designated area before you specify the type size for the titles.

5. Create all the graphs in the drawing program.

    Because the graphs in this example are bar graphs, which you can
    create easily in a drawing program that offers a wide range of for-
    matting options, using a spreadsheet graphing program is not
    necessary. A template file is created with the drawing program

and copied for each bar graph (see fig. 19.17). The template includes all the basic elements. Only the length of each bar needs to
be adjusted. (Refer to Chapter 11 for a tip on creating bar charts
directly in PageMaker, using the Rectangle tool and the numeric
scaling option in the Control palette.)

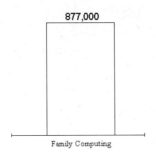

877,000

Family Computing

Fig. 19.17

Graph template
from the drawing
program.

6. Place each graph in PageMaker. Crop the graph titles entered in
   the drawing file and then re-create them using the dummy title
   text from the PageMaker template pasteboard.

7. Copy the tabbed dummy-number text block onto each page, and
   then edit the numbers (see fig. 19.18).

	Totals	COMPUTE!	Competitor
UNW GT	75	4	0
<000>	455	45	0
VERT%	0.27	2.37	0.00
HORZ%	100.00	9.89	0.00
INDEX	100	889	0

Fig. 19.18

Tabbed numbers
and grid created
with PageMaker
tools.

8. Save the file each time you complete a page.

As in Example 19.1, the list of graph file names in the Place Document
dialog box is in sequential order (see fig. 19.19). This order means using
01, 02, 10, and so on, rather than 1, 2, 10, and so on. (Otherwise, the file
GRAPH11 would precede GRAPH2 in the list of figures in the Place
Document dialog box.) If the presentation is large, you can use the Link
command to manage the graphs as external files, rather than store
them as part of the PageMaker publication.

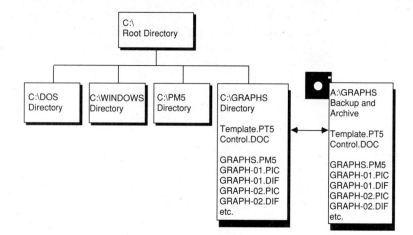

Fig. 19.19

Disk-file organization for a series of tables and graphs.

Example 19.3. A Series of Transparencies with Varied Formats

Frequently, you may want to combine different formats in a single presentation. For example, you may need an opening page with a scanned image or a list of points to be presented. You then may want to include graphs, tables of different sizes, and more explanatory material. This example shows you how to combine formats into a unified presentation.

Description

This set of overheads presents topics and concepts in a variety of formats (see fig. 19.20). The graphics include figures from a drawing program and bit-mapped screen dumps. The grid has been changed from page to page to accommodate page-wide captions as well as titles and narrow figure labels.

Design Principles

Most of the design principles listed at the beginning of this chapter are demonstrated in this set of transparencies, but two exceptions merit some discussion. As mentioned previously, guidelines are just that: guidelines. At times, you will have valid reasons for exceptions. Two principles for which exceptions are demonstrated in this example are repeated here in bold italic.

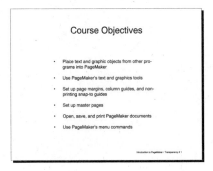

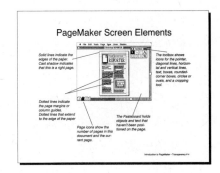

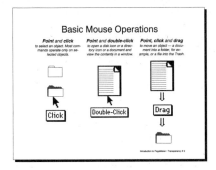

Fig. 19.20

An example of varying formats in a single presentation.

Try to limit the text on each transparency to 25 words. For this example, the number of words was extended to 50 to accommodate some of the detailed bulleted lists and figure captions. This exception to the rule is acceptable in this case because of the classroom setting in which these transparencies are to be used. Each transparency will remain projected on the screen for several minutes as the instructor describes the concepts in detail, and the same information will be available in the students' printed materials.

Use a large point size for text in slides or overhead transparencies. The smallest point size used in these transparencies was 16 (see fig. 19.21). In all the figures, Helvetica was used in four different sizes: 40, 26, 20, and 16 points. The relatively small 16-point captions still are easy to read because Helvetica is a sans serif typeface with individual characters that actually are larger than the same characters in 16-point Times.

Style name

Type specifications

Figure Title

40-point Helvetica, centered

(all other elements will be flush left)

Subhead

26-point Helvetica, flush left

Bulleted lists

20-point Helvetica, flush left

Captions

16-point Helvetica Italic
Auto leading used throughout

Production Tips

An important trick in this example is using automatic page numbering
to number the set (as in every example in this chapter). The other primary production tip is to use the Column Guides command (Layout
menu) to change from one column to four columns as needed for each
transparency, as the production steps later in this section explain.

The Template

The template for this example, shown in figure 19.22, consists of a master page with the basic grid laid out in ruler guides. Dummy text for
each type of element was stored on the pasteboard. A spacing guide is
provided for positioning text and graphics on a page. The running foot
on the master page includes the page numbers.

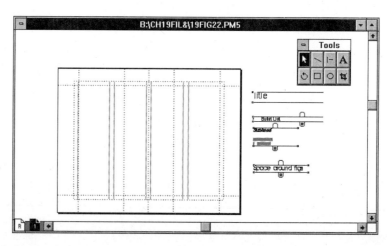

Production Steps

The steps for producing this series of transparencies are similar to those for developing other transparencies. Before you begin production, create the text blocks you need and store them in the pasteboard. Proceed with the following steps:

1. Develop the complete list of figures, and then decide which ones require placement of files from the drawing program or from bit-mapped screen shots.

2. Determine the maximum size for each figure, and then draw the figures to size in the drawing program.

3. Make the screen shots using a screen-shot utility such as Hot Shot, Collage, or Tiffany.

4. Open the PageMaker template and begin building each page. Clone the main heading text from the pasteboard first.

5. Place figures from other programs on each page before typing the captions. Use the Standoff option in the Text Wrap dialog box (Element menu) to set the graphic boundary around the figures; clone the quarter-page-width text blocks from the pasteboard and then type the appropriate text.

6. Make a rough layout of figures with captions to decide how many vertical grid lines are involved, and then use the Column Guides command (Layout menu) to lay out the vertical grid. The column guides help you position the figure labels, not define the width of the labels.

7. Determine the final layout of figures with captions.

8. Save the file each time you complete a page.

All screen shots and figures from the drawing program should be saved under file names that appear in the proper sequence in the Place Document dialog box. This order means using 01, 02, 10, and so on, rather than 1, 2, 10, and so on (see fig. 19.23). If the presentation is large, you can use the Link command to manage the figures as external files, rather than store them as part of the PageMaker publication.

Example 19.4. A Handout Showing a Table with Shaded Columns

This example shows how a shaded box created with PageMaker's Rectangle tool can be used to highlight information that otherwise might be lost in a sea of numbers. As in the first two examples in this chapter, the repeated use of the same format (with different figures on each page) enables you to position the gray box once on the master page, along with the ruled lines that set off the figures.

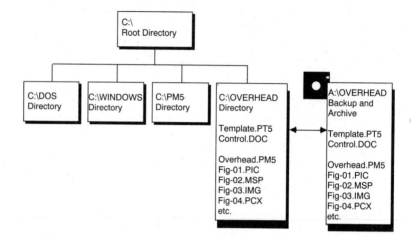

Fig. 19.23

Disk-file organization for a series of transparencies with varied formats.

Description

This presentation series consists of two tables of figures with the same column and row headings (see fig. 19.24); each table shows the figures for a different period. A gray background highlights the figures for the presenter's product against those of its competitors. In such a case, you must use a very light gray background (no more than 10 percent) for readability.

HOME/PERSONAL COMPUTERS
SPRING 1986 MRI

		TOTALS	READ BYTE	READ COMPUTE	READ FAMILY COMPUTING	READ PERSONAL COMPUTING
TOTALS						
	UNWGT	20330	231	218	186	342
	(000)	170599	1466	1898	1517	2655
	VERT%	100.00	100.00	100.00	100.00	100.00
	HORZ%	100.00	0.86	1.11	0.89	1.5
	INDEX	100	100	100	100	100
HOUSEHOLD OWNS						
	UNWGT	2480	114	194	103	158
	(000)	19958	782	1175	877	1321
	VERT%	11.70	53.34	61.91	57.81	49.76
	HORZ%	100.00	3.92	5.89	4.39	6.62
	INDEX	100	456	529	494	425
APPLE COMPUTER						
	UNWGT	339	22	17	14	24
	(000)	2471	162	209	141	181
	VERT%	1.45	11.05	11.01	9.29	6.82
	HORZ%	100.00	6.56	8.46	5.71	7.32
	INDEX	100	763	760	642	471
COMMODORE						
	UNWGT	738	25	63	41	51
	(000)	6208	222	537	376	575
	VERT%	3.64	15.14	28.29	24.79	21.66
	HORZ%	100.00	3.58	8.65	6.06	9.26
	INDEX	100	416	779	681	595
IBM						
	UNWGT	206	19	8	8	21
	(000)	1557	95	34	50	122
	VERT%	0.91	6.48	1.79	3.30	4.60
	HORZ%	100.00	6.10	2.16	3.21	7.84
	INDEX	100	710	196	361	503

December 1, 1986
1118/TmChart/dk7

HOME/PERSONAL COMPUTERS
SPRING 1986 MRI

		TOTALS	READ BYTE	READ COMPUTE	READ FAMILY COMPUTING	READ PERSONAL COMPUTING
GRAPHIC TABLET						
	UNWGT	123	6	6	5	8
	(000)	928	30	30	18	39
	VERT%	0.54	2.05	1.56	1.19	1.47
	HORZ%	100.00	3.23	3.23	1.94	4.20
	INDEX	100	376	291	218	270
PLOTTER						
	UNWGT	58	3	3	1	3
	(000)	411	21	15	2	15
	VERT%	0.24	1.43	0.79	0.13	0.56
	HORZ%	100.00	5.11	3.65	0.49	3.65
	INDEX	100	596	328	55	235

For more information on how **COMPUTE!** best serves your advertising needs in reaching the home market of personal computer owners, please call:

1. *New England & Mid-Atlantic*
   Bernard J. Theobald, Jr 212 315-1665
   Tom Link 212 315-1665
2. *Southeast & Foreign including Canada*
   Harry Blair 919 275-9809
3. *Midwest, Southwest, West & British Columbia*
   Jerry Thompson Chicago 312 726-6047
   Lucille Dennis Texas 713 731-2605 • Colorado 303 595-9299 • California 415 348-8222

COMPUTE! Publications Inc
825 Seventh Ave, New York, NY 10019

*Source: Spring 1986 MRI

December 1, 1986
1118/TmChart/dk7

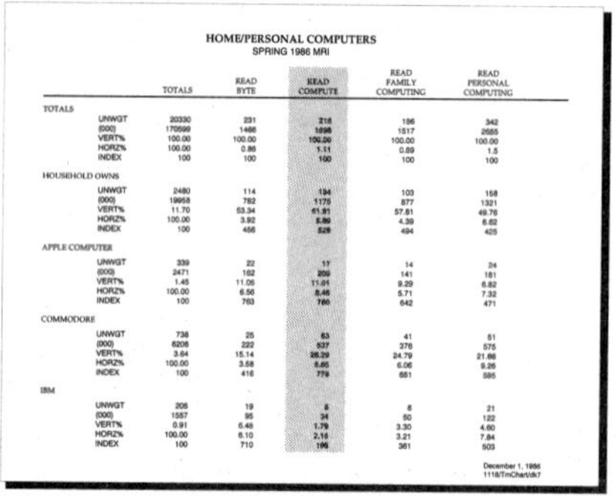

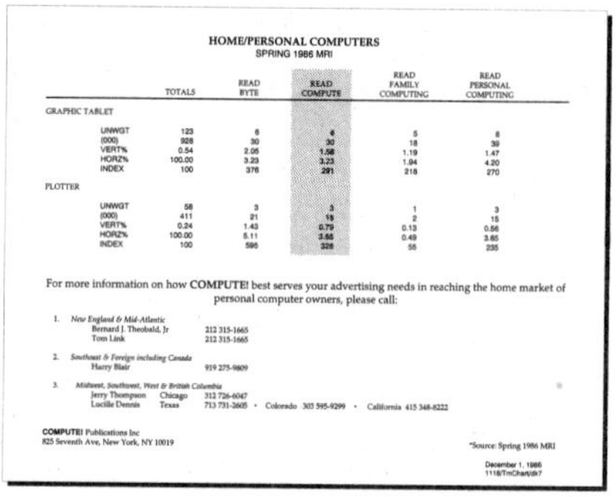

Fig. 19.24

Printout of tables.

Production Tips

One production tip in particular is emphasized in this example: type titles and column headings with PageMaker's tools, but use a word processing program to prepare the rows of data. This tip is especially important because the table has so many rows and columns of data. (Remember that you can reposition tabs in PageMaker, if necessary.) The time required to produce this set of handouts could double if you use PageMaker to prepare all the text.

The Template

The template in this example includes the table title, the column headings, and the slug at the bottom of the page (see fig. 19.25). A ruled line separates the headings from the rest of the text. Ruler guides show the positions of the rows of data and the time-period subhead. Dummy text for the time-period entry was stored on the pasteboard.

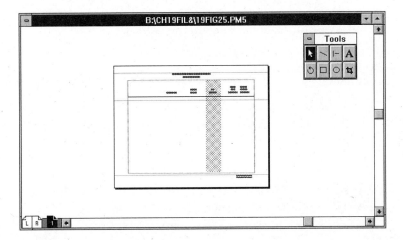

This design uses Palatino and Helvetica in a limited variety of sizes and styles (see fig. 19.26).

Production Steps

Because of the columns and the shading, constructing this handout involves more steps than the preceding examples. For good results, work carefully through the following steps:

Style name	Type specifications
MAIN HEAD	14-point Palatino Bold, 14-point leading, all caps, centered on page
SUBHEAD	12-point Helvetica, all caps, centered on page
COLUMN HEADS	11-point Palatino, all caps, centered in column
PRODUCT NAMES	11-point Palatino, 18-point leading, all caps, flush left
Numbers	11-point Helvetica, 12-point leading, flush right in column
Slug (at bottom of page)	9-point Helvetica, flush left

Fig. 19.26

Type-specifications table for a table with shaded columns.

1. Collect the data and then determine the number of columns and rows of data required for each table. Create one sample table in a spreadsheet or the Table Editor before building the PageMaker template.

2. Open a PageMaker publication and place the sample table on the master page for use in setting up the guides.

3. If the table is imported as text, you can set the text with the desired type specifications and then use PageMaker's Indents/Tabs command (Type menu, or Ctrl+I) to set the tabs that distribute the columns evenly across the page. Tabs can be aligned to the right of the text or on the decimal points. Change the leading to make the rows fit the page length. If necessary, change the type specifications to make the data fit the width of the page. Make a note of the tab settings you use in PageMaker, and set the same tabs in the word processing program.

4. Draw a gray box (10 percent) to cover the column to be highlighted on each page, and then use the Send to Back command (Element menu) to place the gray box behind the text.

5. Type the column headings at the top of the text block on the master page. Delete the text of the sample table from the master page.

6. Add the text of the table title at the top of the master page.

7. Type the dummy text for the time period on the pasteboard. Use horizontal ruler lines to mark the positions of the time-period text and the top of the tabular text on the page.

8. Draw a two-point rule below the column heads. Type the slug at the bottom of the master page.

9. In the spreadsheet program, type the data for all pages of the presentation. Save the data as a single file, and then save the file as text-only.

10. Open the template, and then begin placing the tabular data on the first page. Set tabs as noted in step 3. Be sure that the tabs are the same throughout the document.

11. Continue placing data on all the pages, saving the publication at regular intervals.

This publication has five files: the original spreadsheet data, the text-only spreadsheet data, the formatted word-processing file, the PageMaker template, and the finished publication (see fig. 19.27). If this set of materials is used only for this presentation and will not be re-created with different data, the template file can be the final publication, leaving only one PageMaker file in the system.

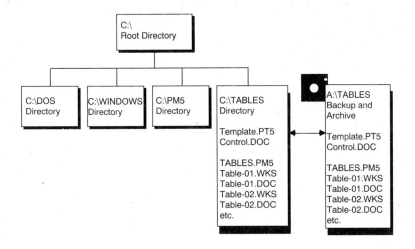

Fig. 19.27

Disk-file organization for a handout showing a table with shaded columns.

When you archive the files, you can discard the text-only file. If, however, you expect to change the figures extensively for next year's presentation, save the spreadsheet data. Replacing old entries in each column with new entries should be easy as long as the row and column headings remain the same. If you expect minor changes, you can update the PageMaker file directly. If you expect to change many entries in scattered rows and columns, save the formatted text file for those changes.

FROM HERE...

For Related Information

◄◄ "Saving a Document or Template," p. 165.

◄◄ "Editing Text," p. 275.

◄◄ "Working with Reverse Text," p. 466.

◄◄ "Creating Color Publications," p. 531.

◄◄ "Organizing Your Disk Files," p. 627.

Summary

Transparencies, slides, and handouts are used frequently in almost all business settings. PageMaker enables you to create effective presentation materials in less time and at less expense than you could if you used other methods. As demonstrated in the examples in this chapter, few limitations exist as to the formats and combinations you can use. You also can save the files so that you can use the same templates to create new transparencies.

Creating Brochures, Price Lists, and Directories

This chapter shows you how to use PageMaker to create brochures, price lists, and directories, examples of which are shown
in figure 20.1. These documents are grouped together here because
they are promotional materials; however, they appear in a wide variety
of forms.

Brochures frequently are designed to fit on 8 1/2-by-11-inch paper
folded into three panels, or as four (or more) 8 1/2-by-11-inch pages
printed on 11-by-17-inch paper and folded in half. These formats are
economical because they don't require special cutting, and they fit
neatly into standard business envelopes.

In a PageMaker file, brochures usually are only one or two pages long,
although the finished document may be folded into four or more panels, as illustrated in Example 20.1. Example 20.2, which is a four page
brochure, is printed on 11-by-17-inch paper and folded in half.

Example 20.1

8 ¹/₂ x 14 Page

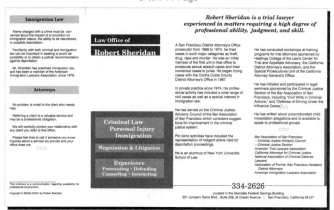

Example 20.2

8 ¹/₂ x 11 Page

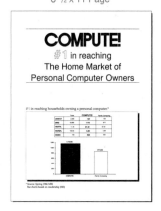

Example 20.3

4 x 9 Page

Example 20.4

4 ¹/₂ x 6 ¹/₂ Page

Example 20.5

11 x 17 Page

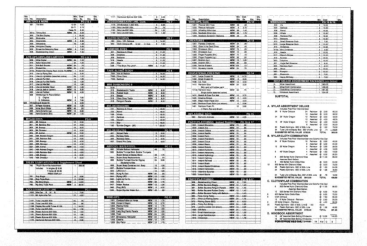

Fig. 20.1

Examples of documents discussed in this chapter.

This chapter includes tips that you can use to produce longer brochures, such as the booklets in Examples 20.3 and 20.4. (Refer to Chapter 17 for more guidelines on producing longer documents.)

Price lists, which are usually mailed in standard business envelopes, are often produced in one of the formats demonstrated in this chapter, unless the lists are very long and in booklet form. The tabbed-list format shown in Example 20.5 (a tabloid price list) can be used for restaurant menus, wine lists, parts lists, inventories, telephone lists, and many other documents. Long price lists can be derived from spreadsheet data or database files, just as the membership list in Example 20.3 and the product list in Example 20.4 were derived.

Directories and membership lists are usually longer than brochures and price lists, and some lists are bound as books rather than stapled as booklets. Example 20.3 (a membership directory) shows how a database file can be converted to a directory format.

Regardless of the final trim size, PageMaker easily handles all these formats.

Design Principles

Many documents in these categories follow the basic design principles recommended throughout this book (particularly in Chapters 15 through 19); however, you will find exceptions to the guidelines when they are applied to brochures in general (and to the publications discussed in Chapter 21).

Two design principles merit a full discussion in this chapter: the use of white space and the limit on the number of different typefaces used.

Don't be afraid of white space.

White space is especially important if the publication presents your product or service to your clients and the general public. A price list, for example, may also serve as a detailed catalog of your products, with illustrations to attract the readers' interest or to explain the value of a special offer. Increased white space can improve the overall effectiveness of the publication as a sales tool.

If you put too many words in a brochure or list of members or services, you may limit the effectiveness of your document. A document that doesn't use white space effectively appears uninviting, but if you create white space simply by making the text smaller, you might lose those readers who ignore anything written in small type.

When you work with a small format, opening up white space may translate into writing less copy or using fewer illustrations. If you are creating a brochure for a small business, you probably want to give the readers as much information as possible but, at the same time, save printing and postage costs by holding down the number of pages. If you are writing your own copy, follow the example of professional copy writers who can make a point in the number of words specified by the designer. By choosing your words carefully, you can get a few important points across and influence the reader to call for your service or come to your store.

If you start with a specific number of pages as a goal and find that this page limit creates a crowded design, you can try any of the tricks described under "Copy Fitting" in Chapter 8, but also check into the cost of adding pages. Adding pages to your publication design sometimes can be done without significantly increasing the printing or production costs.

This guideline is often relaxed in functional reference listings such as telephone directories for an association, a company, or a department, and long inventory or price lists used for reference rather than for marketing. If you have a great deal of information in a repetitive format, as in a price list for a large store or warehouse, the reader can find a specific product more easily if the information is compact.

Use only one or two different typefaces in a document.

The choice of typeface sets the tone of the piece. The typeface you choose can convey a sense of seriousness, elegance, or frivolity. Brochures, for example, often use decorative or unusual typefaces for the headings and sometimes for the body copy. If you are not sure how different typefaces affect the reader, use the traditional faces rather than experiment with more decorative ones.

Traditional typefaces (and their modern adaptations) include American Typewriter, Avant Garde, Bookman, Galliard, Garamond, Goudy, Helvetica, Korinna, Lubalin Graph, New Baskerville, New Century Schoolbook, Optima, Palatino, Times, and Trump Mediaeval. Decorative typefaces include Benguiat, Friz Quadrata, Machine, Souvenir, and Zapf Chancery.

Table 20.1 shows some of the typefaces used for the types of publications presented in this chapter. Notice that brochures can use almost any typeface, and lists are usually limited to typefaces that are readable in small sizes.

Table 20.1 Typefaces Used for Brochures, Price Lists, and Directories

Typefaces	Brochures	Price Lists	Directories
Arial**	Y	Y	Y
ITC American Typewriter	Y	N	N
ITC Avant Garde*	Y	Y	Y
ITC Benguiat	Y	N	Y
ITC Bookman*	Y	N	N
Courier* or Courier New**	N	N	N
ITC Friz Quadrata	Y	N	Y
ITC Galliard	Y	N	Y
ITC Garamond	Y	N	N
Glypha	N	Y	Y
Goudy Old Style	Y	N	N
Helvetica*	Y	Y	Y
ITC Korinna	Y	N	N
ITC Lubalin Graph	Y	N	N
ITC Machine	Y	N	N
ITC New Baskerville	Y	Y	N
New Century Schoolbook*	N	Y	Y
Optima	Y	N	N
Palatino*	Y	Y	Y
ITC Souvenir	Y	N	N
Times* or Times New Roman**	Y	Y	Y
Trump Mediaeval	Y	Y	Y
ITC Zapf Chancery*	Y	N	N

(Y = used; N = not used, * = Standard LaserWriter font, ** = TrueType font packaged with Windows 3.1)

In addition to the preceding principles, you might also use the following guidelines (discussed in more detail in Chapters 17 and 19) for promotional materials:

- ■ Use all capital letters as a deliberate design strategy rather than as a method for emphasizing text or showing a heading.

- ■ Treat all figures consistently: fonts, line weights, and fill patterns.

- ■ Be sure that the space between text and graphics is the same for all figures.

- ■ Use the same graphic elements to carry the theme throughout the document.

- ■ Use ruled lines to help set off the grid of the pages.

- ■ All columns on all pages should bottom out at the same point.

These principles, and the principles discussed in detail in the following paragraphs, are repeated in the examples along with comments about their applications to the specific examples.

FROM HERE...

For Related Information

◄◄ "Creating a Grid System," p. 683.

◄◄ "Planning Your Design Specifications," p. 708.

Production Tips

The first production tip is mentioned repeatedly throughout this book, but the second tip is unique to the list formats in this chapter. The application of these tips to promotional materials is described generally in this section. In the "Examples" section, specific tips are repeated with explanations of their applications to the specific examples.

Use templates if you are producing more than one brochure.

If you are designing a series of brochures that describe different products offered by the same company, you can develop one template and clone it for each brochure. If you are a designer with many clients, however, you may want each brochure to be unique; therefore, you should not use a template system.

Regardless of how the details of the designs change from one brochure to another, you still can create a template for any series of brochures that use the same paper size and number of folds. Figures 20.2 and 20.3 show two types of templates for folded brochures. The text typed on each page of the template shows the sequence of the panels when the brochure is folded.

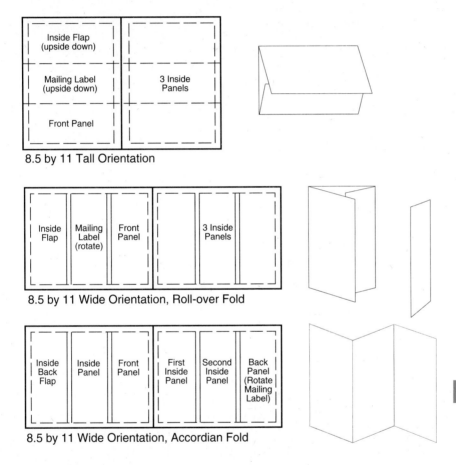

8.5 by 11 Tall Orientation

8.5 by 11 Wide Orientation, Roll-over Fold

8.5 by 11 Wide Orientation, Accordian Fold

Fig. 20.2

Templates for three-panel brochures.

If your laser printer forces a wide margin around large paper sizes, you can solve this problem by using the trick described in the discussion of Example 20.1. In the template for the four-panel, legal-size brochure, 8 1/2-by-11-inch paper was used to get around the margins imposed by the laser printer. See the production tips for the four-panel brochure for an explanation of why this procedure was required.

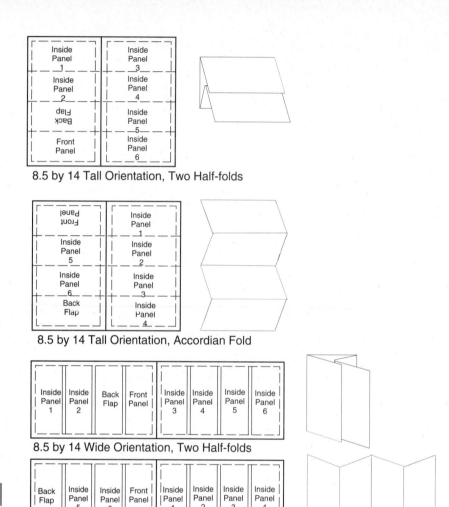

8.5 by 14 Tall Orientation, Two Half-folds

8.5 by 14 Tall Orientation, Accordian Fold

8.5 by 14 Wide Orientation, Two Half-folds

8.5 by 14 Wide Orientation, Accordian Fold

Fig. 20.3

Templates for four-panel brochures.

Compensate for ragged-right text by setting unequal right and left margins.

The need for a balanced appearance is evident in all the examples. Because of the ragged-right text, the right margin may appear to be different from the left. You can compensate for this visual difference by using a wider left-margin setting or a narrower right margin.

For brochures containing mostly graphics with little text, add text to the page after you position your graphics.

In many brochures, graphics are the major design element. When the graphics are the most important factor of the page layout, you can save time by changing the text to fit the graphics instead of trying to change the graphics to fit the text.

Before you complete the specifications for a long list, test run the complete production cycle, using only a small amount of data from a spreadsheet or database.

If you are converting data from a spreadsheet or a database, run a small sample of the data through the production steps before you complete your design specifications. In this way, you can develop a list of required steps and learn how many design specifications can or must be handled in the database or spreadsheet. Examples 20.3 and 20.4, which use database lists, provide discussions outlining the steps required to convert the data into text for PageMaker.

Use black boxes to reserve space for halftone photographs dropped in by the printer, and use white boxes to reserve space for line art to be pasted in before being sent to the printer.

Brochures, price lists, catalogs, and service directories can be illustrated with photographs or computer art. For handling artwork in these examples, use the preceding production tricks (described in more detail in Chapters 17 and 18).

Assigning Style Names in a Spreadsheet

There's a trick for adding style names in a spreadsheet when you want each row broken into two or more lines using different formatting in PageMaker. Suppose, for example, that the row in the spreadsheet contains the following:

firstname   lastname   company   address   city   state   zip

and you want the final format in PageMaker to be this:

firstname lastname

company
address, city, state zip

You can insert a blank column in front of the "firstname," "company," and "address" columns, fill each blank column with a different bracketed style tag name framed in brackets (< >). The columns might resemble the following:

<name>	firstname	lastname	<company>	company	<street>	address	city	state	zip
<name>	Elizabeth	Davis	<company>	Infantium	<street>	123 Joliet St	WA	DC	20833
<name>	Linda	Oates	<company>	Ray Co.	<street>	37 Oak Way	SF	CA	94133
<name>	Theodore	Moore	<company>	Big-I Inc.	<street>	400 Main	RC	CA	90845

Then export the spreadsheet data as ASCII text and use any word processor to globally search for a right bracket (<). Change the bracket to a carriage return followed by a right bracket. Then import the text into a PageMaker publication where the styles have already been set up with the same names, and check Read Tags in the Place dialog box.

For Related Information

FROM HERE...

◀◀ "Creating a Grid System," p. 683.

◀◀ "Production Tips," p. 741 and p. 779.

Examples

The examples in this chapter demonstrate the wide range of formats PageMaker can produce. You also learn how to use databases to produce different kinds of promotional and informative publications. The following examples are presented in this chapter:

- *Example 20.1.* A Four-Panel Brochure with Screens and Bleeds

- *Example 20.2.* A Four-Page Brochure Consisting of Many Repeated Elements

- *Example 20.3.* A Two-Column Membership Directory Derived from a Database

- *Example 20.4.* A Single-Column List of Products with Descriptions, Prices, and Suppliers

- *Example 20.5.* A Tabloid Price List with Horizontal and Vertical Rules

Example 20.1. A Four-Panel Brochure with Screens and Bleeds

The brochure in this example is designed to be printed on two sides of 8 1/2-by-14-inch (legal-size) paper and folded into four panels. Special work-arounds were devised to accommodate the design that required bleeds extending beyond the maximum print area of the printer, and additional steps were taken to mark the final publication for screening by the print shop (instead of using PageMaker's screens). The same work-arounds used here can be adapted for any publication having design elements that bleed beyond the print area of your printer or that use tinted screens. (Refer to figures 20.2 and 20.3 and the accompanying discussion to see how templates can be used for folded brochures.)

Description

This brochure may surprise you. Even though the final brochure is printed on 8 1/2-by-14-inch paper (a size PageMaker supports), the page size is 8 1/2 by 11 inches. The final printouts are pasted on the 8 1/2-by-14-inch layout. The screens behind some of the text in the final printed piece are created by a photographic halftoning process (see fig. 20.4). Although PageMaker creates screens, they are used in this example for draft reviews only, not for the final camera-ready printouts. The production tips for this four-panel brochure describe why PageMaker's screens were not used.

Design Principles

Two design principles merit special mention in this case. The use of white space gives a pleasing uncluttered appearance, and unity is achieved by repeating the graphics.

Don't be afraid of white space. Keep text to a minimum. This brochure violates this guideline. The writer on this project was given no word count at the beginning, and the designer had no idea how long the delivered text would be. As a result, in early drafts of this brochure, the text filled every page from margin to margin. After seeing the first draft, the designer worked closely with the writer to reduce the number of words to fit the space and leave more white space on each page, but the pages are still slightly crowded.

Side one

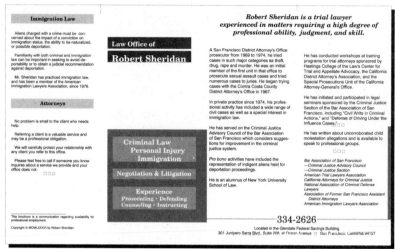

Side two

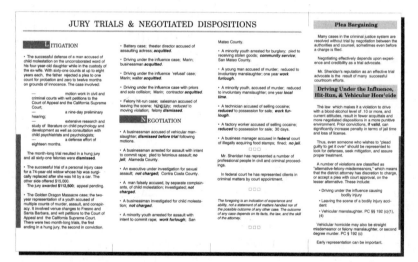

Fig. 20.4

Printout of pages
of a four-panel
brochure.

***Let the same graphic elements carry the theme throughout the
document.*** In this case, shaded backgrounds are used throughout
the brochure. This simple graphic element unifies the panels. These
screens are created with PageMaker's rectangle tool for the draft review cycles, but they are removed for the final printout and added as
halftones by the offset printer.

Production Tips

The trick to producing this brochure is to create it as four 8 1/2-by-11-inch pages. The pages are pasted in place manually before the document is reproduced. You may wonder about the advantage of using an 8 1/2-by-11-inch page because PageMaker has an option for producing 8 1/2-by-14-inch pages—the final size for this brochure. The answer is not obvious until you consider the way the different printers work.

This brochure is designed to be printed on an Apple LaserWriter printer, which does not print to the edges of the paper. One edge of the paper is used by the grippers inside the printer. (Offset printers also require 0.25 inch at the edge of the paper for the grippers on the press.) The other three edges of the paper are defined by the PostScript code inside the printer.

Apple's engineers originally designed the LaserWriter printers this way to conserve memory (though the problem has been corrected in the LaserWriter IINTX). The larger the image area, the more memory used. The engineers, therefore, made the maximum image area for the printer slightly larger than 8 inches by 10.5 inches—taking about one pica from the top and bottom of a page and about 1.5 picas from the sides. In printer's terms, this allowance yields a maximum of 300 pixels per inch, or 90,000 pixels per square inch. When this 90,000-pixel limit is applied to 8 1/2-by-14-inch pages, the margins around the edge become even wider (see fig. 20.5).

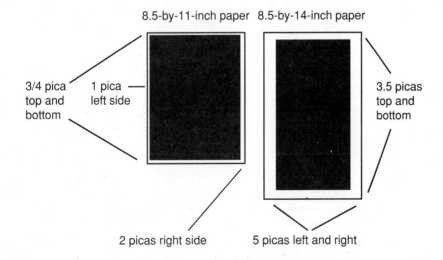

8.5-by-11-inch paper   8.5-by-14-inch paper

3/4 pica top and bottom

1 pica left side

3.5 picas top and bottom

2 picas right side

5 picas left and right

Fig. 20.5

Printing full-page black boxes to determine printer-imposed limits on a page.

Test the Print Area of Your Printer

You can view the print area dimensions in the Print dialog box, as described in Chapter 10. However, to really see how the print area fills the paper, try this exercise: Open a new PageMaker document, set the page size to the paper size in the printer, draw a black or shaded box that covers the entire page, and print the page.

On a LaserWriter Plus printer, the 8 1/2-by-11-inch pages have margins of 1 pica at top and bottom and 1.5 picas on the sides. The 8 1/2-by-14-inch pages have top margins of 3.5 picas and side margins of 5 picas. On a Hewlett-Packard LaserJet Series II printer, these margins are even wider. On a Linotronic typesetter the printer might use, however, an image larger than 11 by 17 inches, without a forced margin around the image, can be printed. Other printer models will have different print areas depending on the model, the resolution, and the printer driver installed.

Although these limitations are not a problem for most documents, when you are designing a small brochure, you want to be able to come within 0.25 inch of all sides—the same limit imposed by the offset printer unless you pay for printing *bleeds* (elements that cross a cut edge in the final document). (The problem is eliminated with printers and imagesetters that handle larger paper sizes, such as the Linotronic typesetter, which has no limits and uses 12-inch-wide film.)

Figure 20.6 shows the Page Setup dialog box for this brochure. Notice that the template uses a page size of 8 1/2 by 11 inches and Wide orientation. If the laser printer could have handled the full-size page layout, as a Linotronic typesetter can, the template would have been set up with a page size of 8 1/2 by 14 inches and Wide orientation. To center each panel in the completed folded brochure, the space between columns is entered (in the Column Guides dialog box) as twice the size of the outside margins.

T I P   Bleeding across Paste-Up Lines

When designing pages that will be pasted together for final reproduction, do not cross seamed edges with gray fill patterns: use solid white or black only. Otherwise, when you paste the pages together, you can see the seam where two edges of a gray pattern meet. Figure 20.7 shows thumbnails indicating how the parts of Example 20.1 are printed.

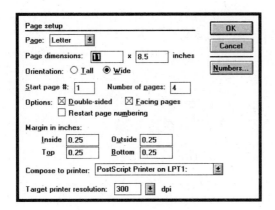

Fig. 20.6

The Page Setup dialog box for a four-panel brochure.

Fig. 20.7

Thumbnail printouts showing how pages are divided.

Production Steps

The production steps for this brochure follow much the same pattern as those for other publications. You need to pay close attention, however, to the order of the pages so that the text flows in the correct sequence after the layout is pasted up (see step 3). To create this brochure, use the following steps:

1. Open the template for this brochure and save the template under the brochure's name.

2. Type and format all text in the Story Editor, using a style sheet. In this case, the text is typed as 5 stories: the cover, the back cover, the two columns that end up on the right of side 1, the 3 columns that end up on the left of side 2, and the last column of side 2 (refer to fig. 20.4). See Chapter 8 for information on formatting text using style sheets.

3. Close the story window by clicking the Control menu icon in the upper left corner. Working in Fit in Window view, place all text on all panels of the template.

   Notice that the text flows through two columns on page 1 that in the final will be pasted up with the two columns on page 4, and the three columns on page 3 will be pasted up with the one column on page 3. If the text is typed as one story and is manually flowed in the sequence that the readers will follow as they open the brochure, it flows from column 2 of page 4 (the front cover), to columns 1 and 2 of page 1 (the facing-page view when the first fold is opened), to the three columns on page 2 and the one column of page 3 (the four columns that compose side 2 of the final), and finally to column 1 of page 4 (the back cover when the brochure is folded).

4. Starting with the first page, go through the document in Actual Size view and make adjustments, adding black or screened boxes behind text.

5. To create the screens in the design, use PageMaker's Rectangle tool and shading for the draft versions. Delete these shaded boxes for the final printout.

6. Print the final document on 8 1/2-by-11-inch paper, and paste the pages in the correct locations to create the 8 1/2-by-14-inch master for reproduction.

Using Screens for the Four-Panel Brochure

Chapter 19 recommends that you use gray screens instead of solid black areas for slides and transparencies if the final output is produced on a laser printer. If you use offset printing to produce a large quantity of brochures, however, gray screens may not produce the effect you want.

If you create gray screens using PageMaker and have your brochure offset printed, the text or the screen may not print clearly. When the camera is set to pick up a fine screen—a 10-percent fill pattern, for example—the photographic process may darken each character of the text and blur the edges of characters. If the camera is set to sharpen the text, the 10-percent screen may disappear in the photographed image. In other words, if the image includes very light gray tones or a wide range of gray tones, you will have trouble finding a camera setting that picks up the 10-percent screens and also produces the correct darkness for text and for screens darker than 10 percent.

If your final output will be offset printed, use tissue overlays and let the offset printer's camera operator make the screens rather than use PageMaker's shading, as done with the brochure in figure 20.8. Also, with this method, you can produce screens of a higher resolution (more dots per inch) than the 300-dpi resolution of the laser printer.

Preparation for Reproduction

Instead of using PageMaker's fill patterns to create the gray tones on the page, you can let the offset printer use a camera to create the percentage screens as halftones. After the initial proofing and editing rounds of the brochure with mixed percentages of fill patterns, change all the boxes in the PageMaker version to solid black (behind reverse type) or white (behind black type) and use tissue overlays to tell the camera operator what percentage screen to use (see fig. 20.8). This adjustment adds only a small charge to the printer's bill.

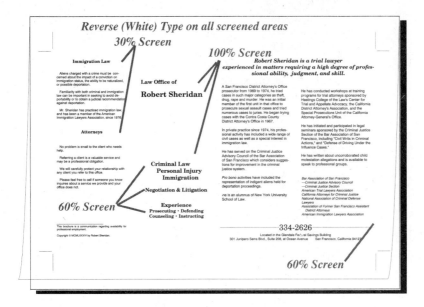

Fig. 20.8

Brochure marked for screening by the camera operator at the print shop.

Example 20.2. A Four-Page Brochure Consisting of Many Repeated Elements

This 8 1/2-by-11-inch brochure is printed on 11-by-17-inch paper and folded in half. Because of the many duplicate elements in the brochure, this example illustrates the use of dummy text and graphics stored on the pasteboard of the template. You can apply the design and production tips to any publication that uses the same elements on every page (with changes to the text or content but not to the format).

Description

This four-page brochure is composed of text and graphics created using PageMaker's tools and graphs from Lotus 1-2-3 (see fig. 20.9). All text was typed directly into PageMaker. The logo, COMPUTE!, was kerned manually. The final 8 1/2-by-11-inch pages are offset printed on 11-by-17-inch sheets folded in half.

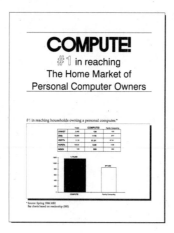
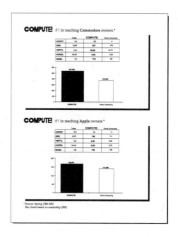
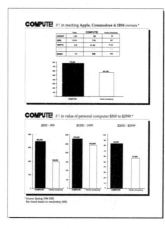
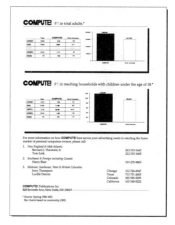

Fig. 20.9

Printouts of pages of a four-page brochure with repeated elements.

Design Principles

Many of the design principles described at the beginning of this chapter and in Chapters 15 through 19 are applied in this publication. The four principles best illustrated by this example are repeated and described in this section.

Use all capital letters as a deliberate design strategy rather than as a method for emphasizing text or showing a heading. In this case, the word "COMPUTE!" is in uppercase, and the letters are kerned to meet the designer's specifications. This customization of the text creates a unique logo.

The logo is kerned once, duplicated, and scaled to various sizes. Whenever this logo is used, the same relative kerning adjustments are applied. The kerning adjustments are preserved when text is sized in PageMaker. (For more information about kerning in PageMaker, see Chapters 8 and 16.)

Treat all figures consistently: fonts, line weights, fill patterns. The same two fill patterns are used in every bar graph in this example. All graphs are scaled to the same size, and all line weights and labels are the same size. This consistency helps highlight the significant differences—the data variations—in the figures.

Use the same graphic elements to carry the theme throughout the document. Each graph is framed in a drop-shadow border. This border helps the reader group related information on the page.

Select only one or two typefaces and use the same sizes for headings and other text on all images. If you are producing a long brochure, consider using style sheets to make the document consistent in appearance. The brochure uses only two typefaces and seven fonts, as outlined in figure 20.10. Except for the axis labels on the bar graphs, which are generated by 1-2-3, all text is typed directly into PageMaker and "cloned" from the pasteboard elements.

Style name	Type specifications
Front Cover: **COMPUTE!**	Various sizes, hand-kerned in PageMaker
 on front cover	48-point Helvetica outline, from Illustrator
Opening text	36-point Helvetica
On each chart: **Large table of figures** Small table of Figures	8-point Helvetica Bold, and 6-point Helvetica
Byline	14-point Palatino
Source	10-point Palatino
Back Cover	12-point Palatino

Fig. 20.10

Type specifications table for four-page brochure with repeated elements.

Production Tips

The graphs are created in 1-2-3. All options for the size of the graphs, size of the axis labels, and fill patterns are specified in advance, and the same specifications are used for every graph. When placed in PageMaker, the graphs are cropped down to the axis labels, and the titles and legends are removed. The drop-shadow border and all other text are added in PageMaker. See Chapter 11 for a tip on creating bar charts directly in PageMaker by using the Rectangle tool and the Numeric Scaling option on the Control palette.

The Template

The template is set up as a double-sided document, but the Facing Pages option is not used (see fig. 20.11). This technique leaves a wider pasteboard area for storing the standard drop-shadow box and table of data that appear on every graph (see fig. 20.12). The pasteboard holds dummy text for all text elements repeated on every page, including the tabular information framed in ruled lines created with PageMaker's Constrained-line tool. A spacing guide is provided for positioning the bar graphs within the drop-shadow borders.

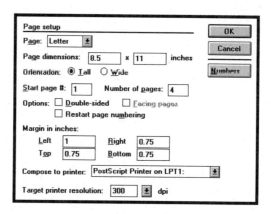

Fig. 20.11

The Page Setup dialog box for brochure with repeated elements.

Production Steps

This type of publication uses the pasteboard to great advantage. To produce this brochure, work through the following steps:

1. Open a new publication to build the template, and set up the following margins, as shown in figure 20.11:

Inside	1.00
Top	0.75
Outside	0.75
Bottom	0.75

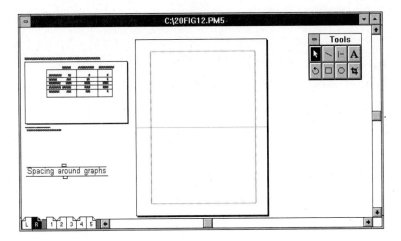

Fig. 20.12

The template with spacing guides and drop-shadow boxes on the pasteboard.

2. Type the logo on the pasteboard in 127-point Helvetica and manu-ally kern the letters to tighten the entire word. Then make two copies of the logo. Change one copy to 14-point and one to 8-point Helvetica, using the Type Specs command from the Type menu. Store all three sizes on the pasteboard.

3. Type the dummy text for the byline and for the source for the graphs, and place these two text blocks on the pasteboard.

4. Using PageMaker's text tools, tab settings, and the dummy data, create the table for the first graph. Draw a box around the text and add horizontal and vertical rules. Place the entire table (text and graph), shown in figure 20.13, on the pasteboard. (Although you can use the Table Editor to create the data instead, typing the data directly into PageMaker is just as fast when the tables are small, simple, and numerous.)

	Totals	COMPUTE	Competitor
UNW GT	75	4	0
<000>	455	45	0
VERT%	0.27	2.37	0.00
HORZ%	100.00	9.89	0.00
INDEX	100	889	0

Fig. 20.13

A tabbed block of text framed by PageMaker's ruled lines.

5. Save the template.

6. Go over each page in Fit in Window view. Copy and paste the drop-shadow box, its contents, and the title dummy text from the pasteboard to the page, and use the Place command to import each graph.

7. Go back to the first page and, working in Actual Size view, edit the text as needed to adapt it to each graph.

8. Save the publication.

Preparation for Reproduction

If you can, print the final version of this brochure on a Linotronic type-setter to produce solid black drop-shadows. If you use a laser printer for the final output, use a coated paper stock for the best image or spray the final pages with a matte finish to darken the solid black areas before you send the document to the offset printer. You can purchase matte-finish spray in any local, art supplies store. (Hair spray also pro-duces the matte effect.)

During production, all the 1-2-3 PIC files are stored on the hard disk in the same subdirectory as the PageMaker document (see fig. 20.14). Later, you can copy these files to the same backup disk. If you use the Link command to link the graphs to external files, you can periodically update the graphs and rebuild the brochure quarterly or annually, us-ing new data.

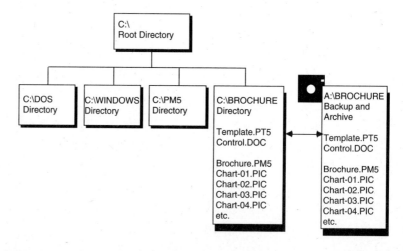

Fig. 20.14

Disk-file
organization
for brochure
with graphs.

Example 20.3. A Two-Column Membership Directory Derived from a Database

This directory is designed as a two-column layout on narrow pages. The list of names and addresses is converted from a database format into text. You can apply the design and production methods used in this example to any directory, regardless of the page size or number of columns. You also can adapt the conversion steps used for the database information for any publication that uses a database or spreadsheet file as a primary source of text.

Description

This 80-page booklet lists the names, addresses, and telephone numbers of more than 1,500 members of a professional association (see fig. 20.15). The information is converted from a database to a word processing file and then formatted before being placed in PageMaker.

Design Principles

The design principles discussed throughout this book are generally followed in this example. Two principles in particular merit comment here.

Don't be afraid of white space. In this document, the white-space guideline is relaxed because the final product is a functional reference list, like a telephone directory. Most of the white space is achieved by leaving a wide bottom margin between the lists and the running foot. A blank line (two carriage returns) is left between entries.

Use only one or two different typefaces in a document. The typeface used throughout this list is Helvetica, as outlined in figure 20.16. This typeface is clean-looking and easy to read in small point sizes.

Style name	Type specifications
Main Title	14-point Helvetica
Level 1 Head	12-point Helvetica Bold, flush left
Level 2 Head	10-point Helvetica Bold, centered
Level 3 Head	8-point Helvetica Bold Italic, flush left
Listings	8-point Helvetica

Fig. 20.16

Type specifications table for two-column membership list.

Production Tips

The primary production trick involves making a detailed list of the required steps before going through the full production process.

NOTE The rather convoluted process demonstrated by this example can be considered a worst-case scenario in terms of data conversion. Some database programs offer the option of saving data formatted as a mailing list so that the word processing step is not required, and some programs even have the capability of switching the order of the data and adding new fields without going through a spreadsheet.

Before you complete the specifications for a long list, test run the complete production cycle, using only a small amount of data from a spreadsheet or database. The text-preparation steps in this project require many global search-and-replace operations in the word processing file. Because of the large volume of data in this project, each global search takes nearly 20 minutes. One wrong global replacement adds at least 40 minutes to the total production time (20 minutes to reverse the changes, 20 minutes to perform the correct replacements). Run a short selection of the data through the production cycle. From this run, prepare a detailed list of steps to reduce the risks of major mistakes in text preparation and of increased production time.

Initially, the data is stored in a database format. Converting the data to a spreadsheet format provides a convenient way to switch the order of the information and to add three columns for the title, secondary specialty tag, and a comma between city and state (see fig. 20.17). After the data is sorted by the column labeled Specialty 1, print the data from the spreadsheet program as a reference during production. Delete the Specialty 1 column, save the data as text-only, and format it with a word processing program.

Last Name	First Name	Initial	Building/Suite	Street	City	State	Zip	Phone	Specialty 1	Specialty 2	
Miller	Stuart	L	Suite 708	12 W. 6th	New York	NY	10010	345-1234	Cardiology	Vascular	

Title	First Name	Initial	Last Name	Building/Suite	Street	City	State	Zip	Phone	Tag	Specialty 2
Dr.	Stuart	L	Miller	Suite 708	12 W. 6th	New York	NY	10010	345-1234	Second Specialty:	Vascular

Fig. 20.17

Changing the order of the fields and adding columns in a spreadsheet program.

The Template

The template is set up on a 4-by-9-inch page with the inside margin slightly larger than the outside margin (see fig. 20.18). Because the lists have a ragged-right margin, the column margins have been shifted by dragging them manually to the right of the page margins on each page. This technique gives a balanced appearance (see fig. 20.19). Otherwise, the text appears to be left of center.

Production Steps

Producing this two-column list from database material requires more steps and more attention to detail than the other examples given in this chapter. The following steps guide you through the entire process.

 NOTE The dBASE and Excel filters can do the same "sorting" and data conversions as done in the following steps (see "Importing Unformatted Text" in Chapter 6).

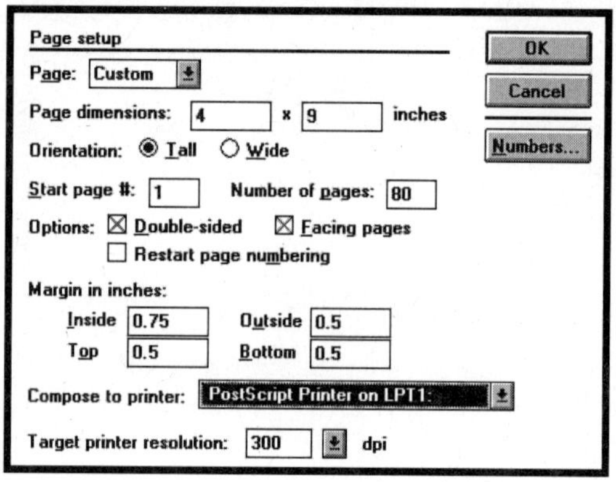

Fig. 20.18

Page Setup dialog box for the membership list.

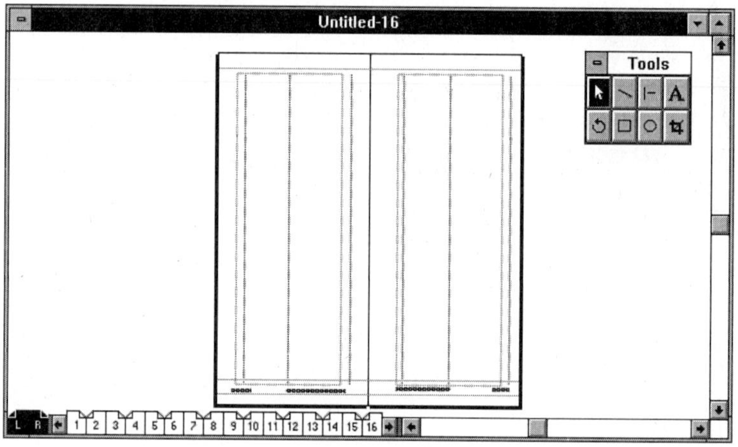

Fig. 20.19

The template for the membership list, with column margins manually shifted to the right.

1. Select a small portion of your data and take it through the entire process, carefully noting the steps required for full database conversion.

2. Use the small sample of data to estimate the number of pages required for different designs and type specifications. The final design specifications are tempered by considerations of white space, readability, function, and printing costs. The final design in this example accommodates about 16 names per page set in 8-point Helvetica (see fig. 20.20).

3. Convert the data to a spreadsheet format (refer to fig. 20.17). Save the data as text-only information.

Fig. 20.20

Printing one-page sample to estimate the full page count.

If this conversion results in commas between the items of information, use a word processor and globally change the commas to tab characters. The spreadsheet program interprets each tab as a new column.

4. Open the spreadsheet file and move each first name and initial to precede the last name; then insert three new items: the title, Dr., before each name; the comma between city and state; and the phrase "Secondary Specialty" where applicable.

5. Sort the data by Specialty 1 and print the list from the spreadsheet for use as a reference. Save the spreadsheet.

6. Delete the Specialty 1 column. Before each data column, add a blank column (before Building/Suite, City, Phone, and Tag). Each blank column begins a new line in the final version. Under a new file name, save the data from the spreadsheet as text-only information. If the text were to be formatted using different styles for name and address and other fields, you can add columns of style tags in this step, as described in the Production Tips at the beginning of this chapter.

7. Open the template and go through the document in Fit in Window view, placing the text in columns on each page.

8. Perform global changes and detailed edits in the Story Editor. In this case, the following four global searches are required:

■ To add a blank line after each entry, change all single carriage returns (type **^p** in the Find What Area of the Change dialog box) to two carriage returns (type **^p^p**).

■ To convert the blank columns inserted in step 6 to carriage returns in the word-processed files, change each double tab (type **^t^t** in the Find What area of the Change dialog box) to carriage return (type **^p** in the Change To area of the dialog box).

■ Change the column of commas between city and state (added in the spreadsheet) from tab-comma-tab (type **^t,^t**) to comma-space.

■ Change all remaining tabs to spaces.

9. Scroll through the document in Actual Size view. Enter the subheads as needed. In most cases, exactly 16 names fit on each page; but if any entry is broken across columns or across pages, adjust the bottom windowshade to force the whole name and address into the next column or page.

Note that if you choose to edit the text using a word processor—before placing the text in PageMaker—you can tag the subheads in the word processing program so that they look like this:

<SUBHEAD>Neurology

See the section "Assigning Style Names in a Spreadsheet" earlier in this chapter.

10. Print the pages so that you can proofread them for accuracy (compare this printout with the spreadsheet printout from step 5) and for formatting.

FROM HERE...

For Related Information

◀◀ "Importing Unformatted Text," p. 250.

Example 20.4. A Single-Column List of Products with Descriptions, Prices, and Suppliers

The product list in this example is designed as a catalog for a fund-raising auction. You can adapt this format for any directory including sentences or paragraphs of descriptive information in addition to names and addresses, or for a product catalog including product descriptions, prices, and product numbers. The list of products easily could have been a list of people, with descriptions of achievements or skills; a list of companies, with descriptions of services or product lines; a list of restaurants, with reviews of what they offer; and so on.

Description

This 48-page booklet lists more than 100 products to be auctioned in a fund-raising event (see fig. 20.21). The listing for each product includes the product name, list price, a brief description, and the name and address of the supplier. Text is wrapped around the large-type item numbers. The page size is designed to accommodate paid advertisements exactly the size of a standard business card (2 by 3 1/2 inches).

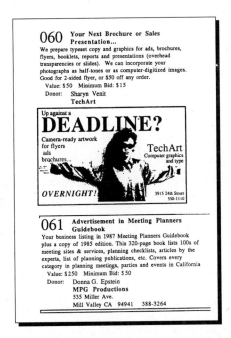

Fig. 20.21

Printout of one page of a list of products.

Design Principles

Besides the general rules related to consistency in design, two principles deserve special mention here.

Don't be afraid of white space. The white space on these pages is produced by indenting the name and address of the donor for each product. Product descriptions are allowed a maximum of five lines each.

Use only one or two typefaces in a document. The Times typeface is used for text throughout this booklet, and Helvetica is used for product numbers (see fig. 20.22). This simplicity helps balance the variety of typefaces in the business cards and display ads supplied by advertisers and pasted in manually on the final printouts.

Fig. 20.22

Type specifications table for single-column product list.

Style name	Type specifications
000	Product numbers, 24-point Helvetica
Product Title	10-point Times Bold
Product Description	10-point Times
Company Name	10-point Times Bold

Production Tips

The original data is stored in a comma-delimited file, which is the source file. A word processing program is used to merge print the data for the product lists into a merge-print file (see fig. 20.23). The trick in this case is that the merge-print file is sent to a disk instead of to the printer. (Keep in mind that not all word processing programs can print to a disk.)

Because the data already has been edited and corrected, little processing is required. The same data is used to send form letters to the donors to confirm their participation, to send formal invitations and complimentary tickets to the event, and to send thank-you notes after the event. This data also is used to merge print all the materials used on the night of the auction, such as item tags (produced on mailing labels) and item lists for the auctioneer and the staff members collecting the payments.

Comma-delimited format

001,Your Next Brochure,"We prepare typeset copy and graphics for
ads, brochures, fliers, booklets, reports, and presentations (overhead
transparencies or slides). We can incorporate your photographs as
half-tones, or as computer-digitized images. Good for 2-sided flier, or
$50 off any order.",50,15,Grace Moore,TechArt,3915 24th Street,San
Francisco,CA,94114,(415) 550-1110

Merge-print file

001

Your Next Brochure
We prepare typeset copy and graphics for ads, brochures, fliers, booklets,
reports, and presentations (overhead transparencies or slides). We can
incorporate your photographs as half-tones, or as computer-digitized images.
Good for 2-sided flier, or $50 off any order.

Value:	$50 Minimum bid: $15
Donor:	Grace Moore
	TechArt
	3915 24th Street
	San Francisco,CA,94114
	(415) 550-1110

Fig. 20.23

Data stored in comma-delimited format and the merge-print formatted file.

The Template

The PageMaker template is set up to print three items per page in a
small (4 1/2-by-6 1/2-inch) booklet format (see figs. 20.24 and 20.25).
The 0.5-inch margins result in a column width of exactly 3.5 inches, the
width of a standard business card and the size of the ads used throughout the booklet. A ruled line is stored on the pasteboard of the template and placed between the product entries. A 2-by-3 1/2-inch border
also is stored on the pasteboard and used to mark the positions for ads
to be pasted in manually.

Production Steps

Unlike other examples, this publication requires steps to merge the
data before you place it in PageMaker. You may need to adapt these
steps to meet the requirements of your own word processor.

1. Enter the data in the merge format used by your word processor.

2. Merge print the formatted data to a disk file, including carriage
   returns and character-formatting specifications (refer to
   fig. 20.23).

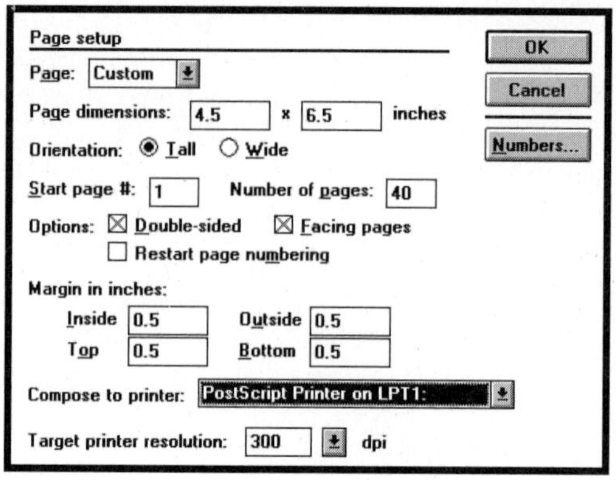

Fig. 20.24

Page Setup
dialog box for
the product list.

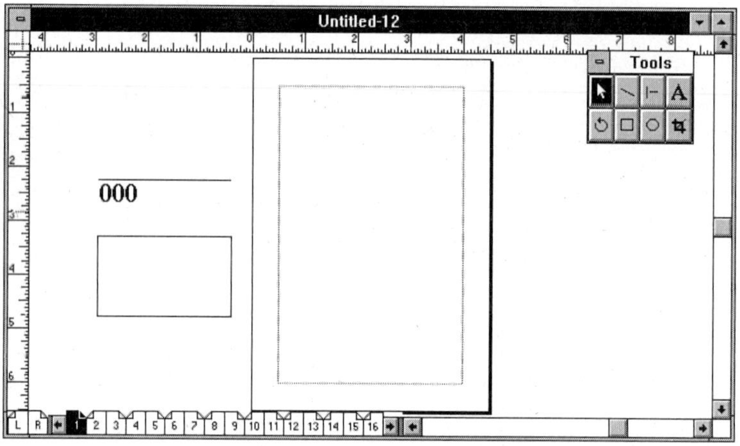

Fig. 20.25

The template for
the product list.

3. Create the boxes used to mark the positions of the ads. Store these boxes and the necessary rules on the pasteboard.

4. Place the formatted text in the PageMaker template. Break the product number and description into separate text blocks and use the techniques described in Chapter 11 to wrap the text around each product number (refer to fig. 20.21).

5. Copy and paste the boxes from the pasteboard to the appropriate pages to reserve space for the advertisers' cards that will be pasted in manually.

6. Print all the pages and proofread the results before pasting business cards on the final version.

Preparation for Reproduction

Advertisers' business cards are pasted by hand into the boxes reserved for them. (Business cards supplied by advertisers should be white cards with black text and graphics. Cards in colored inks or on colored paper may require Photostatting to get a good black-and-white image.)

Example 20.5. A Tabloid Price List with Horizontal and Vertical Rules

The order form in this example is organized into seven columns: quantity ordered, product number, description, minimum quantity, unit price, total price, and quantity shipped. You can adapt the same design principles and production tips to any tabbed list format, including restaurant menus, wine lists, telephone lists, inventory lists, or other price lists. The only absolute requirement is that all the data for each entry fit on one line.

Description

The price list in this example is formatted using PageMaker's paragraph rules (see fig. 20.26).

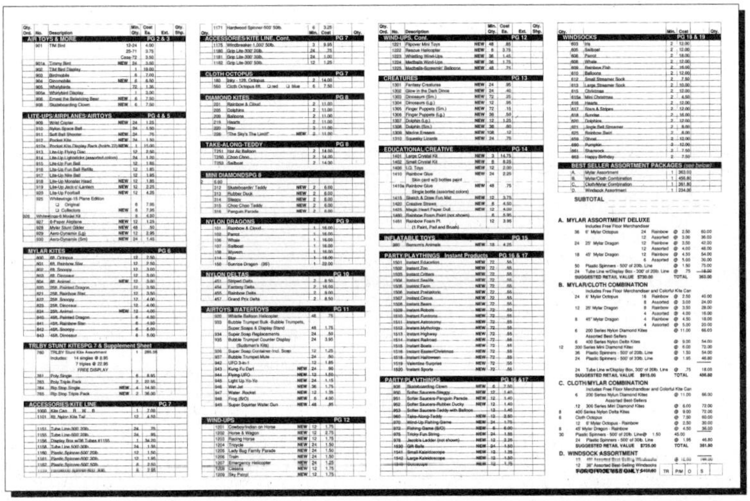

Fig. 20.26

Printout of pages of the tabloid price list.

Production Steps

Follow these steps to create the listing:

1. Set up the simple template shown in figure 20.27 and place the text in PageMaker.

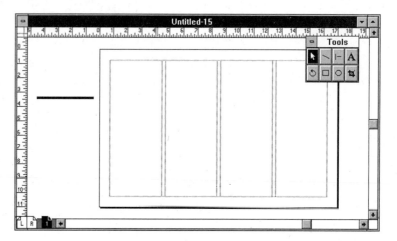

Fig. 20.27

The template for the tabloid price list.

2. Format the text in the Story Editor, setting left, right, center, and decimal tabs as needed. Set up horizontal rules between lines as appropriate by using the Rules option through the Paragraph command. The reverse type is set in PageMaker in a later step.

3. Scroll down each column in Actual Size view to make adjustments as necessary before you reverse the heading type and add the black boxes and hairline rules required by this design.

4. Draw a hairline border around one column, and copy and paste the border to the other columns. You can adjust the length of the box to create two different borders in the first column of the price list.

5. Draw one vertical hairline down one column, and copy and paste the same line in the correct position across the column. Copy and paste this set of lines to all other columns.

6. After you position all the vertical hairlines, go back to the beginning and scroll down each column in 200% Size view, deciding where to put the black boxes behind reverse-text headings.

7. Draw one black box the appropriate size and copy the box to the pasteboard. Paste the box over each heading and use the Send to Back command to position the box behind the text. Don't change the text to reverse type until you position all the black boxes.

As an alternative, you can use the technique described in Chapter 11 for adding black boxes as inline graphics.

8. Scroll through the publication once more with the Text tool selected. Change each heading, now invisible as black type on black boxes, to reverse type. You also can use PageMaker's style sheets to change text to reverse type by tagging the text to be reverse type. Triple-click to select the whole line, and select Reverse Type from the Type menu.

9. Save and print the publication.

For Related Information

◀◀ "Saving a Document or Template," p. 165.

◀◀ "Editing Text," p. 275.

◀◀ "Controlling Spacing of Lines, Words, and Letters," p. 322.

◀◀ "Using Style Sheets," p. 334.

◀◀ "Wrapping Text around Graphics," p. 443.

◀◀ "Working with Reverse Text," p. 466.

◀◀ "Creating Bar Charts," p. 487.

◀◀ "Organizing Your Disk Files," p. 627.

FROM HERE...

Summary

In this chapter, you have seen examples of publications that use unusual formats: folded brochures, small booklets, and tabloid-size price lists. You also have seen how information stored in a database, spreadsheet, or mail-merge format can be converted to text and placed in PageMaker. To meet your specific needs, you can apply and adapt the design principles and production tips illustrated in this chapter to a wide variety of brochures and lists. By studying these examples, you can make your own designs more effective and your production steps more efficient.

Creating Fliers and Display Ads

hroughout this book, the focus has been on multiple-page publications that repeat the same basic master-page elements on every
page and apply the same type specifications throughout. In this chapter, you learn how you can use PageMaker to produce one-page fliers
and display ads like the ones shown in figure 21.1. One example demonstrates how you can transform a simple resume into a marketing tool.
You also see how to use PageMaker to generate a series of different
designs for one flier. Finally, you learn how to create a series of ads for
different franchisers who offer the same product. The fliers and display
ads discussed in this chapter share two important characteristics:

- The documents are usually only one or two pages long in a
  PageMaker file.

- Fliers and ads are often a nonstandard size; the final pages may be
  trimmed and folded.

Example 21.1

Example 21.2

Example 21.3

Fig. 21.1

Examples of fliers
and display ads.

Example 21.4

Design Principles

The design principles in the previous chapters apply generally to the publications in this chapter, but you are likely to find more exceptions to the rules in this category—fliers and ads—than in any other. Some of the common exceptions are described in this section to give you an idea of how and why fliers and ads can break the rules.

Keep text to a minimum.

Following this guideline can be difficult when you work with small formats. When designing a small ad or flier, most people tend to include as much information as possible about the product or service. Too many words in an ad, however, can make the final image uninviting. Readers simply may not read text printed in a small point size. By choosing your words carefully, you can get a few important points across and still convince the reader to call or come to the event or store.

Try to follow the rule of thumb that has evolved from the billboard industry: express the message in seven words or fewer. Examples 21.2 and 21.4 later in this chapter apply this principle. Examples 21.1 and 21.3, on the other hand, are exceptions to this rule. In these cases, a small point size is used to fit the large number of words in a small space and still leave white space on the page or in the ad.

The choice of font sets the tone of the piece.

Ads and fliers often use decorative or unusual typefaces for the headings and sometimes for the body copy. Different typefaces can convey a sense of seriousness, elegance, or frivolity. If you aren't sure how typefaces affect the reader, you should probably stay with traditional typefaces rather than experiment with more decorative ones.

Use only one or two different typefaces in a document.

You can use almost any font in a flier or ad, but the same rule applies here as with all other publications: Use only one or two typefaces. The use of too many fonts in a small space causes the ad or flier to look busy and detracts from the message. Example 21.1, for instance, uses only Helvetica Narrow. The designer calls attention to headings by using reverse type instead of another typeface.

Don't be afraid of white space.

If you skim through any magazine, you are likely to find several full-page ads that leave most of the page blank. These are extreme examples of this principle, but they usually make their point well.

You sometimes may deliberately violate this rule. As already mentioned, Examples 21.1 and 21.3 use small point sizes for the type to gain white space. Some of the variations in Example 21.2 have absolutely no white space because the scanned image fills the whole page, but the impact of the flier is still strong (see fig. 21.7 later in this chapter). The scanned image itself invites the reader's attention, and few words are required to get the message across.

Use all capital letters as a deliberate design strategy rather than as a method for emphasizing text or showing a heading.

You should avoid using all uppercase letters in long blocks of text. Remember that all uppercase text can be difficult to read, especially in sentences.

On the other hand, you can use all uppercase rather than a larger point size to make a few words stand out on the page. You can also use uppercase for a heading rather than change the typeface. The resume in figure 21.1 uses uppercase text and reverse type to emphasize the headings for each section. Uppercase text has the greatest impact if the words or phrases are short. You often can improve the appearance of uppercase text by manually kerning the spaces between certain pairs of letters. (Refer to Chapters 8 and 16 for information about kerning.)

FROM HERE...

For Related Information

◄◄ "Controlling Spacing of Lines, Words, and Letters," p. 322.

◄◄ "Kerning Headlines and Titles," p. 715.

Production Tips

Many production tips that improve productivity when you are creating long documents are irrelevant for one-page documents like those illustrated in this chapter. Other production tips are unique to one-page ads and fliers. Here are some production tips to keep in mind for documents like the resume and ads in this chapter.

Compensate for ragged-right text by setting unequal right and left margins.

The need for a balanced appearance is evident in these examples. Because of the ragged-right text, the right margin may appear to be different from the left. You can compensate for this visual discrepancy by using different margin settings to balance the page.

Store background boxes on the pasteboard to use behind text. Copy boxes to the page as you need them.

Several examples in previous chapters and the resume in this chapter use background boxes. Using the rectangle tool (described in Chapter 6), you can create the box just once, store it on the pasteboard, and paste it on the page in as many different locations as you need.

For ads containing mostly graphics with little text, create your text on the pasteboard and copy text to the page after you have positioned your graphic.

In many ads, the graphic fills most of the available space. As a result, the position of the graphic is the most important factor of the page layout. Text is frequently short and to the point. You can save a lot of time by positioning the graphic before you place the text. Changing the text to fit the graphic is much easier than trying to change the graphic to fit the text.

If your ad includes a border, remember to set the overall ad size— including the border—in the Page Setup dialog box.

If you use a border in your ad, you need to set the page size so that it accommodates the border and the margin surrounding the border.

If your ad includes a border, set margins inside the border narrower than the margins between the edge of the page and the border.

The border should be an integral part of the entire design. If the margins inside the border are larger than those outside, the final product will not be as attractive or unified as it should be.

Examples

Many of you will find this chapter's examples the most useful in the book because one-page fliers and ads you use frequently. With PageMaker, you can easily produce short fliers and ads and modify the designs with only a few additional steps. The examples in this chapter range from a resume to a series of one-page ads. Some examples use scanned images, and others rely entirely on type. Following are brief descriptions of the examples:

- *Example 21.1.* A Photographer's Resume with a Scanned Photograph

- *Example 21.2.* A One-Sided Flier with Several Design Variations

- *Example 21.3.* A Series of Display Ad Designs with Varied Borders

- *Example 21.4.* A Series of Ads in the Same Format for the Same Service

Example 21.1. A Photographer's Resume with a Scanned Photograph

This resume is included under the category of fliers and ads because the creative use of a scanned image and reverse text transforms this list of credentials into a promotional piece. The piece conforms to the 8 1/2-by-11-inch full page that most employers or interviewers are accustomed to receiving from individuals, but the four-column format and the large scanned image in the lower left corner give the resume the impact of a flier or brochure describing a service. This example provides one clear lesson: PageMaker can transform any traditional format—resume, memo, agenda, balance sheet—into a marketing tool that can help sell whatever is being presented.

Description

This resume comes from a photographer, and has been dressed up with a scanned photograph (see fig. 21.2). The final version was printed on a Linotronic typesetter and then sent to an offset printer for reproduction.

Design Principles

Most of the design principles described at the beginning of this chapter are present in this report. The three principles that are especially well illustrated by this example are repeated and described here.

Keep text to a minimum. This design principle is stretched in this example in order to list all the photographer's awards and qualifications. The danger of overcrowding the page is reduced by using a small point size of a narrow typeface: Helvetica Narrow. To compensate for the small size of the section headings, the designer uses all uppercase letters and reverse type. The final effect is a well-balanced composition in a clean, readable typeface with adequate white space.

Don't be afraid of white space. Although the resume contains a great deal of text, the resume uses white space to distinguish the sections and make reading easy. Notice the white space between columns and the four points of leading between each head and following text.

Use only one or two different typefaces in a document. This resume uses Helvetica Narrow throughout (see fig. 21.3). Helvetica Narrow is a compact, clean, readable typeface that helps support the photographer's image as a fine artist and sophisticated technician. Using this typeface also enables the designer to use more text without creating a crowded effect.

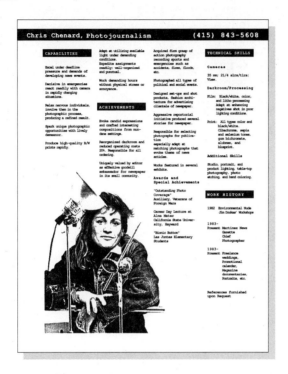

Fig. 21.2

Printout of resume.

Style name	Type specifications		
Banner	14-point Helvetica Bold, reverse type		
Headings	11-point Helvetica Bold, reverse type		
Level 2 Head	9-point Helvetica Bold		
Level 3 Head	9-point Helvetica, 10-point leading, extra line between paragraphs		

Fig. 21.3

Type specifications table for photographer's resume.

Production Tips and the Template

The inside margin of the resume is wider than the outside margin, as specified in the Page Setup dialog box shown in figure 21.4, but both margins appear equal on the page (refer to fig. 21.2). The unequal margin settings compensate for the effect of ragged right text. The pasteboard of the template includes a black box that is copied and pasted behind the reverse text of each heading (see fig. 21.5).

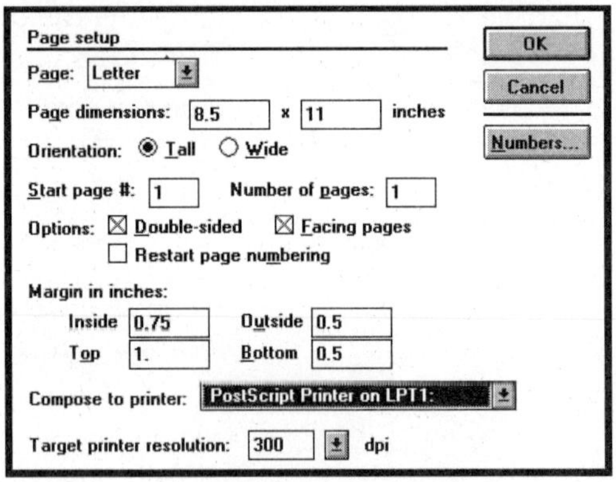

Fig. 21.4

Page Setup dialog box for the resume.

Fig. 21.5

Template for the resume.

Production Steps

As mentioned previously, creating a one-page document is less complicated than creating longer publications. Consult the figures for settings and positions as you complete the following steps for producing this resume:

1. Format the text with a word processing program. Use tabs, not spaces, to indent lines as needed.

2. Scan the image, and use PC Paintbrush, Windows Paint, or the scanning software program to clean up the image. In this case, all the pixels in the background—anything not part of the photographer's head and body or the light stand—are erased to convert the rectangular photo image into an irregular shape that becomes more visually integrated with the text.

3. Open a new PageMaker publication, following the page setup and column settings shown in figures 21.4 and 21.5.

4. Working in the Fit in Window view, place the scanned image in position. Crop and scale the image if necessary.

5. From the Element menu, select the Text Wrap command. Highlight the icon that wraps text rectangularly. (Text is prevented from wrapping on the outside of the graphic if the graphic is next to the outside margin.) Select the Text Flow icon to flow text all the way around the graphic. Create a custom graphic boundary around the graphic, as explained in Chapter 11.

6. In the Fit in Window view, place the text, using the Autoflow command in the Layout menu. If you select Autoflow, text jumps to the top of the next column when a graphic is encountered. If Autoflow is off, text stops at the graphic.

7. Change to the Actual Size view and move down each column, changing the headings to reverse type and adding black boxes as backgrounds for the headings. To reverse the type and add the black boxes, perform the following steps:

   ■ Draw a black box around the first heading in a column. Use the Send to Back command from the Element menu to place the box behind the text, and use the Copy command from the Exit menu to copy the box to the pasteboard.

   ■ Move to each heading and paste the black box from the pasteboard. Position the box over the heading and use the Send to Back command.

   ■ Return to the beginning and use the Text tool to make the headings reverse type.

8. Print drafts on the laser printer.

9. Print the final copy on the Linotronic typesetter to print crop marks and solid black areas that reach the edge of the paper (see fig. 21.6).

Fig. 21.6

Printed resume
with crop marks.

Preparation for Reproduction

You must inform the offset printer that you want part of the image to bleed off the paper. Keep in mind that the bleed adds to the printing charges because of the oversize paper and trimming required. Otherwise, no particular preparation is necessary, because the crop marks are printed by the Linotronic.

T I P   **Printing Black Areas**

Even if your laser-printer cartridge is printing black areas poorly so that they appear unevenly gray, the image often blackens when converted to offset printing plates. True grays are retained when you use gray fill patterns composed of black dots. See the Warning in Example 14.1 about using a wide range of gray tones.

If you aren't using a typesetter to produce solid black images, use coated paper stock in the laser printer. You can also darken the image printed on the laser printer by spraying the page with a matte finish (available in any art supply shop). This trick works best with uncoated paper.

Example 21.2. A One-Sided Flier with Several Design Variations

The approach used in designing this flier can be applied to any one-page document. The trick is to place all the basic elements on the pasteboard and then copy and paste them onto each page of the design publication, making a different arrangement of elements and testing different type specifications and paragraph formats on each page. The result is a series of design ideas that you can review with your team or client.

Description

This flier began as a series of ten designs that used the same text but different layouts of the text and a graphic. In the end, four different designs were selected for reproduction on four different colors of paper (see fig. 21.7). Fliers were mailed to the same individuals on a mailing list at three-month intervals, with a different flier used each month. In this way, the prospective customers were reminded three times of this service, and the variations of the same design helped renew the readers' interest for each mailing.

Production Tips and the Template

The few words required for this piece were typed on the pasteboard of the template. Several different scanned images were candidates for use in the final design. The designer placed each of these images on a separate page and then copied and pasted the text from the pasteboard and modified the text to create different design ideas.

Fig. 21.7

Printouts of a flier with several designs.

You may need to keep track of the series of variations but not want to use page numbers on the ads themselves. You can print thumbnails of the entire design file, as the designer did for this example.

The thumbnails show the design on each page of the template with the corresponding page number (see fig. 21.8). The numbers give quick access to any variation both before and after the final design is chosen. In this way, the full-size printouts of the pages aren't cluttered with page numbers that aren't part of the design.

1

2

3

4

Fig. 21.8

Thumbnails showing the design on each page.

Production Steps

The production steps for this example are easy. The greatest attention is given to placing the different versions of the image and fitting the text with the image.

1. Create a PageMaker publication with the text of the flier on the pasteboard.

2. Go through the document in the Fit in Window view, adding pages as needed. Place a different scanned image on each page, or position the same image in a different location on each page. Some of the scans in this case were deliberately distorted (stretched out of proportion).

    During this step, copy and paste the text from the pasteboard into position on each page, but don't change the type specifications.

3. Go through the document in the Actual Size view. You can work from front to back or vice versa. Change the type specifications and break the type into different blocks on each page to create unique designs.

4. Print thumbnails of all the designs, and choose the one you want.

5. Delete all unwanted variations from the file.

6. Print the variations as you need them.

Example 21.3. A Series of Display Ad Designs with Varied Borders

Like the preceding example, this example demonstrates how to use PageMaker to produce design variations. The new twist in this case is that the final printout is pasted into a larger publication as a display ad. You can apply the recommendations about using special paper for the final printout to any ad or publication that will be pasted manually on larger pages or boards.

Description

This series of display ad designs is similar to Example 21.2 in at least two ways: All the text is predetermined (a list of associates in a law firm), and the size of the ad is predefined (a full-page ad in a booklet). The designer, however, can make variations in the border style and in the type specifications and text layout (see fig. 21.9). For example, the address information is set in different type specifications, and the size of the box is varied.

Production Tips and the Template

Use the Page Size setting in the Page Setup dialog box to define the size of the ad (including the border), and set margins inside the border area (see fig. 21.10). Store the text and a box the size of the ad border on the pasteboard in the template (see fig. 21.11). Both the page setup and the template are straightforward. You can follow the settings shown in the figures without using complicated procedures.

Production Steps

This example leans heavily on the use of the pasteboard. By creating borders and rules and storing them on the pasteboard, you easily can create variations in the final document. The following steps in creating these ads can be used to create similar series of ads or fliers:

1. Open a new publication with the Page Setup specifications shown in figure 21.10, and type or place the text of the ad on the pasteboard. Use PageMaker's Rectangle tool to draw a border (or borders) the size of the ad, and store the box on the pasteboard.

2. On each page of the template, copy and paste the text block from the pasteboard to the page, and change the type specifications as desired.

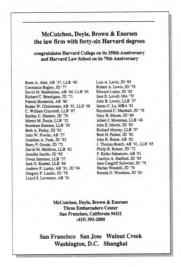

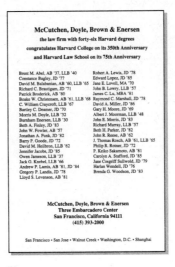

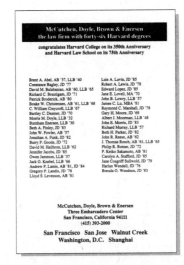

Fig. 21.9

Printouts of the series of display ads.

3. On some pages, copy and paste the box border from the paste-board onto the page, or draw horizontal rules to enhance the design.

4. Print all pages, and choose the final design.

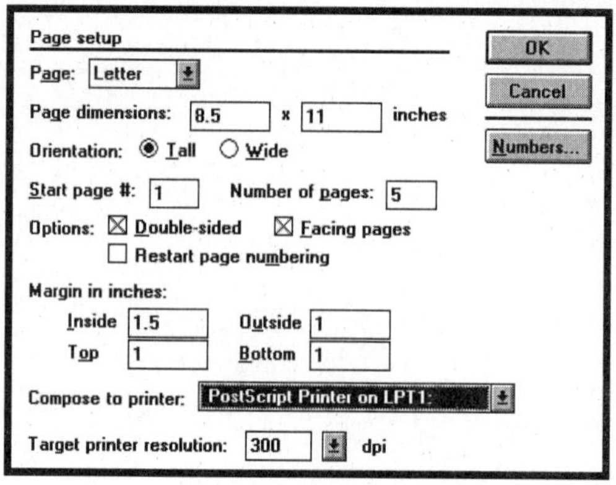

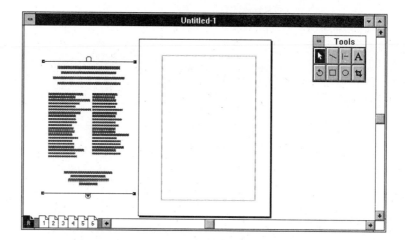

Fig. 21.10

Page Setup
dialog box for
the series of ads.

Fig. 21.11

Template for the
series of ads.

Preparation for Reproduction

Ads to be sent to other publications for insertion should be printed on the Linotronic typesetter or photostated. If you are sending laser-printer output, use laser paper or coated stock to get the best black image and to provide the best surface for pasteup. If you are using regular bond paper, you may want to include a note that the camera-ready copy you are delivering is on regular bond paper. Otherwise, production staff who are unfamiliar with laser printing may think that you are delivering a photocopy instead of an original. (This common misunderstanding should occur less frequently in the future, as more production departments start using laser printers.)

Example 21.4. A Series of Ads in the Same Format for the Same Service

This example demonstrates a new angle in developing a series of ads. Whereas Examples 21.2 and 21.3 develop a series of different designs, this example produces a series of ads that use the same design. Only the store location and phone number are different on each ad. The economy lies in using a central design department to develop ads for dealers in widely separated locations. You can apply the same approach to similar situations in which the same service is offered by different franchisers in different regions, or perhaps when you need to produce a series of announcements for the same seminar or special event that will be held in different cities or on different dates.

Description

Example 21.3 shows a series of ad designs from which only one is chosen. In this case, a series of nearly identical ads is created for different stores that offer the same service (see fig. 21.12).

Production Tips and the Template

The trick is to lay out the basic ad design on the master page (see fig. 21.13). On each page in the document, only the store address and phone number are changed. The template holds the graphic elements and dummy text. Other text is stored on the pasteboard and used as needed.

Production Steps

Because this ad has only one design, only one master page is needed. The variation is achieved with the text. The steps are easy:

1. Lay out the ad design on the master page. For the address and phone lines, store dummy text (set in the correct type specifications) on the pasteboard.

2. On each page of the document, copy and paste the address and phone lines from the pasteboard to the page, and change the information as appropriate.

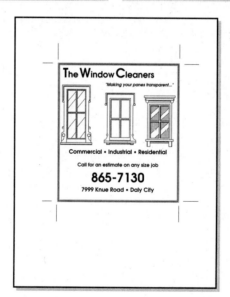

Fig. 21.12

Printouts of
pages for a
series of ads.

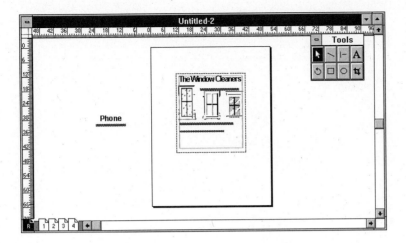

Fig. 21.13

Template for a
series of ads.

For Related Information

◄◄ "Creating a Custom-Shaped Graphic Boundary," p. 446.

FROM HERE...

Summary

The examples in Part V of *Using PageMaker 5 for Windows* illustrate
PageMaker's wide range of uses and helpful features for producing professional documents. No matter what equipment you may be using—
dot-matrix printer, laser printer, or typesetter—PageMaker guarantees
high quality output. Whether your publishing projects are large or
small, PageMaker has the capabilities to produce high quality published documents that just a few years ago could be generated only by
professional designers and typesetters.

With PageMaker, professional quality is available to individuals, businesses, and nonprofit, educational, and government organizations.
Whether you produce books and manuals or single-page fliers and ads,
Part V of this book can help you with each stage: designing, creating,
and printing the professional documents you need for your job. The
examples in this section help you start making PageMaker a true
publishing tool.

System Setup

This appendix describes the requirements for installing PageMaker, the process of installing PageMaker, and the process of installing extra fonts on your system. This appendix supplements the information given in the rest of the book where PageMaker and all the fonts you need are assumed to have been installed.

Reviewing Hardware Requirements

Before you install PageMaker on your system, be sure that your equipment meets PageMaker's minimum requirements. A system equipped to run Microsoft Windows 3.1 usually can run PageMaker if it is equipped with enough memory.

PageMaker runs in the Microsoft Windows environment on a Personal Computer AT or compatible system. Although PageMaker can run on a 286 system, Aldus recommends using a 386 or 486 system for faster operation. PageMaker's 3 1/2-inch version runs on the IBM PS/2 and portable computers that can run under the Windows environment. PageMaker 5.0 must run under DOS version 3.3 or later (version 5.0 or later is recommended) and Microsoft Windows version 3.1 or later and have a minimum of 4M of memory (Aldus recommends 8M), a VGA monitor (Aldus recommends Super VGA), and a hard disk of at least 20M for storage. (Aldus recommends 40M; up to 12M is required simply to install PageMaker along with all filters and tutorial files.) PageMaker also runs on Apple's Macintosh computers.

You should have DOS and Windows 3.1 on your system before you install PageMaker. PageMaker 5.0 will not work with any earlier version of Windows.

Along with PageMaker and a computer running Windows, a full desktop publishing system may include a laser printer for draft or final printouts, a high-resolution imagesetter for final masters, and a scanning device. Other peripherals, such as video digitizers and color printers, add to the flexibility of a desktop publishing system. The following discussion gives you the background you need to make wise hardware decisions for desktop publishing.

Computer Models and Memory

Windows requires at least a 286-based system and 2M of memory. You cannot run PageMaker with this minimum; you need at least 4M of memory. Adding more memory will make your applications run faster. Some graphics programs that you might be using in your publishing efforts can require more than 4M of memory to run. For example, PhotoStyler, another Aldus product, can easily use 8M of memory or more to process high-resolution color images. The speed of the processor becomes more important the larger the volume of pages and graphics. If you are working with many scanned images, you will appreciate the faster performance of a 486 system with 8M or more of memory.

Storage

Besides the temporary storage that is built into any computer (RAM memory), you need to save programs and documents on disks for permanent storage or transportation. Because desktop publishing usually involves the use of several different applications (word processing, graphics, and page composition) and the assembly of files from many sources, the recommended procedure is that you store all your applications and your current document files on a hard disk while you are working and use removable hard disks, optical drives, tape, or floppy disks for backups.

PageMaker requires at least 12M of hard disk space if you want to install all the files that come with the program. Hard disks that are built into the PC usually store between 60M and 500M of information, and you can install additional hard disks to use as your primary hard disk or to use in combination with your internal hard disk.

You will want to invest in a large hard disk if you are working with high-resolution images. In addition, you might want an extra hard disk system just to handle your archived documents. Removable hard disks can be useful for a backup system, but relying on a removable cartridge system for your active daily work isn't recommended.

Monitors

If you do a lot of publishing, a large-screen monitor can increase your productivity by letting you see a full 8 1/2-by-11-inch page of work. Eliminating the need to scroll around the screen can boost your productivity by 50 percent. Even larger monitors that display full views of two facing pages or oversized pages are available.

A color monitor enables you to display high-resolution color images. You can take advantage of PageMaker's color capabilities even without a color monitor by using PANTONE colors and mixing your own colors by entering percentages that you can look up in a color reference book. If you intend to work in color, however, using a color monitor and at least an 8-bit video card is recommended.

Printers Supported by PageMaker and Windows 3.1

The printing devices available for personal computers fall into several broad categories: character printers, plotters, dot-matrix printers, ink-jet printers, laser printers, and phototypesetters or imagesetters, color printers, and color film recorders. Normally, you use laser printers and phototypesetters or imagesetters for the final printing of a PageMaker publication. One reason for this is that laser printers and phototypesetters can handle outline fonts and produce typeset-quality publications. Another reason is that laser printers and phototypesetters can print at much higher resolutions than dot-matrix printers and ink-jet printers. Color printers are used to produce color proofs for review before sending the final publication to an offset print shop for reproduction.

Publications created with PageMaker can be printed on all PostScript printers (such as the Apple LaserWriter II NT and NTX, the IBM Personal PagePrinter, and the QMS ColorScript printer), all PostScript-language imagesetters (such as the Linotronic, the Agfa Pro Set 9400, 9600, and 9800, and the Varityper 4300 and 5300), the Hewlett-Packard (HP) LaserJet series of printers and compatible printers that use HP's Printer Control Language (PCL 4 and PCL 5), non-PCL printers such as the Hewlett Packard InkJet and PaintJet and the Epson LQ series dot-matrix printers, color film recorders such as the Matrix (with AGFA

ChromScript RIP), and continuous-tone color printers such as the Scitex Iris InkJet. You can also print on other printers that are compatible with Windows 3.1, including dot-matrix printers such as the IBM Proprinter and Canon Color Laser copier (when used with Zenographic SuperPaint). PageMaker does not support plotters.

The most widely used page description language (PDL) for desktop publishing is PostScript. PostScript has been implemented in dozens of laser printers and most imagesetters. You can also add a PostScript interpreter on a card that you install in your computer so you can print PostScript to a non-PostScript laser printer. PageMaker also supports PCL—the language used by Hewlett-Packard laser printers—as well as other printers supported by Windows.

Besides the page description language built into the printer, the other variable that is directly related to the price of any printer is resolution. *Resolution* is a measure of the sharpness of the edges of printed characters and graphics. Resolution is commonly measured by the number of dots or spots per inch. Laser printers assemble characters and graphics as a pattern of dots, and they use a fine beam of light (a laser beam) to produce the dots in patterns of 300 dpi (dots per inch) or more. The laser beam puts electromagnetic charges on a drum which then either picks up powdery charged particles of the toner and lays the toner on paper, or transfers the electromagnetic charges onto photosensitive paper. The resulting text and graphics appear very smooth to the naked eye.

Most laser printers offer a standard resolution of 300 dpi, but some toner-based laser printers offer even higher resolutions. (The LaserMaster Unity 1000, for example, offers 1000 dpi.)

Phototypesetters that use the laser technology to set a page image on photosensitive paper or film are available. Linotype, Varityper, Agfa Compugraphic, and other manufacturers offer PostScript laser typesetters that image at various high resolutions. The resolution can be from 600 to 3,500 dpi, and the output is much crisper, of course, than the output from toner-based laser printers.

You can use color printers for printing proof copies of color pages or finished color overhead transparencies or slides.

Your printer choice affects your options for selecting fonts on the menu. Chapter 10 explains printer drivers and fonts and how to choose different printers on a multiprinter network. For specific instructions on installing a particular printer, refer to the documentation provided with your equipment.

Scanners

A full-service publication department will add a scanning device for digitizing photographs, logos, and line art that already exist on paper. A scanner or digitizer is an input device that converts a printed image into computer-readable dots. Digitized images can be saved in one of the paint-type formats supported by PageMaker such as Tag Image File Format (TIFF).

With a scanner, you can incorporate halftones or line art of scanned images into your desktop publishing work as final artwork or as position holders for photographic halftones that will be stripped in later at the print shop. Scanners are a good source of graphics if you are not a fine artist and you have a library of logos, line art, and photographs to which you (or your clients) own the rights.

The software that accompanies scanners can offer many of the features of paint programs, with eraser and pen tools for touching up scanned images. A number of packages are available for editing high-resolution scanned images: Aldus' PhotoStyler, Micrografx' Picture Publisher, or Computer Presentations ColorLab, for example. With the right combination of scanner, page-layout program, and printer, you can produce high-resolution graphics that look like inked line art or halftone photographs. For good results with color photographs, using high quality scanners is recommended. Most "desktop" color scanners, priced for individual use at less than $5,000, are not adequate for high-quality results.

Most black-and-white flatbed scanners accept 8 1/2-by-11-inch or larger pages; color scanners can digitize images from a variety of sources, including 35mm slides, transparencies, or flat color artwork. You can also use a video camera to convert printed or three-dimensional images into computer-readable images. Any scanner requires software to set up the specifications for the input image size, the finished image size, the degrees of brightness and contrast, and the resolution of the stored image.

Most scanners enable you to store the image at 300 dpi or more, and high-resolution images can approach the quality of true halftones when printed on a high-resolution printer. However, a full-page scan can require several megabytes of storage space when saved at high resolutions. You can save scanned images in low-resolution bitmap formats—such as 72 dpi—and still get good quality output from a 300 dpi printer, but if you print the same image on a high-resolution image setter, the image may appear jagged compared with those of high-resolution scans (unless the image is composed simply of horizontal and vertical lines).

Text-scanning (OCR, or optical character reader) technology has improved over the last few years, becoming faster and more accurate. The breakthrough of most relevance for desktop publishers is that some scanners can interpret typeset text in various sizes (whereas in the past, OCRs could read only special characters and typewritten text).

Modems

Files can be telecommunicated over phone lines or through a cable from one computer to another. You can convert files from one application to another type by using communications software that allows you to transfer and translate files. Once the files are transferred, you can edit them using any word processor (if they are ASCII text files), or use the same application that created them to edit or import them directly onto a page in PageMaker.

Modems can be set to send files at different speeds, measured as baud rates (bits per second). A 1200, 2400, or 9600 baud rate is commonly used to send files over phone lines. Higher transmission speeds can be used over direct optical cable connections (rather than over phone lines).

Networks

Desktop publishing in a networked workgroup allows people to share information. This is especially important in a production setting where, for example, one person is responsible for writing copy, another for designing graphics, and still another for laying out the page. Network users can share printers, files, and information.

Several server-based networks are available for the PC, including Novell NetWare, VINES, and Lan Manager. These high-end networks also allow various brands of computers to be used within one work-group. At the lower end of the spectrum, you can connect a few PCs together for less than $500 with DOS-based networks such as LANtastic.

FROM HERE...

For Related Information

◀◀ "Installing the Printer," p. 399.

◀◀ "Selecting the Current Printer," p. 412.

Installing PageMaker

Before you install PageMaker on your system, read this description of the installation process. The Aldus Setup program (ALDSETUP.EXE) leads you step-by-step through the installation process. The installation program offers you the option of installing the full PageMaker package, including tutorial files and templates, or you can choose to install only the PageMaker program and a few filters. Once you have installed PageMaker, you can use the Setup program any time to install additional filters or templates or the tutorial files.

The installation process asks you for the directory names of the Aldus-related software and the PageMaker 5.0 directory. If you don't want to use the directory names suggested by Aldus, you should choose the names of the directories before you start the installation process. The installation program enables you to abort the process if you come to a question that you cannot answer.

The PageMaker package includes either 3 1/2-inch or 5 1/4-inch disks for installation on high-density disk drives. If your package has the wrong size for your disk drives, you can order the correct disks from Aldus.

Before you can install PageMaker, you must have Windows version 3.1 or higher on your hard disk. If you try to install the program without first starting Windows, you get the message `This program requires Microsoft Windows`, and the setup program doesn't start.

To begin installation of PageMaker, you must first enter Windows. You can start Windows in different ways, depending on how it was set up during installation. (Chapters 2 and 4 describe various installation methods.) If you accept all of Windows' defaults during installation, you simply type **win** at the C prompt. If you didn't have the installation program update your CONFIG.SYS and AUTOEXEC.BAT files, you might need to change to the Windows subdirectory before you type **win**. Some computers are configured so that you enter Windows automatically when you turn on the machine. Put Disk #1 into drive A of your computer. When you are in Windows, select the Run command from the File menu in Windows' Program Manager. In the Run dialog box, type **a:\aldsetup**, and then click OK (see fig. A.1). Make sure that the Run Minimize box isn't checked off.

Any time during installation, you can press Alt+X or highlight the Exit box to stop the process and cancel the installation. You usually press Enter or Alt+S to continue installation and view the next screen. The next screen shows you the main PageMaker Installation menu. You can install all the PageMaker options or a specific option, such as the template or tutorial files. The menu enables you to easily modify certain options without reinstalling all of PageMaker.

Fig. A.1

The Run dialog box displayed by the Run command from the File menu in the Windows Program Manager.

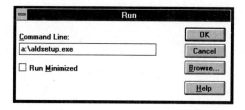

The first screen displayed during the installation process shows you the Aldus Setup Main Window (see fig. A.2). You can choose the Install Everything option, which installs PageMaker and all the filters, additions, tutorial files, templates, libraries, and so on, but requires 15M or more disk space. To customize the installation and use less space, you can select from the following list of categories shown in the dialog box: PageMaker, Tutorial, Filters, Additions, and Printer Files. The Setup program thus enables you to selectively install only parts of the full PageMaker package if you want to save space on your hard disk and you do not, for example, need all the filters. You also can reinstall parts of PageMaker later (if you purchase an update of version 5) or install additional files such as the tutorial files, filters, additions, and new printers, if you did not initially install all these files.

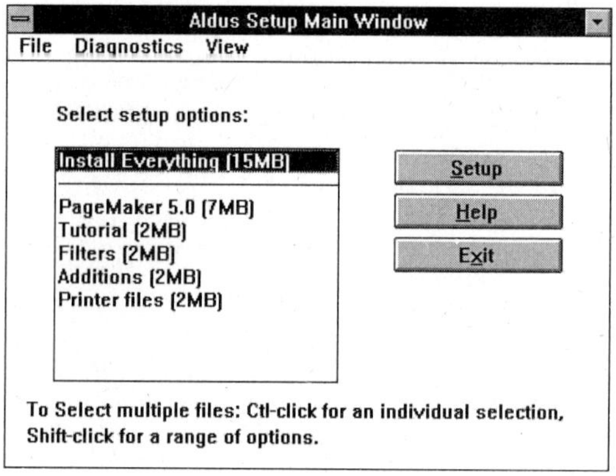

Fig. A.2

The Aldus Setup Main Window.

You select installation options by clicking the selections that you want to install. If you want to cancel a highlighted selection, click the option, and it is deselected. After you have chosen the categories you want to install, click the Setup box, or press Alt+S.

Naming the PageMaker Directory

If this is the first time you are installing PageMaker 5, the next screen displayed during the installation process prompts you to select the directory that you want to use for the PageMaker program and related files. You can create a new directory or use one on your hard disk. If you use an established directory, specify the full path name of the directory. Type the name of the directory you want, or accept the suggested default path of C:\PM5. Press Enter.

After you select a directory for the PageMaker files, the installation program asks you for your name, company, and the serial number of your PageMaker program. Your serial number is printed on the master disks. Type the numbers and dashes exactly as they are listed. If you don't type the number correctly, the program will prompt you to try again, and the installation cannot continue without the correct serial number. If you cannot locate the serial number and you cancel the process, you must reinstall PageMaker from the beginning. The installation will not save the selections made up to this point.

Subsequent screens displayed by the Setup program vary, depending on the options you select. PageMaker then decompresses and copies all necessary files from the PageMaker disks. As the files are copied onto the hard disk, you see what percentage of files have been copied. This process takes 7 to 25 minutes, depending on the speed of your computer and the number of options you install. PageMaker signals you with a beep when it needs a different disk. To continue, you must insert the requested disk and press Enter.

After installing the PageMaker program, the Setup program asks you whether to append your AUTOEXEC.BAT and CONFIG.SYS files so that your hard disk can find your PageMaker files. These files also tell your computer how many files to work with. If you click Enter, the installation program adds the following commands to your AUTOEXEC.BAT file:

```
PATH C:\PM5;C:\

SET TEMP=C:\PM5
```

The PATH command causes DOS to search all listed directories when you enter a command that isn't found in the current directory. You can then enter the command **win PM5** from any directory to start PageMaker. The installation program also changes your CONFIG.SYS file to enhance the performance of PageMaker.

If you don't want PageMaker to make the changes, you can click No and modify the files yourself. You can also edit your AUTOEXEC.BAT and CONFIG.SYS files to make these changes yourself.

Finally, the Setup program asks whether you want to exit Setup and reboot to take advantage of the changes made during installation.

Selecting Filters, Additions, and Other Options

During either the initial installation or later, after PageMaker is installed, you can use the Setup program to selectively install filters, additions, libraries, and other options. In either case, PageMaker displays a screen containing a scrolling list of the available options. You select an option by clicking it in the list.

If you select the filters option, for example, either during initial installation or later, when you want to add more filters, PageMaker displays a scrolling list from which you can choose the filters you want installed. You can select a few specific filters or all the filters listed. (Remember that PageMaker has the capability to use text and graphics from other programs. Because each program is different, PageMaker provides filters that can be used to import and export text and graphics. To import text from dBASE IV, for example, you must install the dBASE filter in PageMaker. PageMaker then can import the dBASE files, read them, and correctly place them into your document.)

On the bottom of the screen, the Select Filters dialog box shows you how much space is needed to install the selected filters and how much space you have left on your hard disk (see fig. A.3). After you have selected the filters that you want, press Enter or Alt+S. Screens that display lists of other options, such as additions and libraries, also display information about the disk space required.

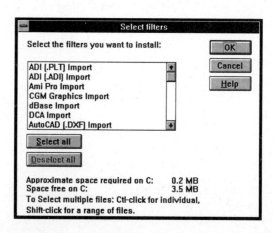

Fig. A.3

The Select Filters dialog box.

Managing Files

PageMaker requires a hard disk system to run on an IBM AT or a compatible system. You should use a hierarchical system of directories to organize all your files. You also should organize your program files and your data files.

As you install PageMaker, the installation program sets up a directory structure for you. In the typical PageMaker setup, the directories named PM5 and ALDEO are created for you. The PM5 directory includes a subdirectory named TUTORIAL, where tutorial files are stored. The ALDEO directory includes a subdirectory named USENGLSH, with additional subdirectories named ADDITION, with the Aldus Additions; COLOR, with color libraries; FILTERS, with the filter files for programs that are imported or exported; PPD, with printer description files; SETUP, with all of the setup files; and UTILITY, with additional utilities such as a dictionary editor.

You usually have plenty of storage space when you work with a hard disk, but you can easily create so many files that you cannot view the complete list of files on-screen at once. More than one screen of file names can be an inconvenience. A more serious production problem is that you cannot track all the files used to create documents. You should create a separate directory or subdirectory outside the PM5 and WINDOWS directories for each project or long document. A directory map set up for a busy production network is shown in figure A.4.

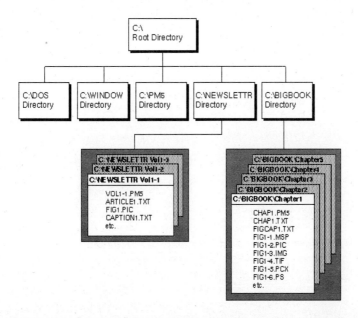

Fig. A.4

A directory system with subdirectories devoted to specific projects.

For more information on directory and file management, refer to Chapter 14 of this book as well as your DOS or Windows manual, or see Que's *Using MS-DOS 6*, Special Edition, or *Using Windows 3.1*, Special Edition.

FROM HERE...

For Related Information

◄◄ "Starting PageMaker," p. 43.

◄◄ "Opening a Publication," p. 133.

◄◄ "Installing the Printer," p. 399.

For more information on directory and file management, refer to the Chapter 14 sections "Memory and System Resource Management," "Organizing Your Disk Files," and "Managing a Workgroup" as well as your DOS or Windows manual; or refer to Que's *Using MS-DOS 6*, Special Edition or *Using Windows 3.1*, Special Edition.

Installing and Using Fonts

Windows comes with a set of TrueType fonts, but you can install other fonts on your system. Installing a new font is usually a two-step process:

1. Install the new font so it appears on PageMaker's Font submenu and in the Type Specifications dialog box (for example, as a screen font) by using the Windows Control Panel.

2. Install the new font on the printer.

The following sections tell you how to install fonts on your computer and printer.

Adding and Deleting Screen Fonts and TrueType Fonts

You add a typeface or font to the list in PageMaker's Type Specifications dialog box by adding a *font* to the system—through the Windows Control Panel, through a type manager such as Adobe Type Manager, or by selecting a printer that has built-in fonts. Of the fonts installed through Windows, the PageMaker font list displays only those fonts for which printer fonts are installed for the target printer (the printer listed in the Page Setup dialog box). To add new fonts using the Fonts utility that comes with Windows, start Windows and choose Main from the Window menu (if the Main window is not already displayed). Double-click the Control Panel icon displayed in the Main window. The Control Panel window displays a number of icons (discussed in Chapter 2), including the Fonts icon (see fig. A.5).

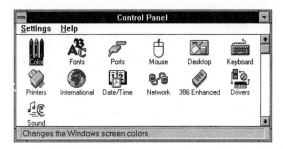

Fig. A.5

The Control Panel window shows the Fonts icon.

Double-click the Fonts icon to display the Fonts dialog box, which shows the list of currently installed fonts (see fig. A.6). The Remove and Add buttons on the right of the dialog box enable you to remove a selected font from the list (delete it from the WIN.INI file) or add a new font or size.

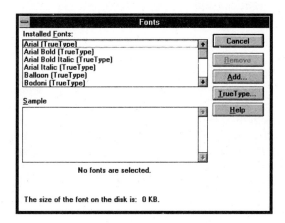

Fig. A.6

The Fonts dialog box.

To delete a screen or TrueType font from the list, first click on the font name to highlight it; then click the Remove button. If you click the Add button, PageMaker displays a dialog box through which you locate the fonts to be installed (see fig. A.7).

The Add Font
Files dialog box.

If you are not using a Type Manager (discussed in the section "Using a Type Manager," in Chapter 13), you may want to install every size of each font you plan to use. Otherwise, fonts may appear distorted on the screen.

Be aware, however, that screen fonts can take up a great deal of space on your hard disk, and fonts currently being used require a lot of memory. You can create and print a publication without using a type manager and without having matching screen versions of every printer font you use. If you do not have a screen version of a printer font, Windows supplies the screen font that most closely matches it. Even when font substitution occurs, line endings and page breaks on-screen are accurate.

If you add screen fonts through Windows, you must make sure that you add the equivalent printer fonts for your printer (as described in the next section) to display the fonts on PageMaker's menus.

As you install Windows 3.1, several TrueType fonts also are installed, and you can install more through the Control Panel, as described earlier in this section. If you plan to use PostScript fonts, some experts recommend that you disable the TrueType fonts. You can do this by clicking the TrueType button in the Fonts dialog box. Click Enable TrueType fonts to turn this option off or on.

Adding Printer Fonts

For a printer to print any font correctly, the printer must have information about how to compose the font's letters. Unlike the screen, however, which uses a relatively low-resolution bit-mapped font, the printer uses a high-resolution bit-mapped font or an outline font (determined by a curve-fitting formula). Available fonts vary from printer to printer. Essentially, three types of *printer fonts* are available, each with its own method of installation: built-in fonts (built directly into the printer), cartridge fonts (stored on a font cartridge), and soft fonts or downloadable fonts (transferred from the computer's memory, or downloaded, into the printer's memory).

If the printers you have installed use only built-in fonts or font cartridges (see "Knowing Your Printers: Types of Fonts," in Chapter 10), you can begin printing publications immediately. Many printers, however, also use downloadable fonts (such as TrueType fonts) that come in the form of software included with some applications or printers or that can be purchased from various sources. These fonts are called *soft fonts* because they aren't "hard-coded" into chips in the printer or in the printer font cartridge. They also are called *downloadable fonts* because you must either send, or download, them to the printer before printing begins or let Windows and PageMaker automatically download them as needed during the printing process. Before you use soft fonts, you must first install them and decide whether to download them permanently or temporarily; these processes are described later in this appendix.

Built-In Printer Fonts

Built-in printer fonts are installed by the manufacturer. They are always available for any publication. Ideally, every font would be built into the printer. Unfortunately, fonts take up space, so most printers have few or no built-in fonts.

Many PostScript printers come with the same set of fonts as were originally built into Apple's LaserWriter Plus and are now built into the LaserWriter NTX: Times, Helvetica, Courier, Symbol (primarily Greek letters and mathematical symbols), Avant Garde, Bookman, New Century Schoolbook, Helvetica Narrow, Palatino, Zapf Chancery, and Zapf Dingbats (all symbols). Figure A.8 shows the LaserWriter Plus typefaces. Each of these fonts, except Zapf Chancery, can be printed in any size or style listed on the menu.

The Linotronic Model 100 and 300 typesetters come with Times and Helvetica built-in. All other typefaces are downloaded as the pages are being printed. The number of typefaces that you can download at one time is limited by the amount of memory in the typesetter (see the discussion of downloadable fonts in this section), unless you are using fonts permanently downloaded to a hard disk attached to the typesetter.

Fig. A.8

LaserWriter Plus's 11 built-in typefaces.

Cartridge Fonts

Cartridge fonts are similar to built-in fonts but are built into removable cartridges rather than hard-wired into the printer. The number of fonts available for a specific publication depends on the cartridge installed at the time of printing. Chapter 10 explains how to tell Windows and PageMaker which cartridge is installed.

The older models of the Hewlett-Packard LaserJet (through Series II) are examples of cartridge printers. Dozens of different font cartridges for the LaserJet are available; many cartridges include groups of fonts suitable for a particular purpose, such as publishing newsletters. If you don't have a cartridge, the default font is 12-point Courier (which is a built-in font). The Hewlett-Packard LaserJet Series II is a cartridge printer with expanded memory that enables you to download fonts to the printer. The LaserJet Series III can accept cartridges, but it also comes with two built-in scalable fonts (Times and Helvetica) and a megabyte of random-access memory (RAM) for downloading more fonts.

Downloadable Fonts

Downloadable fonts differ from both built-in and cartridge fonts in that they aren't coded directly into hardware. Instead, they take up memory space (in RAM) when downloaded to the printer. PageMaker supports most of the downloadable fonts sold by various manufacturers, such as those from Adobe Systems, Inc. (which offers a wide range of downloadable fonts for PostScript printers) and Bitstream (which also makes downloadable fonts for Hewlett-Packard printers and others).

You can download additional fonts to any printer that has built-in RAM, but the printer's memory and the typefaces selected determine the number of downloadable fonts the printer can handle at once. Normally, PageMaker temporarily downloads fonts to the printer as it prints each page. The downloaded fonts remain in the printer's memory unless the space they are using is needed by another font or a large graphic, in which case the font is flushed from the printer memory, and downloaded when it is needed again.

If the printer's memory is very limited or if your publication page is very complex, you can run into memory overload problems that cause printing problems. (Chapter 13 discusses how to diagnose printing problems. See also "Choosing the Fonts" in the "Planning Your Design Specifications" section of Chapter 16.)

If your printer's memory isn't too limited, or if your publications aren't too complicated, you can save printing time by downloading fonts to the printer "permanently"—before printing from PageMaker—as explained later in this appendix, in the section "Downloading Permanently or Temporarily."

Installing Soft Fonts

In order to have access to a soft font in PageMaker, you must let the Windows environment "know" that the new font is available. To do so, you must have a printer font metrics (PFM) version of the font. PFM files aren't themselves downloadable printer fonts, but they contain the character spacing and kerning information PageMaker or a Type Manager needs to space characters proportionally on-screen and in print.

Often, the font installation program supplied by the font manufacturer or the printer manufacturer installs the fonts in Windows for you. Follow the manufacturer's instructions for copying the PFM fonts from the manufacturer's disk to your hard disk. Copy the fonts into the WINDOWS directory or into a new font subdirectory you create. Make a note of the identification numbers the installation program assigns during this process.

If you are planning to print the final version of your publication on another system—or send it to a service bureau for printing—you don't need the printer fonts. If you are printing the final version on your own system, you need the actual printer fonts for your printer in order for those fonts to appear in your printed output.

If you don't have a particular PFM file, the printer driver that comes with Windows can generate a generic PFM file, but the printed results aren't as clear as those from a custom PFM file.

Updating WIN.INI

In most cases, the list of installed fonts is expanded in the WIN.INI file whenever you install a new font using the Windows Control Panel, a Type Manager such as Adobe Type Manager, or a Windows-compatible font installer program such as the Soft Font Installer for PCL printers. Sometimes you are asked to specify which fonts you want to install when you install a new printer or Windows application that comes with fonts, but in many cases that installation process simply loads all the fonts that come with the product.

If the installation program doesn't update WIN.INI for you, or if you use DOS copy commands to copy fonts into the system, you need to update WIN.INI yourself. Before you update your WIN.INI file, be sure that you have either followed the printer installation procedure during the Windows setup program or configured at least one active Post-Script printer through the Windows Control Panel (see "Adding a Printer Driver" in the "Installing the Printer" section of Chapter 10).

T I P   **Editing WIN.INI**

You can use the Windows System Configuration Editor to edit SYSTEM.INI, WIN.INI, CONFIG.SYS, and AUTOEXEC.BAT. Open the Windows System Configuration Editor by choosing Run from the File menu of the Program Manager and typing SYSEDIT.EXE. The System Configuration Editor displays windows with SYSTEM.INI, WIN.INI, CONFIG.SYS, and AUTOEXEC.BAT as editable text files that can be searched, printed, and saved by using commands on the System Configuration Editor menu bar. Click the WIN.INI menu bar to activate that window so you can edit the file, and then choose Save from the File menu.

After editing WIN.INI—by this or any other means—you must restart Windows for the changes to take effect.

Before making any changes to your WIN.INI file, make a backup of the original file and store it in a safe place. If Windows refuses to launch from the edited WIN.INI, you can copy your original WIN.INI back into your Windows directory.

To edit your WIN.INI manually, locate the section in your WIN.INI that lists the soft fonts available to your printer and port. This section appears in brackets. (Several lists may appear in the file, so make sure that you get the correct port.) Following is an example of a printer entry in a WIN.INI:

```
Postscript,LPT1_softfonts=2 \pfm\fub_____.pfm

softfont2=c:\psfonts\pfm\fuh_____.pfm,c:\psfonts\fuh_____.pfb
```

Soft font entries must be numbered consecutively. The total number of soft font entries must equal the number listed in the softfonts= statement. The first directory statement in the soft fonts entry displays the name and location of the printer font metrics file. The second directory statement, which follows the comma, displays the name and location of the printer font file. Each font that you use in a document must contain both the printer font metric (PFM) and, if you want to temporarily download the font to the printer with each print job, the printer font (PFB) file listing. If your document prints in Courier, you probably do not have the PFB file listed. (If you installed screen fonts by using the Fonts dialog box in the Windows Control Panel, or if you use a version of Adobe Type Manager earlier than 2.0, you may need to add complete soft font entries that include both the PFM and PFB font files for each of your downloadable fonts.)

In the preceding example, softfont1 does not have the PFB entry. To temporarily download that font, you must edit the softfont entry to read as shown in the following example:

```
softfont1=c:\psfonts\pfm\fub_____.pfm,c:\psfonts\fub_____.pfb
```

If you need to add a font (Futura Bold Oblique, for example), you must add a soft font entry and update the softfonts= statement to reflect the total number of fonts in the soft fonts list.

Your edited entry for this PostScript printer entry would appear as shown in the following example:

```
Postscript,LPT1
softfonts=3
softfont1=c:\psfonts\pfm\fub_____.pfm,c:\psfonts\fub_____.pfb
softfont2=c:\psfonts\pfm\fuh_____.pfm,c:\psfonts\fuh_____.pfb
softfont3=c:\psfonts\pfm\fubo____.pfm,c:\psfonts\fubo____.pfb
```

If you already have PostScript soft fonts installed, then other soft font entries may already exist in the printer sections of the WIN.INI file. To avoid conflict, you need to edit WIN.INI, using Notepad, to include the additional lines in continuous, numerical order. Suppose, for example, that two fonts already exist in the WIN.INI printer sections, introduced by a line that reads:

```
softfonts=2
```

You need to enter the text for the additional soft fonts after the two existing fonts; then edit the softfonts= line to show the new total number of fonts.

Finally, edit the new lines of text that follow to reflect the correct numerical order (for example, softfont1 through softfont24).

 NOTE You should have no more than one softfonts= line to indicate the total number of soft fonts in each PostScript printer port section.

Unfortunately, every installed font takes up space in memory and can thus make applications run more slowly. Some applications, such as PageMaker, are slowed even further by the fact that they read the specifications of every font in the list when you use a command that references the list of fonts. The longer the list, the longer the command takes to execute.

You can add and delete fonts through the Windows Control Panel, and you should delete fonts that you never use. If you normally produce many publications using different fonts, you can create a different WIN.INI file for each publication or set of related publications that uses a different font set.

Creating Multiple WIN.INI Files

The following memory-saving trick is not recommended by Microsoft, but many people do it anyway. To create different WIN.INI files, first make lists of the fonts that you need for each set of publications. Suppose, for example, that publication set A (reports) uses only Times and Helvetica, and that publication set B (a newsletter) uses only Palatino. To each list of fonts add Helvetica, which is the font used in most Windows dialog boxes; without Helvetica, the dialog boxes are difficult to read.

Next, start Windows. Make a copy of the WIN.INI file that includes all of the installed fonts and name the copy WIN.ALL. Use the Windows Control Panel to delete all the fonts except those that are used in publication set A. The WIN.INI file is automatically updated with the new font list. Make a copy of the new WIN.INI file and name it WIN.A.

Repeat this step for each publication set. In this two-set example, you would next use the Windows Control Panel to delete all the fonts in the WIN.ALL file except those that are used in publication set B (do not delete Helvetica). Again, the WIN.INI file is automatically updated with the new font list. Make a copy of the new WIN.INI file and name it WIN.B.

You now have three different versions of the WIN.INI file—named WIN.ALL, WIN.A, and WIN.B—each with a different set of fonts. Whenever you want to start Windows with one of these font sets, make a copy of the file and name it WIN.INI (replacing the current WIN.INI) and restart Windows.

Using the Soft Font Installer for PCL Printers

Windows provides a Soft Font Installer to install soft fonts on your PCL printer. Open the Main program group in the Program Manager, and double-click the Control Panel icon. Double-click the Printers icon, and select (highlight) a PCL target printer. Click Setup to see the printer-specific dialog box . Click the Fonts button to display the HP Font Installer dialog box (see fig. A.9).

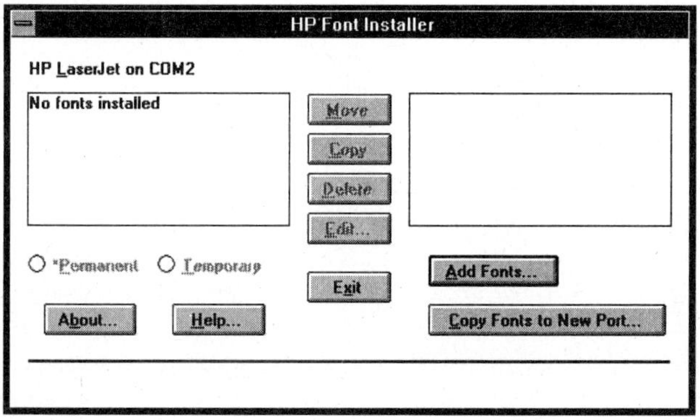

Fig. A.9

The HP Font Installer dialog box for PCL printers.

Next, click Add Fonts. The Add Fonts dialog box asks you where the program can find the fonts that you want installed. In the scroll box to the right, the installer lists the names of all the soft fonts in the path you specify. Select the font you want by clicking it. If you want to install more than one font, hold down the Shift key as you click. Hold down the Ctrl and Shift keys and click the mouse if you want to select all the fonts listed.

After you select the fonts, PageMaker asks you to specify which directory the fonts should be copied to. The installer copies the fonts and the PFM files to your hard disk. You can specify that you want the fonts to be loaded permanently to your hard disk by clicking the Permanent option in the dialog box; click Temporary if you want the fonts to be loaded only when they are used. If you select Permanent, PageMaker updates your WIN.INI file. Click the Copy Fonts to New Port button if you want the fonts to be available through ports other than the one to which the currently selected printer is attached. Remember: Turn on your printer before you start Windows if you use permanently downloaded fonts. To view the new fonts on-screen, you must use a Type Manager program or add the screen fonts through the Windows Control Panel. See "Adding and Deleting Screen Fonts" earlier in this appendix.

Downloading Fonts through Adobe Type Manager

To add fonts to the download list under Adobe Type Manager, double-click the ATM Control Panel icon in the Windows Program Manager. The ATM Control Panel dialog box appears. Click Add, and the Add ATM Fonts dialog box appears. In the Directories scroll list, double-click [psfonts]. Subdirectories now appear; double-click [pfm]. Select all the fonts in the Available Fonts scroll list, and click Add. You also can edit your WIN.INI manually to add or remove soft fonts from the list.

Downloading Permanently or Temporarily

If you want to use fonts that are not built into your printer, these fonts must be sent—or downloaded—to the printer before you print the page or document. Windows does this automatically when printing, as long as the printer fonts have been installed and listed in the WIN.INI file, but you can control whether the fonts are downloaded permanently or temporarily.

To say that a font is "permanently downloaded" is a slightly misleading statement. The only truly permanent fonts are those that are hard-coded into the printer; these fonts, by definition, are not downloadable. They are resident in the printer's ROM or in a cartridge.

The term *permanently downloaded fonts* actually means that those fonts are available during an entire work session. At the beginning of a session, you download a font into the printer's memory, where the font remains until the printer is turned off. Because permanently downloaded fonts remain in the printer's memory, it can print publications more quickly. The amount of memory remaining for processing each page, however, is limited by the number of fonts downloaded. You may experience problems printing pages with graphics if several fonts are downloaded.

Temporarily downloaded fonts, on the other hand, are those fonts that are sent to the printer's memory while a publication is being printed. After the printer finishes printing the publication, the temporarily downloaded font is flushed out of the printer's memory. Printing tends to be slower with temporarily downloaded fonts, because the fonts are downloaded each time the publication is printed. Temporarily downloaded fonts have the advantage of releasing memory space when the font is not being used.

Permanently downloaded fonts are used most often for body text in smaller sizes (10, 12, or 14 points). Temporarily downloaded fonts usually are specialty fonts, such as headlines or decorative fonts, which are used less frequently.

Downloading Fonts Permanently

You can add lines of instructions in your WIN.INI file to download fonts to your printer at the start of your workday. (See the procedure for updating WIN.INI outlined in "Installing Soft Fonts" in this section.) If you use this method, you need to turn on your printer before you start Windows so that the printer accepts the downloaded fonts.

Permanent downloading is advisable if you normally use the same number and style of fonts in your publications, such as company letters or documents that always use a specified type style.

Erasing Permanent Fonts

If you permanently download any fonts at the beginning of the day, and you run into memory problems when you print pages with graphics that don't use those fonts, you can flush the fonts out of the printer's memory by turning off the printer. When you turn the printer back on, print the pages with graphics first, before you permanently download the fonts again.

Most printers can handle no more than 16 soft fonts per page and 32 soft fonts per publication. (Even this maximum depends on the size of the font; larger fonts take up more memory.) These limits are considerably smaller for printers with limited memory available. For example, as much as 512K of printer memory may be necessary to hold only 10 text fonts that are 9 or 10 points in size. Most printers require at least 1M to be able to print a PageMaker publication. The advantage of temporarily downloading fonts is that the printer's memory is completely cleared between print jobs. With permanently downloaded fonts, you must turn the printer off, then on again, to clear the memory.

As noted in Chapter 8, a font is a particular combination of typeface and style (and sometimes point size). Some printers require that each combination of typeface, style, and size be downloaded as a separate font; other printers—PostScript printers, for instance—can print any size of a specific typeface and style after the font is downloaded. To use the entire family in the Palatino typeface on a PostScript printer, for example, you need to download only four different styles: normal, boldface, italic, and boldface italic. For design suggestions, along with a discussion of other production considerations such as the choice of fonts for publications, see Chapter 10.

Using Soft Fonts

After you install a soft font in your system and let Windows know where it is, try using the font in a publication. Select the font in the Type Specifications dialog box, which is displayed when you select the Type Specs command on the Type menu. If you have trouble printing the publication, one of two problems may be the reason:

■ The page has graphics that cannot be processed when the fonts are permanently downloaded.

■ You have used too many fonts on one page or in one publication.

Remember that different typefaces, styles, and sizes take up different amounts of memory and that different types of graphics also make different demands on memory. Before you design a long publication with downloadable fonts, try printing one or two sample pages with representative graphics as well as text that uses all the fonts called for in the design. If you have trouble printing these sample pages, change your design by reducing the number of fonts you use or by simplifying the specifications for illustrations. Chapter 13 offers a more comprehensive discussion of printing problems and how to solve them.

For Related Information

◄◄ "Knowing Your Printers: Types of Fonts," p. 396.

◄◄ "Installing the Printer," p. 399.

◄◄ "Managing Fonts," p. 592.

◄◄ "Troubleshooting Problems in Printing Fonts," p. 613.

FROM HERE...

For design suggestions, along with a discussion of other production considerations such as the choice of fonts for publications, see "Working with PageMaker's Font List" and "Choosing the Fonts" in the "Planning Your Design Specifications" section of Chapter 16.

Quick Review: Summaries of Steps

T his appendix provides concise, quick-reference summaries of many of the procedures described in this book. Chapters that describe these procedures in detail are referenced.

Producing a Publication

The next sections list the basic steps in producing a publication, divided into nine categories: General Steps (from Chapter 1), Starting PageMaker (Chapters 2 and 4), Opening a Document (Chapter 4), Finding a File Name in a Dialog Box (Chapter 2), Changing Views of the Page (Chapter 5), Defining Page Setup (Chapter 4), Building a Master Page (Chapter 5), Creating Document Pages (Chapter 5), and Saving a Document or Template (Chapter 4).

General Steps (Chapter 1)

The typical steps in the production process are the following:

1. Gather the team (see Chapter 1).
2. Write the text (see Chapter 6).
3. Sketch or list illustration ideas (see Chapters 9 and 15).
4. Determine final output device and resolution (see Chapter 10).
5. Develop design specifications (see Chapters 15 and 16).
6. Conduct several editorial reviews.
7. Edit and format the text (see Chapters 7 and 8).
8. Create graphics (see Chapter 9).
9. Organize your project files (see Chapters 2 and 14).
10. Start a new PageMaker document (see Chapters 4, 5, and 15).
11. Add text and graphics (see Chapters 5 through 9 and 11).
12. Print the publication (see Chapter 10).
13. Archive files (see Chapter 14).

Starting PageMaker (Chapters 2 and 4)

To start PageMaker through the Program Manager, complete the following steps:

1. Open the Windows Program Manager.
2. Double-click the Aldus program group icon to open it.
3. Double-click the PageMaker application icon.

To start PageMaker through the File Manager, perform the following steps:

1. Open the Windows File Manager.
2. Click the PM5 directory icon in the left half of the window to display its contents in the right half of the window.
3. Double-click the PageMaker application icon.

To start PageMaker by opening a document, complete the following steps:

1. Open the Windows File Manager.

2. Click the PageMaker document's directory icon—the name of the directory in which the document is saved—in the left half of the window to display its contents in the right half of the window.

3. Double-click the PageMaker document icon in the right half of the window.

To start PageMaker through the Windows Run command, perform the following steps:

1. Open the Windows File Manager or the Program Manager.

2. Choose Run from the File menu.

3. Type **pm5.exe** in the Run dialog box and press Enter or click OK.

To start PageMaker through DOS, if your PATH line in the AUTOEXEC file shows PATH C:\PM5;C:\DOS;C:\WINDOWS;C:\ALDUS, type **win pm5**.

To start PageMaker automatically whenever you start Windows, add the PageMaker application icon to the Startup program group under the Program Manager. (Refer to the Windows Users Manual.)

Opening a Document (Chapter 4)

To open a document use one of the following methods:

Choose the New command from the File menu (Ctrl+N) to start a new publication.

or

Choose Open from the File menu (Ctrl+O) to open an existing publication or template.

Finding a File Name in a Dialog Box (Chapter 2)

To choose the name of the file you want from the dialog box that appears after you select Open or Place from the File menu (Ctrl+O or Ctrl+D), complete the following steps:

1. If the list of file names (the list on the left in the dialog box) is longer than fits in the window, scroll bars appear at the right of the list, and you can click on an arrow to scroll up or down the list.

2. Click C:\ in the directory list (the right side of the dialog box) to view the list at the next higher directory level.

3. Click a directory name to view the list at the next lower directory level. Double-click on a directory name to view files within a subdirectory. If the directories list is longer than fits in the window, scroll bars appear at the right of the list, and you can click on an arrow to scroll up or down the list.

4. To view files on another drive, click the down-pointing arrow under Drives to display a drop-down list, and click a drive name such as A:, B:, or C: to view the lists of files on other drives.

5. Click Cancel to stop the Open command.

6. Click the file name to highlight the file. To open a copy of the document, click Copy in the Open dialog box to make a duplicate of the file as you are opening it, and then click OK. Or, to open the original publication, you can just double-click the file name. PageMaker displays the page that was displayed when the file was last saved.

Changing Views of the Page (Chapter 5)

To change views of the page from the View submenu of the Layout menu, perform the following steps:

1. Click a page number icon at the bottom left of the document window to turn to the page you want to view.

2. Choose a command from the View submenu of the Layout Menu to change the magnification of the page display on-screen.

Keyboard shortcuts for commands on the View submenu are listed in Appendix C.

To change to Actual Size view using the mouse and keyboard shortcut, or to toggle between Actual Size and Fit in Window, perform the following steps:

1. From any view except Actual Size, position the mouse pointer over the portion of the page you want to center on-screen and click the secondary mouse button (usually the right mouse button) to view that portion of the page in Actual Size.

2. From Actual Size, click the secondary mouse button to view the page in Fit in Window view.

To change to 200% Size view using the mouse and keyboard shortcut, or to toggle between 200% and Actual Size, perform the following steps:

1. From any view except 200%, position the mouse pointer over the portion of the page you want to center on-screen and hold the Shift key as you click the secondary mouse button (usually the right mouse button) to view that portion of the page in 200% Size.

2. From 200% Size, hold the Shift key as you click the secondary mouse button to view the page in Actual Size view.

Defining Page Setup (Chapter 4)

To define page setup for a new document, complete the following steps:

1. After starting PageMaker, choose New from the File menu (Ctrl+N) to start a new document.

2. Make entries in the Page Setup dialog box.

To define page setup for an existing document, perform the following steps:

1. After starting PageMaker, choose Open from the File menu (Ctrl+O) to open an existing document.

2. Choose Page Setup from the File menu to change the original specifications.

3. Make entries in the Page Setup dialog box.

Building a Master Page (Chapter 5)

To build a master page, complete the following steps:

1. Click one of the Master Page icons at the bottom left corner of the Publication window, or choose Go to Page from the Layout menu (Ctrl+G) to turn to a master page.

2. Set the column guides.

3. Display the rulers and position guides that are part of the grid, including horizontal guides for positioning the running headers and footers on the master pages.

4. Type the running header between the column guides; then drag the running header to the top of the page.

5. Type the running footer between the column guides; then drag the running footer to the bottom of the page.

6. Add graphic elements.

Creating Document Pages (Chapter 5)

To place text and graphics on each page, perform the following steps:

1. Verify that the master-page elements are appropriate for the current numbered page. If column guides or ruler guides need to be changed for this page, adjust them as needed before placing text and graphics on the page.

2. If your design specifications limit you to one or two variations in text and graphic formats, you can change the default settings to match the most common specifications or set up a style sheet so that each text variation has its own tag. Remember that you change the default settings for text and graphics by making menu selections while the Pointer tool is selected.

3. Place text and graphics on the page. The following are general guidelines:

   - Work in Fit in Window view at first to lay out the entire page. Change to Actual Size view to make fine adjustments.

   - Use the Snap To Guides feature to help you position text and graphics against the guides on the page.

   - Use the drag-place feature to scale a graphic as you are placing the graphic or to override the column width when placing text.

4. Save your work often. Press Ctrl+S to execute the Save command, or click the current page icon to cause a minisave.

Saving a Document or Template (Chapter 4)

To save a document or template, complete the following steps:

1. Save your files often by using the Save command from the File menu or by pressing Ctrl+S.

The first time you use the Save command on a new document, a dialog box displays in which you can specify the name of the document and the disk drive or directory to which you want to store the document.

2. Click C:\ to change to the next higher directory level, or click the down-pointing arrow under Drives to display a drop-down list, and click a drive name such as A:, B:, or C: to save the file on one of the other drives.

   Click a directory name to change to the next lower directory level.

   Type a file name without an extension, and choose Publication or Template from the Save as options. PageMaker automatically adds PM5 as the extension for publications, and PT5 as the extension for templates.

3. Choose whether you want to copy no additional files into the same directory, all files required for remote printing, or all linked files.

4. Click OK to save the document.

To save a document or template with a changed name, format, or drive/directory location, perform the following steps:

1. Choose Save As from the File menu.

2. Make entries as appropriate in the Save As dialog box (see steps 2-4, in the preceding steps).

Working with Text

The next sections summarize the steps in working with text, including Typing Text (Chapter 6), Switching to Story View (Chapter 7), Importing Text (Chapter 6), Changing the Position of Text Blocks (Chapter 6), Selecting Text (Chapter 7), and Searching and Replacing Text (Chapter 7).

Typing Text (Chapter 6)

To type text as a new story with the width of the page margins, complete the following steps:

1. With a document open and the page displayed on which you want to type, click the Text tool to select it from the Toolbox.

2. To position the blinking text insertion cursor, click the I-beam pointer in any of the following locations:

   ■ Within the margins on the top left corner of a blank page

   ■ Anywhere that is not already occupied by another story

   ■ Anywhere on the Pasteboard

3. Begin typing.

To type text as a new story with custom margins, perform the following steps:

1. With a document open and the page displayed on which you want to type, click the Text tool to select it from the Toolbox.

2. Drag the I-beam pointer to the width you want, anywhere that is not already occupied by another story.

3. Begin typing.

To type text as a new story using the Story Editor, complete the following steps:

1. Open a new, empty story window by choosing Edit Story from the File menu (or by using the keyboard shortcut Ctrl+E) when no text is selected and the text insertion point is not positioned in a text block in Page Layout view. Alternatively, while a story window is displayed, choose New Story from the Story menu.

2. Type the text.

3. Double-click the Control menu icon at the top left corner of the story window to close it.

   PageMaker displays a dialog box asking whether you want to Place or Discard the story.

4. Click Place.

   PageMaker returns to Layout view of a document page.

5. Position the loaded text placement icon on an empty area of the page where you want the text to appear, and click to place the text.

To type text on the page as part of an existing story, perform the following steps:

1. With a document open and the page displayed on which you want to type, click the Text tool to select it from the Toolbox.

2. Click the I-beam pointer at the position where you want to insert new text within a story.

3. Begin typing.

To type text as part of an existing story, through the Story Editor (Method 1), complete the following steps:

1. With a document open and the page displayed on which you want to type, click the Text tool to select it from the Toolbox.

2. Click the I-beam pointer at the position where you want to insert new text within a story.

3. Choose Edit Story from the Edit menu (Ctrl+E).

4. Begin typing.

To type text as part of an existing story, through the Story Editor (Method 2), complete the following steps:

1. The quickest way to switch to Story view is to triple-click a text block with the Pointer tool.

2. Click the I-beam pointer at the position where you want to insert new text within a story. (You can use the Find command under the Utilities menu (Ctrl+8) to find the text location quickly.)

3. Begin typing.

Switching to Story View (Chapter 7)

To switch to Story view, the following methods are available:

Method 1: The quickest way to switch to Story view is to triple-click a text block with the Pointer tool.

Method 2: Use the slower method of clicking the text block once in Page Layout view and then choosing Edit Story from the File menu (or use the keyboard shortcut Ctrl+E).

Method 3: Open a new, empty story window by choosing Edit Story from the File menu (or by using the keyboard shortcut Ctrl+E) when no text is selected and the text insertion point is not positioned in a text block in Page Layout view.

Method 4: If a story window is already open but hidden behind another story window or the publication window, click a visible part of the story window to bring it to the front. Alternatively, you can choose the window by name from the Window menu.

Method 5: Use the first three methods to open multiple story windows. You can also open a new, empty story window while a story window is displayed by choosing New Story from the Story menu.

Method 6: To automatically open Story Editor Windows for every story in a document, choose Edit All Stories from the Aldus Additions submenu under the Utilities menu.

Importing Text (Chapter 6)

To import text as a new story with the width of the page margins, complete the following steps:

1. If you are placing the text as a new story, cursor location and tool selection don't matter, but turning first to the page on which you want to place the text is a good idea.

   If you want to replace a whole story, select the Text tool from the Toolbox and click the pointer anywhere within a text block that is part of the story.

   If you want to replace part of a story, select the text to be replaced.

   If you want to insert new text within a story, select the Text tool from the Toolbox and click the pointer within the text at the point where you want to insert.

2. Choose Place from the File menu (Ctrl+D), and select the text file you want to import from the Place dialog box.

3. If your text file doesn't have an extension that is recognized by PageMaker, a dialog box with the message Do not know how to place text appears. Specify the word processing program that the text came from by double-clicking the format.

4. The pointer changes to the manual or the automatic text flow icon (the next step discusses text flow options). Position the text icon where you want the text to appear, and then perform the appropriate step:

   ■ If the manual flow icon is displayed, click once to flow the text to one page only (see step 5a, manual flow), or Ctrl+click to flow the text continuously onto new pages (see step 5b, automatic flow).

   ■ If automatic flow is selected, click once to flow the text continuously onto new pages (see step 5b), or Ctrl+click to flow the text to one page only (see step 5a).

■ In either case, you can Shift+click to control the continuous flow (see step 5c, semi-automatic flow).

■ If you use the drag-place feature—holding the mouse and dragging the text icon to outline a text block—manual text placement is activated (see step 5a).

5a. Under the manual text flow option, when the page is filled but the last block still shows a down arrow in the bottom handle, you can continue the text to the next page by clicking the last handle on the page to get the text icon. You then have the following options:

■ Click the icon of the page number to which you want to go.

■ Select the Go to Page command from the Layout menu (Ctrl+G).

■ Select Insert Pages from the Layout menu to create a new page.

When the next page is displayed, position the text icon on the page and click (see step 4).

or

5b. Under the Autoflow option, text stops flowing when you click the main mouse button, when the text runs out, or when the publication reaches 999 pages.

If you stop the automatic text flow by clicking the main mouse button, you can extend or shorten the last text block by dragging the bottom windowshade with the pointer. You can resume the flow at any time by clicking the down arrow in the windowshade that marks the bottom of the flowed text when the text is selected with the Pointer tool. This method yields a loaded text icon that you can click at the margin to continue the flow (see step 3).

or

5c. Under semiautomatic flow, the text flows to the bottom of the column and stops, but the text placement icon remains loaded and ready for you to position. You then just click to continue the flow (step 3).

To import text as a new story with custom margins, complete the following steps:

1. With a document open and the page displayed on which you want to type, choose Place from the File menu (Ctrl+D), and choose the text file you want to import from the Place dialog box.

2. Drag the text placement icon to the width you want, anywhere that is not already occupied by another story.

To import text onto the page as part of an existing story, perform the following steps:

1. With a document open and the page displayed on which you want to type, click the Text tool to select it from the Toolbox.

2. Click the I-beam pointer at the position where you want to insert new text within a story.

3. Choose Place from the File menu (Ctrl+D), and choose the text file you want to import from the Place dialog box.

To import text as part of an existing story, through the Story Editor, complete the following steps:

1. With a document open and the page displayed on which you want to type, click the Text tool to select it from the Toolbox.

2. Click the I-beam pointer at the position where you want to insert new text within a story.

3. Choose Edit Story from the Edit menu (Ctrl+E).

4. Choose Place from the File menu (Ctrl+D), and choose the text file you want to import from the Place dialog box.

To import text as OLE-linked or embedded text, complete the following steps:

1. First create the text in the other application; then select it and choose Copy from the Edit menu (Ctrl+C).

2. Open a PageMaker publication.

3. If you want to import the text as a new story, select the Pointer tool and turn to the page on which you want to place the text.

   If you want to replace part of a story, select the text to be replaced.

   If you want to insert new text within a story, select the Text tool from the Toolbox and click the pointer within a text at the point where you want to insert.

4. Choose Paste or Paste Special from the Edit menu to import the text. If you choose Paste Special, PageMaker displays a dialog box offering a list of available formats in which the text can be imported. In either case, the text comes in as a new text block or as part of an existing text block, depending on the action you take in step 3.

Changing the Size of Text Blocks (Chapter 6)

To change the size of a text block, perform the following steps:

1. Select the Pointer tool from the Toolbox and click the pointer on the text block to be moved or scaled.

2. Position the pointer over the corner of a windowshade and hold down the mouse button to display a two-headed arrow.

3. Drag the mouse pointer in the direction you want to shape the text block.

4. Release the mouse button when the text block is the shape you want.

To break a text block into two blocks, complete the following steps:

1. Use the Pointer tool to select the block to be broken up to display its handles.

2. Drag the bottom handle up to shorten the block.

3. Click the plus sign in the bottom handle to get the text placement icon.

4. Click the text placement icon anywhere in the column below the top block.

Selecting Text with the Text Tool (Chapter 7)

To select with the Text tool, perform one of the following steps:

1. With a document open and the page displayed on which you want to type, click the Text tool to select it from the Toolbox.

2. Click once to position the cursor where you want to insert new text, or select text that you want to delete, replace, or format using one of the following techniques:

   ■ Click next to the first character you want to select and drag to select a range of text character-by-character or line-by-line.

   ■ Double-click a word to select it, or double-click and drag to select a range of text word-by-word.

■ Triple-click a paragraph to select it, or triple-click and drag to select a range of text paragraph-by-paragraph.

■ Click at one end of text; then move the I-beam and Shift+click at the other end of a range of text to select all the text between two insertion points.

■ Click anywhere in a text block and type Ctrl+A or choose Select All from the Edit menu to select a whole story.

To Edit Selected Text (Chapter 7)

To delete selected text, use one of the following methods:

■ Press Backspace or Del, or choose Clear from the Edit menu.

■ Choose the Cut command from the Edit menu (Ctrl+X).

To replace selected text, just begin typing the new text.

To cut or copy and paste a block of text, perform the following steps:

1. Select with the Text tool the text to be cut or copied.

2. Choose the Cut or Copy command from the Edit menu (Ctrl+X or Ctrl+C).

3. Select the placement for the new text by positioning the text insertion point within an existing text block (to insert the text), or by selecting a range of text to be replaced, or by clicking or drag-placing the text tool icon on a page or on the pasteboard (to create a new text block).

    If you select the Text tool when you paste, the pasted text appears at the text insertion point. If the Pointer tool is selected when you paste, the pasted text appears in the center of the screen in a new text block.

4. Choose the Paste command from the Edit menu (Ctrl+V).

Searching and Replacing Text (Chapter 7)

To search text for a phrase or specific text format that you want to replace with a new phrase or format, complete the following steps:

1. Choose the Change command from the Utilities menu, or press Ctrl+9.

2. In the Change dialog box, type the phrase you want to find in the Find What text box.

3. Type the phrase with which you want to replace found text in the Change To text box.

4. Click the Match Case check box if you want to find only those instances where the capitalization matches what you have typed in the Find What text box. Leave the Match Case box unchecked if you want PageMaker to search for all matches, regardless of case.

5. Click the Whole Word check box if you want to find only those instances where the Find What text is preceded by a space and followed by a space or a punctuation mark (such as a period). Leave the Whole Word check box unchecked if you want to find all the places where the combination of letters occurs.

6. Under Search Document, you can search the current publication only, or all open publications.

7. Under Search Story, you can search the currently selected text only (if you selected text before choosing the Change command), search the current story only, or search all stories. Note that if you chose to search all open publications in step 6, then all stories are automatically searched.

8. You can click Attributes to display a second dialog box. You can use the Change Attributes dialog box to find and change the paragraph style (if a style sheet was used in formatting the text) or to find and change individual font/size/style combinations.

9. Click OK to exit the Change Attributes dialog box and return to the Change dialog box. Click Find to find the next occurrence only (and go on to step 10), or click Change All to substitute all occurrences of the found text with the text you entered in the Change To box.

   If no text was entered in the Change dialog box, all occurrences of the text attributes are changed as specified in the Change Attributes dialog box. If you entered text in the Change dialog box, only text that matches both the entered phrase and the text attributes is changed. If no text attributes are entered, any text that matches the entry in the Change dialog box is changed, and the text takes on the attributes of the found text.

10. If you clicked Find (rather than Change All), you selectively can keep or change each found occurrence; when PageMaker finds the next occurrence of the Find What text or attributes, that area is highlighted in the story window. You can click Find again if you do not want to change that text, or you can click Change or Change & Find to change the text as described in step 9.

Working with Graphics

The next sections summarize the steps used in working with graphics, including Drawing Graphics in PageMaker (Chapter 9), Importing Graphics (Chapter 9), Selecting Graphics (Chapter 9), Scaling Graphics (Chapter 9), Wrapping Text Around Graphics (Chapter 11), and Creating an Inline Graphic (Chapter 11).

Drawing Graphics in PageMaker (Chapter 9)

To use one of PageMaker's four drawing tools, perform the following steps:

1. Select one of the tools from the Toolbox: the Rectangle tool, the Ellipse tool, the Line tool, or the Constrained-Line tool. The pointer changes to a crossbar.

2. Position the crossbar on the page or pasteboard and hold down the mouse button as you drag the crossbar. The object appears on-screen as you drag.

   Hold down the Shift key while you drag the crossbar to create a perfect square with the Rectangle tool, a perfect circle with the Ellipse tool, or a line constrained to a 45-degree angle (when using the Line tool; the Constrained-Line tool does this automatically).

   As long as you hold the mouse button, you can keep adjusting the size of the object.

3. Release the mouse button to finish the object.

To change the size or position of a completed graphic, you must switch to the Pointer tool. See "Selecting a Graphic" later in this Appendix.

Importing Graphics (Chapter 9)

To import graphics from other programs into PageMaker, complete the following steps:

1. If you want to place the graphic as an independent element on the page, choose the Pointer tool before choosing the Place command.

If you want to place the graphic as an inline graphic (for example, as part of a text block), select the Text tool from the Toolbox and click the pointer within a text at the point where you want to insert.

2. Select the Place command from the File menu (Ctrl+D).

3. In the Place File dialog box, find the name of the text file you want to place—but *don't* click the file name until reading the next step.

   If the name of the file you want does not appear in the list, try one of the following techniques to check all the directories and disk drives on your system.

   - If the file name is not visible because there are more files in the directory than can fit in the scroll list on the left side of the dialog box, drag the scroll bars to move down the list.

   - Click C:\ in the scroll list on the right side of the dialog box to view the list at the next higher directory level on the current drive.

   - Click a directory name and click OK or press Enter to view the files in the subdirectory. Alternatively, double-click the directory name to view the files in the subdirectory.

   - Click the arrow at the right of the Drives area to view a drop-down list of all drives, then click A:, B:, C:, or another drive (if more drives exist) to view the list of files on another drive.

   NOTE If the file name still doesn't appear after checking all directories and disk drives, then your disk does not contain the graphic file or PageMaker does not recognize the file. You must install the correct filters for each file format you will be using by going through the installation procedures described in Appendix A.

4. After you find the name of the file you want to place, double-click the name if you want to import the file without changing any options in the Place dialog box, and perform this and the next step simultaneously.

   Otherwise, click once on the name to select it and choose from the following options:

   - Place the file as an independent graphic.

■ Replace an entire graphic that you selected before you chose the Place command.

■ Place file as an inline graphic in a text block where you positioned the text cursor before you chose the Place command.

5. Click OK to close the dialog box and place the file.

If the graphic to be imported is larger than 256K, PageMaker displays the following message:

```
The graphic in the document would occupy ___ KBytes
in the publication. Include complete copy in the
publication anyway?
```

The actual size of the graphic is shown in the dialog box. Click Yes or No.

6. If the Text tool is selected and the text insertion point is positioned within a text block when you choose the Place command, the graphic is imported immediately and becomes an inline graphic.

Otherwise, place the graphics placement icon where you want the top left corner of the graphic to appear and click once. Let the snap-to column guides help you position the graphic placement icon.

Selecting Graphics (Chapter 9)

Use one of the following techniques to select a graphic on a page:

■ Select a single graphic: First, select the Pointer tool from the toolbox; then click the Pointer tool on any part of the object. Two handles appear on a line; eight handles appear on a box or ellipse.

■ Select two or more objects: Select the Pointer tool, hold down the Shift key, and click each object.

■ Select all objects within a rectangular area: Hold down the mouse button as you drag the Pointer tool diagonally from one corner of the area to the opposite corner.

■ Select a layered object: If the graphic is on a layer below other graphics or text blocks, your first click with the pointer selects only the object on the top layer. Press Ctrl as you click again to select the object on the next layer down, and continue Ctrl+clicking until the graphic you want is selected.

Scaling Graphics (Chapter 9)

To scale graphics, follow these steps:

1. Select the Pointer tool from the Toolbox and click once on the graphic to select it and display the handles.

2. Position the pointer on a handle of the selected object and drag to scale (stretch or shrink) the graphic. The pointer becomes a two-directional arrow when you hold down the mouse button to scale a graphic.

   ■ When you use the Pointer tool to change the length of any line, you can also change the angle of the line. You can use this technique to change the angle of a line that was originally drawn with the Constrained-Line tool.

   ■ You can change the shape and size of a box or ellipse using the Pointer tool to select the object and drag one of the handles. Drag the corner handles in any direction to change both dimensions of the box simultaneously. Alternatively, drag the handles in the middle of each side of the box or ellipse horizontally or vertically to change one dimension.

If you hold down the Shift key while dragging a corner handle, you can create several effects:

   ■ If you used PageMaker's tools to draw the graphic, lines become or remain constrained to a 45-degree angle; rectangles become or remain squares; and ellipses become or remain circles.

   ■ If you imported the graphic from another program, you size the graphic proportionally.

> **NOTE** You can also make changes to the Control palette values that affect the size of the selected object.

Wrapping Text Around Graphics (Chapter 11)

To jump text over a graphic, perform the following steps:

1. Position and size the graphic on the page. Use the Pointer tool to select the graphic.

2. Choose Text Wrap from the Element menu.

3. Select the icon for a rectangular graphic boundary—the middle icon in the top row. Set the Text Flow icon for text jumping over the graphic—the middle icon in the second row. In the Standoff in Inches text boxes, type the amount of space that you want between the graphic and the text, the *graphic boundary*.

4. Click OK to close the dialog box and view the effects (if the graphic is already in text), or proceed with step 5.

5. Using the Place command dialog box from the File menu (Ctrl+D), select a text file in the Place dialog box and flow your text on the page. The text continues after the graphic.

To wrap text around a graphic, perform the following steps:

1. Place and size the graphic in the column. Use the Pointer tool to select the graphic.

2. Choose Text Wrap from the Element menu.

3. Select the icon for a rectangular graphic boundary.

4. In the Standoff in Inches text boxes, type the amount of space between the graphic and the text.

5. Set the Text Flow icon to wrap around the text—the third icon in the second row.

6. Place the text.

To create a custom-shaped graphic boundary, complete the following steps:

1. Click the graphic and highlight the Text Wrap command in the Element menu.

2. Select the second Wrap Option, the rectangular boundary in the Text Wrap dialog box. Click the last Text Flow option, which forces the text to wrap on all sides of the graphic.

   Click OK. Diamond-shaped handles appear around the graphic boundary.

3. To change the shape of the boundary, drag the diamond-shaped handles to form a new shape.

   You can add more diamond-shaped handles by clicking the graphic boundary where you want the new handles to appear.

   To erase a handle, drag it on top of another handle.

4. After the custom boundary is in place, use the Text Flow option to choose whether you want the text to flow around part or all of the graphic.

Creating an Inline Graphic (Chapter 11)

To create an inline graphic from a graphic that is already part of the PageMaker publication, perform the following steps:

1. Select a graphic that is already part of the PageMaker publication and choose Cut (Ctrl+X) or Copy (Ctrl+C) from the Edit menu.

2. Select the Text tool and position the text insertion point in the text where you want the inline graphic to appear.

3. Choose Paste (Ctrl+V) from the Edit menu.

To create an inline graphic in Layout view from an imported graphic, complete the following steps:

1. Select the Text tool and position the text insertion point in the text where you want the inline graphic to appear.

2. Choose Place from the File menu (Ctrl+D).

3. Select the graphic you want to import as an inline graphic from the Place dialog box.

To create an inline graphic in Story view from an imported graphic, perform the following steps:

1. Position the text insertion point in the text where you want the inline graphic to appear.

2. Choose Place from the File menu (Ctrl+D).

3. Select the graphic you want to import as an inline graphic from the Import dialog box.

Printing a Publication (Chapter 10)

The Print command—located on the File menu (Ctrl+P) and available only in Layout view—is used throughout the production process to print preliminary versions and final copies of publications. The printing process uses several dialog boxes that vary depending on the type of printer selected and is summarized briefly here from Chapter 10.

1. Choose Save from the File Menu (Ctrl+S). This step is optional but highly recommended.

2. Choose Print from the File menu (Ctrl+P). The Print Document dialog box appears.

3. In the Print Document dialog box, you specify the number of copies and range of pages to be printed, as well as other special options. Three buttons at the right side of the dialog box—Setup or Paper, Options, and Color—access additional dialog boxes.

4. Click the Document button to display the Print Document printing options. Click Paper to display the Paper printing options if printing to a PostScript printer, or click Setup to display the Printer Setup dialog box if printing to a non-PostScript printer. Click Options to display the Printing Options selections. Click Color to display the Color printing options.

5. Click the Print button to print the publication, or click Cancel to end the Print command without printing and without saving any changes made to the options in the dialog box. You can click the Reset button to reverse any changes you make in the dialog box.

Keyboard Shortcuts

Keyboard shortcuts work on all standard 101 keyboards. Some clone keyboards and particularly laptop and notebook keyboards will not support all the shortcuts.

Selecting a Tool from the Toolbox

Click the mouse on a tool to select it, or use these keyboard alternatives:

Tool Selection	Shortcut
Line tool	Shift+F2
Constrained-Line tool	Shift+F3
Text tool	Shift+F4
Rotating tool	Shift+F5
Rectangle tool	Shift+F6

Tool Selection	Shortcut
Ellipse tool	Shift+F7
Cropping tool	Shift+F8
Toggle between any tool and the Pointer tool	F9

Using the Pointer Tool

The techniques and shortcuts described under the next headings involve using the pointer tool.

Selecting Text Blocks and Graphics

Selection	Action
Text blocks	Point anywhere in the text block and click
Graphics	Point anywhere in the line, shape, or graphic and click
Any combination of text and graphics	Point to a blank area of the page or paste-board, and drag diagonally to create a flashing boundary box completely around the items you want to select, or click to select the first item, then hold down the Shift key and click to select the additional items
Overlapping items	Hold down Ctrl, click to select the overlapping item, click again to select the layer immediately below, and so on
All text blocks and graphics	Choose Select All from the Edit menu, **or** press Ctrl+A

Adjusting Graphics

Task	Action
Restore a distorted non-PageMaker graphic to its original proportions	Shift, point to any handle, and hold the left mouse button down as you drag
Change a PageMaker rectangle to a square	Shift, point to any handle, and hold left mouse button down
Change a PageMaker oval to a circle	Shift, point to any handle, and hold left mouse button down
Limit PageMaker lines to 45-degree increments	Shift, and drag either handle
Proportionally resize a graphic	Shift, and drag any handle
Proportionally resize a paint-type graphic so that it best fits the resolution of your printer	Ctrl+Shift, and drag any handle

Canceling a Selection

Task	Action
Cancel any selected items	Select something else, or click a blank area of the page or pasteboard, or click any tool in the toolbox
Cancel an item in a group	Hold down the Shift key, and click each item whose selection you want to cancel

Activating Menu Commands

Click the mouse on a menu name to open the menu, and then click on a command to activate it, or use these keyboard alternatives:

File Menu

Task	Shortcut
Create a new document	Alt+F+N or Ctrl+N
Open a document	Alt+F+O or Ctrl+O
Close a document	Alt+F+C
Save	Alt+F+S or Ctrl+S
Save as...	Alt+F+A
Save all open documents	Shift+Save All
Revert to previously saved document	Alt+F+V
Export	Alt+F+E
Place...	Alt+F+L or Ctrl+D
Use the Links option	Alt+F+K or Ctrl+Shift+D
Use the Book... option	Alt+F+B
Preferences	Alt+F+R
Use the Page setup... option	Alt+F+G
Print	Alt+F+P or Ctrl+P
Exit the program	Alt+F+X or Ctrl+Q

Edit Menu

Command	Shortcut
Undo	Alt+E+U or Alt+Backspace or Ctrl+Z
Cut	Alt+E+T or Shift+Del or Ctrl+X
Copy	Alt+E+C or Ctrl+Ins or Ctrl+C
Paste	Alt+E+P or Shift+Ins or Ctrl+V
Clear	Alt+E+L or Del or Backspace
Multiple paste	Alt+E+M
Select all	Alt+E+A or Ctrl+A

Command	Shortcut
Paste link	Alt+E+K
Paste special	Alt+E+S
Insert object	Alt+E+I
Use Edit Story	Alt+E+E or Ctrl+E
Edit original	Alt+E+O
Close Story window	Ctrl+Shift+E

Utilities Menu

Option	Shortcut
Aldus Additions	Alt+U+A
Find	Alt+U+F or Ctrl+8
Find next	Alt+U+X or Ctrl+Shift+9
Change	Alt+U+H or Ctrl+9
Spelling	Alt+U+S or Ctrl+L
Index entry...	Alt+U+E or Ctrl+; (semicolon)
Show index...	Alt+U+W
Create index...	Alt+U+I
Create TOC...	Alt+U+T

Layout Menu

Option	Shortcut
View	Alt+L+V
Fit in Window	Alt+L+V+W or Ctrl+W
Show pasteboard	Alt+L+V+P
Change document to 25% size	Alt+L+V+S or Ctrl+0 (zero)

continues

Option	Shortcut
Change document to 50% size	Alt+L+V+5 or Ctrl+5
Change document to 75% size	Alt+L+V+7 or Ctrl+7
Change document to actual size	Alt+L+V+A or Ctrl+1
Change document to 200% size	Alt+L+V+2 or Ctrl+2
Change document to 400% size	Alt+L+V+4 or Ctrl+4
Guides and rulers	Alt+L+A
Rulers	Alt+L+A+R or Ctrl+R
Snap to rulers	Alt+L+A+N or Shift+Ctrl+Y
Zero Lock	Alt+L+A+Z
Guides	Alt+L+A+G or Ctrl+J
Snap to guides	Alt+L+A+S or Ctrl+U
Lock guides	Alt+L+A+L
Scroll bars	Alt+L+A+B
Column guides...	Alt+L+C
Go to page...	Alt+L+G or Ctrl+G
Insert pages...	Alt+L+I
Remove pages...	Alt+L+R
Display master items	Alt+L+D
Copy master guides	Alt+L+M
Autoflow	Alt+L+F

Other Layout Shortcuts

Task	Shortcut
Toggle between Actual Size and Fit in Window views	Click right mouse button

Task	Shortcut
Toggle between Actual Size and 200% views	Shift+click right mouse button
Show entire pasteboard	Ctrl+Shift+W
Activate magnifying tool	Ctrl+spacebar+click or drag
Activate reducing tool	Ctrl+Alt+spacebar+click or drag

Type Menu

Task	Shortcut
Select a font	Alt+T+F
Choose font size	Alt+T+Z
Choose leading	Alt+T+L
Set Width	Alt+T+W
Set tracking	Alt+T+R
Set type style	Alt+T+Y
Open Type specs... dialog box	Alt+T+T or Ctrl+T
Open Paragraph... dialog box	Alt+T+P or Ctrl+M
Set indents/tabs	Alt+T+I or Ctrl+I
Open Hyphenation... dialog box	Alt+T+H or Ctrl+H
Set alignment	Alt+T+A
Choose a style	Alt+T+S
Open Define styles. . . dialog box	Alt+T+D or Ctrl+3

USING PAGEMAKER 5 FOR WINDOWS, SPECIAL EDITION

Element Menu

Element	Shortcut
Line	Alt+M+L
Fill	Alt+M+F
Line and fill	Alt+M+A
Bring to front	Alt+M+B or Ctrl+F
Send to back	Alt+M+S or Ctrl+B
Remove transformation	Alt+M+T
Text wrap...	Alt+M+W
Image control...	Alt+M+I
Rounded corners...	Alt+M+C
Define colors...	Alt+M+D
Restore original color	Alt+M+R
Link info...	Alt+M+N
Link options...	Alt+M+O

Window Menu

Menu Item	Shortcut
Arrange icons	Alt+W+A
Tile	Alt+W+I
Cascade	Alt+W+D
Toolbox	Alt+W+T or Ctrl+6
Style palette	Alt+W+S or Ctrl+Y
Color palette	Alt+W+C or Ctrl+K
Control palette	Alt+W+P or Ctrl+' (single quote mark)
Library palette	Alt+W+L

Help Menu

To Use	Shortcut
Contents...	Alt+H+C or F1
Search	Alt+H+S
Shortcuts	Alt+H+H
Using PageMaker Help...	Alt+H+U
Learning PageMaker 5.0...	Alt+H+L
About PageMaker®...	Alt+H+A

Other Help Shortcuts

To Open	Shortcut
Menu-sensitive help	Press Shift+F1
List installed filters	Hold the Ctrl key while using the mouse to select the About PageMaker command

Story Menu (Only in Story Editor)

Menu Item	Shortcut
New story	Alt+S+N
Close story	Alt+S+C or Shift+Ctrl+E
Display ¶	Alt+S+D
Display style names	Alt+S+S

Making Dialog Box Entries

Use the mouse to select a field, or use any of these keyboard alternatives:

Task	Action
Jump to any field	Hold down the Alt key and press the letter that is underscored in the field title
Make a selection from a drop-down list	Release the Alt key and press the up- or down-arrow key to select from the list
Jump to a text box entry	Hold down the Alt key and type the letter underscored in the field name
Select radio button fields or check mark fields	Hold down the Alt key and type the underscored letter in the field name
Toggle (select or deselect) check mark fields	Hold down the Alt key and type the underscored letter in the field name

Using Special Shortcuts

Task	Action
Use Fast index entry	Press Ctrl+Shift+; (semicolon)
Create proper name index entry	Press Ctrl+Shift+Z
Open the Edit style dialog box	Press Ctrl, and click style name from Styles dialog box
Open the Edit color dialog box	Press Ctrl, and click color name from Colors dialog box
Use the Story Editor	Triple-click with the pointer tool in the text you want to edit
Toggle between Actual size and Fit in window	Press Ctrl+Alt, and click the mouse

Task	Action
Search for next index marker	Type ^; (caret semicolon) in the Find dialog box
Display/hide Control palette	Press Ctrl+' (single quote mark)
Activate Control palette	Press Ctrl+` (accent)

Turning Pages

Task	Action
Jump to the page number indicated on the icon	Click a page icon in the lower left corner
Activate the Go to Page command	Press Ctrl+G
Page through publication	Shift while choosing Go to Page command from menu, then click anywhere to stop
Jump forward one page (or two pages in a double-sided publication with facing pages)	Press F12
Jump backward one page (or two pages in a double-sided publication with facing pages)	Press F11

Working with Text

The techniques and shortcuts described under the next set of headings apply to the current text selection when the text tool is selected, or to the next text typed at the text insertion point.

Flowing Text

Task	Action
Change the default from manual flow to automatic	Choose Autoflow from the Options menu
Temporarily change automatic to manual	Press Ctrl, and click icon to place
Temporarily change manual to automatic	Press Ctrl, and click icon to place
Temporarily change automatic to semi-automatic	Press Shift, and click icon to place
Cancel text flow	Click any tool in the toolbox

Moving the Text Insertion Point

With the Text tool selected, you can click the mouse within a text block to position the text insertion point, or use any of these keyboard alternatives:

Task	Action
Select next point of insertion	Click once for new text from the keyboard

To Move the Insertion Point	Press
One character at a time to the left or right of the current point	Left arrow, Right arrow
One word at a time to the left or right	Ctrl+left arrow or Ctrl+right arrow
One line at a time	Home or up arrow
One sentence at a time	Ctrl+Home, Ctrl+End
One paragraph at a time	Ctrl+up arrow, Ctrl+down arrow

To Move the Insertion Point	Press
A fixed distance determined by the view and the resolution of your screen	PgUp, PgDn
To the beginning or end of the article	Ctrl+PgUp, Ctrl+PgDn
To beginning of line	Keypad Home or keypad 7
To end of line	Keypad End or keypad 1
To beginning of sentence	Ctrl+keypad Home or Ctrl+keypad 7
To end of sentence	Ctrl+keypad End or Ctrl+keypad 1
Left one character	Left arrow or keypad 4
Right one character	Right arrow or keypad 6
Left one word	Ctrl+left arrow or Ctrl+keypad 4
Right one word	Ctrl+right arrow or Ctrl+keypad 6
Up one line	Up arrow or keypad 8
Down one line	Down arrow or keypad 2
Up one paragraph	Ctrl+up arrow or Ctrl+keypad 8
Down one paragraph	Ctrl+down arrow or Ctrl+keypad 2
Up a screen	Keypad Page Up or keypad 9
Down a screen	Keypad Page Down or keypad 3
To top of story	Ctrl+keypad Page Up or Ctrl+keypad 9
To bottom of story	Ctrl+keypad Page Down or Ctrl+keypad 3

Selecting Text

Selection	Action
Next point of insertion for new text from keyboard	Click once
A range of text character-by-character or line-by-line	Click+drag

continues

Selection	Action
Whole word	Double-click
A range of text word-by-word	Double-click+drag
Whole paragraph	Triple-click
A range of text paragraph-by-paragraph	Triple-click+drag
All the text between two insertion points	Click+Shift+click
A large amount of text	Click at one end of the text, hold down Shift, and click at other end of text
A whole story	Click anywhere in the story and press Ctrl+A or choose Select All from the Edit menu

Extending or Decreasing the Selection

Each of the selection methods in the preceding section sets the anchor point from which the following keyboard commands operate:

Task	Shortcut
Extend or decrease the selection one character at a time to the left or right of the anchor point	Shift+left arrow, Shift+right arrow
Extend or decrease the selection one word at a time to the left or the right	Shift+Ctrl+left arrow, Shift+Ctrl+right arrow
Extend or decrease the selection one line at a time	Shift+Home or Shift+up arrow, Shift+End or Shift+down arrow
Extend or decrease the selection one sentence at a time	Shift+Ctrl+Home, Shift+Ctrl+End
Extend or decrease the selection one paragraph at a time	Shift+Ctrl+up arrow, Shift+Ctrl+down arrow

Task	Shortcut
Extend or decrease the selection a fixed distance determined by the view and the resolution of your screen	Shift+PgUp, Shift+PgDn
Extend or decrease the selection to the beginning or the end of the article if the article ends or begins on the same page where the cursor is located	Shift+Ctrl+PgUp, Shift+Ctrl+PgDn

Changing Type Specifications

Task	Shortcut
Return text to normal style	F5 or Ctrl+Shift+spacebar
Boldface text	F6 or Ctrl+Shift+B
Italicize text	F7 or Ctrl+Shift+I
Underscore text	F8 or Ctrl+Shift+U
Strike through text	Ctrl+Shift+S
Reverse text	Ctrl+Shift+V
Align on left	Ctrl+Shift+L
Align in center	Ctrl+Shift+C
Align on right	Ctrl+Shift+R
Justify text	Ctrl+Shift+J
Force justify	Ctrl+Shift+F
Set automatic leading	Ctrl+Shift+A
Set normal character width	Ctrl+Shift+X
Turn off tracking	Ctrl+Shift+Q
Make text superscript	Ctrl+Shift+\

continued

Task	Shortcut
Make text subscript	Ctrl+\
Make text all caps	Ctrl+Shift+K

Changing Type Size

To Make Selected Text	Press
One point smaller	Ctrl+Shift+< (less than)
One point larger	Ctrl+Shift+> (greater than)
The next-smaller standard type size	Ctrl+< (less than)
The next-larger standard type size	Ctrl+> (greater than)

Tracking and Kerning Text

Task	Action
Eliminate track kerning (no track)	Click insertion point, then press Ctrl+Shift+Q
Clear manual kerning (layout view)	Click insertion point, then press Ctrl+Shift+0 (zero)
Fine kern apart (1/100 em) (layout view)	Click insertion point, then press Ctrl+Shift+keypad+ (plus)
Fine kern together (1/100 em) (layout view)	Click insertion point, then press Ctrl+Shift+keypad– (minus)
Coarse kern apart (1/25 em) (layout view)	Click insertion point, then press Ctrl+Shift+Backspace or Ctrl+keypad+ (plus)
Coarse kern together (1/25 em) (layout view)	Click insertion point, then press Ctrl+Backspace or Ctrl+keypad– (minus)

Typing Special Characters

Example	Description	Enter in Text Block	Enter in Dialog Box
"	typographer's open quotation marks	Ctrl+Shift+[	^{
"	typographer's close quotation marks	Ctrl+Shift+]	^}
'	typographer's single open quotation mark	Ctrl+[	^[
'	typographer's single close quotation mark	Ctrl+]	^]
LM.RM	page-number marker	Ctrl+Shift+3	^3
•	bullet	Ctrl+Shift+8	^8
®	registered mark	Ctrl+Shift+G	^r
©	copyright mark	Ctrl+Shift+0	^2
¶	paragraph mark	Ctrl+Shift+7	^7
§	section mark	Ctrl+Shift+6	^6
◘	index entry	n/a	^;
	em space	Ctrl+Shift+M	^m
	en space (1/2 em)	Ctrl+Shift+N	^>
	thin space (1/4 em)	Ctrl+Shift+T	^<
	nonbreaking space	Ctrl+Shift+H	^s
-	nonbreaking hyphen	Ctrl+Shift+ - (hyphen)	^~
-	discretionary (soft) hyphen	Ctrl+ - (hyphen)	^-
—	em dash	Ctrl+Shift+=	^_ Shift+ - (hyphen)
–	en dash	Ctrl+=	^=

continues

Example	Description	Enter in Text Block	Enter in Dialog Box
/	nonbreaking slash	Ctrl+Shift+/	^/
	tab	Tab	^t
↵	soft return	Shift+Enter	^n
¶	end of paragraph	Enter	^p
	white space or tab	Space or Tab	^w
?	question mark	?	^?
^	caret	^	^^

Shortcuts in the Show Index Dialog Box

PageMaker offers five keyboard shortcuts for deleting and restoring index entries through the Show Index dialog box.

Reversing Recent Actions

Task	Action
Delete all entries added since last choosing Accept or opening the Show Index dialog box	Press Alt and click the Add X-ref button
Restore all entries deleted since last choosing Accept or opening the dialog box	Press Alt and click the Remove button

Removing Index Entries Globally

Task	Action
Delete all page references	Press Ctrl+Alt and click Remove
Delete all cross-references	Press Ctrl+Shift and click Remove
Remove all index entries	Press Ctrl+Alt+Shift and click Remove

Glossary

Actual Size. A command on the View submenu under the Layout menu. Displays in the publication window a view of the page (or a portion of the page) in approximately the same size at which that page is to be printed, depending on the screen's characteristics.

Additive primary colors. Red, green, and blue. The three colors used to create all other colors if direct, or transmitted, light is used (as on television, for example). See also *Primary colors* and *Subtractive primary colors*.

Alignment. The positioning of lines of text on a page or in a column: aligned left (flush left, ragged right); centered; aligned right (flush right, ragged left); or justified (flush on both left and right).

Ascender. The part of a lowercase letter that rises above its main body. Technically, only three letters of the alphabet have ascenders: *b*, *d*, and *h*. Uppercase letters and the lowercase letters *f*, *k*, *l*, and *t* also reach the height of the ascenders. See also *Descender*.

ASCII. A standard format for storing text files. ASCII stands for American Standard Code for Information Interchange. The form in which text is stored if saved as Text Only, an Export command option in PageMaker as well as a Save command option available for most databases, spreadsheets, and word processors. ASCII files include all the characters of the text itself (including tabs and carriage returns) but not the non-ASCII codes used to indicate character and paragraph formats. See also *Text-only file*.

Autoflow. Text placement in which the text continuously flows from column to column and page to page, with PageMaker creating additional pages as needed until all the text is placed. See also *Manual text flow* and *Semiautomatic text flow*.

Bad break. Term referring to page breaks and column breaks that result in widows or orphans, or to line breaks that hyphenate words incorrectly or separate two words that should stay together (for example, *Mr. Smith*). See also *Nonbreaking space* and *Orphans/widows*.

Baseline. In a line of text, the lowest point of letters, excluding descenders. (The lowest point of letters such as *a* and *x*, for example, but not the lower edges of descenders on *p* and *q*.)

Bit map. A graphics image or text formed by a pattern of dots. PC Paint, Windows Paint, and PC Paintbrush documents produce bit-mapped graphics as well as scanned or digitized images. Low-resolution images are sometimes called *paint-type* files, and these images usually have a lower number of dots per inch (dpi) than high-resolution images.

Bleed. Term used to describe a printed image extending to the trimmed edge of the sheet or page.

Block. See *Text block*.

Blue lines. A preliminary test printing of a page to check the offset printer's plates. This test printing is done by using a photochemical process (instead of printer's inks) that produces a blue image on white paper. See also *Prepress proofs* and *Press proofs*.

Blue pencil/blue line. Traditionally, a guideline drawn with a blue pencil or printed in light blue ink on the boards and used as a guide for manually pasting up a page layout. The blue ink is sometimes called *nonrepro blue* because the color is not picked up by the camera when a page is photographed to make plates for offset printing. In PageMaker, you can create nonprinting margins, column guides, and ruler guides on-screen to help you position text and graphics; these lines do not appear when the page is printed.

Board. A sheet of heavyweight paper or card stock onto which typeset text and graphics are pasted manually. See also *Blue pencil/blue line*.

Body copy. The main part of the text of a publication, as distinguished from headings and captions. See also *Body type*.

Body type. The type (font) used for the body copy. Generally, fonts that are used for body copy, as distinguished from display type. See also *Body copy*.

Boilerplate. See *Template*.

Book. In PageMaker, a series of PageMaker publications that are associated through the Book command, so they can be printed with sequential page numbers and listed in one Table of Contents and Index generated by PageMaker.

Bounding box. Space defined by dragging the mouse diagonally. Used to place or type text.

Brochure. A folded pamphlet or small booklet.

Build Booklet. A command on the Aldus Additions submenu under the Utilities menu that assembles pages as spreads—that is, side-by-side pairs as required for offset printing signatures that will be folded and stapled or bound.

Callouts. In PageMaker, text that points out and identifies parts of an illustration. Also, headings that appear in a narrow margin next to the body copy. See also *Pull-out quote*.

Camera-ready art. The complete pages of a publication assembled with text and graphics and ready for reproduction. Literally refers to pages ready to be photographed as the first step in the process of making plates for offset printing. See also *Mechanicals* and *Offset printing*.

Caps (All Caps and Small Caps). PageMaker offers the capability to set text in All Caps, in which all characters of the selected text are automatically converted to capital letters, regardless of how they were typed, or Small Caps, in which the letters that were typed as lowercase are set as uppercase letters smaller than normal capitals. These options are available through the Type Specs command under the Type menu (as the Case option in the Type Specifications dialog box, or through the Control palette in Character view).

Caption. Descriptive text that identifies a photograph or illustration. See also *Callouts*.

Carriage return. A line break you insert by pressing the Enter key at the end of a line or paragraph. Sometimes called a hard carriage return to distinguish it from the soft carriage returns that result from word wrapping at the right margin of a page or right edge of a column. The term originated from the typewriter, which actually had a carriage that "carried" the paper back and forth in front of the keys and "returned" the paper to the left margin position when you pressed the Return key (now the Enter key on computers).

Chained text. Blocks of text that are connected across the columns on a page and across pages from the beginning to the end of an article. PageMaker chains all text blocks that are part of a story—from a text file you place or text you type as a new story. As you edit chained (or threaded) text, PageMaker moves words from one text block into the next text block in the chain to adjust to the new text length. See also *Text block*.

Check box. The small square to the left of certain options in dialog boxes; you click the check box to turn an option on or off (to select or deselect it). An X appears in the check box after it is selected, or turned on. The check box is empty if it is deselected, or turned off.

Cicero. A unit of measure equivalent to 4.55 millimeters, commonly used in Europe for measuring font sizes. Use the Preferences command from the Edit menu to select Ciceros as the unit of measure for your ruler lines and dialog box displays. You also can enter a value in Ciceros in any dialog box by inserting a *c* between the number of Ciceros and the number of points; for example, *3c2* indicates 3 Ciceros and 2 points. See also *Measurement system*.

Click. To press and release a mouse button quickly.

Clipboard. A feature of Microsoft Windows; temporarily stores text or graphics cut or copied by the commands on the Edit menu. The Paste command brings the contents of the Clipboard to the page. The Clipboard command displays the contents of the Clipboard.

Close. To choose the Close command from the File menu and stop work on the current publication, or to choose the Close command from the Control menu and leave PageMaker.

Coated stock. Paper that has a light clay or plastic coating. A glossy or slick paper is coated. The color you want often depends on the type of stock on which you are printing.

Collated. Printed in numerical order with the first page on top of the stack that comes out of the printer. An option in the Print dialog box. Multiple copies are grouped into complete sets of the publication.

Color keys. A color overlay proofing system produced by the 3M Company. See also *Overlay proofs*.

Color separations. In offset printing, separate plates used to lay different colors of ink on a page printed in multiple colors. With PageMaker, you can create masters for color separations by preparing different pages, each containing the elements to be printed in one color. If the colors do not overlap, you also can use a tissue overlay to specify colors to the offset printer. See also *Overlay*.

Column guides. Dotted vertical nonprinting lines that mark left and right edges of columns, created by choosing PageMaker's Column Guides command.

Column rules. Vertical lines drawn between columns by using PageMaker's Perpendicular-line tool.

Command button. A large rectangular area in a dialog box that contains a command such as OK or Cancel. You can activate command buttons surrounded by a thick black line by pressing the Enter key.

Comp. Traditionally, a designer's comprehensive sketch of a page design, showing the client what the final page is to look like after being printed. Usually a full-sized likeness of the page, a comp is a few steps closer to the final than a pencil rough and can be composed by using ink pens, pencils, color markers, color acetate, pressure-sensitive letters, and other tools available at art supply shops. A comp created by using PageMaker resembles the finished product, featuring typeset text, ruled lines, and shaded boxes created in PageMaker. The comp can be used as a starting point in building the final document.

Condensed type. A narrow typeface having proportionally less character width than a normal face of the same size. Although you can achieve this effect by graphically scaling characters from the normal font, condensed characters are usually individually designed as a separate font. Condensed typefaces are used where large amounts of copy must fit into a relatively small space (such as in tabular composition). See also *Kerning*.

Constrain. To restrict the movement in drawing or moving an object to an angle that is a multiple of 45 degrees. You constrain the movement by holding the Shift key as you drag the mouse. See also *X-axis* and *Y-axis*.

Continued line. See *Jump line*.

Continuous-tone image. An illustration or photograph, black-and-white or color, composed of many shades between the lightest and the darkest tones and not broken up into dots. Continuous-tone images usually need to be converted into dots, either by scanning or by halftone, to be printed in ink or on a laser printer. See also *Halftone*.

Control menu. The Microsoft Windows menu listing commands for working with windows, getting PageMaker Help, using the Clipboard, and leaving PageMaker.

Control menu box. Small square displayed in the upper left corner of the publication window. You click this box to select the Control menu.

Control palette. A movable window in PageMaker that enables you to manipulate the selected object through numeric entries.

Control Panel. A Microsoft Windows application program used to add or delete fonts and printers, change printer connections and settings, and adjust mouse and screen settings.

Copy fitting. Determining the amount of copy (text set in a specific font) that can fit in a given area on a page or in a publication. Making copy fit on a page in PageMaker by adjusting the line spacing, word spacing, and letter spacing.

Corner style. See *Rounded-corners* command.

Crop. To use PageMaker's Cropping tool to trim the edges from a graphic to make the image fit into a given space or to remove unnecessary parts of the image.

Crop marks. Lines printed on a page to indicate where the page is to be trimmed after the final document is printed and bound. PageMaker prints these marks if the page size is smaller than the paper size and if the Crop Marks option is selected in the Print command dialog box. See also *Printer's Marks*.

Cropping tool. Tool used to trim a graphic.

Crossbar. The shape of the pointer after one of PageMaker's tools for drawing lines and shapes has been selected. See also *Pointer*.

Custom. In PageMaker, a word to describe unequal columns, which you can create in PageMaker by dragging column guides to the desired position.

Custom color. An ink color that you assign to objects in your publication. Using custom color, you produce one negative for each color used in the artwork. Treated the same as spot color. See also *process color*.

Cutout. See *Knockout*.

Cyan. The subtractive primary color that appears blue-green and absorbs red light. Used as one ink in four-color printing. Also known as *process blue*. See also *Subtractive primary colors* and *Process color*.

CYMK. Shorthand notation for cyan (C), yellow (Y), magenta (M), and black (K). See also *Subtractive primary colors*.

Default. The initial setting of a value or option when you first display it (as when a dialog box opens). Default settings usually can be changed by the operator.

Descender. The part of a lowercase letter that hangs below the baseline. Five letters of the alphabet have descenders: *g, j, p, q,* and *y*. See also *Ascender* and *Baseline*.

Deselect. In PageMaker, to select another command or option or to click a blank area of the pasteboard to cancel the current selection. Also to turn off (remove the X from) a check box. See also *Select*.

Desktop. The menu bar and blank area PageMaker displays if no publication is open.

Desktop publishing. Use of personal computers and software applications such as PageMaker to produce copy that is ready for reproduction.

Diagonal-line tool. Tool used to draw a straight line in any direction.

Dialog box. A window that appears in response to a command that calls for setting options. See also *Window*.

Digitize. To convert an image to a system of dots that can be stored in the computer. See also *Scanned-image files*.

Dingbats. Traditionally, ornamental characters (bullets, stars, flowers) used for decoration or as special characters within text. The laser-printer font Zapf Dingbats includes many traditional symbols and some new ones.

Directory. A named area reserved on the hard disk where a group of related files can be stored together. Each directory can have subdirectories. See also *Hierarchical filing system*.

Discretionary hyphen. A hyphen inserted when Ctrl+- (hyphen) is pressed. Identifies where PageMaker can divide a word to fit text in the specified line length if Hyphenation is on (as specified in the Paragraph dialog box). The hyphen appears on-screen and on the printed page only if the hyphen falls at the end of a line. See also *Hyphenation*.

Display type. Type used for headlines, titles, headings, advertisements, fliers, and so on. Display type is usually a large point size (several sizes larger than body copy) and can be a decorative font.

Dots per inch (dpi). See *Resolution*.

Dot-matrix printer. A printer that creates text and graphics by pressing a matrix of pins through the ribbon onto the paper. These impact printers usually offer lower resolution (dots per inch) than do laser printers and are used only for draft printouts from PageMaker.

Double-click. To quickly press and release the main mouse button twice in succession.

Double-headed arrow. The shape of the pointer tool as a handle, ruler guide, or column guide is being dragged. See also *Pointer*.

Double-sided publication. An option in the Page Setup dialog box for creating a publication to be reproduced on both sides of the sheets of paper. The front side of a page is an odd-numbered page, and the back side is an even-numbered page. See also *Facing pages*.

Drag. To hold down the main mouse button, move the mouse until the object is where you want it, and then release the button.

Drag and drop. Dragging a selected item from one open publication to another open publication.

Drag-place. To drag the mouse diagonally to define the width of a graphic or text as you place it and so override the column guides.

Draw-type files. See *Object-oriented files.*

Drop-down menu. See *Pull-down menu.*

Dummy publication. Traditionally, a pencil mock-up of the pages of a publication, folded or stapled into a booklet, that the offset printer uses to verify the correct sequence of pages and positions of photographs. PageMaker's thumbnails can serve the function of a dummy publication. See also *Build Booklet*, *Template*, and *Thumbnail.*

Ellipse. A regular-shaped oval created by using PageMaker's Ellipse tool, as distinguished from irregular ovals, which are egg-shaped.

Ellipsis. Series of three dots in text (...) used to indicate that some of the text has been deleted (usually from a quotation). An *ellipsis* appears after every PageMaker menu command that opens a dialog box (for example, Open... on the File menu).

Em. Unit of measure equaling the point size of the type; for example, a 12-point em is 12 points wide. The width of an em dash or an em space. See also *En.*

Emulsion. The photosensitive layer on a piece of film or paper. Emulsion side up or down may be specified in the Print command dialog box.

En. One-half the width of an em. The width of an en dash or an en space. See also *Em.*

Encapsulated PostScript (EPS) format. A file format that describes a document or graphic written in the PostScript language and that contains all the codes necessary to print the file.

Enter key. Key you press to break a line if the Text tool is active or to confirm the selected options in a dialog box. Also called the Return key. Usually has the same effect as the Return key on a typewriter. See also *Carriage return.*

Export. To send PageMaker text to a word processing file.

Export filter. A process that tells PageMaker how to convert its files so that the files can be understood by the word processing program that imports them.

Facing pages. The two pages that face one another if a book, brochure, or similar publication is open. Also an option used in double-sided publications. Facing pages have an even-numbered page on the left and an odd-numbered page on the right. See also *Double-sided publication.*

Fill. To paint an area enclosed by a border with a gray shade or color. You can do this to a rectangle or ellipse created in PageMaker by using the Fill command or the Fill and Line command from the Element menu.

Film. Photosensitive material, generally on a transparent base, that receives character images and may be chemically processed to expose those images. In phototypesetting, any photosensitive material, transparent or not, may be called film.

Flow text. To click the mouse button to discharge a loaded text icon and place text on a page.

Flush. Aligned with, even with, coming to the same edge as. See also *Alignment.*

Flush right (or right-justified). Text in which lines end at the same point on the right margin. Opposite of ragged right or left-justified. See also *Alignment.*

Folio. Page number on a printed page, often accompanied by the name of the document and date of publication. See also *Running head* and *Running foot.*

Font. One complete set of characters (including all the letters of the alphabet, punctuation marks, and symbols) in the same typeface, style, and size. A 12-point Times Roman font, for example, is a different font from 12-point Times Italic, 14-point Times Roman, or 12-point Helvetica. Screen fonts (bit-mapped fonts used to display text accurately on-screen) can differ slightly from printer fonts (outline fonts used to describe fonts to the laser printer) because of the difference in resolution between screens and printers.

Footer. See *Running foot.* See also *Folio.*

Format. Page size, margins, and grid used in a publication. Also the character format (font) and paragraph format (alignment, spacing, and indentation).

Formatting. Using the type and paragraph attributes to modify the page.

Four-headed arrow. Shape of the pointer if used to drag a selected text block or graphic. See also *Pointer.*

Ghosting. The shift in ink density that occurs when large, solid areas interfere with one another. Also, a procedure in which two images are combined together electronically. The images are given specific weight in relation to each other to create the effect.

Grabber hand. A PageMaker icon; appears after you press the Alt key and as you drag the mouse to move around in the window.

Graphic. A line, box, or circle that you draw in PageMaker. An illustration brought into a PageMaker publication from another application.

Graphic boundary. The dotted line around a graphic that limits how close text can get to the graphic.

Greek text (greeked text). Traditionally, a block of text used to represent the positioning and point size of text in a designer's comp. Standard greeked text used by typesetters looks more like Latin: "Lorem ipsum dolor sit amet...." See also *Greeking*.

Greeking. The conversion of text to symbolic bars or boxes that show the position of the text on-screen but not the real characters. Text usually is greeked in the Fit in Window view in PageMaker; small point sizes may be greeked in closer views on some screens. See also *Greek text*.

Grid. The underlying design plan for a page. In PageMaker, the grid consists of nonprinting horizontal and vertical lines (margins, column guides, and ruler guides) that intersect to form a grid.

Gripper. The top part of a page, where the printing press grabs the paper. Nothing can be printed in this area.

Guide. A nonprinting line (margin guide, ruler guide, or column guide) created to help align objects on a page. In PageMaker, nonprinting guides look like dotted lines, dashed lines, or blue lines, depending on the screen's resolution and color settings.

Gutter. The inside margins between the facing pages of a document; sometimes describes the space between columns. In some word processors, the gutter measure is entered as the difference between the measures of the inside margin and the outside margin. See also *Margin*.

Hairline. The thinnest rule you can create, usually 0.25 point. (Some laser printers do not support hairline rules.) See also *Rules*.

Halftone. The conversion of continuous-tone artwork (usually a photograph) into a pattern of dots or lines that looks like gray tones when printed by an offset printing press. See also *Continuous-tone image*.

Handles. The eight small black rectangles enclosing a selected shape; the two small rectangles at the ends of a selected line; the small black rectangles at the four corners and the loops at the center of the top and bottom of a selected text block. You can drag the handles to change the size of the selected object. Also called *sizing squares*. See also *Windowshades*.

Hanging indent. A paragraph in which the first line extends to the left of the other lines. You can use a hanging-indent format to create headings set to the left of the body copy. See also *Indentation*.

Hard carriage return. See *Carriage return*.

Hard disk. Disk storage that is built into the computer or into a piece of hardware connected to the computer. Distinguished from removable floppy disk storage.

Header. See *Running head*. See also *Running foot* and *Folio*.

Headline. The title of an article in a newsletter, newspaper, or magazine.

Hierarchical filing system. A disk storage system in which files can be stored in separate directories, which, in turn, can contain subdirectories. See also *Directory*.

Highlight. To distinguish visually. Usually reverses the normal appearance of selected text, graphics, or options (black text on a white background, for example, appears as white text on black background after it is highlighted).

Hyphenation. Hyphenation can be achieved in several ways: (1) Page-Maker automatically hyphenates text (based on a built-in dictionary) as you place or type text on the page; (2) PageMaker recognizes hyphens inserted by the word processing program; (3) you can activate prompted hyphenation through the Paragraph command and insert hyphens in words that PageMaker displays in a dialog box as the text is being placed on the page; and (4) you can insert *discretionary hyphens* (displayed only if they fall at the end of a line) by pressing Ctrl+- (hyphen) within a word. See also *Discretionary hyphen*.

I-beam. The shape of the pointer after the Text tool is selected. See also *Pointer*.

Icon. Graphic on-screen representation of a tool, file, or command.

Image area. Area inside the margins of the page; contains most of the text and graphics.

Import. To bring text or graphics into PageMaker from other programs, such as text from a word processing program.

Import filter. A process that tells PageMaker how to convert files from other programs for use by PageMaker.

Increment. Distance between tick marks on a ruler. See also *Measurement system*.

Indentation. Positioning the first line of a paragraph (or second and following lines) to the right of the left column guide (to create a left indent), or positioning the right margin of the paragraph to the left of the right column guide (to create a right indent), relative to the other text on the page. In PageMaker, you set indentation through the Paragraph command dialog box or by choosing the Indents/Tabs command. See also *Hanging indent*.

Insertion point. A blinking vertical bar where text is to be typed or pasted.

Inside margin. Margin along the edge of the page that is to be bound. In single-sided publications, this is always the left margin. In double-sided publications, the inside margin is the left margin of a right-hand page or the right margin of a left-hand page. See also *Gutter* and *Margin*.

Integral proof. A color proofing system that bonds all four process colors to a single sheet.

Italic. Letters that slope toward the right, as distinguished from upright, or Roman, characters.

Invert. See *Reverse*.

Jump line. Text at the end of an article indicating on what page the article is continued. Also, the text at the top of a continued article, indicating from where the article is continued. Also called a *continued line*.

Justified text. Text that is flush at both the left and right edges. See also *Alignment*.

Kern. To adjust the spaces between letters, usually to move letters closer together. See also *Kerning*.

Kerning. The amount of space between letters, especially certain combinations of letters that must be brought closer together to create visually consistent spacing around all letters. The uppercase letters *AW*, for example, may appear to have a wider gap between them than the letters *MN*, unless a special kerning formula is set up for the *AW* combination. In PageMaker, letters larger than the point size specified in the Paragraph command's dialog box are kerned against a table of kerning pairs. You also can adjust the space between letters manually by using the Text tool and pressing Ctrl+Backspace to decrease space or Ctrl+Shift+Backspace to increase space. See also *Kern*.

Knockout. A generic term for a positive or overlay that "knocks out" part of an image from another image. The most obvious example of this is white type on a black background. The white type is knocked out of the background.

Landscape printing. The rotation of a page to print text and graphics horizontally across the longer measure of the page or paper (usually 11 inches). In PageMaker, the Wide option appears in the Page Setup and Print Document dialog boxes for page orientation, and as the Landscape option in the Windows Printer Setup dialog box for paper orientation. See also *Orientation* and *Portrait printing*.

Laser printing. Term used to describe printing on a toner-based laser printer. These printers use laser technology—*l*ight *a*mplification by *s*timulated *e*mission of *r*adiation—to project an intense light beam in a narrow band width (1/300 inch in 300 dpi printers). This light creates on the printer drum a charge that picks up the toner and transfers it to the paper. Some typesetters (such as the Linotronic 300 and 500) also use laser technology in their photochemical processing, but usually are referred to as phototypesetters rather than as laser printers. See also *Phototypesetting*.

Layer. To place objects in layers that are in front of one another.

Layout. The process of arranging text and graphics on a page. A sketch or plan for the page. Also the final appearance of the page. (In plate-making, a sheet indicating the settings for the step-and-repeat machine.)

Layout grid. See *Grid*.

Layout view. In PageMaker, the display of the page on-screen exactly as it will appear when printed. Distinguished from Story view, in which only the text is displayed, and only in one font. See also *Story view*.

Leaders. Dotted or dashed lines that can be defined for tab settings. PageMaker offers three types of tab leaders, plus a custom leader option, set through the Tabs/Indents command.

Leading. Historically, the insertion of thin strips of metal (made of a metal alloy that included some lead) between lines of cast type to add space between the lines and to make columns align. In modern typography, the vertical space between the baselines of two lines of text. In PageMaker, leading is measured from ascender to ascender between two lines of text and is entered in points in the Type Specifications dialog box. To give an example of the terminology, 12-point Times with 1 point of leading added is called 13-point leaded type, also called 12 on 13 Times, and sometimes written as "12/13 Times."

Letter spacing. Space between letters in a word. The practice of adding space between letters. In PageMaker, unjustified text has fixed letter spacing; justified text has variable letter spacing, which is adjusted within the limits entered in the Spacing Attributes dialog box. See also *Kerning* and *Word spacing*.

Library. In PageMaker, a collection of commonly used text and graphic elements stored in a PageMaker Library, displayed in the Library palette.

Ligatures. Character combinations that are often combined into special characters in a font. Some downloadable fonts, for example, come with the combinations *fi* and *fl* as special characters.

Line break. The end of a line of text, created by automatic word wrap and hyphenation. See also *Carriage return*.

Line length. Horizontal measure of a column or a line of text.

Line spacing. See *Leading*.

Line style. Appearance of the border of a shape or a line drawn in PageMaker; selected through the Lines submenu.

Linked file. In PageMaker, a graphic or text file that has been imported by using the Place or Paste command in conjunction with the option to Link the original file to the PageMaker publication, rather than store it as part of the publication. Linked files can be managed through the Links command under the File menu, and the Link Info and Link Options commands under the Element menu, to view or change the location of the linked file and update the element in the PageMaker publication when the externally linked file is modified. See also *Object Linking and Embedding*.

List box. Area in a dialog box that displays options.

Lock. In PageMaker, using the Lock Guides command to anchor column guides and ruler guides on the current page or to anchor the zero point of the rulers. Locked guides cannot be inadvertently moved while laying out text and graphics.

Logo. A company trademark. Also, the banner on the front cover of a magazine or newsletter. See also *Masthead*.

Manual text flow. Manually placing text on the page so that the text flows to and stops at the bottom of the column or the first object that blocks the text. See also *Autoflow* and *Semiautomatic text flow*.

Magenta. The subtractive primary color that appears blue-red and absorbs green light. Used as one ink in four-color printing. Also known as *process red*. See also *Subtractive primary colors* and *Process color*.

Magic stretch. PageMaker feature whereby you hold the Ctrl key while scaling an imported TIFF image in order to jump to the best incremental sizes for printing, without introducing Moiré patterns. See also *Moire patterns* and *Scale*.

Margin. Traditionally, the distance from the edge of the page to the edge of the layout area of the page. In PageMaker, page size and margins are defined in the Page Setup dialog box. The margins in PageMaker are normally used to define the limits of text. Running heads, running footers, and column rules usually fall outside the margins. See also *Gutter* and *Inside margin*.

Margin guides. Dotted nonprinting lines displayed near the borders of the screen page to mark the margins of a page as specified in the Page Setup dialog box. See also *Margin* and *Nonprinting master items*.

Marquee. A dashed rectangular region that appears when you drag the pointer tool to select objects.

Master items. Items on a master page; may include text (running heads), graphics (rules), and nonprinting guides (column guides). See also *Master page* and *Nonprinting master items*.

Master page. Page containing text, graphics, and guides you want repeated on every page in a publication. Opened by clicking the L or R page icon in the publication window. A single-sided publication has only one master page. A double-sided publication has two master pages: left-hand (even-numbered) and right-hand (odd-numbered). See also *Master items*, *Double-sided publication*, and *Single sided*.

Masthead. Section of newsletter or magazine giving its title and details of staff, ownership, advertising, subscription, and so on. Sometimes the banner or wide title on the front cover of a magazine or the front of a newsletter or newspaper. See also *Logo*.

Measurement system. Units chosen through the Preferences command on the Edit menu: inches, decimal inches, millimeters, picas and points, or ciceros and points. The chosen units appear on the rulers and in all dialog boxes that display measurements. You can enter a value in any unit of measure in a dialog box, regardless of the current Preferences selection, by typing the abbreviation for the unit in your entry. For example, 3.5i indicates 3.5 inches, 3p2 specifies 3 picas and 2 points, 3.5m indicates 3.5 millimeters, and 3c2 specifies 3 ciceros and 2 points. See also *Cicero* and *Pica*.

Mechanicals. Traditionally, the final pages or boards with pasted-up galleys of type and line art, sometimes with acetate or tissue overlays for color separations and notes to the offset printer. See also *Camera-ready art* and *Offset printing*.

Mechanical separations. Color separations made based on black-and-white art. If using CMYK process color separations, for example, each of four plates represents a different color (cyan, magenta, yellow, and black) but is given to the press/printer as a black-and-white print on paper or film.

Memory. Area in the computer where information is stored temporarily while you work; also called RAM, or random-access memory. PageMaker saves a publication from the computer's memory onto a disk whenever you turn a page or click a page icon; these saves are called *minisaves*. You also can copy the contents of the memory onto disk by using the Save or Save As command. See also *Minisave*.

Menu. A list of choices presented in either a pull-down or pop-up window, from which you can select an action.

Menu bar. Area across the top of the publication window where menu titles are displayed.

Minisave. PageMaker's automatic save of a publication whenever you turn a page or click a page icon. Minisaves create temporary documents on disk and do not overwrite the publication file. Use the Save command to overwrite the last saved version of the publication. See also *Memory*.

Mirror. To create a mirror image of an object.

Moiré pattern. An undesirable grid pattern that may occur if two transparent dot-screen fill patterns are overlaid or a bit-mapped graphic with gray fill patterns is reduced or enlarged. PageMaker's magic-stretch feature (in which you hold down the Ctrl key as you drag) can help eliminate this effect.

Mouse buttons. The main, or primary, mouse button (usually the left button) is used to carry out most PageMaker actions. Use the Control Panel to specify the main button as the left or right button of a two- or three-button mouse. Some PageMaker commands also use the secondary mouse button on a two- or three-button mouse. See also *Control Panel* and *Secondary mouse button*.

Negative. A reverse image of a page, produced photographically on a clear sheet of film as an intermediate step in preparing offset printing plates from camera-ready mechanicals.

Nonbreaking space. A special character inserted between two words so that they are not separated by a line break. See also *Bad break* and *Orphans/widows*.

Nonprinting master items. The ruler guides and column guides on a master page. See also *Guides*, *Margin guides*, *Master page*, and *Ruler guides*.

Object Linking and Embedding (OLE). A feature of Windows 3.1 (and later versions), whereby objects created in one application that supports OLE can be pasted into another application that supports OLE either as embedded objects (that is, part of the document into which they are pasted) or as linked objects (that is, linked to the external source and updated when the source changes). In either case, the objects can be edited by double-clicking them, thereby activating the application that originally created them. See also *Linked file*.

Object-oriented files. Draw-type files consisting of a sequence of drawing commands (stored as mathematical formulas). These commands describe graphics (such as mechanical drawings, schematics, charts, and ad graphics) that you would produce manually with a pencil, straightedge, and compass. Usually contrasted with paint-type files or bit maps. See also *Bit map*.

Offset printing. Type of printing done using a printing press to reproduce many copies of the original. (In PageMaker, the original is printed on a laser printer.) The press lays ink on a page according to the raised image on a plate created by photographing the camera-ready masters. See also *Camera-ready art*, *Laser printing*, and *Mechanicals*.

OLE. See *Object Linking and Embedding*.

Option button. The round area to the left of certain options in a dialog box; you click the option button to turn on, or select, its option. Selecting one option button deselects, or turns off, all other option buttons in the group. Also known as a *radio button*.

Orientation. Page position options: Tall or Wide. In Tall orientation, text runs horizontally across the narrower measure of the page, and columns run down the longer measure of the page. In Wide orientation, text runs horizontally across the wider measure of the page, and columns run down the shorter measure of the page. See also *Landscape printing* and *Portrait printing*.

Orphans/widows. The first line of a paragraph is called an orphan if separated from the rest of the paragraph by a page break. The last line of a paragraph is called a widow if forced to a new page by a page break and separated from the rest of the paragraph. Most publishers generally consider widows and orphans to be bad page breaks (or column breaks). The term widow also is used to describe bad line breaks that result in the last line of a paragraph having only one word, especially if it falls at the end of a column or page. See also *Bad break* and *Nonbreaking space*.

Outline font. A printer font in which each letter of the alphabet is stored as a mathematical formula, as distinguished from bit-mapped fonts that are stored as patterns of dots. PostScript fonts, for example, are outline fonts. See also *Bit map* and *Font*.

Outside margin. The unbound edge of a publication. In single-sided publications, the outside margin is the right margin. In double-sided publications, the outside margin is the right margin of a right-hand page and the left margin of a left-hand page. See also *Inside margin* and *Margin*.

Overhead transparency. An image printed on clear acetate and projected onto a screen for viewing by an audience.

Overlay. A transparent acetate or tissue covering a printed page; contains color specifications and other instructions to the offset printer. Also, an overhead transparency that is intended to be projected on top of another transparency. See also *Color separations*.

Overlay proofs. A color proofing system that uses transparent overlays for each of the four process colors.

Overprint. To specify that a colored object show through another colored object that overlaps it. Normally, the object underneath is hidden by the object in front.

Oversized publication. Publication in which page size is larger than paper size. See also *Page size*, *Paper size*, and *Tile*.

Page icon. An icon displayed in the bottom left corner of the publication window. Icons represent the master pages and every regular page. See also *Icon*.

Page number marker. A series of characters (Ctrl+Shift+3) entered on a master page (displayed as 0) or on a regular page (displayed as the current page number). Instructs PageMaker to number pages automatically.

Page size. The dimensions of the pages of your publication as set in the Page Setup dialog box. Page size can differ from paper size. See also *Margin* and *Paper size*.

Paintbrush icon. Shape of the pointer as a bit-mapped (or paint-type) file is being placed. See also *Bit map* and *Pointer*.

Paint-type file. See *Bit map*.

Pair kerning. The PageMaker option that changes the amount of space between two letters to create visually consistent spacing between all letters.

Pantone Matching System. A popular system for choosing colors, based on ink mixes.

Paper size. The size of the printer paper. Standard paper sizes are letter (8 1/2 by 11 inches), legal (8 1/2 by 14 inches), European A4 (210 by 297 millimeters), and European B5 (176 by 250 millimeters).

Pasteboard. The on-screen work area surrounding the pages on which you are working. You move text and graphics to the pasteboard, where they remain after you turn to another page or close the publication.

Paste-up. See *Mechanicals*.

Pencil icon. Shape of the pointer as an object-oriented (draw-type) file is being placed. See also *Pointer*.

Perpendicular-line tool. Tool used to draw a straight line at any 45-degree increment.

Phototypesetting. Producing a page image on photosensitive paper, as when documents are printed on a Linotronic 300 or 500. This process is sometimes referred to as *cold type* to distinguish it from the older method of casting characters, lines, or whole pages in lead (called *hot type* or *hot metal*). See also *Laser printing*.

Pica. A unit of measure equal to approximately 1/6 inch, or 12 points. Use the Preferences command from the Edit menu to select picas and points as the unit of measure for the ruler lines and dialog box displays. You also can enter a value in picas and points in any dialog box by typing a *p* between the number of picas and the number of points: for example, 3p2 specifies 3 picas and 2 points. See also *Cicero*, *Point size*, and *Measurement system*.

PICT format. A format used to store graphics on a Macintosh computer. Usually converted to PIC format when transferred to an MS-DOS/Windows system.

Pixel. The smallest unit on a computer display. Monitors can have different screen resolutions (pixels per inch) and different sizes (total number of pixels).

Place. Command used to bring into PageMaker a text or graphics file created in a word processor or graphics program.

Point. To place the mouse pointer on an object on-screen.

Point size. The smallest unit of measure in typographic measurement and the standard unit of measure for type. Measured roughly from the top of the ascenders to the bottom of the descenders. A pica has 12 points; an inch, approximately 72 points; a point equals 1/12 pica, or 1/72 inch. See also *Cicero*, *Pica*, and *Measurement system*.

Pointer. The on-screen icon that moves as you move the mouse.

Pointer tool. The PageMaker tool used for selecting and manipulating text and graphics. If the Pointer tool is selected, the pointer looks like an arrow. See also *Pointer*.

Portrait printing. The normal printing orientation for a page: horizontally across the shorter measurement of the page or paper (usually, 8 1/2 inches). In PageMaker, the Tall option appears in the Page Setup and Print Document dialog boxes for page orientation, and as the Portrait option in the Windows Printer Setup dialog box for paper orientation. See also *Orientation* and *Landscape printing*.

PostScript. A page-description language developed by Adobe Systems, Inc., and used by the LaserWriter, the IBM Personal PagePrinter, and other high-resolution printers and typesetters.

PPD and PDX files. PostScript Printer Description and Printer Description Extentions files. These files provide information used by PageMaker to set the default information for the type of printer you are using.

Preferences. The PageMaker command on the Edit menu used to select the unit of measure displayed on ruler lines and in dialog boxes. See also *Measurement system*, *Cicero*, and *Pica*.

Prepress proofs. Sometimes called blue lines, these proofs are made by using photographic techniques. See also *Press proofs* and *Blue lines*.

Press proofs. A test run of a color printing job through the printing press to check registration and color. See also *Prepress proofs* and *Blue lines*.

Primary colors. The elemental colors of either pigments or light. Red, green, and blue are additive primaries. White light is produced when red, green, and blue lights are added together. Cyan, magenta, and yellow are subtractive primaries, the inks used to print in the three-color process (or four-color process with black). See also *Additive primary colors* and *Subtractive primary colors*.

Print area. The area on a piece of paper where the printer reproduces text and graphics; always smaller than the paper size. See also *Margin*.

Print Manager. A Microsoft Windows application for sending files to the printer. PageMaker's Print command sends the publication to the Print Manager—a spooler—not directly to the printer. The Print Manager holds files in the print queue and prints them in the order in which they were received. You can continue working on other files while a file is being printed. The Print Manager is Windows' spooler. See also *Print queue*.

Print queue. Files in the spooler waiting to be sent to the printer. Files are sent in the order received. See also *Print Manager*.

Printer font. A bit-mapped or outline font installed in the printer or downloaded to the printer as a publication is printed. Usually distinguished from the screen font, which displays the text on the computer screen. See also *Bit map*, *Font*, and *Outline font*.

Printer's Marks. An option in the Print command dialog box that results in crop marks and—if you are printing color separations or a color composite—registration marks, a density control bar, and color-control strips.

Process color. One of the four colors—cyan, magenta, yellow, and black—blended to produce colors in the four-color process. By using process color, you produce a maximum of four negatives, regardless of the number of colors used in your artwork. See also *Custom color*, *Spot color*, and *Subtractive primary colors*.

Process separations. Four-color separations made from color artwork.

Proofread. To read a preliminary printout of a page and check for spelling errors, alignment on the page, and other features that are not related to the technical accuracy of the content.

Proofs. See *Prepress proofs*, *Press proofs*, and *Blue lines*.

Publication. A collection of pages created in PageMaker by integrating text and graphics files created in other applications and in PageMaker.

Publication window. Window appearing after you start PageMaker. Displays a view of one or two pages, the pasteboard, page icons, pointer, scroll bars, title bar, menu bar, and toolbox window.

Pull-down menu. A list of commands that appears after you select a menu. In PageMaker, the menu titles appear on the menu bar along the top of the screen, and the menu commands drop down in a list below the selected menu title.

Pull-out quote. Quotation extracted from the text of an article and printed in larger type, often set off by ruled lines.

Radio button. See *Option button*.

Ragged right. Text in which lines end at different points near the right margin. Opposite of flush right or justified text. See also *Alignment* and *Flush right* (or *right-justified*).

RAM. See *Memory*.

Rectangle tool. PageMaker tool used to create squares and rectangles.

Registration. The accuracy with which images are combined or positioned, particularly in reference to multicolored printing where each color must be precisely aligned for the accurate reproduction of the original.

Registration mark. A mark that is added to a document for color printing to line up copies of the same page to aid the printer in positioning color overlays.

Release. To let go of a mouse button.

Resolution. Number of dots per inch (dpi) used to create an alphanumeric character or a graphics image. High-resolution images have more dots per inch and look smoother than low-resolution images. The resolution of images displayed on-screen is usually lower than that of the final laser printout. Laser printers print 300 dots per inch or more; typesetters print 1,200 dots per inch or more.

Reverse. Text or a graphic on the printed page that appears opposite of normal. Usually, text and graphics are black on a white background; if reversed, they are white on black.

RGB. Shorthand notation for red, green, and blue. See also *Primary colors* and *Additive primary colors*.

Right-justified. See *Flush right* (or *right-justified*) and *Alignment*.

Roman. Upright text styles, as distinguished from italic. Sometimes used to refer to Normal style, as opposed to Bold or Italic, on PageMaker's Type menu.

Rotate. To revolve an object about a given point.

Roughs. Traditionally, the preliminary page layouts done by the designer using pencil sketches to represent miniature page design ideas. You can use PageMaker's Thumbnail option in the Print command dialog box to produce the equivalent of roughs. See also *Thumbnail*.

Rounded-corners command. PageMaker command used to adjust the degree of roundness of the corners of squares and rectangles.

Ruler guides. Nonprinting extensions of the tick marks on the rulers, which form horizontal and vertical dotted, dashed, or blue lines on the page. Used to align text and graphics on the page. Select the Rulers command to display the rulers, and then drag the Pointer tool from a ruler onto the page to create a guide. See also *Guide* and *Nonprinting master items*.

Rulers. Electronic rulers, one of which is displayed across the top of the publication window and one down the left side. Also, the text ruler displayed by the Indents/Tabs command on the Type menu. Rulers show measures in inches, picas, millimeters, or Ciceros. Use the Rulers command to display or hide the rulers. Use the Preferences command on the Edit menu to select the unit of measure displayed on the ruler lines and dialog box displays. Increments (tick marks) on the rulers depend on the size and resolution of your screen, as well as on the view (Actual Size, Fit in Window, 200%, and so forth). See also *Measurement system*.

Rules. Black lines added to a page—between columns, for example—to improve the design or increase readability of a publication. Created by using PageMaker's Perpendicular-line or Diagonal-line tool. The Lines submenu sets the thickness and style of the rules.

Run-around. See *Text wrap*.

Running foot. One or more lines of text appearing at the bottom of every page. In PageMaker, the running foot is entered on the master pages. Also referred to as the *footer*. See also *Folio*.

Running head. One or more lines of text appearing at the top of every page of a document. In PageMaker, the running head is entered on the master pages. Also referred to as the *header*. See also *Folio*.

Sans serif. Typefaces without serifs, such as Helvetica and Avant Garde. See also *Serif*.

Scale. To change the size of an object vertically, horizontally, or both. In PageMaker, you scale a graphic by selecting it with the pointer tool and then dragging one of the square handles. In scaling a rectangle or an ellipse drawn in PageMaker, hold the Shift key to force a square or a circle. In scaling an imported graphic, hold the Shift key to maintain original proportions. In scaling an imported TIFF image, hold the Ctrl key to activate the magic stretch feature that jumps the graphic to its optimum sizes for printing without Moiré patterns.

Scanned-image files. Bit-mapped files created by using hardware that digitizes images (converts a two- or three-dimensional image to a collection of dots stored in the computer's memory or on disk). Page-Maker reads the scanned-image files directly from disk. See also *Digitize* and *Bit map*.

Scanned-image icon. Shape of the pointer as a scanned-image file is being placed. See also *Pointer*.

Scanner. An electronic device that converts a photo, illustration, or other flat art into a bit map. A video camera is a scanner that converts three-dimensional objects into bit maps.

Screen. Gray tone usually identified as a percentage. A 100-percent screen is solid black; a 10-percent screen is light gray. Also, any of the other line patterns on the Shades submenu.

Screen font. See *Font*.

Screen ruling. The number of lines per inch in a screen tint or halftone. See also *Halftone*.

Screen tint. A screened percentage of a solid color.

Script fonts. Type designed to look like handwriting or calligraphy, such as Zapf Chancery. See also *Font*.

Scroll bar. Gray bars on the right side and bottom of the publication window. Scroll arrows at both ends of each bar enable you to scroll the document horizontally or vertically. Each scroll bar has a scroll box that you drag to change the view within the publication window. List boxes also can have scroll bars for viewing long lists of files or options.

Secondary mouse button. On a multiple-button mouse, the button that is not the main button. (Usually the right button.) See also *Mouse buttons*.

Select. To click or drag the mouse to designate the location of the next action. Also, to turn on (or place an X in) a check box (or other options) in a dialog box. See also *Deselect*.

Selection area. Area of a text block or graphic defined by the handles displayed after you select that text block or graphic. See also *Handles*.

Selection marquee. A dashed rectangular region drawn by dragging the Pointer tool to enclose and select more than one graphic or text block at a time. See also *Drag*.

Semiautomatic text flow. Text placement in which the text flows to the bottom of the column and then stops until the text-placement icon is placed at a new spot. See also *Autoflow* and *Manual text flow*.

Serif. A line crossing the main stroke of a letter. Typefaces that have serifs include Times, Courier, New Century Schoolbook, Bookman, and Palatino. See also *Sans serif*.

Shade pattern. Pattern selected on the Shades submenu to fill an object drawn in PageMaker. See also *Screen*.

Shape. An object drawn in PageMaker: a square, a rectangle, a circle, or an oval.

Signature. In printing and binding, the name given after folding to a printed sheet of (usually) 16 pages. The term is sometimes applied to page spreads printed adjacent to each other in the sequence required for offset printing of smaller booklets—such as the spreads created by PageMaker's Build Booklet command.

Single sided. An option in PageMaker's Page Setup dialog box that is used to set up a publication so that pages are reproduced on only one side of each sheet of paper. See also *Double-sided publication*.

Size. To make a graphic smaller or larger by dragging the handles. See also *Handles*.

Skew. To slant an object vertically.

Small caps. See *Caps*.

Snap-to. The effect of various types of nonprinting guidelines, such as margin guides, ruler guides, and column guides. These guides exert a "magnetic pull" on the pointer, text, or a graphic that comes close to the guides. Useful for aligning text and graphics accurately.

Snap-to guides. PageMaker command that, after turned on, causes margin guides, column guides, and ruler guides to exert a "magnetic pull" on the pointer or any text or graphic near the guides.

Soft carriage return. See *Carriage return*.

Spacing. The amount of space, in points, that is added or removed between every pair of characters or lines in a type block. Spacing affects the amount of white space in a type block. See also *Leading*, *Type block*, and *White space*.

Spacing guides. A PageMaker object used to help measure and standardize the spaces between text and graphics, between headings and body copy, or between any elements on a page. In PageMaker, spacing guides can be stored on the pasteboard. See also *Pasteboard*.

Spooler. See *Print Manager*.

Spot color. A process that adds solid areas of colored ink to a publication.

Spot-color overlay. A page prepared so that each color on the page is printed separately and then combined by a commercial printer to form the completed page.

Stacking order. Order in which overlapping text and graphics are arranged on the page and on-screen.

Standoff. Distance between the graphic boundary and the graphic.

Story. All the text from one word processing file; all the text typed or compiled at an insertion point outside existing text blocks. Can be one text block or several text blocks threaded together. See also *Text block*.

Story view. In PageMaker, the display activated when you choose Edit Story from the Edit menu, in which only the text is displayed, and only in one font. Distinguished from Layout view, in which the page is displayed on-screen exactly as it will appear when printed. See also *Layout view*.

Style. One of the variations within a typeface, such as roman, bold, or italic. See also *Font* and *Typeface*.

Style sheet. A list of all the tag formats that can be applied to text in a document. See also *Tag* and *Format*.

Subtractive primary colors. Cyan, yellow, and magenta. The three colors used to create all other colors if reflected light is used (for example, in printed material). See also *Additive primary colors*, *Primary colors*, and *CYMK*.

Tag. Formatting applied to a particular paragraph. See also *Format* and *Style sheet*.

Target printer. The printer on which you intend to print the final version of your publication. If no target printer is selected, PageMaker uses the default printer chosen when Windows was installed.

Template. A PageMaker publication containing only the layout grid, master pages, estimated number of pages, and boilerplate text and graphics for a periodical or book. Serves as the starting point for creating many similar documents, such as chapters of a book or issues of a newsletter. You add variable items—text and graphics that are not common to all chapters or issues—to the template document and save it under another name so that the original template remains unchanged.

Text block. A variable amount of text identified, when selected with the text pointer tool, by handles (small squares at the four corners of the text block) and windowshades (two horizontal lines, each with a loop, at the top and bottom of the text block). See also *Handles*, *Story*, and *Windowshades*.

Text box. The area in a dialog box in which you type text.

Text icon. Shape of the pointer after it is loaded with text when using the Place command or after clicking the plus sign in the bottom handle of a text block selected with the Pointer tool. See also *Pointer*, *Autoflow*, *Semiautomatic text flow*, and *Manual text flow*.

Text-only file. Text created in another application and saved without type specifications or other formatting. PageMaker reads text-only files directly from disk. See also *ASCII*.

Text tool. Tool used to select text for editing. After this tool is selected, the pointer looks like an I-beam. See also *Pointer*.

Text wrap. Automatic line breaks at the right edge of a column or at the right margin of a page. Also, the capability to wrap text around a graphic on a page layout. In PageMaker, you can wrap text around a graphic by changing the width of a text block (dragging the text handles) or by using the Drag-place feature. See also *Carriage return*.

Threaded text. See *Chained text*.

Thumbnail. A miniature version of a page that is created by using the Thumbnails option in the Print command dialog box. Used to preview publications. PageMaker prints up to 64 thumbnails on a page. See also *Roughs*.

Tick marks. Marks on the rulers showing increments of measure. See also *Measurement system*.

Tile. Used in oversized publications. A part of a page printed on a single sheet of paper. For a complete page, the tiles are assembled and pasted together. See also *Oversized publication*.

Time-out error. Printer stops because it has not received information for a while. Usually occurs while you print complex pages, and the printer takes a long time to print a large bit-mapped image. Saving before printing helps reduce chances of data loss.

Tint. A percentage of one of the process or custom colors.

Toggle switch. An on/off switch, command, or option. Used to describe cases in which the same command is invoked to turn a feature on and off. On PageMaker menus, these commands display a check mark if they are on.

Tones. The shades of a photograph or illustration that is printed as a series of dots. Tones are percentages of black; lower percentages produce lighter tones.

Toolbox window. Window that overlaps the publication window and contains icons for the tools you use to work with text and graphics.

Transparency. See *Overhead transparency* and *Overlay*.

Trap. Overlap needed to ensure that a slight misalignment or movement of the color separations does not affect the final appearance of the job.

Triple-click. To quickly press and release the main mouse button three times in succession. In PageMaker, for example, triple-clicking on Text with the Text tool selects a whole paragraph. See also *Click*.

Typeface. A single type family of one design of type, in all sizes and styles. Times and Helvetica, for example, are two different typefaces. Each typeface has many fonts (sizes and styles). Sometimes the terms typeface and font are used interchangeably. See also *Font* and *Style*.

Unit of measure. The units marked on PageMaker's rulers, such as inches, picas and points, millimeters, or Ciceros.

Uppercase. See *Caps*.

Vector graphics. See *Object-oriented files*.

Vertical justification. Dragging the bottom windowshades to adjust the length of a text block, or adjusting the spaces between lines of text (leading) in fine increments to make columns and pages end at the same point.

View. The size of the pasteboard and page as displayed in the publication window. View is determined by selections on the View submenu under the Layout menu. The smallest view (Fit in Window) shows either a complete page or two pages (for a double-sided publication with facing pages). The largest view (200%) shows text and graphics in twice the size at which they print.

White space. Empty space on a page, not used for text or graphics.

Widow. See *Orphans/widows*.

Window. On-screen area in which a Windows application runs, or a dialog box. Each application window has a title bar, a menu bar, and scroll bars. Some dialog boxes also include a title bar. See also *Dialog box*.

Windowshades. Horizontal lines, each with a small black square at each end and a loop in the center, that span the top and bottom of a text block. See also *Handles*.

Word spacing. The space between words in a line or a paragraph. In PageMaker, unjustified text has fixed word spacing; justified text has variable word spacing, which is adjusted within the limits entered in the Spacing Attributes dialog box. See also *Kerning* and *Letter spacing*.

Word wrap. The automatic adjustment of the number of words on a line of text according to the margin settings. The carriage returns that result from automatic word wrap are called soft carriage returns to distinguish them from hard carriage returns, which are entered to force a new line after you press the Enter key. See also *Text wrap* and *Carriage return*.

Wrap. See *Text wrap* and *Word wrap*.

WYSIWYG. "What-You-See-Is-What-You-Get" (or "wizzy-wig"). Term describes systems such as PageMaker that display full pages with all text and graphics on-screen. Some systems are more WYSIWYG than others in the accuracy of the display.

X axis. The horizontal reference line to which objects are constrained. See also *Constrain*.

X-height. A distinguishing characteristic of a font. The height of lower-case letters without ascenders or descenders, such as *x*, *a*, and *c*. Also called the body of the type.

Y axis. The vertical reference line to which objects are constrained. See also *Constrain*.

Yellow. The subtractive primary color that appears yellow and absorbs blue light. Used as one ink in four-color printing. See also *Subtractive primary colors* and *Process color*.

Zero point. The intersection of the two PageMaker rulers at 0 (zero). The default zero point is at the intersection of the left and top margins, but can be moved.

Zoom. To magnify or reduce your view of the current document.

0

How the Control Palette Changes an Object

To select the reference point:

Click to select the point that does not move.   OR   Double-click to select the point that moves.

Action	Reference Point	Changed Object
Move the object by changing the X and Y values.		
Scale the object by changing the W and H values.		
Rotate the object by changing the rotation angle (negative=clockwise).		
Skew the object by changing the skew angle (positive number slants top of object to the right).		
Crop an imported graphic by clicking on the cropping icon in the Control palette and changing the W and H values.		

How the Apply Button Changes

Object or Tool Selected	Apply Button
Pointer tool selected, no objects selected	
Line, Rectangle, or Ellipse tool selected	
Placing text	
Placing a graphic	
Graphic selected	
Text block selected	
Multiple objects selected	
Rotating tool selected	
Cropping tool selected	
Dragging a ruler guide	
Dragging a column guide	
Dragging the ruler's zero point	
Text tool selected, Character mode	
Text tool selected, Paragraph mode	

Que Corporation
11711 N. College Ave., Ste. 140
Carmel, IN 46032
1-317-573-2500